A HISTORY OF RUSSIA

A HISTORY OF Russia

BY GEORGE VERNADSKY

RESEARCH ASSOCIATE IN HISTORY IN YALE UNIVERSITY

NEW REVISED EDITION

NEW HOME LIBRARY • NEW YORK

The New Home Library Edition Published April, 1944
By Arrangement with Yale University Press
Reprinted May, 1944

The New Home Library, 14 West Forty-ninth Street,
New York, N. Y.

CL

PRINTED IN THE UNITED STATES OF AMERICA

AUTHOR'S NOTE

FIFTEEN years have passed since the first publication of this book—and what years! During their span the whole world—Russia included—has passed through a complete historical cycle. From an era of peace and prosperity—or so we thought—we were first plunged into a crippling economic crisis, and then for a number of years were forced to stand helpless before the onward march of dictators and the inexorable growth of their power. Then came the shock of the second World War. Today we may look to the future with sufficient confidence, but the dawn is only beginning to break and winning the peace may prove to be an even more difficult task than winning the war.

For Russia those fateful fifteen years have had, perhaps, even more significance than for the rest of the world. When the first edition of this book appeared in 1929, and perhaps a little more clearly while it was being revised the following year, one could faintly discern the beginning of a new era in Russia, but no one could rightly interpret the new trends at that time. The First Five Year Plan was just then getting under way, and whether one was enthusiastic or skeptical about its possibilities, he could certainly not have foreseen the full significance of the change. Only now, after Russia has for nearly three years withstood a terrible test by blood and fire, have we come to understand something of her real strength.

We may approve of Russia's methods of government or disapprove of them. But any evaluation of the Soviet system should be based upon an honest and realistic attempt to approach Russia without bias of any kind. Having taken power under the banner of international revolution, Soviet leaders were later forced to shift to a policy of "building socialism in a single country." Collectivism thus necessarily became part of Russia's national economy. The fact that collectivist policies have made Russia strong does not imply that Russian methods should be adopted in other countries with a different historical background, or even that for Russia herself there had not been—prior to 1917—other roads that might have been followed. However, the historian's business is history and not political or moral speculation. He has to describe a country's development as he understands it—whether he likes its trends or not.

It is only natural that our interpretation of the Russian Revolution today should differ from any approach we may have had fifteen or twenty years ago. Therefore, all the later chapters of this book, from Chapter XV on, have been rewritten for the present edition and new material has been added to bring the story up to date. Chapter I was completely revised to include new evidence which has accumulated during recent years. The author also wished to include the results of his own research in the field which had been carried out in the preparation of his other book, *Ancient Russia.* The text of all other chapters has also been carefully checked and revised wherever necessary. Mr. Melvin Evans has edited the new material in this edition. I express to him here my warmest gratitude.

G. V.

New Haven, Connecticut.
January 14, 1944.

CONTENTS

MAPS

RUSSIAN WEIGHTS AND MEASURES

The metric system has been introduced by the Soviet Government.

1 kilometer = 0.9 *versta* = 3,280.8 feet
1 hectare = 0.9 *desiatina* = 2.5 acres
1 metric ton = 61 *pud* = 2,204.6 lbs.

RUSSIAN CURRENCY VALUES

1 *ruble* = 100 *kopeks* = $0.515
1 *chervonets* = 10 *rubles*
1 American dollar = 1.94 *rubles*

A HISTORY OF RUSSIA

RUSSIAN HISTORY

INTRODUCTION

I.

RUSSIAN history is sometimes thought to be unduly long and complicated. It isn't. It is no longer than the history of most modern nations and the complications are more apparent than real. It is true that geographically Russia covers a vast and varied territory which may be unfamiliar to many readers. It is also true that within that country live many peoples whose origins are likely to be obscure to most Americans and whose names nearly always have an outlandish sound to non-Russian ears. But these are at most surface difficulties: a good long look at a map, the repetition aloud of a few names, and a brief consideration of the broad framework of Russian history will do much to remove them. The first two suggestions will be left to the reader, but it will be the business of this introduction to provide the third—a brief and general survey of the material of Russian history.

Today the Union of Soviet Socialist Republics is the largest country in the world. Nearly three times the size of the United States, it includes within its boundaries roughly one-sixth of the land surface of the earth, an area of 8,819,791 square miles spread over the vast expanse of two continents from the North Pacific to the Gulf of Finland. Its population was estimated in 1940 to be more than 192,000,000, and though representatives of over a hundred nationalities contributed to this total, more than 150,000,000, or nearly four-fifths, are ethnically Russian. The vast number of the Russian people and the tremendous area which they occupy have today made Russia a major force in world history.

The development of Russia as a great factor in the world scheme is, historically, comparatively recent. A thousand years ago the Russian people numbered but a few million and occupied only a fraction of the land now within the borders of the Soviet Union. Their history is a varied one but throughout it centers around one dominant and striking fact—the extraordinary growth of this comparatively unimportant group of people and their expansion over such an enormous part of the earth's surface.

But the Russians are more than prolific. They are a gifted people whose contributions to world culture in the fields of literature, music, the fine arts, the theatre, and the ballet have long been appreciated by all those who have more than a passing acquaintance with the history of the arts. Russian names are inscribed throughout the annals of science, and the achievements of Russians in such fields as medicine and the abstract sciences are now universally recognized. Even in modern technology—a field in which the world long considered the Russian backward and inept—it is today generally admitted that the Russians may claim a substantial share in the invention of the steam engine and the electric light, for example, and that they have established a definite priority on the invention of the radio. Only the rapid and successful industrialization of Russia during the last fifty years—and particularly during the last twenty—has fully revealed Russian capabilities in this field. It is, perhaps, one of the nicer ironies of history that this spectacular development, based so solidly in skills supposedly alien to the Russian spirit, has done more than anything in recent history to establish a somewhat belated recognition of Russian potentialities and to demonstrate the innate adaptability of the Russian people to the requirements of the new technological age.

2.

IT is wise, perhaps, to begin the story of Russia with a word about her people. The Russians are basically Slavs, a part of the greater Slavonic family belonging to the Indo-European group of peoples—a family which includes, among others, the Czechs, the Poles, the Serbs, and the Bulgarians. Their language, like all Slavonic languages, has many characteristics in common with Lithuanian, German, Greek, Iranian, and other Aryan tongues.

This great Slavonic family to which the Russians belong can be divided roughly into three parts: a western section which includes the Czechs and the Poles; a southern segment made up of a group of Balkan Slavs; and a large eastern section, the Russians. Like all modern peoples, the Russians have, through the centuries, acquired a certain admixture of alien blood. During the course of the eighth and ninth centuries A.D. they fell under the control of Norsemen who swept down upon them from Scandinavia, but these Norse invaders

—Varangians, as they were then called—were comparatively few in number, certainly not more than 100,000, and were consequently easily and rapidly absorbed by the Slavs. Both before and after the Norse invasion the eastern Slavs mixed freely with peoples of the Ural-Altai family—the Mongols, the Turks, and the Finns. Though there is not, of course, any way of estimating the extent of the Ural-Altai admixture, it is clear that in any case it was not sufficiently large to change appreciably the racial characteristics of the Slavs.

The Russians remain, therefore, essentially a Slavonic people. In time there grew up among them certain cultural and language differences which resulted in their division into three major branches: the Great Russians who today comprise about 65 per cent of the total; the Ukrainians (or Little Russians, as they were once called), something more than 25 per cent; and the balance, less than 10 per cent, White Russians (Byelo-Russians). The beginnings of this subdivision have been traced as far back as the twelfth century and its persistence has in large part been due to political events. From the fourteenth to the eighteenth centuries the Russians were divided between two states, the eastern, or Moscow Kingdom and the western, under the domination of the Poles and the Lithuanians. Though parts of Little and White Russia were annexed to the Moscow Kingdom about the middle of the seventeenth century, other parts were added only at the end of the eighteenth century at the time of the partition of Poland. Thus it was not until the nineteenth century that the three branches of the Russian people were reunited in a single state. Naturally enough, the Polish influence to which the Ukrainians and Byelo-Russians had been subjected for several centuries was reflected both in their culture and in their language. Even in the twentieth century the political separation of the Russian people was not completely ended, for after the Revolution of 1917 the question of their partition arose once more and from 1921 to 1939 a considerable part of the Ukrainian and White Russian population again came under Polish rule.

3.

THE outward manifestation of this division of the Russian people is the language differences which have developed among them. In discussing these variations, however, it is important to make a distinction between the literary or written languages and the spoken languages or folk dialects of the people. In Russia as elsewhere dialects are not confined by national or provincial boundaries. Within each of the three Russian groups the popular speech varies considerably from section to section—so much so, indeed, that it is impossible to speak of any one dialect as the language of Great Russia, or of Ukraine, or White Russia. Since the branches of the Russian people are not separated one from the other by impenetrable partitions, their languages tend to merge by gradual stages and are differentiated largely on the basis of usage and custom.

The literary languages, however, are separated by a more distinct line of demarcation. Prior to the nineteenth century there was but a single Russian language which was based primarily on the old church Slavonic and the Moscow dialect of the Great Russians. It included, however, many elements of Ukrainian origin which had been absorbed into the language during the late seventeenth and early eighteenth centuries when the Ukrainians played an important role in church and state. Because of these additions and modifications it became to a considerable degree an all-Russian tongue rather than merely the language of the Great Russians.

Nevertheless, during the nineteenth century movements were instituted by both Ukrainian and White Russian intellectuals to create separate and distinct languages for the two smaller Russian groups. By the end of the century Ukrainian had emerged as a recognizably different language, but White Russian began to be shaped only at the time of the Revolution and even today cannot be regarded as having acquired a final character.

In their original inspiration, at least, both the new languages seem to have stressed differences which were partly artificial. New terms were frequently invented or borrowed from foreign languages for the sole purpose, apparently, of providing forms distinct from the Russian; this was especially true of scientific terms and technical modes of expression. However, both languages seem to have enlisted popular support and today have been adopted officially by the Ukrainian and White Russian Socialist Soviet Republics.

4.

DURING the eighteenth and nineteenth centuries German and Russian geographers devised a purely arbitrary division of Russia into two parts, so-called "European Russia" and "Asiatic Russia." This

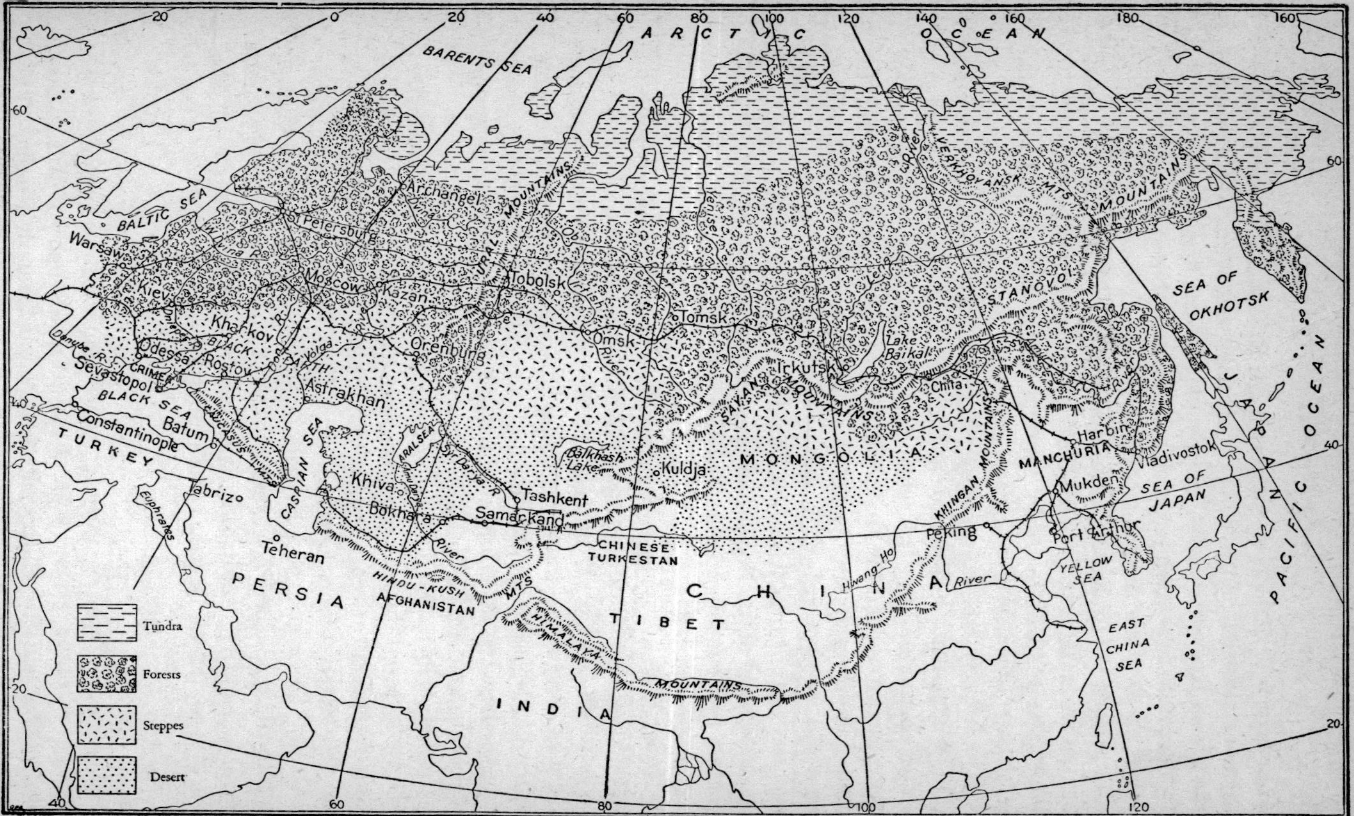

THE NATURAL ZONES OF EURASIA

conception of a two-part Russia is not only historically unjustified and unreal but is also geographically false and misleading. According to this theory, the Ural Range was to be considered the eastern limit of "European" Russia, but a moment's consideration will show that the Urals are in no sense a "natural boundary" and that they cannot even be made to look like one. No amount of rationalization can alter the plain fact that geographically European and Asiatic Russia are one and the same, that on both sides of the Urals there stretch the same zones of tundra, of forest, and of steppe that have played such an important role in the development of the Russian people. Far from separating the country, the Ural Range by its topographical and geological peculiarities has actually bound the eastern and western parts of Russia together into the only real unity possible, "Eurasian Russia."

The Russia that we are to consider is a single geographical unit, Eurasia, and it is worth understanding that term in order to clear up misconceptions which have grown up around it. As we shall use it, Eurasia refers not to a vague socio-historical combination of Europe and Asia but rather to a specific geographical area of the great central continental land mass. It is made up of a series of large, interlocking plains—the White Sea-Caucasian, the Western Siberian, and the Turkestan. This great area is in turn divided into several long latitudinal strips which are distinguished one from the other largely by variations in vegetation and soil. Since much of Russian history hinges on the relationship of these bands, it is well to get them clearly in mind at the very beginning. The first, stretching along the whole shore of the Arctic Ocean, is the tundra, a bleak, unforested, and untillable land; immediately below it lies a zone of deep forests, the southern boundary of which extends from the southern Carpathians approximately along the line of Kiev-Kazan-Tiumen to the Altai Mountains and from there along the northern edge of the Mongolian steppes and deserts; south of the forests lie the steppes, vast plains spreading over the black earth and chestnut soil belts; the fourth and southernmost strip is the desert zone of the Aral-Caspian and Mongolian area which, like the northern tundra, is broad in the east and grows narrower and finally disappears altogether in the west.

All the vast expanses of this Eurasian area have been occupied by the Russians in the course of a long historical process. When first the

Russian people came upon the stage of history, in the period between the third and ninth centuries, they occupied only the extreme western corner of Eurasia north of the Black Sea. From this small corner they spread eastward against the sun until in the middle of the seventeenth century the flow of Russian colonization had reached the Pacific and two centuries later had touched Tien Shan in central Asia. Both in this enormous eastward expansion and in the remarkable persistence with which they meanwhile held their western frontier along the Carpathian Mountains against the ferocious attacks of their neighbors, the Russian people have demonstrated an extraordinary fortitude and determination.

The fundamental urge which directed the Russian people eastward lies deep in history and is not easily summarized in a paragraph. It was not "imperialism," nor was it the consequence of the petty political ambitions of Russian statesmen. It was in the last analysis, perhaps, simply the inevitable logic of geography which lies at the basis of all history.

5.

ALL civilizations are to some extent the product of geographical factors, but history provides no clearer example of the profound influence of geography upon a culture than in the historical development of the Russian people. Eurasia is, as we have seen, divided into four distinct zones, and in the central two of these—the forests in the north and the steppes spreading southward below them—there developed the two dominant culture patterns upon which Russian civilization is based. Today there is little to differentiate these bands which through the centuries have been welded into a single broad agricultural area, but in ancient times the forests and the steppes were sharply divided. Rugged, difficult, and sometimes almost impenetrable, the forest area was inhabited originally by a hunting people widely dispersed and organized into small, independent states. The steppes, on the other hand, were vast open areas over which herdsmen wandered with comparative ease and where, in time, they were able to establish huge states based upon their nomadic way of life.

The part played in history by nomadic cultures deserves some special mention. Too often the cultural level of nomads is thought to have been invariably low, and their part in the development of modern society is frequently represented as a purely negative one. Such generalizations are, of course, false and dangerous. The cultural level of nomads, like that of any other group, has no constant and absolute limits. It has varied with peoples and times and places. The Mongolian tribes, to take a convenient example, clearly made considerable progress in political and social forms and organizations during the course of the twelfth and thirteenth centuries. History is filled with cases of two or more groups of nomads living side by side, each in a distinctly different stage of cultural development. It is well to remember, therefore, that in the cultural sense "nomadic" is not a qualitative measure but rather a descriptive term, that it is used only to indicate a *type* of civilization and not its relative state of development.

The role of the nomadic peoples in the cultural history of Eurasia—and, indeed, of the whole ancient world—was of great significance. There were, in those days, three principal centers of agricultural civilization in the world: one in the far east, in China; another farther west in the central Asian area called Khorezm; and a third in the Mediterranean basin in the southwest. Though these regions may well have been connected with one another in the prehistoric era, later evidence indicates that they had but the slightest association and that each led a comparatively independent life within its own sphere.

Beside and between these areas of settled populations lay the steppes, the realm of the nomads. This vast storm-swept region—which along its southern border blended imperceptibly into the desert—served the nomads as the sea served maritime peoples. Near at hand it was a fertile and hospitable source of livelihood, and beyond the horizon a shifting, dangerous highway over which hardy traders fared on peaceful missions and bands of warriors rode on swift, stabbing raids for plunder. But whether they came in peace or war, the nomads maintained through the centuries the cultural links between the scattered outposts of civilization. The horses, cattle, hides, and wool which were the products of the herdsmen's flocks were essential to the economy of their far-flung neighbors, and in return for them the nomadic traders received the grain and other agricultural produce that they needed. In addition to these primary items of commerce, wealthy herdsmen and tribal chieftains often dealt in artistic wares, precious cloth, gold and silver vessels, jewelry and ornaments of all sorts. At times large workshops were developed within the tribal organizations and craftsmen were engaged in the manufacture of weapons, utensils, harness, and richly ornamented gear. By trade and by plunder tribes were able occasionally to accumulate great riches in their tents, but whatever their economic condition they roamed the length and breadth of the steppes and in their trains traveled cultural elements of all the civilizations which they touched.

Beyond the normal and constant contacts developed within this pattern, the steppes were from time to time swept by great waves of migrations. Before the beginning of our era the central region lying between the Black Sea, the Caucasus, and Khorezm was occupied by the Scythians, while the eastern connecting link between Khorezm and China was held by the Turks and the Huns. In the fourth and fifth centuries the Huns, surging west under the leadership of Attila, attempted to seize control of the whole area of the steppes and thus to become the sole intermediary between the extreme east and west. Centuries later the Mongols aspired to the same position, and under Genghis Khan and his descendants in the thirteenth century were able to found an empire which stretched from the Pacific Ocean to the Adriatic Sea. Each of these invasions brought new cultural patterns and each, when it retreated years or centuries later, left its imprint indelibly in the land that was to become Russia.

6.

EURASIA is a single geographical unit, and from time immemorial it has been united under a single state. In the earliest times a federation of Turko-Mongolian tribes established an empire of the steppes and their rule, extending along the fringes of the forest zone, brought the Russian tribes under their dominion as vassals and subjects. Later, however, the Turko-Mongolian power waned. The Russians gradually absorbed the Eurasian territories which had been under the domination of the nomadic empire, and as they subjugated the Turks and Mongols the center of the state was shifted from the steppes to the forests.

This movement of the center of power which occurred during the formation of the Russian state was an event of primary importance for it resulted in the obliteration of the barrier that had separated the two great central zones. Prompted by economic necessity and directed in part by the new cultural patterns which they had drawn from neighboring and vassal tribes, the Russian people in this period greatly altered the natural character of primitive Eurasia. Agricultural customs spread rapidly through the whole region, and, as the area of cultivation crept outward from the steppes into the forest lands, the northern and southern zones gradually became indistinguishable. This identity was bought at a terrible price in natural resources, but the Russians—like all people engaged in the task of remolding a land to their needs—had no time to reckon the cost. Great forests were slashed away and burned over, fur-bearing animals were hunted down and exterminated, and streams were half emptied of their fish. The transformation went on to its natural end, and when the smoke and dust of the destruction rose above a cleared land the Russians united again in the building of a new economy. The plow bit into soil that had never been broken, the forests fell away to the north, and cattle grazed where hunters had stalked wild game. All over Eurasia there appeared new trades and new industries; the black earth began to yield its riches in agricultural produce and minerals; new and permanent lines of communication drove outward to the remote ends of the land and provided new opportunities for trade and commerce. The Russians had seized the vital connecting zone between the forest and the steppe and by their occupation and utilization of the new territory had assured themselves of the control of the whole vast sweep of Eurasia.

7.

POLITICALLY the Russian people were the successors of the Turko-Mongols. Culturally they were the heirs of Byzantium. Very early in their history the Russians established contact with the powerful empire in the south, but it was not until the ninth and tenth centuries, when Byzantine culture had reached its most brilliant expression, that there occurred the great and decisive turn in the cultural development of Russia—the conversion of the Russian people to Orthodox Christianity.

At that time Byzantium was one of the cultural capitals of the world and the fundamental inspiration of western civilization was drawn from the churches and libraries of ancient Constantinople. Consequently, Russian acceptance of Christianity was in its early stage a move in the direction of a common Russo-European culture since both for a time drew their sustenance from a common source.

All the principal elements of Byzantine civilization, literature, and art entered Russia with the teachings of the Church, and though the transplanted culture was received by the Russian people only after many modifications, it did lay the basis for a closer relation between Europe and Eurasia. This unifying influence was, however, of comparatively short duration, for Russian adherence to Greek Orthodoxy at the time of the breach between the Roman and Byzantine churches again tended to separate Russia from the Western peoples. The separation was further widened by the constant military pressure exerted against Russia's borders by her western neighbors—the Poles, the Germans, and the Swedes. This new cleavage between the east and west persisted until the end of the seventeenth century when the necessity of acquiring the technical skills which the Europeans had developed led to another attempt at cultural affinity. But by this time the breach had so widened that even the sternest measures of the Russian Government could at first do little more than force outright imitation. The circumstances of this final merging of Russia with the west were, perhaps, the primary sources of the dualism and crises in the religious and national psychology of the people which were evident throughout the course of the eighteenth, nineteenth, and twentieth centuries.

8.

History is a constant and continuing process. It does not pause at regular intervals for the convenience of the student and any divisions which we set up must, of course, be purely schematic and arbitrary. Nevertheless, history can be studied only in segments, and the necessary separation of the subject into periods can have positive value if it is not merely mechanical but has its foundation in significant events of the historical process. The preceding sections have been intended to indicate in the broadest outlines the objective and subjective events upon which the divisions of the present history will be based. A recapitulation of those events with reference to their relative positions in the development of the Russian people may provide for the reader a historical perspective which will be useful in the chapters to follow.

The fundamental basis for the divisions adopted in this history is the shifting relationship between the forest and the steppe zones, a relationship which will be considered largely from the standpoint of its sociological implications and effects. On the eve of Russian history, efforts had already begun to unify these two areas so that both might benefit through the exchange of the natural wealth of each. These first elemental attempts, begun long before the appearance of Russia as an independent historical entity, were made by the inhabitants of both the forests and the steppes, and after the emergence of the Russian people were carried on first by the Khazars and later by the Varangian princes. The final attempt at unification during this period was directed by Prince Sviatoslav who strove to unite under his power the Dnieper, the lower Volga, and the lower Danube. This first period, the end of which was important also as the time of the gradual approach of the Russians to Christianity, came to a natural conclusion with the crumbling of Sviatoslav's empire after his death in 972.

The era between the middle of the tenth century and the middle of the thirteenth century—or, more exactly, 972–1238—was characterized by the bitter struggle between the forest and the steppe. Relations between the two zones were broken off during this period of savage fighting between the Russian princes and the Cumans who drove across the steppes and gradually forced the Russians back into the forests. In spite of the hardships endured by the Russian people during nearly three centuries of desperate struggle for existence, their cultural development, though retarded, never quite came to a standstill. Agricultural pursuits took root throughout the area under their control and cultivation spread slowly into the forest region. At the same time foreign contacts were never completely severed, and the association with Byzantium was particularly important for it further stimulated Russian adherence to Greek Orthodoxy.

The third great period of Russian history (1238–1452) began with the Mongolian invasion which at last brought to an end the long conflict between the forest and the steppe. The victory of the invading nomads was, indeed, a decisive victory for the steppes and resulted in the formal unification of the several Russian states under the domination of the "Golden Horde." Though western Russia during this time was held by Lithuania and Poland, the people of eastern Russia were at the end of the period strong enough to align themselves under the Moscow state and to seize the power of the Mongolian Khan when his empire began to disintegrate. With the founding of a vassal Tartar princedom in Kasimov in 1452, Moscow had signaled its assumption of the role of successor to the "Golden Horde."

The internal peace which the Mongolians were able to enforce during the greater part of two centuries was conducive to rapid cultural changes involving almost every aspect of life from the development of civil law to the further extension of agriculture. Particularly important was the religious independence which the Russians attained toward the end of this period. The Russian church had been greatly strengthened when the Mongolian Khan chose to give it his patronage, and the gradual weakening of the Byzantine Empire further freed the Russians from administrative dependence on Constantinople. The Russian church enhanced its position still more when at the time of the Florentine union of 1439 it remained independent while the Byzantine church submitted temporarily to the authority of the Pope. With the collapse of the Byzantine Empire and the capture of Constantinople by the Ottoman Turks in 1453, Russia assumed in the eyes of her people the position of the leading state in Orthodox Christendom.

The fourth period was characterized by the great Russian expansion southeast toward the Turko-Mongolian frontier and the consequent reassertion of the power of the forest zone over the nomadic culture of the steppes. The two and a half centuries following 1452 witnessed the conquest of Kazan, Astrakhan, and Siberia as well as the reoccupation after many centuries of the mouth of the Don. The taking of Azov by Peter the Great in 1696 brought this era to a close. The chief events in the field of religious development were the division of the Russian church into two metropolitan districts—Moscow and western Russia—and the development of the patriarchate in the Moscow Kingdom; the defense of Orthodoxy against the pressure of Roman Catholicism from western Russia; and the schism of the "Old Ritualists" in Moscow.

The fifth period, extending from 1696 to the Revolution of 1917, saw the gradual expansion of the Russian state almost to the natural boundaries of Eurasia. It was the age in which the final unification of forest and steppe was achieved and the two great zones were finally welded into a single economic unit. Agriculture reached a dominant position throughout all Eurasia, and as the area of cultivation spread across the continent industries sprang up to exploit the tremendous natural resources discovered and developed in the land. The cultural history of the time was marked by resurgent conflicts and fermentation and the spiritual life of the day was stirred by a severe crisis in the religious consciousness of the people at the time when the church, in its administrative branches, became subject to the authority of the state.

The present era of Russian history began, of course, with the Revolution of 1917. In its earlier stages it was a time of violent activity, incredible hardships, and bewilderingly rapid readjustments. Its later developments have led toward gradual stabilization, enormous internal and industrial expansion, and single-minded preparation for the titanic conflict of the Second World War.

CHAPTER I.

THE ORIGINS OF THE RUSSIAN STATE

(to 972 A.D.)

1.

THE Russian state came into existence in the western corner of the area we have called Eurasia, where, at least by the third century the territory lying between the Baltic Sea, the Don River, the Black Sea, and the lower Danube had been settled in part by east Slavic tribes. In the course of the eighth and ninth centuries these tribes were united under the Norsemen who had penetrated to the mainland by way of the Baltic, and it is this event which is commonly taken as the date of the founding of the Russian state. In fact, however, political life in the territories occupied by the eastern Slavs had originated much earlier in southern Russia in the social and political forms centering around the trade between the wooded regions and the pasture lands of western Eurasia, the Black Sea, and the East.

2.

THE first inhabitants of the southern Russian steppes of whom we have definite knowledge were the Scythians, a tribe belonging linguistically to the Iranian peoples but in its mode of life closely similar to the Turko-Mongols. In fact, it is probable that even at this time there had been a mixture of racial groups and that among the Scythians there was at least a sprinkling of Mongols.

These Scythians—whose favorite occupation seems to have been war and whose closest companion was the horse—appeared in southern Russia sometime during the seventh century B.C. On the Eurasian steppes they found themselves neighbors of the Turks who inhabited Altai and Mongolia, and together these two groups maintained the connecting links between China and Greece. The northern shore of the Black Sea was occupied at that time by Greek colonies—Olbia at the mouth of the Bug, Chersonesus close to the present city of Sevastopol, Panticapaeum on the site of the city of Kerch, and many others—and the Scythians conducted a lively trade with these outposts of Greek civilization. Greek artisans and craftsmen made household articles for the Scythian kings and for the wealthier classes, and many examples of Greco-Scythian art, some of which are now in the Hermitage Museum in Leningrad, have been found by excavators in southern Russia.

Greek authors have left us interesting information about the life and customs of the Scythians. Herodotus, the fifth-century Greek historian, in a description of Scythia tells us that it extended from the mouth of the Ister (the Danube) up the rivers Borysthenes (the Dnieper) and Tanais (the Don) far to the north and east of the Black Sea. From the data available on the Scythians and particularly from the information on the volume of their trade with the Greeks to the south and the Mongols and Chinese to the east, it seems probable that they succeeded at times in uniting under their power not only the steppes but also part of the wooded north, and indeed there exists archaeological proof that trading settlements were founded along the boundary of this forest area.

3.

At the beginning of the fourth century B.C. another Iranian people, the Sarmatians, began to press upon the Scythians, and by the end of the second century B.C. they had occupied the shores of the Black Sea.

Among the Sarmatians the most powerful tribe was the Alans who, until the coming of the Huns, were considered the best horsemen of the steppes. They are described in contemporary accounts as tall and handsome, blond and fair. For centuries they were famous as highly skilled armorers and jewelers and many of their favorite weapons, a long spear and a long iron sword, have been uncovered in the barrows of the North Caucasus and southern Russia. They developed a peculiar artistic style of their own, a variation of the Scythian "animal style" in which the lavish use of enamel and precious stones for incrustation was characteristic. The famous treasure of Novocherkassk which was discovered in 1864 is thought to represent a part of the riches of an Alanic queen who lived, presumably, during the first century A.D.

Though the Alans were originally typical nomads, in time some of their clans settled down and, as they mixed with the native agricultural population, gradually came to dominate several of the east Slavic tribes. Many of the early Slavic princes bore Alanic names, and the old name of the strongest of the east Slavic tribes—the Antes—is itself of Alanic origin. The Caucasian Alans were called *As* or *Os*—a name which their descendants, the Ossetians, still bear—and *Antes* was the plural of *As*. One clan was known as *Rukhs-As*—"the light (or brilliant) Alans," and it is from this name that *Ros* or *Rus* (hence, Russia, Russians) presumably derives.

These *Rus* (in the variation *Rhos*) are first mentioned in a Syriac chronicle of the middle of the sixth century; at about the same time the Goth historian Jordanes, who wrote in Latin, speaks of the *Antes* in connection with events of the fourth century when they had already developed an organized state. Archaeological and linguistic evidence leads us to believe that the Antes—who must have existed in southern Russia as a Slavic tribe under the domination of Alanic chieftains since the third and possibly since the second century A.D.—early reached a comparatively high degree of civilization. They were engaged in both agriculture and cattle breeding; they had orchards and vegetable gardens; they developed handicrafts such as weaving and ceramics; they forged iron tools and weapons. At times the smaller clans and family communes bound themselves together in larger tribal unions and associations, and there can be no doubt that they held well-defined ideas about social order and organization. It is interesting to remember in this connection that the words for "justice" (*pravda*) and "law" (*zakon*) are among the oldest in the Slavic vocabulary.

From time immemorial the Slavs had been an artistic people who were known for their particular fondness for music and singing. Their religion was a conglomerate system of beliefs drawn from a variety of sources originally involving the worship of clan ancestors and natural forces such as lightning and including rivers and trees which were considered the abodes of nymphs and spirits. Subsequently a more elaborate system developed under the influence of Iranian religious beliefs on the one hand and of Norse mythology on the other. While the Slavic Perun, god of thunder and lightning, resembles the Teutonic Thor, other deities of the early Russian pantheon are more akin to the Iranian gods and genii. Throughout the Sarmatian period the worship of the Great Goddess of the Scythians was continued, and her image imprinted itself firmly in Russian folk art, becoming, for instance, a prominent motif in early embroideries. The "Mother Earth" of Russian folklore is another interesting example of the persistence of the memory, in another form, of this same Iranian age.

According to the sixth-century Byzantine historian, Frocopius of Caesarea, the Antes lived originally in a political democracy in which all public affairs were discussed in clan or tribal assemblies. From other sources, however, it is known that at a later date some of the Antic princes were endowed with considerable personal authority, and apparently an aristocratic class gradually came into being as the chieftains enriched themselves with war booty and prisoners. A rich hoard of gold and jewelry which is thought to have been part of the treasury of one of these princes was found at Pereshchepino in Poltava province and is now in the Hermitage Museum. Various less spectacular ornaments which apparently belonged to ordinary members of the tribe—plaques and rings of bronze, silver, and gold—have been found and serve as additional evidence of a highly developed artistic sense and skill among the people.

4.

IN the third century A.D. the Sarmatian domination over the southern Russian steppes was displaced by German tribes of Goths who descended from the north along the rivers Dniester, Bug, and Dnieper. Having conquered this western corner of the Eurasian steppes, the Goths soon acquired both the nomadic customs and the material culture of the people they had displaced. They themselves became in time mounted warriors and about the middle of the fourth century organized a strong military power under the leadership of Ermenrich. For a time, as they succeeded in subduing one after another of the east Slavic tribes and forcing the peasants to work for them, it seemed that they were about to achieve a permanent subjugation of the Slav by the Teuton.

However, toward the end of the fourth century a new invasion from the east in turn destroyed the power of the Goths. This time the invaders were the Huns, a Turko-Mongol tribe led by a militaristic Mongolian aristocracy similar to the Mongol-Tartars who overran Russia much later during the thirteenth century.

The Hunnic Khan first made vassals of the Alans and then turned against the Goths whom he easily defeated. Shamed by this defeat, Ermenrich, the Goth king, committed suicide, and the tribe began a retreat toward the west in the direction of the lower Danube. However, in the Bug area which lay between them and their refuge there lived a tribe of the Antes, and the refusal of this group to allow the Goths to pass through their territory resulted in a bloody conflict. The Goths crushed one of the Antic armies and Ermenrich's successor ordered their king, Boz, all of his sons, and some seventy boyars crucified. By this time, however, the Hunnic Khan had given permission to the Alans under his rule to come to the rescue of their kin, the Antes, and the Goths were again defeated and driven farther west. Even then they did not completely escape Hunnic suzerainty, for the Huns eventually followed them westward and under the reign of Attila brought most of central Europe under their control.

During the last years of his life the center of Attila's power lay in Pannonia, the western outpost of the Eurasian steppes, now known as Hungary. Strategically situated for marauding expeditions against the Mediterranean coast, Rome, and Byzantium, Pannonia was long the favorite goal of nomadic invasions and it was finally occupied by the Magyars at the end of the ninth century. Though the empire of Attila at one time extended over an enormous area from east to west, following his death it rapidly fell apart and made way for the formation of new political organizations and the remnants of the Huns eventually retired to the Azov area where they came to be known as the Bulgars.

5.

WHILE the nomadic Iranian and Mongolian tribes were displacing each other on the southern Russian steppes, the forests on both sides of the Ural Mountains were being occupied by Finnish tribes. The Finns were of the same racial stock as the Mongols and the Turks and constituted the northern or Ural branch of the Ural-Altai peoples whose southern group was made up of Magyars, a group culturally related to the Altai branch of nomadic Mongols. These northern Finnish tribes lived submerged in the forest regions and were, consequently, a hunting and fishing people; fish was their chief food and furs served them both as clothing and as the major article of trade with their neighbors. Since their contact with each other was limited to a tenuous one along the rivers and waterways, they did not succeed in establishing a strong military power and when the wave of Slavonic colonization started northward they were unable to resist its pressure. As the Slavs advanced into their territory, the Finns either retreated or were gradually absorbed by the ever-increasing number of invaders.

At the same time there lived in northwestern Russia, in the basins of the Western Dvina and Nieman rivers, a group of Baltic or Lithuanian tribes who were related linguistically to the Indo-Europeans. The country they occupied was chiefly forest land not unlike that of the Finns, but even in this early period parts of it had been cleared and numbers of the people were engaged in agriculture. These early Lithuanians appear to have lived not in the village communities common to the time but on isolated farms just as their descendants did much later in the sixteenth and seventeenth centuries. The basic social unit was the family whose head wielded an absolute authority over its members and the household servants they held. In the event of external danger several of these family clans would unite in common defense, and it was from these unions that the larger Lithuanian tribes were eventually constituted. In time they became a mounted, warlike people, and the barrows of that region have yielded many examples of iron halberds, spears, and swords as well as bits, stirrups, and various other trappings for their horses.

6.

DURING the time of the Hunnic predominance the Antes had occupied the region around the Donets and the Bug rivers and had also sent out settlements and enclaves into the area of the Lower Don, the Crimea, and possibly even as far as the North Caucasus. Advancing toward the southwest in the period following the dismemberment of the Hunnic Empire, certain groups of the Antes swept over Bessarabia and in the course of the sixth century joined with other Slavic tribes—ancestors of the Serbs and the Croats—in devastating raids on the Byzantine possessions south of the Danube.

In a maneuver typical of Byzantine diplomacy, the emperors of the southern power endeavored to check the Anto-Slavic menace by both diplomatic and military measures. Seeds of discord were assiduously sown to induce strife between various ethnic and social groups and at times the stratagem worked so well that the Antes and the "Sclaveni" (Serbs) forgot the common enemy, Byzantium, and fell upon one another instead. On the whole, however, Byzantium was forced to rely chiefly upon its armed forces, part of whom, it is interesting to note, were hired "Barbarians" of the same racial stock as the enemy. Many of these mercenaries held high administrative and army positions, and it was to one of them—Chilbudius, a general of Antic ancestry—that Emperor Justinian I entrusted the defense of the Danubian fortified line. Though Chilbudius fought loyally and valiantly against the Anto-Slavs, dealing them severe blows in a campaign north of the Danube, he was eventually killed in battle (534). However, some years later a rumor spread among the Antes that Chilbudius had not been slain but had secretly deserted to his kin with whom he lived in hiding. In due time a man who called himself Chilbudius was indeed produced and acclaimed by the whole tribe as their leader, but this first of a long line of pretenders in Russian history failed miserably. Lured to Constantinople under the pretext of negotiations, he was treacherously arrested on the way and so disappeared from the stage of history. In spite of this episode, however, the Antes later allied themselves with the Empire for a short time.

About 560 the political equilibrium of the Pontic steppes was again upset by two more nomadic tribes driving westward. The leading group was a tribe of Avars, and as they appeared on the east they were being hotly pursued by a tribe of Turks who had originally inhabited the Altai region. When the Antes in Bessarabia valiantly resisted their attempts to break through, the Avars offered to negotiate for a passage. This offer, however, proved to be merely a ruse, for in the midst of negotiations the Antic envoy was killed and the Avars suddenly renewed the attack in the hope of catching the Antes unawares. Though the Antes were not completely annihilated at the first shock as the Avars had hoped, they were so badly disorganized that the attackers were finally able to cut their way through their lines into Pannonia (568) and to subjugate a substantial part of the Pannonian and Balkan Slavs.

While these attacks and counterattacks in southern Russia were in progress, however, the Slavs as a whole continued a steady pressure against the Byzantine possessions to the south of the Danube and during the course of the seventh century were eventually able to occupy most of the Balkan Peninsula to the Aegean and the Adriatic.

7.

THE Altaic Turks who had driven the Avars across southern Russia now established themselves on the steppes between the lower Volga and the Don and in the North Caucasian area. Out of the mixture of Turks and conquered Hunno-Bulgar tribes and Caucasian aborigines there grew a new people, the Khazars, who by the middle of the seventh century had established a stable state. Those Bulgar tribes who were unwilling to submit to Khazar rule were forced to emigrate and spread north and west from the new state. One Bulgar horde settled along the middle course of the Volga and in the Kama basin, while another, driving westward into the lower Danube region, defeated the Byzantines and gradually extended their control over the whole western Balkan Peninsula. Though they defeated the Antic and Sclavenian tribes who held this region, they themselves fell under the influence of Slavic culture and in time even adopted the language as their own. Thus, while the name Bulgar originally applied specifically to this ruling horde of conquerors, it later came to mean that heterogeneous Slavic people who emerged from this mixed background—the modern Budgarians.

At the same time another "Barbaric" horde, the Ugrians or Magyars, was pushed north from the Caucasus. They first settled the territory along the upper Donets River and, while they themselves recognized the suzerainty of the Khazars, they in turn compelled the Antes who had long lived in that region to submit to their rule. Later the Magyars moved on to the Bug and from there, at the end of the ninth century, migrated to Pannonia which became their permanent home under the name of Hungary.

Meanwhile the Alans and Slavs of the lower Don and Azov area —the old *As* and *Rus* tribes—also became Khazar subjects. In a sense they were really allies, for they were allowed an unusual and considerable degree of autonomy. In times of danger they were obligated to send auxiliary troops to the assistance of the Khazars, but these troops retained their identity and fought under their own officers. The whole Alano-Slavic brigade was led by a commander known as *As-Tarkhan,* "the chieftain of the Alans," and it was presumably from this title that the city of Astrakhan derived its name.

During this period Khazar power reached its height in a state extending from the Caspian Sea and the lower Volga to the Dnieper and the Black Sea. Authority was legally divided between two chieftains, the Kagan (or *khagan,* literally, the great khan) and the *beg.* While the Kagan held formal authority in matters pertaining to the state and to religion, it was the *beg* who exercised the real power since he was the recognized head of the army.

Though the Khazars had by this time developed considerable agricultural skill—they were engaged in cattle breeding, cultivation of the land, and fishing enterprises—their principal interest lay in trading activities. The great trade route of the north lay along the upper reaches of the Volga, through Bulgar territory to the Caspian, and on across the Caucasus into the Near and Middle East which at that time (the end of the seventh century) was under Arab rule. It was along this route that the Khazars developed a thriving commerce between the Far East and the Black Sea on one hand, and between the Arabian south and Slavonic north on the other.

One of the results of these commercial contacts with such widely divergent peoples was the variety of religious influences to which the Khazars were subjected. Though the Arabs offered them Islam and the Greeks Christianity, the Khazar Kagan, possibly for political reasons, was reluctant to accept either, fearing that a foreign faith might well be followed by foreign domination. The Kagan eventually solved the dilemma by choosing a neutral faith, Judaism—a faith which carried with it no political threat.

From the middle of the seventh century onward the Khazars and their allies, the Alans, had waged a series of protracted and inconclusive wars against the Arabs to the south. Repeatedly they had gathered sufficient strength to drive a wedge into Transcaucasia only to be driven out by the Arabs. In 737, however, the Arabs finally were able to administer a crushing defeat to the Khazars and, sweeping on through the North Caucasus, penetrated as far north as the Don. Some twenty thousand Slavs were taken prisoner in the campaign and transported to Syria. The political results of this invasion were far reaching, for both the Alans and the Slavs—the *As* and the *Rus* allies and vassals—lost faith in the ability of the Khazars to protect them and began a search for new allies whom they eventually found in the invading Norsemen.

8.

THE Norsemen—or Vikings, as they are sometimes called—had at this time long established a reputation as intrepid mariners and pirates, traders and explorers. As early as the sixth and seventh centuries the Swedes in particular had explored the eastern shores of the Baltic and eventually, ranging up the Dvina waterway, they reached the central Russian "Mesopotamia," the region of the upper Volga and the Oka rivers. By the end of the seventh century they had established themselves firmly around Yaroslavl, Rostov, and Suzdal and were sharing the control of the native Finnish tribes with Slavic settlers from Novgorod and Smolensk. The record of this colonization is amply confirmed by archaeological discoveries of numerous objects such as iron clasps and swords which are unmistakably Scandinavian in origin.

Since further progress down the Volga was barred by the presence of the Bulgars in its lower reaches, the Swedes now turned west up the course of the Oka River. Using the portages between the tributaries of the southern Oka and those of the upper Donets, the Swedes penetrated to the Donets region which had been held since the end of the seventh century by a group of the Antes who were subject to the Magyars. Documentary sources are vague on the history of this period, but the little information available, bolstered by archaeological evidence, indicates that the Swedes soon defeated the Magyars, subjected a part of them to their authority, and drove the main horde southwest to the Bug.

The Antes who were thus freed from the Magyar yoke must certainly have acclaimed the Swedes as liberators, and the news of the Norse deliverers must before long have spread to the Alans and the Slavs of the lower Don and the North Caucasus. They naturally turned to the Swedes for protection after the devastation of the Arab raid of 737.

The Swedes, however, were not numerous, and since they mingled freely with the peoples whom they now ruled they soon fell under the influence of the native culture and even assumed the name *As* and later *Rus*. Though the country beyond the Don was for a time known as "Great Sweden," the capital which they established and which seems to have been situated somewhere on the Taman Peninsula was called *Asaheim* or *As-Grad,* "City of the As." The Swedes assumed for a time the same obligations toward the Khazars that the Alans had previously fulfilled, substituting a Swedo-Slavic brigade for the earlier Alanic auxiliary unit and changing the commander's title from the old *As-Tarkhan* to *Rus-Tarkhan,* "Chieftain of the Rus." However, profiting by the weakening of the Khazar power after another Arabian attack, about the year 825 the Swedish-Russian commander defied the authority of the Khazar and proclaimed himself independent. Assuming the title of Russian Kagan, he established new headquarters, presumably at Tmutorokan in the Taman Peninsula.

This first Russian Kaganate captured from the Khazars and the Volga Bulgars the international trade in which they had been engaged and, in carrying it on, fulfilled the same sociological and economic functions. Their chief articles of trade appear to have been finely wrought swords, which were produced mainly in Scandinavia, and precious furs from the forests of northern Russia. The area lying along the southern shore of Lake Ilmen and centering in a town which still bears the name "Old Rus" (*Staraia Russa*) became an important northern trading outpost for the Russian Kaganate. A steady flow of merchandise was sent down the Oka and Donets-Don waterways and a lively export trade was instituted not only with Byzantium but also with the Orient where the records of the postmaster general of the Caliphate indicate that during the ninth century Russian merchants were regular visitors to such cities as Bagdad.

The political emancipation of the Russians and their economic competition were regarded by the Khazars as nearly equal threats. As a defense against both, the Khazar Kagan appealed to the Byzantine emperor to send architects and engineers to erect a chain of forts along the course of the lower Don and Donets rivers. The emperor was pleased to grant the request and by 835 the Byzantines had built on the Don near the present town of Tsymlianskaia a formidable fortress called Sarkel (in Ugric, *White House* or *White Tower*) which is mentioned in early Russian chronicles. Protected by these fortifications the Khazars were now in a position not only to control the Russian routes to the east but to sever the connections between the Taman Rus and northern Russia as well. Using this advantage skilfully, within a few years of the building of Sarkel the Khazars had conquered the Slavs of the Oka region and had established their Magyar vassals in control of the Kiev area.

Finding himself thus virtually encircled, and having experienced the results of the negotiations which his enemies, the Khazars, had carried through with the Byzantine emperor, the Russian Kagan decided in 838 to send his own envoys to Constantinople. The emperor, however, was cold to his proposition, and not only declined to conclude a treaty with the Russians but delayed the envoys and prevented them from returning to their homes. Using as a pretext the troublesome political situation which had by that time developed around the lower Danube, he urged the envoys to return by a more roundabout way and at last advised them to travel with an embassy of his own which he was just then dispatching to the Frankish emperor, Louis. According to the so-called *Bertinian Annals,* the envoys arrived in Ingelheim, Franconia, with the Byzantine embassy on January 17, 839. Even then their difficulties had not ended for when they proved to be Swedes by birth rather than Russians, Emperor Louis became suspicious of them and ordered them arrested pending investigation. How long they were held is not known, but it does appear that at last they were allowed to return to Russia.

It is hardly surprising that the Byzantine emperor's treatment of the Russian envoys aroused the resentment of the Kagan, who must immediately have set about devising a suitable retaliation. There are indications that about 840 the Russians raided Amastris, a Byzantine city on the southern shore of the Black Sea, and twenty years later Constantinople itself came under Russian attack. This last raid, however, seems to have been made in coöperation with another Russian group which had in the meantime risen in the north, and it is to the origins of this second branch that we must now turn our attention.

9.

THE aggressive Khazar policy which, as we have seen, resulted in the severance of commercial relations between the Taman Russians and the producing areas to the north, affected not only the Russian Kaganate but also Staraia Russa and the whole Lake Ilmen region. It soon became obvious that the sending of a strong expeditionary force from the north to re-establish the trade routes was the only feasible solution to the serious economic crisis which had rapidly developed throughout that area. That plan, however, could not be immediately carried out for there were not, apparently, enough Norse troops available in north Russia to attempt such a serious undertaking. That shortage of troops seems to have been the reason for the "calling of the Varangians from over the sea" which for centuries has been considered "the beginning of Russian history"—according to tradition in 862, but actually about 856.

The call was answered by Riurik (in the Frankish Annals, Roric), the famous Norse adventurer and pirate who, as vassal of the Emperor Lothaire, was then the ruler of southern Jutland and Friesland. Though he soon restored order to north Russia and established himself firmly in Staraia Ladoga and later in Novgorod, he displayed no interest in extending his dominions southward as the Russians had hoped. His chief concern continued to be the developments in western Europe and on several occasions he was forced to rush west in order to secure his holding in Friesland. While Riurik himself did nothing to relieve the Swedish-Russian merchants of Staraia Russa, he raised no objections to their organizing an expedition on their own account. This they did, and about 858 a band of their warriors succeeded in reaching Kiev and in establishing themselves there under an agreement with the Magyars. From Kiev they were able to rejoin forces with the Taman Russians and with them to make the attack of June 860 on Constantinople which was mentioned in the preceding section.

However, even this union of the two Russian groups did not provide sufficient military strength to attain their objectives and they were at length forced to retire. Nevertheless, there was one important indirect result of this campaign, for the Byzantine Patriarch Photius seized the opportunity to send missionaries after the retreating Russians. Several years later a considerable part of the Russians were baptized and in 867 they accepted a bishop whose see was probably at Tmutorokan on the Taman Peninsula.

When Riurik died about 873, his successor, Oleg, who was a Norwegian by birth, shifted his attention to the south. Some five years later he entered Kiev at the head of a strong force and, after killing the leaders of the Swedish Rus who had been in control there, set himself up as an independent ruler. Thus a new state, the so-called Kievan Russia, came into being.

The Kievan state, military and trading in character, was based economically on the control of the Dnieper waterway instead of the Azov area. It continued as the intermediary between the wooded north, the southern steppes, and Byzantium, and the Russians tried also to keep open the old trade route to the Arabians. Twice during the first half of the tenth century they staged military campaigns in the Caucasus and along the southwestern shores of the Caspian Sea —campaigns which had an additional and secondary commercial aspect in the loot they yielded.

The trading character of the new state was exemplified in more orthodox fashion by the relations with Byzantium which were, on the whole, of a more organized character. Every spring expeditions of Varangian and Slavonic traders set out down the Dnieper from Kiev in crude long boats hewn from the trunks of trees. They carried furs, wax, honey, and slaves and in Constantinople received in exchange fine wines and rich fabrics. The military protection necessary for such a valuable cargo was provided by the prince and his *druzhina,* and consequently the prince participated in the undertaking as one of the largest shareholders and chief beneficiaries.

In spite of their commercial connections with Constantinople, the Russians several times during the first half of the tenth century launched military campaigns against the Byzantine Empire. While several of these raids were instituted purely for plunder, others were intended to protect the rights of the Russian traders and to defend their freedom to trade in Byzantium. Throughout this period the Russians seem to have worked assiduously to develop trade alliances in the south and in 911 and again in 944 were able to conclude treaties with the Greeks.

However, Byzantium, which had first attracted Russian warriors and traders by its riches and by the brilliance of the court and the capital, affected them in a more general way as well. Soon those Russians engaged in the southern trade began to fall under the influence of Byzantium's spiritual culture and by the middle of the tenth century a considerable number had been converted to Christianity. That these conversions created a delicate diplomatic situation is indicated by the treaty of 944 which specifically provided that a part of the Russian traders were to perform their rites according to the Christian customs while the rest continued in the old pagan manner. Later, however, the Princess Olga herself was converted and received by the Court in 957 where, according to the "Ceremonial Book" of Emperor

Constantine Porphyrogenitus which contains a detailed description of her reception in the great Byzantine palace in Constantinople, she was recognized as the head of the Russians but, following Byzantine custom, was not accorded the highest honors.

10.

THE real expansion of the Kievan state began with the reign of Olga's son, Sviatoslav, a man of extraordinary strength and resourcefulness and certainly one of the most energetic characters in early Russian history. Though he took over the reigns of government during the lifetime of his mother, there was little to interest him in the internal administration of the country which he left almost completely in Olga's hands. He preferred to spend almost the whole of his reign, from 964 to 972, campaigning far from the capital.

Sviatoslav seems to have gloried in the hard life of the military campaigner. When his mother entreated him to accept Christianity, he is said to have replied, "How can I alone change my faith? The *druzhina* would laugh at me." In the words of the old chronicler, he was as brave and quick as a panther. In the field his armies moved without baggage trains, and Sviatoslav himself shared the hardships of his men: he ate no boiled meat, but cooked horseflesh or game over the coals of the campfire; he carried no tent but slept in the open on a saddle cloth and used a saddle for a pillow. When he attacked, he scorned the use of stealth but instead sent messengers ahead announcing, "I come against you."

Sviatoslav's first campaigns were against the Khazars. After he had conquered one of their vassal Slavonic tribes along the Oka River, he attacked the Khazars themselves and by 965 had completely despoiled their empire and captured their chief towns, Sarkel on the Don and Itil on the Volga. In contrast to the marauding expeditions which the Russians had conducted during the first half of the tenth century primarily to obtain plunder, Sviatoslav's campaigns were essentially political in character. Having overthrown the Khazar Empire, he intended to entrench himself on the lower Volga and erect a new empire on the ruins of the old, and had he been content to remain there it seems likely that he would have become the natural successor to the Khazars. Incidentally, at this point we come again to one of those abrupt turns which make the study of history so fascinating. The Russian chronicles of the time record the efforts of the religious leaders of the Khazars and Volga Bulgars to convert Sviatoslav's son, Vladimir, to Judaism and Islam, and it is interesting to speculate on the possible course of history had the Russian princes after him adopted either of these faiths instead of Christianity.

However, Sviatoslav was a restless character, and when the Byzantine emperor called on him for aid against the Bulgars on the Danube, he left Itil—after stationing a small force, perhaps, to guard the newly conquered territory. His campaign against the Bulgars in 967 proved highly successful, and when he had occupied the town of Pereyaslavets on the Danube he was satisfied to entrench himself and give up dreams of further conquests. "I desire to live in this place on the Danube," he said. "Here is the center of my lands. Here are to be had all good things: gold, cloth, wines, and fruits of the Greeks, silver and horses of the Czechs and Hungarians, and furs, wax, honey, and slaves from Russia."

Indeed, with the conquest of the Bulgars Sviatoslav had carried to completion a political plan of broad vision. He had become the successor of the nomadic emperors and so occupied a unique and strategic position.

At that time he controlled an empire of tremendous proportions, far greater than that of the Avars or Khazars, for it included within its sweep the mouths of both the Volga and the Danube. In size it could be compared only to the Hunnic Empire of the fourth and fifth centuries, but to the central steppes which the Huns had ruled Sviatoslav had added the tremendous expanses of the forest states of Kiev and Novgorod.

After the conquest of the Khazars, it is probable that Sviatoslav assumed the title of Kagan to follow in the tradition of the first Russian Kaganate. We know that his successors bore the title and there is a record of the Metropolitan Bishop Hilarion ascribing it in the middle of the eleventh century to Vladimir the Saint and Yaroslav the Wise.

The empire of Sviatoslav first began to crumble in the east. Following the decline and later dissolution of the Khazar power, there appeared in the south of Russia a new force, another Turkish tribe called the Pecheniegs. Taking advantage of the absence of Sviatoslav with the main Russian armies, they besieged Kiev and forced him to return hastily from the Danube to save his mother and the citizens of the beleaguered city. He relieved Kiev, but after the death of Olga in 969 did not remain long in the capital, preferring to establish his sons as rulers of the principal towns while he himself returned to the Danube. But by now the whole eastern frontier of the empire was aflame with revolt. In addition, the Greeks could never reconcile themselves to the fact that by enlisting Sviatoslav's aid against the Bulgarians they had merely replaced one enemy by another, the Russians. Finally, the Emperor John Tsimiskes, one of Byzantium's most brilliant military leaders, personally led a campaign against Sviatoslav, defeated him, and besieged him in a fortress. In 971 Sviatoslav was forced to accept peace terms which included the condition that he leave Bulgaria and the following year, while the dispirited Russian armies were returning to Kiev, they were surprised and defeated by the Pecheniegs. In the battle Sviatoslav was killed and—so the old story goes—a Pechenieg prince afterward made himself a drinking cup of his skull.

CHAPTER II.

THE STRUGGLE WITH THE STEPPE

(972–1238)

I.

AT the end of the tenth century the Russian people occupied almost the whole of the great area from the Finnish Gulf and Lake Ladoga in the north, to the lower Danube, the Black Sea, the Azov Sea, and the Caspian Sea in the south. From east to west the territory stretched from the Oka and the Don rivers to the Tisa and the Marosh rivers, within the boundaries of present-day Hungary. But from the end of the tenth to the middle of the thirteenth centuries the area occupied by the Russian people did not remain unaltered. The changes consisted principally in the gradual loss of the southern steppe zone and the loss of communication with the southern seas. The nomadic peoples of the steppes wedged themselves in between the southern seas and the territories occupied by the Russians. Bitter struggles characterized the whole period. The Russian princes at times attempted to fight against Turkish tribes with the help of Turkish allies. They were not always in agreement among themselves; and many of them, during such quarrels, hired Turkish mercenaries. The Russian princes attempted to fortify themselves against the steppe by the construction of trenches and forts. From the point of view of the basic unity of the process of Russian history it is significant that later on similar lines of defense against the steppe were built by the tsars of the sixteenth to eighteenth centuries. But in spite of all their efforts the Russians of the Kievan period were forced to retreat to the north.

In the middle of the thirteenth century the southern frontier of Russian people followed a line from Moldavia to the lower course of the Oka and northeast to Viatka. The losses of territory in the south may be illustrated by the example of the town Tmutorokan. In the eleventh century Tmutorokan, near the straits of Kerch, was a strong Russian center. In the chronicles of the twelfth century it is no longer mentioned. The Russians, however, remained strongly entrenched in the southwestern corner of Eurasia, the Carpathian Mountains, and Moldavia, in spite of the ferocious attacks of the Magyars on one side and the Pecheniegs on the other. Russian settlements on the lower Danube as late as the twelfth century were included in the Byzantine Empire and later in the Bulgarian Kingdom.

North of the Carpathians the Russians were subjected to the pressure of the Hungarians and the Poles, but successfully resisted them and the boundary was moved westward. Farther to the north the Russian land, prior to the thirteenth century, was in a relatively peaceful state. The former line from the Nieman to Lake Peipus and along the river Narov to the Gulf of Finland was retained. In the eleventh century the town of Yuriev (now Tartu) was founded west of Lake Peipus. In the north and northeast the Russians moved forward and occupied new territories. The White Sea, the Arctic Ocean, and the Ural Mountains were reached. Similarly Russian colonists in the east moved during the nineteenth century to the lower course of the Oka and the middle Volga.

2.

THE death of Sviatoslav was followed by the collapse of his ambitious plan of uniting the forests and the steppes and controlling the trade of both the Black Sea and the Caspian Sea. The Russian princes were forced to concentrate almost all their attention upon the internal organization of their states and upon defense against the invaders of the steppes. The nomadic tribesmen who, like the Khazars, in earlier times had united the forests and the steppes under one rule, now became again a dangerous enemy. One wave succeeded the other; after the Pecheniegs there appeared the Cumans. For a long time neither the forest nor the steppe succeeded in completely crushing the other. The forces of the Kiev state and the nomadic tribes in the south of Russia were approximately equal, and their struggle was long and indecisive.

After the death of Sviatoslav his sons fell into dispute. Victory came to Vladimir in 980. The most important event during his reign was his conversion to Christianity and the institution of

Christianity as the official religion not only of the princely house but of the whole Russian people. The baptism of the Princess Olga some years earlier had not had this result.

As we have seen above, part of the Russian people were converted to Christianity in the ninth and tenth centuries. The pagan religious ideology was broken down. There was a need for a new faith. The ancient Russian chronicles contained an account of Vladimir's christening after a long period of indecision. According to the chronicler, in 986 Vladimir was visited by religious missions of different faiths and churches: Mohammedans from the Bulgars of the Volga, Roman Catholics from Germany, Khazars professing Judaism, and a Greek philosopher of the Orthodox faith. Incidentally, the division of the Roman and Greek churches finally took place in 1054, but there was a division in fact in 867. The picture presented by the chronicler was not a mere rhetorical figure but an exact reflection of the facts. These different religions were professed partly by neighbors and partly even by inhabitants of the Kiev state.

The acceptance of one or another of these faiths must necessarily have determined the future cultural and political development of Russia. The acceptance of Islam would have drawn Russia into the circle of Arabian culture—that is, an Asiatic-Egyptian culture. The acceptance of Roman Christianity from the Germans would have made Russia a country of Latin or European culture. The acceptance of either Judaism or Orthodox Christianity insured to Russia cultural independence of both Europe and Asia.

Political arguments could be mustered equally in favor of Judaism and Orthodoxy. On the one hand, there were the same arguments that converted the Khan of the Khazars to Judaism, that is, the desire to secure political and religious independence from the strongest churches and states of the eastern Mediterranean. On the other hand, in favor of Orthodoxy, there were arguments of a different nature—the advantages of a cultural union with Byzantium, which already had close trade relations with Russia. Aside from political calculation the question of faith had also to be decided with regard to spiritual needs, for the question of a new faith had arisen in view of the inadequacy of the old Russian paganism. According to the chronicler, Vladimir, after listening to the representatives of the various religious missions, seemed to be favorably impressed by the Greek philosopher. Before making a final decision, however, he dispatched his emissaries to the neighboring countries in order to observe "by whom and how God was worshipped." The accounts of his emissaries finally determined Vladimir to accept baptism into the Orthodox church. The Russian emissaries, in telling of how they attended a service in Saint Sophia in Constantinople, related that they did not know whether they were on earth or in heaven.

Prior to the official conversion of Russia to Christianity, there occurred political complications with Byzantium. Vladimir undertook a campaign against the Greek town Chersonesus. Following a prolonged siege the city surrendered to the Russian prince. The Byzantine emperor agreed to give Vladimir the Byzantine princess, Anne, in marriage. Upon his return from the Chersonesus campaign, Vladimir organized a general christening of his subjects (about 989 A.D.). At the same time the people of Novgorod were likewise christened, but with them force had to be used, since their paganism was more strongly entrenched. The Christian churches were built upon the former places of pagan worship. A few years after the conversion of Vladimir, the legal position of the church was fixed by the order regarding the collection of a tithe for the benefit of the church of the Our Lady in Kiev, about 996, and the statute regarding church courts in 1010.

3.

FOLLOWING the death of Vladimir the Saint, just as in the case of Sviatoslav, an internecine strife broke out among his sons. Victory lay at first with his eldest son Sviatopolk. To protect himself against his brothers Sviatopolk took recourse to murder. At his orders, Boris and Gleb, later venerated by the Russian church as saints, were put to death. But Sviatopolk did not succeed in getting rid of his most dangerous rival, likewise his brother, the prince of Novgorod, Yaroslav. Between Sviatopolk and Yaroslav there began a struggle. Yaroslav received support from his subjects and the Varangians, whose forces were augmented by mercenaries brought from across the sea. Sviatopolk concluded an alliance with his father-in-law, the Polish king, Boleslav the Brave. While Yaroslav remained true to Orthodoxy, Sviatopolk found support from western Roman Catholicism. The struggle between the brothers took on a far wider significance than a family disagreement. The victory of Sviatopolk would have subjected Russia to Polish and Catholic influence.

After a long period of indecisive struggle Yaroslav finally defeated his brother in 1019. Sviatopolk was killed during his retreat. Following this victory over his brother and the subjection of Kiev, Yaroslav entered into a conflict with his other brother, Mstislav. The latter was an interesting figure in the history of ancient Russia. He had attempted on a smaller scale to recreate the empire of his grandfather, Sviatoslav. In doing so he started not from the north but from the south. He ruled over the eastern corner of the Black Sea coast from the city of Tmutorokan and attempted to extend his power northward. In this respect his policy followed the tradition of the Khazar Khans of adding the forest regions of the Dnieper to their empire of the steppes. The two-year war between the brothers resulted in the victory of Mstislav. Yaroslav was forced to agree to a division of the Russian state along the line of the Dnieper. Several years later Mstislav died and in 1036 Yaroslav became head of both parts of the Russian lands. In the same year Yaroslav completely defeated the Pecheniegs who had advanced again on Kiev. From this time on the Pecheniegs never again attacked this town.

The internal policy of Yaroslav was of great significance. During his reign the first laws regulating procedure were drawn up. This collection of laws was known as the Russian Law. Yaroslav first granted the laws to his Novgorod subjects as a reward for their aid in his struggle against Sviatopolk. Later, the law was also promulgated in Kiev. The laws of Yaroslav attempted to limit the prevailing custom of blood vengeance for murder, by empowering only certain relatives to avenge a murder, in whose absence the murderer was fined by the treasury of the prince. The Russian Law was the product of a combination of Norman and Slavonic customs. A jurist having acquaintance with the Roman and Byzantine law took part in its formulation. Yaroslav, furthermore, defined the powers of the church courts and the property rights of the church, thus adding to the ecclesiastical legislation of Vladimir.

Imitating the Byzantine emperors, Yaroslav wanted to make

Kiev an imperial city similar to Constantinople. He embellished the city with beautiful buildings, some of which, like the church of St. Sophia, were constructed by Greek masters. In St. Sophia of Kiev Yaroslav brought together a collection of books. He also organized schools for the children of the *druzhina.* During his own life or that of his immediate successor, the World History of the Greek chronicler, George Hamartolos, and the collection of laws regulating ecclesiastical matters (*nomokanon*) were translated into Slavonic. In his reign there appeared a remarkable leader in the Russian church, Hilarion, the first Metropolitan of Russian origin (1051). He was fully educated in Greek ecclesiastical matters, and his profound wisdom and oratorical power are evidenced by one of his surviving addresses in which he spoke of the significance of Russian conversion to Christianity. Hilarion, even before he became Metropolitan, was known for his deeply religious life. In his earlier days he had dug for himself a cave in a hill near Kiev, for spiritual meditation. He may therefore be regarded as the founder of the Kiev Monastery of the Caves, which flourished under the sons of Yaroslav. Less than one hundred years following the conversion of Russia, the church could boast of such Christian leaders as Anthony and Theodosius of the Kiev monastery.

4.

After the death of Yaroslav in 1054 Russia was divided into principalities ruled by his sons. As the royal house increased with each generation, these principalities were broken up into a greater number of parts. The subdivision of the Russian land under the descendants of Yaroslav, however, was not permanent. The princes frequently moved from one town to another. The eldest of the family always tried to occupy the throne of Kiev which was regarded as the highest. Following the death of each Kiev prince, a general movement of princes took place. The power was vested in the whole royal family and was constantly being reallocated between members of the family—a custom that corresponded to the principles of property ownership in ancient Russia. There is much in common between this custom and the later customs of the peasant commune.

As might be expected, the distribution of power was frequently complicated by the personal ambitions of individual princes. Of considerable moment, likewise, were the desires of the population of the large towns. The popular council or *vieche* frequently refused to accept a new prince and called in another following its own wishes. However, in most cases the prince was selected from the dynasty of Yaroslav.

Principally in view of this custom, Russian history from the second half of the eleventh century to the first half of the thirteenth century is full of civil strife between princes. To strengthen their power, some of these princes frequently allied themselves with foreigners—Hungarians, Poles, or Cumans. At the end of the eleventh century and the beginning of the twelfth century, efforts were made to form an alliance among the princes. A family *seim* or council was called on several occasions. The idea of a general alliance of princes was supported by one of the best men of the time, a grandson of Yaroslav, Vladimir Monomakh, prince of Kiev. His death in 1125 brought to an end the efforts to form an alliance. Russia began to fall apart. In place of a single cultural and national center in Kiev, in the middle of the twelfth century a number of local centers came into existence: the Galician principality in the west; Novgorod in the north; the Vladimir-Suzdal principality in the northeast; and Kiev in the south. The importance of Kiev was shaken in 1169 when it was captured from Vladimir by the armies of Prince Andrei Bogolubsky. The city also suffered severely from the sacking of Constantinople by the Crusaders in 1204. The Greek Empire never quite recovered from this. A Latin empire was founded in Constantinople and lasted until 1261 when the Greeks overthrew it; but the Greek Empire never regained its strength. Prior to these events in Byzantine history the Greeks had played an important part in the political life of the Russians. Byzantium sent to Kiev metropolitans who then headed the Russian church and constantly attempted to secure alliances with Russian princes by marriage with Byzantine princesses or aristocrats. The mother of Vladimir Monomakh was a Greek princess, and the mother of Andrei Bogolubsky was also a Greek.

Byzantium attempted to employ the Russian princes in its own politics. Thus, in the twelfth century, during a war with Hungary, Byzantium sought to form an alliance with the Galician princes for the purpose of attacking Hungary from the northeast. As the

Galician princes were unfriendly with the Kiev princes, Byzantium attempted to raise the enemies of Kiev in Suzdal to counterbalance Kiev. On the other hand, in the second half of the twelfth century, when the Galician princes allied themselves with Hungary, Byzantium sought an alliance with the Kiev princes, setting them up against the Galician princes.

A constant struggle was waged by the Russian princes against the Cumans, nomadic tribesmen in the steppe zone who made frequent raids upon the Russian principalities, subjecting them to terrible destruction and enslaving the inhabitants. The Russian princes from time to time undertook campaigns against the Cumans; but although they occasionally defeated the mounted nomads, the Cumans invariably saved themselves by flight. The Russians could not completely subdue their nomadic enemy; and sometimes the Russian campaigns in the steppes were terminated by catastrophic defeat. The Cumans would trap the Russian armies and surround them on all sides. One of these unfortunate campaigns in 1185 is the subject of an old Russian epic poem "Tale of the Host of Igor."

In the thirteenth century the pressure of the Cumans was weakened and the alliances between separate Russian princes and Cuman Khan's increased in frequency. At this time new enemies arose —in the northwest, the Germans, Swedes, and Lithuanians; and in the southeast, the Mongols.

The Germans appeared at the mouth of the Western Dvina in the middle of the twelfth century, their first contacts with the natives being peaceful. Most of them were traders and missionaries. In 1200 Bishop Albert founded the town of Riga at the mouth of the Dvina. The inhabitants of the region, Lithuanians and Letts, were converted to Christianity with difficulty. Then there came warriors in support of the missionaries. An order of knights similar to those who fought against the Moslems in the Holy Land was organized. This order was known as the Sword-Bearers, their distinguishing mark being a cape with a red cross and a sword on the shoulder. The Sword-Bearers were subject to the orders of their master and were responsible to the Livonian bishop. They extended their power rapidly eastward from Riga in the direction of Pskov and Polotsk. The region southwest of the Livonian Order of Sword-Bearers, between the Nieman and the Vistula, was occupied by the Teutonic Order of Knights, wearing a black cape and white cross. The Teutonic Order first came into existence for the purpose of fighting the Moslems, but in view of the hopelessness of the struggle in the Holy Land the Order moved in 1230 to the Baltic Sea at the invitation of a Polish prince, who asked them to protect him against the attacks of a Lithuanian tribe of Prussians. The Knights conquered the Prussians and created a German state, later Prussia.

Tribes of Letts and Lithuanians united to struggle against the German knights. For the most part they were unsuccessful, and the result was a movement of Letts and Lithuanians eastward into the Russian lands. Thus arose the threat of Lithuanian conquest in the northern principalities. Meanwhile the civil strife among the Russian princes continued. A leading part was played in the early thirteenth century by Prince Mstislav the Daring, a brilliant fighter, but unsuccessful in his policies. Mstislav took part in the wars between Smolensk and Kiev, Novgorod and Suzdal. He was allied with the Cumans and defended the Galician principality against the Hungarians, but nowhere did he achieve permanent political conquests. The glory of fighting was all he desired; everything else was unimportant. In character he resembled many of the western knights of his time, being perhaps most akin to Richard the Lion-Hearted.

While the Russian princes continued their endless feuds, a new danger appeared in the east. A wave of nomadic peoples with unprecedented force was advancing westward. This wave flooded the Russian land, submerging the princes and their quarrels.

In 1223 the Mongols or Tartars appeared in the southeast. Fleeing from the Mongolian advance, the Cumans sought the aid of the Russian princes. Khan Kotian, father-in-law of Mstislav the Daring, said: "Today they have taken our land; tomorrow they will take yours." Mstislav undertook the organization of an alliance of Russian princes against the Tartars. The emissaries sent by the Mongols to the Russian princes were killed. It was decided at a conference called in Kiev not to await the enemy but to go out and meet him in the midst of the steppes. The meeting took place on the river Kalka near the Azov Sea. The Russian troops fought bravely but without coöperation among themselves or with the Cumans. Meanwhile, the Mongolian armies were led by the experienced generals Djebe and Subutai. The Mongolians first defeated the Cumans and part of the Russian troops before the Kiev warriors could take part in the struggle. The Kiev prince then shut himself up in an armed camp on the shore of the Kalka. For three days he resisted the enemy, but was forced to buy his freedom and retreat. But the Mongolians did not abide by the convention and killed all their enemies. The Prince of Kiev was crushed to death under planks.

Following their victory the Mongolians did not advance upon the Russian territory but turned back. During the following fifteen years Russia heard nothing of the Mongolians. The chronicler wrote of those "evil Tartars": "Only God knows whence they came and whither they went."

5.

THE political organization of the Russian principalities in the pre-Mongolian period was a combination of monarchical, aristocratic, and democratic government. The monarchical element was to be found in the person of the prince, who in ancient Russia was, however, not an autocratic ruler. His chief function was military. His duty was to defend the town from enemies outside. Another important function of the prince was judicial. He appointed special agents to render judgment in litigations among his subjects.

The aristocratic element was to be found in the prince's council. Every prince had a council composed of the higher officers of his *druzhina*. This council discussed the most important questions of government and generally took part in legislation.

The democratic element of government was to be found in the popular gathering known as the *vieche*. This was not a representative body, but consisted of all the adult males of the population of each town. Unanimity was necessary before the *vieche* could arrive at a decision. In practice this requirement frequently led to armed encounters between the opposing groups in the *vieche*, after which the defeated side would acquiesce in the decision of the victors. The *vieche* of the capital of the principality had authority over the smaller towns.

These three elements of power appeared in all Russian principalities of the Mongolian period, but the relative importance of each differed from place to place. The *vieche* was especially powerful in the large trading city of northern Russia—Novgorod. During the Mongolian period its population grew very rapidly and was estimated at over two hundred thousand. The peculiarities of the form of government in Novgorod became fixed only in the end of the thirteenth and the beginning of the fourteenth centuries. Their origin, however, went back to the eleventh and twelfth centuries. The prince was served by two elected aides—the *Posadnik* (mayor) and the *Tysiatsky* or Chief of the Thousand—the militia commander—without whom he could make no decision. A custom also developed gradually by which the prince in assuming power was required to kiss the cross of Novgorod as he took his oath. The Novgorod *vieche* had a permanent chancellory—the *vieche* house. In practice the affairs of the city were managed by a council of merchants. Novgorod was divided into five sections. These sections were in turn divided into "hundreds" and the "hundreds" into streets. At the *vieche* the people were organized along these lines of division. When unanimity was not reached and the opposing sides fought, they usually met on the bridge over the Volkhov River.

The aristocratic element was particularly strong in southwestern Russia, in the principalities of Galicia and Volyn. The council of *boyars* dominated the political life of these principalities. It is possible that one of the causes of the aristocratic domination in western Russia was the influence of western feudalism coming through Poland and Hungary. The prince was forced to submit to the *boyars* or to fight them. One of the energetic princes of southwestern Russia said about the *boyars*—"without crushing the bees the honey cannot be eaten." This refers to the custom of keeping bees in hollow tree trunks, which necessitated killing the bees to obtain the honey.

The monarchical element was particularly developed in northeastern Russia. The development of princely power was greatly aided by the dominating personality of Prince Andrei Bogolubsky, who was killed in 1175.

Notwithstanding all the differences in the political organization of separate principalities, the *vieche* and the council of *boyars* may be found in all of them. The only question was which of these elements was strongest.

The social stratification of the old Russian principalities was also almost identical. Ancient Russian society was divided into two basic groups, the freemen and the slaves. The chief reason for slavery was economic necessity. A man sold himself into slavery when he had no more means with which to subsist. Besides, almost all war prisoners were made slaves. Between the slaves and the freemen was an intermediary class of people, *zakupy,* half slaves and half free, who were forced to work in return for borrowed money.

Among the freemen there were no fixed classes and it was easy to pass from one group or occupation to another. It is therefore possible to speak only roughly of the groups into which free society was divided. They were four in number: the Church, including priests and monks; the *boyars*—the officers of the prince's army and the large landowners; the townsmen—traders and craftsmen; and finally, the peasants.

During the period between the tenth and the twelfth centuries the clan system of old Russia broke down. Individuals took on a greater and greater significance. The chief elements of economic life were foreign trade and agriculture. The society of the time was organized on the basis of private property vested in the individual or in the family. The oldest land deed found, of the year 1147, shows freedom of purchase and sale of land. The contemporary law was greatly influenced by Byzantium. Byzantine law, which was in fact Roman law, penetrated to Russia through the church.

6.

THE spiritual culture of ancient Russia came, together with the church, from Byzantium—a culture principally religious. The church, therefore, was the chief cultural force of ancient Russia.

Following the conversion of the Russians under Vladimir, paganism was stamped out in the towns very quickly, but stubbornly maintained itself in the country districts. Pagan influences long persisted in the popular beliefs. Little is known of the organization of the Russian church in the first fifty years following the conversion. It was only after Yaroslav became the sole ruler of Russia that he was in a position properly to organize the church administration. Thus the Russian church took definite form only in 1037. It was a metropolitan district of the ecumenical patriarchate of

Constantinople. The metropolitan was nominated by Constantinople and was usually a Greek. There were only two exceptions to this rule, in the cases of Metropolitan Hilarion in the eleventh century and Metropolitan Clement in the twelfth century. The bishops were sometimes Greek, but for the most part Russian. In the time of Yaroslav there were ten bishops. Later the number increased. An important center of spiritual life in pre-Mongolian Russia was the Kiev Monastery of the Caves.

The first literary work in Russia was the edition of the books of church ritual and of church law translated from the Greek to serve the purposes of the Russian church. Some of these books were translated into Slavonic in Russia; others were brought from Bulgaria in Slavonic translation. The church Slavonic language of Bulgaria was the literary and church language of ancient Russia. At this time the difference between the Russian language and the south Slavonic language was much less than at present. The church Slavonic language in Russia was itself gradually changed by the infiltration of Russian. Religious literature rapidly came into existence: the sermons of the Russian bishops and the lives of the first Russian saints and monks. The church at this time was not a secluded organization, but stood at the head of national thought. It was within the monastery walls and the church circles that the first chronicles of contemporary events both of the church and lay world were compiled. At the end of the eleventh century one of the monks of the Kiev Monastery of the Caves wrote the first all-Russian chronicle on the basis of the records of Kiev and Novgorod. In the beginning of the twelfth century this chronicle was given literary form. Thus came into existence the first history of Russia, known as the *Poviest vremennykh let* (Annals). It has come to us only in manuscripts of the fourteenth and fifteenth centuries. This history is filled with the idea of the cultural and racial unity of the Russians and of their relationship to the whole Orthodox Christian world. The Kiev history led to the development of similar writings in every principality. Every prince and bishop had a chronicler record events in his domain. These ancient Russian annals are saturated with religious thought and the causes of historic events are usually ascribed to the struggle between Christianity and the evil forces in the human soul. Together with the church literature there grew up also a lay literature. This type of writing originated in the society of the military aristocracy, the *druzhina,* and is characterized by its requirements and tastes. For the most part the lay literature is an epic description of military feats of various princes and warriors. The most famous is the "Tale of the Host of Igor," a song of the heroic though unsuccessful campaign against the Cumans by Prince Igor in 1185. Many other epic songs, the so-called *bylinas,* were composed in this period as well as in the course of succeeding centuries. These *bylinas* were still chanted by peasants in remote villages of northern Russia in the beginning of the twentieth century.

While the literature of ancient Russia developed rapidly and began to free itself practically from church influence, the art of ancient Russia remained completely dependent upon the church. The architecture, painting, and vocal music of the period were produced to satisfy the demands of the church. Instrumental music was not used in the services of the Orthodox church. Prior to the fifteenth century, singing in Russia was in unison. Only in the fifteenth and sixteenth centuries was harmony developed. Sculpture, which had found some place in the Greek church, was rarely used in the Russian church. In the eleventh century the principal towns of the time, Kiev, Novgorod, and Chernigov, built large stone churches. These were at first constructed by foreign masters from the Byzantine Empire. In these churches the influence of the architecture of Constantinople and the Byzantine provinces in the Near East may be observed, but in some examples, as in the Church of St. Sophia in Novgorod, certain changes from Byzantine prototypes are to be noted, made apparently to satisfy the tastes of the Russians.

In the twelfth and thirteenth centuries German masters appeared, but at the same time craftsmanship was developed among the Russians themselves. Of great artistic importance are the twelfth and thirteenth century churches of northeastern Russia. The architectural decoration of these churches shows the influence of the Orthodox East—Armenia and Georgia. They also have many features in common with the western Romanesque architecture.

Religious painting of ancient Russia was likewise influenced by Byzantium and the Near East. Contemporary painting took two forms, frescoes on the walls of churches and portable icons. Both these forms came from Byzantium and as in the case of architecture, were executed at first by Greek masters and only later by Russians. Some icons were imported directly from Byzantine. Mosaics were also used in ancient Russia. The remains of some fine examples exist in St. Sophia in Kiev.

Icons were a characteristic expression of the customs of the Orthodox church. They represented Jesus Christ, Our Lady, the Saints, or scenes from their lives. The icon, however, is not a portrait but an object of veneration. This use of the icon was recognized following the defeat of the iconoclastic party in Byzantium in the middle of the ninth century. The Orthodox believer places his icon in a prominent place in his home, in Russia usually in a corner. A wick is lighted before it and prayers are said facing the icon. It is in fact a symbol or a reminder of the spiritual world to the believer, and its purpose is to raise corresponding emotions in the soul. For this reason ancient Russian iconography had a much more powerful psychological influence than ordinary painting. The old icon-painters approached their task with religious feeling and in this likewise differed from lay artists.

CHAPTER III.

RUSSIA UNDER THE SWAY OF THE STEPPES

(1238–1452)

I.

THE Mongolian period is of enormous significance in Russian history. The invasion began the separation of the eastern and western parts of the Russian people. Finding themselves divided politically between the Mongols and the Lithuanians, the Russians split into two sections culturally distinct. The territorial distribution of the Russians remained, however, practically the same as in the preceding period. In the thirteenth century, following the ruin caused by the first Mongolian invasion, a movement of population from the middle Dnieper region took place northeastward into the region of the upper Volga and Oka rivers; but the general retreat of the Russians from the southern steppes to the north practically ceased. The Russians settled where they were in the thirteenth century, on the border of the steppes, preparing to advance into them again.

Progress into the steppe regions was most rapid in the southwest, where in the second half of the fourteenth century the Russians in the Grand Duchy of Lithuania reached the Black Sea between the Dniester and southern Bug rivers. In the southeast other Russians from Moscow and Suzdal penetrated peacefully, moving far down the Volga and Don. A considerable number of Russians settled in Sarai, as is witnessed by the formation of an Orthodox bishopric there. Russian merchants in considerable numbers visited the northern Caucasus. Furthermore, Russian soldiers recruited by their Mongolian masters frequently took part in engagements in China. Simultaneously, the colonization of the north continued. Novgorod merchants pushed farther and farther into the northern forests.

2.

At the end of the twelfth century, as on several earlier occasions, the Mongolian tribes of eastern Eurasia experienced a great intensification of national energy. Among their chieftains there appeared a man of unusual power of will and vision, Temuchin, the "barbaric genius." Born in 1155 of a noble family, he made himself leader of the Mongolian aristocrats, who desired to create a powerful state in the steppes. He was elected "Khan" of this group and named Genghis, Heavenly Emperor. This name, connected with the Altaic religion, indicated his complete autocracy. Upon his appointment as Khan, Genghis immediately set about organizing his forces. The fighters were divided into "tens," "hundreds," and "thousands." He carefully selected his assistants among men he knew well. Attention was paid to the supply of the army. The most important part of his army was the Guard, who served as the personal troops of the Khan and were the picked portion of the whole army. They were organized along strictly aristocratic lines, and a special "thousand" within the Guard was composed of "brave fighters." Over all his troops Genghis wielded an iron discipline.

When the organization of the Mongolian army was finished, the world expansion of the Mongols commenced. War was decided upon at the meeting of the elders (*Kurultai*) at the source of the river Orkhon in 1206. The *Kurultai* appointed Genghis Khan Master over the whole Mongolian people. He first led his forces eastward toward the kingdom of northern China. The long war which followed brought Genghis into touch with Chinese statesmen familiar with ancient administrative and governmental customs. Following the capture of Peking in 1215, Ye-liu Chu-tsai, one of the outstanding statesmen of the time, a poet and scholar, astronomer and astrologer, who possessed an extraordinary talent for organization, became a close associate of Genghis. While the military organization of the Mongolian Empire must be attributed to Genghis Khan, it owed its administrative mechanism to Ye-liu Chu-tsai.

Having achieved decisive success in the east, Genghis Khan turned to the west. At this time there existed under the name of Khorezm an enormous Moslem kingdom consisting of Turkestan, Afghanistan, and Persia. With this kingdom Genghis Khan desired rather permanent trade relations than war; but the Mongolian envoys and traders were killed in 1218 in Otrar, an important town of Khorezm. This made war inevitable. Before it began, in the spring of 1219, Genghis Khan called the *Kurultai* to discuss the details of the coming conflict and to give orders to all the chiefs. In the autumn of 1219 Genghis took Otrar and in the beginning of 1220, Bokhara. The shah of Khorezm fled to Mazenderan.

The force sent to capture the fleeing shah was ordered to reconnoiter the lands already marked for conquest. The Mongolians under Djebe and Subutai passed from northern Iran to Transcaucasia. The Georgians made an effort at resistance which resulted in the destruction of the Georgian knights in battle. The Mongolian force crossed the Caucasus and passed into the steppes of the Don and the land of the Cumans. As we have already seen, the Russian princes came to the help of the Cumans and a battle took place on the river Kalka, following which the Mongolians turned back. The expedition had accomplished its purposes; but, as has been said, the sudden appearance and disappearance of the Mongolians seemed to the Russians of the time quite inexplicable. It is doubtful that the question arose among the Russians of that day, whether the appearance of the Mongolians in 1223 was accidental, what forces had caused it, and whether it would be repeated. No information was available as to what transpired in the depths of Eurasia. No one took into consideration the calculations of the framers of Mongolian policy.

Genghis Khan died in 1227 in the midst of a successful campaign against a tribe of Tanguts, but his death did not mean the breakdown of the military organization of the Mongolians. His son Ugedey was appointed his successor. Ye-liu Chu-tsai now rose to a position of unparalleled importance.

The first stage of the Mongolian program of conquest was completed during the life of Genghis Khan in the twenties of the twelfth century. The preparation for the second stage began ten years later. When all the internal arrangements were completed a further advance was decided upon at the *Kurultai* which met at Karakorum in 1235 and determined that the Mongolian armies should move in three directions: China, Persia, and Russia. At the head of the Russian expedition was placed Batu, grandson of

Genghis, and nephew of Ugedey. Batu was accompanied by representatives of other descendants of Genghis Khan. Military control was in the hands of Subutai personally, one of the most talented of all the leaders of Genghis Khan. He had under him from 120,000 to 150,000 horsemen, and in 1236–37 he completed their concentration on the Volga.

Batu turned first of all against the Bulgarians of the Volga who refused to recognize the Mongolian power. Having vanquished them, he crossed the Volga in the end of 1237 and approached the boundaries of the principality of Riazan. He demanded submission and money tribute. Riazan refused and was conquered. Then, having subjugated the principality of Vladimir, the Tartars pursued its prince, George Vsevolodich, and crushed his army, George being killed in battle. The Tartars moved westward through Tver toward Novgorod. They came within sixty miles of the latter and then suddenly turned southward, fearing snows and floods.

After the north Russian expedition, Batu settled on the lower Don and Volga—that is, in the same place which several centuries earlier had been the center of the Khazar Empire. He then moved westward, and in 1240 the Mongolians conquered Kiev after a desperate defense by the Russians. Many a Russian *bylina* of the time glorified the Russians' last stand at Kiev and invoked the protection of Our Lady for the Russian people.

Following the occupation of Kiev the Mongolian armies divided into two. One army advanced against Poland, defeated the Poles as well as the Germans who had come to their aid, and then turned south and invaded Hungary. The other army, led by Batu and Subutai, attacked the Magyars of Hungary and completely defeated them. The Hungarian king fled to the Adriatic Sea and Subutai sent a small mounted band after him. Batu reached Vienna and was in Klosterneuburg near Vienna when he received news of the death of Khan Ugedey. This news stopped the advance of the Mongols. Batu gave the order of retreat. The question of appointing a new Khan required his presence in Mongolia. He returned to the Black Sea through Bulgaria, thus completing a circle.

The great campaign of Batu of 1237–41 ended with his return to the Volga steppes. It had resulted in the conquest by the Mongolians of an enormous territory. Batu had brought under his sway not only the southern Russian steppes and the northern Russian forests, but also the lower Danube. Hungary remained a Mongolian province only for one year, but Bulgaria and Moldavia became a part of the Mongolian Empire for a century.

At approximately the same time, the eastern armies of the Mongolians completed the conquest of northern China and the southern army conquered Transcaucasia. Their empire in the middle of the thirteenth century included a huge region from the Pacific Ocean to the Adriatic Sea.

3.

THE great Mongolian Empire rapidly began to fall apart into *ulus* or principalities of the descendants of the house of Genghis Khan. Nominally a certain unity of the empire continued up to the middle of the fourteenth century. The Mongolian emperor in China, Kubilai, who reigned from 1257 to 1298, and his descendants, were regarded as the leading rulers in the system of Mongolian kingdoms. However, this did not prevent animosity between individual Mongolian states. Russia became part of Djuchi's *ulus* or the "Golden Horde," whose center was the town of Sarai on the lower Volga. This city was situated at the junction of the steppe and the desert zones. The Don and the Volga, which come very near to each other at this point, formed an advantageous location with regard both to Russia and to the Black Sea. It would not be amiss to explain here that the kingdom of Batu was known as the Djuchi's *ulus* after his father, Djuchi. Later on, when Djuchi's descendants became independent rulers, their state became known as the "Golden Horde," the connotation being that of wealth and power.

The first century of the existence of the "Golden Horde," up to the middle of the fourteenth century, was the time of its highest development both in respect to international politics and to internal order. The "Golden Horde" maintained close diplomatic relations with Egypt and Byzantium, while the Genoese colonies in the Crimea were the intermediaries in a lively commerce with Europe. The towns of Solkhat in the Crimea and Sarai attracted the traders of many countries, including Russia. The internal policy of the Khans of the "Golden Horde" was chiefly concerned with the protection of trade routes and the creation of strict order in their domains for this purpose.

Of considerable importance in the policy of the Mongolian

Khans was their attitude toward religion, in which they accorded complete toleration. They even acted as patrons of all religious organizations without preference. The first Mongolian Khans were Shamanists. The son of Batu who ruled the "Golden Horde" for a very short time was a Christian. The brother of Batu was a Moslem. The next Khan was again a Shamanist. Uzbek, who ruled from 1314 to 1341, was a Moslem, and only from this time on did Islam become the official religion of the Khans of the "Golden Horde." But even then the policy of toleration continued. The Russian church was not only free from oppression under the Mongolian rulers, but was especially patronized by the Mongolian Khans. In the capital city of Sarai a Russian bishopric was founded, and the bishop received freedom to preach and the right to proselytize his faith.

A different condition prevailed with respect to Russian governmental institutions. The princes were forced to recognize their complete submission to the Khan. They had to go to the Horde to receive permission to be crowned. At first they had to travel not only to Sarai but also to the great Mongolian Khan in Karakorum in Mongolia. But on these conditions they retained their power as agents of the Khan. When they fell into dispute among themselves as in the past, the deciding factor was the Khan. Frequently the quarreling princes would go to the Horde to be judged, each accusing the other of insubordination to the Khan, who judged the cases and punished offenders, at times by death.

Next to the Russian princes the Mongolians appointed their own agents in the principal Russian towns during the first years of their rule. These agents collected revenue and enlisted soldiers. Part of the recruits entered the army of the "Golden Horde" and part were sent to the Great Khan in China. Russian soldiers took part in the conquest of southern China under Kubilai Khan. At times the Horde appointed representatives with full powers on special missions to Russia, such as the punishment of a prince or a town for insubordination to the Horde. These representatives were accompanied at times by a military force.

Among the Russian princes there prevailed two general ideas as to how to regard the Mongolian power. Some princes espoused the policy of loyal submission to the Mongolian rule. This allowed them to defend the Russian lands from western attack and to strengthen their own authority. Examples of this policy were the princes of northwestern Russia. Moscow, for instance, which was first mentioned in the chronicles of the twelfth century, began to acquire great significance in the fourteenth. An outstanding instance of a prince who followed this policy was Alexander Nevsky, who died in 1263 and was later canonized by the Russian church. He succeeded in stopping the advance of the Swedes, Germans, and Lithuanians upon the northwestern territories of Russia.

The policy of other Russian princes consisted in attempts to free themselves from the Mongolian yoke with the help of the west. This attitude was particularly characteristic of such western Russian princes as Daniel of Galicia. He expressed his readiness to recognize the authority of the Pope and in return received a crown in 1255. But a crown was not in itself sufficient, and military assistance did not arrive, so that Daniel was forced in the end to submit to the Tartars. The Mongolian power up to the fourteenth century thus encompassed both eastern and western Russia.

4.

IN the middle of the fourteenth century the power of the Khans of the "Golden Horde" began to fail. Continuous internal strife agitated the center of authority. One pretender rose against another. The decline of the "Golden Horde" is explained partly by the indecision of the Khans in their cultural policy. The other Mongolian kingdoms which formed the Mongolian Empire gradually transformed themselves under the cultural influence of the locality they occupied. In China the Mongolian Khan became converted to Buddhism and the Chinese rapidly absorbed the Mongolian invaders. In Persia the Khan accepted Islam, and the Mongolian Kingdom was transformed into the Persian Empire. If the Mongolian Khans in Russia had become converted to Orthodoxy they would in all probability have converted their kingdom into a Mongolo-Russian state. This, however, did not take place. With all their patronage of the Orthodox church, the Khans of the "Golden Horde" eventually became converted not to Orthodoxy but to Islam. This circumstance prevented the foundation of a Russian state with its center in Sarai, and led to the long historical process of development of the Russian state centering in Moscow, which was to include in its population a portion of Turko-Mongols.

Moscow rapidly gained strength under the power of the "Golden Horde" and in the end of the fourteenth century occupied the leading position among the eastern and northern Russian principalities. But, simultaneously with the creation of this internal Russian center at Moscow, an external center came into existence in the west in the form of the Lithuanian state. The Lithuanian tribes began to unite in the second half of the thirteenth century. The concentration of power in the person of the Grand Duke originated at the beginning of the fourteenth century. The Lithuanian princes, taking advantage of the waning power of the "Golden Horde," succeeded in the middle of the fourteenth century in occupying a considerable portion of western Russia. Russian princes and towns frequently submitted to the Lithuanians without resistance, in order to free themselves from the Tartar yoke. In the sixth decade of the thirteenth century, the Grand Duke of Lithuania, Olgerd, not only occupied all the Russian principalities west of the Dnieper, but extended his sway as far as the Black Sea.

Russian influence was very strong in the Lithuanian state. The Orthodox culture of the Russians was at a higher level of development than the pagan Lithuanian culture. Russians served in the army and in the palace of the Grand Duke of Lithuania. But the Lithuanian principality was not converted to Orthodoxy, due to the fact that at the end of the fourteenth century Lithuania fell under Polish influence when the Grand Duke Yagailo was offered the Polish throne. He accepted the offer and was converted in 1386 to Roman Catholicism. At first the union between Poland and Lithuania was only personal, each state living an independent political life. But the union had great political consequences. The pagan nobility of Lithuania was rapidly converted to Catholicism and took on Polish characteristics. A part of the Russian nobility in Lithuania followed the same course. An important consequence of this was that there were no religious and cultural ties between the Lithuanian nobility and the greater part of the population of the principality.

The unification of Poland and Lithuania had great importance in the defense of both these states against the German Teutonic Knights. In 1410 the united Polish and Lithuanian-Russian forces defeated the German Knights in a decisive battle at Tannenberg, at the same spot where the Russian army of General Samsonov was crushed by the Germans in 1914.

5.

In the middle of the fourteenth century internal dissension began to disrupt the Horde. Several pretenders to the throne of the Khan appeared and finally one of the pretenders, Mamai, succeeded in seizing the supreme power. During the weakening of the Horde, Moscow grew in strength and finally revolted. In 1380 Dimitri, Grand Duke of Moscow, defeated Mamai in a bloody battle at Kulikov Meadow on the upper reaches of the river Don. Thereafter Dimitri was surnamed Donskoi (of the Don).

The victory had immense psychological significance, but at the same time it was not decisive. The Russian losses in the battle were very large, as was the expense of the struggle. Meanwhile, there was the prospect of a long-drawn-out conflict with the Tartars.

Soon after the battle of Kulikov, a revolt occurred in the Horde and Mamai was overthrown by a new pretender, Tokhtamysh. The new Khan was a vassal of the Turko-Mongol conqueror, Timur, who like Genghis Khan was an outstanding general and military organizer. Tokhtamysh was greatly strengthened by the patronage of Timur, and soon after his triumph in the Horde undertook a campaign against Moscow. On this occasion Dimitri Donskoi did not venture to struggle with the Tartars but retreated from Moscow to the north of Russia. Moscow was taken by the Tartars and pillaged in 1382. Dimitri was forced to submit again to the Horde.

The authority of the Horde over Moscow continued from this time for some scores of years; but submission protected Moscow from Lithuanian conquest, for the Horde undertook the struggle against the Lithuanian-Russian army. A terrific defeat in 1399 on the river Vorskla brought an end to the Lithuanian invasion near the spot where in 1709 Peter defeated the Swedes.

But the support of Timur did not long give strength to the "Golden Horde." He died in 1405 and soon after, in the early fifteenth century, the Horde was again torn by internal dissension. Several Tartar princes transferred their allegiance to Moscow and Lithuania, bringing their armies with them; others pursued an indecisive policy between the Horde and Moscow, fighting sometimes against the Horde and sometimes against Moscow. In 1445 the Grand Duke Basil of Moscow was captured by Ulu-Makhmet. Khan of an independent Tartar group. This event was quite unexpected even to the Tartars themselves, and they apparently did not know what to do with Basil. Finally he was released from captivity on condition that he collect a large ransom. To collect the ransom Basil was accompanied to Russia by many Tartar princes with their supporters. It appears that some of them entered his service at that time. The Grand Duke Basil was accused in Moscow of bringing the Tartars to the Russian land, of giving them towns and counties for exploitation, of loving the Tartars, and of oppressing the Russians and taking gold and silver from them to give to the Tartars.

The Tartars who had originally come to Russia as agents of a distant power now appeared in the capacity of servants of the Russian government of the principality of Moscow. The Grand Duke Basil was to satisfy the Tartar princes with Russian towns and counties. In return they supported him. The more farsighted among Russian statesmen understood that this general admission of the Tartars to service in the government of Moscow signalized the end of the Horde. About the year 1452 Basil gave to one of his faithful Tartar aides, Kasim, the life tenancy of a town on the river Oka. The creation of a vassal Tartar state on the southeastern frontier of the Grand Duchy of Moscow was a threat to the newly created Tartar kingdom at Kazan. The ruler of Kazan, Makhmutek, and Prince Kasim were brothers, but their close relationship seemed only to stimulate their enmity, Kasim being prompted by revenge for his murdered father. The kingdom of Kazan was thus weakened at the very outset of its existence. The Horde was crumbling. Besides Kazan, another new Tartar kingdom came into being in the Crimea. The "Golden Horde" continued to occupy Sarai for several decades, but was now very weak. The Grand Duke of Moscow, Basil, ceased to be its vassal.

6.

As we have seen, the Mongolian yoke bore for a longer time on the northeastern half of Russia than upon the southwestern half. For this reason Mongolian influence exercised was stronger in Moscow than in Lithuania. It found expression in many aspects of the Russian governmental and social structure. The most substantial effect was felt in the political thought of the Russian people. The Mongolian state was built upon the principle of unquestioning submission of the individual to the group, first to the clan and through the clan to the whole state. This principle was in the course of time impressed thoroughly upon the Russian people. It led to the system of universal service to the state which all without differentiation were forced to give. Under the influence of Mongolian ideas, the Russian state developed on the basis of universal service. All classes of society were made a definite part of the state organization. Taken altogether, these ideas amount to a peculiar system of state socialism. The political theory developed into a finished plan later, in the Moscow Kingdom and the Russian Empire; but the basis of the idea of state service was laid down during the period of Tartar domination.

The Mongolians also introduced a new view regarding the power of the prince. The power of the Khan was one of merciless strength. It was autocratic; submission to it was unqualified. This view of the authority of the prince was transferred to the Grand Duke of Moscow when the rule of the Khans was weakened. When the last threads of Tartar control were broken by Moscow, the dukes of Moscow openly regarded themselves as absolute monarchs and considered their people completely subject to their will. All lands within the boundaries of his state were claimed by the duke to be devoted to the interests of the state. The current theory was that the prince was the sole owner of the land, and that all other persons merely had the tenure and use of it temporarily.

Besides the general influence upon the conceptions of sovereignty, the Mongolian domination brought with it a number of administrative changes. Under Mongolian influence a new system of taxation was evolved in Moscow. Many Russian financial and administrative terms were borrowed from the Tartars. The Mongolian census of the population was the basis for the later census of the Moscow state. The Mongolians also introduced a postal system. Finally, Moscow borrowed its military organization from the Mongols. Cavalry was the basic military force. The division of the mounted army into five corps and the arms borne were all copied from the Tartars.

7.

THE Mongolian influence, both psychological and administrative, was felt principally in Moscow. With the gradual expansion of the Moscow principality the Mongolian practices in political organization began to spread all over northeastern Russia. In Moscow itself the Mongolian ideas were only accepted after a struggle with the old Russian ideas. Thus, for example, the new theory of the state was in the course of development for two centuries following the first Mongolian invasion. During this time the authority of the Grand Duke of Moscow over the eastern territories of Russia grew. In the fourteenth and the first half of the fifteenth centuries, the Moscow Grand Duke was only one of the eastern Russian princes. His power, however, waxed greater with each decade. Political authority in the Russian lands was divided among a great number of princes, and in every principality the prince had direct authority only over part of its territories, the rest being controlled by nobles or monasteries. The nobles, or *boyars,* served the prince, but in turn were served by others. There resulted a complex system similar to the feudal organization of western Europe; but Moscow feudalism was accompanied by less division of power. The forces of union were stronger than the forces of division. With each decade the ascendancy of the Moscow prince increased, leading to the creation of the Moscow monarchy.

The slow assimilation of Mongolian ideas was particularly noticeable in the development of civil law. In the fourteenth and fifteenth centuries, even in Moscow itself, the old principles of civil law were strong, and during this period the old ideas continued unmolested in northwestern Russia in the city states of Novgorod and Pskov. These ideas were clearly expressed in the *Court Laws* passed by the Pskov *Vieche* in 1467. This interesting monument of jurisprudence was a direct continuation of the ancient "Russian Law." In northwestern Russia as late as the fifteenth century, private ownership of land was the dominant system. The ancient traditions of pre-Mongolian Russian law were retained in southwestern Russia. The old customs were supported by the influence of Roman and Byzantine law which penetrated into western Russia through Poland and Moldavia.

8.

The Mongolian period is of great importance in the history of the Russian church. As we have noted above, the Mongolian Khans acted as patrons of the Orthodox church. The Russian metropolitans received from the Khans their licenses (*yarlyki*), by which the rights of the church and the integrity of church property were guaranteed. The organization of the Russian church in the Mongolian period remained for the most part unchanged. It continued to form one metropolitan district, but the metropolitan shifted his residence from the southwest to the northeast. Cyril III, who died in 1280, lived during the greater part of his tenure of office in Vladimir. Metropolitan Maxim, who held the office from 1283 to 1305, moved the seat of the metropolitanate definitely from Kiev to northeastern Russia. Under Metropolitan Peter Moscow became the permanent seat of the head of the church and it was officially made so under Metropolitan Alexis. But the metropolitanate long continued to bear the name of "Kiev and All-Russia." Following the transfer of the metropolitan seat to Moscow and the formation of a separate political organism under the Grand Duke of Lithuania in southwestern Russia, efforts were made to organize a separate western Russian metropolitan district. At the same time the founding of a bishopric in Sarai, the capital of the "Golden Horde," was of great importance. The Bishop of Sarai played an important part in the Russian church, especially in the second half of the thirteenth century and the first half of the fourteenth century.

The fourteenth and fifteenth centuries were characterized by the multiplication of monasteries in northeastern Russia. The severity of the Mongolian rule led to a widespread desire among many men to leave the world and devote themselves to a spiritual and ascetic life. The monk went into the forests, built a cell for himself; there he and sometimes two or three disciples would spend their time in religious exercises and prayer. If the monk were a man of high moral outlook and spiritual purity, capable of exercising an influence upon other people, the news of his exalted life spread to neighboring villages and other monks joined him to assist in his religious exercises. The monks were also followed by laymen in search of consolation and advice. This led to the creation of villages around the monasteries. Contributions of money and of land were made to the monasteries to induce the monks to pray for the souls of the contributors. The monasteries continued to grow and prosper even after the founders died. Stone churches and walls were built to protect the monks from robbers. Such was the usual development of many north Russian monasteries, the most important of which was St. Sergius Trinity Monastery forty miles from Moscow.

The monks were the pioneers of colonization in northeastern Russia and their influence was of great cultural importance. The old Russian monastery was also a wayside inn, a school, and a hospital. If the monastery was wealthy, it also became a bank. Monasteries had libraries and so were frequently centers of study to which the princes and statesmen turned for religious, historical, and legal information. The cultural rôle of the Russian monasteries continued through to the sixteenth and seventeenth centuries. In the eighteenth century as the spiritual demands of the Russian people changed and the knowledge which the monasteries contained was less sought, their importance decreased. In the middle of the eighteenth century a great number of monasteries were closed by the Imperial Government, and in 1918 the Soviet Government closed those remaining.

To a greater degree than before the Mongolian invasion, the church and the monasteries directed the intellectual life of Russia, affecting literature and art. During the Mongolian period painting reached a high point of development—that is, religious icon-painting. Especially popular were the icons of Novgorod. The most famous of Russian icon-painters of the time, Andrew Rublev, who died about 1427, was a monk of the Trinity Monastery. His art has some features in common with that of the Italian Fra Angelico, a contemporary. Russian icon-painting of the fourteenth to sixteenth centuries may be regarded as one of the highest artistic expressions of mankind.

CHAPTER IV.

RUSSIA FROM THE MIDDLE OF THE FIFTEENTH TO THE END OF THE SIXTEENTH CENTURY

(1452–1598)

I.

IN the middle of the sixteenth century the Russian people began an advance upon the south and east. This colonizing movement is connected with the expansion of the Polish, Lithuanian, and Moscow states, but also continued independently of these states. On the extreme southwestern frontier, the Russian people, as has been noted, reached the Black Sea at the end of the fourteenth century, but they were pushed back from it at the end of the fifteenth century by the Crimean Tartars. The Russians, however, retained a firm hold over the Dnieper River as far as the cataracts. Along the Don and Volga they advanced rapidly during the sixteenth century, and Russian armies conquered the middle and lower Volga.

A line of towns connected by fortified works supported the colonizing activity of the Moscow state. The expansion continued particularly in the region of the Ukraine following the absorption of Little Russia by the Moscow state in the seventeenth century. The Cossacks, meanwhile, advanced to the east of the Volga. The southeastern boundaries of Russia were populated both through the efforts of the state and the natural process of migration. People fled from state taxes and serfdom. In the second half of the seventeenth century migration was further increased by the persecution of religious dissenters.

On the northeastern front, in the course of less than a century, from the middle of the sixteenth century to the middle of the seventeenth century, Russian colonists occupied the enormous area of Siberia as far as Kamchatka.

2.

In the second half of the fifteenth century the Grand Duke of Moscow, Ivan III, succeeded in annexing almost all the hitherto independent cities and principalities of northern Russia—Novgorod, Tver, and the small principalities on the upper Oka. The Duchy of Moscow became a powerful military state and under the able direction of Ivan III extended its influence far into the Islamic world. Emissaries of Moscow penetrated as far as Herat.

In the fifteenth century, as we have seen, the Tartar kingdoms of Kazan and Crimea broke free from the "Golden Horde," while in Kasimov another Tartar kingdom was formed under the suzerainty of Moscow. Ivan III succeeded in stirring up enmity between the Tartar kingdoms, and profited by the struggle between Kasimov and Kazan, as well as by the struggle of Crimea against the "Golden Horde." In the year 1480 Ivan shook off the last vestiges of his own subjection to it.

In the sixteenth century the situation changed. Moscow failed to maintain its alliance with the Crimean Kingdom, and found itself confronted by an alliance between Kazan and the Crimea directed against the Duchy of Moscow. But the Kasimov Tartars remained faithful to Moscow and with their assistance Ivan the Terrible, grandson of Ivan III, annihilated the kingdom of Kazan and annexed the whole of Kazan to Moscow in 1552. Following this conquest, Astrakhan was subjugated in 1556. Siberia paid homage to Moscow in 1555. The real annexation of Siberia, however, took place later, following the expeditionary campaign of a Cossack force under the command of Yermak in 1584.

While expanding rapidly in the east, Moscow also fought bitterly for the restitution of Russian lands held under the dominion of Lithuania. The rulers of Moscow were descendants of Vladimir the Saint, and laid claim to the western lands which he had possessed, as their heritage. Moscow's struggle with Lithuania was long and stubborn. Years of peace were the occasion only for preparation of new wars. At first success lay with Moscow, and in the beginning of the sixteenth century its army occupied Smolensk. Pskov and Riazan were also annexed by Moscow at that time.

The danger of conquest by Moscow threw Lithuania into a closer alliance with Poland. During the fifteenth century and the first half of the sixteenth century, Poland and Lithuania were united only by the bonds of a dynastic union in the person of a common king. Even this bond was temporarily broken when the unity of rulership was interrupted. The joint activities of Poland and Lithuania during this period were those of two allied countries rather than those of a single power. In the middle of the sixteenth century the situation changed. Poland, taking advantage of Lithuania's difficulties with Moscow, urged the complete unification of the two states. The union took place in 1569 on conditions disadvantageous to Lithuania. Prior to the final agreement of union, the Ukrainian lands were transferred from Lithuania to Poland. Under the treaty of union, Poland and Lithuania were to have a single king to be elected by a joint session of the representative bodies (called the *Seim*) of the two states. Each retained its own army, taxes, and laws.

Following the union of Poland and Lithuania, the latter disappeared as an independent political force. In 1791 the last vestiges of Lithuanian independence were destroyed by Poland. Lithuania later was annexed by Russia in the third partition of Poland. In 1918 Lithuania regained her independence, but in 1920 Polish forces seized the city of Vilna and the territory around it, which the League of Nations later awarded to Poland. The united Polish-Lithuanian Commonwealth, under the leadership of Poland, became Moscow's chief enemy in the west. Meanwhile Ivan the Terrible was engaged in war not only with Lithuania but also with the Baltic states which interfered in Russia's communications with Europe through the Baltic Sea. This drew Russia into war with Sweden. The situation became acute for Moscow, when Stephen Batory, one of the greatest military leaders of his time, occupied the Polish throne in 1576. For several years thereafter the Russians were defeated by the Poles and were forced to retreat. Moscow was saved only by the heroic defense of Pskov, which repelled the fierce attack of Batory. In 1583 Ivan the Terrible was forced to conclude a disadvantageous peace both with Poland and with Sweden. Moscow lost all the lands conquered from Lithuania with the exception of Smolensk, as well as the gains in the Baltic area. Sweden received in addition a portion of the Baltic coast which had long belonged to Russia. This portion was returned to Moscow several years later but was lost again during the "Time of Trouble."

3.

In the pre-Mongolian period of Russian history, as we have seen, three principles underlay the organization of Russian political authority: the monarchical, the aristocratic, and the democratic. These three principles became identified with three regions in Russia. The monarchical principle triumphed in Moscow, the aristocratic principle in Lithuania, and the democratic principle in northwestern Russia—Novgorod and Pskov—from the twelfth to the fifteenth centuries. But at the end of the fifteenth century Novgorod was annexed by Moscow and the power of the *vieche* was destroyed. In the sixteenth century the same fate was suffered by Pskov, and the last remnants of the independence of Novgorod were eradicated by Ivan the Terrible.

The democratic principle did not disappear, however, with the annexation by Moscow of the northern dominions. It reappeared in the south of Russia. The Cossack communes were governed on a democratic basis. They originated in the south of Russia in the middle of the fifteenth century. During the weakening of the Turko-Mongol state, the intervening region between the "Golden Horde" and Russia was occupied by Russians and Tartars who desired to break away from the restrictions imposed upon individuals by both states. These settlers not only occupied themselves with peaceful labors but were also obliged to be ready for armed defense of their homes. They further took advantage of their occupation of the frontier regions to rob the trade caravans which connected Russia with the "Golden Horde." The Tartars called these independent frontiersmen Cossacks. This name was also adopted by the Russian frontiersmen. The Cossacks gradually formed themselves into groups in order to increase their military force. In the middle of the sixteenth century two Cossack states came into existence, formed by the merger of separate groups and communes: the Host of the Don in southeastern Russia; and the Zaporog Host in southwestern Russia. *Zaporog* means literally "beyond the cataracts," i.e., those of the Dnieper River. These Cossack states were pure republics. In each of them authority was vested in a chief, elected by the whole Host. He was called Ataman by the Don Cossacks and Hetman by the Zaporog Cossacks. He possessed no independent power but was merely the executive of the Cossack popular council, called the Circle or *Rada.* Only during campaigns did the Ataman acquire dictatorial power over the whole Host; but with the termination of the campaign he had to give a full account of his administration to the Circle. The Circle chose, also, an assistant to the Ataman and the Chancellor of the Host. The Circle was the highest judicial authority and wielded unlimited power over the life and death of the whole population of the state. The usual punishment for serious offenses was death by drowning in a river. In the Cossack republics there were no class differences; all were regarded as equal. There was no private property in land; all the land belonged to the whole Host and individual Cossacks were given only the right of temporary use of the ground they occupied.

The absence of class differences attracted a constant stream of people of the lower classes of Poland and Russia to the Cossack lands. The number of settlers from Moscow increased especially during the second half of the sixteenth century when the institution of serfdom made its appearance. At first agriculture played only a small part in the life of the Cossacks. Their customary occupation in peace time was hunting and fishing. They bought grain from Moscow, and in later times received grain as a subsidy. In the seventeenth century classes began to form in the Cossack state. The old settlers on the Don, having permanent homes, came to be called "house-owning" Cossacks, while the newcomers who possessed no property were called *golytba* or shelterless (literally "naked"), and formed the unsettled element. The *golytba* often played an active part in the political difficulties of Moscow, as during the "Time of Trouble" from 1605 to 1613, and during the revolt of Stephen Razin in 1671. In the seventeenth century the Cossack state gradually lost its independence. The Host of the Don in 1614 became the vassal of Moscow; and in return the Moscow Government furnished the Cossacks with firearms and supplies for the struggle against the Turks. But during the whole of the seventeenth century the Host of the Don had complete control over its internal affairs.

4.

In the Russian territories which became part of the Grand Duchy of Lithuania and the kingdom of Poland, there developed an aristocratic society. From the end of the fifteenth century the power of the Lithuanian Grand Duke was limited by an aristocratic council of *boyars* known as the *Rada.* The council comprised the nobles (*Pany*) who were the hereditary rulers of large feudal estates. The nobles retained all the important posts in the government: those of Hetman or commander of the troops; of chancellor or keeper of the royal seal; and of financial controller. Besides the *Rada* there was also an assembly known as the *Seim,* composed of all the landowners both large and small, as well as a small number of representatives from the towns. But actually the nobles had a preponderating influence in the *Seim.* Only the landowners and a part of the townsmen had political representation in Lithuania. The peasants were subject to limitations in their rights, which gradually restricted their freedom, particularly on privately owned estates. From the middle of the fifteenth century the peasants were forbidden to move from privately owned land to state lands. Their condition rapidly approached that of slaves.

The social structure of the Russo-Lithuanian state was defined in the code of laws known as the Lithuanian statutes. This was drawn up in the first half of the sixteenth century, but was twice revised. In 1588 the statutes were printed in Russian. They represent a fully developed, systematically written code, having great juridical significance. Concerning themselves largely with questions of civil rights and property interests, they indicate a high degree of juridical knowledge and a considerable development of the principles of civil rights in the Russo-Lithuanian state. But like the political structure itself, the legal principles were chiefly to the advantage of the upper class of landowners and townsmen.

5.

Moscow developed the third type of Russian political organization of the sixteenth and seventeenth centuries—the type destined to become the basis of Russian political evolution in the eighteenth and nineteenth centuries. As we have seen, the concept of absolute power of the Moscow ruler was borrowed from the Mongols. But besides this, the influence of Byzantine ideas was also observable—such as the sanctification of the state by the church, and close union between the church and the state. The coronation of Ivan IV in 1547 reflected these ideas. The promotion of the Moscow metropolitan archbishop to the rank of a patriarch in the late sixteenth century was the next step toward Byzantinization. The creation of this dualism of tsar and patriarch was a limitation upon the independence of the Moscow rulers, which led in the seventeenth century to a conflict between church and state.

In the sixteenth century the Moscow rulers engaged in a stubborn struggle with the upper class in Moscow society. The *boyars* of Moscow were composed of different groups. There were first the old *boyar* families—some closely related to the Moscow princes—which had been in Moscow before it became the center of the Russian lands. Second, there were the descendants of other Russian princes, but not of the Moscow dynasty. Finally, there were the *boyars* of the annexed principalities. The former independent princes, now brought to Moscow in the capacity of *boyars* of the Moscow tsar, could not reconcile themselves to the loss of their political power and were ready at all times to join in movements against him. Inasmuch as many of these princes and *boyars* were large landowners and controlled great numbers of armed supporters, their opposition could easily lead to armed conflict. However, Ivan took the offensive. He organized the *Oprichnina,* a band of faithful servants, and crushed the *boyars* and princes before they revolted against him. It was only following the defeat of the *boyars* that the Moscow tsar could consider himself an autocrat.

The autocracy of the Moscow tsars was of a peculiar character. The political structure of their kingdom was not identical either with that of Byzantium or with that form of absolutism which later developed in St. Petersburg, along western lines. The peculiarity of the Moscow Government consisted in the close contact between the rulers and the people. The state combined a strong central power with independence of the local *mir* or commune. This form of self-government was less a privilege of the inhabitants than their duty to the state—which explains the fact that the electors were responsible to the central government for those elected.

Local self-government in Moscow had two main functions—judicial and financial. In each department of the Moscow state there was an annual congress of all the representatives of the inhabitants. At these congresses a judicial commission was elected for one year to suppress crime. The chief of this commission was an elder chosen from among the landlords. There also operated in the sixteenth century a financial commission having powers over townsmen and peasants, but not over the landowning classes. Financial committees were elected locally, and the landowning classes over which they had no authority took no part in the elections. Thus self-government was more restricted in character in the financial than in the judicial sphere.

The principle of self-government was applied by the Moscow state, not only in respect to local affairs, but also to general concerns of the whole state. In the second half of the sixteenth century the tsar from time to time called in Moscow a popular congress or *Zemsky Sobor.* These congresses reached their fullest development, however, only in the seventeenth century.

6.

The sixteenth century was a period of great social changes in the Moscow state. Three important tendencies in development must be noted: the decline of the former landed aristocracy or the *boyars;* the creation of a new order of landholders, or *pomiestchiks;* and the restriction of the freedom of the peasants to move from the land they occupied. These tendencies were closely related. The *Oprichnina,* organized by Ivan, was the connecting link of the whole system. Its formation was one of the most dramatic incidents of Ivan's struggle against the *boyars.*

Late in 1564 Ivan unexpectedly and secretly left Moscow and moved to a village called Alexandrovskaia Sloboda near the Trinity Monastery, and from there dispatched word to Moscow that he had abandoned the tsardom because of the treachery of the *boyars.* In reply there came a delegation from the terrified citizens of Moscow with a request that he remain their tsar. Ivan agreed on condition that he be given absolute power and authority to pursue the "traitors." He demanded an extension of customary authority by the creation of a private household and a separate domestic guard for himself. The word *Oprichnina* means exactly "separate" or "private" household or court. The new courtiers, known as the *oprichniks,* became the chief weapons of Ivan the Terrible in his struggle with the *boyars.* The significance of the *Oprichnina* was that it permitted Ivan to lead an entirely new sort of life. The "traitorous" *boyars* were not admitted to the new court. Ivan chose his courtiers from the younger generation, without regard to seniority or nobility. Having thus modified the character of the state, Ivan could freely deal with anyone whom he suspected of treachery, and particularly with the *boyars* and princelings. Wholesale executions took place. In 1570 the city of Novgorod was raided. While the executions disposed of individuals, Ivan's economic reforms ruined entire families of *boyars.* Gradually he appropriated all the towns and counties where the *boyars* and princes had ancestral estates. He deported the former owners to frontier zones where they were unknown. Their lands were distributed among the *oprichniks* of the tsar. Thus Ivan the Terrible destroyed the former social and governmental organization of Russia, the patrimonial *boyar* system, and created the new order of *dvorians* or courtiers. The new court was organized along the lines of a monastery, where humble prayer alternated with wild orgies, and where the *oprichniks* or court adherents were "brothers" and wore black garments.

The *oprichniks* ran riot for almost seven years, during which time they accomplished their purpose of weakening the aristocratic *boyars.* The further activity of the *Oprichnina* by this time threatened the Government itself. While able to suppress traitors, it was helpless against the foreign enemy, without the aid of the old landowning class or *zemschina.* In 1571 the Crimean Khan, Devlet Girei, managed to occupy Moscow and after plundering the town to burn it. When in 1572 he repeated the invasion, the forces of the whole Russian state were mustered and he was defeated. Following these events the *Oprichnina* declined. A reaction set in. The former landowners received back their lands, and the *oprichniks* received other lands instead.

The activity of the *Oprichnina* may be compared with that of the Communist party during the initial years of the Russian revolution. The difference is that the terror of the *Oprichnina* was directed against the higher *boyars,* while the communists attacked the whole *bourgeoisie.* The rule of the *Oprichnina* was accompanied, as has been pointed out, by the creation of a new landowning class, or *pomiestchiks,* the holding of land being made dependent upon service to the tsar. This was called *pomiestie* and replaced the former patrimonial estate.

As a result of this method of land distribution, Ivan the Terrible succeeded in creating a new ruling class, which remained the basic political force in the Russian state until the middle of the nineteenth century. The land given to the *pomiestchiks* was populated by peasants. In the middle of the sixteenth century these peasants were freemen—that is, they had the right to move from their land, following the autumn harvest, to lands belonging to other proprietors. This freedom of migration proved unprofitable to the *pomiestchiks* and the Government began to limit the peasants' right to move freely. During a period of economic hardship due to the Lithuanian war, the Government proclaimed certain years as "prohibited." The peasants were deprived of the right to move from the estate of one landowner to that of another during such years. This law was first applied in the year 1581. Following the death of Ivan a census of the population and a survey of lands in the Moscow state were made; and the peasants were registered as being fixed to the land which they then occupied, and were thenceforth regarded as serfs. The compulsory attachment of the peasants to the soil was reinforced by their indebtedness to the landowners which had already been tending to have the same effect. The majority of the peasants of any estate borrowed from the owner to build houses, purchase cattle, and so forth. The peasants were thus fixed to the land, but not to the proprietor. The serf was not the personal property of the landowner, or a slave, as were the house slaves or *kholops.* Even after the institution of serfdom, the peasant retained his civil rights: he could sue in court, and own both land and slaves.

7.

One of the consequences of the political division of Russia in the sixteenth and seventeenth centuries was a separation of the Russian church into two parts: the Moscow and the Lithuanian branches. As we have seen, unity of church organization in Russia was retained during the Mongolian period, but during the struggle between Moscow and Lithuania the preservation of this unity became increasingly difficult. In the middle of the fifteenth century Lithuania succeeded in establishing a metropolitan district in Kiev, independent of Moscow and dependent directly upon the patriarch of Constantinople. Thus the Russian church broke into two metropolitan districts, that of Kiev and that of Moscow, both of which, however, formed part of the patriarchate of Constantinople. Actually the Moscow church became autonomous, and the metropolitans were elected by a congress of Russian bishops following the year 1448.

With the fall of Byzantium, Moscow began to regard itself as the chief center of Orthodoxy. The Moscow church experienced during the sixteenth century a profound emotional upheaval and together with this an intensification of religious and nationalistic problems. The internal peace of the Moscow church was, however, greatly disturbed by the dispute over church property and the relation between church and state in the first half of the sixteenth century. One party, headed by Nil Sorsky, opposed the ownership of land and other forms of wealth by the church and the monasteries, and took a stand against close relationship between church and state. A second party, headed by Joseph Volotsky, defended the right of the church to own land and advocated close relationship between the church and the state. Permission to monasteries to own property was motivated not by considerations of personal interest, but by the social value of the monasteries and their benefit to the state. The struggle was won by the second party, and in the middle of the sixteenth century the principle of close relationship between church and state became firmly established. An important exponent of this view was Metropolitan Makary, one of the leading Russian churchmen who stood at the head of widespread cultural movement. Under his direction, and partly with his personal assistance, religious and secular historical material was collected. Metropolitan Makary called a congress of churchmen in 1551 to correct evils in the church, which were openly admitted in the resolutions of the congress. The congress was known as *Stoglav* or "Hundred Chapters," from the number of resolutions. The religious and political views of Metropolitan Makary were derived from Byzantium. He believed that the Orthodox state should have two heads, the tsar and the patriarch. The institution of tsardom originated in Russia at the time of the coronation of Ivan the Terrible in 1547. In accordance with the Byzantine doctrine of the time, Makary urged that Moscow should have a patriarch—that is, that the metropolitan of Moscow should be raised to that dignity. In view of the fact that a long preparation in Constantinople was necessary before the program could be executed, the patriarchate was introduced in Moscow only following the death of Makary. In 1589, Jeremiah, the patriarch of Constantinople, agreed to the foundation of a patriarchate in Russia. During the next year a congress of eastern patriarchs in Constantinople confirmed the action of Jeremiah. The patriarchate of Moscow and All-Russia was placed in the fifth or last category. The order of patriarchates was as follows: Constantinople, Alexandria, Antioch, Jerusalem, and Moscow.

At the time that the Moscow church was experiencing its national and spiritual revival, the Metropolitanate of Kiev was fighting a battle for existence. The second half of the sixteenth century was marked in the history of Europe by the sudden revival of Catholicism. The order of Jesuits gave militant Catholicism new life and succeeded in regaining many countries where Catholicism seemed to have become so weak as to be obliterated by the reformed churches. Among these countries was Poland. Popular feeling in Poland changed rapidly in the middle of the sixteenth century. The Jesuits advanced Catholic propaganda in an energetic struggle with Lutheranism. They succeeded in arousing religious fanaticism in Polish society. This emotional upheaval coincided with the military success of Stephen Batory against Moscow. Batory patronized the Jesuits, considering their activity of great assistance to the energetic foreign policy of the Polish-Lithuanian state against Moscow. The Jesuits turned from a struggle against Protestantism to one against Orthodoxy. The situation of the Orthodox population in Poland became difficult. The political unification of Lithuania and Poland in 1569 was completed at a time when the Lithuanian and Russian Orthodox population had no cause to fear religious oppression on the part of Poland; but following the victory of the Jesuits in Poland, such oppression became inevitable.

The nomination of Orthodox bishops was interfered with by political interests of the Polish state. The king chose bishops, not from among the best of the Orthodox, but frequently from among the worst. The highest religious authority, the patriarch of Constantinople, was too distant and too powerless to protect his subjects. The protection of the Orthodox church was left to the laymen. Some nobles who had remained Orthodox, such as Prince Ostrozhsky, and principally merchants in the cities, began to form unions or brotherhoods to support the church. The Ostrozhsky family gave it contributions and organized a printing establishment for the publication of church books. The Orthodox bishops, however, were dissatisfied with the excessive interference of laymen in church matters. The western Russian bishops met at a congress in Brest in 1591 and complained to the king. Two of them secretly announced to the king that they were ready to accept the authority of the Pope. In the end of 1594 several bishops signed a declaration expressing the desirability of union of the churches. At the end of 1595 the two bishops who had addressed the king at the Brest congress were received in Rome by Pope Clement VIII. Following their return the Polish king issued a manifesto announcing the union of the churches and called a church congress in Brest.

The congress met in October, 1596, and the irreconcilability of the Orthodox and Uniate churches became immediately evident. The Orthodox representatives broke away from the congress and met separately. The advocates of unity passed their resolution of submission to the Pope. The advocates of Orthodoxy denounced submission. There were thus two congresses at Brest in 1596, each having its own resolutions. Instead of unity there took place a schism of the western Russian church into Uniate and Orthodox groups. In the eyes of the king and of the Polish and Lithuanian governments, the Uniate congress at Brest was the only one that received official recognition. Basing his policy upon the resolutions of this congress, the king could pursue his bitter struggle against the Orthodox church.

8.

RUSSIAN literature of the Mongol and post-Mongol period concerned itself with the political and religious problems which agitated the society of the time. We must distinguish during this period between the literature of Moscow and that of western Russia. The literature of Moscow was saturated with national feeling. Following the victory of Dimitri Donskoi over the Mongols at the Kulikovo Meadow in the upper Don region (1380) a poem was composed to glorify the deeds of the Russian warriors. Known as *Zadonshchina* ("Beyond the Don River"), it was an imitation of Prince Igor's song of the twelfth century. Other popular poems (*byliny*) portrayed Tsar Ivan IV and his struggle with the Khanate of Kazan.

The most important historical work of the time was the "Book of Degrees" (*Stepennaia Kniga*), i.e., of generations. This work is not a mere chronological account of Russian history but a carefully analyzed Russian history, tracing the course of national and religious development.

In the seventeenth century a new form of literature appears which may be called the historical novel. Examples are the semi-realistic story of the seizure of Azov and its defense by the Don Cossacks (1637–41) and the semi-fantastic story of the young merchant Savva Grudtsyn who allegedly took part in the campaign against the Poles in 1632. Of a quite different nature is the story of Frol Skobeiev written at the very end of the century. It is a realistic and even cynical story of a successful rascal, in a sense already a forerunner of the nineteenth-century realistic satire.

In the popular literature of western Russia the Cossack ballads (*dumy*) of the sixteenth and seventeenth centuries play a particularly important role. Vivid chronicles of the Cossack-Polish wars and other tempestuous events of the period may likewise be mentioned here. Another branch of west Russian literature was devoted to the problems of religious life. Western Russia, as we have seen, was forced to conduct a constant internal struggle in order to preserve its own church and nationality from the incursion of Catholicism and Polish nationalism. This struggle created a need for religious and historical literature. Another favorite subject was the analysis and rebuttal of arguments advanced by Catholic propaganda. The development of Russian theology was advanced by the foundation of seminaries. In the beginning of the seventeenth century a theological academy was founded in Kiev, following the model of the Jesuit colleges. In 1682 a Greek seminary was founded in Moscow, which five years later became known as the Greco-Slavo-Latin Academy.

The development of natural and mathematical sciences in Russia was progressing rather slowly during the sixteenth and seventeenth centuries.

Printing, which was the new technical means of advancing literature and education in general, came to Russia long after its invention in the west. The first printed Slavonic books were published in Cracow, Poland, in 1491 and in Prague, Bohemia, in 1517–19. In 1525 printing began in Lithuanian Russia in the town of Vilna. In the end of the sixteenth century there were ten printing establishments in western Russia. They worked slowly, however. The first printing establishment in Moscow was founded in 1553. Its work was soon suspended and started again only in 1568, after which it developed very slowly. Prior to 1600 hardly a score of books were published in Moscow. In the seventeenth century, following the "Time of Trouble," the work of the Moscow printers developed more rapidly. From 1613 to 1682, almost five hundred books were published, most of which were of a religious character and a smaller proportion of lay interest.

9.

WHILE Russian painting attained notable development during the fourteenth and fifteenth centuries, the sixteenth century witnessed high achievements in architecture. Before the sixteenth century, Russian church architecture reflected for the most part Byzantine influences and, to a lesser degree, influences from the Near East. In the fifteenth century several Italian masters were called to Moscow, the most famous of whom was R. Fioravanti, nicknamed Aristotle. They were ordered to follow the existing architectural forms. For this reason the Moscow cathedrals of the fifteenth century are to a certain extent copies of the cathedrals of Vladimir of the twelfth and thirteenth centuries. Italian influence was more prominent in lay architecture, as witnessed by the style of the walls and towers of the Moscow Kremlin, and the palaces of the Moscow Grand Duke. A direct result of the labor of the Italian masters was the extraordinary beauty of the Kremlin, constructed in the Italo-Byzantine style. In the sixteenth century Byzantine influence in architecture disappeared. Russian churches of the next two centuries belong to an entirely new style of architecture, distinguished by a turret-like structure. The new Moscow architecture was a copy in stone of wooden buildings. Contemporary architecture in wood had developed in accord with the influence of popular tastes and needs. The Moscow architecture of the sixteenth and seventeenth centuries, therefore, is profoundly national in character; but the influence of the Near and Middle East cannot be denied, particularly in some of the architectural details. These influences came through Turkestan and probably also through the Crimea.

Russian painting did not pass through changes as far reaching as did architecture. The Novgorod school of icon-painting fell into decay with the general decline of Novgorod. A new center was founded in Moscow. In the seventeenth century the Moscow school became more and more subject to western, and particularly to Italian, influences. The icons of Simon Ushakov, who lived from 1626 to 1686, represent an effort to combine the new Italian and the old Byzantine styles of religious painting.

CHAPTER V.

RUSSIA IN THE SEVENTEENTH CENTURY

(1598–1696)

1.

THE unceasing wars of the sixteenth century had an exhausting effect upon the Moscow state. The internal situation of Russia at the end of the sixteenth century was greatly confused. The social reforms of Ivan the Terrible had resulted in governmental patronage of the middle classes at the expense of the upper and lower classes. These reforms aroused keen dissatisfaction in both these classes: the *boyars* were discontented with the diminution of their political and social influence; the lower class, the peasantry, was discontented with the institution of serfdom.

Popular discontent was expressed in the events of the "Time of Trouble" in the beginning of the seventeenth century. An uprising occurred which appeared to be purely fortuitous. But the events leading to it were effective only because the ground had been prepared. In 1598, following the death of the childless Tsar Fedor, son of Ivan the Terrible, the old dynasty came to an end. This circumstance was of great importance in the eyes of people of the time. If the dynasty had continued, it could have endured for a long time by mere inertia; but the change of dynasty opened the doors to political speculation. The *Zemsky Sobor* elected a new tsar, Boris Godunov, in 1598. He had been the actual ruler during the last years of the reign of Ivan IV and the whole of the reign of the weak-willed Fedor. Godunov was one of the organizers of Ivan's social and administrative system and the policies of government therefore did not change when he ascended the throne. But Boris did not have the authority of the former tsars, despite his election by the *Zemsky Sobor*. Immediately following his election, the *boyars* commenced to plot against him. Their intrigues, becoming connected with foreign complications, endangered his position.

The Moscow *boyars* provided a new candidate for the throne, a young man of no prominence, who had been brought up under the delusion that he was the Tsarevich Dmitri, youngest son of Ivan IV. The true Dmitri had been in fact killed when a child, in 1591, under circumstances giving rise to the belief that Boris Godunov was responsible for the murder. The Pretender Dmitri announced himself in Poland. The Polish king and the Jesuits saw in him a powerful weapon for the furtherance of Polish diplomacy and Catholic propaganda. With Polish aid, the Pretender organized a small army of Russian refugees and Cossacks. Greatly inferior to the regular army of Moscow, it none the less succeeded, in view of the widespread discontent in Moscow, in reaching the capital. Boris, meanwhile, died, and Dmitri was victorious. The victory of the Pretender led to further uprisings. The original intrigue of the *boyars* and the Poles, having shaken the Government's authority, resulted also in stirring up a revolt among the lower classes against the middle and upper classes. In the ensuing conflicts, the false Dmitri was killed and the throne was occupied by a representative of the *boyar* party. Disorder, however, continued, and a new false Dmitri—a candidate not of the *boyars* but of the lower classes—advanced against the *boyar* tsar.

The social uprising had two phases: first, a radical movement of peasants and slaves, which was not unlike the Communist Revolution of 1917, whose object was to annihilate all the more wealthy people in the country. At the head of the uprising was a runaway slave, Bolotnikov. His army was, however, defeated by the troops of Moscow and he was executed. The second phase of the movement was of a more moderate character, and was conducted by the Cossacks, who succeeded in occupying half of the Moscow state. The civil war continued until the tsar, who was supported by the *boyars,* was forced to abdicate; the second false Dmitri was killed, and Russia fell into a frightful state of anarchy. Armed bands wandered about the country, robbing everyone on their way. The Poles and Swedes took advantage of the civil war to occupy Russian territory; the former seized Moscow and Smolensk, the latter occupied Novgorod. The patriarch of Moscow, Hermogen, having refused to recognize the legality of Polish dominion in the capital, was imprisoned by the invaders and died of starvation. The seizure of the capital by the Poles and the death of the head of the church, brought about a nationalistic and religious reaction. At the initiative of K. Minin, a Nizhni-Novgorod merchant, an army was mustered from among townspeople of the Volga and north Russia. The army was commanded by Prince Pozharsky who succeeded in securing the support of the Cossacks and with their aid in defeating the Poles and occupying Moscow in 1612. In the beginning of 1613 a *Zemsky Sobor* was called, which elected a young *boyar,* Michael Romanov, tsar of Russia.

2.

THE suppression of the uprising was effected primarily through the initiative of government officials and townspeople, that is, the middle classes of society. Thus it may be said that the social program of Ivan the Terrible and Boris Godunov triumphed in spite of all difficulties. The new government, however, ceased to struggle against the upper class or *boyars*. They had no important political position in the seventeenth century, but retained their social privileges. The *boyar* Duma or council continued to function, but its composition was changed by the admixture of recently created noblemen.

The new government was on friendly terms with the Don Cossacks, assisting them with grain and weapons, but it continued the earlier policy toward landowners and peasants. The members of the government service class were supplied with land. Control over all lands was vested in a special estates office in Moscow (*pomestny prikaz*). This government agency controlled both the *pomesties* and the patrimonial estates (*votchiny*). Thus aristocratic landownership was combined with the *pomestie* system. The Government demanded military service from each land category.

In 1619 a new census of all the holdings in the state was made to bring order into the land question following the confusion of the "Time of Trouble." The state support of the land tenure was connected with the binding of the peasants to the land. As we have seen, in the end of the sixteenth century the Government had declared certain years "prohibited" (*zapovedny*), that is, it refused to permit peasants during these years to move to other lands. The same policy was pursued during the first half of the seventeenth century and freedom of movement was entirely forbidden to peasants in 1649. This led to increased peasant desertion. Escaping from serfdom, many peasants made their way to the Don or to eastern Russia, which at that time was sparsely populated and was a welcome hiding place from the Government.

It was only due to the discontent of the peasant masses and to the large numbers of outlawed peasants that the revolt of Stephen Razin could assume such large proportions. Razin was the ataman of the *golytba* of the Don. In search of plunder and food, a large number of Don Cossacks, headed by Razin, forced their way down the river Volga to the Caspian Sea and, crossing it, entered the mouth of the river Yaik (subsequently Ural) in 1667–68. They established friendly relations with the Kalmyks, and in 1668 attacked the Persian possessions on the southwestern shores of the Caspian Sea. The Cossacks occupied an island near the Persian shore and in the course of several months brought there a tremendous booty. In 1669 they returned with their booty to the Don. The representatives of the tsar in Astrakhan allowed them to pass and took only a number of the guns captured by the Cossacks. Razin returned to the Don with the reputation of a brilliant ataman. He now regarded himself as sufficiently strong to attack Moscow. In 1670 he opened his campaign on the Volga. The towns of Tsaritsyn, Astrakhan, Saratov, and Samara were taken. The government officials and all representatives of the central power were tortured and put to death by Razin. The lower classes were conscripted into the Cossack army. To give the appearance of legality to his movement, Razin spread rumors that he was accompanied by the tsarevich of Moscow and the patriarch. The revolt of Razin extended over an enormous area, including all the middle and lower Volga. The Cossacks were joined by peasants and by non-Russian tribes in these regions. Razin advanced as far as Simbirsk, where he was defeated by government troops. He fled to the Don, but was seized by the house-owning Cossacks and handed over to Moscow. In 1671 he was executed.

3.

FOLLOWING the disturbances of the beginning of the seventeenth century the importance of the *Zemsky Sobor* or assembly, which had been organized in the middle of the sixteenth century, grew considerably. The *Zemsky Sobor* was called by Minin and Prince Pozharsky when they were organizing their army in 1612. It elected a new tsar in 1613 and convened thereafter almost uninterruptedly until the middle of the century. Later on the meetings of the council became rarer and its existence was terminated in 1682. The council concerned itself with questions of foreign policy, such as the declaration of war and the conclusion of peace, as well as questions of internal policy, such as taxation and legislation. It had also the important right of petition, which it exercised freely. The *Zemsky Sobor* was divided into two *palaty* or chambers. The *boyar* Duma acted as the higher chamber in lay matters and the *Sobor* or assembly of churchmen in church matters. The lower chamber was composed of representatives of the people, chosen on a basis of combination of two different principles—representation of classes and professions as well as geographical representation. The *Zemsky Sobor* contained members of all classes of society—state employees, landowners, traders, craftsmen, and peasants—and also delegates of the provinces of which the Moscow state was composed. The franchise was given to house-owning heads of families.

The powers of the *Zemsky Sobor* were determined not by law but by custom. The tsar called it because he felt he needed its practical assistance. Especially important in the internal development of the Moscow state was the *Sobor* of 1648–49, by which the new code of laws was passed. The code of 1550, drawn up under Ivan the Terrible, had become antiquated. Especially following the "Time of Trouble," a great many new *ukazes* or decrees of the tsar and *boyar* Duma had accumulated. Part of these were inscribed in the books, but the books were inaccessible. The disorder in the recording of laws was the cause of irregularity in the courts. The malpractice of the courts evoked serious discontent among the people. Acceding to repeated petitions, the Tsar Alexis organized a commission under Prince Odoevsky to formulate a new code of laws. The code was examined and passed by the *Zemsky Sobor* and immediately published in two thousand copies. This work was a great novelty, as the previous code had never been printed. The code of Tsar Alexis Michaelovich was drawn up under the influence of Lithuanian statutes and Byzantine law. The material in it was arranged strictly according to chapters and sections. The code had an immense significance in the history of the Russian state as well as in Russian law. It was the basis of Russian legal relations for almost two centuries until superseded by the code of 1832.

4.

In the seventeenth century the economic development of Russia entered a new phase, for which conditions had been prepared in the sixteenth century and which reached its peak in the eighteenth to twentieth centuries. Prior to the sixteenth century the principal occupations were hunting, fishing, agriculture, and cattle raising. Handicrafts of various kinds such as weaving, embroidery, wood carving, metal casting had likewise been popular in Russia since the middle ages. Central Russia was extensively cultivated in the sixteenth century. The soil was becoming poor and required a great deal of fertilization. The three-field system of agriculture, a more intensive form than the single field system, was widely applied in Russia during this period and remained the prevailing system among the peasantry to the twentieth century.

During the middle ages, in the thirteenth to fifteenth centuries, Russia traded primarily with central Europe through the Hanseatic League. The center of this trade was Novgorod. After the middle of the sixteenth century the Moscow state entered into closer trade relations with western Europe. Those responsible for the improved contact were foreigners, principally the English, Dutch, and Swedes. The pioneers of sea trade with Moscow were the English. In 1553 an English expedition was organized to discover a northern sea route to India. Three ships, under Sir Hugh Willoughby, left England. Two were lost, but the third, under Richard Chancellor, succeeded in entering the White Sea and reaching the mouth of the northern Dvina. Instead of India the expedition "discovered" Muscovy. Chancellor visited Moscow, where he was received by Ivan the Terrible, and from that time close relations were maintained between Moscow and England. A new town, Archangel, sprang up shortly at the mouth of the Dvina, and in England the Muscovy Company was organized for trade with Russia. Ivan the Terrible gave this company the privilege not only of free trade with Russia but also of transit trade with Persia. Archangel was also visited by the Dutch and the Swedes, who received certain privileges but less than the English. Gradually the Dutch outstripped the English. In 1582 nine English ships entered Archangel to six Dutch, while in 1638 out of eighty ships entering Archangel, only four were English and the majority of the rest were Dutch.

In the middle of the seventeenth century, urged by the demands of Russian merchants, the Government took away from foreigners the greater portion of their privileges. The English lost the right to free trade. The foreigners were also deprived of the right to retail trade. Russian merchants desired to be the exclusive intermediaries between foreign merchants and the Russian consumers and producers.

The principal exports from Russia during this period were forest products, pitch and gum; the products of cattle raising, skins, fat, and bristles; of hunting, furs; of agriculture, grain and linen; and to a lesser extent manufactured articles, cloth and burlap. The chief imports into Russia were manufactured articles and arms. The annual volume of trade through Archangel during the second half of the seventeenth century probably reached the sum of a million rubles. The purchasing power of a Russian ruble at the end of the seventeenth century equaled approximately seventeen rubles of the twentieth century prior to the World War, or about $8.50.

The development of industry in Moscow owed a great deal to the enterprise of foreigners. In 1632 a Dutchman, Vinius, organized a metallurgical establishment near Tula. All the ammunition produced at the Vinius works was supplied to the state. Following this, other similar factories soon grew up. In the middle of the seventeenth century foreigners started several paper factories near Moscow. During this time native industries rapidly developed in the Moscow state, particularly small-scale peasant shops known as *kustarnaya* industry. This name is said to be derived from the German *kunst*. In the northern wooded regions the peasants and other enterprising individuals extracted pitch and potash; in Yaroslavl they manufactured burlap; and in many places the peasants made nails and various metal articles. The productivity of Russian industry in the seventeenth century was, of course, not very great, but its steady growth cannot be questioned.

5.

THE "Time of Trouble" was terminated by the election of Michael as tsar of Russia in 1613; but the struggle with foreign enemies, the Poles and the Swedes, continued for several years longer. A peace was concluded with Sweden in 1617, by which Novgorod was returned to Russia but Sweden retained Ingria on the southeastern shore of the gulf of Finland. The Moscow state was thus cut off from the Baltic Sea, and Archangel was its only port for direct communication with Europe.

A year after the peace with Sweden, the Government of Moscow concluded a temporary settlement with the Poles. Smolensk remained in the hands of Poland and another war in 1631–32 failed to change the situation. It was evident that the strength of the two opponents was approximately equal and the continuation of the struggle seemed to bring no benefit to either. The Polish state, however, was shortly afterward weakened from within. Following the Polish-Lithuanian union in 1569, a considerable area of western Russian lands was absorbed by Poland. The Ukrainian peasants became the serfs of Polish landlords; and in addition to social oppression, the Ukrainian population suffered religious persecution in view of the fact that the Orthodox church was regarded as an illegal organization after 1596. The Polish Government further attempted to subject the Zaporog Cossacks to its control. The policy pursued by Poland stimulated hatred against Polish rule among the Russian population. This eventually led to a general uprising along the river Dnieper, headed by the Zaporog Cossacks with their Hetman, Bogdan Khmelnitsky, who had succeeded in concluding an alliance with the Crimean Khan against Poland (1648).

At first the fortunes of war favored the Cossacks, but in 1650 the Crimean Tartars betrayed Khmelnitsky and he was defeated. A peace was concluded with Poland under terms which accorded to the Cossacks certain privileges but limited their numbers to 20,000. The peasants meanwhile were to remain in a state of serfdom.

The peasants were unwilling to accept this settlement and began to migrate in large numbers to the Moscow state, settling in unoccupied lands along its southern boundaries. Finding no other way out, the *Rada* or council of the Ukrainian Cossack Host, which met in Pereyaslavl in 1654, unanimously decided to offer its allegiance to the Moscow tsar. Khmelnitsky wanted to secure recognition of the autonomous position of the Ukraine as a condition of allegiance to Moscow, but the Moscow envoy refused to accept conditional submission. The Cossacks abandoned their reservation and swore allegiance to the tsar. Later Cossack envoys went to Moscow and the tsar agreed to Ukrainian autonomy, granting special privileges to the Cossack Host. The union with Ukraine was a very important event in the political history of Russia. It made the Moscow tsar the nominal tsar of all Russia and, moreover, gave Moscow a decisive superiority over Poland.

Poland could not agree to the loss of the Ukraine without war. At first Russia was successful in the conflict, but misunderstandings arose between the Moscow Government and the Ukrainian Cossacks. Hetman Ivan Vygovsky, who succeeded Khmelnitsky, passed over to the side of the Poles. The changes in Cossack policy were due to internal dissension. The Cossack officers favored an agreement with Poland, as they were in sympathy with the aristocratic organization of Polish society and hoped to receive from Poland the privileges of their class. The mass of the Cossacks sympathized rather with Moscow. The pro-Polish policy of Vygovsky was, therefore, not supported by the Cossack troops. A considerable portion of the Host remained faithful to Moscow and elected a new hetman. These events greatly lengthened the war with Poland, and it was only in 1667 that an agreement was signed to maintain peace for thirteen and a half years. Moscow abandoned its claims to Lithuania, but retained Smolensk and acquired the left bank of the Dnieper as well as the city of Kiev.

6.

THE extension of Moscow's control over southwestern Russia coincided with an acute crisis in the religious and political consciousness of the people. This was connected with the activities and the personality of Patriarch Nikon. The controversy took two forms: first, in regard to the relationship between church and state, or the tsar and the patriarch; and secondly, in regard to church ritual, resulting in the dissension of the "Old Ritualists."

The Metropolitan of Novgorod, Nikon, was elected patriarch in 1652. He was of peasant origin and started life as a village priest. He later came to Moscow where, following the death of his children, his wife entered a convent and he entered the Solovetsky Monastery in the White Sea. Subsequently Nikon was made *Igumen* or Abbot of the Kozheozero Monastery, and later *Igumen* of a monastery in Moscow. During his second sojourn in Moscow, Nikon acquired an extraordinary influence over the tsar, and ascended the patriarchal throne with thoughts of organizing an orthodox state on the basis of close coöperation between the tsar and the patriarch. His high opinion of the patriarchal power found expression in the conditions which he presented before accepting the throne. The tsar and the whole ecclesiastical *Sobor* or assembly promised Nikon "to obey him in everything as a shepherd and a father." Nikon officially took the title of Great Sovereign.

Nikon's conditions were accepted by Tsar Alexis. The policy of the state and the policy of the church were to be completely coördinated. Both were guided by the same ideas; both were conducted in harmony.

The delicate question of church policy was that of the Ukraine, which was a metropolitan district of the patriarchate of Constantinople. In the first half of the seventeenth century the Metropolitan of Kiev, Peter Mogila, brought about some changes in the ritual of his church, attempting to bring it closer to the Greek church. In order to unite western Russia with Moscow, Tsar Alexis and Patriarch Nikon had to create conditions which would induce the western Russian church to accept the sphere of authority of the Moscow patriarch. To do this it was necessary to alter the ceremony of the Moscow church along the same lines as that of Kiev. This reform in ritual was undertaken by Patriarch Nikon simultaneously with the efforts of Moscow diplomacy to bring about a union with Ukraine.

The first steps toward reform of the Moscow ritual were undertaken in the spring of 1653. One of the changes urged by Nikon was that the believers while crossing themselves should join three fingers symbolizing the Trinity, and not two fingers symbolizing the dual nature of Jesus Christ as was the ancient custom in Russia. This question became a burning issue within the church and was more important to the masses than the reform of the service books carried through by Nikon. In 1654 a church council was called in Moscow which approved the reforms of Nikon in church books and ritual.

The reforms, however, aroused deep indignation among the Russian Orthodox masses, and the most devoted church people were the most irritated. The measures carried through by Nikon were directed against the whole idea of the "Third Rome" which dominated the Russian consciousness since the fifteenth century. Moscow, it was argued, was the Third Rome—Rome, Constantinople, Moscow. How could Moscow, the center of religious life, admit of mistakes which were to be corrected following the model of the Greeks, who from the time of the Florentine union were suspected of Romanism?

Nikon did not pay any attention to the opposition but used his authority to carry through his policies. The opponents of the ecclesiastical reforms were threatened with exile. But Nikon did not long remain patriarch. In the end of the sixteen-fifties he came into sharp conflict with Tsar Alexis, not so much over personal differences as over differences in principle. Nikon jealously held to the views which he had advanced regarding the authority of the patriarch at the beginning of his reign. He believed that his importance was no less than that of the tsar, and regarded it as his right and duty to take a hand not only in church affairs but also in the affairs of the state. He played an important part in the *Zemsky Sobor* and wished to have the tsar consult him in all important matters. Nikon's pretensions to power soon displeased Tsar Alexis and he began to drift away from the patriarch. When Nikon realized that Alexis had ceased to regard the patriarch as of equal power with the tsar, he protested by refusing to fulfil his functions as patriarch. He left Moscow for a monastery which he had constructed some thirty miles away. It was impossible to elect a new patriarch, as Nikon had not abdicated. The management of the Russian church passed to Tsar Alexis. In 1660 the ecclesiastical *Sobor,* by a majority of votes, deprived Nikon of patriarchal powers; but a minority protested so energetically that Tsar Alexis did not confirm the decision of the majority.

A "Great *Sobor*" was called in Moscow in the autumn of 1666, all the eastern patriarchates taking part. The patriarchs of Alexandria and Antioch came in person. The patriarchs of Constantinople and Jerusalem sent their representatives. The complainant against Nikon was Tsar Alexis himself. The *Sobor* unanimously decided against Nikon and deprived him of his patriarchal authority. He was exiled to a monastery in northern Russia. Later on he was permitted to move to his monastery near Moscow, in 1681, by Tsar Fedor Alexievich. He died in making the journey, near Yaroslavl. His condemnation was the outcome of the political questions arising from the relationship of tsar and patriarch. But the reforms in ritual begun by Nikon were not stopped, and after he was deposed the struggle with the "Old Ritualists" continued.

7.

THE schism of the "Old Ritualists" had far-reaching consequences in the spiritual development of the Russian people. The dissension consumed the most vital forces of the Orthodox church. To the reader of today the causes of the schism must seem small and unimportant, but to the Orthodox believer church ritual was the symbol of religious emotion. The feeling of the faithful was associated with the details of church ceremony. The alterations in ritual were made by Nikon in dictatorial and sudden manner. It was not surprising, therefore, that many believers defended their right to worship in their own way against the measures of either church or lay authorities. The opposition to "Nikonianism" spread not only among ecclesiastics but also widely among laymen. The Government met the dissenters with oppressive measures. The principal leaders of the opposition were exiled—such as Bishop Paul of Kolomna, who protested against Nikon at the *Sobor* in 1654, and Archpriest Avakum, the leader of the earliest "Old Ritualists," whose autobiography is one of the outstanding works of old Russian literature. Following the anathematizing of the opposition at the *Sobor* of 1666–67, repression was redoubled. Some of the most stubborn dissenters were burned, among them Archpriest Avakum. The executions were carried out by the lay authorities.

When the monks in the Solovetsky Monastery in the White Sea refused to accept Nikonianism, troops were dispatched which subjected the monastery to a siege which lasted eight years from 1668 to 1676.

The governmental persecution did not succeed in suppressing the movement, but on the contrary evoked a greater religious enthusiasm. The triumph of Nikonianism in the official court resulted in desperation among the dissenters. Great numbers of "Old Ritualists" began to think that the end of the world was coming and that the Antichrist was due to appear, and some began to wish that—since the end must come—it might be hastened. This tendency led many of the "Old Ritualists" to burn themselves. Many scores or hundreds of people would confine themselves together with their spiritual leaders in wooden barns and then set fire to the walls. Such acts of self-immolation were sometimes undertaken upon notice of the approach of government troops sent to arrest the "Old Ritualists"; but sometimes there was no ascertainable external cause. During the seventeenth century over twenty thousand people lost their lives by burning themselves to death; but toward its end the wave of suicidal hysteria began to pass.

8.

Due to the schism of the "Old Ritualists," the Orthodox church lost many of its leaders. The gaps were filled by churchmen from southwestern Russia. These Ukrainian bishops, priests, and monks filled the churches and monasteries of the Moscow state. Their education bore a Polish impress. Having conducted a constant struggle with the Roman Catholic church, the southern Russian ecclesiastics had unconsciously acquired in part the mentality of their opponents. They brought with them the devices of formal argumentation and theological scholarship. The influence of the southern Russian churchmen imported into Moscow the culture of the Catholic church. But Polish influence had penetrated to Moscow independently. As a result of the long years of Russo-Polish warfare in the second half of the seventeenth century, Poland—defeated—won a spiritual victory over Moscow. Many of Russia's military and diplomatic officers, having been in constant contact with the Poles, were subjected to this influence. This relationship was strengthened by the conclusion of a diplomatic and military alliance with Poland in 1686. Polish customs became the fashion in the Moscow court in the seventies and especially in the eighties of the seventeenth century. Once the national isolation of Moscow was broken, it was clear that the penetration of western influences would not be limited to the relations with Poland. It was possible to foresee the influence of central and western European powers as well. In Moscow of the seventeenth century there was a suburb where citizens of German and Anglo-Saxon countries lived. They were officers, doctors, craftsmen, and traders. A few foreigners had penetrated to Moscow in the fifteenth and sixteenth centuries, but in the seventeenth century they were numerous. At the end of the seventeenth century many of the Russian political leaders were in contact with foreigners. A decisive moment arrived when these influences reached the tsar himself.

9.

Tsar Alexis was married twice. He had several children by his first wife and Peter, born in 1672, was a son by his second wife. Following his second marriage the court was divided into two parties, the first composed of those related to Alexis by his first marriage, the Miloslavskys, and the second of those related to him by his second marriage, the Naryshkins. Both groups had their followers. Each tried to secure the support of the Moscow garrison, called the *Streltzy*. These were infantry regiments organized by Ivan the Terrible. In their free time they engaged in trade and crafts. This created a close contact between them and the city population of Moscow, but it prevented the maintenance of strict discipline among the *Streltzy*. At the time of the death of Tsar Alexis in 1676, the discipline of the garrison was extremely lax. The nervous tension in Moscow caused by the religious disputes of the time was also felt by the *Streltzy*, who thus represented a convenient field for propaganda. Alexis' eldest son, Fedor, who succeeded his father, was a sickly and unenergetic man. Following his death in 1682 an encounter took place between the two court parties. The Naryshkins called the Moscow population to the Red Square to act as a substitute for the *Zemsky Sobor* and "elected" their candidate, the youngest son of Alexis, the ten-year-old Peter, to the throne. They passed by the seventeen-year-old Ivan, Alexis' son by his first marriage.

Two weeks later the opposing party of the Miloslavskys succeeded in arousing the *Streltzy* to mutiny. They broke into the palace, killed several influential members of the Naryshkin party, and demanded that Ivan be named tsar. As a compromise the Moscow throne was occupied by two co-tsars. Actually, power passed to the Miloslavsky party.

Tsar Ivan was a weak man, incapable of ruling. His eldest sister, the Tsarevna Sophia, a woman of remarkable intellectual energy, was named regent. She attempted to introduce western Russian and Polish influences in carrying out a gradual cultural reform of the Moscow state. Polish influence found expression in questions of foreign policy. In 1686 Moscow concluded a perpetual peace with Poland and an alliance with her against the Turks and the Tartars. Moscow thus joined the great coalition of Christian states of eastern and southern Europe directed against Turkey. Venice and Poland played the leading role in the coalition. In 1683 the Polish king, Jan Sobieski, defeated the Turks before Vienna, thus delivering the first blow to the gradually declining power of the Turks. Moscow undertook to destroy the Crimean Tartar state, but the two campaigns of the Moscow troops failed to achieve their object.

Simultaneously with the failure in the south, Moscow's foreign policy suffered defeat in the Far East. During the first half of the seventeenth century Moscow was continually increasing its possessions in the east. Tradesmen and Cossacks, as well as government representatives, rapidly penetrated eastward. Their chief interest was in valuable furs, secured either by trapping or from natives by purchase or taxation. Following the individual pioneers, the administrative system of the Moscow state organized the new territories. As early as 1632 the town of Yakutsk in northeastern Siberia was founded, and in the sixteen-forties the pioneers reached the Sea of Okhotsk. At the same time, they penetrated to the valley of the Amur River, but here they soon met Chinese troops. In 1689 the Moscow state concluded a treaty with China by the terms of which the river remained Chinese. The Russians returned to the valley of the Amur only in the middle of the nineteenth century.

10.

THE failures in foreign policy resulted in a loss of popularity for Tsarevna Sophia's government. Meanwhile, Sophia realized that with each year the younger of the tsars, in whose name she ruled, Peter was nearing his majority. She knew, as did all her courtiers, that Peter was endowed with extraordinary energy, intellectual curiosity, and a lively temperament. It was clear that as soon as he became of age he would seize power for himself.

During Sophia's rule Peter lived in a village near Moscow. He grew up outside the influence of official royal education, and left to his own resources he made the acquaintance of German technicians from the German suburb at Moscow. Alert and informal, he learned from them all that there was to know about shipping matters, which greatly interested him. Peter also studied arithmetic and geometry. He organized among his playmates unofficial regiments, similar to the Boy Scouts, and put them through military maneuvers.

This period of Peter's life was brought to an end by the news that the party of Tsarevna Sophia was preparing an attempt against his life. He was only seventeen years old at this time but he succeeded in carrying out a *coup d'état* with the help of part of the *Streltzy*. Tsarevna Sophia was arrested and shut up in a convent in 1689.

Peter began to occupy himself on a larger scale with military and naval matters. He did some sailing in the White Sea near Archangel. The direction of governmental affairs fell into the hands of Peter's mother and her group of supporters. An important part was played by the patriarch. The new policy was a reaction against western Russian and Polish influences. But the reaction did not last long. In 1695 came a new war with Turkey. It gave Peter the opportunity to apply his military and technical knowledge. He was anxious to avoid the military errors of Sophia's administration and chose for his point of assault the Turkish fortress of Azov at the mouth of the river Don. Peter attacked Azov with his new disciplined regiments which had formed from the play regiments of his boyhood. In Voronezh he rapidly constructed ships to descend the Don. The first attack upon Azov was unsuccessful, but in the following year, 1696, Peter succeeded in taking the fortress. The capture of Azov he regarded as a successful test of his new army and his new military methods.

From this time on Peter took the reins of power into his hands and carried through a policy of close political contact with Europe. The new policy was not merely to open the doors to Polish influence, as under Sophia, but to the countries of central and western Europe.

CHAPTER VI.

THE RUSSIAN EMPIRE IN THE EIGHTEENTH CENTURY

I.

THE reign of Peter the Great opened a new period in Russian history. Russia became a typical state following the European pattern. The administration and the judiciary, the army, and social classes, were reorganized along western lines. The industry and trade of the country developed rapidly, and a great improvement in technical training and sciences took place.

The Russian people in the course of the eighteenth and nineteenth centuries reached the natural geographic limits of their expansion: the Baltic and Black Seas in the west, the Pacific Ocean in the east, and the Pamir Plateau in the south. With the exception of the inhabitants of the regions in the southwest—Galicia, Bukovina, and Ugro-Russia—all the branches of the Russian people were united during these centuries in one single state.

But the great triumphs of the imperial period in the history of Russia were accompanied by profound internal disorders. The chief crisis was in the development of the national psychology. The Europeanization of Russia brought with it new political, religious, and social ideas, which were absorbed by the governing and upper classes of society before they reached the masses of the people. Consequently a split occurred between the top and the bottom of society, between "the intellectuals" and "the people." The chief psychological basis of the old Russian state, found in the Orthodox church, was shaken in the course of the seventeenth century, and was gradually losing its influence from the beginning of the eighteenth until the Revolution of 1917, when it underwent a serious crisis. Together with the religious problem, political and social problems took on an acute character. The political emergency was brought about by the cessation of the *Zemsky Sobors* after

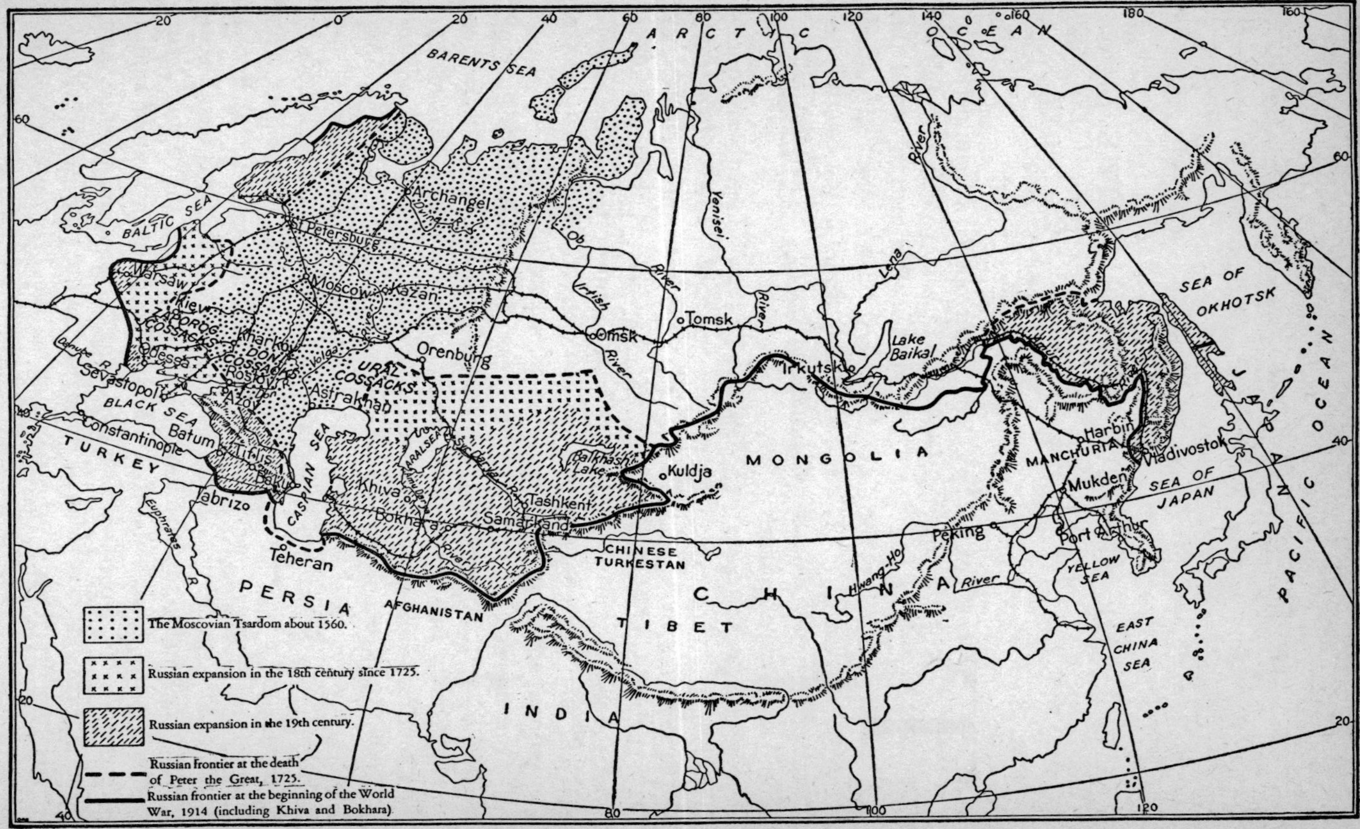

THE GROWTH OF RUSSIAN EMPIRE TO 1914

1682, which deprived the people of political power, and the abrogation of local self-government in 1708.

The Government keenly felt its lack of contact with the people following the reforms of Peter. It soon realized that the majority did not sympathize with the program of Europeanization. To carry out its reforms, the Government was consequently forced to act harshly, as, in fact, Peter the Great did. Later the concept of absolutism became habitual and traditional. Meanwhile western political thought influenced the Europeanized circles of Russian society, which absorbed ideas of political progress and rapidly became ready to fight absolutism. Thus the reforms of Peter set in motion political forces which the Government later was not capable of controlling.

The political crisis was complicated by social instability. The barriers between classes became sharper as time went on, and the stage was finally reached where only autocratic government was capable of mediating between the various groups in society.

2.

THE character of Peter the Great reached its full development following the Azov campaigns in 1695–96. His chief traits were enormous physical energy and persistency combined with intellectual activity and determination. Peter had no respect for traditions and authority. His mind was as constantly in search of knowledge as his hands were of work. Peter could not be inactive for a moment. He was not content with theoretical knowledge, he wanted to try everything himself. For this reason he worked as a carpenter on the docks when he was building the new Russian navy, and pulled teeth when he wanted to learn medicine. But for all that, Peter was of an imperious nature that brooked no contradiction. He demanded that everyone submit without question to his will, and he was capable of great cruelty.

Primarily his concern was the good, not of the Russian people, but rather of the Russian state. His famous order before the Battle of Poltava illustrates this principle: "Do not think of Peter, the only thing that matters is that Russia remain alive." He made exacting demands both on himself and on others, and stopped at nothing in pursuing the interests of the state as he conceived them.

Having acquired a great respect for European sciences and technology, Peter expected the same from all his subordinates. Peter acted impulsively. He succeeded in doing great things: he created a first-class army and the best state chancellery that Moscow had ever had. He also turned his attention to details: he demanded that all his subjects dress in European clothes and shave off their beards. Peter succeeded in this only as far as the military officers and civil servants and nobles were concerned. He personally supervised the exact execution of his orders, making no distinction between large matters or small, and threatened severe punishment for their nonfulfilment.

In carrying out his reforms, Peter completely overlooked the national psychology. For this reason both his admirers and his enemies regarded him as a man foreign to the Russian spirit. But with all his apparent opposition to Russian tradition and habits, Peter was a typical Russian.

3.

THE capture of Azov was the first test of the new "regular" army. Peter realized that Russia was capable of fighting Turkey and securing a foothold on the coast of the Black Sea. He wanted to continue the war with Turkey on a large scale and for this purpose considered it essential to enter into alliances with European states. Thus arose the idea of the Extraordinary Russian Embassy which was to tour the chief courts of Europe. The Embassy left Moscow in the spring of 1697. The personnel included Peter, who traveled *incognito* under the name of Peter Michailov. The route taken by the Embassy was first, Riga, at the time a Swedish town, then Courland, the Electorate of Brandenburg (Prussia), Holland, England, and back through Holland to Vienna. From Vienna Peter was to have continued to Venice, but news arrived from Moscow that the *Streltzy* had revolted, and Peter hurriedly returned to his capital in the summer of 1698.

The Embassy was not successful in accomplishing what had been planned by Russian diplomacy, namely, the creation of an all-European alliance against the Turks. The moment was ill-chosen. Europe was occupied by the struggle between the Hapsburgs and the Bourbons. The only state directly interested in the struggle against the Turks was Venice, and it was just this state that Peter failed to visit. While not succeeding in its purpose, the Embassy of 1697–98 had important consequences. It brought a number of talented Russians into direct contact with Europe and particularly influenced Tsar Peter. He had the opportunity of satisfying his thirst for learning European technique. In Holland and in England, Peter had time to study shipbuilding—in Holland he worked as a carpenter in the shipyard. The Embassy made decided advances toward the cultural Europeanization of Russia.

The Embassy also had diplomatic consequences. It drew the attention of Peter away from the Turks to other matters. He observed that in a number of Baltic states, among them Brandenburg (Prussia), Poland, and Denmark, there was growing the idea of a war with Sweden which then controlled the greater part of the coast of the Baltic Sea. Peter decided to take advantage of this situation and to participate in the struggle. Thus it turned out that Peter went to Europe with the idea of fighting the Turks and returned with the idea of fighting the Swedes.

On his return to Moscow in August, 1698, Peter first investigated the uprising of the *Streltzy,* which had been suppressed before his return. He then began to prepare for a war with Sweden. A treaty was concluded with the Polish king, Augustus II, and King Christian of Denmark, but Peter refused to begin a new war before making peace with the Turks. In the summer of 1700, a Russian plenipotentiary concluded a treaty of peace with Turkey in Constantinople, under which Azov was annexed by Russia. Immediately upon receiving news of peace with Turkey, Peter moved an army to the Swedish town of Narva in the Gulf of Finland. This was the customary move of Moscow in all its wars with Sweden.

The war with Sweden began very unfavorably for Peter and his allies. The young king, Charles XII, vanquished Denmark at one stroke and then turned against Russia. The Russian army was defeated at Narva. Charles, thinking that he had finished with the Russians, then turned against Augustus. This drew him away from Russia, and in the expression of Peter, "He got 'stuck' in Poland." This circumstance was the salvation of Peter. The defeat at Narva did not break his military ambition, but on the contrary gave it a powerful stimulus. There began the feverish activity of

Peter in organizing the Russian army along new lines. He dispatched auxiliary forces to Poland and Lithuania to aid Augustus, but his attention was chiefly directed to the Baltic coast.

In the course of 1701–04, Peter conquered Ingria. In May, 1703, he founded the new city of St. Petersburg. Its construction in the swamps of the Gulf of Finland, the conscription of recruits for the army, the supply and transportation of foodstuffs for the army—all demanded great sacrifices from the population. Peter demanded constantly more money and men. Popular discontent found expression in a series of revolts. In 1705 an uprising took place in Astrakhan against the *boyars* and "the Germans," the term *Niemetz* (German) in popular parlance meaning any foreigner. At the same time another occurred among the Bashkirs, which was suppressed only in 1709. In 1707 the Don Cossacks rose when Peter sent an army to the Don to recapture escaped robbers and runaway slaves. The poorer Cossacks under the leadership of Bulavin overpowered the house-owning Cossacks and the uprising took on a threatening aspect. Peter was forced to send large forces to the Don. Bulavin was caught in Cherkassk, where he committed suicide in 1708. His accomplices took refuge in the Kuban. All these uprisings were suppressed with great difficulty. At one time it seemed that the whole of the southeast of Russia would revolt. The situation was saved by the Astrakhan Kalmyks, whose Khan sent a large military force of over twenty thousand men to aid in restoring order.

Simultaneously the foreign danger grew. Charles drove Augustus from Poland, pursued him to the boundaries of Saxony, and compelled him to conclude a separate peace in 1707. Poland elected a new king, Stanislav Leszczynski, under the pressure of Charles whom he supported. At the end of 1707 the Swedes moved against Russia. In the beginning of 1708 Charles took the town of Grodno and the Russian army barely escaped a crushing defeat. From Grodno Charles attacked Mogilev; Peter expected a further advance against Smolensk and Moscow, and Moscow was hurriedly fortified. But Charles unexpectedly turned south to the Ukraine without awaiting the arrival from Latvia of an auxiliary corps that accompanied large quantities of military supplies and provisions, only relying upon the assistance of Hetman Mazepa, who, planning to abandon Peter, opened negotiations with the new Polish king Stanislav as early as 1707. Charles wisely planned to supplement his military attack upon Russia by an organized political uprising against the Russian Government. In this respect the Austro-German forces during the First World War followed his example. But he overestimated the strength of Mazepa, who joined him with an insignificant force of Cossacks. By not waiting at Mogilev, Charles had committed a great mistake. In September, 1708, Peter defeated the auxiliary force near the village Lesnaya and captured the whole Swedish supply train.

In 1709 came the climax. Peter considered it necessary to save Poltava from Charles and Mazepa, for this city was the key to the route to Voronezh, the chief base of Peter's southern fleet, containing large reserve stores of grain. The battle of Poltava was decided principally by the superiority of Peter's artillery. The Swedish army was completely defeated. Several days afterward, the remnants gave themselves up to Menshikov who overtook them at the crossing of the Dnieper. Only Charles and Mazepa succeeded in crossing the Dnieper with a small following and escaped to Turkey. The victory of Poltava had great consequences. Stanislav Leszczynski was forced to leave Poland and Augustus, regaining the throne, declared war upon Sweden.

Charles did not hasten to return from Turkey to Sweden, but attempted to use his presence there to draw Turkey into war with Russia. His intrigues met with success. Toward the end of 1710 Turkey declared war upon Russia. Peter decided to undertake an offensive war. A European alliance against Turkey proving impossible, Peter returned to the program of his predecessor, Alexis Michaelovich, and utilized for his purpose the sympathies of the Orthodox subjects of the Sultan—the Slavs, Rumanians, and Greeks. He received promises of assistance from the princes of Moldavia and Wallachia, and moved toward the Danube with a small army of not more than forty thousand men. His troops soon began to suffer from lack of provisions which had been promised by the princes but which never came. Having reached the river Pruth, Peter found himself surrounded by a great Turkish army of 200,000 men. He considered it a stroke of luck that the Turkish vizier agreed to enter into peace negotiations, in which he had to cede to the Turks the town of Azov, secured earlier with such extraordinary efforts.

The Turkish campaign of Peter undermined the military prestige he had acquired by the victory at Poltava, and this protracted the Swedish war. Peter, however, continued it with great energy. In 1714 the Russian fleet was completely victorious over the Swedish fleet at Gangut. Peter also captured the Aaland Islands, and from them he was able to threaten Stockholm. This was the turning point of the war. In 1717–18 peace parleys began between Peter and Charles, who meanwhile had returned to Sweden from Turkey.

These negotiations were broken by the death of Charles, and the war continued for another three years. In the end Sweden was forced to conclude peace. The treaty of Nystadt of August 30, 1721, ceded Ingria, Esthonia, and Latvia to Russia. St. Petersburg—which in the words of Peter was "a window to Europe"—was formally secured. Russia gained easy access to the shores of the Baltic Sea. The struggle of centuries, it seemed, had at last given her a favorable position. By the Brest-Litovsk peace of March 3, 1918, Russia lost all the Baltic acquisitions of Peter with the exception of Ingria.

The Senate presented Peter with the titles of "Father of his Country, Emperor, and Great" (Pater Patriae, Imperator, Maximus). The Byzantine idea of the tsar was exchanged for the Latin idea of the emperor. Peter hastened to make secure the position of Russia in the Baltic Sea by a series of diplomatic marriages. One of his nieces was married to the Duke of Courland, and another niece, Catherine, to the Duke of Mecklenburg. Peter also arranged the marriage of his daughter Anne to the Duke of Holstein. These Baltic relations of the Russian imperial house later gave the nation considerable anxiety and frequently exercised an unfortunate influence upon Russian foreign policy.

4.

THE great tension caused by Peter's policy of unceasing war called forth constant disorders, first in Moscow, as in the uprising of the *Streltzy* in 1698, and later in the provinces those led by Bulavin, Mazepa, and others. All these rebellions were successfully suppressed by Peter, thanks to the new organization of the army and of the state. Peter had combined the new European technique with the old Muscovite organization of the army. The secret of the discipline of his army lay in the exceptional importance of the Guards regiments, composed entirely of nobles.

The organs of government were also reformed to comply with European state principles. Russia was divided into governmental provinces in 1708. The Senate was placed at the head of the administration in 1711. Later, to direct the separate functions of the central government *"collegia"* were formed which were supervised by councils and not by individual Ministers.

In 1716 the Army Statutes were published. They were based on Swedish and German models. The harsh rules of military procedure were applied to criminal and civil offenses in general. Prior to these reforms, the new direction of policy was symbolized by the transfer of the capital from Moscow to St. Petersburg. The "regulated" state created by Peter was based upon the strictest subjection of all persons and classes to its interests. Peter regarded himself as its first servant. The nobility was called upon to give unlimited military service, the merchant and manufacturing classes to give economic assistance, the peasants to supply recruits and supplies to the army and all services connected with it, and also the workmen and horses for the construction of new towns and factories. Taxes were levied upon them. Peter regarded both the privately owned and government-owned peasant serfs as state property. Those belonging to the *pomiestchiks* merely paid smaller state taxes, since they had already had to pay a part to their masters so that these in turn could serve the Government.

The increasing burden of services to the state created extensive dissatisfaction among the people. This reaction was perhaps even more dangerous to Peter than open uprisings. Both the lowest and the highest classes were seething with discontent. The higher circles of the Moscow aristocracy—the *boyars*—were especially disturbed because Peter did not pay respect to seniority, but only to individual capacities. This attitude of Peter was later formulated in the Table of Ranks published in 1722. The lowest rank as an officer, that of lieutenant, conferred hereditary nobility on the holder. The aristocracy of service or *dvoriantsvo* replaced the aristocracy of birth. Naturally the hereditary nobles were displeased with Peter's reforms.

The church was also disaffected, as its position was lowered by

Peter. He was not an atheist, but his faith was not the traditional Russian faith. Greatly influenced by Protestantism, he believed that the Russian church should be reorganized in accord with the new European models. Protestantism, furthermore, helped to subject the church to the emperor—"*Cujus regio, ejus religio.*"

Under the influence of Protestantism, Peter came to the conclusion that the independence of the church was harmful and that the church should be subordinated to the civil power. Following the death of Patriarch Adrian in 1700, Peter refused to allow the election of a new patriarch. The patriarchal throne remained vacant, and only a guardian for it was appointed.

In reorganizing the higher branches of administration during the second half of his reign, Peter introduced a clerical *collegium* for the government of the Russian church. This body was later renamed the Holy Synod, but its character did not change. Thus, the highest organ of church government became a bureaucratic agency subject to the emperor. The number of the clergy was limited, and Peter passed a number of laws against monasticism. An "all-comic and all-drunken Council" was organized for the amusement of Peter, a grotesque parody of the church ritual. Its principal characters were "Prince Pope" and "Prince Patriarch." All this explains the opposition of the church to Peter.

However, the opposition of the church, the nobility, and the peasantry was not sufficiently well organized to lead to an uprising against Peter. But it did find a leader very close to the emperor. This was the Tsarevich Alexis, son of Peter by his first marriage. Peter soon separated from his wife and began living with a Latvian prisoner, Skavronskaya, whom he later married and who took the name of Catherine Alexeievna. Peter's daughters Anne and Elizabeth were the children of this second marriage. The political rivalry led to a family tragedy. Following a quarrel with his father, Alexis fled abroad. Fearing that some foreign power would take advantage of Alexis as a means to disturb the internal situation in Russia, Peter sent agents who succeeded by means of fraudulent promises in persuading Alexis to return to Russia. There Alexis was arrested, tried and sentenced to death in 1718. The Tsarevich died several hours before the time set for the execution from nervous shock and the effects of torture. A number of his followers were tortured and executed. After this the opposition subsided, and even following the death of Peter in 1725 it did not immediately re-awaken.

5.

At the insistence of the Guards regiments, the widow Catherine was named Peter's successor, but sovereignty passed in fact to the Supreme Secret Council which comprised the leading personages of Peter's new aristocracy, Menshikov, Tolstoy, Osterman, and others. Only one member of the council, Prince Golitsyn, belonged to the old aristocracy. The Supreme Secret Council continued to control governmental affairs even after the death of Catherine in 1727, but very soon the political situation changed. The new emperor, Peter II, the son of Alexis, was only twelve years old. His coronation was followed by a reaction. The old opposition to Peter's reforms raised its head. The church and *boyar* parties reappeared in the political arena. The imperial court moved to Moscow, although St. Petersburg did not cease to be the capital. The membership of the Supreme Secret Council was completely changed by the intrigues of the reactionary group which succeeded in driving out its members one by one. The new members of the council were of the old aristocratic party. Soon, with the exception of Osterman, all the members of the council were of the Golitsyn or Dolgoruky families. When the young emperor died from smallpox before his coronation in 1730, the Supreme Secret Council acted as regent. It decided to invite to the throne one of the Baltic nieces of Peter the Great, Ann of Courland.

Prior to being vested with the imperial power, Ann was called upon to sign certain "Conditions," according to which the actual power in the state passed from the empress to the Supreme Secret Council. The Russian Empire thus became an oligarchy. The news of the "Conditions" in favor of the council aroused excitement among the Guards officers who had assembled in Moscow in great numbers to attend the coronation of Peter II. The city became the scene of unusual political activity; meetings were called; plans were made for a Chamber of Nobles in the Government to assist the Supreme Secret Council. It soon became apparent that the majority of the Guards officers were opposed to the oligarchical privileges of the council. They were greatly concerned with questions affecting the limitation of military service, and desired to end the service of nobles as ordinary soldiers in the Guards regiments. Under Peter the nobles were compelled to serve in the army without time limit. They likewise desired to repeal the restrictions upon the inheritance of noble estates. The new empress knew how to take advantage of the discontent of the officers, and promised them civil and economic privileges. The "Conditions" were torn up, the Supreme Secret Council dismissed, and autocratic power triumphed again.

6.

THE reign of Empress Ann was marked by the ascendancy of the Baltic German party at the Russian Court. The favorites of the empress were now Biren, Duke of Courland, Osterman, and Field Marshal Münnich. After the death of Empress Ann, during the short reign of Ivan VI, grandson of her sister Catherine, Duchess of Mecklenburg, the members of the ruling German group began to intrigue against each other. This circumstance made a *coup d'état* possible. The officers of one of the Guards regiments called Peter's daughter Elizabeth to the throne and the youthful emperor, Ivan VI, was arrested on January 5, 1742.

The leading members of the group supporting Elizabeth—the Vorontsovs, the Shuvalovs, Chernyshevs, and others—belonged to the Russian gentry. The triumph of the "Russian" party over the "German" did not bring with it a return to the national ideals that prevailed before Peter's time. The German cultural influence at court was exchanged for French culture. Henceforth French, English, and German influences maintained themselves at court to the middle of the nineteenth century.

Russia during the reign of Ann and Elizabeth was not faced with any definite foreign problems and did not succeed in achieving permanent results with respect to Europe. Austrian and, later, French policies exercised their pressure upon Russia and in part determined Russian activity. During the reign of Ann, Russia interfered in Polish affairs and opposed the French candidate to the Polish throne. This struggle did not affect Russia's interests. War with Turkey also resulted in nothing, despite the brilliant victories of Münnich.

During the reign of Elizabeth, Russia participated with Austria and France in the Seven Years' War against Prussia. The war was favorable to Russia. Eastern Prussia was occupied by the Russian army under General Saltykov who, together with the Austrians, inflicted a decisive defeat upon Frederick the Great at Kunersdorf in 1759. Russian troops occupied Berlin, but the death of Elizabeth in 1762 put an end to Russia's gains. The successor of Elizabeth, a nephew from Holstein, Peter III, was an ardent admirer of Frederick and immediately concluded a separate peace. Peter III desired to go even further and to send an army to the help of Prussia against Russia's recent allies, Austria and France. This intention, however, gave rise to an officers' riot, and the Russian throne was given to Peter's wife, Catherine, by birth a German, Princess of Anhalt-Zerbst, in 1762.

The period of almost forty years from 1725 to 1762 between the death of Peter the Great and the coronation of Catherine II was of little significance in the foreign policy of Russia with respect to Europe. Unproductive also in internal changes, it nevertheless had a great significance in the eastern policy of Russia. Precisely at this time a sound basis was laid for the new period of Russian expansion in the east. The main lines of the new eastern policy were laid down by Peter the Great, who set up the guideposts for it in both the Far and Middle East. He attempted to enter into relations with China. He sent a Russian embassy to Peking in 1720–22. He also entered into relations with Japan. When Russian Cossacks occupied Kamchatka in 1697, they met a Japanese survivor of a shipwreck. Peter called him to Moscow and ordered him to teach several Russian children Japanese. After the death of Peter Russia concluded a permanent treaty with China. Trade relations between the Russians and the Chinese were limited to a single point—Kyakhta-Maimachin on the Siberian-Mongolian border; Russia received the permanent right to have a religious mission in Peking, which was at first also a diplomatic mission.

Peter further organized the Behring Expedition which was sent to discover whether Asia and America were joined. The fact that this problem had already been solved by Dezhnev in 1648 was not known in St. Petersburg. Behring's first expedition in 1724–30 had few practical results, but in 1732 the navigator Fedorov and the geodesist Gvozdev stumbled upon the "Great Land," the American continent, at Alaska. In the course of the next decade, from 1733 to 1743, the Russian Government organized the so-called "Great

Northern Expedition," which was of immense scientific importance and one of the most remarkable undertakings in the history of science. In 1741 Captain Behring reached the shore of America at latitude 58° 28′ N. Captain Chirikov, in charge of another ship, also reached America at latitude 56° N., but was not able to make a landing. From the islands near Alaska, Chirikov's crew brought many valuable furs, which stimulated the initiative of Siberian merchants. The first "merchant sea voyage" was undertaken in 1743, to be followed by many others.

The Middle East attracted Peter's attention no less than the Far East. The objective of his policy in this region was to establish direct trade relations with India. This was not easy to achieve. Peter's first plan consisted in attempting to conquer the central Asiatic Khanates, Khiva and Bokhara. The plan was unsuccessful. A Russian division of troops sent to Khiva was betrayed and destroyed in 1717. Equally unsuccessful was the attempted expansion of Russia into the Middle East from the Irtysh River. But the failure did not put an end to Peter's hopes, and in 1721 a Russian envoy was sent to Khiva and Bokhara.

The policy pursued by Peter aroused the fears of Persia, which led to a war in 1722. Persia he regarded as a step on the road to India. One of his contemporaries expressed his policy as follows: "The hopes of His Majesty were not concerned with Persia alone; if he had been lucky in Persia and were still living, he would of course have attempted to reach India or even China. This I heard from His Majesty myself."

The Russian army moved from Astrakhan southward along the western shore of the Caspian Sea, occupying the cities of Derbent and Baku. By the peace of 1723 Russia received from Persia all the western and southern shore of that sea. After the death of Peter the Russian Government renounced these acquisitions in view of the great expense of defending them. They were returned to Persia (1729–35). Following the Persian war Peter thought of opening a sea route to India. In December, 1723, two warships were sent out from Revel. The commanding vice-admiral received two instructions, one ordering him to seize Madagascar, the other to sail to the East Indies and Bengal. The vessels were to sail secretly in the guise of trade ships. The expectation, however, was not carried out as they turned out to be unfit for such a long voyage—one ship sprang a leak as soon as it entered the open sea.

At the time of Peter's death the frontier of the Russian Empire in the Middle East formed an angle from the Altai Range down the Irtysh River to Omsk, and from Omsk to the upper reaches of the Yaik River and thence along the Yaik to the Caspian Sea. The Middle Eastern steppe was at the very Russian frontier. The Yaik was a feeble barrier and the untamed steppe peoples entered and left the territories of the Russian Empire without even being aware of it.

Three leading ethnographical groups had to be taken into consideration at the time by Russian policy. The Bashkirs, the Kalmyks, and the Kirghiz moved over a huge area lying approximately between the Volga River and the Altai and T'ien-shan Mountains. The Kirghiz were divided into three hordes—the eldest, the middle, and the youngest. Pressure from the Kalmyks forced them to seek aid from the Russians.

Ivan Kirilov, one of the most outstanding Russian statesmen of the eighteenth century, took advantage of this situation. Kirilov regarded the Kirghiz horde as the key to all Asiatic lands, and insisted upon building a town at the mouth of the river Or in the southern Urals. His plan was to extend Russian domination to the east of the Aral Sea, and he dreamed of "picking up the provinces of Bokhara and Samarkand"—that is to say, of occupying Turkestan.

Empress Ann approved the policy of Kirilov, and he was made leader of the expedition to the river Or. He first suppressed an uprising of Bashkirs who opposed the extension of Russian dominion to the southern Urals and laid the foundation of a new town at the junction of the rivers Or and Yaik in 1736, which was named Orenburg and later Orsk.

Kirilov died in the spring of 1737, but his program was not abandoned. In 1742 the new government agent, who was also a pupil of Peter's, moved the town to another site near the mouth of the river Samara, and fortified lines from Orenburg to Samara and to the Caspian Sea were constructed to enforce the obedience of the Bashkirs, the Kalmyks, and the Kirghiz. In 1754–55 in view of the oppressive measures of the Russian Government against the

Mohammedans, there occurred another Bashkir uprising under the leadership of Batyrsha, who attempted without success to arouse the Kirghiz. Nepliuev, the successor of Kirilov, succeeded in gaining the support of the people who occupied the Bashkir lands as tenants, but although he carried on the ideas of his predecessor, he did not succeed in advancing Russian power to the Aral Sea.

7.

THE reign of Catherine II, from 1762 to 1796, raised new problems in Russian foreign policy, and transferred the attention of Russian diplomacy from the Far and Middle East to the Near East and the west. The Far East was left to the initiative of individual traders. In the second half of the eighteenth century they founded Russian settlements in America, in Alaska, and the neighboring islands. Special energy was shown by the merchant Gregory Shelekhov, nicknamed "the Russian Columbus." He had migrated to Siberia at the age of twenty-eight; in 1777 he had chartered his first ship to the Kuril Islands, and then made voyages to the Aleutian Islands. In 1784 Shelekhov formed a trading company with the brothers Golikov and occupied the island Kadiak near Alaska. From this center the Shelekhov company rapidly increased its possessions on the continent. Its chief activity was the purchase of the valuable furs of seals and beavers from the natives.

In the Middle East the Government of Catherine II aimed primarily to maintain peace among the Turkish peoples by officially supporting the Mohammedan faith, in contrast to the Russian policy during the reign of Empress Elizabeth. In 1785 Catherine published a charter of religious toleration. The Russian Government began immediately to take a great interest in the education of the Kirghiz, and school books were published in the Kirghiz language together with Russian. Mullahs from Kazan were appointed teachers of the natives, in the absence of trained candidates among the Russians and Kirghiz. These measures led to the artificial encouragement of Mohammedanism and medieval Mohammedan learning among the Kirghiz.

8.

IN the west Catherine's foreign policy falls into two distinct periods. The first period, prior to 1780, was characterized by the existence of the so-called "northern alliance" between Russia, England, Prussia, and Sweden. The second period was marked by an understanding between Russia and Austria. The turning point between the two periods of Catherine's diplomacy was the "Act of armed neutrality" of 1780. It was published in connection with the American War of Independence and favored the revolutionary colonies against England. It insisted upon the right of neutral ships to enter into trade with belligerent states and to import all goods with the exception of arms and munitions.

The European policy of Catherine was determined by the Polish and the Turkish questions. Her first problem was to determine the fate of the western Russian lands, a large part of which were in the possession of Poland in the beginning of the eighteenth century. The second was to extend the territories of Russia to the shores of the Black Sea, which formed the natural boundary of the Russian state.

The Polish question first arose with respect to the rights of the Orthodox population of Poland and Lithuania. During the diplomatic *rapprochement* between Russia and Poland in the late seventeenth and early eighteenth century, the Orthodox population of Poland was subjected to Polonization and forcible conversion to Uniate Church. The Prussian king, Frederick II, was protecting the rights of the Protestants in Poland. Russian diplomacy consequently sought an agreement with Prussia. Meanwhile, the Polish *Seim* rejected the petition of rights of the "dissenters," that is, the non-Catholic portions of the population. This led to quarrels between the various parties of the Polish nobility, which in turn brought about an intervention of the powers and a partition of Poland. Prussia received western Poland, which was populated chiefly by Poles; Austria received Galicia, populated by Poles and Ukrainians; Russia took Polotsk, Vitebsk, and Mogilev, populated by White Russians. Nineteen years later under the influence of revolutionary ideas coming from France, great changes took place in Poland. On May 3, 1791, the *Seim* adopted a new constitution. The right of *liberum veto* was rescinded; the central power was strengthened. The Constitution of May 3d turned the former loosely knit Polish state into a new centralized state. The Grand Duchy of Lithuania was formally incorporated in Poland. In the development of Poland, this Constitution was a great forward step, but with respect to Lithuania and western Russia, it marked the culmination of the policy of forcible Polonization. While the Constitution protected the rights of Polish citizens, it disregarded those of the Lithuanian and Russian population. The publication of the Constitution provoked a civil war in Poland. The conservative sections of the Polish nobility, displeased with the Constitution, requested Catherine to intervene. Russia sent troops into Poland and occupied Warsaw. The second partition of Poland took place in 1793. Russia took a considerable portion of the western Russian lands—Minsk, part of Volhynia, and Podolia. The boundary between Poland and the Soviet Union from 1921 to 1939 corresponded approximately to the Russo-Polish boundary after the second partition. Prussia occupied Poznan. What remained of the Polish Kingdom was forced to rescind the Constitution of May 3d. In 1794 uprisings took place in Warsaw and Cracow, organized by Polish patriots, in protest against the plight of their country. The Russian garrison was forced to retreat from the city when about two thousand sleeping soldiers were killed in the night by rioters. A Polish revolutionary government, headed by Kosciuszko, was formed. This government declared war upon Prussia and Russia. Catherine sent the best Russian troops, headed by Suvorov, against Poland. In 1794 Suvorov occupied Praga, a suburb of Warsaw. Kosciuszko was previously taken prisoner by another detachment of the Russian army. After this Poland ceased to exist as a separate state. By the third partition in 1795, Prussia received Mazowia, with the city of Warsaw; Austria took Little Poland, with the city of Cracow; Russia took Courland, Lithuania, and the western part of Volhynia—that is, territories populated by Ukrainians, Lithuanians, and Letts. As a result of the partitions of Poland, Russia retook possession of all the southwestern Russian lands, with the exception of Kholm, Galicia, Karpato-Russia, and Bukovina.

9.

A SOLUTION of the Black Sea question was essential to Russia, both for economic and political reasons. Only by reaching the Black Sea and destroying the Crimean Khanate could southern Russia be freed from constant dangers which hindered economic development. As late as the middle of the eighteenth century, Crimean Tartars still made destructive incursions into the Ukraine. The expansion of the Russian state to its natural frontier at the Black Sea demanded great efforts, and took the greater part of the eighteenth century. Under Empress Ann the Government, following the old Moscow custom, constructed a fortified barrier. In 1731–35 the so-called Ukrainian barrier between the Dnieper and the northern Don was constructed. Twenty regiments of territorial militia were settled along this line. The fortress of St. Ann was constructed on the lower Don. This was later renamed for St. Dmitri of Rostov and is now known as Rostov-on-the-Don.

In 1736 a war with Turkey broke out. It was especially burdensome to Russia in view of the difficulty of conducting campaigns at great distances in the Crimea and Moldavia, but the Russian troops under the leadership of Field Marshal Münnich achieved a series of important victories—the capture of Perekop, Ochakov, Azov, and the battles of Stavuchany and Khotin. The peace of Belgrade of 1739, however, did not adequately repay the enormous effort and the brilliant successes of Russia in the war. All Russia received was a portion of the steppe from the Bug River to Taganrog. It was agreed that the fort of Azov should be torn down and a neutral strip of territory left between Russia and Turkey. Russia, moreover, did not receive the right to have a fleet in the Black Sea. The Government of Elizabeth strengthened the southern boundary of Russia by extensive military colonization. In 1752 sixteen thousand Serbs settled on the right bank of the Dnieper, and were organized into two regiments. In 1759 new Serbian settlements were established at Lugan and Bakhmut, the settlers receiving liberal allowances of land.

The first Turkish war of Empress Catherine was connected with the Polish complications of the 1760's. When the Polish disorders drew away Russia's forces, Turkey decided to seize the moment for revenge. In 1768 she declared war upon Russia. Though completely surprised, Catherine succeeded in arousing great enthusiasm among her subjects for the conduct of the war. A daring plan of campaign both on land and sea was drawn up. The army under Count Rumiantsev moved to the Danube, while a fleet was sent from the Baltic Sea around the whole of Europe to the Mediterranean. In 1770 considerable success was achieved on both military fronts. Rumiantsev twice defeated the Turkish army, while the fleet occupied the Aegean archipelago, the Turkish fleet being destroyed in the Bay of Chesme. The Russian fleet did not succeed, however, in passing the Dardanelles. An effort to provoke a Greek uprising against the Turks in Morea did not meet with success. The Turks suppressed the rebels with great severity. The Russian forces landed in Morea were too feeble to oppose the Turks.

In spite of the great success of the Russian army and navy, Turkey was far from destroyed. She did not plead for peace, and it was necessary to continue the war. It was concluded only in 1774 by the peace of Kuchuk Kainardji, a village beyond the Danube.

The terms of this treaty were of great importance in Russo-Turkish relations. Russia gave back Moldavia and Wallachia, occupied by the troops of Count Rumiantsev, and also abandoned the Aegean archipelago. She received, however, the mouths of the Bug and the Dnieper on the northwestern shore of the Black Sea, as well as the mouth of the Don and the Straits of Kerch on the northeastern shore of the Black Sea. The Crimean and Azov Tartars were recognized as independent of Turkey. Russian traders in Turkey were accorded special privileges. As a matter of principle it was of great importance that the Sublime Porte in one of the articles of the treaty promised "protection to Christians and to their churches," while Russian envoys were given power to confer with the Sultan upon affairs concerning the Orthodox church. Following the Kuchuk Kainardji treaty, Russia established herself firmly on the Black Sea, both from a military and a diplomatic point of view. G. Potemkin was made head of the *Novorossiisky Krai* ("New Russian Territory") and showed unusual energy in organizing the territories and developing their economic resources. Security for southern Russia was further advanced by the destruction of the stronghold of the Zaporog Cossacks in 1775 and by the seizure of the Crimea in 1783. Russia sent armies to the Crimea at the request of the Khans, following an intrigue in the affairs of the Crimean Khanate. Several years later, in 1787, under the influence chiefly of English diplomacy, Turkey declared a new war upon Russia. Thinking that Russian forces would be diverted to the south, Sweden also declared war on Russia in 1788. Prussia likewise prepared to attack Russia. Finding herself surrounded by enemies, Empress Catherine II demonstrated a remarkable presence of mind and strength of character. All attacks by the Swedish fleet on St. Petersburg were repulsed in 1788–89. After a preliminary struggle on the coast of the Black Sea the Russian armies, under Suvorov, advanced beyond the Pruth River. Suvorov was victorious at Fokshany and Rymnik in 1789 and he stormed the chief Turkish fortress on the Danube, Izmail, in 1790. With respect to Prussia, Catherine succeeded well in taking advantage of the international situation. She directed the attention of Prussia to a struggle against France where the revolution had just broken out in 1789. Meanwhile, a peace was signed with Turkey in 1792. Russia expanded her possessions along the shores of the Black Sea and the Azov Sea, including the Taman Peninsula. The Crimea remained Russian, and new territories in the Kuban were settled by Zaporog Cossacks brought from the Dnieper.

10.

As has been said above, the Empress Catherine II was raised to the throne by an uprising of Guards officers. The Guards consequently became a "Praetorian" group, possessing power to dispose of the Russian throne as it saw fit. Having attained the throne, Catherine made it her object to strengthen her autocratic power and to free herself from all outside influences. She approached this objective first by making every effort to strengthen the state's initiative both in internal and foreign policy. According to her political views, the state was called upon to be the chief moving force in Russian education and progress. Second, Catherine attempted to make the imperial power the arbiter in conflicts of interest between the various classes in Russia.

From the very beginning of her reign, Catherine faced powerful political opposition from the nobility. Prior to her accession to the throne, under Peter III, a law had been passed giving its members the right to serve or not to serve in the army as they chose. This manifesto of 1762 also contained promises of political privileges in their favor. When Catherine overthrew Peter III, she had to take into consideration this promise. The nobility meanwhile was preparing plans for a Council of Nobles similar to that of 1730. Catherine, however, did not agree to adopt these plans, and so aroused widespread discontent among the nobles. A series of conspiracies took place, and Catherine decided to counterbalance the political ambitions of the nobility by those of other classes. In 1767 a commission in the nature of a national congress was called to draw up a new code. This commission contained representatives from the nobility, the towns, and the state peasants. It was divided by a struggle between the nobles and the representatives of the towns. At the initiative of Catherine, one of the more liberal nobles raised the question of revising the laws concerning serfdom. The commission was dissolved in 1768 without having come to any agreement.

For a time public opinion was diverted by questions of foreign policy rising out of the first Turkish war. Later, Russia entered into a critical period. The whole southeast of Russia, and the middle and lower Volga and Ural districts were stirred by a Cossack and peasant uprising under the leadership of Emelian Pugachov. An uneducated, illiterate Cossack, he declared himself to be the Emperor Peter III, saved from death. In his name Pugachov announced the abolition of serfdom, and the nationalization of all the peasants belonging to the estate owners. His movement had deep roots in the social unrest of the time, but it was doomed to failure in view of the absence of intelligent leadership. The troops collected by Pugachov were defeated. They had scarcely any officers, for the officer class on the whole remained loyal to the existing *régime*. Isolated peasant uprisings were suppressed. Pugachov himself was seized in flight, brought to Moscow, and executed in 1775.

The Pugachov rebellion had unexpected political consequences. Under the influence of the social danger, a reconciliation took place between the empress and the nobility. Catherine declared herself the "first landowner." The nobility abandoned their political opposition and received compensation in the form of a number of elective posts in local government and the courts established by the laws of 1775. After this the personal and class privileges of the nobility were confirmed by a special charter in 1785. Simultaneously a charter of privileges was issued to the cities.

The Pugachov rebellion made evident to many Russian statesmen the necessity of solving the peasant question. A new group was formed in opposition to Catherine's policy. This group may be called the conservative opposition. Its leaders believed it necessary to limit serfdom and the privileges of the nobility while strengthening the imperial power. They grouped themselves around the Tsarevich Paul, who was officially regarded as Catherine's son by Peter III, Catherine herself in her diary names her favorite, Saltykov, as his real father, but it is necessary to note that both physically and mentally Paul closely resembled Peter III. It is also possible to find resemblance between many of the descendants of Paul and the ancestors of Peter III. A political situation was created similar to that in the time of Peter the Great and the Tsarevich Alexis. Paul feared for himself the fate of Alexis. As a matter of fact Catherine was preparing a manifesto depriving him of the succession and naming as heir to the throne her grandson, Paul's son Alexander. But her death in 1796 came before she had time to put this plan into execution.

CHAPTER VII.

SOCIAL AND ECONOMIC DEVELOPMENT OF RUSSIA IN THE EIGHTEENTH CENTURY AND FIRST HALF OF THE NINETEENTH CENTURY

I.

THE outstanding fact of the social history of Russia, in recent times, is the extremely rapid growth of her population. In this respect Russia was second only to the United States, but greatly exceeded all European states. In the sixteenth and seventeenth centuries the Russian population numbered approximately fifteen million. This figure varied from time to time in view of wars and revolutions, but the general total remained approximately the same. There was no accurate census of the population of Russia prior to the eighteenth century. During the first quarter of that century the population did not increase; in fact, it probably decreased in view of the hardships of Peter's reign and its unceasing wars. At the time of Peter's death in 1725, Russia had a population of about thirteen million. In the beginning of the nineteenth century, the total rose to forty million, while by the middle of the nineteenth century it had reached almost seventy million.

This rapid growth of population is partly explained by the annexation of new lands to the Russian Empire, but parallel with this there was a natural increase. The great majority of the people of Russia in the eighteenth and nineteenth century lived in the country and engaged in agriculture; only a small part lived in cities. The urban population increased rapidly, however, both in absolute figures and in proportion to the whole population. At the beginning of the eighteenth century the population of the cities was only 325,000, of which Moscow had 200,000—that is, no more than 3 per cent of the whole population. In the middle of the nineteenth century, the town population had risen to 3,500,000—that is, 6 per cent of the whole population.

2.

DURING the century and a half following 1700, the area of cultivated land had greatly increased. Not only had the agricultural population increased in size, but also new areas were invaded by the agriculturalists. The most important area so to be occupied was the black earth belt in the southern Russian steppes, which was cultivated following the conquest of the north shore of the Black Sea.

But at the same time the importance of industry also rapidly increased. In 1725 there were less than two hundred factories in Russia; in the beginning of the nineteenth century there were about twenty-five hundred factories employing a hundred thousand workmen; and in the middle of the nineteenth century, ten thousand factories and five hundred thousand workmen. Metallurgy and mining increased in importance from the time of Peter the Great. The chief metals worked were iron, copper, lead, and in later times, gold. The study of natural science in connection with the foundation of the Academy of Science in 1726 had considerable influence upon the development of mining enterprise in Russia.

An important branch of industry was the manufacture of woolen cloth, and in the nineteenth century cotton goods. Simultaneously with the expansion of industry there developed peasant craftsmanship, brought into being chiefly by climatic causes. The long winter, especially in the north of Russia, gave the peasants an opportunity to employ their spare time in home industry. They did not need any complicated machinery in view of the primitive nature of their work. There were other reasons for the growth of this kind of small industry. The craftsmen were well acquainted with the needs of the peasant market and were quick to supply them. They manufactured a great variety of goods—wooden utensils, wheels, sleds, textiles, harness, knives, and small metal objects. Peasant craftsmanship continued to develop through the nineteenth century.

With the progress of agriculture and industry, trade also increased. The trade turnover of the port of Archangel in the beginning of the eighteenth century reached 3,000,000 rubles. Following the transfer of trade to St. Petersburg, the importance of Archangel diminished, toward the end of the reign of Peter I, to 300,000 rubles, but the trade of St. Petersburg at the same time rose to 4,000,000 and that of Riga to 2,000,000 rubles. The annual turnover of Russian foreign trade in the middle of the eighteenth century reached about 15,000,000 rubles, and in the beginning of the nineteenth century about 120,000,000 rubles. It must be noted that the value of the ruble in the middle of the eighteenth century was almost double what it was in the beginning of the nineteenth century.

In addition to the goods which Russia supplied to the world in the seventeenth century, she added all kinds of forest products and pig iron during the eighteenth century. In the nineteenth century, following the acquisition of the black earth belt of the south, Russia began to export grain. In 1760 this export reached over 8,000 tons, valued at 822,000 rubles, and by the beginning of the nineteenth century it had risen to around 260,000 tons, valued at 12,000,000 rubles.

During the eighteenth and the beginning of the nineteenth centuries, the inland water routes were improved. The main rivers were joined by canals, but the construction of ballasted roads was commenced only in 1817. In 1813 the first Russian steamer was constructed in St. Petersburg, but steam navigation along the Volga River started only thirty years later. The construction of railroads was first contemplated in 1835. The earliest railroad to be opened ran between St. Petersburg and Tsarskoe-Selo. It was built by a private company and opened in 1838. In 1842 the construction of a railroad joining St. Petersburg and Moscow was commenced by the state. In 1851 telegraphic communication was established between St. Petersburg and Moscow.

3.

In its economic policy, the Imperial Government had to take into consideration the peculiar social structure of the Russian state of the time. The social and economic tendencies noted in the Moscow state of the sixteenth and seventeenth centuries were now finally crystallized. The whole economic system of Russia was regulated primarily by the needs of the state. The first of these at the time was a permanent regular army, whose maintenance called for considerably larger funds than had the army of the Moscow state. The number of men in the permanent army under Peter reached two hundred thousand, that is, 1.5 per cent of the population. By the first quarter of the nineteenth century, the size of the army had reached eight hundred thousand, that is, 1.75 per cent of the population. The soldiers had to have weapons, clothes, and food. For all these commodities were necessary, and money with which to pay for them. The state treasury was consequently one of the largest purchasers in the Russian internal market, and the largest patron of Russian industry. The supply of products of agriculture and industry to the treasury was the typical form of Russian economic turnover. The state needed iron, pig iron, and steel for army munitions, which led to patronage of the metal industry. The state needed cloth for the soldiers' uniforms, which led likewise to patronage of the cloth factories. The state required enormous amounts of grain, meat, and other foods for the army, and this brought about the organization of large farms—that is, an agricultural economy dominated by great landowners. Following the army-supply laws of 1758, these *pomiestchiks* received the exclusive right to supply the agricultural demands of the state. The needs of the army, moreover, were the chief cause of the financial reforms of Peter. In the year of his death, 1725, 65 per cent of the Russian budget was being expended upon the army and navy. To cover these costs, Peter introduced a head tax. The financial needs of the army were calculated at 4,000,000 rubles, and this sum was distributed over a male population of about five million, each of whom had to pay eighty kopeks a year. The head tax in 1725 made up 54 per cent of the state revenues.

The collection of the head tax from the individual subjects of the state was impossible in view of the inadequate development of the administrative organization. For this reason the Government encouraged the formation of peasant communities (*obshchiny*), and conducted its financial affairs directly with them. On the estates of private landholders, the tax was collected by assessing them for the number of "souls" they owned. Thus they became both the economic and financial agents of the Government. But in spite of all efforts, the Government was not able to purchase necessary supplies at the market price, assuming that there existed a free market for labor. For this reason the state was forced to supply the factories and the landowners with cheap labor in the form of serfs. In the course of the eighteenth century, about 1,300,000 peasants were forcibly apportioned to factories and estates. Almost half of Russia's economy during the eighteenth century and the first half of the nineteenth century was based on serf labor.

4.

In the seventeenth century the holders of the *pomiestie* estates were chiefly military agents of the Government. In the eighteenth century, on the other hand, the landowning nobles considered themselves primarily the economic and financial agents of the Government. They also bore administrative responsibilities. In the words of a government official of the beginning of the nineteenth century, each *pomiestchik* was a "free policeman." In particular the *pomiestchiks* were responsible for supplying recruits to the army from their estates. These functions explain to a considerable degree the Government's encouragement of the growth of the landowners' authority over the peasants during the eighteenth century. The institution of serfdom in the eighteenth century was completely different from what it had been in the seventeenth century, when it merely consisted in fixing the peasant to the soil but not to the person of the landowner. As we have seen, this policy toward the peasants was motivated by the needs of the state. Peter the Great, even more than his predecessors, stressed the importance to the state of the institution of serfdom. But beginning with his reign, serfdom was rapidly transformed into slavery. The peasants became bound not to the land, but to the landowner. One of the reasons for this was the merging of the serfs and the former slaves or *kholops* into one social category. We have seen above that in the Moscow state there were both serfs and real slaves; the latter had no juridical identity and were regarded not as individuals but as chattels. For considerations of fiscal policy, Peter ordered that in drawing up the head tax, slaves were to be listed with serfs. The *pomiestchiks* paid the tax for both, and thus, first in practice and later by legislation, received complete authority over both groups. In the middle of the eighteenth century, the *pomiestchiks* received the right to punish their serfs and to exile them to Siberia, and laws were passed giving them the right to sell serfs. Only in 1827 was a law passed making it necessary to insure a sufficient quantity of land for the serfs; and in 1833 another forbade the partition of families by sale. Although the laws provided that the *pomiestchiks* should not misuse the power of punishment, the serfs were completely defenseless. They were divided into two groups—the "house serfs" who lived in the household of the owner, and the peasants. The position of the house serfs was particularly burdensome, and they were completely unprotected. The peasants were usually better off for the reason that their owner cared for them at least because of their economic value. The arable land of an estate was usually divided into two parts, the owner's personal fields and the peasants' fields. In large estates the peasants of each village usually formed a separate community (*obshchina*), with an elected elder at its head. The elections were confirmed by the *pomiestchiks*. All the duties of the individual serfs were allocated by the *obshchina*. The peasant duties consisted either in payment of a rent—this being the custom in northern provinces of Russia—or in working on the owner's land during a fixed number of days a week, usually three.

Serfdom reached its fullest development in the last quarter of the eighteenth century, after which the Government began to take measures modifying the institution.

5.

In view of the evolution of serfdom in the eighteenth century and the prevailing system of recruiting and supplying the army, the Government became dependent upon the nobility. At times such dependence was a great inconvenience, because of the political opposition which frequently arose among the nobles. This explains the efforts of the Government during the first half of the nineteenth century to free itself from dependence upon the nobility in matters concerning the army. The most significant of these efforts were the so-called "military settlements" introduced by Alexander I.

The plan was that the army should support itself economically and supply itself with recruits. This was to be the function of the military settlements. They could be created by two means: either by settling soldiers on farms and making them agriculturalists, or by militarizing the peasant villages and making the peasants into soldiers while they continued to be peasants. In either case the life of the peasant-soldier was subjected to strict discipline. The military command had authority not only over military instruction but also in the household of the soldier. The settlements were an experiment in a sort of military socialism. In a sense they were the forerunners of the military labor communes of 1920.

The application of strict military discipline to peace-time life made existence in the military settlements very hard, and they were consequently shaken on many occasions by terrible riots. The Government suppressed the riots with great cruelty, and did not abandon its policy. At the end of the reign of Alexander I, one-third of the Russian army, more than two hundred thousand men, were transferred to military settlements. The system remained in existence during the reign of Nicholas I and was terminated by Alexander II.

6.

THE military settlements were the most obvious expression of the general tendencies of the Russian Government during the eighteenth and nineteenth centuries in the direction of state socialism, together with which there developed an opposite tendency toward middle-class individualism. The spread of the idea of property in land is indicative of the growth of the latter movement. We have seen that in the early Moscow state there were two types of property in land: the patrimonial estates (*votchiny*) and the tenure estates (*pomestia*), which were held on the condition of government service. In the seventeenth century these two types practically merged into one, for the Government then demanded service both from the patrimonial estate and from the *pomestie,* while on the other hand temporary and conditional possession of the *pomestie* was gradually being transformed into hereditary ownership. In the beginning of the eighteenth century, the two types of possession were finally merged by legislation. By the law of 1714 a single concept of real property was introduced.

Neither under Peter the Great nor under his immediate successors, did the owners of real property have full possession of it. The legislation of Peter and Ann introduced material limitations upon the right of property. Thus title to subsoil rights was vested in the state, and their exploitation was granted to all who desired on the payment of a small sum to the owner of the land. Timber suitable for the construction of ships was also declared government property. The owner of the land had no right to fell oak on his own land, under the threat of the death penalty. These examples demonstrate how circumscribed was the right of private property in land in the first half of the eighteenth century, and to what an extent the state interfered in private matters. Only in the second half of that century were protests heard against this interference, and in 1782 Catherine II rescinded the limitations. It was at this time that the modern Russian word "property" (*sobstvennost*) first appeared in Russian jurisprudence.

The struggle which this legislation involved affected only the nobility, for in the middle of the eighteenth century the right to private property in land became a privilege of the nobility. The Cossack lands and the lands of the state peasants were not owned by individuals. The next phase was the extension of property rights to other classes of society. In 1801 Alexander I issued a manifesto granting the right to own land to individuals of all classes, except serfs. From this time on the only remaining privilege of the nobility was the right to private property in "populated" lands—that is to say, to own land with serfs.

This was a tremendous step forward in the development of modern juridical concepts and in the creation of a new type of middle-class society. The recognition of the right of all classes, except the serfs, to private property in land was evidence of the fact that new groups in Russian society were acquiring full civil status. The tenth volume of the *Russian Code of Laws* of 1832, devoted to civil rights was to a certain degree an echo of the Napoleonic *Code Civile*. The principles of the tenth volume were in contradiction to the institution of serfdom.

7.

THE social changes of the eighteenth and nineteenth centuries intimately affected the Russian state budget. The constant growth of population and of the national economy permitted a steady increase in the whole budget, together with which the relative weight of budgetary items underwent modification. While the expenses of the army grew, its proportion to total expenditure steadily decreased. Military expenses in 1725 swallowed up 65 per cent of the budget. In 1801 the proportion had decreased to 50 per cent and in 1852 to 42 per cent. Thus it may be said that the Russian budget gradually became demilitarized. This greatly relieved the Government of anxiety about sufficient means for the support of the army.

The sum derived from the head tax decreased in importance as a source of revenue. In 1725 the head tax brought in 54 per cent of all state income. In 1801 it only accounted for 30 per cent of the income, and in 1850 for 24 per cent. In place of direct taxation the chief income was made up by indirect taxation, and, in particular, the tax on spirits. The changes in the budget made the former system of state economy less necessary and permitted the Government to undertake the fundamental reconstruction of the whole social system begun by the reforms of Alexander II.

CHAPTER VIII.

SPIRITUAL CULTURE OF RUSSIA IN THE EIGHTEENTH AND THE FIRST HALF OF THE NINETEENTH CENTURIES

I.

THE Europeanization of Russia, begun under Peter, consisted primarily of the secularization of Russian culture. The church, which had played such a leading part in Russian life before his time, gradually lost its importance. The upper circle of society, which came under European influence, no longer needed a church, or, at any rate, the church definitely lost its position as the chief source of cultural life. In the eighteenth century, the aristocratic and official classes of Russian society were educated in the spirit of French "enlightenment." They were devoted to Voltaire and had no real respect for the church.

For the lower classes of society the church also lost its original meaning. Following the schism of the "Old Ritualists" of the seventeenth century, almost half the population of north Russia turned away from it. Thus, the Orthodox church in the eighteenth century lost the support of a large part of the noble classes and a considerable portion of the trading and peasant classes.

It has been pointed out above that the church was made subservient to the state by Peter's reforms. The management of the church became one of the functions of a special government department. Important positions in the new ecclesiastical hierarchy were given to supporters of Peter's reforms, such as Archbishop Theophan Prokopovich, who drew up the new "Spiritual Regulation" which determined the activity of the Holy Synod. A government appointee, the Over-Procurator of the Holy Synod, had almost complete authority in church administration. In the eighteenth century, the Government ceased to value the church as a moral authority either with regard to its own activities or as a force in society at large. The church was considered essential only for the moral education of the lower classes.

A change in the Government's attitude toward the church took place at the end of the eighteenth century during the reign of Emperor Paul. But Paul, while recognizing the moral value of the church, regarded it as subject to his authority. It was he who gave voice in 1797 to the formula that "The tsar is the head of the church." This formula under Nicholas I found its way into the laws of the Russian Empire in the form of a note to one of the articles of the basic law, with the comment that it was intended to define the rôle of the tsar as the protector of the interests of the church and not in any wider sense.

Throughout the whole eighteenth century the Government did not hesitate to limit the material rights of the church. Its land was secularized by Empress Catherine II in 1764. The Archbishop of Rostov, Arseni Matseevich, who protested against this measure, was deprived of his office and imprisoned in a fortress where he subsequently died. At the same time a large number of monasteries were closed. But while the Government itself felt no compunctions in its dealings with the church, it demanded obedience from the masses of the people to the institution whose moral authority it was itself destroying. "Old Ritualists" and the sectarians who desired to leave the church were subjected to government oppression during the greater part of the eighteenth century. It was perfectly natural that these forcible measures did not prevent the further widening of the schism and the growth of sectarianism.

The movement of the "Old Ritualists," by the end of the seventeenth century, ceased to be a unit and broke into several separate sects. It was essentially a protest against the innovations of Nikon by defenders of the old ritual; but the break-up of the old organization of the church forced the "Old Ritualists" to enter upon paths of even greater innovation. Thus, it became necessary to decide in a new manner the election of priests. The Greek Orthodox church held that only the bishop could name new priests and that the priest could not transfer his office to another person. Meanwhile, the "Old Ritualists" had no bishops. The priests named before the schism were gradually growing old and dying and there was no way in which to secure new ones. The "Old Ritualists" were faced with the possibility of remaining without priests. This question served as a basic ground of difference between the two chief sects of "Old Ritualists." One decided to be consistent in its conservative beliefs and to remain without priests. The other sect sought a bishop outside of Russia. It was only in the nineteenth century that they succeeded in creating a bishopric beyond the limits of the Russian Empire, in Bukovina, which in the nineteenth century formed part of Austria.

The break-up of the "Old Ritualists" into sects was only one of the sources of weakness of the opposition to the Russian church. Another source was the rapid growth of various other sects. One of the very oldest Russian sects, the "*Khlysty*" (flagellants), originated at the end of the seventeenth century. The *Khlysty* were mystics who believed in the possibility of the permanent incarnation of God in the individual. They repudiated the official church and its organization and also denied marriage. They organized secret meetings in which they attempted to call forth the presence of the Holy Spirit by means of ecstatic dances. These meetings at times terminated in orgies. Gregory Rasputin, who played such a tragic rôle in the fall of the imperial *régime* in Russia, was associated with the *Khlysty*.

At the other extreme, seeking liberation from the darker aspects of the *Khlysty* sect, was "Spiritual Christianity," the *Dukhobors* who arose in the middle of the eighteenth century in central and southern Russia. In the last quarter of the eighteenth century, among the Spiritual Christians of the Tambov province, there originated a sect of "Evangelical Christians" who received the name of *Molokane,* that is, people who drank milk during Lent, which was forbidden by the rules of the Orthodox church.

Prior to the nineteenth century, the "Old Ritualists" and the sectarians converted many of the trading and peasant classes. In the beginning of the nineteenth century, under Alexander I, sectarianism, especially the *Khlysty,* began to penetrate into the higher circles of society. Branches of *Khlysty* were organized in the time of Alexander I by the higher groups of society in St. Petersburg.

All the dissenters, as has been said above, were subjected during the eighteenth century to constant repression on the part of the Government. The leaders of the *Dukhobors* in southern Russia were sentenced to be burned as late as 1792, but Catherine II replaced the death sentence with exile to Siberia. The Government began to be more tolerant toward the "Old Ritualists" in the second half of the eighteenth century; but the repression of sectarians was terminated only at the beginning of the nineteenth century under Alexander I, on the advice of Senator Lopukhin, who conducted an investigation in one of the southern governments in 1801. Under Nicholas I, in the middle of the nineteenth century, a reaction set in and the Government again pursued the policy of repressing religious dissenters.

2.

THE secularization of Russian culture in the eighteenth century was noticeable first in education. In the early Moscow state, education was of a narrow religious character. Practical needs during the reign of Peter the Great brought about a new system of education which was to serve the purpose of preparing officers for the army and the navy. In 1700 he founded in Moscow a "School of Mathematics and Navigation" and invited a Scotchman, Henry Fargwarson, to direct it. In 1715 the school was moved to St. Petersburg and named the Naval Academy. The pupils of the Academy became teachers in the mathematical schools instituted in the principal cities of Russia. In these schools children were taught arithmetic and geometry. In the last years of the reign of Peter there were about forty of them, with two thousand pupils, part of whom came of their own free will while others were taken forcibly from soldiers' and civil servants' families.

In Peter's reign plans were made for the foundation of an Academy of Science which was to direct the new scientific training. The project was carried out after the death of Peter in 1726. The first academicians were called from abroad, chiefly from German states. They were accompanied by eight students to be instructed in the University opened by the Academy. This University, however, was soon closed. The Academy also opened a "Gymnasium" or upper school where a number of Russian boys, chiefly the sons of government servants and merchants, received their education. The nobility showed more willingness to send boys to the Cadet Corps or military school opened in 1730 to prepare officers for the army. Further steps in public education were made in the second half of the eighteenth century. In 1755 the University of

Moscow was founded. This was the first real Russian university. In the beginning the professors were chiefly Germans, but later Russian professors also appeared. The Moscow University had as adjuncts two gymnasiums—one for the children of nobles and one for those of all other classes. In 1782 a Commission for the Creation of Public Schools was called. This Commission, under the direction of Jankovich de Mirievo, a Serbian educator brought over from Austria, drew up a plan for the development of public teaching in Russia. High schools were to be opened in the chief cities and primary schools in the small cities; but this was prevented by inadequacy of funds. The obligation of maintaining the schools was left to philanthropic departments of the provincial governments, whose budgets were very small. By 1800 there were in Russia 315 schools with twenty thousand pupils, for the most part children of merchants and craftsmen. At the beginning of the nineteenth century, the Ministry of Public Education was founded, in 1802, and Russia was broken up into six educational districts, each of which was placed under a superintendent. The first appointments to these posts were very successful and the reform greatly helped the development of education. According to the plan, in each educational district there was to be founded a university; in each provincial capital a gymnasium; and in each county (*uyezd*) a school. This program was practically completed toward the end of the reign of Alexander I. Russia then had 6 universities (Moscow, Derpt, Vilna, Kazan, Kharkov, and St. Petersburg), 48 gymnasiums, and 337 schools. There were 5,500 students in the gymnasiums and about 30,000 in the schools. The University of Derpt was German until the end of the nineteenth century. The University of Vilna, prior to its closing after the Polish rebellion in 1831, was Polish. Instead of it, a Russian university was opened in Kiev in 1833. The chief progress compared with education in the eighteenth century was in the development, not of primary, but of secondary and higher education. Private initiative aided the Government in the educational movement, for instance, in opening the Kharkov University. Furthermore, two higher schools, the Demidov Law School in Yaroslavl in 1805 and the Historico-Philological Institute of Prince Bezborodko in Niezhin in 1820, were opened by private means. During the reign of Nicholas I, several technical schools were opened, among them the Institute of Technology of St. Petersburg in 1828 and the Institute in Moscow in 1844. Several military schools of secondary education were founded. There were eleven of these in the reign of Nicholas I.

3.

THE organization of the Academy of Science before that of either universities and schools seems at first sight to have been an impractical idea; but it had a great influence upon the development of Russian learning, and particularly in mathematics and natural science. Russian scientists had a center of organization at a time when the west was beginning a particularly intensive study of the natural sciences. The Academy immediately took an important place in the world of learning of the eighteenth century. The first members of the Academy were imported from abroad, chiefly from German states. Among them were two well-known mathematicians, Bernouilli and Euler. But very soon there appeared learned men of Russian origin, among them an outstanding and universal genius, M. V. Lomonosov, the son of a peasant shipbuilder from the north of Russia, who lived from 1711 to 1765, and made himself equally proficient in chemistry, physics, mineralogy, history, philology, and poetry.

Of immense importance was the work of the Academy of Science in making a geographical survey of Siberia, and its support of the great Siberian expedition of 1733 to 1743. It also contributed to the spread of technical education in Russia, thus preparing the ground for important inventions. A Russian technician, Ivan Polzunov (1730–66), conducting his experiments simultaneously with James Watt but independently, constructed a steam engine which was used in the Barnaul metallurgical plant in the Altai region in 1766.

The greatest Russian scholar of the first half of the nineteenth century was not an academician but a university professor from Kazan, N. I. Lobachevsky, who lived from 1793 to 1856. He began teaching in 1811. At first his new ideas were not understood by his contemporaries, either in Russia or abroad. It was only after some time that his originality was understood. Lobachevsky's mind was one of the most productive in the history of mathematics. He created a new geometry which uses a hypothesis of space differing from that of Euclid.

The study of social sciences and history was less developed in the eighteenth and the beginning of the nineteenth century, than the natural sciences. The Academy of Science produced in the eighteenth century an energetic collector of historical documents, G. F. Mueller, a naturalized German. The greatest Russian historians of the period were, however, not professional men of learning. During the eighteenth century, one of Russia's historians was an administrative official; another, a politician; and a third, a military man. The leading Russian historian of the nineteenth century, N. M. Karamzin, who lived from 1766 to 1826, was also unassociated with any institution of learning. The publication of his exhaustive *History of the Russian Empire,* the first edition of which appeared in 1816, was a great event in the spiritual life of Russia. The breadth of his learning and his deep knowledge of sources were combined in a masterly literary presentation. The saying was current that Karamzin had discovered ancient Russia as Columbus had discovered America.

Evidence of the growth of interest in science in Russian society, at the end of the eighteenth and the beginning of the nineteenth century, is to be observed in the foundation of several learned societies. Such were: "The Free Economic Society," founded in St. Petersburg in 1765; "The Friendly Society of Learning" of Moscow, founded in 1782; and "The Society of Russian History and Antiquity" and "The Society of Experimental Science," both opened in 1805. Very significant, also, was the activity of private individuals in organizing scientific investigations. Particularly noteworthy was the work of Chancellor Count N. P. Rumiantsev, in the beginning of the nineteenth century. He was a man of unusually wide interests both in the fields of geography and history. At his initiative and expense, a valuable collection of ancient Russian documents was brought together and published. Rumiantsev gave his money for geographical expeditions and historical research. He conducted an extensive correspondence with many Russian scholars, took an interest in the details of their work, and stimulated them to further activity. The collections acquired by

Count Rumiantsev are housed in the Rumiantsev Museum in Moscow, now known as the Lenin Library.

4.

BEFORE the reforms of Peter the Great, literature and art had an equal appeal to the upper and the lower classes of Russian society, as both groups had a religious training. Conditions, however, had completely changed. The upper circles of society had broken away from the church, whose creative powers had at the same time been materially weakened. The upper classes began to create for themselves a new art and literature, while the lower classes remained without the leadership they had formerly had in their aesthetic life. The new literature had already come into demand by the great mass of Russians in the middle of the nineteenth century. The rift between the "intellectuals" and the people, in literary matters, was being gradually closed. But in the eighteenth century, this literature was available only to the highest groups of society educated in cities—the nobles and the merchants. A characteristic "poet of nobility" in the eighteenth century was Derzhavin who, in some of his verses, achieved real artistic merit. The first half of the nineteenth century saw the rise of a number of writers and poets who attracted wide circles of readers, among them Pushkin, Lermontov, and Gogol.

A. S. Pushkin, who lived from 1799 to 1837, the "Sun of Russian Poetry" as he was justly called, is the greatest genius of Russian literature. Pushkin wrote chiefly in verse, and for this reason he is more difficult to appreciate in translation than Russian prose writers. This partly explains the fact that his works are little known outside Russia. Pushkin had an unusually harmonious personality. He was endowed with a sharp and brilliant mind. He could both feel and express the most intimate experiences of the human soul, as well as manifestations of group life. Pushkin had a great interest in history and in contemporary political questions. His political ideas passed through two phases. During his youth, up to the second half of the reign of Alexander I, he was filled with sympathy for liberalism, being close to many of the so-called "Decembrists." During his later life, in the reign of Nicholas I, he held moderately conservative views. But, both in his youth and in later years, Pushkin was to the highest degree a sincere humanitarian. At times, he was unhappy in the world of politics and personal intrigue which characterized the higher Russian society of the day. He was ultimately ruined by intrigue. Defending the honor of his wife, he was killed in a duel at the age of thirty-seven.

M. Y. Lermontov, who lived from 1814 to 1841, was a brilliant poet, but a more one-sided individual than Pushkin. An ancestor of his was George Learmont, a Scottish adventurer who, in the early seventeenth century, entered the Russian service. In his poetical work, Lermontov was strongly influenced by Byron. The source of his poetic inspiration was the Caucasus, with its natural beauty, the primitive customs of its mountaineers, and its state of constant war. Lermontov took part in the Caucasian War as an officer of the Russian army. He was transferred to the Caucasus in punishment for his verses "On the Death of Pushkin," blaming court society for the death of the poet. His most famous poem, "The Demon," is set in the Caucasus. The Demon was the Spirit of Negation and Doubt which had fascinated Lermontov from his early youth. Lermontov died in a duel as did Pushkin, at the age of twenty-seven.

N. V. Gogol, who lived from 1809 to 1852, was of Ukrainian origin and introduced many Ukrainian words and idioms into the Russian language. In his first stories, he chose for his subjects incidents in the life of the people of southern Russia. Later he described the world of *pomiestchiks* (landowners) and *chinovniks* (civil servants) in his comedy, *The Government Inspector* (*Revizor*), and in his novel, *Dead Souls*. The characteristics of Gogol's work are realism and humor. But behind his humor lies a profound sense of grief for the imperfection of human society. It is laughter through tears. Through his realism in the description of the external world, one feels his search for spiritual values as the real basis of life.

Pushkin, Lermontov, and Gogol laid the cornerstones of the foundation upon which all subsequent Russian literature arose.

5.

The art of ancient Russia, even more than literature, was dependent upon the church. Architecture, painting, and music served first of all the needs of the church. For this reason instrumental music and sculpture were very little developed in ancient Russia. Russian art did not cease to serve the church in the eighteenth century, but religious art became only one of the branches of a general development.

Imperial palaces and the houses of nobles in town and country became the chief objects of the endeavor of artists. This explains partly the character of Russian art during the eighteenth and the first part of the nineteenth century. Catering to the tastes of society, it became subject to western influences. An important rôle in the development of the fine arts in Russia was played by the Academy of Arts, founded in 1757, which introduced the technique and ideals of western art.

Western architects and painters, among them many Italians and Frenchmen, were called by the court to construct and decorate the imperial palaces and, to a certain extent, the churches as well. Among the western architects working in Russia were the well-known Italian, Rastrelli, and the Scotchman, Cameron. Many of them became naturalized, like Rossi in the nineteenth century, and must be regarded as Russians. Gradually native Russian artists and architects appeared, possibly the most gifted one of this period being Bazhenov. The new architecture was exemplified first in the new capital, St. Petersburg, as well as the imperial palaces in the surroundings of the capital. The favorite style of architecture during the eighteenth and nineteenth centuries was classical. Columns of different types became an essential part both of lay and church architecture of this time. The style set by the imperial palaces was followed by the nobles. During this period many of the noble estates were adorned by architectural masterpieces. The design of Russian manorial houses of this period was similar to the colonial style in the United States, but was often executed in stone. The classical style of architecture soon became adapted to the Russian environment and ceased to appear foreign. In the beginning of the nineteenth century, a Russian variant of this style, known as Russian "Empire" style was developed.

The most famous sculptural work of the time was the monument to Peter the Great in St. Petersburg, cast by two French sculptors, Falconet and Marie-Anne Collot. Russian sculptors contributed several good pieces of sculpture of less renown. The portrait busts of Shubin were talented pieces of work, as were the monuments of Martos. Russian sculpture, like the architecture of the period, was inspired by classicism. Kozlovsky represented Marshal Suvorov as a youthful Mars, while Martos represented Minin and Pozharsky, the heroes of 1612, as citizens of ancient Rome.

Several remarkable portrait painters appeared, among them: Levitsky, Borovikovsky, and Kiprensky, and a landscape painter of great talent, Shchedrin, who died at an early age. The most famous painter of the early nineteenth century was K. P. Brullov, who painted in 1830 the "Last Day of Pompeii," a theatrical and cold picture, which nevertheless produced a great impression. More important than Brullov, and more profound in his work, was A. A. Ivanov, who was moved by deep religious sentiment. His picture "Christ Appearing before the People" combines depth of feeling with high technique. Ivanov spent more than twenty years, from 1833 to 1855, in completing this work.

6.

In the seventeenth century, new melodies entered into the Moscow church service, which came from the south—Kiev and Greece. These were accepted by the Russian church universally at the end of the seventeenth century, and were only rejected by the "Old Ritualists," who retained the ancient forms.

In the eighteenth century, church singing fell under Italian influence. An Italian operatic troupe performed in St. Petersburg and the court singers took part in the choruses. Italian influence may be noted in Russian spiritual compositions of the period. The most famous and competent composer of the period was Bortniansky, who lived from 1751 to 1825, and was trained in St. Petersburg by an Italian master and studied in Italy. In 1796 he was appointed director of the court choir. This choir had succeeded even before his appointment in reaching a high degree of excellence, so Bortniansky directed his attention to the selection of voices and to the perfection of the *ensemble*. He sought singers in southern Russia and the Ukraine, where the people were famed for their voices. As a result he achieved enormous success. His successor as director of the choir was Lvov, the author of the Russian national anthem composed in 1833. The French composer, Berlioz, when he heard the choir under Lvov, found it superior to the papal choir.

During the eighteenth century, secular music, both instrumental and vocal, flooded Russia from the west. The music of the eighteenth century was valued in Russia as an entertainment, accompanying banquets, dinners, balls, and performances of all kinds. Many landowners, imitating the court, organized orchestras and choirs among their serfs. In 1735, in the reign of Empress Ann, the Italian Opera was invited to visit St. Petersburg. Soon afterward the first attempts were made to organize a Russian opera, combining the Italian manner with Russian songs. In the nineteenth century, the musical life of Russia became more serious and significant. In 1802 the Russian Philharmonic Society was founded. Following the War of 1812, many operas of a patriotic character were written. Textbooks on music became available; the number of serious professional musicians increased; and musical education improved.

This atmosphere of interest and creativeness in music made possible the appearance of the real founder of Russian national music, M. I. Glinka, who lived from 1803 to 1857. He occupies in the history of Russian music the same central position that Pushkin holds in the history of Russian literature. They were contemporaries; and Glinka, who had a great respect for Pushkin, composed music for a number of his poems. The Composer was of an aristocratic family from Smolensk province. His first musical impressions were received in listening to an orchestra of serf musicians belonging to his uncle. From childhood Glinka had heard Russian popular songs sung in the country, and they had a great influence upon the character of his later work. He studied in Berlin, and having acquired high proficiency in musical technique, he developed a Russian symphonic and operatic style entirely his own in conception. He composed two operas, *A Life for the Tsar* (now called *Ivan Susanin*), in 1836, and *Ruslan and Ludmila,* in 1842, the latter with a libretto based on a poem by Pushkin and expressing a brilliant eastern theme of fantasy.

A decade later than Glinka was born the second great Russian composer, A. S. Dargomyzhsky, who lived from 1813 to 1869. He is representative of realism and of the declamatory style in music. He sought a perfect union between speech and music. As he expressed it: "I desire that the sound directly express the word. I desire the truth." His highest achievement in this direction was his opera based on the poem of Pushkin, *The Stone Guest.*

CHAPTER IX.

THE DEVELOPMENT OF RUSSIAN INTERNAL AND FOREIGN POLICY UP TO THE MIDDLE OF THE NINETEENTH CENTURY

(1797–1857)

I.

EMPEROR PAUL, who reigned five years from 1796 to 1801, came to the throne with many brilliant conceptions in mind concerning Russian policies, domestic as well as foreign, but his despotic caprices marred all efforts to realize these plans. At the time of his accession Paul was mentally unbalanced. The program of the conservative circle which was formed around Paul before his coronation, primarily intended to procure fundamental laws which would define the imperial power, was carried into execution by the acts of April 5, 1797. The following laws were promulgated: the Law of Succession to the Throne, laws Concerning the Imperial Family (the internal organization of the imperial house), and, finally, an *ukaz* which limited serf labor for the landowner to three days a week. This last law was the first serious attempt at imperial legislation to limit selfdom. The *ukaz* was of small practical importance, as the Government did not have enough agents to secure enforcement. However, it had great significance as a matter of principle. Simultaneously, the privileges granted by Empress Catherine to the nobility were suspended. The Government of Emperor Paul also began reforms in the governmental departments, to replace collective responsibility by personal leadership.

Foreign policy under Emperor Paul was significant, particularly with respect to the Black Sea and the Mediterranean. The anti-Turkish policy of Empress Catherine had secured for Russia a part of the coast of the Black Sea. This had very great value for the development of Russian trade and the prosperity of agriculture in the south. Meanwhile there appeared the possibility of developing relations with Turkey on entirely new lines. The Government of Emperor Paul succeeded in taking advantage of this opportunity in a manner which gave its foreign policy special importance in the history of Russian diplomacy. Its guiding principle was the extension of Russian influence in the eastern part of the Mediterranean Sea, by means not of war but of cordial relations with Turkey. In 1798 Russia and Turkey joined England, Austria, and the Neapolitan Kingdom in a coalition against France, motivated by the common purpose of resisting her expansionist policy which had brought Switzerland, northern Italy, and the Ionian Islands under her sway.

In 1798 France sent General Napoleon Bonaparte to Egypt to seize the route to India. Russia concluded a special convention with Turkey for united action. The Turks agreed to allow the Russian fleet to pass through the Bosporus and the Straits of the Dardanelles, while undertaking to hold them closed to the warships of other nations. The Russian Black Sea squadron, under Admiral Ushakov, together with certain Turkish vessels, were sent into the Adriatic Sea. He drove the French from the Ionian Islands, where he organized a republic formally under the patronage of Turkey, but actually under the control of Russia.

Ushakov succeeded in securing great influence in the Adriatic Sea. In 1799 Montenegro offered its allegiance to Russia. Thus policy under Emperor Paul led to the foundation of a firm Russian base in the Adriatic Sea, from which actual control over the Orthodox and Slavonic peoples of the Balkans could be secured. Desirous of extending Russia's power still further in the Mediterranean Sea, Paul became patron of the order of Knights of St. John, known as the Maltese Knights, who owned the island of Malta.

The naval campaign in the Mediterranean Sea was supplemented by a military campaign. Emperor Paul sent to Austria's aid in 1799 Russia's best general, Suvorov, who succeeded in a short time in defeating the French armies in Italy and forcing them to retreat. He was ready to invade France but instead was ordered by Paul, who yielded to the advice of Austria, to eject the French troops from Switzerland. Consequently Suvorov entered

Switzerland after an extremely difficult march across the Alps by the St. Gothard Pass.

The brilliant activities of Suvorov were not sufficiently appreciated by Austria. Paul became convinced of the selfishness of both Austria and England, and not wishing to be a toy in their hands he broke relations with them. Russia then began to enter into close relations with her recent enemy, France. Paul's sympathy for Napoleon Bonaparte followed his return from Egypt, to become First Consul of France.

Russia's change of policy with regard to France, however, did not lead to altered relations with Turkey. The alliance of Russia and Turkey continued, and the Adriatic base was retained for the further development of Russian policy in the Balkans. The alliance with Napoleon automatically led to a complete break with England. Paul imposed an embargo upon all English goods in Russia and the Don Cossacks received an order to enter upon the conquest of India. This, however, only proved the unbalanced condition of Paul's mind. The march of the Don Cossacks was ordered without any preparation. They had not even maps, and the Cossacks before reaching the Russian frontier lost half their horses in the desert. The march was not a serious undertaking and necessarily failed. The Cossacks were ordered back immediately following the assassination of Paul.

England's reply to Paul's new policy was the dispatch of the British fleet to the Baltic Sea. At the same time the British representative in St. Petersburg attempted to utilize the discontent, which Paul's *régime* had aroused in court circles and among the officers, to organize a *coup d'état*. This plan did not prove difficult of execution. Paul's insanity expressed itself in constant attacks of wild fury from which none about him could feel entirely secure. For a mistake at a military parade, Paul would send the responsible officers into exile; the most highly responsible governmental officials were constantly in fear of retirement and displeasure. Paul used to say, "In Russia he is great with whom I speak, and that only while I speak with him." The result was an unceasing change of personnel in high military and civil posts.

It is not surprising, in view of these circumstances, that the courtiers and officers who plotted against Paul were led by the Military Governor of St. Petersburg, Count Pahlen. In the night of March 24, 1801, Paul was assassinated by conspirators who succeeded in entering his bedroom.

The new emperor was Paul's son Alexander. He had given his consent to the overthrow of Paul, but had not supposed that this would be carried out by means of assassination. There is evidence to the effect that Alexander suffered a nervous collapse when he received the news of the assassination. He was brought back to himself by the angry remark of Count Pahlen, *"C'est assez faire l'enfant, allez régner."*

2.

ALEXANDER I had one of the greatest political minds of his time. Its power found expression in his judgment on questions both of internal and foreign policy. He had few equals if any among the contemporary diplomats. The outstanding traits of Alexander's mind and character were his ability to visualize plans of the widest scope and to execute them without the knowledge of those around him.

He has been regarded as a weak man, frequently changing his policies. On the contrary, Alexander was unusually stubborn in reaching his objectives, but he did so, not by direct means, as did Peter the Great and Alexander's chief opponent, Napoleon, but by devious methods—first instilling his ideas into the minds of those around him and then pretending that he was following their views. Alexander had an unusual ability of charming his auditors. He was particularly attractive to women and succeeded in attaining many results with their aid. Only a few contemporaries saw through his diplomatic methods. Hence the accusation, "Alexander is as sharp as a pin, as fine as a razor, and as false as sea foam." Napoleon referred to him as a *"Grec de Bas Empire"* (Byzantian).

The principal concern of Alexander's diplomatic activity during the first half of his reign, from 1801 to 1815, was his struggle with Napoleon. This required the conclusion of a series of alliances, sometimes with Austria, sometimes with Prussia. It was broken by periods of friendship with France, the most important of which followed the failure of the first coalition against Napoleon and the Peace of Tilsit in 1807. The struggle was decided by a gigantic duel between Alexander and Napoleon in 1812 and concluded by the organization of an all-European coalition against Napoleon which led to his downfall.

Alexander succeeded in finding a great principle on which to base his struggle with Napoleon. As opposed to Napoleon's world empire resting on the principle of civil equality, Alexander brought forward the idea of a liberal federation of national states. This he expressed clearly in a remarkable document of 1804—the diplomatic instructions to Novosiltsev for his extraordinary mission to England.

Alexander did not succeed in realizing his program fully, but, nevertheless, the long period of struggle with Napoleon was concluded by the creation of the first European League of Nations, the Holy Alliance. Though it later became a reactionary combination of emperors against peoples, it originally—and particularly in the eyes of its founder, Alexander—did not have this character.

A part of Alexander's general program of federation was his policy with respect to the Slavs. The southern Slavs in the Balkans and Poland were to be freed from Turkish, Austrian, and Prussian rule, and to form a federation under the leadership of Alexander. These ideas were at the foundation of Alexander's policy up to the Congress of Vienna, 1815, but the actual course of events prevented their realization. The inevitable military alliance with Austria and Prussia made it impossible to raise the Polish question in all its breadth prior to the Peace of Tilsit, but the south Slavonic question was raised in connection with Russia's policy in the Mediterranean Sea.

The Mediterranean policy of Paul lay at the basis of Alexander's policy. It is true that on June 5, 1801, a convention of friendship was concluded with England whereby Russia abandoned her pretensions to Malta, and this renunciation constituted a material breach in Russia's Mediterranean front. But in general Paul's program was not abandoned. The principal factor was now the Ionian archipelago which became the center of Russian diplomatic and military interest. In September, 1805, a small Russian squadron under Admiral Seniavin left the Baltic Sea. In January, 1806, Seniavin reached the island of Corfu. With the Ionian Islands and Montenegro as bases, he fought against the superior forces of France and Turkey for a year and a half. Turkey declared war upon Russia at the end of 1806. In June of 1807 Seniavin defeated the Turkish squadron in the Aegean Sea near the island of Imbros.

However, the Peace of Tilsit between Napoleon and Alexander in 1807 brought about a complete collapse of Russian plans in the Mediterranean Sea. The Ionian Islands were handed over to France. But Alexander did not abandon Paul's hope of realizing Russia's aspirations in the Balkans and the Adriatic Sea and of improving the lot of the Balkan Slavs by means of direct agreement with Turkey. It was precisely this mission that Admiral Chichagov was to fulfil in replacing Kutuzov in 1812 as chief of the Russian army on the Danube. But Kutuzov, prior to the arrival of Chichagov, had had time to make peace with Turkey without concluding an alliance.

Because of the Tilsit agreement, Russia was enabled to settle her differences with Sweden. As a result of the Russo-Swedish War of 1808–09, she annexed Finland.

The Peace of Tilsit, insincere both on the part of Alexander and Napoleon in spite of the advantages which each of them received from the agreement, was broken by the War of 1812. That war was carefully prepared by Napoleon from the point of view of military technique. The march of Napoleon to Moscow was strategically brilliant, but the great battle of Borodino was a draw and due to the strategic skill of the Russian commander-in-chief, Kutuzov, Napoleon did not succeed in destroying the Russian army.

With the active force of the Russian army still undefeated and all classes of Russian society aroused by an enormous patriotic outburst, Napoleon could conquer Russia only by bringing about a social revolution. The elements for such a revolution were then present even to a greater extent than in 1917, particularly in view of the existence of serfdom. Among the Russian people there were still alive eyewitnesses of the Pugachov rebellion. It is now known that several Russian statesmen of the time feared war, especially for the reason that they expected Napoleon to bring about another similar rising. If he had succeeded in this, he would of course have subjected Russia to his control, at least for some time.

There were evidences of unstable conditions among the Russian peasants in 1812. Several revolts occurred among the recruits. Napoleon either did not wish, or did not know how, to take advantage of this situation. Moreover, he did not have at hand a "fifth column" in Russia. Incidentally, the unfounded and unjustifiable arrest and exile immediately prior to the War of 1812 of a leading Russian statesman, "the right hand of Alexander," Speransky, may be explained by the panicky fear of the ruling group in Russia that in him Napoleon had a man capable of organizing a revolution in Russia. But without organizing a social revolution, Napoleon could not hold Moscow, hundreds of miles away from his base. Retreat was inevitable. It became a rout, with the French soldiers exposed to hunger and cold and to the attacks of the Russian army and cf guerilla bands. Russian society regarded Napoleon's expulsion as the end of Russia's part in the war. The further struggle with him must be attributed to the personal initiative of Alexander. He was the soul of the European coalition against Napoleon, and the chief manager of all military activities. His adviser was the Russian general Barclay de Tolly, a descendant of a Scottish family, Kutuzov having died on April 28, 1813. The resistance of Napoleon was broken only after a stubborn struggle. The Russians and the allied troops entered Paris in the summer of 1814. The forces of Napoleon, following his return from Elba, were defeated by the British and the Prussians before the Russian troops had arrived at Waterloo, 1815.

The Russian foreign policy during the first half of the reign of Alexander also extended to the Pacific Ocean. Under Paul in 1798 Shelekhov's trading company was reorganized into the Russo-American Company and received a trading monopoly, as well as the power to administer justice in the Russian colonies on the Pacific Ocean. Under the charter granted by Paul, the chief director of the company had to be a member of the Shelekhov family. N. P. Rezanov was appointed, but the leading rôle in the company was played by the manager of the company, A. A. Baranov.

In 1805 the fortress Novo-Archangel was built and became the chief center of Russia's possessions in Alaska. Baranov was not content with Alaska, but formed extensive plans. In 1812 he organized a Russian colony in California and dreamed of making the Pacific Ocean a Russian sea. In 1815 he sent an expedition to the Hawaiian Islands. However, this expedition failed. In 1818 Baranov was to retire; he died while returning to Russia on a ship of the Russo-American Company in the Sunda Straits, and was buried at sea according to custom. The far-reaching Pacific policy of Baranov was not continued after his death.

3.

THE constant state of war with Napoleon did not draw Alexander's attention wholly from questions of internal policy. The eighteenth century left two problems to be settled in the course of the nineteenth—political reorganization of the state, and the condition of the peasantry. During the reign of Alexander I, the solution of both these problems was considerably advanced. The reorganization of the structure of the state was attacked in two ways: first, in improvement of the bureaucratic organization of many of the Government departments; second, in partial agreement as to the principles underlying the reorganization of the state.

With respect to the first point it is necessary to note the new organization of the Senate and the Ministries in 1802. The Senate became primarily a judicial body. Its reorganization was completed along these lines by the judicial reform of Alexander II in 1864. The creation of ministries completed the reform commenced by Paul. Finally, an improvement in the technique of preparing laws was secured by the creation of the State Council in 1810. In addition there were the reforms affecting local government, which consisted of subdividing the territories of Russia into provinces under the control of governors-general in 1819 and the reorganization of local administration by the creation of special councils to advise the governors in 1823.

The second point concerns the constitutional reorganization of the state. Several projects of reform were made. The basic purpose of all these programs was the introduction of representative government in legislative matters. The projects were prepared under the influence of Anglo-American or French political experience. It is necessary to mention those of Speransky in 1809 and of Novosiltsev, the latter known as the Constitutional Charter of the Empire, in 1819–20. According to the plan of Speransky the representative body, the state Duma, was to be composed of deputies indirectly elected by the population. Each township was to elect a Duma, each township Duma was to elect a delegate to a county Duma, each county Duma to a provincial Duma, and each provincial Duma to an imperial Duma. This plan served a hundred years later as the basis for the elective system of the Soviet Government.

Besides the creation of an imperial Duma, it was proposed to create an imperial Council. This bureaucratic organ would have as its chief function the coördination of the work of the various government organs. The Council was, as we have seen, brought into existence in 1810. The rest of the plan was not executed.

Speransky's plan was based upon the idea of a centralized state. The plan of Novosiltsev, on the other hand, had as its basic concept the creation of a federal state within the territories of the Russian Empire. The plan was partly inspired by the example of the United States of America. Aside from the influence of books on the subject of federal government, there was also a personal influence. In 1806 Emperor Alexander entered into correspondence with President Jefferson of the United States about the question of the governmental structure of the United States. According to Novosiltsev the Russian Empire was to be divided into provinces or states. The fundamental idea of Novosiltsev was the coördination of the original Russian Empire with the later accessions, particularly those which possessed local rights and peculiarities, such as the Baltic provinces and the region of the Don Cossacks, and those which were in fact constitutional states, such as Finland from 1809 and Poland, annexed at the Vienna Congress in 1815. As early as 1807, under the Treaty of Tilsit, Napoleon organized the Grand Duchy of Warsaw out of those parts of Poland that had been seized by Austria and Prussia in the partitions of the eighteenth century. Following the defeat of Napoleon in 1812, the Grand Duchy of Warsaw was occupied by Russian troops, and according to the resolutions of the Vienna Congress the greater part of the Duchy was annexed by Russia, while the smaller part was returned to Prussia and Austria. Alexander granted Poland a constitution on November 27, 1815, which was considered one of the most liberal European constitutions of the time.

According to the plan of Novosiltsev, the border states were to be joined to the states of the new federated empire. The plan of Novosiltsev, just as the plan of Speransky, was not put into practice, but in 1819 preparatory steps to its execution were taken in reforming local government. Novosiltsev's plan was not completely abandoned until the death of Alexander in 1825, and if Alexander had continued to reign it might have been put into practice.

The social policy of Emperor Alexander I was important. As under Catherine II, the peasant question was a weapon in the hands of Alexander against the aristocratic movement of constitutionalism. The frightful after-effects of the Pugachov rebellion were forgotten in the nineteenth century, and the political opposition of the nobles again expressed itself in 1802 in demands that the Senate be made a Council of Nobles, and even in advocating a limitation of imperial power. In the decree concerning the reorganization of the Senate in 1802, Alexander did not follow the plans advocated by the nobles, but he did leave the Senate a shadow of a political authority. This was the right to protest against imperial decrees which were at variance with the established laws. Something in the nature of the *droit de remontrance* of the French parliament of the eighteenth century.

The Senate soon desired to take advantage of its right when it felt that the Government was destroying the privileges of the nobility. In December, 1802, the Council of Ministers approved, and the emperor confirmed, a report of the Minister of War which demanded that nobles who had served in the army without securing promotion to the grade of officer could not retire until they had served at least twelve years as non-commissioned officers. The report was sent to the Senate for publication. A few days later one of the Senators expressed the opinion that the new regulation was at variance with the fundamental privileges of the nobility. At the end of January, 1803, the Senate supported this opinion. In March a deputation of Senators was received by the emperor who told them dryly that special legislation would be promulgated. At the beginning of April, 1803, a decree was published announcing that the right of the Senate to protest was limited to laws and decrees published before 1802. The decrees submitted following that year were to be accepted without qualification.

In answer to the pretensions of the Senate and to warn the nobles, Alexander raised the peasant question. On March 4, 1803, a decree was published regarding "free landowners." This decree concerned the rules for emancipating serfs with land; the granting of liberty was left to the free will of the estate-owners.

The practical significance of the decree was not great. The total number of serfs freed following its publication was about fifty thousand, but it had great significance in principle. The nobles saw the possibility of Alexander's granting privileges to the peasants to counterbalance the privileges of the nobility. The nobles retired, and Alexander remained victor in the political duel. After that time nobles desiring to advance a practical political program were forced to include in it a solution for the peasant problem. This was done by the "Decembrists" at the end of the reign of Alexander I.

The law on free landowners was obviously only a first step. Alexander had to take further steps to deal with the peasant question. Without this it was impossible to advance political reform, plans for which were supplemented by plans for the solution of the peasant question. In the Baltic provinces the emancipation of the serfs—without land—was actually carried out in practice in 1819.

4.

THE attempts at internal reorganization during the second half of the reign of Alexander I were accompanied by changes in his foreign policy. The central factor of this policy was the "Holy Alliance." Its purpose was the unification of the policies of the European states. It was based upon a religious foundation—the unification of the Christian states without differentiation between creeds. While the Holy Alliance represented Alexander's mystical idealism, international policies were at this time actually controlled by the so-called Quadruple Alliance (Austria, Great Britain, Prussia, and Russia) to which later on France was also admitted (Quintuple Alliance). During the first years of its existence, the Alliance met in several Pan-European congresses: Aachen in 1818; Troppau (Opava) in 1820; Laibach (Ljubljana) in 1821; and Verona in 1822. The Alliance succeeded in preventing war between member states for a long period of time. There were no important wars in Europe for almost forty years, from 1815 to 1853.

The policy of the Alliance with respect to the internal affairs of its members was the subject of a keen difference between the more liberal group headed by Alexander I and the reactionaries led by the Austrian Minister Metternich. During the first years of its existence, the Liberal party was paramount. The years 1819–20 were ones of crises. Alexander threatened even to *"lâcher la bête,"* to release Napoleon from his captivity at St. Helena. However, the reactionary party triumphed and the Alliance gradually became an alliance of kings for the suppression of the liberal movements in various countries. Alexander made one concession after another to Metternich. The opinion was expressed that Alexander had completely lost any independence of view. This seemed to be confirmed by the events of the Greek revolution against Turkish rule. The revolution broke out in 1821. Public opinion in Russia demanded support of the movement. Metternich, on the other hand, saw in it only a rebellion of the subjects of the Sultan, their legal ruler, and on this basis the Alliance expressed itself against support of the revolution.

Alexander did not want to quarrel with the Alliance, which had come into existence at his own initiative, but his diplomacy during this period sought for independent means of expression outside the Alliance. He sought separate agreements with its members.

Simultaneously, in view of the possibility of war with Turkey, Russian troops were concentrated in the south. In the midst of the new diplomatic and military policy, Alexander fell sick of a fever which he contracted in the Crimea and died in Taganrog on December 1, 1825. The unexpectedness of his death gave rise to a popular legend that he had not in fact died but had taken the disguise of a pilgrim who many years later appeared in Siberia as an old man under the name of Fedor Kuzmich.

5.

THE death of Alexander almost led to a revolution in Russia. During the second part of his reign, there had been a high degree of restlessness among the nobles and the officers. The extraordinary part played by the Russian army in the European wars of 1813–14 had aroused patriotic feeling among the officers. The subsequent policy of Alexander seemed to the majority of them contrary to the interests of Russia. His concessions to Metternich were severely criticized. The rôle of "policeman" in suppressing popular movements in Europe, which Russia was supposed to play in the Quintuple Alliance following 1821 was not attractive to the Russian officers. Finally, the refusal to aid the Greek revolution was taken to be a betrayal of the interests of the Orthodox church. Also fears were current regarding alleged pro-Polish inclinations of Alexander.

These considerations drove the younger officers into political opposition. Soon after 1815 secret societies having as their object the reorganization of internal affairs in Russia began to be formed. These societies were organized partly under the influence of Masonic lodges and in some connection with them. The lessons of history were not missed by the Russian liberal nobles who formed the opposition. The program of all the secret societies included the abolition of serfdom and the solution of the land question. Among the secret societies, two had especial importance, the Southern Society which was composed of officers of the southern army and was headed by Colonel Pestel, and the Northern Society of St. Petersburg. The plan of a future Russian constitution drawn up by Pestel was known as the *Russkaia Pravda* (Russian Law). Pestel visualized the future Russian state as a centralized republic with democratic or even socialistic policies. He also recognized the necessity of a powerful dictatorship in the revolutionary government. In these matters Pestel was the pupil of the French Jacobins and a forerunner of Lenin. The Northern Society had planned a constitution written by Colonel Muraviev. This plan considered it possible to retain a liberal monarchy, but gave primary importance to the rights of the individual. According to this plan Russia was to be organized along federal lines. The constitution of Muraviev was written under the direct influence of the constitution of the United States of America.

The secret societies waited several years for a convenient time to start a movement. The proper occasion arose at the time of the death of Alexander. The reason for this was confusion in the matter of the succession to the throne. According to the law of succession of 1797 Alexander, who died childless, should have been succeeded by his brother Constantine, who held the post of commander-in-chief of the Polish army after 1815. But Constantine, being happily married to a Polish lady, was not inclined to accept the responsibilities and risks of the imperial office.

At his request, Alexander signed a manifesto in 1823 confirming the refusal of Constantine to assume the throne, and appointed as his successor a third brother, Nicholas. For unknown reasons, Alexander did not publish this manifesto but deposited three copies in sealed envelopes in various places. One of the reasons for such secrecy may have been his fear of irritating the officers and bringing about an uprising which Alexander hoped to prevent by publication of the constitutional project of Novosiltsev. Nicholas was very unpopular among the officers in view of his Prussian contacts and sympathies, since he was married to a Prussian princess, as well as for his conservative point of view.

At the time of Alexander's death, Constantine was in Warsaw and Nicholas in St. Petersburg. Both of them knew of Alexander's manifesto, but only Constantine acted in accordance with it. Upon receiving news of the death of Alexander, he ordered the military and civil officials of Warsaw to swear allegiance to the new emperor, Nicholas, who on the other hand, having been informed by the military governor of St. Petersburg of his unpopularity among the officers of the Guard, did not dare to demand allegiance to himself in St. Petersburg and had the officials take their oath to Emperor Constantine.

With no telegraph service or railroads, connections between St. Petersburg and Warsaw being maintained by post horses, the crisis was drawn out over a long period of time. The news of Alexander's death was received in St. Petersburg, December 8, 1825. Only two weeks later was the correspondence between Nicholas and Constantine concluded, and Constantine renewed his categorical refusal to accept the throne. The 26th of December was appointed as the day for taking the oath of loyalty to Emperor Nicholas I. This moment was chosen by the plotters for an uprising. For this reason the participators in the movement are known as "Decembrists." The plotters succeeded in convincing the soldiers of several regiments that the oath demanded of them was illegal and that it was necessary to uphold the rights of Emperor Constantine and to demand a constitution. The anecdote was current that some simple soldiers thought that "Constitution" was the name of the wife of Constantine.

The rebels occupied the Senate square and efforts to send negotiators to them failed. The military governor of St. Petersburg, one of the heroes of the War of 1812, who approached them to enter into negotiations, was killed. The rebels, however, displayed no plan of action and limited themselves to forming a square in the middle of the city. Nicholas succeeded in bringing together the remaining loyal troops and in planting cannon at the important points in the capital. The rebels had no artillery. When toward evening they were asked to surrender and refused, they were fired upon with case-shot. The square broke, and the rebels fled. The uprising was immediately suppressed. The attempt at a military uprising in southern Russia also failed.

Immediately, arrests and investigations were started. A hundred and twenty men were committed to trial, among them many members of leading noble families in Russia. The decision of the Court was commuted by Nicholas. However, five of the prisoners were hanged, among them Colonel Pestel; thirty-one were condemned to hard labor in Siberia; the remainder were exiled to Siberia or committed to prison for various periods of time.

6.

NICHOLAS I was quite unlike his elder brother Alexander. He had a very much more primitive nature, with more limited interests and not the slightest shade of liberalism in his political views. He was not lacking entirely in diplomatic ability in his relations with people, but even here his capacities were very limited. He loved to play the rôle of a simple, honest officer and servant of the state.

His political wisdom consisted primarily in imposing strict discipline in military and civil matters. Nicholas was guided by the same idea of a "regulated" or "policed" state as was Peter the Great, but of course he was a far less capable man than Peter. A contemporary of Nicholas, the great Russian poet Pushkin said of him: *"Il y a beaucoup d'enseigne en lui et un peu de Pierre le Grand."* Nicholas undoubtedly felt responsible before the bar of history and desired to be of service to Russia, but as he had received no education except in military matters, he was unprepared for the task of ruling. Nicholas, nevertheless, attempted to take part in all the departments of government. He did not share the liberal ideas of his brother. As he distrusted liberalism in general, he brought to an end all preparations for constitutional reform and in connection with this revoked the new experiments in the realm of local administration. None the less, it is impossible to deny his efforts to introduce improvements in the governmental and social organization of Russia. He ordered that a summary of the views of the "Decembrists" regarding the need for change in governmental affairs be drawn up, and studied them carefully.

One of the principal deficiencies of the Russian political system in the eyes of the "Decembrists" was the absence of any system in the laws and the consequent confusion of procedure in the courts. In order to correct this deficiency, Nicholas called a committee to codify the law and to compile the *Svod Zakonov* (Code of Laws). One of the greatest Russian statesmen and jurists, Speransky, was placed in charge of this work. As we have seen above, Speransky was exiled in 1812. In the second half of the reign of Alexander, he was admitted into the Civil Service in the provinces; he became governor-general of Siberia in 1821–22, and later was allowed to return to St. Petersburg but did not have the same importance as before. Nicholas tested his loyalty by appointing him one of the judges in the trial of the "Decembrists." After several years of concentrated work, Speransky succeeded in publishing forty-two volumes of *The Complete Collection of Russian Laws* in their chronological order from the Code of Tsar Alexis Michaelovich of 1649 to the coronation of Emperor Nicholas. On the basis of this work, a systematic Code of Laws of the Russian Empire was compiled in 1832. A second edition of this Code was published in 1842 and a third in 1857. Thus under Nicholas I was accomplished the codification of laws which neither Catherine II nor Alexander I had been able to achieve.

Another serious deficiency in Russian life noted by the "Decembrists" was the institution of serfdom. We have seen how, under Alexander I, the Government thought seriously of abolishing or at least limiting serfdom. Nicholas I continued to work in the same direction. To both Alexander and Nicholas the peasant question was of political importance in the struggle with the opposition of nobles. Nicholas was distrustful all his life of the political intrigues of the nobility following the "Decembrists" movement which was primarily a movement of the nobility.

Under Nicholas I several measures were taken to limit serfdom. One was the law of 1827 forbidding the purchase of peasants without a sufficient quantity of land for their sustenance; another was the law of 1833 forbidding the separation of families by sale. The Government was motivated by the idea of regulating the exploitation of peasant labor by the landowners. The law concerning peasants bound to the land, proclaimed in 1842, was in accordance with this purpose. It called for a definition by the landowners of the duties of the peasants, but left the matter to their good will. The attempt to impose fixed responsibilities in respect to serf labor was made only in certain districts of Russia. In the kingdom of Poland the so-called "tables" were introduced in 1846. This law was passed in view of the peasant uprisings in Austrian Galicia. In the southwestern provinces "inventories" were introduced in 1853. Both "tables" and "inventories" were lists of peasant liabilities. Everything pointed to a general peasant reform, but this actually took place only in the next reign.

Another evil in the governmental system of Russia pointed out by the "Decembrists" was the confusion in finances, and the depreciation of the ruble caused by the paper money inflation as a result of the prolonged wars under Alexander I. The financial reforms of Nicholas were carried out by Kankrin, his Minister of Finance. The first measure introduced by him was the stabilization of the value of paper money in 1839 at the rate of 3½ paper rubles to one stabilized ruble. Following this, new paper currency backed by a gold reserve and maintained at parity was introduced; the old bills were purchased by the State Treasury.

After acceding to many of the wishes of the "Decembrists" in carrying out reforms in the judicial and administrative machinery of the state and in accepting some of their suggestions regarding social and economic matters, Nicholas reasserted the principle of autocracy. All manifestations of liberalism were mercilessly suppressed. The press was limited; the universities were placed under strict supervision; a special "Third" division of the imperial chancellory was organized for the suppression of political unrest. This particular body was known as the *gendarmerie*. The slightest suspicion of political untrustworthiness terminated the career of any civil or military official, however talented. As a result of this, the proportion of capable officers and civil servants in higher posts decreased considerably. Arrest and exile threatened anyone having independent political views. The brilliant conservative political thinker belonging to the "Slavophile" group, George Samarin, was imprisoned for a short time in 1851 for opposing the German party in the Baltic provinces. The young author Dostoievsky, a genius of the first rank, was exiled to Siberia in 1848 for being a member of a group interested in French socialism.

The system of Nicholas I was enforced harshly and without right of appeal. When the military collapse of Russia in the Crimean War showed it to be poor, its creator was incapable of surviving it. Nicholas I died in the midst of the war, on March 2, 1855, ostensibly from a cold but actually from nervous fatigue. There was a rumor that he poisoned himself.

7.

In his foreign policy Emperor Nicholas I followed the same firm principles as in his internal policy. The basic concept of his foreign policy was legitimism, hence his opposition to all liberal and revolutionary movements. His first move in foreign policy—the Russo-Turkish War of 1828–29—was not, however, in complete consistency with this principle. In supporting the Greek revolution he was guided not by his general principles of foreign policy, but by the traditional objectives of Russian diplomacy in the Balkans. Moreover, the war had been prepared in the preceding reign. Nicholas really followed his brother by inertia, also probably because of his desire to divert the attention of Russian society from the effects of the "Decembrist" uprising by a foreign war. In 1827 an agreement was concluded by Russia, England, and France to aid Greece. In the autumn of 1827 the combined Russo-Anglo-French squadron destroyed the Turko-Egyptian fleet at Navarino. The immediate consequence of this was a war between Russia and Turkey in 1828–29.

According to the plan of Emperor Alexander, the Polish army was to take part in the war in the Balkans, the object of which was to free the southern Slavs. But the Grand Duke Constantine did not consent to the dispatch of the Polish army to the Balkans. Its participation in the war, however, was symbolized by the presence of an Extraordinary Mission of Polish officers. The war progressed slowly in 1828; only in the course of the next year did the Russian commander-in-chief, General Diebitsch, deliver a telling blow to the Turks at Kulevche and cross the Balkans. At the same time General Paskevich succeeded in capturing Erzerum on the Caucasian front. Turkey was forced to conclude peace at Adrianople.

According to the treaty of peace, Russia took possession of the mouth of the Danube and improved her position along the Caucasian coast of the Black Sea. The independence of Greece was secured as well as the autonomy of Serbia, Moldavia, and Wallachia, the Danubian principalities.

The conditions of the Peace of Adrianople astonished the diplomats of Europe by their moderation. This was not the result of weakness or of error, but of farsightedness and strength. It was a continuation of the Turkophile policy of Emperor Paul. The moderation of the Peace of Adrianople bore fruit several years later in the famous Treaty of Unkiar-Skelessi between Turkey and Russia. Several years after the Peace of Adrianople, Turkey found herself on the verge of disruption in view of civil war. The Egyptian Pasha, Mechmet-Ali, rose against the Sultan, and his son Ibrahim succeeded in defeating the Sultan's army. Turkey was saved by the intervention of Russia. A small corps was sent under the direction of General N. N. Muraviev to the Bosporus for the defense of Constantinople against the Egyptian army.

General Muraviev was one of the most outstanding military personages of the reign of Nicholas. He had prepared himself for activity in the east by learning several oriental languages, which enabled him to carry on conversations without interpreters. The result of his expedition to the Bosporus was the conclusion of the Unkiar-Skelessi treaty which placed Russia in the position of protector with respect to Turkey. The gist of the treaty consisted in the provision that the Straits of the Bosporus and the Dardanelles were to remain closed to all military vessels except those of Turkey and Russia. The Treaty of Unkiar-Skelessi was a great victory for Russian diplomacy, but Russia did not succeed in utilizing its benefits. Emperor Nicholas tied his own hands with an agreement concluded the same year with Austria at Münchengrätz. Later on, Russia adhered to the London conventions of 1840 and 1841, according to which the Straits were closed to military vessels of all nations, under international guarantee.

Even prior to the conclusion of the Unkiar-Skelessi treaty, Nicholas had the opportunity of demonstrating the true nature of his foreign policy. This was the revolution of July, 1830, in France, which overthrew the legitimate power of the Bourbons and replaced it by the liberal monarchy of Louis-Philippe of Orleans.

Nicholas decided to intervene in favor of the Bourbons and prepared to dispatch Russian troops to the Rhine. The intervention was prevented, however, by a revolution in Poland. This uprising cannot be explained by the Polish policy of Nicholas, for while he never sympathized with constitutional principles, he was particularly careful to maintain the Polish Constitutional Charter. But the nationalistic policy pursued by Nicholas made it evident to the Poles that there was no hope of the annexation to the Polish Kingdom of the Lithuanian and the western Russian provinces for which they still had hope during the reign of Alexander I. The Polish uprising was suppressed only in 1831, after a year of heavy fighting. The Polish Constitution was then repealed. The Organic Statute of 1832 left Poland with only a few political privileges. Thus, contrary to the original intentions of Russia, a considerable portion of Poland was annexed. This further confused the Polish question both in the opinion of Russians and Poles.

The reactionary foreign policy of Nicholas found expression a second time in 1848–49, when the whole of the European continent was swept by a new wave of revolution. On this occasion he took part in its suppression. Following the personal request of the young Austrian emperor, Francis Joseph, Nicholas moved an army of one hundred thousand Russians under General Paskevich to suppress the Hungarian uprising against Austria in 1849. Paskevich soon succeeded in forcing the Hungarian army to surrender. Austria was saved. The Austrian Minister Schwartzenberg immediately took steps to forestall excessive Russian influence upon the subsequent policy of Austria. His expression is famous: "Austria will surprise the world with her ingratitude." An opportunity for this soon arose with a new turn in international affairs.

It was easy already in the 1840's to foresee a complete breach between Russia on the one hand and England and France on the other, over the Eastern Question. The French Revolution of 1848 completely disrupted the relations between Russia and France. The situation was not improved when the French Republic became the Empire of Napoleon III. On the other hand, Napoleon attempted to strengthen his internal power by an effective foreign policy. In the hope of attracting the French Catholics to his side, he demanded that Turkey grant privileges to Catholics in the Holy Land. The keys of the Church of Bethlehem were taken away from the Orthodox Greeks and given to the Catholic church. Emperor Nicholas, in his capacity of patron of the Orthodox population of Turkey, under the provisions of the Treaty of Kuchuk-Kainardji of 1774, demanded the reëstablishment of the rights of the Orthodox church. Having been refused by the Sultan, he sent Russian troops to the autonomous principalities of Moldavia and Wallachia, which were under the suzerainty of the Sultan.

In the autumn of 1853, Turkey declared war against Russia. In November the Russian Black Sea squadron destroyed the Turkish fleet at Sinope. Following this the British and French squadrons entered the Black Sea and a breach occurred between Russia and the western European states. England and France were later joined by Sardinia. The position of Russia became difficult when Austria demanded the evacuation of the principalities of Moldavia and Wallachia. This was the beginning of Schwartzenberg's prediction regarding the ingratitude of Austria. Nicholas submitted to the demands, as he considered that Russia was not prepared to fight Austria as well, the more so since Prussia was acting in an unpredictable manner.

War on the Danube, which formed the basis of the Russian military plan, became impossible. The chief forces of the Russian army were brought back for the defense of the Russian frontiers against the possibility of attack by Austria. Meanwhile, the Russian fleet could not oppose the united and incomparably stronger Anglo-French fleet. The Russian fleet consisted of sailing vessels while the fleet of the allies contained a number of steam vessels. During the autumn of 1854 the allies landed their troops in the Crimea near Eupatoria and moved against Sevastopol. The city was hurriedly fortified by General Todtleben, and the Russian fleet was sunk at the entrance of the harbor to prevent the entrance of the Anglo-French fleet. The siege of Sevastopol began. The city could have been saved, perhaps, if Paskevich had agreed to send reinforcements from the main Russian army which was defending the Russian frontier against Austria, but Paskevich did not agree to take this risk.

On March 2, 1855, Emperor Nicholas I died, but the accession of Alexander his son, was not accompanied by a change in military plans. Sevastopol was in fact left to take care of itself. On September 8, 1855, the French succeeded in taking Fort Malakoff, the key to the fortress of Sevastopol. After this the Russian troops left the southern side, which comprised the principal part of the fortified town, and crossed the bridge to the northern side.

After the fall of Sevastopol, the Russian troops were victorious on the Caucasian front, where General N. N. Muraviev took by storm the fortress of Kars, regarded as impregnable by the Turks. Russia had taken Kars in 1829, but it had been returned to Turkey by the Treaty of Adrianople.

In the beginning of 1856, by the invitation of Austria and Prussia, peace negotiations were opened between Russia and her enemies. The Treaty of Paris was concluded on conditions highly unfavorable to Russia. Russia received back Sevastopol in return for Kars, but lost the right to maintain a fleet in the Black Sea. The Straits of the Bosporus and the Dardanelles were closed to military vessels of all nations. The southern part of Bessarabia was taken from Russia and annexed to Moldavia so as to deprive Russia of any access to the Danube River. Finally, Russia had to abandon the right of exclusive protection over Orthodox peoples in Turkey. All the Christians in Turkey were placed under the protection of the Great Powers.

The foreign policy of Nicholas I thus ended in a complete catastrophe. The military prestige of Russia was destroyed. The extraordinary influence exercised by Russia in European affairs was terminated. This was a severe blow to national self-esteem. Russia's defeat in the Crimean War was one of the causes of the series of internal reforms which were carried out by Alexander II.

sequently natural that the reforms of Alexander II should start with this matter, the more so because the solution of the question had been prepared during the reign of Nicholas I.

In January, 1857, a secret Committee on Peasant Reform was organized. It was composed of several of the highest officials of the Government, but the fear of taking decisive action retarded its work. A decisive step was taken at the initiative of Alexander in the late autumn of 1857, when the emperor authorized the governor-general of Vilna to organize "Provincial Committees" of the nobility in the Lithuanian provinces for the discussion of the terms of the proposed peasant reforms on December 2, 1857. Following this move there was no possibility of retreat; the reforms became inevitable. The nobles of other provinces were forced to request the Government's authorization to form similar committees. Their motives were clearly expressed in the famous speech of Alexander II to the nobility of Moscow: "Better that the reform should come from above than wait until serfdom is abolished from below."

The working out of a general plan of reform and of detailed provisions for its execution occupied more than three years. The work of the Provincial Committees was revised by special commissions in St. Petersburg. These "Revising Commissions" consisted primarily of partisans of reform. They were composed of government officials, from ministries directly concerned in the proposed reform, and experts drawn from progressive estate-owners. Y. I. Rostovtzev was at the head of the Commission until his death in 1860. One of its leading members was the Vice-Minister of Internal Affairs, N. A. Miliutin. Great influence was exercised by several leaders of the Slavophile movement notably Prince V. Cherkassky and G. Samarin. The Revising Commission showed the greatest initiative in developing the project of reform which went much farther than the proposals of the majority of the Provincial Committees. The project of the Committee was partly reduced in the "Main Committee," and by the State Council. After this the project was confirmed by the emperor in a manifesto regarding the abolition of serfdom which was signed on March 3, 1861.

1861 Reforms

The basic principles of the reform were as follows: Household serfs were to be freed within a period of two years without redemption, but were to receive nothing on gaining their freedom. Peasant serfs were to receive not only their personal freedom, but also certain allotments of land. In determining the dimensions of each peasant's share, the amount of land worked by peasants for their own use under conditions of serfdom was taken into consideration. The serfs had worked both their own lands and the lands of their owner. The area of the allotments granted to the peasants following the reform was equal approximately to the area retained by the landowner. Thus, under the terms of the reform of 1861, the peasants received grants of land which, prior to the reform, had absorbed only half of their labor.

By the terms of the emancipation, the land which the peasants received did not become their private property. It continued to be regarded as the property of the landowner, but was held for the benefit of the peasant. The peasants, though now freedmen, were called upon to pay for the use of this land or to perform certain services for the landowner. The Government, however, was willing to help, if both the landowners and the peasants desired to terminate this relationship. Help was provided in the form of a long-term credit to purchase the land. In those cases where estate-owners agreed to sell the land to their former serfs, the Government paid the landowners the cost of the land with an interest-bearing bond, and this sum was imposed upon the peasant in the form of deferred payments over a period of years. The cost was computed on the basis of the annual payment of the peasant, being worth 6 per cent of the cost of the land. The deferred payments were added to the head tax of the peasant. The appointed period was forty-nine years. Within twenty years following 1861 about 85 per cent of landowners actually sold to the peasants their part of land in each estate with the above-mentioned assistance of the Government. Even in this case the peasant did not receive the land in complete personal ownership, but each peasant commune or village received the whole area of land in communal ownership under collective responsibility for the redemption payments of all the members of the commune. Special government agents named for the purpose of putting the reform into operation, called mediators, drew up charter deeds for the land in the name of a whole commune. The commune itself divided the land among its members according to the size of families. These subdivisions took place periodically every few years.

Thus, even following the reforms, the peasant did not become an individual property owner or an individual possessing full civil rights, but remained subject to the authority of the commune. Actually the peasants became dependent upon those government bureaucratic agencies which concerned themselves with peasant affairs. It is necessary to add that outside of the commune each peasant could purchase land on the basis of full ownership. This situation is important for the understanding of future events. It explains the continued juridical isolation of the peasants even following the reform. It also preserved in their consciousness the memory of serfdom. The firm bonds of the commune did not permit changes in the manner of owning land. The peasants never forgot that the commune had only half of the former estate. The reform of 1861 seemed incomplete and they dreamed of completing it. Another idea connected with the land commune was that the land was not the property of individuals but was granted in the form of an allotment to serve the uses of the individual. Thus, land within the whole state was regarded by the peasant as a fund which could be drawn upon for further allotments until it was used up. These were the embryonic ideas of the subsequent revolution.

The reform of 1861 was tragically inadequate. There were two ways of really solving the question finally. The first was to leave the possession as well as the ownership of the land with the landowner. The peasant in this case would have received merely his personal freedom. In the majority of cases, however, under the pressure of necessity, the landowner would have been forced to sell part of his land to his former serfs. The Government could have assisted in this transaction, in the favor of the individual peasants, and not of the communes. The actual result would have been almost the same as it was by the reform of 1861, but the psychological results would have been quite different. Instead of thousands of peasant communes there would have been created millions of peasant landowners. The ideas of a "general fund" and of "allotments" would have been avoided. It was toward this result that the later reforms of Stolypin were directed, but the reforms of Stolypin came forty-five years too late (1906).

The other possibility, in introducing the reform of 1861, was to take all the land away from the estate-owners and to divide it among the peasants. This would have been the simplest solution, which would have prevented all the later upheavals in Russia. If the partition of land had been completed in 1861, there would have been no need for it in 1918 and in that case the Russian revolution would never have been accompanied by such riots as it actually was.

However, in spite of its incompleteness, the reform of 1861 was an ambitious effort which changed the whole old order. After the peasant reform, it seemed easier to start with other reforms which, taken together, completely changed the nature of the Russian state. The other leading "great reforms" of Alexander II were the reforms of the Zemstvo, the towns, the courts, and the military service.

The reform of the Zemstvo in 1864 created for the first time since that of the early Moscow state, real local self-government without regard to class. The basis of the reform consisted in granting to elected representatives of each county (Uyezd) control over the schools, medical affairs, and roads. The elective law provided for the division of electors into three *curias:* the private landowners (nobles and merchants); peasant communes; and townspeople. The representatives elected an "Executive Committee" known as the *Uprava* for a term of three years. The representatives of the Uyezd formed a provincial assembly which elected a provincial Zemstvo Committee (*Uprava*). Following the general spirit of the Zemstvo reforms, similar measures were introduced for town government in 1870. The electors were likewise divided into three *curias,* according to a property census; the amount of taxes paid was totaled and divided into three equal parts, each having an equal number of representatives. Both the Zemstvo and the town authorities succeeded in carrying out work of great cultural importance in Russia prior to the Revolution of 1917.

Of no less significance was the new judicial reform of 1864, of which S. I. Zarudny was the chief promoter. Its basic principles were: the improvement of court procedure; the introduction of the jury and the organization of lawyers into a formal bar. Despite some drawbacks of the Russian courts following 1864, they undoubtedly reached considerable efficiency, and in this respect Russia could be favorably compared with the most progressive European countries. It is necessary, however, to note here the difference between the façade and the foundation of the new Russian state. The peasants in the vast majority of small civil litigations did not use the new courts and had to be content with the "volost" courts, especially organized for them, and from the reign of Alexander III until 1912, they also had to accept the jurisdiction of the "Land Captains." The last of the major reforms was the introduction of universal military service in 1874. The law of military service was practically the only one of the laws of this time which affected equally all the classes of the Russian people. Here there was no difference between the façade and the structure; it was profoundly democratic in spirit. The recruits were granted privileges only according to their family position. The only son, the only grandson, or only supporter of a family, received full privileges and were registered in the reserve of the second category, that is, in practice, prior to the World War, they were never called into service. With respect to the term of service and promotion, special privileges were recognized in favor of individuals having secondary education. Class differences were not in any way reflected in privileges of military service, with the exception of the selection of the Guards officers from the aristocratic circles of society.

The society created by the reforms of Alexander II lasted in its general character until 1905, and in part until 1917.

2.

THE foreign policy of Emperor Alexander II may be divided into two main periods. During the first, Russian policy was inspired primarily by the idea of revising the Treaty of Paris of 1856 and particularly of abrogating the humiliating clause regarding the prohibition of maintenance of a Russian fleet in the Black Sea. Taking advantage of the Franco-Prussian War of 1870, Russia succeeded in overthrowing the limitations of the Treaty of Paris. Then began the second period of Alexander's foreign policy. Russia's policy now sought further success in the Near East. But the union of Europe against Russia at the Berlin Conference in 1878 deprived Russia of the fruits of her efforts. This marked a new turn in Russia's policy.

Finding herself thrust out of the Near East as a result of the Crimean War, Russia attempted to carry on an active policy in the Caucasus, in the Middle East, and in the Far East. In all these directions the preparations had been made during the reign of Nicholas I. The Government of Alexander II succeeded in achieving its most important successes in the Caucasus and in the Middle East. The conquest of the Caucasus had been commenced by Alexander I. General Ermolov, appointed viceroy in the Caucasus in 1816, had gone far in the conquest of Caucasia and Transcaucasia in the second half of the reign of Alexander I. Ermolov was one of the prominent Russian statesmen of the nineteenth century and had a recognized talent for military and administrative matters. Personally of a modest and simple nature, he was known as a harsh man when he considered such action necessary in the interests of Russia. However, neither Ermolov nor his immediate successors succeeded in finally subjecting the Caucasus to Russia. Throughout the reign of Nicholas I Russia was forced to maintain troops in the Caucasus to protect its possessions from incursions of the mountaineers. An exhausting mountain war continued for many years.

The conquest of the Caucasus was concluded only in the reign of Alexander II. In 1857 the new viceroy in the Caucasus, Prince Bariatinsky, began a methodical advance into the hills of Daghestan against the leader of the mountaineers, Shamil. Shamil conducted a heroic defense which was, however, overcome by the Russian armies. In 1859 Shamil was taken prisoner. After conquering the eastern Caucasus from the Georgian military road to the Caspian Sea, Bariatinsky turned to the western part of the Caucasus. The Circassian tribe was ordered either to move to the valleys where it could be controlled or to move out into Turkey. About two hundred thousand went to Turkey.

The renewal of Russian activity in the Middle East commenced, as has been said above, during the reign of Nicholas I. The energetic governor-general of Orenburg, Count Perovsky, in the winter of 1839–40, opened a campaign against Khiva in order to punish the Khivans for their raids. The campaign, however, ended in failure, owing to the severity of the winter. But in 1847, a Russian army reached the Syr-Darya, not far from its mouth in the Aral Sea. Here a fortress, Aralsk, was constructed. This event marked the turning point in Russia's policy in the Middle East.

The fortress of Aralsk became the basis of Russian domination of the Aral Sea. Two military vessels were brought in sections from Orenburg, and a Russian flotilla was organized on the Sea of

Aral. The dream of Kirilov of seeing the Russian flag float over the Aral Sea became a reality in less than a hundred years.

In view of the incursions of Khokands, it was decided to move up the Syr-Darya to the fortress of Ak-Mechet. This was seized and renamed Fort Perovsk in 1853. Following the conquest of the lower Syr-Darya and the bringing of a flotilla into the Sea of Aral, the Russian frontier moved from Orenburg to the boundary of Turkestan. The fortified line of Orenburg became obsolete. At the same time the eastern Kirghiz line was advanced by the occupation of the basin of Balkash Lake. The frontier was carried from Irtysh to Semirechie. Thus, less than one hundred and twenty years after Kirilov, the provinces of Bokhara and Samarkand could be annexed. But these provinces were no longer lacking in unity as they had been in the time of Kirilov. In the beginning of the nineteenth century a new dynasty of Khans in Bokhara had succeeded in strengthening their power by means of a cruel despotism. The new center of government was in the valley of the Fergan where one of the local Uzbek princes took the title of Khan, having founded his capital in Khokand. The Khanate of Khokand was a troublesome neighbor. The Khokands attempted to conquer the Kirghiz, who had long ago become Russian subjects. The ensuing struggle made it necessary for Russia to intervene and connect the Syr-Darya and the Semirechensk lines. In 1865 the occupied territories were united to form the province of Turkestan and were made part of the region under the control of the governor-general of Orenburg. General Cherniaiev was made head of the new territories. On June 27, 1865, he captured the largest Khokand city, Tashkent. The capture of Tashkent by a small force had a tremendous effect upon the whole of Turkestan and decided the further course of the struggle. The emir of Bokhara attempted to assist the Khokands and demanded that the Russian troops immediately leave the territories they occupied. A struggle began with Bokhara which was conducted by General Kauffmann, who had been appointed governor-general of Turkestan in 1867. In 1868 Kauffmann occupied Samarkand, and the emir of Bokhara recognized the suzerainty of the Russian tsar.

The attention of the Russian Government and public opinion was attracted to the Far East in the 1840's. At this time the basin of the Amur River, ceded to China at the end of the seventeenth century, had not been occupied by the Chinese. It was an almost uninhabited region. In the beginning of the 1840's, the academician Middendorf headed a scientific expedition into Siberia. On his way home he passed through the region of the Amur and was convinced that it was actually not occupied by anyone. Middendorf's report created a strong impression in St. Petersburg. In 1847, in appointing N. N. Muraviev governor-general of eastern Siberia, Emperor Nicholas I mentioned the "Russian" river Amur. In the naval and diplomatic circles of Russia, the Amur was not regarded as having a great value, since it flowed only into the Sea of Okhotsk and Sakhalin was believed to be connected with the mainland, so that the Sea of Okhotsk seemed to have no direct outlet to the south. Captain Nevelskoy, sent to the Sea of Okhotsk on the brig "Baikal," decided to investigate at his own risk the mouth of the Amur and the shores of Sakhalin. Nevelskoy left Petropavlovsk (Kamchatka) June 11, 1849, and sailed to the eastern shore of Sakhalin. On September 15 he passed through the Straits of Tartary to the Bay of Aian. Sakhalin was proved to be an island and the importance of the river Amur as a line of connection became evident. On August 19, 1851, Nevelskoy raised the Russian military flag at the mouth of the river Amur. For these acts "of the greatest impertinence" he was sentenced to be demoted to a sailor's rank. Only the personal intervention of Nicholas I saved him from the punishment. Nicholas I said at that time: "Where once the Russian flag has flown it must not be lowered." The region of Amur was occupied by Russia in 1858 by the Treaty of Aygun, while in 1860 the northeastern half of Sakhalin and the region of Usuriisk were granted to Russia. The southern part of Sakhalin remained in the possession of Japan up to 1875 when it was granted to Russia in exchange for the Kuril Islands.

Russian success in the Middle and the Far East increased the international importance of Russia and aroused concern among the Great Powers, particularly Great Britain. This situation was attested by the events of 1869 when Great Britain, increasingly concerned at the success of Russia in Turkestan, entered into negotiations with the Russian Government. Great Britain proposed to form a neutral zone between Russian and British possessions in the Middle East, providing that Afghanistan would be included in the sphere of British influence and that the sphere of Russian influence would extend to the river Amu-Darya. The Russian Government long refused to answer this offer, perhaps awaiting an offer of compensation in the Black Sea.

Meanwhile, the desire to secure allies against the European powers induced Russian diplomats to reach an understanding with the United States. The tradition of Russo-American *rapprochement* goes back to the eighteenth century. During the Crimean War of 1853–56 the United States Government gave moral support to Russia. On its part, Russia gave a similar support to the Union forces during the Civil War of 1861–65. The Russian fleet was sent to the northern states as an expression of sympathy and support of the Federal Government in its struggle against the Confederate South. When Alexander II barely escaped an attempted assassination in 1866, the United States Assistant Secretary of the Navy, G. V. Fox, was sent to Russia to extend congratulations on account of Alexander's escape from death. The social life of the two countries at this time had certain common characteristics. Serfdom had just been abolished in Russia while slavery had been abolished in the United States. This circumstance, it seemed, led to a mutual understanding and sympathy. The desire to meet the interests of the United States was one of the basic reasons for Russia's sale of her American possessions. In 1867 Alaska was sold to the United States for $7,200,000, a nominal sum considering the natural wealth of Alaska. The Russian colony in California—Fort Ross—had already been sold by the Russo-American Company to J. A. Sutter in 1844.

The *rapprochement* of the United States, however, could not serve as a firm support to Russia against Great Britain and France in her Near Eastern policy. Russia took advantage of the helpless condition of France during the Franco-Prussian War in 1870 in order to announce her determination to abrogate the Black Sea clauses of the Treaty of Paris. Great Britain alone, without France, was not feared by Russia. Alexander II also attempted to strengthen his position in European diplomacy by means of an understanding with Germany and Austria. (The League of Three Emperors, 1872.)

Having achieved success in the Black Sea, Russia was ready to make concessions to Great Britain in the Middle East and it agreed to the British demands. Prince Gorchakov announced Russia's willingness not to seize Khiva. Events, however, proved otherwise. A struggle with Khiva was unavoidable in view of increasing raids of the Khivans. In 1873 thirteen thousand Russian troops under the command of Kauffmann moved against Khiva from Turkestan and the Caspian Sea. The country was conquered. Part of its territory was merged with Russia and part became a vassal state. At the taking of Khiva a great number of Persian slaves were released. In 1871 the Kuldja region on the Chinese frontier was occupied on account of the disturbances which threatened the peace of the Kirghiz. Uprisings of Dungan (Chinese Mohammedans) and of Taranchis (Sarts) took place against China. The Chinese Government proved itself unable to suppress them. Kuldja was occupied by Russia for ten years and in 1882 was returned to China. In the middle of the 1870's the Khokand Khan rose against Russia. The uprising was suppressed and the Khanate was incorporated in Russian territory. In 1876 the Fergan region was organized.

The attention of Russia was again directed toward the Near East in the latter 1870's. The Russo-Turkish War of 1877–78 was caused by serious internal complications in the Balkans. The Turkish oppression of the Slavs in collecting taxes led to uprisings against the Turks in Bosnia and Herzegovina, as well as in Bulgaria. The Turks attempted to suppress the uprising with extraordinary cruelty. As the Great Powers did not intervene, Serbia and Montenegro declared war on Turkey in 1876. The Serbian Government invited General Cherniaiev, famed for his Turkestan campaigns, to command the Serbian army. Cherniaiev was accompanied by an inconsiderable number of volunteers from Russia; but the forces of the Serbs and the Turks were too unequal, and after a heroic resistance at Alexinac, Cherniaiev was forced to retreat. Serbia was saved from a complete defeat by the timely intervention of Russia. When Turkey refused to carry out the demands of the conference of European diplomats in Constantinople in 1876 respecting the reform of government over the Slavonic lands, Alexander II declared war on Turkey, April 24, 1877. Russia was joined by Rumania, a Principality formed in 1859 from the union of Moldavia and Wallachia. The war was difficult, especially because it began when the reorganization of the Russian army on the basis of universal service was far from completed. In the autumn of 1877 Russian troops achieved considerable success both on the Balkan and Caucasian fronts. At the end of November Kars was taken by the Russian troops for the third time in the nineteenth century. In December, Plevna, where the main Turkish army of Osman Pasha was besieged, fell to Russia. During the winter Russian troops crossed the Balkans. In February, 1878, they neared Constantinople. The success of the Russian armies led to the interference of Great Britain. The British fleet entered the Sea of Marmora. On March 3, 1878, at a small village, San Stefano, near Constantinople, the preliminary conditions of peace between Russia and Turkey were signed. Turkey agreed to form a new princedom, Bulgaria, including the river Vardar and the whole of Macedonia, of its Balkan possessions between the Danube and the Aegean Sea. Turkey further agreed to recognize the independence of Serbia, Montenegro, and Rumania. Russia received the southern part of Bessarabia, ceded by her in 1856, Batum, and Kars in Transcaucasia. It may be noted that Kars was returned to Turkey by the Treaty of Brest-Litovsk in 1918. But the Treaty of San Stefano aroused the opposition of Great Britain and Austria. The creation of a big Bulgaria was contrary to the provisions of the secret conventions between Austria and Russia, concluded in 1876 and 1877. Russia was threatened with a new war. Desiring to avoid it, Alexander II accepted the mediation of the German Chancellor, Bismarck, and agreed to revise the conditions of the treaty at a European Congress in Berlin. The Congress of Berlin was a complete defeat of Russian diplomacy. The territory of Bulgaria was reduced to half, Macedonia being left to Turkey. Furthermore, this territory was cut in two forming the Principality of Bulgaria and the Autonomous Province of Eastern Roumelia, both remaining vassal to Turkey. Furthermore, Bosnia and Herzegovina were "temporarily" occupied by Austria. The foreign policy of Alexander II terminated in failure.

3.

THE internal policy of Alexander II did not bring about political peace in Russia. In spite of his far-reaching social and administrative reforms, he had to face bitter political opposition and direct revolutionary movements. The political opposition to the Government came primarily from the nobility. The idea was current that the nobility, having been deprived of its social and economic privileges, should receive in exchange political privileges, that is, a part of the governing power. This idea appeared during the preparation of the peasant reforms among members of the Provincial Committees who were discontented with the radicalism of the Revising Commission. In addition to the political programs of the nobles, other plans, looking to the reorganization of Russia along constitutional and democratic lines, were advanced, as a continuation of "Decembrist" tradition.

The revolutionary idea was chiefly current among the "Raznochintsi"—that is, individuals of no definite class: the children of peasants and merchants having received secondary or higher education; the children of the clergy who did not desire to enter the church; the children of small civil servants who did not desire to continue the vocation of their fathers; and the children of impoverished nobles. These Raznochintsi rapidly formed a new social class, the so-called "intelligentsia," which included many members of the nobility. The intellectuals grew rapidly with the reforms of Alexander II. The institution of the legal bar, the growth of newspapers and magazines, the increased number of teachers, etc., contributed to the growth. The intelligentsia consisted of intellectual people in general, but at first it consisted primarily of people connected with the publication of papers and magazines or connected with universities. The university students contributed the greatest number of radical and revolutionary leaders. The majority of the students consisted of men who had no means whatsoever. The average student lived in a state of semi-starvation, earning his way through the university by giving lessons or by copying. The majority of the students had no notion of sport and no taste for it. Lack of physical exercise and consequent ill-health had a crushing effect upon the psychology of the students. The leaders of the intelligentsia desired not only radical political changes but also a social revolution, in spite of the fact that Russian industry was too undeveloped to supply a firm basis for socialism. The Government was criticized for not being radical enough. The more moderate criticism was expressed in the legalized press, while the more bitter criticism appeared in revolutionary organs published abroad, the best known of which was *Kolokol* (The Bell), published by Herzen in London. Revolutionary propaganda against the Government immediately took a harsh tone. In 1862 there appeared a proclamation to the youth of Russia calling for terrorism and the murder of members of the Government and supporters of its policy. The appearance of this proclamation was contemporaneous with a number of cases of incendiarism in St. Petersburg. The Government took decisive steps; several individuals were arrested and exiled. At the same time the Polish revolutionary leaders were preparing an uprising in Poland. The activity of the Russian revolutionary leaders was connected with the Polish movement. The Polish revolution broke out in 1863. Just prior to this uprising the Russian Government had started a more liberal policy in Poland. The introduction of the reform had been put in the hands of a prominent Polish statesman, Marquis Wielopolski. The radical elements in Poland decided to *sabotage* the policy of moderate reform. The uprising was suppressed by military force, after which the last remnants of Polish independence were abrogated. Instead of the "Kingdom of Poland" the official title of the territory became the By-Visla Provinces. At the same time, a land reform was introduced in Poland in 1864 under the management of Miliutin and Cherkasky, who had been the chief figures in the Russian reform movement. They succeeded in carrying out the land reform in Poland more successfully than in Russia. Thanks to this measure, the great mass of Polish peasants, almost to the World War, remained loyal to the Russian Government.

The Polish uprising had an important influence on the evolution of the opposition and revolutionary movements in Russia. It aroused the patriotic feelings of the great majority of the Russian people and thus strengthened the position of the Government. The Russian revolutionary leaders who had been connected with the Polish uprising rapidly lost all prestige in Russia. The circulation of Herzen's *Kolokol* fell from three thousand to five hundred. Following the Polish uprising, the revolutionary and opposition movements in Russia for some years did not receive the support of any important groups in Russia. The attempt of Karakozov against Emperor Alexander II in 1866 was an isolated fact and the work of a very small group of conspirators.

A new wave of antigovernment activity arose in the 1870's. Among the liberal circles of society, the desire grew for elective representation not only in local self-government (Zemstvos and towns) but also in the central agencies of government. The institution of a parliament was to complete the unfinished reforms. This movement became particularly strong following the Turkish War of 1877–78, when the liberated Bulgaria received a constitution. The desire for a constitution in Russia became clearly expressed. The activity of the revolutionary organizations in Russia during this period likewise increased. Their activity may be divided into two periods. From 1870 to 1875 the radical intellectuals abstained from direct struggle against the Government, but undertook preparatory propaganda among the masses of the people. Many members of the intellectuals of that time went "to the people," living among the peasants and workmen, teaching schools or becoming agricultural or industrial laborers.

The Government, fearing the results of the propaganda, oppressed the movement by arresting participants in it. At times the peaceful members of the movement suffered arrest together with the real propagandists. In many cases persons were tried and imprisoned or exiled on the mere suspicion and action by the police. The Government's measures aroused the bitterest feeling among the radical intellectuals. In the middle of the 1870's, the revolutionaries began to use terrorism and to make attempts against members of the Government. In 1879, in Lipetsk in central Russia, the leaders of the revolutionary movement met in secret conference. An Executive Committee was elected at this meeting for the purpose of opposing the Government. This Executive Committee decided to abandon all attempts against individual members of the Government and to bend every effort upon assassinating the head of the Government, Emperor Alexander II. From that time on, Alexander II was the object of a man hunt by revolutionaries. Attempts were made in rapid succession, one after the other, but were without success until the attempt made in St. Petersburg in the spring of 1881, which resulted in the death of Alexander II on March 13, 1881.

The assassination of Alexander II occurred on the very day when the emperor signed a *ukaz* calling for Representative Committees to advise the State Council. This was the "constitution" drawn up by Loris Melikov, the Minister of the Interior. Melikov's idea was that the revolutionary activity of the intellectuals could not be stopped by police measures alone. In his opinion the revolutionaries had the moral support of the moderate classes of society who were discontented with the autocratic policy of the Government. Melikov believed that the Government should placate the moderate elements of the opposition by means of granting a moderate constitution. This measure, he believed, would deprive the revolutionaries of the moral support of these classes. The assassination of Alexander II prevented the execution of this plan. His son and successor, Alexander III, withdrew the constitution of Melikov, and the *ukaz* signed by Alexander II was never published.

4.

THE impression made upon Alexander III by the assassination of his father lasted during his life. He retained a distrust for all popular movements and influenced by Constantine Pobiedonostsev, expressed a firm belief in the infallibility of the principle of autocracy. The political program of Alexander III was extremely simple. It consisted in opposing all liberal and revolutionary movements in Russia and in satisfying, to a certain degree, the urgent economic demands of the Russian people. These principles of policy were handed down by Alexander to his son Nicholas, who ascended the throne on the death of his father in 1894. It was only under the pressure of the revolution of 1904–5 that Nicholas agreed to grant a constitution; but up to the second revolution of 1917, and probably to his very death in 1918, Nicholas retained a belief in the principles of policy laid down by his father.

During the twenty-five years between 1881 and 1905, the political program of the Russian Government remained unchanged; but while the general policy remained unchanged, the actual course of events took different directions during the reigns of Alexander III and Nicholas II. Both father and son had common traits: simplicity in their private life and a love for their home. Both Alexander and Nicholas were model husbands and fathers. Coupled with these qualities was a certain cautiousness and stubbornness. In spite of these similarities, the son did not closely resemble the father. Alexander III had a masterful nature and knew how to secure obedience both from his ministers and from the members of the imperial household—the grand dukes. Alexander was not particularly well educated, but he had the instinct and the tact of a statesman and could grasp without difficulty the essential points of questions presented to him. Alexander had a simple nature; but he was a born emperor.

Nicholas II, on the other hand, had a more complex and delicate personality. His education had not been very complete, but he loved knowledge and books. In private life Nicholas II could have succeeded easily in applying his knowledge and his gifts; but he totally lacked the qualities of a statesman and a leader. Nicholas had a weak will and was not interested in political matters. His mind slipped along the surface of political questions and seized only their superficial aspects. Nicholas never attempted to penetrate into the substance of the matters submitted to him. Not having a firm will, Nicholas, as many weak men, attempted to hide this fact by stubbornness.

Soon after Nicholas' coronation, intrigues sprang up among his ministers and the grand dukes, whom Nicholas never succeeded in mastering and putting in their proper place. Nicholas did not like to admit that anyone exercised any influence upon him. In fact, however, he was constantly under someone's influence, until he became completely dominated by his wife, Alexandra Feodorovna. An episode illustrating Nicholas' character took place in Moscow during his coronation. Because of the incompetence of the police, a panic occurred at the distribution of gifts in honor of the occasion, in which over one thousand people were crushed to death. This accident took place at the very height of the coronation festivities. There is no doubt that if it had occurred at the coronation of Alexander III, he would have immediately canceled all further celebration. Nicholas, however, had the idea of showing his firmness and made no change of plans. Even the ball at the French Ambassador's the same evening was not canceled. As a matter of fact this was not firmness but tactlessness.

While it is possible to define the internal policy pursued by Alexander III, the same cannot be done for the reign of Nicholas II. His policy consisted simply in continuing by inertia the policy of his father. The internal policy of Alexander III consisted first of all in strengthening governmental control in all directions where free public opinion could be expected to manifest itself. Pursuant to this policy, the laws regarding local self-government were revised. The power of the Government, in the person of the provincial governors, was strengthened as against the power of the Zemstvos. According to the new laws of 1890, the peasants elected only candidates for the Zemstvo, while the governor chose representatives from among these candidates. This law was repealed in 1906. In order to extend governmental supervision over the peasants, the office of "Zemsky Nachalnik" or Land Captain, appointed by the Government from the nobility, was created in 1889. The Zemsky Nachalniks had administrative power in local affairs as well as the function of judge over the peasantry.

Many measures were also taken to repress the intellectuals. The universities were reorganized in 1884. Education became subject to government control. Censorship of the press was strengthened and the majority of newspapers and magazines became subject to the "preliminary censorship" of government agents. The political tendencies of the intellectuals became subject to redoubled watchfulness by the police. Persons who were suspected were subject to police supervision. Attempts at political conspiracies were mercilessly crushed. In 1887 the police discovered a plot to assassinate Alexander III. The guilty parties were executed, among them Alexander Ulianov, Lenin's eldest brother. In order to grant the police greater freedom, many provinces of Russia were declared in a state of "special protection." This enabled the administration to suspend the normal laws of procedure with respect to political prisoners. Several of the territories of Russia, inhabited by non-Russian peoples, also fell under suspicion. The Government began a policy of forcible "Russianization." This policy was applied particularly to Poland. Measures were also taken against the cultural dominance of the Germans in the Baltic provinces where they formed a minority of the population. Only the landowning class, the Barons, were Germans. The religious life was also subject to restrictions. The Christian dissenters, the evangelical sects, Stundo-Baptists, and Catholics were equally affected. Particular suspicion was leveled against the Jews.

The Jewish question had arisen in Russia in the eighteenth century. A great many Jews had become subjects of the Russian state, following the division of Poland and the annexation of the southwestern Russian territories, which had a large Jewish population. According to the laws of 1804, the Jews were forbidden to settle in the central Russian provinces. The statutes fixed a "pale of settlement" where alone Jews could live. This included the western and southern provinces. Under Alexander III the conditions under which the Jews lived were subjected to further restriction. They were forbidden to settle outside the towns and villages, even within the territories which they might inhabit. The line of demarcation was further restricted in 1887 when the city of Rostov-on-Don was excluded from the pale. In 1891 seventeen thousand Jews were deported from Moscow. Furthermore, a quota of Jews, limited to their proportion of the population, was introduced in government educational institutions. With few exceptions the Jews were not admitted to governmental service.

Seeking to hold the various classes under close observation, the Government searched for a group in society upon which it could itself depend. This group was the Russian nobility. During the reigns of Alexander III and Nicholas II, the Government attempted to secure the support of the nobility by granting it special privileges in respect to local self-government and local justice. In addition a number of financial privileges were granted to the nobility. The dependence of the internal policy upon the nobility was a fatal political error. The Russian nobility was politically dead after the reforms of Alexander II and the beginning of the democratization of Russian life. The attempt to bring it back into political life was an attempt to revive a corpse. Even when the nobility had been a powerful force in Russia, in the eighteenth and the first half of the nineteenth century, the interests of the imperial power seldom agreed with those of the nobility. It was an act of political shortsightedness to seek to establish a close union between the Government and the nobility at a time when the nobility no longer possessed any vitality. This mistaken policy only brought about further discontent with the Government on the part of other classes.

However, it would be unjust to point only to the negative aspects of Russian policy in the last quarter of the nineteenth century for it must be admitted that the Government also carried out reforms improving the social and economic conditions of the majority of the people. Many measures were directed toward the improvement of the condition of the peasantry. First, in the beginning of 1882, a decree was issued ordering compulsory sale to peasants of land on those estates where the sale had not been completed following the emancipation. Furthermore, the instalments to be paid by the peasants for the land were lowered and the head tax was abolished (1886). New regulations were issued making it easy for peasants to rent government lands and aiding them to migrate to the free lands in the eastern part of the Empire. It was partly to further migration that the Siberian railroad was begun in 1892. The reign of Alexander III also marked the beginning of labor legislation in Russia. In 1882 government inspection of factories was instituted and the Government undertook to regulate the conditions of the workers. At the same time the working day of minors and women was limited by law. Labor legislation was continued during the reign of Nicholas II.

The Government also undertook reforms of the finances. We have seen above that the finances of Russia were greatly improved under Nicholas I, but since that time two wars and expensive internal reforms had succeeded in shaking them and the currency had already depreciated. The Government was fortunate in having such a brilliant statesman as Witte. He succeeded in reorganizing Russian finances and in reintroducing gold into circulation in 1897.

All these government measures directed toward improving the economic condition of the country could not, however, outweigh the irritation caused by the police supervision instituted by the Government. The internal policy of Alexander III succeeded in suppressing social discontent and political opposition only for a short time. Actually, in the course of the reign of Alexander III and the first half of the reign of Nicholas II, everything was quiet; but during the second half of the reign of Nicholas II, the accumulated social discontent expressed itself in a violent explosion. The immediate cause of this was the failure of Nicholas II's foreign policy.

5.

THE foreign policy of Russia following the Congress of Berlin of 1878 was characterized by fatigue and disillusionment. The Congress of Berlin was a serious defeat of Russian diplomacy. The sacrifices borne by Russia during the Turkish War of 1877–78 seemed to have been useless. The emancipation of the Balkan Slavs was only halfway accomplished. Furthermore, there soon arose misunderstandings in Bulgaria, which further diminished the rôle of Russian diplomacy in the Near East. The cause of this misunderstanding was partly the tactlessness of the Russian advisers who took too imperious a tone with respect to the Government of Prince Alexander Battenberg, a German nephew of Alexander II who had been placed upon the Bulgarian throne in 1879. In 1879 an alliance was concluded between Austria and Germany, directed against Russian influence in the Balkans. Despite this, Bismarck succeeded in 1881 in reviving the League of Three Emperors (Russia, Germany, and Austria) which had been first organized in 1872. This alliance was concluded only for a period of three years with the option of renewal. It was renewed in 1884, and terminated in 1887 when Austria broke with Russia. The alliance between Germany and Russia continued for three more years. The success of Bismarck may be explained by the fact that Russia at this time was looking for an ally against Great Britain. Relations between Russia and Great Britain each year became worse. The reason for this was the continued advance of Russia in central Asia. In the beginning of the 1880's, a punitive expedition was sent against the Tekins and the capture of the fortress Geok-Tepe by Skobelev took place in 1881. In 1884 the lower reaches of the river Murgab, with the town of Merv, were annexed by Russia. In 1885 Afghan troops were met and defeated on the river Kushk. In 1885–88 the Trans-Caspian railroad from Askhabad was extended to Samarkand. The construction was in charge of General Annenkov, who carried it out with extraordinary rapidity, despite the natural barriers of desert and windswept sands that had to be overcome. The Russian policy of expansion aroused great excitement in Great Britain. The battle of the river Kushk almost led to war between the two powers. Russia was enabled to retain her acquisitions, thanks to her alliance with Germany as well as to the conciliatory policy of Gladstone.

The Russo-German understanding could not, however, be permanent if Germany continued to support Austria in the Balkans. The unreliable character of the German alliance forced Alexander III to seek for other allies. This prepared the ground for a Franco-Russian understanding. The *rapprochement* between Russia and France started in the realm of finance. Russia needed loans to develop her industries and to improve her armaments. Prior to 1880 Russia's foreign loans had been floated chiefly by German bankers.

After 1880 Germany was herself in need of funds for the development of her fleet and colonies, and was, for this reason as well as for other reasons political in nature, less anxious to extend loans to Russia. In 1888 a group of French bankers offered to grant Russia a loan. The offer was accepted, and in 1890 three loan agreements were concluded. After that France repeatedly extended loans to Russia, in 1893, 1894, 1896, 1901, 1904, and 1906. The financial *rapprochement* was followed by a political and military understanding. On July 25, 1891, a French squadron visited Kronstadt. The French sailors were cordially greeted. The visit made a great impression upon Russian society. It seemed strange that the autocratic tsar should order the playing of the *Marseillaise,* which was written during the French revolution in 1789 and is filled with revolutionary sentiment. Among Russian revolutionaries the *Marseillaise* was regarded as their hymn. The Russian text called for a revolution in Russia. A month later a military agreement was concluded between Russia and France, August 22, 1891. After several years of exchange of good feelings, the French Foreign Minister, Hanotaux, disclosed the existence of the Franco-Russian Entente, June 10, 1895. The agreement with France was not, in the eyes of the Russian Government, a direct threat to Great Britain or Germany. It was regarded rather as a measure preventing the possibility of an attack by one European power upon another. For this reason, several years after the conclusion of the alliance with France, Russia made the proposal for a general agreement by the European powers. At the initiative of Russia a peace conference was called at The Hague in 1899. The conference met for two months, May 18 to July 29, but led to no practical results. Its only significance was one of principle. For the first time since the Holy Alliance, an attempt had been made to bring about international peace; and again, as in 1815, the initiative had come from the Russian emperor.

6.

The failure of The Hague Conference was due primarily to the general distrust felt by the Great Powers toward each other. Clashes took place between France and Great Britain and between Great Britain and Germany. In this condition of affairs there was little opportunity for creating international order. Possibly the only way to guarantee peace would have been an understanding between the chief continental powers: Russia, France, and Germany. In Russia this scheme was supported by Witte. But a working agreement between Russia and Germany was rendered difficult by the competition in the Balkans between Russia and Germany's ally, Austria, not to speak of the difficulties in the way of a Franco-German understanding. The efforts of German diplomacy were consequently directed toward transferring Russia's attention from the Near East to the Middle and Far East. At the same time Germany attempted to restrain Austria and to discover a *modus vivendi* between Russia and Austria in the Balkans.

To a certain extent German diplomacy was successful. In 1897 there began in the Balkans a decade of coöperation between Russia and Austria. Meanwhile, even without German encouragement, Russia's economic interests attracted her to the Middle and Far East. Here, too, Witte stood as the chief exponent of Russia's new policy. Witte's policy was to encourage Russia's economic penetration in the east. In the early 1890's Witte first directed attention to Russia's economic interests in Persia. A Russo-Persian bank was organized, supported by the Russian Government. This bank was interested in financing Russian concessions in Persia and in aiding Russian trade with Persia. Somewhat later, Witte turned his attention to the Far East. In 1894 a war took place between China and Japan. Japan was victorious and China was forced to cede the Liaotung Peninsula to Japan. China's finances following the war were completely disrupted. Witte urged Russia's interference in favor of China. Both France and Germany backed Russia, thus giving an example of the possibility of a Russo-Franco-German understanding as advocated by Witte. Japan was forced to abandon the Liaotung Peninsula; and with the aid of France Russia extended China a loan of 400,000,000 francs. Germany and Great Britain also granted Chinese loans of £16,000,000 each. The Russian loan was at the rate of 4 per cent, the British 4½ per cent, and the German 5 per cent. Soon after this, upon the occasion of the visit of the Chinese Minister, Li Hung-chang, to Russia, a treaty of friendship between China and Russia was concluded (1896). Russia undertook to aid China in case of aggression by a third power, it being understood that the treaty had special reference to Japan. At the same time China agreed that

Russia should have the right to construct a railroad through northern Manchuria, connecting Chita and Vladivostok. A company was organized for this purpose, known as the Chinese Eastern Railroad Company, controlled actually by the Russian Government.

Russian diplomacy, however, did not confine itself to economic penetration, as it was advised by Witte. At the suggestion of Germany Russia took a more aggressive tone. Germany advanced the idea that the European powers should guarantee their financial interests in China by occupying several Chinese ports. Germany took Kiao-chao, leaving the Liaotung Peninsula to Russia and Weihaiwei to Great Britain. Russian diplomacy fell into the German trap. The Liaotung Peninsula was forcibly occupied by Russian troops and taken from China under the terms of a twenty-five-year lease, March 27, 1898. This move, as might well have been expected, aroused the keenest dissatisfaction in China. All the favorable effects of the Russo-Chinese Treaty of 1896 were obliterated.

The next Russian move in the Far East occurred when the Russian forces in 1900 took part, together with the forces of the European powers, in suppressing the Boxer Rebellion. At this time Manchuria was occupied by Russian troops. These events did not advance friendly relations between Russia and China. They resulted, moreover, in straining Russo-Japanese relations. Japan had been deeply offended by Russia's seizure of the Liaotung Peninsula. She also feared Russia's economic competition in Korea. These fears were stimulated by the activities of an irresponsible group of Russian concessionaires on the river Yalu, as well as by the aggressive policy pursued by Admiral Alexeiev, the Russian viceroy in the Far East. Russia did not succeed in solving her difficulties with Japan by peaceful means. On February 9, 1904, without any declaration of war Japanese armed vessels attacked Russian armed vessels in the outer harbor of Port Arthur.

7.

THE war with Japan in 1904–1905 resulted in a series of defeats for Russia. The Japanese fleet showed itself to be considerably stronger than the Russian, whose vessels were less well constructed and had weaker armaments. The Japanese fleet soon succeeded in blockading Port Arthur. Soon after the Japanese troops were landed on the mainland.

The Russian army was considerably stronger than the Japanese in numbers. As regards quality, the Russian troops were not inferior to the Japanese. Nevertheless, the war on land was as unfortunate for Russia as the war on the sea. The first failures might be explained by the difficulty of rapidly concentrating Russian troops at the distant battlefield. The whole army depended upon the Siberian railway, which was not even completed. There was no line around Lake Baikal. But the subsequent defeats must be explained on psychological grounds. The Russian army went into battle without enthusiasm. The deep dissatisfaction of the Russian people with the Government could not fail to be reflected in the army. The war was unpopular in Russia from the very beginning. Its objects were not understood by the Russian people. It did not seem to them to affect the vital interests of the country, while every Japanese soldier understood that the war concerned the vital interests of Japan.

The Russian army was led by inferior commanders. At its head was General Kuropatkin, who had a high reputation, having been chief of staff for the popular general Skobelev in the reign of Alexander III. But while he had been an excellent chief of staff, he did not possess the qualities of a commander-in-chief. He had neither the necessary initiative nor the strategic ability. A leading Russian general said to a friend who expressed his opinion that Kuropatkin was made commander-in-chief because he had been chief of staff for Skobelev: "Who, then, is going to take the place of Skobelev?" After several failures Kuropatkin was dismissed and his place was taken by the old general Linevich, a much better strategist; by that time, however, the Government was already thinking of peace.

Soon after the beginning of the war, the Japanese succeeded in cutting off Port Arthur and forcing the Russian army back to the north. A great battle at Liaoyang in the autumn of 1904 was lost by the Russians as a result of Kuropatkin's mismanagement. Early in 1905 Port Arthur surrendered to the Japanese, and several months afterward Russia suffered two new setbacks. The army was defeated at Mukden, and the fleet, sent under the command of Admiral Rozhdestvensky from the Baltic Sea to the Far East around Africa, was destroyed by the Japanese in the battle of Tsushima,

The defeats in the war led to internal disorders in Russia. The financial condition of the country was greatly disturbed. These conditions led the Russian Government to accept the mediation of President Roosevelt and to agree to negotiate with the Japanese at Portsmouth. At the head of the Russian peace delegation was Witte, who succeeded in concluding peace on more favorable conditions than were generally expected. He was subsequently granted the title of Count in recognition of his services. As to the provisions of the treaty, Japan abandoned her original demand for a money indemnity; but Russia agreed to cede to Japan the southern half of Sakhalin. Russia also ceded to Japan the "lease" to the Liaotung Peninsula but retained her control over the railroads in northern Manchuria. The Peace of Portsmouth of September 5, 1905, was concluded just in time to save the Russian Government from a complete internal catastrophe. Russia was already in a state of revolution.

CHAPTER XI.

THE REVOLUTION OF 1905 AND THE CONSTITUTIONAL EXPERIMENT

(1905–1914)

I.

THE Japanese war was the outward cause of the first Russian revolution. Its inner causes lay very deep in social conditions. The widespread dissatisfaction among the most diverse groups of the population in Russia during the period preceding 1905 has already been described. In 1904–1905 this dissatisfaction showed itself in overt acts. Political parties were formed, but in view of the long period of suppression of all parliamentary government and the absence of freedom of political expression, it was impossible to establish large political groups. Consequently, political organizations in Russia were illegal or "underground" agencies. The programs and the activity of these groups did not express the real needs of the people, but were in the nature rather of theoretical declarations. Political platforms originated primarily among the intellectuals, who were isolated from the actualities of life and were often forced into exile for their activities against the Government. Russian Jews played an important rôle among political *émigrés* abroad. This resulted partly from the fact that the number of Jews permitted to enter the universities in Russia was limited by their proportion to the whole population. This number, being small, forced many Jews to seek education abroad. Many of them attended foreign universities in Germany, Switzerland, and France.

The conditions of the period of "underground" development of Russian parties go far to explain their activities. Because of this imposed secrecy and restriction they were forced to stress theoretical discussion rather than to face practical problems. The Russian political parties did not seek to understand or to express the real desires of the people, but rather to utilize popular emotion in order to achieve success for their programs.

The first Russian political party was the Workers' Social Democratic party, organized in 1898, on the model of the German Social Democratic party, which followed the teachings of Karl Marx. The party attempted to get into touch with the workers through party "cells" in the principal industrial centers of Russia. The party "cell" was a peculiar form of political organization in Russia. It was a secretly organized group of trusted party members who maintained contact with the party organization. Its purpose was to diffuse the ideas of the party among non-members.

At the convention of 1903, the Social Democratic party split into two groups. The radical group, subsequently known as Bolsheviks, sought to realize a social revolution in Russia by violent means. The moderates, subsequently known as Mensheviks, insisted that before the social revolution could be effective, a *bourgeois* or democratic *régime* had to develop. At the head of the Bolsheviks was Vladimir Ulianov, whose pseudonym was Lenin. He was born in 1870, the son of a nobleman, and both he and his brother engaged in revolutionary activity at an early age. Lenin's brother became a well-known terrorist and was executed for his connection with a plot against the life of Alexander III. In 1900 Lenin left Russia and remained abroad until 1905.

At the head of the Mensheviks was Plekhanov, a theoretical Marxist, who during almost the whole of his political career was in opposition to the policies advocated by Lenin. While the attention of the Social Democratic party was directed exclusively to the workers, another socialist group, calling itself the Social Revolutionary party, undertook to defend the interests of the peasants. They tried to organize "cells" among the peasantry. In their policy of opposition to the Government, they differed from the Social Democrats. The latter advocated a mass movement; the former contented themselves with terrorist acts against government officials. The theory of the terrorism practiced by the Social Revolutionaries was that the people would be stirred into activity mainly by example. Their revolutionary theory was derived not from Marx, but from French socialism of the "utopian" school as well as from some Russian writers.

Both of these socialist groups succeeded in obtaining a large following among university students of both sexes; they also attracted members of the professions: lawyers, doctors, and teachers.

In 1903 liberal groups also organized an illegal party consisting primarily of professors and liberal estate-owners. The real *bourgeois* classes, the merchants and manufacturers, did not enter into any political organizations at this time. In 1905 this illegal union formed the Constitutional Democratic party. Their program was based not upon Marx and western socialism, but upon the political teachings of constitutional and democratic groups of western Europe and America. This party attempted, not to reach the masses of the people, but to influence the thought of the government employees and the petty *bourgeoisie* in the cities. It was the political organization of the middle classes.

All these parties were united in desiring the end of autocracy and the introduction of a representative government elected by universal, direct, equal, and secret ballot. But between the programs of these political parties and the concrete needs of the people, there was no relation. The Social Democrats regarded themselves as the representatives of the workers, but were interested only in the propaganda of socialism among the workers; the Social Revolutionaries regarded themselves as representing the peasants, but advocated the nationalization or socialization of all land, including that of the peasants, in spite of the fact that the peasants desired only the division of the large estates among themselves. The Constitutional Democrats advocated a parliamentary government following the French or British model, and the undermining of centralized executive power, while the interests of Russian democracy in fact dictated a combination of popular representation and strong government.

In view of the theoretical character of the activities of these parties the Imperial Government could easily have continued to dominate by rapidly and energetically introducing political reforms; but being under the influence of the reactionary nobility, the Government was incapable of undertaking this task. The Government always retreated in the face of overwhelming criticism, but never undertook action on its own initiative. Its indecision was the principal factor in the success of the revolutionary groups.

2.

The revolutionary sentiments of the Russian people in 1904–1905 expressed themselves in the most diverse forms. The political activity of the intellectuals took the form of lectures on politics, the organization of societies of a semipolitical nature, and, in some cases, of riots on the part of students. The liberal landowners, members of the local (Zemstvo) administration, organized conferences to discuss reforms and a deputation from one of these congresses was sent to the emperor on June 19, 1905. The workers took recourse to strikes, the chief aims of which were political, rather than economic, reforms. The discontent of the peasantry found expression in agrarian riots, which resulted frequently in the destruction of landowners' houses or even in the murder of the landowners. Finally, following the termination of the Japanese war, disorder spread to the army. The soldiers were affected by socialist propaganda and in many cases revolted against their officers. Socialist agitators urged the formation of councils composed of soldiers, an idea which in 1917 proved fatal to the Russian army. Riots spread from the army to the navy, and on the battleship *Potemkin* the sailors succeeded in temporarily seizing control in June, 1905. The whole period was characterized by a series of assassinations of governmental officials by terrorists. The Government first attempted to deal with the revolutionary sentiments of the people by suppressing disorders with armed force and by disrupting the revolutionary organizations. The Department of Police introduced secret agents in revolutionary organizations for the purpose of securing evidence against their leaders. The government agents sometimes became leaders of the revolutionary parties and took so active a part in the movement that it became impossible for the Government to determine where revolution began and where provocation ended. It was under circumstances of this kind that the Minister of the Interior, Plehve, was assassinated. The Department of Police also attempted to get control over the workers' movement by satisfying their economic demands and thus drawing them away from political activity. Zubatov, an agent of the secret police, succeeded in the spring of 1902 in organizing the workers along purely economic lines in Moscow and was ordered by Plehve to introduce his system all over Russia. Following the death of

Plehve and the dismissal of Zubatov, the workers' organization continued to develop of its own momentum. Its new leader, the priest Gapon, thought of petitioning the tsar in person to effect the reforms demanded by the workers. On January 22, 1905, a huge crowd of workmen made their way to the Winter Palace in St. Petersburg to appeal to Nicholas II. The day had a tragic end, for, notwithstanding the fact that the workmen were peacefully inclined and unarmed, the crowd was dispersed by gunfire, as a result of which several hundred people were killed or wounded. "Bloody Sunday," as this day came to be called, became a decisive turning point in the history of the opposition of the working classes. It had as its immediate result their alliance with the socialist working class parties. The Government by this time realized that it had no plan to alleviate the situation and no firm support among the people. It consequently decided upon concessions in the matter of political reform. But even in this it moved unwillingly. On August 19, 1905, the order was given to call a national congress, the imperial Duma, which was to have deliberative, but not legislative, functions. This was, however, a half-measure which satisfied no one. In the autumn of 1905, the situation became critical. A general strike was called throughout Russia. In the cities even the electricity and water supply were cut off; all railroads came to a standstill, with the exception of the Finland Railway. The leadership of the revolutionary group in St. Petersburg was taken by a special council composed of the leaders of the Socialist parties and representatives of the workers. This was the so-called Soviet of Workers' Deputies which was to take a prominent part in the events of 1917. At the first session of the Soviet the number of workers' representatives was only forty. It was increased later to five hundred. The chairman of the Soviet was a lawyer, Khrustalev-Nosar, but the actual leader was the vice-president Bronstein, subsequently known as Trotsky. It should be noted that the pseudonyms employed by many revolutionary leaders were assumed for self-protection against the espionage of the government police. All revolutionary instructions were signed by fictitious names.

The majority of the Soviet was in the hands of the Mensheviks, of whom Trotsky was a prominent member. The Bolsheviks failed to capture control of the first Soviet and regarded it with suspicion. Soviets were formed in some other cities, Moscow, Odessa, and elsewhere; but before they achieved any important results, the Government decided to make far-reaching political concessions. At the initiative of Count Witte, a manifesto, which amounted practically to capitulation by the Government, was issued October 30, 1905.

By this manifesto the imperial Government promised that it would grant to the Russian nation: (1) the fundamental principles of civil liberty—inviolability of person, and liberty of thought, speech, assembly, and organization; (2) democratic franchise; (3) the principle that no law could henceforth be made without the consent of the Duma. A new Prime Minister, Count Witte, with power to appoint assistants from opposition circles, was named to carry the manifesto into effect. This was the first time in Russia that a united cabinet was formed.

The manifesto was an embodiment of the principal demands of the liberal opposition. The hope was that it would stop the revolutionary activity of this opposition. In this regard the manifesto was an attempt to unite the Government and the Liberal parties against the imminent social revolution. For this reason leaders of the social movement who desired revolution at all costs were opposed to the manifesto. Their arguments were that the Government was not sincere in its promises, that it desired only to stop the revolutionary movement, and that as soon as conditions permitted, it would rescind the manifesto. The Government indeed did hope that the manifesto would stop the revolution; but it was not true that it wished to withdraw the concessions. In fact, it did not do so after its real victory over the revolutionaries. Count Witte, the head of the Government and the author of the manifesto, personally believed in the necessity for reform and had naturally no intentions of retraction. Only the inexperience of the leaders of the Russian liberal movement can explain the decision of the liberal groups to decline all the invitations of Count Witte to enter his ministry. The result was that the manifesto of October 30 did not stop the revolutionary movement at once.

The Socialist parties desired only the triumph of their revolutionary doctrines. The leader of the Bolsheviks, Lenin, who came to Russia following the manifesto of October 30, became the staunchest opponent of the Government's policy. The strikes went on; a second railroad strike lasted from the end of November to the middle of December, and an armed insurrection occurred in Moscow at the end of December, 1905. The irreconcilable policy of the revolutionaries was not supported, however, by the majority of the people, who were fairly well satisfied with the program set forth in the manifesto. The Government was enabled to retake control of the situation. The Soviets were disbanded and the riots were suppressed by force. In several cities *pogroms* against Jews took place, organized by the so-called "Union of the Russian People," a reactionary group whose ideology was of the same pattern as that of German Nazism.

The insurrection at Moscow was not fully suppressed when the Government published a decree on December 24 on the procedure for elections. At the beginning of March, there appeared a manifesto concerning the organization of the new Parliament, which was to be formed of two Houses: the state Duma and the state Council, the first consisting of members elected by the nation, and the second of members half of whom were appointed by the emperor and half elected by the nobility, Zemstvos, and university faculties. The electoral law gave the right of suffrage to the majority of the people, but it was neither equal nor direct. The voters were divided into groups: The workers in several large cities chose their electors to the Duma separately; the peasants chose electors who formed electoral colleges together with the electors chosen by the large landowners. These councils selected the deputies to the Duma. The electoral law artificially isolated the peasants and the workers and gave them a considerable rôle in the elections. This policy was prompted by the desire on the part of the Government to draw the peasants and the workers away from the opposition parties. As a further means of appeasing the peasantry, Count Witte had the idea of expropriating the large estates and handing over the lands to the peasants. This project was developed by one of Witte's ministers, Kutler, who subsequently took a prominent part in the financial reorganization of the Soviet Government. The expropriation of large land holdings, however, was bitterly opposed by the estate-owners. Witte did not have enough power to insist upon the measures he proposed, and was forced to cancel his project. This failure reacted upon the operation of the electoral law which was primarily a bid to the peasantry. Just as in the case of the earlier attempts to organize the workers in a manner favorable to the Government, it merely succeeded in stirring up social movements without either satisfying or being able to control them.

3.

THE elections to the first Duma took place in March, 1906. On May 10 the state Council and Duma were opened by Nicholas II. The majority of the Duma consisted of opposition deputies; of 490 members, 187 belonged to the Liberal party and 85 to the moderate labor group. The Constitutional Democrats, led by I. Petrunkevich (the other leader, P. Miliukov, being removed under a specious pretext from the list of voters), was the strongest party represented. The Socialist parties boycotted the elections, while the Nationalist and Conservative parties were defeated at the polls and secured only a small number of seats. The results of the elections were disappointing to the Government.

Finding a hostile group in control of the state Duma, Nicholas II immediately dismissed Count Witte and appointed Goremykin in his place. The new Prime Minister was a typical civil servant of the old *régime*. He was chosen, not because he had initiative and political convictions, but, on the contrary, because he lacked these qualities and was ready to execute the orders of the emperor. The appointment of Goremykin was a great political error. The relations between the Government and the Duma rapidly took on an unfriendly character.

The principal point of dispute between the Government and the Duma was the agrarian problem. Its discussion in the Duma aroused the passions of all groups. An agrarian bill, sponsored by the Constitutional Democrats, proposed the expropriation of the large estates and the transfer of land to the ownership of the peasants, granting compensation to the owners. This led to increased agitation against the Duma by the reactionaries. Nicholas II faced the problem of either submitting to the Duma and displeasing the nobility, or of dismissing it and provoking the hostility of the Liberals. On July 21 the Duma was dissolved. As a concession to the Liberals, Goremykin was dismissed and a new man, Stolypin, was appointed Prime Minister. Stolypin had been Minister of the Interior in the Cabinet of his predecessor in office. He began his service to the Crown as a governor of one of the southern provinces. Before that he had managed his own estates. He had a profound comprehension of the agrarian problem in Russia and possessed the qualities of an outstanding statesman. He was firm, patriotic, and a man of ideas. The opposition parties did not support Stolypin and his program, but they were obliged to reckon with him. Following the dissolution of the Duma, the opposition groups were undecided as to their course. Their psychology was not that of peaceful parliamentary opposition, but that of revolution. They dreaded the possibility of the Government's canceling the whole program of reform and plainly distrusted the emperor. After the dissolution, members of the Duma issued an appeal to the Russian nation to resist the Government by refusing to pay taxes and to refuse conscription into the army. The appeal had no effect upon the people. Its only result was that its authors lost the right of voting in the subsequent elections.

Stolypin first tried to attract some of the leading members of the moderate liberal groups into his Cabinet. They refused to co-operate with him, and he was obliged to draw upon professional bureaucrats. His agrarian policy consisted primarily in destroying the communal ownership of land instituted by the reforms of 1861, and in encouraging peasant ownership of individual farms.

On November 22 the decree abrogating the peasant commune was published. Each peasant was given the right to receive his share of the common land in full ownership. Simultaneously, measures were taken to finance the purchase by the peasantry of Crown lands. Stolypin's measures were an attempt to repair the defects in the reform of 1861 and to create in Russia a new class of small landowners to form the basis for the new state. This program was deemed incompatible with the agrarian bill introduced by the first Duma. The expropriation of nearly all land, the basis of that proposal, was calculated to solve the whole agrarian problem at one stroke. Stolypin's reform required a score of years to produce lasting results.

When the second Duma gathered on March 5, 1907, it proved to be even more hostile to the Government than was the first. The second Duma had a stronger left wing than the first one (180 Socialists); Lenin had abruptly changed his tactics, and the Socialists did not boycott the Duma. The conflict between the Government and the Duma in 1907 was more acute than in 1906. The Government now had a practical program of reform which the

Duma did not possess. Fifty-five socialist deputies were charged with organizing a plot against the emperor and the second Duma was dissolved in June, 1907. In order to suppress similar expressions of opposition, the electoral law was changed. The large landowners were given preference over the peasants in selecting representatives to the electoral colleges. The third Duma, elected in November, 1907, had a membership different from that of its predecessors. The majority of deputies now belonged to parties of the right, and the liberal and socialist deputies were in the minority. The result of the two years of political conflict was the victory of Stolypin and the Moderate parties. The new *régime,* it seemed, had succeeded in entrenching itself firmly. However, it was not a true parliamentary government that emerged from the revolutionary period of 1905–1906.

4.

Simultaneously with the internal political struggle, important events were shaping Russia's foreign policy. In the beginning of the twentieth century, the international situation had not as yet taken the form of alliances of mutually antagonistic states. Germany was allied to Austria and Italy, Russia to France, but Great Britain had no political ties with Russia. Germany was seeking an agreement with Russia. During the Japanese war, Russia needed an ally to counterbalance Great Britain which, in 1902, had entered into an alliance with Japan. A commercial treaty was signed with Germany in July, 1904, greatly favoring German trade and quite unprofitable to Russia. This treaty was an expression of Russia's fear of Great Britain. It had as its result the strengthening of German foreign policy. In the spring of 1905, the German Government demanded an open door in Morocco against the privileges of France. This gave rise to the famous Tangier incident. In July, 1905, Emperor William II visited Nicholas II at Björkö and concluded a secret alliance with Russia. Nicholas II regarded this as a move against Great Britain and not against France. The Björkö agreement was to take effect immediately following the Japanese war, but after the conclusion of the Portsmouth peace, it became evident that the friendship of France would be lost if the Björkö agreement was maintained. In choosing between the two, the interests of Russia following the war dictated a French alliance for purely financial reasons. The expense of the war and the economic instability caused by the revolution, made foreign borrowing absolutely necessary. A tentative effort made by Count Witte to secure funds in the United States did not lead to success. Russia's strained relations with Great Britain closed the London market. Only France could supply the necessary loans. As compensation for financial support, France demanded Russian support against Germany. The result of this international tangle was Russia's decision to cast her lot with France. At the Algeciras Conference Russia and Great Britain supported France, and Germany was forced to recede before the united pressure of the three powers. Nine days after the Algeciras Conference, France agreed to extend the necessary loans to Russia.

The French loan of 1906 exceeded two billion francs. It came at a critical moment in the Russian Government's struggle with the political opposition, and served to strengthen the bonds that tied Russia to France. At the same time, Russo-British relations took on a more favorable character. Russia's position in the Far East had been materially weakened by the Japanese war. The weakening of Russia's military prestige also affected Great Britain in central Asia. In August, 1907, a convention was signed between Great Britain and Russia concerning Persia, Afghanistan, and Tibet. Afghanistan was recognized as being within the exclusive sphere of British influence; Persia was divided between Great Britain and Russia into two spheres of influence; and Tibet was recognized as being neutral territory. By this convention Russia openly abandoned her pretensions in central Asia and opened the way to further agreements between the two countries.

At the suggestion of President Roosevelt, a second world peace conference was called at The Hague. Pursuant to this suggestion, in 1907, Nicholas II invited the representatives of all the powers to discuss the problem of disarmament. The Hague Conference failed to achieve its purpose and gave evidence only of the new political alignments in Europe. On one side stood Germany and Austria; on the other France, Russia, and Great Britain. A clash between the two groups was now almost inevitable.

5.

FOLLOWING the revolutionary period, characterized by the bitter struggle between the Government and the Duma, there began a period of relative quiet. The third Duma sat without interruption through the whole period of its legal existence, from 1907 to 1912, and the elections of 1912 resulted in a triumph of the conservative nationalist groups.

While the political conflict between the Government and the Duma was temporarily solved by the reformed electoral law of 1907, there remained the more troublesome question of dealing with the aftermath of the revolutionary spirit of 1905. The dissatisfaction of that period found continued expression in a number of assassinations of prominent government officials. Premier Stolypin adopted a course of merciless suppression of revolutionary terrorism. Those accused of political crimes were subject to trial by a court-martial, and when found guilty were punished by death. Stolypin's policy in this regard met with severe criticism from the opposition, but was supported by the majority of the conservative members of the Duma. The greatest number of executions during this period occurred in 1908, when the total number reached 782. After this year the number steadily decreased, and in 1911 seventy-three sentences were passed.

Just as political equilibrium seemed to have been reached, Stolypin was assassinated in September, 1911. His place was taken by the Minister of Finance, Kokovtsev. Like his predecessor, he was a Moderate Constitutionalist. He was faced with the constitutional problem of overriding the power of veto vested in the state Council organized at the same time as the Duma, and consisting only partially of elected members. One-half of the members of the Council were appointed by the emperor, and the Prime Minister had little influence in their selection. The Court circles of reactionary aristocrats were irreconcilably opposed to the Duma and succeeded in carrying out their policies without consulting the Prime Minister by direct influence upon the emperor. But notwithstanding irritating incidents of this kind, the Duma proved itself capable of bringing about many favorable changes in the country. Of great importance was the legislation concerning the peasantry, by which the precarious legal status of the peasants was done away with and their civil rights were equalized with those of other citizens.

The reform of local justice was an important measure in this connection. By virtue of the law of June 28, 1912, the general judicial system was to be gradually extended over the peasant population. The Land Captain was displaced in judicial matters by a justice of the peace. The Duma also undertook to organize the educational system and provided for an annual increase of 20,000,000 rubles in the educational budget, which grew steadily from 44,000,000 in 1906 to 214,000,000 in 1917. The number of pupils in the primary schools rose from 3,275,362 in 1894 to 8,000,000 in 1914. Thus on the eve of the war over half of all children of school age in Russia were receiving instruction. It was estimated by the educational committee of the Duma that universal education in Russia would be reached in 1922. The war and the revolution, however, prevented realization of this program.

6.

THE defeat of Russia in the Far East and her agreement with Great Britain in matters concerning central Asia had the effect of stimulating Russian diplomacy in the Near East. Great Britain now showed signs of abandoning her traditional fear of Russia's seizure of Constantinople. This may be explained in part by the fact that Great Britain now feared Germany more than she did Russia. This change in policy became evident following the Turkish revolution of 1908, which brought a pro-German group into power in Turkey. In the autumn of 1908 the Central Powers opened a diplomatic offensive in the Balkans. On October 6, 1908, Austria, supported by Germany, announced the annexation of Bosnia and Herzegovina. The leader of Austria's foreign policy, Aehrenthal, used some preliminary parleys with the Russian foreign secretary, Izvolsky, very skilfully. Izvolsky was himself surprised by Austria's step. France and Great Britain were caught fully unawares; not one of the members of the Triple Entente desired war or was prepared for it. Meanwhile it appeared that any effective protest against the Austrian move might lead to war. Nothing could be done but to accept the *fait accompli.*

The incident, however, had one important consequence—the beginning of an armament race between the two groups of powers. In 1911 Germany decided to interfere again in Morocco and dispatched the gunboat *Panther* to Agadir to protect German interests. The diplomacy of the Entente on this occasion, however, was more effective than in 1908 and presented a united front to Germany. The result was that the German Government was forced to recognize a French protectorate in Morocco.

The tension in Europe increased following this incident. A new move by the Central Powers was to be expected, and did in fact take place three years following the Agadir incident. In July, 1914, Austria presented an ultimatum to Serbia which led to the First World War.

CHAPTER XII.

THE INTERNAL DEVELOPMENT OF RUSSIA FROM THE MIDDLE OF THE NINETEENTH CENTURY TO THE FIRST WORLD WAR

(1857–1914)

I.

A GREAT change occurred in Russia between the reigns of Nicholas I and Nicholas II. In half a century, Russia underwent a complete social reconstruction. The Russia of Nicholas I had a *régime* based upon serfdom and *sui generis* state socialism. As a result of the reforms of Alexander II, there arose on the ruins of the earlier *régime* a capitalist economy. The tenth volume of the *Code of Russian Laws* now became a reality and was made to correspond with the actual structure of society. The change was witnessed by the abolition of the head tax in 1886. As we have seen, the financial importance of the head tax fell rapidly in the middle of the nineteenth century, when it comprised only 24 per cent of the total income. In the beginning of the 'eighties its importance was lessened; but its complete abolition had great importance. This tax was directly associated with the old *régime;* the repeal of the tax terminated the division of the people into two radically different classes; the head-tax payers (*podatnoe sostoianie*) and those exempt from paying this tax. However, with the rescission of the tax there appeared a substitute in the form of payments for the lands given to the peasantry at the time of their emancipation. These payments were the chief financial reason for the continuation of the special legal condition of the peasantry. For this reason, notwithstanding the reforms of Alexander II, a considerable part of the Russian people was isolated from the new citizenship and placed in a special category. This was the chief social anachronism of Russia prior to the Revolution of 1905. The introduction of complete legal equality for the Russian peasantry was directly connected with the discontinuance of payments for land. These, by calculations of the Treasury, were not to end until 1931, but in 1905 a revolution took place which led to far-reaching changes in the social structure of Russia and in 1906 the Stolypin legislation concerning the peasantry went into effect. An inevitable part of this legislation was the termination of the payments for land, in 1906. This step was followed by the replacement of Land Captains by justices of the peace, in 1912. Thus it was only after the Revolution of 1905 and the legislation of Stolypin and the Duma that the Russian peasantry became fully endowed with equal rights of citizenship. It was only on the eve of the First World War that the Russian people became a society of citizens with full equal rights.

2.

THE creation of the new capitalist structure was accompanied by a rapid economic development of the country. The basic factor of economic development, as in the preceding period, was the rapid growth of population. From the middle of the nineteenth century to the beginning of the twentieth century, the population of Russia doubled. During the first fifteen years of the twentieth century, the population increased 30 per cent. In 1914 it totaled 175,000,000.

Particularly significant was the growth of city population. In 1851 there were less than three and a half million people in the towns or less than 6 per cent of the total population. In 1897 the town population had risen to sixteen and one-third millions or 13 per cent of the whole population, and in 1914 to 17.5 per cent. These figures indicate the growth of the industrial population as compared with the agricultural. According to the census of 1897, 74.2 per cent of the population was agricultural, and 13.3 per cent industrial. Thus, in spite of the growth of the cities and of industry, about three-quarters of Russia's population before the First World War was occupied in agriculture.

Agriculture remained the foundation of the economic life of Russia. The area under cultivation increased rapidly. In 1905 it amounted to around 100,000,000 hectares; in 1914 this had risen to around 120,000,000 hectares. The grain harvests in Russia were considerably smaller than in other countries. However, they gradually increased, thanks to the introduction of modern methods of cultivation. The average annual harvest of grain in European Russia in the decade 1861–70 was half a ton per hectare. In the decade 1901–10 it increased to five-sixths of a ton per hectare.

The total production of grain in 1913 reached over 92 million tons. In view of the occasional droughts, the harvest of grain in Russia was not steady but subject to wide variation. The years of poor harvest led to insufficiency of food or even to starvation of part of the population, as in 1891, 1906, etc. The tragic extent of the famine of 1921–22, however, was due not only to natural but also to social and political conditions.

Russian economic life up to very recent times was dependent directly upon "his excellency the harvest," as the Minister of Finance Kokovtsev said in one of his speeches in the Duma in 1911.

The ownership of land in Russia, following the peasant reforms of 1861, underwent great changes. Land rapidly passed into the ownership of the peasants. The peasantry not only retained the lands distributed in 1861, but also acquired new lands by purchase. Thus, simultaneous with the growth of area under cultivation in Russia during the fifty years preceding the First World War, a radical change in the social structure of the agricultural population took place. As a result of the Stolypin reforms of 1906, the peasant communes began to disintegrate, and in 1911 six million households had acquired personal possession of the land. Russia was moving with great strides toward small landownership by citizens possessing equal rights with the rest of the population.

3.

THE industrialization of Russia which began in the second half of the nineteenth century increased rapidly until 1914, and in some branches of industry until 1917. We will trace this process briefly in three of the most important branches of Russian industry: textiles, metallurgy, and food products.

The Russian cotton industry, prior to the First World War, occupied fourth place in world production. It was exceeded only by Great Britain, the United States, and Germany. In 1905 the Russian cotton industry employed 7,350,683 spindles and 178,506 looms. By 1911 the productive forces of the industry had grown to 8,448,818 spindles and 220,000 looms. The increased production of Russian cotton factories was absorbed partly by the home market and partly by foreign trade. The increase of internal consumption may be illustrated by the fact that in 1890 the per capita consumption of cotton cloth in Russia was 2.31 pounds and in 1910, 4.56 pounds. The principal foreign market for Russia's cotton industries was Persia where they competed successfully with British goods. The cotton exports from Russia to Persia in 1906–1907 totaled 10,189,000 rubles. British exports to Persia for the same period totaled 13,999,000 rubles. In 1912–13 Russian exports rose to 16,180,000 rubles as against British exports of 14,238,000 rubles. The growth of cotton manufacture in Russia led to a rapid increase in the area of cotton cultivation in Turkestan and Transcaucasia, where, prior to the war, over 600,000 hectares were planted in cotton.

The metallurgical industries showed a similar development. In 1900, around 1,500,000 tons of pig iron were produced in Russia. By 1914 production had grown to over 3,500,000 tons.

The principal products produced by Russian food manufacturers were sugar, alcohol, flour, and tobacco. Sugar was an important commodity both of internal consumption and of export. In 1909–10 over 80,000 tons of sugar were exported. In 1911–12 exports reached 500,000 tons.

The growth of industrial production was reflected also in mining. Eighty-five per cent of the coal used in Russia was of domestic extraction. The chief center of coal mining was the Donets basin which supplied 55 per cent of Russia's needs for coal. In 1900, 11,000,000 tons were mined in the Donets basin and in 1913 the production rose to 25,000,000 tons.

The exploitation of forests served both domestic needs and foreign trade. In 1904, 13,200,000 rubles worth of lumber was exported. By 1913 exports reached 164,900,000 rubles. Of great importance also was the production of oil, chiefly in the neighborhood of Baku. In 1860 oil production in the Baku area hardly exceeded 160,000 tons. In 1905 production rose to over 7,000,000 tons and in 1913 to around 9,000,000 tons. As world production of oil in the twentieth century grew by gigantic strides, the proportion of Russian production to the total fell during the years preceding the war. In 1905 Russia supplied 27 per cent of world production, but in 1913 only 16.5 per cent.

Even more rapid than the expansion of industry was the development of railroads in Russia. In the middle of the nineteenth century, the total length of railroads in operation in Russia did not exceed 660 miles. In 1912 the Russian railroad system comprised 40,194 miles and was second only to that of the United States. The greatest achievement was the completion of the great Trans-Siberian Railroad, from 1892 to 1905. Its construction was one of the most daring railroad projects of our time. The length of the line from Moscow to Vladivostok is 5,542 miles. In the construction of this line it was necessary to overcome the greatest natural and technical difficulties—the frozen subsoil and the wildness of the territories penetrated. The cost of the Trans-Siberian Railroad exceeded $200,000,000. It was originally a single-track line, but during the First World War a second line was laid down.

4.

THE rapid expansion of Russian industry was accompanied by the creation of a working class on a scale previously unknown in Russia. Gradually the social character of the Russian laboring class changed. In the beginning of the twentieth century, the majority of Russian workers were still connected with the peasantry. They were in fact peasants temporarily engaged in factory work. This partly explains the psychology of the Russian worker, who had little interest in his occupation or his factory. The worker almost always could, if he wished, return to his village where he could secure an allotment of land. But with every year conditions changed. The Stolypin reforms, in creating a new class of small landowners, cut off the village peasants from those who had become factory workers. Thus they stimulated the growth in Russia of a city proletariat. Among Russian workers a stable professional psychology was only beginning to be formed when the First World War broke out.

The organization of labor unions also was very recent. For this the Government was at fault in fearing any kind of organization. It was only in 1902 that the Government assented to the legalization of some unions and it was only after the Revolution of 1905 that labor unions were permitted on a large scale by the Law of March 4, 1906.

The Government artificially retarded the development of labor unions and thereby unwittingly fostered the formation of illegal revolutionary organizations. But while restricting the development of labor unions, the Government made efforts to satisfy the principal needs of the workers by means of legislation. Labor legislation in Russia goes back to the 1880's in the reign of Alexander III. In 1897 day work was limited to eleven and a half hours and night work to ten hours. Night work was forbidden for children under seventeen, and children under twelve were not allowed to engage in industrial work of any kind. The legislation of the twentieth century introduced workers' accident compensation in 1903, health insurance in 1912, and accident insurance in 1912. The condition of the working class gradually improved, thanks to increasing wages, particularly in Petrograd and Moscow. At the end of the nineteenth century, the average wage of the Russian worker was only 187 rubles a year. By 1913 it had risen to 300 rubles and in some branches of industry in Petrograd and Moscow to five times this sum. In many factories the low money wages were augmented by free lodgings, hospital services, and factory schools.

5.

DURING the reign of Alexander II, the Government apparently desired to refrain from interference in economic matters and to allow the highest degree of private initiative. These principles were expressed in the policy stimulating the construction of railroads by private companies on the concession basis. A number of government-owned factories in the Urals were sold to private individuals and the salt mines in the southeast were leased to private capital. At the same time a policy of free trade was instituted in 1865. The Government's policy, however, led to confusion in many branches of Russian industry. In railroad administration chaos reigned. In 1871 the unpaid obligations of the private railroad companies to the Treasury amounted to 174,000,000 rubles. The sum rose in a few years to 500,000,000 rubles. As a result of this, the Government changed its policy. In 1876 the tariff on imports was raised and continued to be raised steadily until the First World War. The Government also started buying up private railroad lines and undertook the construction of new railroads. In 1889 23 per cent of the railroads were Government controlled, while in 1900 60 per cent were. The Government constructed the Trans-Siberian Railroad and the Orenburg-Tashkent Railroad in Turkestan. It also reassumed its position as factory owner.

The most energetic organizer of government control was the Minister of Finance Witte, in the period from 1892 to 1903. Following Witte's initiative, the Government undertook the ambitious scheme of introducing the alcohol monopoly. The reform begun in 1894 gradually spread over the whole country. The consumption of alcohol in Russia in 1905 totaled 200,000,000 gallons and in 1913 280,000,000 gallons. The income from the monopoly in 1905 was 443,200,000 rubles and in 1913, 675,100,000 rubles. Closely allied to the industrial policy pursued by Witte was his financial policy. The state was the chief banker of Russia and under his administration the State Bank assumed the leading position in the money market. The State Bank was made a "bankers' bank." Its turnover in 1909 amounted to 162,324,000,000 rubles and in 1913 to 234,009,000,000 rubles.

The steady growth of the budget was a reflection of this economic policy. Government expenditures in 1900 were 1,889,000,000 rubles and in 1913, 3,382,000,000 rubles. About one-third of the budgets of the twentieth century were appropriated for government-operated industries and less than one-quarter for the army and navy. If the budgets of the Russian Empire in the time of Peter I could be called military budgets, the budgets under Witte may be termed industrial budgets. In the twentieth century the Government regained the position of leadership in economic matters that it occupied in the eighteenth and the beginning of the nineteenth century.

6.

In the eighteenth and the first half of the nineteenth century, Russian culture centered chiefly around the large cities and the nobles' estates. From the middle of the nineteenth century, the basic elements of modern civilization, as, for example, education and medical care, spread far and wide, reaching the lowest levels of the city population and the peasant huts. A prominent part in this movement was played by the Zemstvos and city organizations introduced by the reforms of Alexander II. Notwithstanding the imperfections in the electoral law, local self-government in Russia in the half century preceding the First World War fulfilled an immense cultural task. The Zemstvos were first introduced in thirty-four provincial governments. The reform did not extend to Turkestan, Siberia, the Caucasus, Poland, the Baltic provinces, the western Russian provinces, or the Cossack domains. By the Law of 1864 the Zemstvos were given the task of supervision of public education, public health, charity, care of roads, fire insurance, in fact, all questions relating to local life and economy. The budget of the Zemstvos was organized along the lines of self-assessment and was derived chiefly from the taxation of real property.

The Zemstvos first directed their attention to the development of public education and to matters of sanitation. The population of the country districts of Russia which, prior to the reforms of Alexander II, had been almost entirely illiterate and lacking in medical care, was gradually provided with schools, hospitals, and dispensaries. In 1895, in the regions having Zemstvos, there was one hospital bed to every 6,500 inhabitants, while in the regions where there were no Zemstvos there was only one hospital bed to every 41,000 inhabitants. The expenditure of the Zemstvos on public health increased each year. In 1892 the average expenditure on medical assistance was thirty-four rubles per hundred inhabitants and in 1904 it rose to fifty-six rubles per hundred inhabitants.

The same tendency may be observed in the activity of the Zemstvos in public education. In 1911, in provinces having Zemstvos, there were forty-six pupils in Zemstvo schools for every one thousand rural inhabitants. In non-Zemstvo provinces of European Russia there were thirty-four per thousand receiving schooling and only eighteen per thousand in Siberia. By the laws of 1911–12, Zemstvos were introduced in nine additional provinces.

The total budgets of the Zemstvos steadily grew. In 1875 the expenses of all the Zemstvos in thirty-four provinces totaled 28,870,000 rubles. In 1905 the expenditures rose to 124,185,000 rubles. In 1914 the budget of the Zemstvos of forty-three provinces reached 347,512,000 rubles and if the sums expended upon the commercial undertakings of the Zemstvos and insurance be included, the 1914 budget approximated 400,000,000, i.e., one-ninth of the total state budget.

Over two-thirds of the expenditures of the Zemstvos were for public health and education. The Zemstvo department of Public

Health in 1914 expended 82,000,000 rubles. The rural population, prior to 1864 when the Zemstvos were introduced, was almost wholly lacking in medical care. Fifty years later, at the eve of the First World War, the Zemstvos had covered the rural territories with hospitals and dispensaries. The average radius of the medical districts was ten miles. In 1914, in the forty provinces having Zemstvos, there was a total of 3,300 medical districts. Many Zemstvos introduced special organizations for the supply of medical materials—pharmacies and stores of medical supplies—and in some cases stations for vaccination against smallpox and rabies. Sixteen of the twenty-nine Pasteur laboratories in Russia were under the management of the Zemstvos or city organizations.

The expenditure of the Zemstvos on public education in 1914 was 106,000,000 rubles. Most of these sums were expended upon primary schools. In 1914 there were fifty thousand Zemstvo schools with eighty thousand teachers and three million school children. The Zemstvos paid particular attention to the construction of new schools corresponding to modern pedagogical ideas and hygienic requirements. Besides primary education, the Zemstvos also organized their own system of secondary education for the training of teachers and organized courses for the improvement of teaching methods. The Zemstvos likewise organized extension courses and built libraries. In 1914 there were 12,627 rural public libraries in thirty-five of the forty-three Zemstvo governments.

Besides their activity in public hygiene and public education, the Zemstvos undertook to assist the population in agriculture, insurance, and the development of roads and telephones. In 1914 they were authorized to open 219 telephone systems and there were 163 systems already in operation with a total length of about 42,900 miles of lines and 100,000 miles of wire.

The work of the Zemstvos, in spite of its undisputed usefulness, was at first little appreciated by the peasant population for whose benefit it was directed. This may be explained partly by the poverty of the Russian peasant, who first of all thought of the Zemstvos in connection with the payment of new taxes. Moreover, as has been explained above, the electoral law on the basis of which the Zemstvos operated until 1917, gave little actual responsibility to the peasants in the election of representatives in the Zemstvos. In view of the deficiencies of the electoral law, the Zemstvos and city organizations did not have a real contact with the masses. In spite of the fact that the Zemstvos were operating for the benefit of the people, they were often regarded not as popular, but as aristocratic, organizations.

The coöperative societies reached nearer to the popular masses than the Zemstvos. Their rapid development, however, began only in the last years preceding the war. On January 1, 1915, there were 32,300 coöperatives with a membership of twelve million, most of whom were peasants.

7.

THE development of higher education in Russia during the half century preceding the Revolution of 1917 was likewise of considerable importance. First of all, the number of students increased. In the second half of the nineteenth century, three new universities were founded (Odessa 1865, Warsaw 1869, Tomsk 1888). In the twentieth century one more was opened prior to the First World War and one during the war (Saratov 1909, Perm 1916). The University of Simferopol (Crimea) was opened during the revolution in 1918. During the war Warsaw University was transferred to Rostov and Yuriev University to Voronezh.

The total number of universities in Russia in 1917 was eleven, to which must be added a number of technical schools which were separated from the universities: institutes of technology, mining academies, land survey institute, institute of roads and communications, institute of forestry, and several law schools and philological schools, several women's universities and four theological academies.

The character of the instruction in Russian universities in the twentieth century reached a very high level and cannot be considered inferior to the universities of Europe and America. Nearly all the above institutions were under state control, although some received assistance from private individuals. The Shaniavsky University in Moscow, the Makushin Science School in Tomsk, and several others were municipal or private universities. The number of students of both sexes in the universities of Russia in 1912 totaled one hundred and thirty-seven thousand. The universities of Russia played an important part, not only in extending higher education, but also in the political development of the country. The professors mostly took part in the liberal movement and a considerable portion of the students were Socialists. In 1905 some liberal groups were organized by students, but in 1917 the political rôle of the universities was of little importance.

The control over university life under Alexander III was closely regulated by the Law of 1884. In 1905, however, the management of the universities was handed over to the professors. The restrictions remaining in the academic organization of the universities in 1905 led in 1911 to a dispute between the Government and the professors, which resulted in the resignation of the greater number of the professors of Moscow University.

The Academy of Science at the end of the nineteenth century likewise participated actively in the development of Russian culture. The various institutes of the Academy of Science, prior to the war, grew into large institutions enjoying a high degree of autonomy in their scientific research. At the end of the nineteenth century many learned organizations came into existence. Their activity spread, not only to the natural sciences and mathematics, but likewise to historical and philological fields. In the beginning of the twentieth century, Russia was covered with a network of the most diverse learned societies, and Russian science held an important place internationally. In the learned circles of various countries, such names as those of the chemist Mendeleiev and the physiologist Pavlov, have acquired high prestige.

Russian scientists contributed their share to the technological inventions of the modern age. In 1874 A. N. Ladygin, then a student of the University of St. Petersburg, applied electricity for illumination purposes and built a lamp which was perfected by two other Russian physicists, demonstrated in Paris in 1875, and later tested in the Siemens-Halske plant in Berlin. Simultaneously Paul Yablochkov (1847–94) constructed his carbon arc "candle" which was commercially produced in 1876. Incidentally, it was only in 1878 that the news of Thomas Edison's incandescent lamp was reported in American press. In the 1890's Alexander S. Popov (1859–1905) entered the then entirely new field of radiotelegraphy. Having constructed a new device for receiving electromagnetic waves—the antenna—he demonstrated his apparatus for wireless transmission at a meeting of the Russian Physical Society in St. Petersburg in 1895. He applied to the Ministry of the

Navy for funds to enlarge his researches but was granted only the paltry sum of 300 rubles ($150.00). Nevertheless he continued his experiments and in 1897 was able to operate transmission stations at a distance of five kilometers. By that time, however, Guglielmo Marconi, who knew of Popov's experiments, came to the fore with his paper on radiotelegraphy, and it is with his name that most people usually associate the invention of the radio.

8.

The flowering of Russian literature in the second half of the nineteenth century was an event which has been fully recognized both in Europe and in America. The works of the Russian authors, Tolstoy, Dostoievsky, and Turgeniev, have been translated into all languages and doubtless have found their way to the hearts and minds of foreign readers. It is consequently unnecessary to give here any characterization of these writers. Of sufficient note also are some Russian authors of the end of the nineteenth and the beginning of the twentieth centuries, e.g., Anton Chekhov and Maxim Gorky.

Of less fame abroad are the Russian poets of this time. In the late nineteenth century and in the beginning of the twentieth century, Russian poetry was dominated by a movement known as symbolism. The whole world, according to the view of this school, is merely a combination of symbols. The poets of this movement attempt to combine verse and music so that the one supplements the other. The founders of this tendency in Russian poetry were K. D. Balmont (1867–1942), and V. I. Briusov, who lived from 1873 to 1924. At first misunderstood and laughed at by the public, they finally secured recognition. Of the younger symbolist poets the most important was A. A. Blok, who lived from 1880 to 1921. The next generation of Russian poets moved away from symbolism: "We want to admire a rose because it is beautiful, not because it is a symbol of mystical purity." At the head of this movement was M. S. Gumilev, who lived from 1886 to 1921, and Anna Akhmatov, born in 1889. Gumilev was shot by the Bolshevik Government under suspicion of having taken part in a counter-revolutionary organization.

Russian sculptors in the period did not form any recognizable movement. Prominent among them was Prince P. P. Trubetskoy. Russian architecture was at the crossroads and partly engaged in imitating sixteenth and seventeenth century architecture. However, in the period just preceding the First World War new constructive tendencies appeared. As for painting, a certain analogy may be found between its development and that of the new Russian literature. The second half of the nineteenth century saw the rise of a new group of artists who broke with the traditional Academy of Arts in 1870. The ideal of this new movement was to depict historical subjects and scenes of everyday life and history realistically. Some were guided by an inclination to reveal social evils. Among these artists was one of the most famous of Russian painters, I. E. Repin. A special place among these artists was held by V. M. Vasnetzov, who attempted to combine modern realism with the manner of the old Russian and Byzantine religious painting. His murals in the cathedral of St. Vladimir in Kiev, painted from 1885 to 1895, are the best known of his works.

By the end of the nineteenth century, a new movement was to be observed in Russian painting devoted to "pure" art. According to the artists of this school, art must not serve any social or political purpose, but must tend only to beauty. The new tendency in Russian painting centered around the magazine *Mir Iskustva* (*The World of Art*). The group of artists around the *Mir Iskustva* included: V. A. Serov, Russia's greatest portrait painter, M. V. Vrubel, whose *chef d'œuvre* is *The Demon* of Lermontov, A. N. Benois, M. V. Dobujinsky, and N. Roerich, many of whose pictures are now in a special museum in New York devoted to the exhibition of his work. Many of the artists of this group designed stage settings. The Russian theater became known abroad together with Russian painting (*The Salon d'Automne,* Paris, 1906).

Distinct from the "intellectual" painting of the above groups was the popular art. Down to recent times, peasant artists continued painting icons in the traditional manner, particularly in the province of Vladimir. A great interest in this work was shown by the archaeologist N. P. Kondakov. A special committee was organized at his initiative, under the patronage of Nicholas II, to promote the icon painting (1901). The committee succeeded in aiding the peasant iconographers and providing them with special training.

9.

RUSSIAN music in the second half of the nineteenth century entered into a period of great creative activity. In the early 1860's a group was formed in St. Petersburg, having as its object the development of Russian music. This group became known as the "Mighty Band" (*Moguchaia Kuchka*). The leading spirit was M. A. Balakirev, and the group included N. A. Rimsky-Korsakov, M. P. Mussorgsky, and A. P. Borodin. The name of "Mighty Band" given them by their admirers was seized upon by their enemies, who for many years taunted them with it. But time has justified this name and it is now seriously accepted by everyone. The basic idea of the "Band" was, first, the utilization of folk song themes and, second, realism in music. In their first idea the "Band" followed the views of Glinka. Their realism, on the other hand, was a continuation of the views of Dargomyzhsky. They drew upon popular music and popular fantasy for their themes. The operas composed by the "Band" have as their libretto historical or mythological subjects. Russian folk songs and eastern themes were frequently at the basis of their composition.

The leader of the group, M. A. Balakirev, who lived from 1836 to 1910, left several songs, symphonies, and masterly piano compositions. He himself was a remarkable pianist. Balakirev was for many years the director of the court choir.

M. P. Mussorgsky, who lived from 1839 to 1881, is perhaps the most famous of all the members of the "Band." His work had an influence upon modern French music. He opened the way to new paths in music. The operas *Boris Godunov* and *Khovanstchina* have historical plots. The first concerns itself with the troubled epoch of the seventeenth century and the second with the *Streltzy* and "Old Ritualists" of the end of the seventeenth century. Mussorgsky succeeded in giving to his music, which is full of drama, the pathos of great popular movements.

The music of Borodin and Rimsky-Korsakov is more quiet and clear than that of Mussorgsky. Borodin, who lived from 1834 to 1887, was both an outstanding composer and a great scientist. His opera *Prince Igor* is founded on the narrative of the old Russian heroic song "Slovo O Polku Igorevi" ("The Campaign of Igor"). Borodin left three symphonies, the last of which is unfinished, and a symphonic picture entitled *In Central Asia,* where two themes meet, the Oriental and the Russian.

Rimsky-Korsakov, who lived from 1844 to 1909, was the youngest of the members of the "Mighty Band." He was the chief technician of the group and completed as well as orchestrated the unfinished works of Borodin and Mussorgsky. The music of Rimsky-Korsakov is characterized by the brilliance of his instrumentation. Most of his fifteen operas deal with mythical and eastern subjects, such as *Sadko,* based on an old Novgorod trading song, and *The Golden Cock,* based on a story by Pushkin. His best opera, *The Invisible City of Kitezh,* deals with the epoch of the Mongolian invasion of Russia.

Unrelated to the "Mighty Band" P. I. Tchaikovsky, who lived from 1840 to 1893, wrote his great masterpieces. His music is of a totally different character. It concerns itself with the spiritual experiences of a man of the nineteenth century. The music of Tchaikovsky bears fewer national traces in the sense of describing national character and popular movements. Like Dostoievsky, he looks deep into the human soul and expresses the struggles and sufferings there. In the blind and helpless moods of the Sixth Symphony there may be a prophetic and sorrowful utterance of approaching calamities. He composed many songs, some of which are of inferior quality while many demonstrate a remarkable depth of feeling. His operas, *Eugene Onegin* and *The Queen of Spades* are two of the most popular in Russia. His soft lyricism is universally understood and appreciated.

The scene of the activities of the "Mighty Band" was St. Petersburg. Tchaikovsky, on the other hand, lived for the most part in Moscow; the majority of Russian composers of the end of the nineteenth century and the beginning of the twentieth century were also connected with Moscow.

The leading composers of the modern period are A. N. Skriabin and S. V. Rachmaninov. A. N. Skriabin, who lived from 1871 to 1915, was a mystic and a theosophist. He never composed vocal music as he considered it as too materialistic. The finest of his symphonic pieces are the *Poem of Ecstasy* and *Prometheus.* Skriabin attempted to find the relationship between sounds and colors and to complete musical symphony with color. His final objective was to write "Mysteries," which was to lead to the reformation of the world by sound. He did not, however, have time to compose even the prelude to this composition.

S. V. Rachmaninov (1873–1942) is well known in this country, both as a composer and as a pianist. His first opera *Aleko,* with a libretto based on a poem by Pushkin, was composed in 1892. In the beginning of the twentieth century, he produced a number of orchestral as well as chamber compositions.

A decade younger than Skriabin and Rachmaninov, I. F. Stravinsky, born in 1882, was a pupil, though not a follower, of Rimsky-Korsakov. Stravinsky, prior to the First World War, moved to Paris, where in 1911 his ballet *Petrushka* was given for the first time. He is now in the United States.

10.

Most characteristic of Russian religious life prior to the war was the wide spread of evangelical teachings denying the complex dogmatism and ritual of the Orthodox church. The movement of rationalism among the intellectuals took on the form of Tolstoyism, following the religious teachings of Leo Tolstoy. Among the popular masses, especially in the south of Russia, this tendency found expression in a Stundo-Baptist movement. The term "Stunda" was derived from the German *stunde* (hour), and signified to certain German evangelical and reforming groups of the eighteenth century, the hour of religious congregation. The Stundites appeared in the south of Russia in the first half of the nineteenth century and expanded rapidly in the second half. In the 1870's they fell under the influence of the Baptist teachings coming from Bessarabia and Transcaucasia. In the end of the nineteenth century, the Stundo-Baptists spread over more than thirty provinces of Russia.

The Government attempted to put a stop to the movement by means of police measures. In 1894 the sect was recognized as a "specially harmful" one and they were forbidden the right to congregate. The natural consequence of the police measures was to stimulate the growth of the movement. It was only following the Revolution of 1905 that the policy of the Government with respect to dissenters changed. In 1905 a manifesto was issued permitting religious freedom.

The manifesto of 1905 was the beginning of the liberation, not only of the dissenters, but also of the Orthodox church itself. In the years preceding the First World War a great internal upheaval took place in the Orthodox church. This upheaval was a sign of life. The church, notwithstanding the fall of its moral authority in the eighteenth century and the beginning of the nineteenth century, was alive and capable of assuming the religious guidance of its members. A proof of the continued vitality of the Orthodox church, even in the most lifeless period of the eighteenth century, was the appearance of a man of such outstanding character as the Bishop Tikhon Zadonsky, one of the first Russians to raise his voice against serfdom.

In the nineteenth century the Russian church produced a number of outstanding elders who exercised a great influence upon members of both the upper and lower classes by the purity of their moral life. The *startzi* (elders) were monks of strict habits to whom believers came for advice and consolation in their spiritual as well as their practical difficulties. The cell of the elder was always open to anyone coming for such advice, no matter from what class of society. Especially famous in the nineteenth century were the elders of the monastery *Optina Pústyn,* which was visited by Gogol, Dostoievsky, and Tolstoy. The elder Amvrosy served as the prototype of Dostoievsky's character of the monk Zosima in *The Brothers Karamazov.*

In the end of the nineteenth century and the beginning of the twentieth century, the members of the Orthodox church raised the question of calling a council (*sobor*). The purpose was to secure the final liberation of the church from the guardianship of the state and also to carry out internal reforms in its organization. One of the chief internal reforms sought was the right of the congregation to self-government. In times before Peter the Great in Russia the congregations had had self-government. In the eighteenth and nineteenth centuries the congregation became merely a section of people living in the vicinity of a given church and possessing no right of self-government in church affairs. The liberation of the church from government interference also had a bearing on the revival of the institution of the patriarchate abolished by Peter the Great. No Council was called prior to the Revolution of 1917, and up to that time the Russian church continued to be under the official guardianship of the Government through the Holy Synod.

CHAPTER XIII.

RUSSIA IN THE FIRST WORLD WAR

(1914–1917)

I.

THE main features of the diplomatic background of the First World War have already been treated. Russia was destined to participate in the war, since she formed part of one of the great groupings of powers in Europe. After the formation of the alliance of the Central Powers and the triple *entente cordiale,* it became only a question of time as to which would be ready to attack first. In the year preceding the war, Germany felt herself better prepared for war than the Allies. She realized, moreover, that the forces of her two probable enemies, France and Russia, were rapidly growing.

Not only the growth of Russia's military force, but also the rapid economic and cultural development of Russia was obvious to Germany. The execution of the Stolypin agrarian reforms was rapidly strengthening the new social basis of the Russian state in organizing a new class of peasant owners. In 1914 it was still possible to count upon internal difficulties in Russia, as the new constitutional *régime* had not as yet been fully carried out. Within ten years, however, the possibility of a revolution in Russia would have been very slight. The plans of the General Staff of Germany, in the event of a struggle with Russia, took into consideration both the strategic problem and the internal weakness of the Russian state. Germany hoped to take advantage of this weakness in two ways: First, by stimulating separatist feelings among subject nationalities of the Russian Empire; second, by arousing social and economic friction within the Russian state. The most sensitive point in Russia's problem of nationalities was the Polish question, the origin of which may be traced back to the Congress of Vienna. Germany, however, was not free to stress this question since part of Poland had been appropriated by Prussia at the time of the partition of Poland in the eighteenth century. While Austria had encouraged a degree of autonomy to her section of Polish population at the end of the nineteenth century, she, too, could not easily raise the Polish question; she would have met with resistance, not only from Germany, but also from Hungary, which strongly opposed any growth of Slavonic influence in the Hapsburg monarchy.

A more fertile field for German and Austrian activity was to be found in the Ukraine. Galicia and Bukovina were territories of the Hapsburg Empire, populated by Slavonic peoples kindred in blood and language to the population of Russian Ukraine. Austria's policy prior to the war was to patronize the "Ukrainian" cultural movement in Galicia in contradistinction to the Russian policy of stemming the Ukrainian movement within the boundaries of Russia. From the middle of the nineteenth century and through the beginning of the twentieth century, the Russian Government opposed all separatist movements of the Ukrainian people and even tried to suppress all literature published in the Ukrainian language. This policy aroused widespread ill feeling in the south of Russia although the separatist movement was actually confined to a small number of intellectuals. The policy pursued by the Russian Government succeeded only in strengthening the Ukrainian movement. Austria and Germany succeeded in profiting by the mistakes of the Russian Government, but they erred in overemphasizing the danger to Russia of the Ukrainian movement. They repeated the error made by Charles XII in the beginning of the eighteenth century when he relied upon the Ukrainian Cossacks to help his cause. The movement became a reality only following the defeat of Russia in the war, and even then Ukrainian sovereignty existed only so long as it was supported by German arms.

Another weak spot in Russia, in the opinion of the Central Powers, was social unrest. Germany supported revolutionary propaganda against the Imperial Government in Russia during the war. But even the undeniable social weakness of Russia did not bring about the hoped-for results. Germany expected a revolution in Russia at the very outbreak of the war. It occurred, however, only in 1917 at a time when Germany was already greatly enfeebled by the struggle and had little, if any, chance of defeating the Allies.

Within eighteen months of the fall of the Russian Empire, a successful revolution took place in Germany and overthrew the German Imperial Government.

2.

THE whole political atmosphere of Europe in the last years before 1914 was permeated by the presentiment of imminent war. The immediate cause was furnished by events which took place in the Balkans.

Toward the end of the nineteenth century and the beginning of the twentieth century, the diplomacy of Russia and Austria in the Balkans had succeeded in dividing the peninsula into two spheres of influence, Russia being supreme among the eastern Balkan Slavs, particularly in Bulgaria, while Austria was dominant in the west of the Balkans, particularly in Serbia and Bosnia. Rumania had been allied since 1885 to Austria. The situation was changed in 1908 when Austria annexed Bosnia and Herzegovina. The Serbs could not reconcile themselves with this step which resulted in the complete domination by Austria of territories peopled by Serbs. Prior to the annexation, when Austrian influence in Bosnia had not yet been legalized, the Serbs could still secretly hope that the Slavs of the western Balkans would yet achieve unity. The annexation of 1908 deprived them of these hopes and the national feelings of the Serbs against Austria were greatly stimulated.

In view of these circumstances, after 1908, the object of Russian diplomacy became the emancipation of the Balkans from both Austrian and Turkish influence. By 1912 this aim seemed near to realization. Four Balkan states, Serbia, Montenegro, Bulgaria, and Greece, united in an alliance against Turkey. The Balkan War which followed ended in the complete triumph of this alliance. Turkey was deprived of almost all European possessions populated by Slavs or Greeks. Then a disagreement between the allies arose. A second war immediately followed between Bulgaria on the one hand and Serbia and Greece on the other. The enemies of Bulgaria were joined by Rumania. Bulgaria was defeated, and, finding herself alone, turned to look for new allies. Serbia had now gained the patronage of the *Entente,* Bulgaria, therefore, joined the Central Powers.

The diplomatic situation in the Balkans in 1914 was thus radically different from that of the beginning of the twentieth century. Bulgaria was now on the side of Austria, while Serbia and Rumania were on the side of Russia. The general condition was characterized by extreme instability. The Balkans were like a powder magazine ready to explode at any moment. The Bulgarians hoped for revenge against Serbia and Rumania. The Serbs thought only of emancipating their brothers by race from Austrian rule, just as they had succeeded against Turkey. The national feeling in Serbia threatened at any moment to provoke a revolution among the Serbs in Austria. There began a number of attempts at assassinating prominent members of the Austrian Government. One of them was directed against Archduke Ferdinand, the heir to the Austrian throne.

On June 28, 1914, the Archduke Ferdinand was assassinated in a Bosnian town, Sarajevo. A month after the Sarajevo murder, on July 23, Austria presented an ultimatum to Serbia, impelled by the idea that the murder was sanctioned by the Serbian Government.

Serbia's reply was practically a complete submission to Austria's demands. Nevertheless, the Austrian Minister in Belgrade declared the Serbian reply unsatisfactory and immediately left for Vienna.

It was quite clear that Russia would not leave Serbia without help at this moment and remain an indifferent spectator of Serbia's annihilation by Austria. It was also quite plain that in case a war broke out, France would side with Russia against the Central Powers. The position that England would take was not clear, and Germany might have reasonably hoped that she would not enter into the struggle. British diplomacy and Sir Edward Grey, personally, worked hard to avert the war, but the only means which might have succeeded during these fatal days would have been to declare Britain's complete solidarity with France and Russia. This Great Britain did not do.

Russian diplomacy, within the bounds of what was possible, tried to avoid the war. However, all attempts to settle the Austro-Serbian dispute by diplomacy failed, and on July 28 Austria declared war on Serbia. After this had taken place, Russia had the choice either of doing nothing and seeing Serbia invaded, or of ordering the mobilization of the army. The original proposal was to compromise and order only a partial mobilization in the south of Russia, thus clearly directing it only against Austria and not against Germany. Sazonov, the Minister of Foreign Affairs, immediately announced this decision to the governments of Europe. This idea, however, met with vigorous objections on the part of the General Staff and the military experts in Russia. The reason for these objections was that a partial mobilization of the Russian army would, for technical reasons, delay and complicate a subsequent complete mobilization. If after some days Germany were to declare war, it was held that a general mobilization would be disorganized by any partial steps taken earlier, which would considerably weaken Russia's position. The question of Russian mobilization is one which must be approached, not only from the point of view of its effect upon international relations, but also from the practical viewpoint of military efficiency. It must not be forgotten that, granting the instability of the general situation and the high degree of preparedness of all the powers for a general conflict, a delay of a few days or the confusion of a prearranged program of mobilization might have created a situation in which the Power so taken unawares would be incapable of resisting the first onslaught of the enemy.

On July 29 Count Pourtales, the German Ambassador, called at the Russian Foreign Office and informed Sazonov that even a partial mobilization of the Russian army would lead immediately to a German mobilization. In the light of these circumstances, a general mobilization of the Russian army was ordered on July 29 at 5 P.M. At 9.20 P.M. Emperor Nicholas received a telegram from Emperor William promising that he would do his utmost to promote a direct understanding between St. Petersburg and Vienna. Emperor Nicholas immediately canceled the order for the general mobilization and a partial mobilization was substituted instead, orders being given accordingly to the commanding officers of the four military districts of Kiev, Odessa, Moscow, and Kazan, at midnight. On July 30 partial mobilization commenced. Following these orders information was received by the Russian War Office that Germany was already starting secret mobilization. Simultaneously, the last effort of Sazonov to find a satisfactory basis for negotiations was rejected by Germany and Austria. Sazonov, after conferring with the Minister of War, and the Chief of the General Staff, decided to advise the emperor to order general mobilization. Sazonov was received by the Emperor Nicholas at 4 P.M.

on July 30. The emperor reluctantly gave his consent to the general mobilization. Sazonov issued appropriate instructions to the Ministry of War and the General Staff. Thus, on July 31, general mobilization began. This, however, did not mean war—a fact specifically explained in the telegram of Emperor Nicholas to Emperor William II on July 31, and by Sazonov, who, at the initiative of Sir Edward Grey, expressed readiness to continue diplomatic negotiations. All that Sazonov demanded was that Austrian troops should not invade Serbia.

Simultaneously with the order for Russian mobilization, and before the news of this act reached Berlin, the *Kriegsgefahrzustand* was decreed by the German Government. This order, except in name, was the same thing as mobilization. On the morning of August 1, Emperor Nicholas once more telegraphed to Emperor William asking him to give assurance that German mobilization did not mean war. Before anything resulted from this correspondence, at 7 P.M. on August 1, the German Ambassador at St. Petersburg, after demanding that Russian mobilization cease immediately, informed Sazonov that Germany declared war upon Russia.

3.

GERMANY'S declaration of war aroused in the Russian people entirely different feelings from those caused by the beginning of the Japanese war ten years previously. The gravity of the situation was realized by many. In the main cities of Russia, patriotic manifestations took place. A strike that had been taking place in St. Petersburg during the days preceding the rupture of diplomatic relations ceased immediately.

The Duma met in a special session and expressed complete agreement with the policy pursued by the Government. This declaration was evidence of the accord between the Government and the representatives of the people. On August 12 the representatives of the Zemstvos created an All-Russian Union of Zemstvos for the aid of the wounded. Thus the war opened under the best political auspices —all of Russia seemed to be united, for the time being, at least. The rise of national feeling was further aided by the policy of Slavonic emancipation declared by the Government. The war was commenced avowedly to free the Serbs, and at the outset the Russian Commander-in-Chief, Grand Duke Nicholas, called for the liberation of another Slavonic people—the Poles. Russian diplomacy did not avoid this troublesome question, but went straight about cutting the Gordian knot. The Russian proclamation to the Poles promised the reconstitution "of the living body of Poland cut into three parts"—a reference to the three parts in the possession of Russia, Germany, and Austria, which were to be united under a Russian protectorate. A little later an appeal was made to all the oppressed peoples of Austro-Hungary. To satisfy Pan-Slav feelings, the German-sounding name of the capital of the Empire, St. Petersburg, was replaced by the corresponding Slavonic form, Petrograd.

Germany had calculated that disorganization would develop in Russia immediately following mobilization, but the mobilization of the Russian army, following the plan prepared by General Lukomsky, was carried out with unexpected rapidity and with no difficulties. It was materially aided by the promulgation of prohibition of all alcoholic beverages and the closing of all wine shops.

During the course of the first months of the war, it became evident that Russia had profited greatly by her experiences in the Russo-Japanese War. Save for that, the Russian armies could not have withstood the German forces. But in the course of the ten years following the Japanese war, the effectiveness of the Russian army, in view of a complete reorganization, was increased at least threefold.

4.

THE German declaration of war against Russia was followed on August 3 by a declaration of war against France. Within two more days Austria declared war on Russia and, following the German breach of Belgian neutrality, Great Britain declared war on Germany. In October, 1914, Turkey entered the war on the side of the Central Powers. The forces of the *Entente* seemed to be greater than those of the Central Powers, but this inequality of man power and wealth was compensated for by the unity of the Central Powers under the direction of Germany. The forces of the Allies were not united under a general military command and the military activities of the separate *Entente* states were not harmonized. In the beginning the forces of the *Entente* were divided into three unequal parts: one on the western front, composed of France and

Britain; another on the eastern front, Russia; and a third on the southeastern front, Serbia. The Serbian forces were so much weaker than those of the Central Powers opposing them that the Serbian front could be effectively maintained only in case the forces of the Central Powers were attracted by the struggle on the main fronts. The progress of the war, therefore, depended primarily upon the success or failure of the opposing sides on the main fronts.

The principal feature of the German military plan in case of a war against France and Russia simultaneously was first of all to throw almost all her forces against France and leave merely a small force to oppose Russia, and only after defeating France to throw her main forces on the eastern front and engage in what was not expected to be a long campaign against Russia. In view of this it was of the greatest importance to France that, immediately following the commencement of hostilities, Russia should attack Germany and thereby force the German Command to withdraw some of the forces taking part in the western offensive. In accordance with the military convention with France of 1913, Russia undertook in case of war to start an offensive against Germany on the sixteenth day following mobilization. Russia fulfilled her undertaking exactly on schedule. The war started on August 1. On August 17 a Russian army under General Rennenkampf started an offensive in East Prussia. In a few days a second army under General Samsonov advanced into East Prussia from the south. The movement of the Russian armies was hastened by the insistence of the French who by this time were heavily pressed by the German offensive on the western front. In view of the imminent necessity of action on the eastern front, the Russian forces entered East Prussia without effective preparation. The second Russian army was in a particularly precarious situation, having begun to advance before the required quantity of military supplies had been received. The Germans, in accordance with their plan, prepared to retreat beyond the Vistula River, leaving East Prussia to Russia. However, the Russian advance into Prussia had so strong an effect upon German public opinion that the Supreme Command of Germany was forced to change its plan and oppose the Russian attack. A new commander, General Hindenburg, with Ludendorff as Chief of Staff, was appointed on the northeastern front and a part of the troops engaged against France were withdrawn to stem the Russian tide. At the most decisive moment of the German advance against France, six divisions of troops and one cavalry division were ordered to Prussia. Ludendorff succeeded in surrounding and annihilating five Russian divisions of Samsonov's army at the battle of Tannenberg on August 31, 1914, at the same spot where in 1410 the Polish, Lithuanian, and Russian troops defeated the German Knights. During the following weeks Ludendorff succeeded in driving the Russian armies out of East Prussia

The transfer of German troops from the western front directly contributed to Germany's successful repulse of Russia; but it upset the whole plan of German offensive on the western front and had a profound influence upon the general course of the war. The weakening of the German army on the eve of the Marne enabled the French to arrest the German advance.

While the first engagement between Germany and Russia resulted in a German victory, Russia succeeded in defeating the Austrian army on the southeastern front and occupying Galicia. During this operation of General Alexeiev, the Russian army occupied important strategic posts in Austria and took over two hundred thousand prisoners. Following her success in East Prussia, Germany was forced to engage in further operations on the eastern front in order to support Austria. In the end of September, 1914, Ludendorff moved fifty-two divisions of German and Austrian troops in the direction of Warsaw. After nearly a month of bitter fighting, the battle was won by the Russian troops and on October 27 Ludendorff gave the order of retreat. This battle of October, 1914, was the high point of Russia's military effort in the First World War. However, it did not result in a complete defeat of the German troops. In order to undertake an offensive, Russia required preparation; but the French and British military command insisted upon an immediate Russian advance to draw away the German reserves from the western front. The Russian Command yielded to the insistence of the Allies, although the attraction of new German forces to the east at this time did not correspond with the main strategic interests of the common cause of the Allies. This operation was primarily favorable to France and Britain as it enabled them to give their troops a needed rest and to replenish supplies and munitions. Meanwhile, the Russian army, after suffering enormous losses in the course of the first three months of the war, needed rest more than the French and British. Meeting the demands of the Allies, however, the Russian troops were ordered to attack Silesia and Poznan on November 14, 1914, but Germany acted first. Fourteen divisions were drawn from the western front in November, 1914, and thrown against Russia. The proposed Russian advance failed after considerable losses had been suffered.

The failure of German offensive in France led to a reversal of Germany's military plans. It was decided that now Russia would be attacked, and only following success in the east would offensive operations be resumed in the west. In the spring of 1915, following a short suspension of active military operations, Germany brought thirteen new divisions originally intended to be used on the western front, to the eastern front. A great quantity of heavy artillery was concentrated on the Russian front and General Mackensen took charge of operations. It soon became apparent that the Russian troops could not withstand the furious attack of Mackensen in view of an almost complete depletion of supplies. A general retreat during the whole summer of 1915 resulted not only in the loss of all enemy territory occupied, but also of Poland, Lithuania, and Courland, and a huge stretch of Ukrainian and White Russian provinces.

The inadequacy of supplies was keenly felt during the whole of 1915. In August the number of unarmed Russian soldiers reached 30 per cent and the troops had to depend upon the arms of those wounded or killed in order to continue fighting. The German advance came to an end when the increased distances from bases in Germany made it difficult to supply the German troops with sufficient provisions and ammunition. In the autumn of 1915 the German advance stopped along the line Riga-Dvinsk-Tarnopol.

Meanwhile, the supply of munitions of the Russian army, following the great retreat, rapidly improved. The reason for this was the increased production of Russian munition factories and the relative quiet on the line of battle. The supplies from abroad began arriving only in 1916. At no time during the retreat of the Russian army in the summer of 1915 nor during the collapse of Serbia in the autumn of 1915 did the French and British undertake large-scale operations on the western front to draw away the forces of the Central Powers. They tried to help Russia and Serbia by attacking the Dardanelles, but this attack failed. The entry of Italy into the war in May, 1915, could give no more help. Thus, during 1915, Germany had the opportunity of delivering a terrific blow to the military power of Russia. At the beginning of the war the Central Powers had sixty-three divisions on the eastern front and ninety-three on the western. In September, 1915, they had concentrated one hundred and sixty-one divisions against Russia and eighty-four on the western front. While successful in driving back the Russian armies, Germany failed in obtaining its objective—the destruction of Russia's military power. At the same time, the fighting on the eastern front allowed the British and French to concentrate their forces for the continuation of the struggle.

5.

A CRISIS in the supply of munitions was experienced by all warring countries. Not one of the powers engaged in the war had taken due account of the duration of the struggle or of the quantity of materials necessary to conduct it. As it became evident that the war would be prolonged, measures were devised to supply a sufficient quantity of munitions. The result was the militarization of industry in Germany, Great Britain, and France. Russia's position was harder than that of the other powers, as Russian industry, in spite of its great progress in the decades preceding the war, remained comparatively feeble. The Russian army, moreover, being larger than those of the other Allies, was in greater need of supplies. During the first year it was engaged in fighting almost without an interval, while the British and French, following the battle of the Marne, dug into permanent positions. The Russian situation was further complicated by an internal political conflict. The failures of 1915 created a rift between the Government and the Duma. The inadequacy of munition supplies was attributed to the shortsightedness of the Government and the General Staff. This was in part true. Moreover, the retreat of the army led to the evacuation of the abandoned territories by great numbers of the population. This evacuation was undertaken at the command of the army authorities, who followed the policy pursued by Russia during the Napoleonic invasion of 1812. It was, however, a great mistake and brought to the attention of public opinion in Russia the defects in the military Command.

In order to aid the Government in dealing with the problems which it faced, the Union of Zemstvos and towns as well as other public organizations took over the relief of refugees and the furnishing of the army with necessary supplies. Industry was mobilized by a War Industry Committee and the Duma became the center of a vast system whose object was to assist the Government in dealing with its war problems. The work of the various agencies soon brought relief to the army, but as their work grew in popularity, the prestige of the Government fell. In the most of this internal transformation, the Allies found themselves unwillingly on the side of the Duma. They could not help seeing that its activities were of the greatest assistance to Russia in waging the war. The Duma, on the other hand, felt that only the Allies could satisfy Russia's demands for munitions, as Russian industry alone was not capable of dealing with this problem. There grew up an important relationship between the Duma and the public organizations, on the one hand, and the representatives of the Allies, on the other. This aroused political jealousy prompted by justifiable fears in court circles. The political rift was widened by personal animosities. The head of the Government was Goremykin, whose part in the dissolving of the first Duma made him unpopular in duma circles. The Government agreed to a short session of the Duma in August, 1915, and dismissed the Minister of War, Sukhomlinov, who was held responsible for the military setbacks experienced by the Russian army. But very soon Emperor Nicholas showed his unwillingness to accept the leadership of the Duma in directing the organization of the army and the country. There followed a split between the Duma and the Government, reminiscent of the condition during the first two Dumas of 1906–1907. At the initiative of the liberal leader, Miliukov, a progressive "bloc," composed of Moderate Rights, and Liberals, was formed, which controlled a majority in the Duma. The Duma now demanded a Cabinet having the confidence of the country. Nicholas II had only two courses of action open to him: either to yield to the Duma or to end the war even at the cost of betraying the Allies. The emperor could not reconcile himself to betraying the Allied cause and attempted to find a solution of the problem which would avoid yielding to the Duma, by taking over personally the Supreme Command of the Russian armies. It was hoped that this act would raise the prestige of the emperor in the country at large, in the army, and with the Allied Powers. It was, however, a risky undertaking, since further failures would bring popular condemnation upon the personality of the emperor himself. On September 5, 1915, the Grand Duke Nicholas was transferred to the Caucasian front and Nicholas II became Commander-in-Chief of the Russian army. The political atmosphere in Russia thickened. The Duma was called for the shortest possible periods and a supreme effort was made by the emperor to find leaders capable of solving the problems which he faced without calling for aid from the Duma. Nicholas II failed to find competent assistance. For this reason, Ministry supplanted Ministry without apparent reason or improvement. The precarious internal situation in Russia resulted in arousing the suspicions of the Allies, particularly following the dismissal of Foreign Minister Sazonov and the appointment of Sturmer, who was suspected of being pro-German in his sympathies.

Gradually, the emperor found himself politically isolated. He was abandoned by the Left Groups and the Right and finally by the Allies. The Duma felt that he was incapable of conducting the war with sufficient energy. The members of the extreme right faction, on the other hand, desired a separate peace, and everyone secretly suspected that the real source of power was the Empress Alexandra Feodorovna, under whose sway the weak-willed emperor had completely fallen. The empress, in turn, was known to be under the influence of Rasputin, an uneducated peasant "prophet" who was regarded by the empress as a saint. The ascendancy of Rasputin was due to his magnetic personality and the neurotic condition of the empress. The empress credited him with the power to protect the health of the tsarevich, who had suffered since birth from the incurable hereditary disease of haemophilia.

A chain of influence was thus created. In order to secure the confidence of the emperor, it was necessary to secure the favor of the empress, and in order to do this Rasputin's good offices had to be obtained. Unwillingness to ask favors of Rasputin on the part of most reputable individuals resulted in the isolation of the emperor. It was only in the army that Rasputin had no influence. The Chief of Staff under Nicholas II, i.e., the actual Commander-in-Chief of the army, was General Alexeiev, who demanded and secured freedom from outside interference. However, General Alexeiev could not keep secret from the emperor the plans of military operations. The emperor could not fail to impart so much as his own views to the empress. The empress could not hide anything from Rasputin. The question was who wanted the information from Rasputin and to whom Rasputin cared to give it.

On the other hand the army was closely allied to the interests of the whole country and any excitement in the country at large could not help but affect the morale of the troops.

6.

THE prospect of a political conflict between the Duma and the emperor was especially dangerous in that it weakened both sides. The disagreement tended to destroy authority in general and opened the path to the destructive forces of the social revolution which had taken cover since 1906. The situation became favorable for the spread of "defeatist" propaganda by the extreme Socialist parties. During the war the Socialists of all countries had abandoned internationalism in favor of nationalism. Among the Russian Socialists there were many patriots, but there was also a powerful group of Social Internationalists.

The most active agents of Russia's defeat in the war were the Bolsheviks. Their leader, Lenin, had been abroad since 1907, but continued to exercise a great influence over Russian politics. The Bolshevik members of the Duma first expressed their adherence to the "defeatist" policy of their leader in November, 1914. In the spring of 1915 they were arrested, and after trial for sedition, imprisoned or exiled. There is no doubt that their ideas slowly sank into the minds of the mass of Russian labor. Lenin continued his preparatory work in Switzerland and in 1915 proposed the foundation of the Third International. During 1915 and 1916 he succeeded in reasserting his "defeatist" policy at two International Socialist conferences. He now openly advocated civil war of the lower classes against the higher classes to end the "imperialist" war between peoples.

7.

THE political conflict between the representative organs and the Government, which has been referred to, prepared the ground for revolutionary propaganda. In addition to this conflict, the economic condition of the country contributed to the demoralization of the popular morale. The war called for the mobilization of vast numbers of men in all countries. The Russian Government, under the influence of the Allied policy, likewise called to the colors almost all those capable of carrying arms. By the beginning of 1917, over fifteen million men had been recruited. The Government did not have any immediate need for all these men or sufficient munitions to arm them effectively. Millions of soldiers lived in the rear of the battle line in complete inactivity and presented a convenient fertile field for political propaganda. The mobilization of such large numbers led to economic difficulties. The expense of caring for the millions of recruits called for enormous expenditures by the Government and increased the difficulties of transportation and production. The cities, which depended entirely upon foodstuffs imported from the country districts, were the first to suffer. In the autumn of 1916, Petrograd had difficulty in securing sufficient supplies. In calling the reserves, the Government was forced to undertake the support of the families left at home, which increased the administrative and financial burdens of the Government. Finally, the two million refugees from the abandoned areas of western Russia were also dependent upon government aid.

In order to supply the army with munitions, the Government subsidized industry. In the end of 1916 more than 73 per cent of the industrial workers were exclusively engaged in military production. The state expenses increased and the income decreased. The families of those called to the front could not pay the usual taxes, while in introducing prohibition the Government also lost the proceeds of the largest indirect tax.

The Treasury was compelled to issue paper money. In 1915, 2,946,500,000 rubles were in circulation. In 1916 the amount increased to 5,617,000,000. The increased amount of paper money in circulation led to an increase in prices, which in turn necessitated constantly increasing the pay of all officials and workers. The impression of economic insecurity was produced all over the country. This demoralized the population.

8.

FOLLOWING the setbacks of 1915, the condition of the army began to improve. In March, 1916, an offensive against the center of the

German front was tried, but failed in its objective. The plan of attack was ill prepared, being scheduled just when the spring thaw set in. The Russian troops were defeated by mud rather than by the efforts of the German army. The failure of the offensive had bad effects upon the attitude of mind among the Russian troops. The impression was created that the German positions were impregnable.

Operations were undertaken in the summer of 1916 against the Austrian army. The moment was chosen to relieve the pressure of Austria against Italy which in May threatened completely to disrupt the Italian army. In answer to the insistent requests of Italy, an offensive on the Russian southwestern front was started on June 4. This operation was successful to the highest degree. The Russian army under the command of General Brusilov succeeded in smashing the Austrian army and capturing over four hundred thousand prisoners. The Central Powers were forced to withdraw troops from other fronts to stem the Russian advance. In the autumn of 1916, Rumania entered the war against the Central Powers, but was soon defeated. The consequence of the Rumanian defeat was the further extension of the Russian front southward as far as the Black Sea in order to bring relief to Rumania.

The counter offensive against Brusilov and the Rumanian offensive called for extraordinary efforts on the part of Germany. In gaining Pyrrhic victories in the east, the Central Powers failed to secure decisive victory on the western front. In 1917 the position of Germany became critical. Meanwhile, the forces of the Allies in the west, now the principal opponents of the Central Powers, continued to grow. At the same time, owing to the arrival of some supplies from abroad and the reorganization of Russian industry, the Russian army in the spring of 1917 was amply provided with munitions. In spite of all the hardships in the past, it was possible to expect that the new Allied campaign of 1917 would be successful in crushing the Central Powers.

9.

DURING the winter of 1916–17, the conflict between Nicholas II and the Duma became particularly acute. Some solution of far-reaching importance was inevitable. Both sides were embittered. The Duma feared the possibility of an alliance between Rasputin and the reactionary circles for the purpose of concluding a separate peace with Germany. At the session of the Duma of November, 1916, several speeches were made attacking the influence of the empress. Meanwhile, in the highest circles of society, the decision was made to do away with Rasputin, who was regarded as the evil genius of the empire. On December 30 Rasputin was killed by a well-known aristocrat, with assistance of a conservative Duma deputy and of a member of the imperial family. The policy of the emperor, however, did not change following this act. A plot was formed in one of the court circles to overthrow the emperor and to substitute another member of the royal family in his place. However, the moment for such an act had already passed; before a court revolution could be effected a popular uprising took place.

CHAPTER XIV.

THE REVOLUTION OF 1917

I.

THE revolution of March, 1917, broke out while a new Russian offensive against the Central Powers was in course of preparation. The revolution made the success of this offensive impossible, for it was accompanied by a complete collapse of the Russian army and led directly to Russia's defeat in the war.

The revolution was hailed, however, by men who desired to continue the war and who imagined that the overthrow of the autocracy would stimulate patriotic feeling in the Russian people, and thereby add to their effectiveness as fighters. The most influential group in sympathy with the revolution was the upper middle class, looking for leadership to the liberal members of the Duma. Many of the army officers, including the High Command, were also sympathetic. Finally, the revolution found favor with the representatives of the Allies—France and Great Britain.

The political opposition in the Duma conducted by the liberal forces against almost every measure of the Imperial Government, was motivated by the highest patriotic feeling, the common belief being that the best interests of Russia would be served by opposition to rather than by coöperation with the old *régime*. In surveying the history of the Russian revolution one is frequently struck by this curious disparity between the objectives of the various groups and leaders and the actual results of their policies.

The leaders of the opposition in the Duma desired only a political revolution, and not a social one, whereas the extreme tension of the years of war added to the peculiar conditions prevailing in Russia made far-reaching social changes inevitable.

The war broke out before the social reorganization of Russia—following the first revolution of 1905—had reached completion or the agrarian reform had been carried to its necessary conclusion.

The new principles of landownership introduced by Stolypin, sound as they were, had not had time to bear fruit. The land hunger of the peasants remained unsatisfied and their desire to divide the large estates manifested itself as soon as the Imperial Government collapsed. The solution of the land problem always meant more to the Russian peasant than mere political reform.

The Socialist parties immediately following the revolution started propaganda among the masses, advancing a program of extensive social reform. Since the army was composed largely of peasants recruited from the fields this agitation had a serious demoralizing effect. The liberal opposition in the Duma failed to realize the effect of this agitation. They had less contact with the people and completely miscalculated the degree of socialist influence upon the masses.

In view of the restrictions enforced against political organization under the old *régime,* the liberal parliamentary parties were not organized on a large scale. The Socialist parties, meanwhile, had direct contact with the city workers through their chain of secret groups or "cells."

The most serious effect of the radical program of social reform was to destroy the morale of the army. The collapse of the Russian army was not the cause, but the result of the revolution. The first troops to become disorderly were reserve battalions and not the active regiments at the front. The army of 1917 was tired, but it was still able for some time to continue fighting. Supplies were at last adequate, and the morale of the active troops would have made possible an active campaign during 1917. But the agitation of the radical groups soon accomplished its purpose. The collapse of strong government, aggravated by the discussion of far-reaching social questions, completely deprived the troops of any desire to continue the war. Once started, the social revolution was destined to destroy the effectiveness of the Russian army.

2.

THE success of the revolutionary movement was greatly aided by the moral disintegration of the supreme authority in the Russian State. The court circle formed around the Empress Alexandra Feodorovna as we have seen was under the influence of Rasputin. This alienated the best elements from the Government. At the most tragic moment of Russian history, the Government was composed largely of incapable men having neither the ability nor the will to rule.

The murder of Rasputin, on December 30, 1916, did not improve the situation. On the contrary, it resulted in utter disorganization in the imperial household. After the murder of Rasputin the emperor ceased in fact to rule.

The disintegration of the Imperial Government and the attempts to create a new organ of power may be traced chronologically.

The emperor was in Mogilev, the Headquarters of the Russian army, when a telegram was received informing him of the murder of Rasputin in Petrograd. The same day, December 31, 1916, he left for Tsarskoe Selo to join the empress and from then on he took no further interest in political affairs.

It happened that the Chief of Staff, General Alexeiev, had previously fallen seriously ill and was also absent from Headquarters, recovering in the Crimea. He was temporarily replaced by General Gurko. He returned to Headquarters on March 3, 1917, although not completely recovered. Emperor Nicholas returned on March 9. On the following day a telegram came telling of disorders in Petrograd caused by the insufficiency of food supplies. The first telegrams from Petrograd, however, were rather optimistic in tone. But the following days brought more alarming news about the disorders there. The president of the state Duma, M. V. Rodzianko, described the events very gloomily. He requested that a new Cabinet be formed to satisfy the Duma and command the full confidence of the people. On March 12, the Grand Duke Michael Alexandrovich, brother to the emperor, informed General Alexeiev that he believed that this alone could save the situation which had become further aggravated.

A few hours later a telegram arrived from the Prime Minister, Prince Golitsyn, asking for similar measures. It seemed that the only decision open to the emperor was to accept this advice. But he did not do so. The other alternative was to take very energetic measures to crush the uprising. Some measures were taken, but they were wholly inadequate to meet the situation. The new session of the Duma, which opened on February 27, was discontinued by the Imperial *ukaz* of March 11, and General Ivanov was dispatched with one battalion to Petrograd with orders to suppress the revolt. But these measures were not sufficient.

The members of the Duma did not obey the Imperial *ukaz* and gathered on the morning of March 12 in the Tauride Palace. The measures taken having proved insufficient, the emperor could still try to take others more resolute. But at this very moment, the emperor left Headquarters again for Tsarskoe Selo, early on the morning of March 13, not wishing to be separated from the empress during these troublous days. Thus the emperor cut himself off from the current of events. Meanwhile events were developing with extraordinary rapidity.

The acts of the emperor were not sufficient to crush the revolution, but they were quite sufficient to prevent the Duma from assuming control of the forces now in motion. Very soon the Duma was no longer able to guide the revolution.

Neither the leaders in the Duma nor in the Socialist parties had called the soldiers and the workmen into the streets. The immediate cause of the rioting in Petrograd was the insufficiency of food. However, this did not affect the soldiers, who received their normal supply. On the morning of March 12, Petrograd was already overrun by the revolutionary mob. Policemen were killed in the streets, the Kresty jail was forced open, and the courthouse set afire. The soldiers of many reserve battalions staying in Petrograd joined the crowds. Some officers were killed. The Government, the military command, and the chief of police were helpless. Anarchy began.

It seemed that the Duma was the only authority which could control the situation. Crowds of soldiers and civilians rushed to the Tauride Palace where it sat.

About noon the members of the Duma decided to act. About 2 P.M. a Temporary Committee of the Duma was elected to lead the movement. The Committee numbered twelve members, with Rodzianko as chairman. The majority consisted of liberals and moderate conservatives. Besides these, two socialist members of the Duma were elected—Alexander Kerensky and Nicholas Chkheidze. Chkheidze at once refused to serve. This refusal was significant. He wished to have his hands free to advance purely socialistic policies. The socialist leaders arrived at the Tauride Palace at the same time as the Duma members. Instead of joining with the Duma, they tried to create their own government on the pattern of 1905. During all of March 12, the Duma and the socialist leaders hesitated to break with the old *régime*. They merely followed the leadership of the mob, which arrested the Ministers and brought them to the Duma. It was only in the evening that the Temporary Committee of the Duma decided to take power in its hands. Commissaries were appointed to all government offices. It seemed for a moment as though the Duma would succeed in mastering the revolution.

But at the same time the Petrograd Soviet of Workers and Soldiers' Deputies was being organized. Deputies of workmen, one for each thousand, and of soldiers, one for each company, were summoned to gather at the Tauride Palace at 7 P.M. on March 12. The socialist chiefs who led them did not even ask the Duma Committee's permission to occupy the Duma hall. Chkheidze was chosen as chairman of the Soviet at its first meeting.

It was but natural under these circumstances that the emperor had not time to reach Tsarskoe Selo. The railroad staff was already informed of the revolution by a telegram of the deputy appointed Commissary of the Ministry of Communication. The emperor's train was stopped at the station of Dno. On the evening of March 14 the emperor arrived at Pskov. His will was broken and he decided to abdicate.

The Duma Committee was already taking the next step in the revolution. It appointed a Provincial Government of Russia, with Prince George E. Lvov as chairman, Alexander Guchkov as head of the War Office, and Paul Miliukov as head of the Foreign Office. Among other ministers there was one socialist deputy, Kerensky, as Minister of Justice. The Labor Office was offered to another Socialist, Chkheidze, but he refused again.

The first care of the new Government was to eliminate the emperor. On March 15 the new war minister, Guchkov, and the member of the Duma Committee, V. V. Shulgin, left for Pskov to secure his abdication. The emperor did not wish to separate himself from his son. For this reason he did not abdicate in favor of his son and heir apparent, Alexis, but in favor of his brother, the Grand Duke Michael Alexandrovich. Before his abdication, the emperor appointed the Grand Duke Nicholas Supreme Commander-in-Chief of the Army and named Prince Lvov Premier of the

Cabinet. The Grand Duke Michael Alexandrovich did not choose to accept the Supreme Power and passed it on to the Provisional Government. The Romanovs had ceased to rule Russia. The late emperor was soon arrested, with the empress and their children, and then exiled in Siberia.

3.

THE revolution which took place in Petrograd was accepted not only by army Headquarters, but by the whole of Russia. Supporters of the old *régime* made no sign of resistance. The revolution had acquired a legal character, owing to the manifestos of Emperor Nicholas and of his brother. This circumstance completely disarmed the enemies of the revolution. There were, however, a number of cases of suicide by ardent supporters of the monarchy. The overthrow of the empire and substitution of the authority of the Duma were tacitly accepted by the bureaucratic machine of the old *régime* both in the capital and in the provinces. But it soon became evident that the new Government did not possess real authority.

From the first hour of its existence the Provisional Government was hampered by the Workers and Soldiers' Soviets. The first decree it issued, on March 14, was written under the pressure of the Petrograd Soviet.

It laid down the following principles: (1) A general amnesty for all political, religious, and military prisoners; (2) freedom of speech and of the press, freedom for unions and strikes; (3) abolition of all social, religious, and national distinctions; (4) the summoning of a Constituent Assembly; (5) a people's militia to replace the police; (6) elections to be based on universal suffrage; (7) troops that took part in the revolution should remain in Petrograd and not be transferred to the front; (8) soldiers to have the same public rights as civilians when not in active service.

In spite of the fact that this declaration was a compromise between the Provisional Government and the Soviet program, the Soviet issued another declaration independently and without the approval of the Provisional Government.

It was the famous "Order No. 1" of March 14 which was the principal agency in the destruction of the Russian army. The main features of this "order" were the following: (1) Soldiers' committees were to be chosen in each military detachment; (2) each military detachment was to obey the Soviet in its political decisions; (3) orders of the military commission of the state Duma were to be obeyed only if they did not contradict the Soviet's orders; (4) all weapons were to be under control of the soldiers' committees and were not to be delivered to the officers.

This order brought about confusion in the control of the army. It was issued without the consent of the High Command and was directed against the authority of the superior officers. It threatened with immediate destruction the whole organization of the army, by drawing the troops into the turbulent stream of politics and filling them with suspicion of the Duma. It was clear that the authors of this order desired to make the continuance of war impossible. After this order had been issued, the Provisional Government attempted to have it revoked, but this it failed to accomplish. It was now perfectly clear that the real administration was the Soviet and not the Provisional Government. Yet the Soviet did not wish to seize power openly because it feared a reaction among the liberal and conservative elements of society at this moment. The Provisional Government was indispensable to the Soviet because it was still the recognized authority for the country and the army. The Soviet preferred to maintain the Provisional Government in nominal authority as a bait for the anti-socialist groups, controlling it and checking its measures when they conflicted with Soviet policy.

Consequently, there were two governments in Petrograd from the very first days of the revolution: the Provisional Government representing the political revolution, and the Soviet of Workers and Soldiers' Deputies representing the social revolution. And the latter had no responsibility

The helplessness of the Provisional Government is explained partly by the personal incapacity of its members and partly by the difficulty of the problems which it had to face.

Almost all the members of the first Provisional Government were men of education and intelligence, of great and sincere love for their country, but none had a strong will nor the determination to suppress the enemies of order. Some of its members would perhaps have been excellent ministers under normal conditions; but during the war and in the time of upheaval they proved themselves unfit for their task.

The Premier of the Government, Prince Lvov, was a passive

character, incapable of crushing his opponents. He was a Tolstoian type who believed in "nonresistance to evil." He frequently expressed a naïve faith in the "great bloodless" revolution.

The Ministers of War and Foreign Affairs, Guchkov and Miliukov, were perhaps the only men in the Government who supported an active foreign and military policy. It was this that centered the hatred of Soviet circles on these two men, especially Miliukov.

In their political views, most of the members of the Provisional Government belonged to the Constitutional Democratic party. Brought up in the principles of European constitutionalism, they tried to apply these principles to Russia, without taking into account the revolutionary temper of the time, which demanded rapidity of decision and not the minute fulfilment of constitutional procedure.

Both for the purpose of local Zemstvo and national elections, the Provisional Government formulated new laws involving universal, equal, direct, and secret balloting. First of all, reorganized local bodies or Zemstvos were to come into existence, to take charge of the lists of those voting for the members of the Constituent Assembly. Thus the election of representatives was delayed until the autumn of 1917.

The second Government of Russia during this period, as has been pointed out above, was the Soviet of Workers and Soldiers' Deputies. This government, in the beginning, was also unorganized. The Petrograd Soviet consisted of 2,500 workmen and soldiers chosen without any technical formalities in the factories and by military detachments in Petrograd. Besides the real representatives of the soldiers and workers, the Soviet comprised the leaders of the Socialist parties who, ever since 1905, had regarded themselves as the real representatives of the interests of labor. The unwieldy body of the Soviet was actually incapable of carrying on political activity. It therefore formed a Central Executive Committee, consisting almost exclusively of the leaders of the Socialist parties. The principal measures to be taken by the Soviet were decided in an even smaller group—the Praesidium of the Central Executive Committee. Measures were frequently adopted by individual members of the higher organs of the Soviet and were only later subscribed to by the Central Executive Committee. All non-Socialist parties were classified as *bourgeois* or "capitalist" and were not admitted into the Soviet. The greater number of members of the Soviet were Socialist Revolutionaries, who regarded themselves as representing the peasantry. The next group in importance was the Socialist Democratic party which regarded itself as representing labor. This latter party was, as we have seen above, split into "Mensheviks" and "Bolsheviks." After the arrival of Lenin, who came back to Russia from exile in April, 1917, the Bolsheviks finally broke relations with the Mensheviks and organized a separate party which later was called the "Communist" party. Lenin differed from the Mensheviks regarding a basic concept of policy. The latter believed that the socialist revolution in Russia was impossible until the country had become industrialized to a higher degree than it was. The Bolsheviks, on the other hand, desired to bring about socialism in Russia immediately. The partisans of Lenin formed but a small minority of the Petrograd Soviet during the first months of the revolution, but owing to the disorganization of the Soviet and their own tireless activity, they managed to play a part far out of proportion to their numbers. While the more moderate Socialists desired to see the Provisional Government continue in control, the Bolsheviks loudly demanded that all power be given to the Soviets immediately.

The peculiar strength of the Soviet lay in the fact that, despite its clumsy size and heterogeneous membership, it had far closer contact with the masses than the Provisional Government. Very soon every town in Russia formed its Soviet. These were further supplemented by similar organizations in the army and in many villages.

The Provisional Government replaced the officials of the old *régime* in the provinces by the heads of the old Zemstvo Committees. But though generally of a liberal turn of mind, they had almost as little contact with the people as the authorities whom they displaced. But while the former officials had experience in ruling, the new ones had none. The central power in Petrograd thus found itself, from the beginning, without suitable representatives in the provinces. The Commissars of the Provisional Government found themselves forced to share power with the local Soviets. The conditions in Petrograd were reflected in every local capital.

No sooner had Soviets been formed all over the country than the Central Executive Committee called an All-Russian Soviet Congress. Everywhere the Socialists dominated the Soviets. The Congress which brought together all the central committees of the Soviets, was in fact a Congress of the Socialist party leaders.

The convention opened on June 16. The strongest party present was the Socialist Revolutionary party with 285 deputies. The Mensheviks were represented by 248 and the Bolsheviks were in a minority with only 105 delegates.

This Congress, in the eyes of the sympathizers of the Soviet, was the real representative organ of the new Russian state. The Bolsheviks demanded that it immediately seize power, but, being in a minority, they failed to carry through their wish. As a result of this early failure to overthrow the Provisional Government, Lenin set about creating conditions which would make it possible to seize power at the next Soviet Congress.

It must be admitted that the Soviet Congress was much easier to organize than the Constituent Assembly, and consequently it was a more practical organ of power during the revolution. The first success in calling the Soviet Congress forecast its victory over the parliamentary system borrowed from the west and advocated by the Provisional Government.

4.

THE leading political question of the time of the revolution was, of course, the question of war. There were two extreme views with respect to this question. The moderate elements in the Government desired to continue the war to a victorious end. This view was frequently expressed by Foreign Minister Miliukov, in his conversations with the Allied representatives in Petrograd, and in public statements.

The opposite view was held by the Bolsheviks and a number of other Socialist Internationalists. Representatives of these parties argued the need of immediate peace and openly admitted themselves to be "defeatists."

Between these two extremes lay a group composed of a majority of the Socialists in the Soviets. They realized that popular feeling was not in support of a war policy, but they were unwilling as yet to accept the fact of the complete collapse of Russia's military power.

A weighty influence was also wielded by the representatives of the Allied Powers in Russia. It was quite natural that the continuance of Russia in the war was of the greatest interest to the Allies and they insisted that she must not on any account "betray the cause of Allied democracy."

From the very outbreak of the revolution the Allies were closely in sympathy with the new Government of Russia. The United States was the first to grant it official recognition, on March 22, and was soon followed by Great Britain, France, and Italy. But very soon the Allied Powers showed signs of anxiety as to the new Government's capacity to maintain order in Russia and continue the military campaign against the Central Powers. Seeing the success of the socialist leaders in organizing the masses, they urged the Government to compromise its differences with the Soviets and secure a unified and strong government. For this purpose a labor delegation led by Albert Thomas, the French socialist Minister of Munitions, was sent by France, and a similar delegation went from Great Britain, to effect a cordial understanding between the Soviets, the Provisional Government, and the western democratic groups.

The bitter opposition between the two views of Russia's war policy remained unreconciled. On March 18 Miliukov addressed the representatives of the Allies in Petrograd, assuring them that Russia "would fight by their side against the common enemy until the end." On March 27 the Petrograd Soviet issued a proclamation to the people of the world calling for "concerted and decisive action in favor of peace." From this day the socialist leaders began an intensive struggle against the "imperialistic policies" of Minister Miliukov. On May 3 the Bolsheviks organized their first demonstration against the Government under the slogan "Down with Miliukov." This demonstration led to a patriotic counter demonstration on the following night; but, to avoid further conflicts with the Soviet, the Provisional Government accepted the resignations of the two ministers most severely criticized, and on May 17 formed a new Cabinet without Miliukov and Guchkov. The Government on May 18 also accepted the demands of the Soviet that peace with the Central Powers be signed "without annexations or indemnities on the basis of self-determination of peoples."

The new Government retained Prince Lvov as Premier, but its

real leader was Kerensky, who was both War and Marine Minister. Albert Thomas supported Kerensky and, through him, the new Government, which included many Socialists. It was his belief that these were the only political leaders possessing sufficient authority to induce the Russian army to continue the war, but although the Soviets had secured the dismissal of their enemies, their opposition was not calmed.

5.

KERENSKY's program with respect to the army contained two principles: the preparation of a general Russian offensive and a democratic reorganization of its command. The idea of an offensive against the Central Powers did not conflict in the mind of Kerensky with his earlier commitments to a purely defensive war or to his renunciation of imperialistic aims. The chief purpose of the offensive would be to force the Central Powers to abandon the territories of Russia which they then occupied. The chief defect in this policy was the failure to give due consideration to the new attitude of the Russian soldiers subsequent to the revolution.

The proposed reorganization of the army destroyed the last vestiges of discipline. On May 22 Kerensky approved an order to the army and navy known as the "Declaration of Soldiers' Rights." This order confirmed nearly all the points of Order No. 1 issued by the Petrograd Soviet on March 14, and in some respects went even farther.

A new feature in the organization of the army laid down by Kerensky was the appointment of commissars to represent the Government in the army, empowered with its political leadership. The High Command of the army found itself checked from above by the government appointees and from below by soldiers' committees organized at the outset of the revolution.

The High Command of the army received the orders of the Provisional Government without protest after the tsar's abdication. The commanding generals of the Russian army were loyal to the revolution and the Provisional Government following the tsar's abdication. It was not until later that they realized the fact that the Government was subject to the destructive influence of the Soviet. Meanwhile, Kerensky extended the reorganization of the army to the command. General Alexeiev, who had replaced the

Grand Duke Nicholas, was now removed by Kerensky and General Brusilov appointed in his place as Commander-in-Chief.

The dissolution of the Russian army reached a hopeless stage. The authority of the officers collapsed. The army Soviets issued orders contrary to those of the commanding officers, and the troops were subjected to a flood of "defeatist" literature. Very soon the soldiers began to fraternize with the enemy on the front. The German Command decided to suspend military operations, believing that it was the best method of furthering the disintegration of the Russian army. Meanwhile, Kerensky sincerely tried to accomplish the preparation of an offensive. After his tour of the front, which earned him the nickname of "Persuader-in-Chief," a Russian offensive was planned for July, 1917. The first days of fighting were successful. A great breach was made in the Austrian lines and the enemy put to flight, but very soon it became evident that the "reorganized" Russian army could not continue the advance. Whole regiments refused to carry out their military orders and even left the front when they felt tired. The successful phase of the offensive was due only to the enthusiasm of the officers and a small minority of the soldiers, most of whom perished in the first days of the fighting. The offensive was doomed.

A factor contributing to the failure of the Russian offensive was a lack of coöperation between the Allies. The British and French offensives on the western front took place early in May. By July the Allies were exhausted and the Germans succeeded in transferring two divisions from the western front to reinforce the crumbling Austrian forces. A counter-offensive broke the Russian line at a spot where one of the unruly regiments had abandoned the front. A complete collapse was imminent. The German troops stopped advancing after reaching the river Zbruch, but had they wished they could easily have occupied the whole southwest of Russia. The catastrophe compelled one of the commanding officers, General Kornilov, to send a bitter message to the Government requiring the immediate restoration of military discipline and of capital punishment for all deserters. The government commissars supported the demands of General Kornilov.

This produced an immense impression over the whole country. It was the first time firm language had been used since the beginning of the revolution. In one day Kornilov became the center of patriotic feeling. Kerensky also was strongly impressed by his demands and on July 30 appointed him supreme Commander-in-Chief in place of Brusilov.

6.

SIMULTANEOUSLY with the collapse of the Russian offensive an armed uprising took place in Petrograd, the Bolsheviks leading a group of sailors and some of the regiments of the Petrograd garrison in an attempt to overthrow the Government, from July 16 to 18, but a cavalry division summoned from the front by the Provisional Government succeeded in suppressing the movement.

The chief purpose of the Bolshevik uprising in July was to seize power in the name of the Soviets. It had been prepared quite openly, but neither the Government nor the majority of the Soviet, who were in opposition to the Bolsheviks, took any serious measures to prevent the outbreak. On the contrary, the socialist leaders declared that the Government had no right to take any measures against the peaceful propaganda of the Bolsheviks.

The strength of the Bolsheviks lay in the force of their slogans and the efficiency of their organization. Their program contained three points: (1) Immediate peace; (2) immediate distribution of land to the peasants and the seizure of factories by the workers; (3) all power to the Soviets. Though they had only a minority in the Petrograd Soviet and the Soviet Congress, they played a dominant rôle in these bodies. Their activity became particularly effective following the arrival of Lenin and Trotsky from abroad. Both of these leaders were well-known "defeatists." Prior to the revolution Trotsky had been living in the United States. On his way to Russia through England he was arrested by the British as a dangerous propagandist, but was released at the insistence of the Provisional Government and allowed to proceed to Russia. Lenin, since 1914, had been living in Switzerland. He entered into negotiations with the German Government through the mediation of Platten, a Swiss Socialist, with the purpose of being allowed to return to Russia through Germany. The German Government, desirous of using Lenin as a weapon to destroy Russia's military power, agreed to allow him passage from Switzerland to Sweden in a sealed railroad car. Lenin arrived in Petrograd on April 16.

A few days following his arrival, Lenin began to expound his ideas at meetings of workmen and soldiers. He appealed to the Socialists to discard their old-fashioned methods of parliamentary opposition and espoused the class war of communism.

The central ideas of his policies were "peace to the village huts, war against the palaces" and "loot the looters." Lenin's speeches at first merely puzzled the Socialists. His opponents, after hearing him speak, declared: "A man who talks such nonsense is not dangerous. It is a good thing that he has arrived for now he is in full view." Lenin was very much in view. He worked in the open. With undaunted energy he began preaching his views and reorganizing the Communist party.

His attack against the "palaces" was forecast by the forcible seizure of a private house belonging to the dancer Kshesinskaya. Neither the Provisional Government nor the Petrograd Soviet succeeded in evicting him from the house which became the headquarters of the Bolshevik faction. It was only after the July uprising that the house was recaptured by the Government.

The failure of the first Bolshevik uprising might have been a turning point in the history of the Russian revolution. It was the right moment to enforce the authority of the Government in Petrograd. But this opportunity was not seized by the Government. Some Bolshevik leaders, including Trotsky, were arrested; Lenin fled to Finland; but the Bolsheviks were not outlawed in the Soviet. The Government meanwhile was reorganized. Prince Lvov resigned; Kerensky became Prime Minister, and remained head of the War and Marine Ministries. The majority in the Cabinet was now Socialist.

7.

THE disorganization of the army and of the administration was accompanied by an economic crisis. Agricultural as well as industrial production declined, transportation became greatly disorganized, and the finances of the Government rapidly grew worse. The agrarian situation was particularly confused. The Provisional Government hesitated to accomplish the redistribution of land before the convocation of the Constituent Assembly. Meanwhile the leaders of the Democratic and Socialist parties were promising the peasants that they would receive the land. Under such circumstances the peasants were unwilling to wait for the Constituent

Assembly to divide the lands. In many places the lawless seizure of land commenced, accompanied by the destruction of the houses and even the murder of the owners. In many estates, which had supplied the Government with alcohol prior to prohibition in 1914, the cellars were broken into and the mob was driven to greater excesses by drink.

An effort was made by the Government to control the movement by organizing the Committee on Agrarian Reform and local committees composed of government officials and peasants. These committees, however, were helpless in their efforts to restrain the peasants from seizing the land. The Minister of the Interior, Tseretelli, a Socialist, in an official announcement of July 30, characterized the movement as follows: "Everywhere fields are being seized, peasants are making impossible demands upon landowners, live stock is being destroyed, property is being stolen, crops are perishing, forests are being chopped down, lumber and firewood in transit is being plundered. Private owners are leaving their fields unsown and are not reaping the harvest."

The agrarian crisis had an immediate effect upon the food supply. The supply of the troops and the cities during the war had required the careful attention of the Government. Insufficiency of food in the capital had served as the first pretext for the revolution. The Provisional Government attempted to solve the problem of food supply by instituting a grain monopoly on April 11, 1917. Every peasant household was rationed and the balance was to go to the Government at fixed prices. But the depreciation of the currency made the prices established far lower than the market value of the grain and the peasants refused to give up their grain. As a result of this measure and the disorganization of transportation, the proposed quotas of grain supply remained unfilled. The government purchases fell in July to 26 per cent and in August to 10 per cent of the needs of the army and the cities.

The condition of industry was no better. From the very first days of the revolution the workers put through their demands without consulting the management. The eight-hour day was introduced; managers were dismissed by the factory committees composed of workers. The result was the rapid breakdown of discipline and production. The output of the metallurgical industries of Moscow fell 32 per cent by April, 1917; in Petrograd production fell from 20 to 40 per cent; coal mining in the Donets basin had fallen 30 per cent by July. The workers in all branches of industry meanwhile demanded an increase in pay, without any regard to the income of the enterprises concerned. The demand for increase in pay was caused partly by the depreciation of currency, but at the same time it led to further issue of paper currency and to further depreciation.

For example, in some of the enterprises of the Donets basin having a total profit during 1916 of 75,000,000 rubles, the workers demanded additions in pay totaling 200,000,000 rubles.

The decision had to be made whether industries would be run by the workers or by the state. The representatives of foreign shareholders in Russian industries seized upon the idea of "government control" as a protection against the excessive demands of labor. The idea of government control, as introduced in the Allied countries during the war, was supported by the delegate of British labor in Russia, Arthur Henderson, who arrived in Petrograd in May, 1917. The Russian Socialists took advantage of the support offered by Henderson to carry out their program of "social" control—that is, to introduce socialism and hand over the factories to the workers. This program was not in fact carried through under the Provisional Government, but in several instances control over factories passed into the hands of the workers, increasing the general confusion.

The railroads were likewise affected by the general disorganization. By an order of the Minister of Communications, of July 9, 1917, the administration of the Russian State Railways was handed over to the committees composed of railroad employees. An Executive Committee was created at the head of the committees of railroad workers, socialistic in temper and primarily interested in politics. The railroads soon showed the results of mismanagement. The number of locomotives out of repair increased. Car loading decreased. During the first months of 1917, 980,000 fewer cars were loaded than for the same period of 1916.

The general collapse of economic life could not fail to react upon the condition of finances. As we have noted above, each year of war weighed down more heavily upon the state budget. The revolution did not decrease, but, on the contrary, increased the state expenses. The Provisional Government found itself compelled to subsidize industries which, due to the decrease in productivity and the rise in wages, failed to balance accounts. In the Donets basin the subsidy amounted to 1,000,000,000 rubles. The rise in pay to soldiers called for an additional 500,000,000 rubles; the increase in pay of railroad employees exceeded 350,000,000 rubles.

The rise of government expenditures was not accompanied by an increase in government income. The land taxes fell one-third in the first months of the revolution, city house taxes fell 43 per cent. The internal loans of the Provisional Government did not sell well. There remained the only one means of covering the deficit—by printing money. For the first half year of 1917, the issue of new paper currency totaled almost 4,000,000,000 rubles as against 3,500,000,000 for the whole of 1916.

The rate of exchange on Petrograd in London for cheques was (in rubles to £10) in July, 1917, 226.5 (lowest) and in September, 1917, 322.5 (lowest). The economic condition of Russia had become critical.

8.

In the course of the first months of the revolution, the High Command of the army had passively submitted to all the measures of the Provisional Government. But after the collapse of the offensive of July, 1917, and following the appointment of General Kornilov as Commander-in-Chief, the attitude of the army changed. Army Headquarters became a political force. Kornilov accepted the post of the Commander-in-Chief only after laying down his conditions to the Government. These conditions were: (1) The new Commander-in-Chief would have full powers; (2) the Government would not interfere with the military orders of the Commander-in-Chief; (3) military discipline would be restored. Kerensky accepted the conditions proposed by General Kornilov. In order to carry out his promise, it was clear that Kerensky would be forced to break with the Soviet. But even following the suppression of the Bolshevik revolt of July, he was unwilling to do so. The political situation became extremely confused. Prior to the Bolshevik uprising there were two powers in Russia: The Provisional Government and the Soviet. The main strength of the Provisional Government consisted in the loyal support of the army Command. The Soviet's active strength was in its left wing, the Communist party. Now both extreme groups broke away from the moderate forces. The Bolsheviks, while continuing to act in the name of the Soviets, carried out their own policies. The failure of their first uprising did not abate their energy. The army Command likewise prepared to act for itself.

In the past, during the political rivalry between the Provisional Government and the Soviets, it was possible to choose between the tactics of the Moderate Democrats and the Socialists, between Miliukov and Kerensky. But the situation had undergone a radical change. The opposing forces now were Lenin on the one hand and Kornilov on the other—communism versus military dictatorship. The country had to make a choice between the two.

In spite of his growing popularity, General Kornilov was not in a position to rely exclusively upon himself. He had to cloak his moves behind the authority of the Provisional Government, just as the Bolsheviks cloaked theirs behind the authority of the Soviets. Kornilov's plan of reinstating discipline in the army was based upon the coöperation of the Provisional Government. If he had had to deal with the first Provisional Government, headed by Prince Lvov, it is quite likely that his plan of subjecting the Government to his will would have succeeded. But unluckily for him, the head of the Government was no longer Prince Lvov, but Kerensky, who was not sufficiently strong to retain power for himself, but who had enough political cunning to prevent anyone else from taking it from him so long as the Provisional Government continued to exist.

A rift soon opened between army Headquarters and the Government. While Kerensky was eager to end the interference of the Soviet and to allow Kornilov to restore discipline in the army, he feared the complete annihilation of the Soviet, which might lead to his own defeat by Kornilov and his supporters in the army. His fears were justified. The plan of Kornilov was to get rid of the Soviet by means of military force. He tried to win the coöperation of the Provisional Government for this purpose. But if the Government should be afraid at the last moment, Kornilov was ready to get rid both of the Provisional Government and of the Soviet.

On August 27 there was a "National Political Conference" in Moscow. Representatives of the main corporations of the country were summoned. Kornilov attended the Conference. He was applauded with enthusiasm by the conservative members. The socialistic half of the Conference accorded an ovation to Kerensky. Thus, the split was prepared. Both Kornilov and Kerensky foresaw that the announcement of the measures to secure discipline in the army might lead to a revolt of the Bolsheviks in Petrograd. To take care of the emergency, Kornilov, in agreement with the Provisional Government, moved the Third Cavalry Corps toward the capital. At that moment a further complication was brought about by a former member of the Duma, V. N. Lvov (not to be confused with the former Prime Minister, Prince G. E. Lvov), who visited Headquarters in September. He attempted to play the part of an intermediary between the two men, representing to each that he was empowered by the other with full authority to negotiate. From a conversation with Lvov, Kornilov received the impression that Kerensky was prepared to hand over to him, Kornilov, dictatorial power in Russia, while Kerensky himself would be satisfied with a post in the new government. Kornilov approved of this proposal which Lvov advanced in the form of an offer from Kerensky. On his return to Petrograd, Lvov presented the plan as an ultimatum of Kornilov to Kerensky. On September 8 Kerensky called Kornilov by direct wire and asked him to confirm the report that he had actually charged Lvov to convey information of his plans and purposes. Kornilov replied affirmatively, but omitted to ask Kerensky what it was that Lvov had said to him.

On September 9 a telegram from Kerensky informed General Kornilov that he was dismissed from his post and ordered him to proceed immediately to Petrograd. It was an unexpected blow to Kornilov. It was also a violation of the first condition which Kornilov had required when he was appointed the Commander-in-Chief. He decided that it was the right moment to act. On September 10 Kornilov issued a proclamation by telegraph to all Russian citizens refusing to give up the post of Commander-in-Chief and asking for support against the Provisional Government. At the same moment he ordered General Krymov to move the Third Cavalry Corps against Petrograd.

Kerensky meanwhile joined forces with the Left groups of the Petrograd Soviet and ordered the Petrograd garrison to prepare itself to fight General Krymov. All the socialist organizations in

Russia hastened to the support of Kerensky. A particularly important part was played by the Executive Committee of the railroad workers who had control over transportation. A battle between the two groups however was averted.

The official aim of General Krymov's mission was the suppression of the Bolshevik uprising which was expected to take place in Petrograd following the Government's approval of Kornilov's program. Kornilov's program was neither approved nor published and no such revolt took place. Krymov's troops were disconcerted and eager to hear the propaganda of their opponents. Simultaneously, the railroad workers refused to obey Kornilov's orders to transport reinforcements to Krymov. The latter feared to give the deciding order to open an offensive against the capital and accepted Kerensky's offer to report himself in Petrograd. The day following his arrival he committed suicide.

After the failure of General Krymov's mission, Kornilov and his assistants, Generals Denikin, Lukomsky, and Markov were arrested by order of the Provisional Government.

CHAPTER XV.

THE REDS AND THE WHITES

(1917–1920

I.

WITH the collapse of the Kornilov movement the Russian revolution entered a new phase. On the surface Kerensky had triumphed over the two opponents who had threatened his position: Kornilov was under arrest and Lenin had sought refuge outside of Russia. Kerensky's victory, however, was an illusory one. He was no longer the real power but a political ghost no longer able to control or direct the political and economic anarchy which was rapidly overrunning the country. Indeed, the defeat of the Military party itself immediately reacted against the Provisional Government, for thereafter the dominant force was not the alliance of the Government and the army but the alliance of the Soviet and the Bolsheviks.

Kerensky's triumph over Kornilov led to the final collapse of the Government's tottering prestige in the eyes of many of its most ardent supporters. Among the officers and in middle-class circles the conviction grew that his *régime* was no better than that of the Soviet of Workers and Peasants and that Kerensky himself was no more desirable than Lenin. In fact, many reactionary groups actually hoped for the victory of the Soviets at this time, for no one then doubted that such a victory would result in the early collapse and elimination of the Soviets from the political arena. In this atmosphere of bewilderment and turmoil the initiative definitely passed out of the hands of the Provisional Government and into those of the extreme radical faction of the Socialist party. In return for their support against Kornilov, these groups exacted from Kerensky a series of concessions which undermined his position. They were able in time to force the release of the Bolshevik leaders who had been arrested after the July uprising, and these skilled agitators were soon directing the attack. Trotsky was among those thus returned to the struggle, and Lenin, though he did not dare return from Finland openly, secretly attended a number of Bolshevik meetings in Petrograd.

The Government meanwhile had but one hope: to retain at least the forms of power until the Constituent Assembly met. The election of members to the new body had been set for November 25, and the first session of the Assembly was to meet on December 12, 1917. But the Bolsheviks were equally aware of the political importance of these events and, as the dates approached, hastened to summon the Second All-Russian Congress of Soviets in order to forestall the Government. The Congress was to meet on November 7, and the Bolshevik party planned to carry out its *coup d'état* immediately after the official opening and then to secure the approval of the Congress for constituting the new Government.

In preparation for the impending decisive struggle for power the Bolsheviks extended their organization and increased the scope of their propaganda and to a large extent were successful in enlisting support among the workers of Petrograd and Moscow. The city elections were clear indications of their growing power: In Moscow they had controlled only 11 per cent of the votes of the Council elected in July, but by September their control had increased to 51 per cent; in Petrograd they had made similar gains. The results of the city elections were convincing demonstrations that the laboring classes had lost confidence in both the Provisional Government and the parties of the Moderate Socialists. The way was now clear for the Bolshevik party, with its strong organization and its simple program, to harvest the support of the workers as the only political group capable of leading Russia out of the chaos into which she had been plunged.

The Bolsheviks were able to inspire the same feelings among the armed forces. In the confusion following the collapse of the Kornilov movement conditions at the front were neither those of peace nor of war. The Bolshevik solution was direct and simple; they urged an immediate peace and thus promised an end to the crisis. It became increasingly clear to the troops that this was the only powerful group in Russia. Not only did the Bolsheviks succeed in establishing close relations with the army Soviets but they also entered into negotiations with the High Command—a step made possible by Kerensky himself who had previously replaced all of Kornilov's supporters at Headquarters with generals of socialist sympathies.

The determining event in the growth of Bolshevik power was Trotsky's election in October as president of the Petrograd Soviet. The Bolsheviks also succeeded in winning control of the all-important Military Committee of the Soviet which, by the end of October, 1917, they had transformed into an instrument of their party policy. When they had secured, through the Military Committee, the submission of the Petrograd garrison to their authority, they were prepared for the final blow. On the evening of November 4 the Military Committee issued its first order to the garrison: The troops in the capital were to transfer their allegiance to the Committee—that is, to the Bolsheviks. This was an act of open rebellion against the Provisional Government and any competent leadership would have treated it as such. Kerensky made no move. Both he and the leaders of the Moderate parties, with quite incomprehensible blindness, continued their debates without taking any practical measures to defend their authority.

During the night of November 7 the principal government buildings in Petrograd were occupied by Bolshevik troops. Posters which only that morning had come off the presses announced their program: (1) immediate opening of peace negotiations; (2) partition of large estates; (3) control of all factories by the workers; (4) creation of a Soviet Government.

Kerensky at last realized the danger. Leaving the Government under the temporary leadership of one of his fellow Ministers, he fled from Petrograd to rally troops against the Bolsheviks. Since the Petrograd garrison had joined the Bolsheviks, the Government was left without armed defenses; when the Bolsheviks attacked the Winter Palace where the Cabinet was in session, only a few military cadets and a battalion of women attempted resistance. They were quickly crushed and the members of the Cabinet were arrested. The Government had fallen into the hands of Lenin.

When the Second Congress of Soviets opened immediately after the fall of the Provisional Government, Socialist Revolutionary and Menshevik members protested futilely. They did not succeed in blocking the meeting of the Congress, nor were they, on the night of November 8, able to prevent it from approving the program advanced by the Bolsheviks. A Cabinet was formed under the title of the Council of People's Commissars with Lenin as president. Trotsky was appointed Commissar for Foreign Affairs, Rykov Commissar of Internal Affairs, Stalin Commissar of Nationalities, and Lunacharsky Commissar of Education.

The first acts of the Council were the unanimous adoption of the "Decree of Peace" and the "Decree of Land." The first proposed that all warring peoples and their governments begin immediate negotiations for a just and democratic peace without annexations or indemnities. The "Decree of Land" abolished private ownership of the soil which henceforth was to be shared equally by all laborers. Thus, in the night of November 8 alone, the Bolsheviks succeeded not only in organizing the Government but also in proclaiming new revolutionary policies on the most important questions of the day.

Meanwhile, Kerensky reached army Headquarters at Pskov where he found everyone against him. General Cheremisov, Commander of the northern front, was in contact with the local Soviets and flatly refused any aid. General Krasnov, in command of the Third Cavalry Corps, was a stubborn monarchist who disagreed with Kerensky's policies. His troops, moreover, were so scattered that even with the best will it would have been impossible for him to organize an immediate attack—especially since the Executive Committee of Railroad Workers which controlled communications with the capital had refused to coöperate with Kerensky. Krasnov did, however, reluctantly move a small detachment against the Bolsheviks at Tsarskoe Selo, about fifteen miles from Petrograd. There they were halted by superior forces of sailors and armed workers sent from Petrograd, and since Krasnov's contingents received no reinforcements they did not attempt to break through but avoided a decisive engagement. It was typical of the chaos of the moment that Dybenko, one of the Bolshevik military leaders, proposed to the Cossacks that he deliver Lenin to them in exchange for Kerensky. A few days later, on November 12, a group of cadets in the capital made an abortive attempt at a military uprising against the Bolsheviks, but in a brief round of street fighting they were disarmed and killed.

Kerensky, meanwhile, had been warned that Krasnov's troops were plotting to deliver him to the Bolsheviks, and, fearing execution at their hands, he fled. Thereafter he took no part in the struggle between the Bolsheviks and their opponents whose countermoves became increasingly futile. Kerensky's disappearance left the partisans of the Provisional Government without a leader, and neither the army nor the country at large was able to supply the leadership or the organization to provide effective opposition to the disciplined and purposeful Bolsheviks. Kerensky had previously crushed the initiative of the High Command and thereby gained the distrust and hatred of the officer class. After the Kornilov movement of August he had appointed new men to command the military garrisons of various cities, men whose only qualifications were their political sympathies with the Provisional Government. These officials were disliked and suspected by the great majority of the officers under their command. The garrison troops themselves fell into one of two classifications: they were either quite indifferent to the political issues of the day, or they had already been converted by the Bolsheviks and now openly supported the Soviets. Throughout the country the working class as a whole had accepted Bolshevism as a system which promised order and an improvement of their position. The *bourgeoisie* and the intellectuals very generally opposed it, but they were divided among themselves and lacked the organizational mechanisms to make their opposition felt. In this situation a determined minority rose to grasp the power which a confused majority had lost by default.

The only serious opposition which the Bolsheviks met in the early stages of their *coup d'état* was in Moscow. A few thousand military cadets and volunteers, mostly university students, tried to stem the Bolshevik rising but after a week of bloody street fighting they were crushed. With Petrograd and Moscow under their control and with a large part of the army actively supporting their policies, the Bolsheviks had entrenched themselves so that the whole vital central area of the country was now in their hands. The opposition remaining centered in the Cossack regions of southeastern Russia and that offered no immediate threat to the stability of the Government. The Bolsheviks were confident that nowhere in Russia at that moment was there an organized group capable of blasting them from their positions, and they could look forward to a relatively long period in which to secure and consolidate their control over the whole of Russia. They had arrived. In the course of a single week the Bolsheviks had come to power in the largest nation in the world.

2.

The Soviet Government was now faced with the task of translating the proclaimed Bolshevik policies into concrete governmental and administrative terms. The problems before them were pressing: They must terminate the war, and that quickly; they must suppress the rapidly growing counter-revolutionary movement in southern Russia before it had become a challenge too great to meet; they must apply a solution to the economic crisis which held the nation in its grip. So long as the Bolsheviks had been the opposition party, it had been easy for them to criticize the policies of the Government and to make attractive promises to the people. They were now confronted with the necessity of bending the vast government machinery inherited from Kerensky to their will.

In March, 1917, after the first revolution, the functionaries of the central state offices and the local authorities throughout Russia had accepted the leadership of the new Government. The Bolsheviks, however, met only with resistance. Everywhere regular government employees refused to coöperate with the Soviet Government and in Petrograd state employees went out on strike. Indeed, very few of the educated classes anywhere were willing to accept the radical Bolshevik *coup d'état,* whereas most of them had been sympathetic to the Kerensky reforms. Unlike the soldiers and workmen, the intellectuals and the middle classes regarded the Bolsheviks with the utmost distrust; in the eyes of many they were simply agents of the Central Powers who were intent upon the betrayal of both Russia and the Allied cause, a cause to which the *bourgeoisie* in Russia was still devoted. Moreover, almost everyone considered the new Government a wild swing of the political pendulum which would soon be corrected. It seemed that the Bolsheviks would be incapable of holding power for more than two or three weeks, and government employees everywhere felt that it was neither wise nor necessary to throw in their lot with a temporary *régime.* It was enough for them to sit tight and wait for the return of sanity.

In Petrograd it was hoped that Moscow would not fall to the Bolsheviks. In Moscow, meanwhile, it was hoped that army Headquarters or the Don Cossacks would assume control and put an end to these political adventurers and their antics. The strike of government workers was an expression of these vague hopes. Another gesture of the same sort came in the refusal of the employees of the State Bank to obey the orders of the new Government, a stoppage before which the Bolsheviks were nearly helpless since they were totally inexperienced in bureaucratic matters. By and large, the middle classes were content to make gestures and to wait for some redeeming force to sweep them back into power. They waited in vain; there was no determined organization to rescue them, and the expected uprising did not occur. The Soviet Government continued to extend its power and the Council of People's Commissars gradually mastered the situation. New men from the Bolshevik party took over the important posts, some of the recalcitrant government employees were dismissed, and others, moving with the times, submitted and entered the service of the new Government. Within a few weeks the governmental machinery of Moscow and Petrograd was firmly under Bolshevik control.

The Bolsheviks extended their authority from Moscow and Petrograd to the provinces, for the most part without exercising force. The fact that the Soviet Government was a dictatorship of the Communist party was evident only in the capitals. The Bolshevik revolution officially consisted merely in the transfer of power from the Provisional Government to the Soviets, which in the provinces merely meant that the local soviets took the place of the Commissars of the Provisional Government. At this time the authority of the Soviets extended only to the towns; and the village communities, which even under the Provisional Government had shown opposition, were now entirely independent of the central Government and reverted to the rule of the traditional village assembly. Accordingly, the forms of local government varied from province to province and dependence of local soviets upon the national Government was purely nominal until the Bolsheviks gained control of each soviet. This was accomplished in time by dispatching agitators and armed supporters to the sections where support was needed.

The chief instrument used by the Government to suppress disorder was the political police organization. By order of Lenin on December 20, 1917, the Extraordinary Commission for the Suppression of Counter-Revolution (Cheka) came into existence. Under the leadership of Felix Dzerjinsky, the "Red Terror" was proclaimed against all enemies of the state. During the winter of 1917–18 the Cheka claimed a considerable number of victims, but it was not until the autumn of 1918—following the attempts against the lives of the Bolshevik leaders, the manifestations of counter-revolution in the south, and the intervention of the Allies in Russia—that the "Red Terror" reached its height. The atrocities which were committed in its name during this period were not accidental abuses of authority. The "Red Terror" was a recognized and integral element in the process of subjecting the nation to the Bolshevik will. Lenin himself declared, "No dictatorship of the proletariat is to be thought of without terror and violence." Officially the activities of the Cheka were directed at the *bourgeoisie* alone. "We are not waging war against separate individuals; we are exterminating the *bourgeoisie* as a class," said Latsis, one of the leaders. As a matter of fact, however, the Cheka exterminated without discrimination all of those suspected of opposing the Soviet Government. The victims were not confined to the upper or middle classes but included peasants and occasionally even workers as well. The Cheka moved without compunction and ruthlessly. The taking of hostages from the non-communist groups of a community was a favorite method. In the event of an uprising against the Government—and especially if an attempted assassination of communist leaders occurred—the hostages, who were commonly non-political people who themselves had done nothing to oppose state authority, were shot without hesitation. Nor was the Cheka unwilling to resort to torture to obtain confessions or information which it considered necessary. Besides the executions ordered by the Cheka, individual Bolshevik groups in the provinces not infrequently took the law in their own hands and dealt death where they felt it warranted—as in the case of the collective execution of officers in Sevastopol in the spring of 1918. The active period of the "Red Terror" was a bloody one in which the normal processes of justice were supplanted by an all-powerful organization operating on a system of suspicion and summary judgment. Thousands suffered for the crime of opposing the dictatorship and more thousands completely innocent of any political activities suffered with them.

In addition to the political police who were used against dissident groups, the Soviet Government had the active support of the "Red Army," the "Workers' and Peasants' Army" which was organized on February 23, 1918. It consisted at first largely of hired troops recruited from the ranks of the old army and young workmen; the soldiers received good pay and special rations and could be counted upon loyally and zealously to carry out government orders. The discipline of this body was much better than that of the demoralized Imperial Army which was completely disorganized after the opening of peace negotiations and which was finally demobilized after the Brest-Litovsk peace. Using to the utmost the Cheka, the Red Army, and whatever other instruments they could bend to their will, the Bolsheviks succeeded during the winter of 1917–18 in entirely subjecting the governmental machinery to their control.

The solution of the economic crises facing the country was a more serious problem. Not only did the economic difficulties remain unsolved but as time went on they grew increasingly critical. The value of the ruble diminished; prices rose to higher levels than ever before; the condition of the railways became desperate; industrial production slumped after the seizure of control by committees of workers. The only problem partially solved by the Bolsheviks was that of supplying certain groups of the urban population with food, particularly members of the Communist party, employees of Soviet institutions, and workers. This was accomplished by requisitioning all the food available in the cities and all deliveries of foodstuffs from the country and distributing it by means of a system of ration cards to certain categories of inhabitants. Members of the Communist party and workers were placed in the best-fed category; government employees in the medium; and craftsmen and the unemployed in the third group. All others were declared "unproductive elements" and as such were not objects of government care. The average ration was about half a pound of bread a day. It was difficult to purchase any food in excess of the ration by legal means, and to be deprived of a card meant almost certain death by starvation. These circumstances delivered the city population into the hands of the Bolsheviks, for it was they, of course, who controlled the food cards which had virtually become permits to live.

The distribution of food was, however, only one side of the difficulty. The first problem was to obtain the food in the villages. Because of the Provisional Government's inability to supply manufactured goods or to pay for produce in stable currency, the peasants had already refused to coöperate with the Kerensky *régime.* The Soviet Government was even less capable than its predecessor of satisfying the demands of the peasantry. The "Decree of Land" of November 8 had been an attempt to appease the dissatisfied peasantry, but its importance was largely documentary and it had little effect on the attitude of the peasants who on their own initiative had already partitioned a substantial part of the landowners' estates. When the Government found that it could not enlist the voluntary coöperation of the peasants, it did not hesitate to take the grain from them by force. Special "food battalions" of Red Guards and Cheka employees were organized and sent into the villages, and, though the peasants tried to hide their grain or even to destroy it, some quantity was secured and shipped to the cities. The measures which the Government was forced to use in solving the food problem of the city population inevitably produced another problem, the natural and widespread opposition of the peasants. In time this feeling of resentment grew into armed resistance, and the Bolsheviks then had to face a serious threat to their authority precisely in the regions in which they were weakest, in the provinces remote from the center of power.

3.

THE Russian people were so occupied by and absorbed in the catastrophic events of the autumn of 1917 that the war in Europe was almost driven from their minds. The mass of humanity within the boundaries of the former Russian Empire had been profoundly stirred by the national crisis and by this time they were seething with the passions generated by their own experiences. Some hailed the Bolshevik upheaval as the dawn of a new and better era; others cursed the new dictators; all were beset by constant worries about the problems of getting sufficient food and fuel to survive the winter. The Russians were overwhelmed by their own desperate circumstances, and, for all except the more conscientious army officers and a limited cross section of the intelligentsia and the middle class, World War I was psychologically over.

From the legalistic point of view, one may well charge the Russians at that time with deserting the Allies and thus giving the Kaiser one more chance to win the war for Greater Germany. In logic and jurisprudence there is no adequate answer for such an accusation. But one must not forget that in those tumultuous days the Russians had passed the stage in which scholarly logic or legalistic reasoning could materially influence their actions. Finding themselves in the vortex of the greatest social revolution that had ever swept across a nation, they were borne along by elemental feelings and primitive emotions, by idealistic dreams of a Utopian future and violent hatred for their oppressors. For the Russians nothing mattered but the revolution. Russia had become a world in itself, though at the same time in their naïve enthusiasm the Russians believed that the peoples of all nations were prepared to accept the new creed and march with them toward a new world. Yes, it was true there was still a German front; but would not the Germans themselves understand that the play was over? And did not the new Government—the People's Government—promise an immediate peace, not only for Russia but for the whole world?

Though the Soviet leaders were absorbed in "deepening the revolution" during this period, they could not avoid the practical problems of government and the insistent demands of the people. Having promised the Russians peace, they now had to deliver peace; theoretical declarations such as the "Decree of Peace" were no longer sufficient, and it now became necessary in one way or another to approach both the Germans and the Allies.

On November 20, 1917, the Soviet Government ordered army Headquarters to propose to the enemy a cessation of hostilities. The Commander-in-Chief, General Dukhonin, refusing to carry out the order, replied that this was the task of the Government and not of the army. The next day he was dismissed and Ensign[1] Krylenko was appointed Commander-in-Chief in his place. On November 22 Trotsky addressed a note to all the Allied ambassadors in Petrograd proposing "an immediate armistice on all fronts and the immediate opening of peace negotiations." At the same time a similar note was presented to the diplomatic representatives of the neutral nations who were then in the capital. Although the military agents of the Allied Powers in Petrograd immediately protested against the suggestion of a separate peace with Germany, it seems clear that at the time they did not fully realize the seriousness of the

[1] According to the system of rank in the Imperial Russian Army, Ensign (*praporshchik*) was the lowest rank of commissioned officer. It corresponded approximately to the rating of Second Lieutenant in the United States Army.

situation. Some of the representatives appear seriously to have considered the possibilities of the proposal for a general democratic peace, and few of them could bring themselves to believe that the Bolsheviks were quite ready to conclude peace with Germany alone. The belief that Russia could be persuaded to continue the war if she were properly approached was indicated by the visit which Trotsky received on December 1 from the Chief of the American Military Mission, General Judson, who declared "that the time of protests and threats addressed to the Soviet Government had passed, if that time had ever existed."

As a matter of fact, the negotiations for an armistice between the Central Powers and Soviet Russia began on December 3, only two days after General Judson's visit. The November 25 elections to the Constituent Assembly—elections which had been called by a decree of the Provisional Government and had not been cancelled by the new Government—showed that the Bolsheviks were in a decided minority. They controlled only 168 votes in a body of 703 deputies, the majority of whom were members of the Socialist Revolutionary party. It is probable that the results of the election convinced the Germans of the unstable position of the Bolsheviks and alarmed them sufficiently to make them willing to hasten peace negotiations.

The opening of the armistice conversations was no more than the open recognition of the realities of the situation, for the Russian Army had already ceased to exist as an effective organization. The former Commander-in-Chief, General Dukhonin, had been killed, and his Bolshevik successor, Krylenko, had taken over complete authority at Headquarters. The final disintegration of the army was under way, with the masses of soldiers under arms in western Russia and on the Caucasian front already abandoning their posts and racing back to their native villages.

On January 18, 1918, while peace negotiations with the Central Powers were still going on, the Constituent Assembly met in Petrograd. The meeting of the Assembly had been postponed by the Bolsheviks in order to gain time to win over sufficient delegates to thwart the Socialist Revolutionaries who, as a majority, were in a position to create difficulties for the Government. The Bolsheviks were determined to exclude opponents who could not be influenced, and as a first step in this direction they arrested all the non-Socialist deputies, two of whom, being ill, were brutally murdered in a hospital. When the remaining non-Bolshevik deputies still refused to acknowledge the Council of People's Commissars as the legal government of Russia, the Bolshevik delegates withdrew from the conference. In the streets demonstrations broke out against the Government, but they were quickly suppressed. At 1.30 on the morning of January 20 the Central Executive Committee of the Soviet issued a decree disbanding the Assembly. The deputies were ejected from their meeting place and a Bolshevik military force guarding the building refused to allow any further sessions.

Though the disbanding of the Constituent Assembly strengthened the Bolsheviks at home by buttressing their control of the government machinery, it weakened their position in the armistice negotiations in Brest-Litovsk. The Germans, no longer afraid of an imminent collapse of the Bolsheviks, now demanded that Russia renounce her control of Poland, Lithuania, Latvia, and Esthonia. In addition, a delegation from Ukraine also came forward to demand the right of self-determination. These proposals were more than the Bolsheviks were prepared to accept, and in a proclamation on January 23 they protested against the German peace conditions. The time for protests had passed. With her army disbanded, Russia was now helpless before the military power of Germany.

To increase the pressure on the Soviet Government and to insure the complete annihilation of Russia as a military power, the Germans encouraged and supported the Ukrainian separatist movement, and on January 28, 1918, Ukraine proclaimed itself an independent republic. Incidentally, both France and Great Britain recognized the independence of the Ukrainian Republic whose birth had been presided over by the Germans. The history of this Ukrainian state is brief, for on February 8 Kiev, the capital, was occupied by Bolshevik troops.

The peace conference at Brest-Litovsk meanwhile dragged on in a deadlock. Trotsky, who was negotiating for the Soviet Government, refused to accept the German conditions, but on February 10 he announced that the war with Germany was at an end and that the Russian Army was demobilized. This sign of despair, curiously enough, again created apprehension in Germany. It suggested the possibility that the Soviets might be turning to some alternative solution of the crisis; in his *Memoirs* General Ludendorff expresses his belief that Trotsky at this time was acting as an instrument of the *Entente.* Whatever the purpose of Trotsky's proclamation it appears to have miscarried, for the German reply was an order to their troops to advance into Russia. The Soviet Government was forced to abandon its resistance to the peace terms which had been offered and on March 3 signed the Brest-Litovsk treaty.

The peace conditions were disastrous for Russia. Eastern Poland, Ukraine, Lithuania, Esthonia, and Latvia were separated from Russia and taken over by Germany, and after the defeat of the Central Powers the Allies recognized the three Baltic states as independent republics. Previously, in December, 1917, the Soviet Government itself had recognized Finland's status as an independent state. In the south, part of Transcaucasia was ceded to Turkey. Russia's losses were enormous—26 per cent of her total population; 27 per cent of her arable land; 32 per cent of her average crops; 26 per cent of her railway system; 33 per cent of her manufacturing industries; 73 per cent of her iron industries; 75 per cent of her coal fields. In addition to all this, she was to be forced to pay a large war indemnity. Such were the results of a war in which Russian casualties were about 2,500,000 soldiers killed and mutilated.

In spite of the disaster which had overtaken the nation, the Bolsheviks were able to realize some satisfaction from the turn of events. By signing the peace treaty they had gained for themselves a breathing spell which they badly needed and were thus able to build up their own strength so that it was possible for them to break formally with the Moderate Socialists. A small but significant step was taken by the Seventh Convention which approved the ratification of the Brest-Litovsk treaty when it adopted a new name for the party. Until then known as the Russian Social Democratic Party, Bolsheviks, it was now renamed Russian Communist Party, Bolsheviks. The change was a concrete indication that the political dividing line which formerly had been drawn between the *bourgeois* parties and the socialist parties had now been shifted leftward to establish the boundary between the Communists and the Socialists. The change meant, too, that the new *régime* had completed the consolidation of its position, and, to add a final touch to the break with the past, the capital was soon afterward transferred from Petrograd to Moscow.

4.

Though the Soviet Government was able to establish its control over stunned and demoralized Russia with almost incredible rapidity, it could not, of course, completely eradicate all the potential sources of opposition. In order to seize and hold power the Bolsheviks had resorted to harsh and ruthless means which inevitably bred discontent and resentment in certain sections of the country and among various groups of the population. As the feeling of indignation spread in widening circles about the Government, opposition groups were organized and gradually established interconnections. By merging their forces and by recruiting dissident elements antagonized by the new Government, some of these opposition groups in time became strong enough to engage in open revolt against the Soviet Government. The Bolsheviks were thus confronted with yet another crisis—civil war.

The causes of the civil war were many and complex. In the political sphere, the Bolsheviks had openly violated the principle of democracy by disbanding the Constituent Assembly. It was only natural that the duly elected deputies—most of them Social Revolutionaries—not only protested against the action of the Soviet Government but also attempted to form a government of their own in opposition to that of the Bolsheviks. On the military side, a number of the officers of the Imperial Army refused to accept the German peace which they considered detrimental to Russian interests and a betrayal of Russia's allies—a point of view which was very generally shared by intellectuals, especially the university students. This group of officers eventually created the so-called Volunteer Army in the south and set up contacts with the Don and Kuban Cossacks who traditionally had existed as a separate and privileged group within the Russian Empire. Enjoying a measure of self-government and being somewhat wealthier than the average Russian peasant, the Cossacks were in no mood to submit to communist rule without a struggle, and from the very beginning of the conflict became the mainstay of the opposition in the south. Furthermore, certain national groups such as the Ukrainians, the Georgians, the Kalmyks, and others saw in the revolution and subsequent disorganization the opportunity to separate from Russia and establish themselves as autonomous states and were consequently willing to support a movement against the central Government.

As we have already seen, the Government had incurred the enmity of the peasants—the largest single group in the Russian population—when it had embarked upon the policy of outright confiscation of food and the application of drastic measures of suppression. Gratified by the early enactment of the "Decree of Land," the peasants had at first tacitly accepted Soviet rule, in spite of the fact that the Social Revolutionary party had previously developed more support among the peasantry. By the spring of 1918, however, nearly all the available land—including both the large estates of the gentry and the small individual farms created by Stolypin's legislation—had already been divided among the village communities, increasing by only a third the earlier peasant allotment. As the period of free adjustment came to an end and as government agencies, reaching out from the central areas of power, began to apply increasingly stringent controls, the attitude of passive toleration among the peasants began to evaporate. The Government resorted to more and more drastic steps in an effort to provide the cities with food, and the peasants became increasingly reluctant to part with their grain without recompense—recompense which the Government was in no position to provide.

Driven by the absolute necessity to supply food for the army and the city proletariat and faced by the stubborn resistance of the peasants who must provide that food, the Soviet Government had to find an immediate solution for the dilemma. If the Government were to survive, the peasant opposition had to be broken, and a method was therefore devised to neutralize the power of the whole peasant class by dividing the village population into separate categories and setting one group against the other. This division was accomplished by the creation of "Committees of the Poor." The village inhabitants were classified in two groups, one composed of richer peasants (*kulaki,* rich peasants, and *seredniaki,* middle peasants) and the other of poor peasants (*bedniaki,* those who possessed no cattle or stores of grain). The Bolsheviks then delegated authority in village affairs to the poor peasants, who were to form committees to see that the richer peasants did not hide grain from the government collectors and were empowered to seize any surplus grain or cattle discovered. By these measures the Bolsheviks succeeded effectively in planting the "class warfare" of communism in the villages.

The slogan of "loot the looters" with which rich and poor peasant alike had justified the seizure of land from the large landowners was now turned against many of those who had at first profited by it, peasants who owned no more than a few acres of land and two or three head of cattle. The Committees of the Poor worked with a will and within a short time had brought about a serious disorganization in agriculture and great hardships for all classes. For the Bolsheviks, however, this did accomplish one purpose. The revolutionary struggle which had thus been transported to the very heart of the village community completely absorbed the powers of the whole peasant class, and the Government was free to proceed with other plans. In the villages the Committees of the Poor had become the chief support of the Bolsheviks.

In view of the Government's difficulties and the means the Bolsheviks had chosen to handle the situation, the Whites would seem to have been provided with ample opportunity to secure for themselves the support of the "rich" and the "middle" peasants. Almost without exception, however, they failed to exploit their advantages. When they expelled the Reds from an area, the White governments usually re-established the laws that had been valid in the pre-November period. This meant, of course, that the former owners of the large estates were free to return and evict the people who had occupied their land—a step which aroused the indignation of all groups of peasants, rich and poor alike. The peasants were, therefore, caught between two forces, neither of which they were willing to support. In certain agricultural areas they occasionally tried to organize a government of their own which would be neither Red nor White, a "Green" government, as it was sometimes called, intended to serve their interests and protect them from the other contenders. On the whole, however, the peasants remained unpredictable, moving from side to side as the occasion demanded, first supporting the Whites to get rid of the Reds and then turning to the Reds to help drive out the Whites.

One rather curious political fact emerges as we study this period. Though most of the White governments were definitely conservative and though they sprang up in different parts of Russia, were organized along various political lines, and were led by representatives of many different groups, none of them ever attempted to reestablish Tsarism. This may have been partially accounted for by the fact that the overthrow of Tsarism in 1917 had been legalized by the last Tsar himself when he abdicated in favor of his brother Michael. Michael had never accepted the throne, however, and he later disappeared, having been kidnapped and supposedly killed by the revolutionaries. Nicholas II and his wife and children were brutally murdered by the Bolsheviks in Ekaterinburg (now called Sverdlovsk) on July 16, 1918, and other members of the Imperial family were either killed or escaped to exile. Grand Duke Nicholas, the former Commander-in-Chief of the Russian armies, was the only one of the Grand Dukes remaining who enjoyed any real or widespread popularity, but he would not think of accepting the throne. Grand Duke Cyril, who was later to assume the Imperial title among the émigrés, was too cautious to risk taking the lead in Russia in the midst of a civil war. Among the other Grand Dukes there were probably some who would gladly have accepted an offer of the title, but nobody cared to support their claims. Thus it seems that one of the chief reasons that there was no effective movement for a restoration at the time of the civil war was the lack of a suitable candidate. There were other reasons too. At no time did the wide masses of the population exhibit any enthusiasm for the idea of a return of the monarchy. Finally, the most influential leaders of the White armies themselves had no monarchistic inclinations, and those among their followers who had such sympathies were afraid to espouse them openly.

Contrary to the general opinion, which was particularly widespread in the United States, the Whites were not Tsarists, certainly not officially so. The Samara Government of the Members of the Constituent Assembly was clearly republican and even moderately socialist in tone. In the event of victory, it was the intention of the two strongest leaders of the White armies, General Denikin in the south and Admiral Kolchak in Siberia, to establish a strong military government for the transition period and then to convoke a National Assembly. Throughout the whole period, the main struggle of the Whites was against socialism and communism rather than against the constitutional or republican form of government.

5.

The underlying issues and the course of the civil war itself were greatly complicated by foreign intervention. It seems to be a historic law that in a conflict of such range and magnitude as that of the First World War no country bound by alliances can with impunity break off hostilities before the general end of the war. While both the Russian Government and the Russian people imagined that they had succeeded in withdrawing from the slaughter, actually the Germans and the Allies continued to fight over Russia's body on Russian soil. The Allies were greatly irritated by the cancellation of Russia's foreign debts and obligations which was announced by the Soviet Government in February, 1918, and they were even more indignant, of course, about the separate peace which the Soviets had concluded with Germany. Most of the Allied statesmen refused to recognize the peace even after the Soviets had signed the Brest-Litovsk treaty, and proceeded with plans to reestablish the Eastern Front with or without the consent of the Soviet Government and, if necessary, even against the will of the Russian people. This determination went to such lengths that at one time the French even suggested a plan whereby Japan would send her troops through Siberia to fight the Germans, a plan which failed to materialize chiefly because of the opposition of the United States.

Besides these general problems about the attitude of the Soviets, there were certain specific tasks in Russia which demanded the Allies' immediate attention. By the time of the revolution, huge stores of ammunition which had been bought by Imperial Russia from the United States, Great Britain, and Japan had accumulated in Russia's two northern ports, Murmansk and Archangel, and in Vladivostok on the Pacific. The Allies certainly had no desire to see this vast amount of precious material fall into the hands of the Bolsheviks. In addition to the danger that the revolutionaries would take over the supplies, the Germans were now in a position to threaten the capture of the stores in Murmansk. Early in 1918 a civil war between the Finnish Reds and Whites had started, and the Whites, under General Mannerheim, had asked for German assistance. With German help the Reds had soon been crushed, and German troops were now well along in a drive northward toward Murmansk.

It was obviously necessary for the Allies to act quickly, and in April, 1918, Allied troops landed at Murmansk and, a little later, at Archangel.

There was certainly no danger that the Germans would penetrate as far as Vladivostok, yet the Allies were eager to lay hands on the stores in that port as well. A suitable pretext was therefore produced. It was suggested that, according to information available to the Allies, the Soviet Government was believed to be releasing German and Magyar prisoners from the Siberian camps in which they had been confined and arming them for attack against the Allies. Subsequent thorough investigation proved these rumors to have been fabrications: the number of prisoners actually freed was shown to have been insignificant and, in addition, only those who accepted communism and agreed to join the Red Army had been liberated. Nevertheless, Allied contingents intended to forestall this non-existent threat began landing in Vladivostok in April, 1918. By September 15, 1919, there were in the Russian Far East 60,000 Japanese troops, 8,477 Americans, 1,429 British, 1,400 Italians, and 1,076 French.

It must be noted that there was by no means complete agreement between the Allies about the objectives of the intervention as a whole. While originally the motive of guarding the military stores against possible German seizure was kept in the foreground, at a later date the British and French both established close connections with the anti-Bolshevik forces in Russia and talks about a crusade against communism were begun. The attitude of the United States was somewhat different. Considering the presence of American troops in Siberia primarily as a check to Japanese aspirations to establish a base of their own in that area, President Wilson instructed the American commanders to remain neutral in the Russian civil war and to give direct assistance only to the Czechoslovaks. However, since the Czechs themselves were in active opposition to the Bolsheviks until November, 1918, it was difficult to preserve actual neutrality.

The Czech anabasis was one of the most spectacular episodes in the whole course of the civil war. Among the Austrian soldiers captured by the Russians prior to the revolution there had been a substantial number of Czechs who, as subjects of the Austrian emperor, had been conscripted and sent to the front. Inspired by the hope of establishing an independent Czech state, many of them had agreed to form a special brigade to assist the Russian Army and in the summer of 1917 had taken part in the Kerensky offensive against the Central Powers. After Russia's withdrawal from the war, these Czechoslovak troops, who at that time numbered forty thousand, requested that they be transferred to the western front to continue the struggle against Germany and her allies, a movement which required transporting them across the whole width of Siberia as the first leg of their journey around the world. In May, 1918, the first units of the Czech troops reached Vladivostok with the balance of the force strung out across the continent behind them, the last sections not yet having crossed the Volga. Apparently under the influence of the German Ambassador in Moscow, Count Mirbach, Trotsky then ordered the Czechs to disarm. They agreed, but when a new order came from Moscow directing that they again be interned as prisoners of war, they rose against the Bolsheviks. During the early part of June, 1918, they took possession of all the principal cities between Samara and Vladivostok, a stroke which was soon followed by political revolt against the Bolsheviks throughout all of eastern Russia and Siberia.

While the Allies were intervening both in the north and in the Far East—and, through the Czechs, along the whole Trans-Siberian Railroad as well—the Germans lost no time in occupying the southern regions. To be sure, it was not technically an intervention in Russian affairs, since by the treaty of Brest-Litovsk the Soviet Government had recognized the independence of Ukraine. Actually, however, the Ukrainian Reds who were now compelled to retreat before this new German onslaught were part of the all-Russian communist movement. Coming officially to Ukraine in response to the émigré Ukrainian Government's call for assistance, German troops quickly overcame the scattered resistance of the poorly organized Red Army and occupied Kiev while the Austrians captured Odessa in April, 1918. In a further German advance to the Don, the city of Rostov fell on May 8. Thereupon Ataman Krasnov entered into negotiations with the invaders who, anxious to secure an opportunity for the economic exploitation of south Russia, willingly agreed to support him with arms and ammunition in his struggle against the Bolsheviks. While all this was in progress in the south, it is interesting to note that in Moscow the Germans, through their first ambassador, Count Mirbach, were expressing their friendship toward the Soviet Government. On April 23 the German forces of occupation concluded with the

Ukrainian Government an economic treaty which secured for Germany the rights to the rich resources they coveted. They re-established the landowners on their estates and soon accomplished the overthrow of the half-socialistic Ukrainian Government. A little later General Skoropadsky was proclaimed head of a government which was in reality a puppet of Germany.

Though Germany may have had some semblance of a legal justification for the occupation of Ukraine, in the capture of Rostov in the Don area, the seizure of the whole of Crimea, and the excursion into Transcaucasia it clearly and openly violated the boundaries of the Soviet state it had officially recognized. German expansion in the south was a cynical recognition of the fact that the Soviet Government at the time was unable to resist encroachments by force of arms.

6.

THOUGH the total amount of territory subject to the control of the Soviet Government was reduced by the outbreak of counter-revolutionary movements in the south, the southeast, and the east, within that circle of enemies the Bolsheviks had, by the middle of 1918, extended their power not only to the towns but to the rural districts as well. In order to regain the regions in revolt, the communists now began the reorganization of the Red Army which was still not an efficient fighting force. Within a few months the whole structure was thoroughly overhauled. Trotsky was appointed Chief of the Military Revolutionary Committee—the War Office—and in June, 1918, the Government determined to conscript a new army on the basis of compulsory service. The Soldiers' Committees which had been formed in 1917 were abolished and replaced by "communist cells," directed by political commissars and composed of party members, which were charged with the maintenance of strict discipline.

Generals of the old Imperial Army and officers of the former general staff were given the task of reorganizing the Red Army according to the pattern of the army of the Tsar, and, though some communists were promoted from the ranks by the Bolsheviks, the majority of the commissions in the new Red Army were held by line officers of the old army. Even the High Command of the Red Army during the civil war was largely in the hands of these trained soldiers—men like Colonel S. S. Kamenev[2] of the old Imperial General Staff—though there also arose new leaders among whom Lieutenant Tukhachevsky, Sergeant Budenny, and Commander Frunze were the best known. Lack of other means of support, the habit of professional military service, and the fear of the Cheka were perhaps the main reasons which impelled officers of the demobilized Imperial Army to accept service in the Red Army. After they had enlisted, it was a matter of self-preservation to serve in good faith, for in the event of their capture they faced reprisals by the anti-Bolshevik forces—and, indeed, many Red officers were shot when they fell into the hands of the Whites. In addition, these men well knew that treason to the Soviet Government would entail swift retaliation against members of their families who were held by the Cheka as hostages for their loyalty.

Paradoxically enough, it was the civil war itself which transformed the Red Army into a fighting organization and the Soviet Government into a strong centralized power. Even though the conscription of 1918 succeeded in raising only half the number of men called, by November of that year the Soviets had an army of four hundred thousand men under competent leadership. The efforts of the anti-Bolsheviks had actually produced a result diametrically opposed to that which they had intended. By constituting a threat to the stability of the Bolshevik *régime* they had directly provoked the formation of a strong military power in Russia subject to the will of the Soviet Government.

The Don basin and north Caucasian area were the main theaters of military operations in the spring and summer of 1918. During the winter of 1917–18 General Alexeiev and General Kornilov—each of whom had at one time served as Commander-in-Chief of the Russian armies—began the organization of a force to oust the Bolsheviks. Immediately after the November revolution Alexeiev left Petrograd for the Don where he met his personal friend Kaledin, Ataman of the Don Cossacks, who permitted him to recruit a volunteer army in that area, provided that the organization was kept secret. Kornilov, who had been imprisoned by Kerensky after his rebellious attempt of September, 1917, escaped a few weeks after

[2] S. S. Kamenev should not be confused with L. B. Kamenev (Rosenfeld), a prominent communist leader who subsequently became a leading member of the opposition.

the Bolshevik uprising and joined Alexeiev in the Don region. While these two were building their officers' organization in the Don, another officers' division, completely independent of the first, was being formed behind the Red Army on the Rumanian frontier. Both groups of officers who thus entered into the struggle against the Soviet Government had dual reasons for their actions. They were, of course, impelled to a large extent by political convictions which made the Bolsheviks anathema to them. In addition there were professional reasons for their opposition: the aspirations which they still had to rebuild the old Russian Army and continue the struggle against Germany in order to restore Russian national honor in the eyes of the Allies, who, they felt, had been basely betrayed by the Soviet Government.

The Volunteer Army, however, did not grow rapidly. Only about seventy-five recruits per day enlisted, most of them officers, cadets, students, and high-school boys. The army had no guns, rifles, or ammunition, and the uncertain funds it received in private donations from sympathizers in Moscow and other cities dribbled in through difficult secret channels; in all, only about five million depreciated rubles were received by General Alexeiev during the winter of 1917–18. Handicapped as it was, it was not until the early months of 1918 that the Volunteer Army was prepared to open a campaign against the Bolsheviks. The Supreme Command of the anti-Bolshevik movement was at that time delegated to a triumvirate composed of Alexeiev, the principal promoter of the group, Kornilov, Commander-in-Chief of military operations, and Kaledin, Ataman of the Don Cossacks. However, when the Don Cossacks showed themselves unwilling at that time to take a firm stand against the Soviet forces, Ataman Kaledin committed suicide on February 11, 1918. Without the Cossack support which Kaledin had promised, the Volunteer Army, now a ragged group of no more than four thousand poorly armed and ill-equipped men without funds, had no alternative but to retreat southward into the Kuban valley and along the northern slopes of the Caucasian Mountains.

Under the leadership of Kornilov the Volunteer Army on February 22 began a drive into the Kuban district with the object of joining the isolated Cossack forces which had risen there against the Bolsheviks. After more than a month of heavy fighting against enormously superior Red Army forces, Kornilov finally managed to reach the small Kuban army, and, having united the two groups, decided to attack Ekaterinodar (now called Krasnodar), the Headquarters of the Bolshevik Army in the Kuban. The first assault failed, and on the day before the second attempt Kornilov was killed. This second attack, under the leadership of General Denikin who replaced Kornilov as Commander-in-Chief, was also beaten off and the Volunteer Army was forced to retreat from Ekaterinodar into the Don valley where the Bolshevik *régime* had become very unpopular. In spite of the fact that Denikin's army had suffered a severe defeat and sustained heavy losses, because of the steady influx of volunteers it was now larger than it had been at the beginning of the campaign, numbering more than five thousand fighting men in addition to over fifteen hundred wounded who were evacuated with the retreating forces.

In the middle of April the Don Cossacks, who had previously refused to join the opposition, rose against the Bolsheviks and drove them out of Novocherkassk. The city was taken and retaken several times before it was finally secured by the Cossacks, thanks to the timely arrival of a brigade of volunteers who had fought a difficult campaign across the whole of southern Russia from Rumania.

The anti-Bolshevik forces, though somewhat successful militarily at this time, were unable to establish effective coöperation between themselves. On May 11 a Cossack assembly elected General Krasnov Ataman of the Don Cossacks, and he, as we have already seen, hoping to get arms and munitions, entered into negotiations with the Germans. Denikin, the leader of the other important group, was ardently pro-Ally and his feelings were also shared by the Kuban Cossacks. Yet, in spite of the lack of coördination between the Volunteer Army and the Kuban Army on the one hand and the Don Army on the other, during the summer of 1918 the three of them somehow succeeded in clearing the Bolsheviks out of both the Don and the Kuban areas. The Soviet Government was not in a position at the time to throw more troops into the south, for its attention was now occupied by the Czechoslovak rebellion beyond the Volga which was already having important repercussions both in Siberia and in the Volga region.

The plot to overthrow the Soviet Government in Siberia was organized through the close coöperation of two opposition groups, secret associations of ex-officers and the Socialist Revolutionary party which had been excluded from power by the Bolsheviks. Siberia was fertile ground for the opposition. Among the Ural Cossacks there was widespread discontent with Soviet policies, and the Government itself had stirred up the animosity of the peasants by its program for the confiscation of grain. After the Czech rebellion, many of the employees of the powerful peasant coöperatives—the majority of whom were Socialist Revolutionaries—entered into close relations with the Czechs, who were themselves predominantly Socialists. In Samara (now called Kuibyshev) a government composed of thirty-four socialist members of the Constituent Assembly was formed under the leadership of V. M. Chernov who had been president of the 1918 Assembly. This government, though weak, attempted to organize a "People's Army," a fighting force which proved to have all the defects of Kerensky's army. It gained little help from the peasants who refused to trust it because the agrarian program of the Socialists was scarcely distinguishable from the program of the Bolsheviks against which they were revolting.

Although the People's Army was able to enlist the support of the Czechs and the local Cossacks and succeeded in August, 1918, in establishing a fighting line between eastern and western Russia along the Volga and Kama rivers, the deterioration of the anti-Bolshevik forces soon began. The Samara Government had a brief success when, in capturing the city of Kazan, it also seized the $317,000,000 gold reserve of the State Bank of Russia, but the army was soon forced to retreat before a Red Army counterattack. Meanwhile, another government composed of more conservative elements was formed at Omsk and with the support of the peasants' coöperatives in Siberia gradually gained power. This Siberian Government, as it was called, after the defeat of the People's Army in the fall of 1918 took command of the anti-Bolshevik forces over the whole length of Siberia up to Lake Baikal. On September 23 the Samara Government officially united with the Siberian Government in the formation of a five-man Directorate in which the Socialist Revolutionaries were the dominant element. Efforts were to be made to secure General Alexeiev, who was then in southern Russia, as a leader, but he died before any definite moves could be made.

7.

In the autumn of 1918 the position of the Soviet Government seemed quite desperate. Of all the land previously held within the empire, the Bolsheviks now exercised control over only the central part of European Russia. The balance of old Russia was split into small segments divided against each other and the mother state. In the south, Ukraine was under German and Austrian occupation; the Don valley was independent of the Bolsheviks and friendly to the Germans; the Kuban area had been cleared of Bolshevik forces and was opposed to the Germans; the southern Ural region and Siberia were under the control of the Czechs and the Directorate—a potential threat to Germany; the extreme north and the extreme east had been occupied by Allied forces. Russia, under the Soviets, had been reduced to the boundaries of Muscovy of the early sixteenth century. At that moment, when Soviet fortunes were at their lowest ebb, the World War ended with the capitulation of Germany on November 11, 1918.

The armistice produced unexpected results in Russian affairs. On the surface, this sudden turn of events seemed to favor the policy of those among the Allied leaders who had been thinking of a crusade against communism. The whole military might of the Allies seemed now to be available for a crushing blow against the Bolsheviks who, in the eyes of the victors, had betrayed the common cause by signing a separate peace with Germany in March, 1918. And yet, the blow was not to fall. On the contrary, the Bolsheviks greatly profited by the collapse of the Central Powers. Like the Russian Army of the year before, the Germans who had occupied Ukraine and propped up the ephemeral Ukrainian Government now withdrew from this territory in a state of complete demoralization. The anti-Bolsheviks hoped that after the Allies had compelled the Germans to evacuate southern Russia, the Allies themselves would occupy that area rather than let it be exposed to the Bolshevik armies, but contrary to the expectation of the Whites no Allied troops made their appearance. Since the Ukrainian Government under Skoropadsky had not been allowed by the Germans to maintain any armed troops of its own, within a few weeks after the evacuation of the German army of occupation it fell before the socialist Ukrainian leader Petlura. Detachments of French troops did occupy Odessa on December 18, 1918, but by that time the opportunity to seize the control relinquished by the Germans had already been lost. By then considerable force would have been necessary to reconquer southern Russia, and the Allies were in no position to undertake another military campaign.

A number of circumstances made any large-scale Allied intervention impossible. The soldiers of the Allied armies were tired and anxious to return to the ways of peace; they were certainly not eager to enter into a new war. Complications had arisen between the British and French who were unable to reach any agreement on the policy to be pursued in this area. Though they differed in their evaluation of the forces available to them in southern Russia, neither the British nor the French had anything like complete confidence in the anti-Bolshevik movement with which they would have had to work. This division between the Allies most concerned in the situation resulted in scattered and disorganized action.

The whole of southern Russia was divided by the Allies into a British and a French zone of influence roughly separated by the Don area. On their side the British attempted no military operations on any substantial scale but instead limited themselves to an occupation of the Transcaucasian area. At the end of November, 1918, a British detachment occupied Baku, the center of the oil industry on the Caspian Sea, and a month later took Batum, the terminus of the Transcaucasian pipeline. While the British did not themselves engage in serious military operations against the Russians, assistance in the form of war supplies and arms was provided to the Volunteer Army by representatives of the British Government. In the territory under their control, however, the French attempted more aggressive action. On March 13, 1919, they proclaimed themselves the supreme authority in the Odessa area and with the support of local Russian forces began operations against the Bolsheviks. This policy of direct attack against the Soviet armies resulted in complete failure. The French soldiers soon fell under the influence of Bolshevik propaganda and refused to fight against the Red Army. The French Command was at last unable to trust even its own troops, and in time a comparatively feeble Bolshevik army drove them completely out of south Russia.

The armistice on the western front also affected subsequent developments in Siberia. With the termination of the World War the

Allies of course lost interest in the creation of a front along the Volga, and the Czech troops who had been fighting in that area lost heart in their battle with the Bolsheviks, which to them had been nothing more than an episode in their struggle against the Central Powers. They were with difficulty induced to remain in Siberia to protect the Trans-Siberian Railroad while the Allies tried to settle their difficulties with the Russians by diplomatic means. During the winter of 1918–19 the Russian situation was discussed at the Peace Conference in Paris. On January 22, 1919, President Wilson issued an invitation "to every organized group that is now exercising or attempting to exercise political authority or military control in Russia" to send representatives to a conference to be held on the island of Prinkipo in the Sea of Marmora, a truce of arms to be operative meanwhile.

Thus, within a few months the desperate situation faced by the Soviet Government had entirely changed. The Bolsheviks as well as the anti-Bolsheviks were now invited to attend the conference and discuss the future of Russia. The Bolsheviks immediately accepted President Wilson's proposal, for such a conference promised them relief from the terrific pressure they were under both from the opposition within the territories they occupied and from the circle of external enemies which had been drawn around them. All of the anti-Bolshevik forces, however, refused the invitation which they considered insulting. They refused to negotiate with a group which had, they felt, usurped political power within the country, betrayed Russia to the Central Powers, and was at the moment pursuing an intolerable policy within the territory under its control. From their point of view the proposed conference would amount to indirect recognition of the Soviet Government by the *Entente* and in itself would give significant moral support to the Bolsheviks.

8.

EVEN after the Soviet Government had been saved by the end of the World War from what seemed imminent destruction, it still had before it the task of subjecting the whole of Russia to its control. Basically its political position had been improved, but the year 1919 proved to be a critical one from the military standpoint. That the Soviet Government was eventually able to emerge victorious was again due in large part to the lack of coöperation between the two principal leaders of the opposition, Denikin and Kolchak, on the one hand, and between Denikin and the Ukrainians on the other. Denikin, a firm believer in centralized government, was politically so inept that he even tried to curtail the autonomy of the Kuban Cossacks who were his loyal allies. Aided by the failures and blunders of its enemies, the Soviet Government was able to act against each of them separately and to defeat each of them in succession.

In a *coup d'état* on November 18, 1918, Kolchak assumed the leadership of the Siberian Government. He was a brave man and, from his point of view, a patriotic one, but he was not fit for the difficult task of being a dictator. Although a capable naval commander, he was neither a land strategist nor a diplomat, and both skills were necessary for success in his position. Diplomatic subtlety was particularly essential if he was to handle the delicate problems which were constantly arising as he sought to organize the support of the Czech legionaries and the Allies. In addition, Kolchak was unacquainted with Siberia and with the people with whom he had to work. His subordinates were not drawn to him by bonds of personal affection as were those of the commanders of the southern Russian armies. His November *coup d'état* had aroused the opposition of the Socialist Revolutionary party which immediately set about undermining his power by adverse propaganda among the Czechs and the peasants.

In spite of the organizational difficulties which hampered him, Kolchak launched an offensive against the Soviet Government, and during the first months of his dictatorship the fortunes of war favored him. The city of Perm was taken, and in March, 1919, Ufa fell. Following the Bolshevik armies which were then in disorderly retreat, Kolchak's forces reached a line running through Glazov, Buzuluk, Orenburg, and Uralsk.

Kolchak's military success naturally impressed the Allies. On May 26, 1919, the Supreme Council sitting in Paris informed him that the Allies were "disposed to assist the government of Admiral Kolchak and his associates with munitions, supplies and food to establish themselves as the government of all Russia." In return, the Allies asked Admiral Kolchak and his associates to agree to certain conditions under which they would receive continued assistance from the Allied powers. These conditions included the following promises: (1) to summon a Constituent Assembly; (2) to permit immediately throughout their areas free elections in the local assemblies; (3) not to revive the special privilege of any class or order in Russia; (4) to recognize the independence of Finland and Poland; (5) to recognize the Baltic and Caucasian territories as autonomous; (6) to recognize the right of the Peace Conference to determine the disposition of Bessarabia; (7) to enroll the future Russian Government in the League of Nations. Admiral Kolchak answered that the summoning of a Constituent Assembly would be his first order after the Bolsheviks were crushed; that the independence of Poland would be beyond objection, but that the future Russian-Polish frontier, as well as the problem of Finland and Bessarabia, would be decided by the Russian Constituent Assembly. He accepted the autonomy of the Baltic and Caucasian areas, and concerning problems of internal Russian policy gave assurances that no return to the old *régime* would be allowed. The Supreme Council welcomed his response and replied that the Allies were "willing to extend to Admiral Kolchak and his associates the support set forth in their original letter" of June 12, 1919. To cap the success, on the same day General Denikin proclaimed his submission to Kolchak as the supreme ruler.

The diplomatic position of Kolchak was now excellent, but the support of the Allies was not to be the crucial factor in the struggle. The determining point proved to be one of military strategy between Admiral Kolchak and the Soviet leaders. Against 110,000 Soviet troops Kolchak was able to marshal about 125,000 men divided into several units, of which the strongest and best equipped was the northern army under the command of General Gayda, a Czech. Kolchak's master plan called for throwing the major part of his resources behind this army which was to drive through to join the British and Russian forces on the littoral of the White Sea. The adoption of this plan proved to be a mistake. It made it impossible to take any effective action toward effecting a juncture with Denikin's army in the south, and, at the same time, it created a weak spot in the very center of Kolchak's front. Realizing the mistake made by their enemy, the Red Army commanders immediately delivered a successful counterattack against the middle of the line. The Kolchak offensive rapidly collapsed when the northern army, fearing that it might be cut off by the Soviet advance, retreated eastward with the rest of the army.

The victory on the Siberian front allowed the Soviet Government to shift the most trustworthy Red Army troops against Denikin and to begin the second operation against the anti-Bolshevik forces. During the winter of 1918–19 Denikin's Volunteer Army had engaged the Bolshevik troops in southern Russia. In the middle of May, taking advantage of the widespread revolt of the peasants against the Soviet Government, Denikin's armies, which at that time numbered about 150,000 men, were able to direct an offensive at Moscow. During June several important cities in the south—Kharkov, Ekaterinoslav (now called Dniepropetrovsk), and Tsaritsyn (now Stalingrad)—were occupied by the Volunteer Army. It was at this point that the Reds were able to free their forces sufficiently to turn their full attention to Denikin. The Soviet Army's first counterattack failed, however, and by the middle of October the Volunteers had reached the extreme limits of their advance at a line stretching through Voronezh, Orel, Chernigov, Kiev, and Odessa. At the same time, in the north the army of General Yudenich, with its base in Esthonia, occupied Gatchina and launched an attack against Petrograd.

With active fighting in progress on four separate fronts—Siberia, south Russia, Petrograd, and Archangel—the Red Army still was able to crush Denikin's forces. The peasant uprising, which had originally smoothed the way for the advance of the anti-Bolsheviks, now turned against them and forced their rapid retreat all the way to the Black Sea ports where they were finally compelled to ask the British to help evacuate the troops, their families, and the wounded. On March 27, 1920, Novorossiisk was abandoned, and the remnants of the Volunteer Army, as well as most of the Don and part of the Kuban Cossacks, were transported by sea to the Crimean Peninsula. The defeated Denikin resigned his position as Commander-in-Chief and appointed General Wrangel his successor.

Meanwhile, the fate of Kolchak had already been sealed, for the complete disintegration of the forces under his command was obviously only a matter of time. The support of the Allies, upon which Kolchak depended and which had been promised in the declaration of June, 1919, never materialized. Throughout Siberia his Government was harassed by peasant revolts incited by the Socialist Revolutionaries. To add to the confusion, the only means of communication over these vast distances, the Trans-Siberian Railroad, was under the control of the Czechs who had joined the opposition. Cut off from his troops, Kolchak was finally seized by the Revolutionary Committee in Irkutsk with the connivance of the Czechs and the consent of the French general, Janin. A few days later he was shot.

With the arrival of the Red Army troops in Irkutsk two weeks later, the Soviet Government established its control over all the territory west of Lake Baikal and thus divided Siberia into two main areas. The far eastern portion remained under the practical control of Japanese troops. It was only after two more years of alternate fighting and diplomatic negotiation that the Soviet Government was able to complete the occupation of the whole of Siberia.

The collapse of the anti-Bolshevik forces all along the line at last compelled the Allies to alter their stand in regard to the Soviet Government. They began to realize that after two years in power the Bolsheviks had entrenched themselves and were, indeed, growing stronger. As early as November 8, 1919, Lloyd George declared that the Bolsheviks could not be conquered by arms, and on January 16, 1920, the Supreme Council of the Allies voted to withdraw the economic blockade of Russia. A little later Archangel was evacuated and soon thereafter all Allied troops were withdrawn from Russian territory.

9.

DURING the course of the civil war the Soviet Government enjoyed certain advantages over its opponents. The most important of these, perhaps, was that of controlling the central regions of Russia, a circumstance which secured for the Red Army the use of shorter, internal lines of communication. Within their territory, also, the Soviet armies had at their disposal enormous reserve stocks of armaments and munitions which had been accumulated by the Imperial Army for a huge offensive planned for 1917 and which had been only partly used by Kerensky in his abortive advance in July. Politically, too, the Soviet Government was a centralized power with the advantages of unity of purpose and clearness of program, while the many peripheral White governments opposed to it were muddled and divided among themselves. Although the *bourgeoisie* and part of the intelligentsia objected to the communist dictatorship and the peasants remained more or less neutral, the Bolsheviks were able to base their program solidly on the factory workers who, with few exceptions, supported the Soviet Government wholeheartedly.

The policy of the Soviet Government in this period is known as "War Communism." Motivated partly by theoretical Marxist concepts and partly by the grim necessity of circumstances, it set about the task of transforming the whole country into a huge military camp. As we have seen, the land was divided among the peasants in 1917–18. This solution of the agrarian problem was regarded by Lenin and other communist leaders as only a temporary one dictated by considerations of practical expediency. Theoretically, the Bolsheviks were inclined to regard the peasant not as a proprietor but as a workman operating government-owned land. All his produce was considered government property and, as such, whenever necessary was subject to government seizure by means of a levy in kind. Under the circumstances, of course, food requisitioning continued to be necessary for the duration of the war.

In industry the Soviet Government at first introduced the so-called "Labor Control" policy by which representatives of the workers shared the direction of plant operation with the former owners. Since there were constant altercations between the two groups and since the working of the plan became increasingly involved in red tape, the Labor Control system failed to produce adequate results. In the summer of 1918 all large-scale plants were seized by the Government, and from then on the nationalization of industry gradually spread downward to even small machine shops. In 1920 a decree was issued nationalizing all plants which employed more than five workers and used mechanical power and all those without mechanical power which employed more than ten workers.

National production as a whole was thus taken over by the Government which was then to arrange to supply the manufactured articles to the public. At first the distribution of the articles apparently was intended to be gratuitous, a plan which was to apply equally to materials such as fuel and machinery as well as to articles of personal use. The latter were apportioned by means of ration cards which were issued on the basis of a predetermined scale. Trade and commerce were, of course, eliminated under this system of communist economy and in 1918 were officially abolished. Banking having also become an unnecessary function, the banks were nationalized and in their place a "People's Bank" was created in 1918. This organization, a bank in name only, was in reality a department of the Commissariat of Finance, and by the decree of January 19, 1920, it was merged with another branch of the same bureau and became the "Budget Accounting Department."

Money was not abolished but, because of the continual issuance of paper currency, in actual practice it soon became worthless. This condition can be demonstrated graphically in a few figures on money and prices during those years. On March 1, 1917, there were 11,786,000,000 rubles of paper money in circulation. By November 1 this sum had doubled. By January, 1918, it had reached 27,312,000,000 rubles. Two years later the total was 225,014,000,000 rubles, and a year after that, January 1, 1921, it had reached the astronomical figure of 1,168,596,000,000 rubles. At the beginning of 1918 the dollar was worth about 9 rubles; at the beginning of 1919, about 80 rubles; at the beginning of 1920, 1,200 rubles. Naturally, prices soared with this inflationary spiral, and every decline in the value of money led to a corresponding increase in the cost of goods. In 1917 the general index of prices was three times as high as it was in 1913. At the beginning of 1918 it was 23.5 times as high. In 1920 it rose to 2,420 and at the beginning of 1921 to 16,800 times the 1913 figure.

Having destroyed the delicate and sensitive organization of trade and money exchange, the economy of War Communism was now forced to substitute clumsy and bureaucratic systems regulating both the production and distribution of goods. At the head of these organizations was the Supreme Council of National Economy. The real difficulty of this situation lay in the necessity not only to develop a new economic organization but also to provide new psychological incentives for the whole economic machine. In the overthrow of the old *régime* the communist system had also destroyed the natural incentives of individual enterprise which heretofore had been basic in all social schemes. Demand now lost touch with supply. The market for goods no longer depended upon the value of work done but upon membership in one or another category of consumers. No longer able to depend upon the usual incentives which had caused people to work, the Soviet Government was forced to resort to the principle of forced labor. This policy, first proclaimed in 1918, was finally confirmed by the Decree of Compulsory Labor of January, 1920, which stipulated that it was to apply not only to factory work but to agriculture as well. A further step in this direction was taken in the same year when an attempt was made to organize military workers' communes, a move which, from the historian's point of view, was an interesting parallel to the establishment of the military settlements of Alexander I.

The essential difficulty at this time was not that the governmental plans were necessarily faulty but rather that the Government had no means to make them work. The problems were complicated especially by the fact that at the time of the Bolshevik revolution both industry and agriculture in Russia had already been seriously disorganized by the World War. All of these factors now culminated in the steady year-by-year decline in agricultural and industrial production. In order to tighten its control over the workers, the Government moved to restrict the freedom of trade unions which had been legalized in Russia only in 1906. Although the Bolsheviks favored another form of labor organization, the shop committees, trade unions showed a rapid increase in membership under the Provisional Government and the movement was largely captured by the Mensheviks. Only at the First Congress of Trade Unions in January, 1918, did the Bolsheviks succeed in gaining an absolute majority, and, under their influence, the All-Russian Central Committee of Trade Unions was made the agency of factory and shop committees. After that the trade unions became for all practical purposes subordinate to government control. In 1920 the Ninth Convention of the Communist Party passed a resolution to the effect that "the trade unions . . . must gradually be transformed into auxiliary agencies of the proletarian state. The tasks of the trade unions lie chiefly in the field of economic organization and education."

The same method and policy were applied to the coöperative societies which were especially popular among the peasants. Here, too, the normal functions of the coöperatives were gradually transformed, and in 1920 the agencies of the consumer coöperative societies became mere subdivisions of the People's Commissariat of Food Supply.

It was the attitude of the peasants which remained the thorniest problem for the Government throughout the whole period of the civil war. In spite of the establishment of the Committees of the Poor—or rather, precisely because of them—the peasant masses continued to look upon the Soviet Government with suspicion and distrust. Because of the constant opposition in the villages the Bolsheviks decided that some concessions should be made to the "middle peasants" at least. As early as August 8, 1918, Lenin consented to a three-fold rise in the fixed price of grain, but by that time the depreciation in the value made the increase little more than a gesture. The peasants would, of course, have been glad to accept manufactured goods in exchange for their grain, but the Government had no surplus of such articles at its disposal. The whole problem was like that of squaring a circle. "We have no blessings to bestow upon the middle peasant"—such was Lenin's frank avowal before the Eighth Convention of the Communist Party in March, 1919. However, he did suggest certain palliative measures such as improving the apparatus of village administration, correcting the corrosive abuses, and, in general, attempting to establish a working agreement with the "middle peasants." As a sort of moral consolation for this group, a "middle peasant," M. I. Kalinin, was elected as the new chairman of the All-Russian Central Executive Committee—a post corresponding to the position of president in a republic.

Life in Soviet Russia was desperately hard during those troubled years, and even some of the government leaders themselves were at times overcome by despair. That the Government was somehow able to pull through now seems to have been due principally to two forces—Lenin's iron will and the support of the factory workers.

10.

AFTER the defeat and evacuation of the anti-Bolshevik forces in the north and east of Russia, there remained only one center of opposition to the Soviet Government—the remnants of Denikin's army under General Wrangel's command on the Crimean Peninsula. Attempting to reorganize that army and to continue armed resistance to Moscow, Wrangel ordered that the troops be given a rest, discipline reinstated, and severe measures taken against the forced requisitioning of food from the peaceful population. This last order was particularly important to his plans for he relied upon the support of the peasantry of southern Russia and had declared that his basic policy would be the satisfaction of their demands. Another support for his policy was his new agrarian law of June 7, 1920, vesting ownership of the land in the peasants, a reform which was to be carried out by Krivoshein, the former Imperial Minister of Agriculture who had taken a prominent part in the Stolypin reforms. Widening his search for allies against the Bolsheviks, Wrangel made certain overtures both to Poland and to leaders of the peasant movements in Russia. He even dispatched a representative to Makhno, the leader of a group of anarchical peasant bands, in the hope of making an alliance with him. He received no reply, however, and Makhno went so far as to kill the messenger who had brought Wrangel's offer.

Wrangel was convinced that his army, which consisted of only 70,000 men, could not hope to defeat the Soviet Government alone. He did believe, however, that his agrarian policy would secure for him the support of the peasantry when they understood its purpose, and that it would at the same time undermine the discipline of the Soviet armies. But his hopes were not realized, for the peasants, weary of civil war, were not to be won over by new agrarian laws. Indeed, in many localities in southern Russia the news of Wrangel's agricultural reforms never even reached them. An attempted uprising of the Don and Kuban Cossacks against the Soviet Government failed, and the Red Army, at that moment at the high point of moral exaltation, remained completely unaffected by Wrangel's program.

The war against Soviet Russia which was begun by Poland at that time, instead of strengthening the anti-Bolshevik movement, actually had the opposite result. By taking advantage of the national patriotism which had been aroused in Russia by the Polish intervention, the Soviet Government was able to secure the coöperation and assistance of many of its staunchest enemies. At the invitation of the Government the World War veteran, General Brusilov, issued an important and effective proclamation urging all Russian officers to support the Red Army in its struggle against Poland.

The first steps taken in the war by Poland were successful. After a brief campaign, Kiev, the capital of Ukraine, was occupied on May 6, 1920. An immediate counteroffensive by the Red Army, however, drove the Poles out of Kiev and back to the very gates of Warsaw. Finding herself hard pressed, on July 10 Poland appealed to the Allies for assistance, and a French military mission under General Weygand was sent to Warsaw while simultaneously the Allies attempted to reconcile the two warring governments.

Aware of the ever-increasing military power of the Soviet Government, France, however, decided to support General Wrangel, and on August 12, 1920, recognized his administration as the *de facto* government of south Russia. Meanwhile, with the arrival of additional French supplies in Warsaw, the Poles launched another attack against the Soviet armies and drove them back in disorder almost to Minsk. There the advance halted, and, with both sides negotiating for peace, a truce was concluded on October 12, 1920. The peace was finally signed in Riga on March 18, 1921, on terms that were patently unfavorable to Russia. The eastern frontier of Poland was drawn along the line of the German front at the outbreak of the Bolshevik revolution, which meant that several million Ukrainians and White Russians became subject to Polish rule. Though the Soviet Government was compelled to accept the Polish conditions, it could not but consider the peace a harsh and unjust one.

The cessation of military activities on the Polish front in October, 1920, enabled the Soviet Government to throw the Red Army over to the attack against General Wrangel in the south. In November a fierce battle was fought on the Perekop Isthmus connecting southern Russia with the Crimea. Realizing that he could no longer withstand the assault of the Red Army, Wrangel ordered the evacuation of all the anti-Bolshevik elements from the Crimean Peninsula. In all, about 130,000 soldiers and civilians, with their families, took ship and sailed for the Bosporus. The civil war was over.

CHAPTER XVI.

THE PERIOD OF THE NEW ECONOMIC POLICY

(1921–1927)

I.

RUSSIA survived the civil war, but it had taken all her strength to achieve even that bare survival. She emerged from the cataclysm in a state of collapse unique in modern history. She had been devastated from end to end by the combined destruction of three contending forces—the Reds, the Whites, and the foreign interventionists—who had fought along battle lines that had writhed over a vast part of the nation. The blockade had throttled the already crumbling economic system. Peasant opposition to the Government's enforced policy of food seizure had reduced agriculture to a level far below national requirements. The whole industrial system, burdened by a cumbersome and unworkable management scheme, was grinding to a halt. As a nation Russia had endured, but at a fearful cost in human suffering.

The continual decline of industry and the disorganization of transport now led step by step to the total impoverishment of the country. Each year industrial production sank to new levels until in 1920 it totaled no more than 13.2 per cent of the 1913 volume. Transportation reflected the disappearance of manufactured goods and produce of all sorts. In 1916 daily carloadings had totaled 31,164, but in 1920 the number had dwindled to 10,738. This condition could only mean increasing hardship and want for the population. The scarcity reached nearly all articles of daily use. Before the war, for example, the consumption of sugar and molasses per individual amounted in monetary units to 4.87 gold rubles. By 1920 it had fallen to .24 gold rubles. The prewar consumption of textiles per individual was to the value of 6.77 gold rubles. In 1920 it was only .91 gold rubles.

The catastrophic decline in agricultural production was a far more serious condition. All of the arable land had passed into the hands of the peasants at the time of the revolution through their appropriation of the large estates, a shift which had increased their land holdings by about 31 per cent. But though the revolution had given the peasants the land which they wanted, the civil war, with its train of military difficulties driving the Government more and more to the literal application of communist theory, brought them the economic policy of War Communism which they abhorred. To them the new system was a compound of regulation and robbery which took away all of the old incentives for cultivating the land. Since the peasant no longer had any desire to raise more crops than he needed for his own purpose, the total area under cultivation began to shrink. In 1916 there were about ninety million hectares of land under cultivation in the territory later under Soviet control; by 1921 that area had been reduced to sixty million. In addition, the yield per hectare had declined with the destruction of the large estates where production had generally been more efficient, and the collection of grain had consequently fallen off even more than the area of cultivation. In 1916 the harvest had totalled seventy-four million tons of grain. In 1919 it was estimated at only thirty million tons. That was near a starvation scale for the nation; even without allowance for the seed which had to be put aside for sowing, for a population of 137,000,000 it amounted to no more than 500 pounds of grain per capita. Livestock raising inevitably would have been curtailed by the fodder shortage alone, but the economic policies pursued by the Soviet Government hastened and intensified the reduction. The 1916 total of thirty-one million horses had by 1920 been cut to twenty-four million, and during the same time the number of cattle had been reduced from fifty million to less than thirty-seven million.

Because of the already terribly impoverished condition of Russia at the time, the drought of 1920 and 1921 led to a famine which had appalling consequences. The collection of grain in 1920 barely reached eighteen million tons; in 1921 the harvest failed in the whole of southeastern Russia. By the following year nearly thirty-five million people were actually starving and an additional fifteen million were in a state of semistarvation that was only slightly better. The loss of life during the famine years of 1921–22 has been estimated at five million, a figure twice as great as the total Russian casualties in the World War. The death toll would have been even higher had the starvation not been relieved by assistance from outside the country, mainly from the United States. The chief organization engaged in the work of alleviating the suffering was the American Relief Administration which operated under the leadership of Herbert Hoover. This group, together with others, was particularly active in providing aid to Russian intellectuals whose situation otherwise would have been quite hopeless. The total sum administered by the A.R.A. was $61,566,231.53, and the quantity of commodities furnished amounted to 718,770 tons. During August, 1922, the number of persons fed daily by the A.R.A. in Russia reached a high of 4,173,339 children and 6,316,958 adults—a daily total of more than ten million individuals. Besides the food which they supplied, the A.R.A. shipped and distributed $8,072,256.03 worth of medical supplies furnished by the American Red Cross and the American Army.

Devastation, disorganization, chaos, and starvation—such was the legacy which the civil war left to a nation already bled white by the enormous losses of the World War.

2.

THE widespread dissatisfaction which the Russian people felt under the *régime* of War Communism was expressed during 1920–21 in a series of peasant uprisings. There were, in all, a considerable number of these revolts—the most important of them arose in Tambov province under the leadership of Antonov—but all of them were suppressed quickly and many of them with great cruelty. Finally, at the beginning of March, 1921, there occurred a serious outbreak among the sailors of the Red Navy in Kronstadt, a group which had previously been the chief support of the Bolshevik revolution. The principal demands put forward by the rebels were for the calling of a constituent assembly and the reintroduction of freedom of trade. Though the uprising was soon quelled by armed force, the Soviet authorities considered it an ominous symptom. Grasping the seriousness of the situation, Lenin determined to supplement repressive police measures by a change in policy which was calculated to eliminate the causes of discontent.

Here again, as in the question of the Duma elections in 1906,

Lenin showed that he was willing to make a sharp turn in his policy. He was prepared to make any compromise, to adjust his plans to suit the realities of the time, if by so doing he retained command of the situation. "We are in a condition of such poverty, ruin, and exhaustion of the productive powers of the workers and peasants," said Lenin in a speech at the Tenth Convention of the Communist Party in March, 1921, "that everything must be set aside to increase production." With that announcement, Lenin had begun the creation of the New Economic Policy which in time came to be known simply as the N.E.P.

In its beginning the N.E.P. involved a fundamental revision of the policy which had previously been enforced with the agricultural population. In place of the levy in kind which had created violent resentment that found outlets either in armed opposition or in a passive resistance which was even more crippling, the new economic setup substituted a systematic scheme of taxation. At first the tax was an assessment in kind and was collected principally in grain; later it became a money tax. This reform was undertaken, of course, for the purpose of recreating among the peasantry a will and an incentive for the cultivation of their land. The Soviet Government promised the peasants that hereafter it would take only a definite proportion of the produce of their labor in the form of tax and not, as heretofore, the entire surplus in excess of their immediate needs. The peasants were now granted the right to dispose of the surplus as they wished—that is, to sell it in the open market. The decree replacing the levy with a tax opened the way for a thorough alteration of the economic system, for by the restoration of the peasant's right to sell his grain the Government had started a process which led inevitably to the introduction of freedom of trade. Indeed, in July, 1921, before the collection of the harvest there was promulgated a decree sanctioning free trade in internal commerce, though foreign trade, of course, still remained a government monopoly.

Simultaneously with the liberation of agriculture, a similar reform was put under way in industry. The purely socialist form of production was replaced by a new system of "state capitalism." The central, unified management of industry gave way to a system of "trusts" in which the state retained control over large-scale production but allowed smaller productive units to revert partly to private individuals. In a limited sphere the investment of foreign capital was permitted by the introduction of a system of concessions. The plan for supplying raw materials and tools to factories gratis was dropped; every manufacturing plant, whether government owned or privately owned, now had to pay for everything it used. These changes logically led to the reintroduction of currency, in its proper economic function, as well as to the re-establishment of a credit and banking mechanism. At the end of 1921 a State Bank, operating on an orthodox business basis, was set up.

The general retreat from the socialist system in the whole realm of production was necessarily accompanied by the abandonment of socialist principles in the distribution of goods. The state no longer undertook to supply the needs of great sections of the population. The right to receive goods free of charge was restricted to groups roughly similar to those so provided for in nonsocialist countries—members of the Red Army, the Red Navy, and the police forces, as well as prisoners held in confinement. A final and important reform accompanying the extensive economic revisions of the N.E.P. was the abolition of forced labor which had been resorted to in the violent period of War Communism.

3.

During the period of internal dissension and external attack, Russia's windows on Europe had been sealed. Her contacts with the Western world either had been deliberately severed by the Western powers or the Russians had allowed them to wither away because events at home had so completely monopolized the energies of the nation. The Allied intervention in Russia in the years from 1918 to 1920 had been a type of "undeclared war." When the Allied troops were withdrawn from Russia, no formal peace was concluded between the Soviet Government and the major European countries involved in these expeditions. From the legalistic point of view, of course, a peace treaty was both unnecessary and impossible since, technically, no state of war had existed between the belligerents. Nevertheless, it was apparent that the chaotic and disorganized state of affairs which existed could not endure and that some stabilization of the relations between Russia and Europe was essential.

The first step in the direction of a real peace taken by the European states was the lifting of the economic blockade against Russia on January 16, 1920. However, because of the failure of the Allies to reach any agreement on the more basic issues at stake, further moves were impossible. France favored the establishment of a *cordon sanitaire* around Russia's western frontier. By strengthening the newly created or reorganized hostile border states—the Baltic countries, Poland, and Rumania—the French hoped to erect a barrier to any future westward expansion of Russia. Great Britain, on the other hand, was rather indifferent about the settlement of Russia's European border but was preoccupied with an attempt to build a wall along the southern Russian boundary in order to thwart any extension of Soviet influence in the direction of India. Of all the great powers, the United States adopted the most benevolent policy toward Russia. In his note of August 20, 1920, Secretary of State Colby suggested that Russia be guaranteed her prewar frontiers, excepting only that portion of Poland in which the Poles were an actual majority.

The introduction of the New Economic Policy was received favorably and with pleased anticipation by statesmen and business interests throughout Europe. Both groups very generally misunderstood the essential meaning of the revision in Soviet economic policy. To them the N.E.P. meant only the complete capitulation of the Bolsheviks to the capitalistic world, and almost without exception it was interpreted as a sign of weakness rather than the mark of strength and political flexibility which it actually was. On the Continent hopes ran high that the supposed feebleness of the Bolsheviks would provide opportunities for the exploitation of Russia's natural resources by foreign interests. A Soviet Government amenable to "capitulations" and extraterritorial rights similar to those already established by European powers in Turkey and in China was anticipated. The governments of most of the European states nervously edged toward favorable positions from which they hoped to capture the lead in the expected rush for concessions. But here again a failure to reach any common agreement hampered the Allies. Lloyd George, in the true British tradition of free trade, advocated independent action by each individual country, while the French continued to insist that the Allies act only in concert. The Germans, fearful of being left entirely behind, offered their services as middlemen between Russia and the West. It was also proposed that a *Europa Consortium* be organized to facilitate the reconstruction and exploitation of Russia. Though no plan was adopted officially and no agreement reached between Great Britain and France, the main contenders, these tentative moves made it abundantly clear that a thoroughgoing discussion of Russian affairs on an international scale could no longer be postponed.

At the session of the Supreme Council of the *Entente* at Cannes on January 6, 1922, the general terms under which the economic reconstruction of the countries prostrated by the war might be undertaken were discussed. Though not specifically recognized as such, Russia was, of course, the chief subject of the deliberations. The two principal conditions laid down for the work of rehabilitation were: (1) recognition of all previous debts and obligations; (2) development of a normal financial and trade organization. At the same time the Supreme Council affirmed its belief in the principle of noninterference in the economic life of each country.

The succeeding conference which opened in Genoa on April 10, 1922, was the first international diplomatic gathering to include representatives of the Soviet Government. The first declarations of the Soviet delegates were businesslike in tone and led European statesmen to hope that an agreement of some kind might be possible. In tentative and preliminary terms, Chicherin declared himself ready to recognize both the prewar and the war debts of Russia and either to return confiscated property to foreign owners or to give them compensation. In return he demanded immediate *de jure* recognition of the Soviet Government and large credits. In addition, he advanced a number of counterclaims for damages caused by the Allied intervention in Russia during the civil war. Once more the Allies showed by their reaction to Chicherin's proposals that they were hopelessly divided among themselves. Great Britain and Italy were willing to examine the Russian propositions. France and Belgium, however, concerned as they were about the disposition of the concessions they had formerly held in southern Russia, flatly refused even to discuss them. At the same time Lloyd George was attempting to secure advantageous economic privileges for Great Britain through a direct agreement with the Soviet Government by which the entire production and export of Russian oil was to become a monopoly of the Royal Dutch-Shell Company. To put the finishing touches to the snarl, when information of the English negotiations leaked out, the American "observer" warned the conference that the United States would insist that an "open door" policy be applied in exploiting Russian oil.

Although it was basically the conflict of interests among the Allies which caused the failure of the Genoa Conference, the situation was additionally aggravated by the Soviet Government's conclusion of a separate agreement with Germany in Rapallo on April 16, 1922. This treaty disposed of all mutual claims of the two countries for war damages. Germany abandoned the support of claims by her citizens for compensation for property confiscated by the Soviet Government "provided the Government of the Russian Socialist Federative Soviet Republic does not satisfy similar claims of other states." Full diplomatic and consular relations between Germany and Russia were to be resumed. Article V of the treaty further provided: "The Two Governments shall mutually assist each other in supplying the economic requirements of the two countries . . . The German Government declares itself ready to facilitate as far as possible the conclusion and execution of economic contracts between private enterprises in the two countries."

At the conclusion of the Genoa Conference, those questions remaining unsettled had been left to "commissions of experts" which were summoned to meet at The Hague in June and July, 1922. However, by the time this assembly met, Moscow, wearied by the previous failure to come to terms with the "capitalistic" governments, had assumed a much firmer attitude. Because of the uncompromising mood of the Soviet representatives, The Hague Conference also proved to be a failure, even though it appeared at the time that the *Entente* negotiators were prepared to work more willingly for an understanding with Russia.

4.

After the seizure of power by the Bolsheviks, two divergent tendencies, nationalism and internationalism, came to the fore in Russian political policy. As the leader of the Communist party, Lenin was striving to promote revolution throughout the capitalist world. As the governmental head of Soviet Russia, however, his primary concern was in re-enforcing his own control and that of his party in the country and in providing for the defense of the nation against the attack of foreign powers. This duality of purpose inevitably became clearer as the communists grappled with the complexities of national government and foreign diplomacy. In time it expressed itself in the division of responsibility between two agencies. The administration of both the internal and foreign affairs of the Soviet state, as such, remained in the hands of the Soviet Government; the propagation of revolutionary doctrine and the sponsorship of revolutionary movements in the rest of the world became exclusively the province of the Communist party. It should be remembered, however, that Lenin was chairman of both the Council of People's Commissars and the Central Committee of the All-Russian Communist party, and that, though Bolshevik activities were apportioned between the two branches, they were still closely coördinated.

The establishment of the Communist party on an international scale was only the natural translation of the basic concepts of the doctrine into organizational form. Lenin had, in fact, proposed the founding of the Third, or Communist, International as early as 1915 (Chap. XIII, sec. 6), but for obvious reasons it had been impossible to carry out the plan at the height of the World War and it was laid aside until after hostilities had ended. However, the Bolsheviks had profitably used the last months of the war to disseminate communist tenets among prisoners of war in Russia, and immediately after the Armistice they hastened to organize the Third International. The call for the First Congress of the International was issued by Lenin and Trotsky on January 24, 1919—a date which coincided with President Wilson's invitation to the Prinkipo Conference—and the delegates assembled in Moscow in March, 1919. Chiefs of the various departments of the new body were elected, and a long manifesto was issued to the working people of the world.

The first period of activity by the International was characterized by immediate attempts to incite communist revolutions in all countries. Uprisings did actually occur in a few nations, but their existence was brief; the Communist Government of Bela Kun in Hungary lasted from March 21 until August 1, 1919, and a Bavarian Soviet Government, founded on April 7, 1919, held power for an even shorter period. Revolutions were also planned in England and in the United States, though in these countries the "plans" could hardly have been more than vague hopes.

After the failure of the revolutionary movements which sprang up immediately after the war, the Second Congress of the Third International in July, 1920, adopted a new plan. Instead of relying so heavily upon spontaneous insurrection in the capitalist states, the Bolsheviks, through the headquarters of the International in Moscow, launched a systematic program of propaganda all over the world. In order to facilitate the operation of the plan, the globe was divided into special propaganda areas of which no less than six were in Europe. Presumably the sums expended on this scheme of preparation for "world revolution" were considerable, but of course it is difficult to even estimate the total. It is clear, nevertheless, that the Executive Committee of the Communist International was originally intended as the nucleus of a potential Soviet world government, though in actual practice it remained merely a supplement to the Russian Communist party. The existence of the International did, however, definitely establish Moscow as the center of the communist world.

The Communist party was particularly active at that time in efforts to inculcate revolutionary theories among the Asiatic peoples, and the leaders of the party and of the Soviet Government feverishly set about training propagandists to carry on that part of the work. Largely because of their growing resentment against Europeans who possessed special economic and political privileges in the East, the Asiatics were ready to listen to the call. The revolutionary appeals of the Bolshevik agitators first met with considerable success in the Near and Middle East, but they were greatly handicapped in the consolidation of their gains by an excessively literal interpretation of communist doctrine, especially by their insistence on its violent opposition to all religion. At the Congress of Eastern Peoples in Baku in September, 1920, Mohammedanism showed itself to be stronger than communism and adherents to that faith were aroused to indignation by an exceptionally bitter antireligious speech by Zinoviev. In general, nowhere in the Middle or the Near East, in Persia or in Turkey, was the existing social organization suited to the adoption of communism. The Russian revolution had demonstrated that the doctrine of revolution was attractive chiefly to factory workers and a part of the intellectuals. In Persia and Turkey there were no industrial workers and no intellectual class of any political importance.

Farther east, communism met varying degrees of resistance. In

India, where the British had greatly feared the penetration of insurrectionary beliefs, the strong religious feeling of the people served as an effective deterrent to the growth of the communist idea. In China, however, Russian communism achieved greater success than it had in Asia Minor, and a substantial number of Chinese intellectuals, as well as a portion of the laboring class, accepted the belief. The left wing of the Chinese Kuomintang was sympathetic to the movement, and a little later a Chinese Communist party was formed and formally enrolled in the International organization. Having thus sounded out the political and social attitudes of the peoples along the Russian borders, the International was now prepared to frame the elements of a campaign to persuade the working classes to join the new revolutionary order.

5.

DURING this period the Soviet Government was most immediately concerned with the clarification of the position along Russia's vital southern and southwestern border, and it was precisely there that the situation was exceptionally involved in international complexities. By the terms of the treaty of Brest-Litovsk, Russia had ceded Batum, Kars, and Ardagan to Turkey. However, Batum and the whole general area of Transcaucasia were actually occupied first by the Germans and subsequently by the British. Batum itself was later retaken by Soviet troops and eventually was permanently incorporated in the Russian state. Of the territory officially transferred at Brest-Litovsk, only Kars and Adagan ever actually passed under Turkish control.

The position of Great Britain in this area was ambiguous. Although her occupation of Transcaucasia was officially temporary in character, it is obvious that in 1919 British diplomacy had far-reaching ambitions in the Middle East. On August 9, 1919, at Teheran an Anglo-Persian agreement was concluded which virtually introduced a British protectorate over Persia, and in November of the same year Lord Curzon referred in an important speech to "the British lion standing forth as the proud and valiant champion of the rights and liberties of Persia." British troops were stationed at Enzeli and Meshed, and a little later a small force, entering Russian Turkestan, occupied Merv and defeated the Soviet forces at Dushakh. It is clear that at least some British officers were at that time developing schemes for the establishment of English rule over the whole of Turkestan, but the instability of the political situation in England, coupled with the Russian sympathies which the International had been able to arouse among liberal British groups, forced the abandonment of these colonial ambitions in the Middle East. In 1920 British troops were withdrawn from Turkestan, Transcaucasia, and northern Persia, and the enforcement of the 1919 Anglo-Persian agreement—which had not been ratified by the Persian Parliament—was never undertaken.

The departure of the British opened the way for the firm establishment of Soviet rule in the Middle East. In Azerbaijan and in Armenia Soviet republics were organized as early as 1920. At the same time the Republic of Georgia signed a peace treaty with the Soviet Government and the following year, after a communist revolution which, according to some, had been engineered in Moscow, it was proclaimed a Soviet republic. Still later, the Transcaucasian Soviet republics, organized as the Transcaucasian Federative Soviet Republic, were accepted as a unit in the U.S.S.R.

The situation in Turkestan was handled somewhat differently. The Soviet Government was first faced with an uprising of the so-called "Basmachi," a group of natives active in a Pan-Turanian and Pan-Mohammedan movement which was led by Enver Pasha, the famous Turkish general who had entered Turkestan as a friend of the Soviet but subsequently went over to the opposition. The Red Army succeeded in suppressing the revolt in July, 1922, and Enver Pasha was captured and killed. The Soviet Government, after it had regained control of the situation in Turkestan, introduced administrative reforms which granted a certain degree of autonomy on the basis of workers' representation. In the spring of 1921 an autonomous Soviet Government was formed in Tashkent. During 1920–21 the Soviet Union entered into treaty relations with the republics which had been set up in Khiva and Bokhara, though it was not until several years later that these two states were organized as the Turkmen and the Uzbek Soviet Republic and entered the Union of Socialist Soviet Republics.

While she was thus engaged in the re-establishment of her Middle East boundaries, the Soviet Union had also been active in the formulation of a new policy upon which to base her relations with Persia. On February 26, 1921, the Soviet Government concluded an agreement with Persia in which it renounced "the imperialist policy of the former governments of Russia," a principle which was similarly expressed in a treaty with Turkey which was signed shortly afterward. In addition to this political assurance, the Soviet yielded a number of tangible assets to Persia: the railroad from Djulfa to Tavriz, which had been built and owned by Russians; the military roads from Enzeli to Teheran and from Kazvin to Hamadan; the funds of the Loan Bank of Persia—all were relinquished by Russia. The Soviet Government at the same time agreed to withdraw all of its previous claims for Russian loans to Persia. The Soviets retained the right to exploit the fisheries along the southern coast of the Caspian Sea, but the exact commercial terms under which this industry was to operate were left for discussion at a future conference. The Caspian fisheries proved to be a difficult subject which resulted in prolonged negotiations and misunderstandings between the two countries. It was not until October, 1927, that the two parties finally reached a twenty-five-year agreement by which the fisheries were to be worked by a Russo-Persian company under a Persian chairman, the produce being divided equally between the two nations.

After the Greco-Turkish war of 1922–23, near-eastern territorial questions again became the subject of international negotiations. At the Lausanne Conference, to which the Soviet Union had been invited after some hesitation on the part of the British, Russia and Turkey appeared with a common program. Both demanded that the Dardanelles be closed to all military vessels except those of Turkey. The British, hoping to keep the Caucasian ports and especially Batum, the outlet for the oil of Baku, under their control, wished the Straits to remain open to both the military and commercial ships of all nations. As a result of the mediation of France, a compromise between the two positions was finally reached. Warships were to be allowed to pass through the Straits provided their total tonnage did not exceed that of the navy of the principal Black Sea naval power, that is, Russia. When the Turkish delegates accepted this proposal without previous agreement with the Soviet representatives, Chicherin refused to sign the treaty and warned the powers that the question could not be considered solved without the participation of Russia, Ukraine, and Georgia. Although the convention on the Straits, which was attached to the treaty of Lausanne, was later signed by a Soviet representative, it was never ratified by the Soviet Government. The Straits were, however, internationalized and remained so until Turkey demanded the restitution of her rights in the area, a plea which was recognized at the Montreux Conference in 1936.

In spite of the lack of coördination between Soviet Russia and Turkey which had developed in the course of the Lausanne conference, relations between the two countries continued to be friendly, perhaps the most generally satisfactory of any achieved by the Soviet Union at the time. A new agreement with Turkey was signed in December, 1925, and in November of the following year, at a meeting with the Turkish Minister of Foreign Affairs, Chicherin hailed Turkey as the Soviets' faithful ally against imperialism.

6.

In the Far East the Soviet Government faced a complicated situation which, for a number of reasons, was to prove even more difficult than that with which they had to contend in the Near East. The whole area was swept by political cross-currents which made a direct or speedy solution impossible. For a time during the civil war Moscow had been entirely cut off from the whole of Siberia which had, during that time, fallen under the control of the Whites and foreign interventionists. With Siberia lost and the road eastward blocked, the Soviet Government for some time was not in a position to establish direct contact with China. Japan, foremost champion of intervention in the Russian Far East, was, of course, actually a hostile power. Handicapped as she thus was, the Soviet Union was at first limited almost exclusively to issuing reassuring declarations in which she expressed her willingness to cancel all remnants of Russian imperialism such as the various concessions and extraterritoriality rights which the former Russian Government had enjoyed. This attitude was in line with the policy pursued in the Near East, but it by no means represented the total Soviet effort in the Far East which in time proved to be much more vigorous and realistic than it had been in Persia and Turkey.

Even after the defeat of Kolchak in western Siberia, the eastern end remained outside the Soviet Union. The Government was then unable to undertake its conquest by arms since it was entirely occupied with the Polish War and with the struggle with Wrangel in southern Russia. Toward the spring of 1920 the Allied troops and the Czechoslovaks left Vladivostok, the last American withdrawing on April 1 of that year. The Japanese, however, continued their occupation of Vladivostok and the coastal area, and Ataman Semenov, their agent, maintained control of the Transbaikal region. When the Whites' retreat to the Manchurian border released a large territory which they had previously ruled, the Soviet Government decided to incorporate it in a buffer state east of Lake Baikal. Accordingly, on May 14, 1920, the Soviets recognized the "Far Eastern Republic" whose capital was at Chita and whose prime minister was Krasnoshchekov (Tobelson) who, interestingly enough, had formerly been a Chicago lawyer. Immediately after its formation, the Far Eastern Republic protested against the continued presence of Japanese troops in eastern Siberia and against the support granted by the Japanese to the remnants of the White forces. At the same time it called upon the Soviet Union to support it, and in the autumn of 1920 Red Army troops entered Chita.

Japanese policy in Siberia, meanwhile, was vacillating and undecided. In the spring of 1921 Japan gave support to the organization of an anti-Bolshevik government in Vladivostok but insisted upon disarming the remnants of the White armies, which were to be the military forces of that government, before they were admitted to the coastal area. By the fall of 1921 there were signs that Japan was considering relinquishing her hold on Siberia. In September of that year she opened negotiations with the Far Eastern Republic at Darien. When these conversations broke down, they were followed by further conferences at Washington in February, 1922, and at Changchun in September. Japan finally announced that she would voluntarily withdraw her troops from the mainland of Siberia by the end of October, 1922. With the exception of the Japanese claim to the northern part of the island of Sakhalin, this step effectively removed Japan from interference in Russian affairs.

Without active Japanese support the government set up at Vladivostok was incapable of resisting the Bolsheviks. The remnants of the White forces were soon evacuated to Shanghai, and Vladivostok was occupied by Soviet troops. The conquest of Siberia having been completed, the Far Eastern Republic was now of no further use to Moscow, and when, on November 13, 1922, the "National Assembly" of the Republic voted the transfer of all of its powers to a revolutionary committee appointed by the Soviet Government, the Far Eastern Republic ceased to exist.

The Soviet Government formally readjusted its relations with Japan in a treaty signed on January 20, 1925. By this agreement both parties reaffirmed the terms of the Peace of Portsmouth. Japan abandoned North Sakhalin in return for a number of concessions which the Union of Socialist Soviet Republics agreed to grant her in the northern half of the island.

In its relations with China, the Soviet Government had to consider two involved and interrelated problems which it had inherited from Imperial Russia: the question of the Chinese Eastern Railroad and the question of Mongolia. During the World War, in 1915, a tripartite agreement had been concluded among China, Outer Mongolia, and Imperial Russia which had established a joint protectorate of the two powers over Mongolia. During the Russian upheaval in 1919 the Chinese Republic had decided to revise the situation by annexing Mongolia, but even this move failed to prevent the civil war in Siberia from rolling across the border. In the beginning of 1920 when a part of the Russian White armies was driven into Mongolia by the Bolsheviks, the Mongolian and the Chinese authorities were equally incapable of preventing the invasion. Soon afterward Soviet troops intervened to crush the last vestiges of the White forces, and a little later a Moscow-instigated uprising set up a revolutionary Mongolian Government. Shortly thereafter, on November 5, 1921, the Soviet Union concluded with the Mongolian Government a treaty of friendship in which no mention of China was made, a circumstance which provoked considerable indignation among Chinese ruling groups.

The problem of the management of the Chinese Eastern Railroad was intimately bound up with the question of Sino-Russian relations. In the declaration of 1919 the Soviet Government had, of course, renounced its rights in the railway. This declaration, however, had been made at a time when Siberia was under the control of the White armies and when the Chinese Eastern was being managed by an Allied commission. The Soviet Government had then given up something which it did not actually possess, but with the improvement of the Bolshevik position in Siberia in the next year, the attitude of Moscow toward the problem of the railroad was immediately altered. When Soviet troops occupied Vladivostok, the Chinese Eastern again assumed the importance which it had formerly held—that of the shortest route between two portions of Russian territory. In 1922 Joffe, the Soviet representative, frankly informed the Chinese of the new Soviet view of the question. In response, the Chinese Ministry of Foreign Affairs demanded the withdrawal of Russian troops from Mongolia and the recognition of Chinese sovereignty in that region. The two countries remained adamant in their positions, and Joffe's negotiations eventually broke down in this deadlock. Not until 1924 was an agreement concluded when Karakhan, the new Soviet representative, finally yielded on the Mongolian issue. According to Article V of this agreement, the Soviet Government "recognizes that Outer Mongolia is an integral part of the Republic of China and respects China's sovereignty therein." The Soviet Union further agreed to withdraw its troops from Mongolian territory. It must be said, however, that, while the principle of Chinese sovereignty over Outer Mongolia was recognized, actually the Chinese control was not re-established and for practical purposes Mongolia remained a "People's Republic" under Soviet protectorate. As for the Chinese Eastern Railway, the Soviets and China agreed at the same time to regard it as a purely commercial enterprise; the U.S.S.R. recognized China's jurisdiction and police control over the territories owned by the railroad and affirmed China's right to purchase the railroad. The management of the Chinese Eastern was to be in the hands of a board of directors, half of them appointed by the Chinese Government and half by the Soviet Government, with the chairman to be chosen by the Chinese. In addition to this arrangement with China, the demands of Marshal Chang Tso-lin, who was at that time dictator of Manchuria, had to be considered, and on September 30, 1924, the Soviets were able to conclude an agreement with him on substantially the same terms as that with China. Though these arrangements did much to resolve the most vexing problems of the Chinese Eastern, they did not completely clear up the situation since the claims of the creditors of the railroad, including Japan, the United States, and the Russo-Asiatic Bank, were still outstanding.

Just when the older problems which had separated the Soviet Union on the one hand and China and Japan on the other were working toward a settlement, the whole far-eastern situation was plunged into a new crisis by the outbreak of the Chinese revolutionary movement which was directed to a large extent against the special privileges which the British and other foreigners held in China. Russians were comparatively little involved in this resentment which flared up in China. Though the Soviets had preserved their interest in the Chinese Eastern Railroad, its administration had assumed a much more moderate form, and since all the rest of Russia's exclusive rights in China had been given up, the Soviet Union was in a position to enjoy neutrality in the Chinese-British conflict. Nowhere was there any ill-feeling against Russia on the part of the Chinese.

Instead of remaining aloof from the Chinese troubles, however, the Russians eventually became involved in them. Their entanglement in this situation came about less as a result of the policies of the Soviet Government than because of the interference of the Communist International. To the leaders of the International the Chinese revolution seemed to provide a favorable opportunity to undermine the forces of the European capitalist powers since, according to Lenin's theory, the main strength of international capitalism and imperialism lay in their ability to exploit the "colonial and semi-colonial countries." Because China's political and economic conditions fitted this theory so perfectly, it fell to her lot to become the principal battleground of the struggle of the Communist International against European imperialism.

The great Chinese leader Sun Yat-sen, who had been in touch with Lenin and who, although he was not a communist himself, was sympathetic to Russian communism, died in 1925. His work, however, was continued by the party which he had organized under the name of the Kuomintang. In it a labor and peasant movement was united with a nationalist movement which was led by intellectuals and students who opposed the imperialist policies of certain of the European powers. The Kuomintang also included a strong communist wing, and while Sun Yat-sen was still alive his party had entered into close relations with the Communist International in Moscow. The Soviet Government was quite willing to support the southern Chinese movement and during 1925 supplied about a thousand military and political instructors as well as some $3,000,000 which was cleared through the banks of Shanghai and Canton.

A prominent communist, Borodin, was appointed adviser to the Canton Nationalist Government which during 1925 and 1926 continued to expand its sphere of control along the coast toward Shanghai and inland toward the middle section of the Yangtze River. A dictatorship patterned after the Moscow model was introduced in the areas occupied by its armies. When the Nationalists swept into Hankow in September, 1926, the star of Soviet influence in China was rising to its zenith.

This movement seemed to have been so successful that the Communist International now confidently tried to extend its activities from China to the Dutch East Indies, where an abortive communist uprising was organized in November. During a general strike in Hankow early in January of the following year a boycott of foreign goods was proclaimed and violent anti-British demonstrations took place, a mob invading the area of the British concession on January 4. On March 22 the Nationalist forces occupied Shanghai, with the exception of the foreign concessions, and on the next day Nanking was taken. The communists were then at the peak of their power in China.

It was at this point that the development of internal dissension brought to a halt the further expansion of military operations by the Nationalists. Differences between the conservative and moderate members of the Kuomintang and the communist wing had, in fact, arisen as early as the autumn of 1926. By the following spring these differences had grown greater, and antagonism flared up between Chiang Kai-shek, who was then a general in the Chinese Nationalist forces, and the Soviet adviser, Borodin. On April 6, with the written permission of the Dean of the Diplomatic Corps, the police raided the Soviet Embassy in Peking. Documents seized there revealed the close connection between Russian diplomacy and the communist wing of the Kuomintang and plainly established Borodin's dominating position in that party. The publication of these documents led to a full break between Chiang Kai-shek and Borodin, who then tried unsuccessfully to organize a purely communist government in Hankow but was forced to leave on July 27, 1927.

The following December in a communist-aided uprising Canton was seized, but after three days the insurrection was put down by the Nationalist forces. It was suppressed with severity; many revolutionary leaders, among them some Russians, were executed. Indeed, all over China the influence of the Communist International, which had only two years before seemed so promising to the leaders, was relentlessly being crushed.

7.

SOVIET policy in the Orient, as we have seen, was a combination of idealistic principles and realistic political action, the whole sprinkled occasionally with communist propaganda of world revolution. In the West, Russian diplomacy tended in the same general direction. Here, too, the constant and long-term objectives seem to have been the restoration of the former boundaries of the Russian Empire, the establishment of normal relations with neighboring countries, and the safeguarding of the interests of Soviet Russia as a national state. In the West, however, the course which Soviet policy actually followed was necessarily more intricate, and the results, by and large, were less satisfactory.

The failure to achieve the restoration of the old Russian borders in Europe was one which was to have grave repercussions in the future, and without taking some cognizance of it we cannot sufficiently understand Soviet policies during the critical years of 1939 and 1940. The Soviets' boundaries after the World War were the result of several agreements. One of the conditions of the Brest-Litovsk peace of 1918 was the separation of Ukraine from Russia. Nevertheless, both the Whites and the Reds continued to regard Ukraine as an integral part of Russia, and after the collapse of Germany and the withdrawal of her troops Ukrainian territory became a prize which both sides fought to win throughout the civil war. With the victory of the Soviets, Ukraine became part of the federated Union of Socialist Soviet Republics. Bessarabia, on the other hand, was occupied by Rumanian troops in the spring of 1918 and was later officially incorporated in that state. The Soviet Government, however, has always refused to abandon its claim to the disputed territory, and in 1924 it set up within the territory of Ukraine a special Moldavian Soviet Republic which it hoped would serve as a political magnet to the peoples of Bessarabia. Farther to the north, a considerable section of land populated by White Russians and Ukrainians was ceded by the Soviet Government to Poland by the severe terms of the peace of 1921. Northward from

Poland the frontier of the Union of Socialist Soviet Republics followed the lines which she was compelled to accept in the treaty of Brest-Litovsk. In 1920 the Soviet Union concluded treaties of peace with Esthonia, Lithuania, Latvia, and Finland which indicated her willingness to accept the losses in territory which she had sustained, and for the time being stabilized her western boundary.

The task which faced the Commissariat of Foreign Affairs after the frontier lines were drawn was the establishment of normal relations with the great powers. The treaty which was signed at Rapallo in 1922 regularized Russo-German affairs and freed the Soviet Union to concentrate on the clarification of relations with Great Britain, France, and the United States. The Genoa and The Hague economic conferences in 1922 and the Lausanne Conference in 1923, in all of which Moscow participated, to some extent amounted to *de facto* recognition of Soviet Russia by the Western powers. However, they constituted only a partial acceptance, and the Soviet Government was anxious to obtain a *de jure* recognition without which the position of Russia in the community of nations remained at best precarious.

The main difficulty standing in the way of a better understanding between the Soviet Union and the outside world was the activity of the Communist International. The obvious involvement of this organization in world politics continued to prejudice the chances of the Soviet Government to establish itself in a position of equality with the other nations since it was well known that even though the International had been formally separated from the government of Russia, both bodies were actually controlled by the same group of men. There was a certain inner contradiction in this situation, particularly after the introduction of the N.E.P. which was based on the assumption that some compromise with capitalist principles was necessary. The Russians were themselves aware of the paradoxical elements in their attitude. Krassin, the chief promoter of the N.E.P., speaking at the Thirteenth Conference of the Communist Party in January, 1924, argued that the aid of foreign capital was indispensable if the bankruptcy of the Soviet *régime* were to be prevented. "To obtain foreign help, it is necessary, however," he added, "to assume a more peaceful attitude, and to lower the banner of the World Revolution."

The Communist International did not accept Krassin's point of view. On the contrary, Zinoviev, who was its president at that time, expressed the belief that a new wave of international revolution was rising. The Fifth Congress of the Communist International, which met in Moscow during June and July, 1924, fully approved this point of view and adopted an irreconcilable policy embodying it. In spite of this frame of mind among the communist leaders, precisely at this moment European diplomacy began to show some willingness to accord the *de jure* recognition which the Soviet Government wanted. This new turn of events was due, in part at least, to the fact that public opinion in Europe was unaware of the change in communist policy and, indeed, continued to expect still further concessions from Soviet diplomacy.

The granting of recognition to the Soviet Union was hastened by the victory of the Labor and the Radical parties in the British and French elections. As early as the end of 1923 Soviet recognition had been included in the platform of the Labor party in England, and after the victory of that party at the polls the Labor Cabinet of MacDonald voted to fulfil its pledge at its first meeting on February 1, 1924. Within two months Italy, Norway, Austria, Greece, and Sweden had followed the lead of Great Britain. However, the recognition of the U.S.S.R. granted by Britain was by no means unconditional and was followed by a series of prolonged negotiations. First of all, the British note accorded recognition only to those parts of the former Russian Empire which were then willing to accept Soviet authority. Second, the British Government required that the Soviets recognize the pre-Soviet debts of Russia. Finally, it asked the Soviet Government to abstain from anti-British propaganda, especially in the Orient. In April, 1924, a Soviet delegation came to London to discuss the terms of the note, but after several months the negotiations broke down without producing any results. The British continued to demand Soviet recognition of Russian debts, and the Soviet delegates countered by asking for a loan with which Russia could begin to pay them. Not until August 8, 1924, was an agreement finally signed. Even then it was a strange document, for it left unsettled almost all of the important questions and agreed only that the two parties would try to reach a real agreement later.

MacDonald's unsuccessful attempts to enter into friendly relations with the Soviets resulted only in increasing his unpopularity.

On October 8, 1924, he was defeated in Parliament and was obliged to dissolve the House, setting new elections for October 29. A few days before the election English newspapers published what purported to be a secret letter written by Zinoviev and containing instructions for the preparation of a communist uprising in England. The letter was a forgery, but its publication had accomplished its purpose by arousing the indignation of the voters and thus contributing to the defeat of the Labor party. The new Conservative Government cancelled the agreement of August 8, 1924, but it did not withdraw the original recognition which had been accorded to the Soviet Union on February 1. This compromise in Soviet-British affairs, by which the formality of diplomatic recognition was retained, was a highly unsatisfactory arrangement which led only to the further estrangement of the two countries.

In spite of the failure of British negotiations, France followed the example of England and the course of diplomatic events in that country fell into roughly the same pattern. In May, 1924, the Left Bloc headed by Herriot won the elections, and on October 28 the French Government extended *de jure* recognition to the Soviets. The question of Russian indebtedness to France remained unsolved, however, and subsequent negotiations between the two nations proved futile.

Great Britain and France were at this time particularly anxious to achieve some stability in European affairs. Since their recognition of the Soviet Union had not resulted in the establishment of a real friendship between Russia and the West and since they still continued to distrust communist activities, they now turned to Germany and Italy in an effort to organize European relations. An important step in this direction was taken at the Locarno Conference on October 16, 1925. Through it there was built up a system of agreements providing for arbitration as a means for the settlement of disputes. Moscow, however, regarded the conference as an international attempt at the "isolation" of Soviet Russia and the "formation of a united anti-Soviet front." Soviet diplomatic tacticians, looking about anxiously for a method of piercing this front, readily agreed upon Germany as its most vulnerable point. Although Germany had been invited to attend this conference, she had not yet attained equal membership in European diplomatic society, since she had not yet been admitted into the League of Nations. It was, therefore, only natural for the Soviets to attempt to enter into closer relations with Germany, which, in turn, was quite willing to threaten the Western powers with the possibility of a Russo-German alliance in order to hasten her admission into the League. On October 12, 1925, just before the departure of the German delegates for Locarno, Chicherin succeeded in concluding a trade agreement with Germany which, among other points, provided that Soviet Russia was to receive a loan amounting to 100,000,000 marks. Several months after the Locarno gathering, on April 24, 1926, a Soviet-German political treaty was concluded in Berlin; both sides were bound to maintain friendly contact and to remain neutral in the event one of them should face armed attack by a third power. This was Germany's reply to the Western powers for the affront she had received at the March session of the League of Nations, when she was not accepted as a member although her representatives had been summoned to Geneva. In addition to the broad terms of the treaty, a German note attached to the text specifically stated that one of the aims of the pact was to oppose anti-Soviet tendencies within the League. The treaty proved to be a skilful move for both countries; it strengthened the Soviet Union's hand in Europe and led to the admission of Germany into the League of Nations on September 7, 1926.

Following the Locarno Conference, Soviet diplomacy intensified its attack against Great Britain. "Chamberlain believes he encircled us at Locarno," wrote *Pravda,* the official organ of the Communist party in Moscow. "On the contrary, we will encircle him with the masses of labor at his very home."

The labor situation in England at that time was indeed unstable. In September, 1925, the Congress of English Trade Unions at Scarborough, by a vote of 2,456,000 to 1,218,000, passed a radical resolution which was opposed in principle to the development of peaceful methods of settling differences between capital and labor. In December of that year Zinoviev made the following statement at the Fourteenth Congress of the Russian Communist Party: "A huge movement of miners is to be expected in England before May, 1926. A real revolutionary labor movement is beginning in England." In a further elaboration of the communist position, he prophesied in March, 1926, that Britain was on the eve of a social catastrophe. "If the strike really begins, it will be our first task to help it, along the European and international front of industrial war." The rupture of negotiations between the English mine owners and the miners did eventually lead to a general strike which, contrary to communist expectations, soon ended in complete failure. The miners themselves, however, remained out of the pits until the autumn of 1926 and during the whole period of the strike received support from the Soviet workers both in money and propaganda. By May no less than $1,300,000 had been received from Moscow, and by July aid to the striking miners had risen to $2,225,000.

About this time the Anglo-Russian Committee of Trade Unions attempted by mediation to bring about an understanding between the Moscow leaders and the General Council of English Trade Unions. These efforts were fruitless, however, for the General Council was not willing to accept the firmly dogmatic point of view adopted by the Moscow representatives. The communist position was not entirely without support, however. The London Conference of the Minority of English Trade Unions on August 30, 1926, did accept the Moscow viewpoint, but the General Congress of English Trade Unions meeting in Bournemouth the following September rejected it by the decisive majority of 2,416,000 votes.

The English public at large was, not unnaturally, considerably irritated by communist interference with British labor affairs. The participation of Russian communists in a Chinese revolution which also had anti-British implications was an added source of worry for British statesmen. Finally, as a result of growing suspicions in both these groups, a break in Soviet relations was decided upon. Disregarding Russian claims of diplomatic immunity, representatives of Scotland Yard on May 12, 1927, raided Soviet House, the London headquarters of both the Soviet Trade Delegation and Arcos, Ltd., the trading company for the Soviet coöperative societies. The Secretary for Home Affairs justified the raid with the explanation that a document containing military secrets, which had been stolen from the Government, had been traced to these premises. Although this particular document was not found, the police seized other papers which, in the opinion of the British Cabinet, amply justified the action. The Soviet Government protested in a note that the British authorities had violated the immunity granted to the Soviet Trade Delegation by the agreement of 1921. Toward the end of May the whole question was discussed in the House of Commons. Some of the documents seized were laid before the House by Prime Minister Baldwin who declared that they proved "the existence, under the direct control of the Soviet authorities, of a regular system whereby documents of a subversive character from various organizations in Russia were conveyed secretly to various persons engaged in Communist activities in this country and elsewhere."

With these events as a background, a rupture of diplomatic relations with Soviet Russia was recommended by the Ministry and approved by Parliament. On May 27, 1927, the decision of the British Government was communicated to the Soviet *chargé d'affaires* in London, and Baldwin made the following announcement: "I wish to state emphatically that our rupture of diplomatic relations does not in any way mean, or imply, war against Russia." The break was not followed by a serious disruption of normal commercial contact between the two nations. The usual facilities for trade were not disturbed, and after the deportation of certain employees of Arcos, Ltd. the balance of the personnel was allowed to remain and continue its work.

While the British attitude toward the Soviet Government varied thus from time to time, the policy of the United States throughout this period rested firmly on one principle—that of nonrecognition. The break which had developed between Great Britain and Soviet Russia seemed a substantial argument in favor of the continuance of that position. However, some financial circles in the United States, approaching the question from a different point of view, now advanced reasons for the restoration of relations with Moscow. Trade between the United States and Russia in 1927 reached $100,000,000, twice the prewar total, and the prospects of its continued growth constituted a strong inducement to establish diplomatic contacts.

The division among American business interests on the question of Soviet recognition came to a head in the fall of 1927 when a sharp conflict arose between a group of English and a group of American interests over Soviet oil. In July the Standard Oil Company of New York and the Vacuum Oil Company, another member of the Standard group, concluded agreements covering the purchase of oil from the Soviet Naphtha Syndicate. The Standard Oil Company of New Jersey protested against these arrangements, insisting that, prior to any deals with the Soviet Government, former owners who had been deprived of their property rights should receive compensation. An even stronger protest was made by Sir Henry Deterding, the head of Royal Dutch-Shell. At this point representatives of the Soviet Government revealed that both Standard Oil of New Jersey and Royal Dutch-Shell had been trying for some time to obtain a monopoly of the oil exported from Russia, and expressed their conviction that the resentment of these two companies arose from the refusal of the Soviet Government to grant them exclusive privileges. Answering this accusation, Deterding admitted that he had negotiated with the Soviets but at the same time asserted that he had always demanded compensation for former owners. The confusion resulting from this three-cornered dispute was finally resolved in February, 1929, by an agreement drawn up between the Soviet Petroleum Trust and the Anglo-American interests. By this arrangement prices for Soviet oil were fixed sufficiently low to enable the purchasers to build up a fund for the settlement of the claims of former owners.

In 1927, at the end of this period, Soviet relations with the western countries were still in an unsettled state. A number of countries had formally granted full recognition to the Soviets, but their actions were frequently hardly more than gestures. In general, though the Soviet Union had made some progress toward the re-entry into the world community of nations, especially in the field of trade, she was still refused the status of an equal member.

8.

It was largely during this period between 1921 and 1927 that the political forms and the governmental mechanisms which were to prevail in the Soviet Union took shape. In 1917 the Bolshevik revolution seized power under a slogan calling for the concentration of all power in the Soviets, and it was this principle which determined the general character of the new political structure of Russia. The Second All-Russian Congress of Soviets, meeting at the time of the revolution, sanctioned this new political form and itself assumed the functions of the Constituent Assembly which had actually been elected two weeks after the upheaval but was dismissed by the Bolsheviks after its first session. Acting in the capacity of a legislative assembly, the Third Congress then officially confirmed the Government of the Council of People's Commissars which was headed by Lenin.

Lenin's Government did not, however, hasten to define the precise political structure of the state. It had neither the time nor the inclination to present a detailed governmental system. At the time it was nearly overwhelmed with practical problems affecting the very existence of the new state which demanded immediate solutions, problems involving the consolidation of Bolshevik power within the country and the conclusion of the promised peace with Russia's enemies without. It was not until the meeting of the Fifth Congress of Soviets on July 10, 1918, that a new constitution for the Russian Socialist Federative Soviet Republic (R.S.F.S.R.) was adopted.

The Soviet or Council system written into the constitution of this first Soviet republic was the model upon which the governments of the subsequent members of the Union and of the Union itself were based. According to the provisions of this constitution, the highest agency of power was the All-Russian Congress of Soviets, a large and somewhat cumbersome elected body, which met whenever necessary but never less than once a year. This body was not intended to function as the parliament of a constitutional state; it was primarily intended as a kind of assembly of all the electors of the country, and its decisions resembled a universal referendum rather than legislation. The Congress of Soviets elected a Central Executive Committee in whose hands the supreme power reposed between sessions of the Congress. The Executive Committee, a body of more than three hundred members which met regularly, corresponded somewhat roughly to a parliament. Its members were accorded the equivalent of parliamentary immunity; they were not subject to arrest without the consent of the Presidium or the chairman of the Committee and could be tried only upon the authorization of the Committee itself or its chairman.

When the Central Executive Committee was not in session, its power in turn resided theoretically in its Presidium, which was, in effect, a collective president of the Soviet state. Actually, however, the Council of People's Commissars—the Soviet form of a Cabinet—wielded much greater power. At first, indeed, it had been the main agency of government in the Soviet Republics and in the winter of 1917 and during the early part of 1918 issued a number of important laws. The majority of the decrees by which the life of the country was organized came from this agency; between 1917 and 1921, 1,615 were issued in the name of the Council of People's Commissars and only 375 in the name of the Central Executive Committee.

In contrast to the precise limitations set upon the power of each branch of government in European and American states, no distinction was made in the constitutional power of the several higher branches of the Soviet Government. The principle of replacement applied throughout, and rights and duties passed automatically from one body to another. The Central Executive Committee had the same legislative and administrative power as the Soviet Congress when the latter was not in session. Its Presidium was the supreme legislative and administrative branch between the meetings of the Committee. The Council of People's Commissars had the right to assume supreme authority whenever it was necessary to do so.

As the power of the Soviets extended beyond the border of Russia proper, the R.S.F.S.R., other Socialist Soviet republics were founded—the White Russian (Byelo-Russian), the Ukrainian, and others, including the Esthonian, the Latvian, and the Lithuanian; the latter three existed for only a short time in 1918–19 and were restored in 1940. Each of these republics was organized on the pattern of the R.S.F.S.R., and each in turn concluded an alliance with the larger state. Gradually, however, the need for a closer link between the sister republics was felt, and in December, 1922, all of them issued a joint declaration of union. On July 6, 1923, the new constitution of the Union of Socialist Soviet Republics (U.S.S.R.) was passed. At that time the Union consisted of the following four republics: (1) the R.S.F.S.R.; (2) the Ukrainian S.S.R.; (3) the White Russian S.S.R.; and (4) the Transcaucasian S.F.S.R., which included Georgia, Armenia, and Azerbaijan. In 1924 two Central Asia Soviet republics, the Uzbek and the Turkmen, were formed and accepted into the Union. Later on, three new republics were formed in Central Asia, the Tadjik, the Kazakh, and the Kirghiz, and the Transcaucasian Federation was dissolved, each of its three parts receiving the status of a full-fledged constituent republic. As a result of these admissions, by 1929 the number of constituent republics in the Union had risen to eleven.

The constitution of the U.S.S.R. was basically the R.S.F.S.R. constitution elaborated sufficiently to fit it to the necessities of a wider federation. An All-Union Congress of Soviets was elected and it, in turn, elected an All-Union Executive Committee. The latter was composed of two chambers, the Union Soviet and the Soviet of Nationalities. The Soviet of Nationalities consisted of five representatives from each of the allied and autonomous Soviet republics and one representative from each of the autonomous regions of the R.S.F.S.R.

The electoral system adopted by the Soviet Union was a frank expression of the principle of the dictatorship of the proletariat. The factory workers, who constituted only about 15 per cent of the population in the early 1920's, were represented at the rate of one deputy to 25,000 electors; the peasants, who constituted the bulk of the population, were represented by only one deputy for every 125,000 electors. Several million people, including remnants of the *bourgeois* class, the gentry, the clergy, and members of the former police force, were "disfranchised" altogether. Members of this "disfranchised" group were not only denied the right to vote; they were also ineligible for civil service, were prohibited from working in factories, and their children were refused admission to the colleges.

In addition to the fact that it was neither universal nor equal, the electoral system functioned under other restrictions. The elections were not direct but were conducted through several stages (township, district, province), in each of which the members of the assembly elected a certain number of that body to represent them in the next higher body. This system made for the elimination of all opposition, for in each stage voting was by a show of hands and was thus easily controlled by the political police. The task of restraining the voters and of supervising the administration generally was at first entrusted to a force headed by the so-called *Cheka* (Extraordinary Commission to Combat Counter-revolution and Sabotage). In 1922, following the reforms of the N.E.P., the *Cheka* was replaced by the O.G.P.U. (United Department of Political Police) which was supposed to work within certain legal restrictions. The change, however, amounted only to a revision of the name rather than an alteration of policy or method.

Whatever might have been the advantages or disadvantages of

the Soviet system as it was organized in 1918–23, the real power lay at that time not with the Soviets but with the Communist party. In spite of the fact that no mention of the party was made either in the constitution of 1918 or in that of 1923, the control of the country from top to bottom was firmly in communist hands. The party had its branches in each of the republics of the Union; its "cells" operated wherever decisions were made—in every factory, every local Soviet, every army unit. Its rule prevented the rise of opposition or conflict between either the republics of the union or the highest bodies of the Soviet Government itself. It was the only political party allowed to exist in Soviet Russia. In those years the Soviet system was not so much a dictatorship of the proletariat as of the Communist party.

The activities of the party itself were directed by a Central Committee of about one hundred members and a smaller group of nine members called the Political Bureau. Both of these bodies were elected at party conventions and both had authority over party institutions throughout the Soviet Union. The membership of the party was severely restricted, and each applicant had first to pass through a rigorous trial period as a candidate before he gained admission. Besides the party itself, a Communist Youth Movement, the Komsomol, was inaugurated. By 1927 there were about two million party members and candidates and something over a million youths enrolled in the Komsomol. These were considered the elite of the nation to whom was entrusted the creation of the new society. They had—and still have—many privileges in everyday life, but whatever honors and prerogatives they may enjoy are paid for in obedient and strenuous labor for the party. They are members of an organization which prides itself upon the discipline it enforces and they cannot refuse the heavy tasks of administration, propaganda, or military service which are allotted to them. The rewards for success are sometimes considerable, but the punishments for failure are equally great.

9.

The introduction of the N.E.P. in 1921 was an emergency measure forced upon the party by Lenin to save the sick and sinking economy of the Soviet state. It was successful beyond the hopes of most Bolshevik leaders. Reluctant as many of the more zealous communists must have been to admit the achievements of a system which seemed to contradict the very principle upon which the new world was to be built, the beneficial results of the retreat on the economic front were almost immediately evident. In both agriculture and industry production began to recover. The area under cultivation, which in 1921 had fallen to sixty million hectares, by 1923 had risen to sixty-five million hectares and in 1927 almost reached the 1916 level of ninety million. Grain collections, which had sunk to the famine level of eighteen million tons in 1920, increased to thirty-seven million tons in 1924 and by 1926 doubled again to produce a harvest in excess of seventy-four million tons. There was a gradual increase in livestock until in 1926 horses numbered more than twenty-seven million head and cattle fifty-five million. Productivity in the various branches of industry showed similar gains. Coal production, which in 1922–23 had declined to eleven and a half million tons, rose in 1925–26 to twenty-four and a half million. During the same period the manufacture of cotton fabric shot up from five hundred sixty million meters to two billion meters. Released from the suffocating restrictions of War Communism, Russian economy had started on the road to recovery.

The new stability introduced by the economic reconstruction of Russia made possible the reorganization of the currency and establishment of a firm monetary unit. The State Bank, which had been re-established in 1921, was authorized in 1922 to issue chervonets bank notes. The chervonets—equal to ten gold rubles, or about $5.00[1]—was to be backed by a quarter of its value in gold, platinum, or stable foreign currency. The rest of its value was to be guaranteed by readily negotiable short-term obligations. With the issue of the chervonets the old paper currency was not withdrawn, however, and the state treasury, in fact, continued to produce still more of it. Thus, for a time there were two kinds of paper money in circulation—one stable and the other constantly falling in value. The chervonets was quoted on the exchange like pounds sterling and dollars: One chervonets was worth 117 rubles of the 1923 paper currency, and each of these rubles was in turn worth 1,000,000 rubles of any previous issue. The value of the old paper currency sank rapidly; in December, 1923, the chervonets was quoted

[1] The ruble contains 17.424 dolyas of pure gold. One dolya is equal to 0.68576 grains.

at 13,700 "1923 rubles" and in April, 1924, at 500,000 "1923 rubles."

In the spring of 1924 the treasury was authorized to issue small currency notes of one-, three-, and five-ruble denominations. Simultaneously the State Bank announced that it would accept an unlimited amount of new currency notes in payment of all liabilities at the official rate of ten rubles to the chervonets which had been established in 1922. At the same time the further printing of the old paper currency was suspended, and silver and copper coins were put in circulation. On March 17, 1924, the redemption of "1923 rubles" at the rate of fifty thousand to the gold ruble was announced. The end of the circulation of the old currency was set for May 10, 1924, and the final date for its redemption fixed as May 31. The withdrawal of the depreciated paper money left only chervonets, stable currency notes, and metal coins in circulation, and the consequent strengthening of the monetary system greatly increased public confidence in the Government.

The introduction of the N.E.P. was generally regarded outside the Soviet Union as the first step in the direction of the complete return to a capitalist economy. Indeed, had the tendencies implicit in the new policy not been carefully controlled, the reforms might well have led to that conclusion. However, the Soviet Government was entirely conscious of the dangers and made extraordinary efforts to prevent the situation from getting out of hand. In March, 1922, the Eleventh Conference of the Communist Party announced that the "retreat on the economic front" must end. Nevertheless, several further concessions were later made to the N.E.P. in connection with the reintroduction of the produce exchanges and the important annual fair at Nizhni-Novgorod. Toward the end of 1922, however, "the retreat" was actually brought to an end with the exception of the currency reform which was then in progress and a few temporary measures favorable to the peasants which were canceled by 1927. The economic system which prevailed in Russia from this time until 1927 was a bastard plan, neither socialist nor capitalist but something between the two. It differed from a true socialist system to the extent of all the reforms instituted by the N.E.P.; it varied from the capitalist form in that it involved an excessive government control of economic matters, especially foreign trade.

Both government-owned and private industry shared in the increased production of the period, but the relative strength of the state industries increased steadily. The tendencies are clearly shown in the following figures. In 1923–24 the production of government industries amounted to 2,400,000,000 gold rubles in prewar prices, while production by private industry, including foreign concessions, was about one third of that, or 842,000,000 rubles. Two years later state industries produced 5,333,000,000 rubles' worth of goods and private industry 1,252,000,000 rubles, or less than a quarter as much. Although production had been released from the more stringent restrictions of War Communism, the Soviet Government still retained the essential direction. It continued to exercise a monopoly of foreign trade and through the *Gosplan,* or State Planning Commission, to shape the course of Soviet economy for several years in advance.

The agricultural policy of the Soviet Union was directed toward two objectives: an increase in the production of food material and the prevention of the development of private property in land holdings. The provisions of the N.E.P. carefully avoided the reintroduction of the right of ownership in small individual farms. According to the Land Code of 1922 all land belonged to the state and the peasant was merely accorded the free use of it. It was to be cultivated either by the community or by an individual, but Section 27 of the Code categorically forbade the sale, purchase, mortgage, bequest, or gift of the land. The Soviet Government was in no wise committed to the support of the old Commune but in general it gave less encouragement to the peasant to leave the Commune and become an individual tenant than did the Stolypin legislation.

The essential part played by the Commune in opposing peasant individualism was now transferred to the Soviet coöperatives which came into existence with the N.E.P. During the period of War Communism which preceded the reforms, the Soviet Government had attempted to suppress all forms of coöperatives as expressions of *bourgeois* prejudice. Agricultural coöperatives were, however, reinstated by decree on May 7, 1921, and on August 16 of the same year a second decree fully confirmed their right to hold property and officially recognized them as essential instruments in the development of the new system. Their growth was exceedingly rapid; by October 1, 1926, there were 33,500 agricultural coöperatives with a membership of 5,948,760 engaged in the operation of creameries, flour mills, and many other agricultural industries.

The Government hoped that in the coöperative movement it had found a method of achieving the unification of all individual peasant households in an organization which could be controlled and centrally directed. The communist leadership believed, too, that the coöperatives would serve as an efficient means of educating the peasantry toward socialism, that they would be instrumental in leveling out the inequalities still existing between individual peasant households, and that they would prove particularly useful as a means of combating the development of the richer peasant class. The importance of the coöperatives in the Soviet plan was so considerable that it was not unusual for communist leaders at that time to speak of the new policy as agricultural-coöperative-socialism.

The reforms of the N.E.P. so successfully revitalized Soviet economy that by 1927 production in many fields had already reached the levels of 1913 and in some instances, in fact, had slightly exceeded them. For example, in 1913 the value of agricultural goods produced within the territories later held by the Soviets totaled 12,790,000,000 rubles; by 1927 it had reached 12,775,000,000. Industrial production, which in 1913 was valued at 6,391,000,000 rubles, had risen by 1927 to 6,608,000,000 rubles; coal production moved from 29,000,000 metric tons to 30,000,000; oil from 9,000,000 to 10,000,000; and the manufacture of cotton cloth from 2,238,000,000 meters to 2,342,000,000. The N.E.P. was indeed a theoretical "retreat" on the economic front, but it was a retreat that carried the Soviet Union forward on its way to a stable economy.

10.

At the time of the Bolshevik revolution Soviet Communism was a new system, an untried theory without example anywhere in the world. To bring such a system to a backward political country was a monumental task. To accomplish that objective Lenin devised the Communist party. During the early years of the Bolshevik *régime* Lenin was almost an absolute dictator in Soviet Russia, and it was his strength and his political perception that enabled the struggling new government to overcome almost unending obstacles. On May 25, 1922, at the very beginning of the critical period of the inauguration of the N.E.P., Lenin was felled by a stroke. By

October of the same year he had regained his health and resumed his work; but at the end of November his condition again became worse. In March, 1923, a second stroke deprived him of the power of speech and on January 21, 1924, he died.

For a time after his death Lenin's spirit continued to rule over Russia. His tomb was made a communist shrine, and Petrograd, City of Peter (the Great), was renamed Leningrad in his honor. No speech by a party orator could omit a quotation from his work, and his words became the Bible of communism to which his followers returned again and again for political guidance.

The task of directing the destinies of the country and the problems of guiding a world-wide organization made it necessary, however, to find a successor to Lenin—both as leader of the Communist party and as head of the Soviet Government. These duties were at first assumed by a triumvirate consisting of Kamenev, Zinoviev, and Stalin—all three Bolsheviks of long standing. Kamenev, whose real name was Rosenfeld, was the least revolutionary in temper and at the same time the best educated. Zinoviev, whose name was Radomyslsky, was an insolent man without either moral principles or great ability who had attained a leading position in the party chiefly because of his servile attitude toward Lenin. Stalin, a Georgian whose real name was Djugashvili, had already exhibited the firmness of will and undeniable organizing ability which were eventually to bring him to a prominent position in the Soviet Government.

Trotsky, who was the most prominent leader next to Lenin and the most brilliant orator of the Russian revolution, was prevented from sharing power by the "Triumvirate" against whom he soon started an opposition movement. His policy was an amalgam in which personal motives and political principles were intricately combined. He had never been an orthodox communist. In the revolution of 1905 and in the years following it he had wavered between the Bolsheviks and the Mensheviks, in many cases making common cause with the latter. Only after the revolution of March, 1917, did he finally throw in his lot with the Bolsheviks and in the months following he rose rapidly to a position of leadership. Even after the revolution, however, Trotsky had on many occasions expressed views which were not approved either by Lenin or by the majority of the Communist party. That Trotsky should, after Lenin's death, become an exponent of pure communism was an unexpected reversal of his previous position.

Pointing out that Zinoviev and Kamenev had voted against the Central Committee of the Communist party even as late as two weeks before the Bolshevik uprising, Trotsky now charged them with a lack of true revolutionary spirit. Trotsky was an able antagonist. His oratorical ability, combined with his prestige in the party, were such that the leadership was soon involved in intense debates which led to a bitter struggle for the control of the party mechanism. Within a short time various factions had arisen and Trotsky assumed the leadership of a group, soon dubbed the "Trotskyites," who accused the party of *bourgeois* tendencies and proclaimed themselves the true followers of Lenin and the guardians of communism pure and undefiled.

As early as 1922, while Lenin was still alive, the party congress had declared that the "retreat from the economic front" was complete. By the spring of 1925, however, relations between the Soviet Government and the peasants had become so strained that a new series of compromises was necessary. Bukharin, the chief theorist of the Communist party and the editor of *Pravda,* admitted that in spite of the N.E.P. the effects of War Communism were still evident in village economy. The peasantry still had no confidence that their farms would be secure under the Soviet *régime.* Two years later Stalin himself was willing to confess that prior to 1925 the peasant problem had pressed heavily on the Communist party: "Our agents in the villages were killed and their houses set on fire by the peasants. . . . In some places, especially in the border regions, we had to fight the activities of organized bands; and we had to suppress a real peasant uprising in Georgia." Because of these difficulties the Soviet Government decided to adopt a more lenient agricultural policy which the Fourteenth Party Conference approved in the spring of 1925. Defining the party aims at that conference, Stalin said: "The chief problem now is how to rally the middle groups of peasants around labor; we have to conquer the sympathies of the middle groups of the peasants." At the same meeting the policy of providing relief for the peasantry was also strongly supported by Kalinin, Chairman of the Soviet Federation, and Rykov, the Prime Minister of the Soviet Government.

It was against this new peasant policy of the Soviet Government, conceived as a further development of the N.E.P., that the opposition within the Communist party centered its attack. The situation became especially dangerous for the unity of the party when two leading members of the Political Bureau, Zinoviev and Kamenev, also joined the opposition. The critics excoriated the new policy as an example of the abandonment by the Soviet leaders of the principles of pure communism, and when the Central Committee justified its position as a step toward unity with the middle group of the peasants, the opposition accused them of giving relief to the richer[2] peasants.

Besides all of this, the opposition charged the majority leaders with despotism in the party management and asked that the Political Bureau be deprived of its autocratic power. However, in spite of the opposition's vitriolic criticism of the majority during the Fourteenth Conference of the Party in December, 1925, the delegates approved the policy presented by the Central Committee.

Stalin's program had been sustained. Consequently he did not yet consider it necessary to take any punitive measures against the opposition leadership but confined himself to the following warning: "The Party desires unity, and it will achieve it with Kamenev and Zinoviev if they wish it, or without them if they do not wish it."

The victory of the Central Committee of the All-Union Communist Party over the opposition in the Fourteenth Conference of the Party was not final. The defeated leaders, all masters of the techniques of political maneuvering, tried all sorts of measures to increase their influence within the party. By 1926 they had built up their own organization which was guided by its own committee and operated its own secret printing office. In September and early October, 1926, this group tried to win labor over to its side by attacking the Central Committee in meetings of the workers of various large factories in Leningrad and Moscow. However, when the workmen remained loyal to the Central Committee and the results of this revolt appeared to be unfavorable to the opposition, the leaders realized their defeat and on October 16 drafted a petition

[2] It is interesting to know what the Soviet leaders meant by the various classes of peasants. According to the data presented to the Fifteenth Party Conference, the poorer peasants were those with an annual per capita income of $39; the middle group had an annual income of $46; and the richer peasants, $88.

to the Central Committee promising to cease the struggle and to work together with the party majority. Stalin, however, was not ready this time to accept their statement as a *bona fide* recantation and in an address before the Fifteenth Conference of the Party, held in October and November of 1926, subjected the opposition to merciless criticism. He enumerated the following principal "sins" of the opposition: (1) Its leaders had tried to tempt the Communist International to follow the path of revolutionary adventure; (2) they had proposed the greatest possible burden of taxation on the peasants, thus preparing an inevitable split between the peasantry and labor; (3) they had aimed at a relaxation of the party dictatorship over Russia; (4) they had aspired to weaken the dictatorship of the Central Committee by requiring the establishment of a "democratic" *régime* within the party. His conclusion was that, while the opposition leaders were trying to mask their intentions with a pretense of pure communist principles, their policy was in reality permeated with opportunism and tended toward the restoration of a middle-class *régime*. This point of view was accepted by the party conference and approved by the Central Committee.

The peace within the Communist party, however, was not lasting. In the summer of 1927, when relations between the party majority and the opposition again became critical, Stalin decided to inflict penalties on the opposition leaders. Declaring that they were causing a split in the party and consequently endangering the future of the Soviet system, he demanded that Trotsky and Zinoviev, as the two most active leaders, be formally excluded from its rolls. This expulsion was carried out in November, 1927, before a new convention of the party. The purge which Stalin thus achieved secured the dominance of the majority within the party, and although it did not end the conflict with finality, it did assure the party an opportunity to carry out its program with a minimum of internal dissension.

CHAPTER XVII.

THE PERIOD OF THE FIRST FIVE YEAR PLAN

(1928–1932)

I.

THE Fifteenth Convention of the All-Union Communist Party which was called in December, 1927, marked the beginning of a new era in Soviet Russia. It was an event of the first magnitude not only in the development of internal party policy but also in the remolding of the political and economic system under which the Soviet Union itself was henceforth to operate. As subsequent events were to prove, it was the decisions of the Fifteenth Convention which turned the energies of Soviet Russia away from the drive toward international revolution and concentrated them in a movement for national revolution. In its wider aspects, it represented the triumph of the proponents of Russian nationalism over the advocates of uncompromising revolutionary internationalism.

The immediate business of the Fifteenth Convention concerned the conflict which had split the Russian Communist party, and from the first session it was clear that it was to result in the victory of the Central Committee over the opposition. The overwhelming majority of the deputies were followers of the Central Committee, and the recalcitrants were without a leader, since Trotsky had already been expelled from the party. After representatives of the various workers' organizations had delivered addresses supporting the party position and attacking the minority recommendations, the Central Committee proposed the exclusion from the party of all the leaders of the opposition. A member of the Committee who had been appointed to study the problem charged that all the counterrevolutionary elements in the country were beginning to center around this group, and that—to quote his own words—"The opposition leaders have become open enemies of the dictatorship of the proletariat." On December 18 all opposition leaders were excluded from the party and passed into a political oblivion that at the time seemed final. In January, 1928, Trotsky was exiled to the city of Alma-Ata in Turkestan and early in 1929 was deported from Russia to Turkey. Expressing their willingness to abandon their opposition, Kamenev and Zinoviev sought pardon from the Central Committee and thus escaped formal exile. They were assigned for a time to obscure positions in provincial towns of central Russia, and in the summer of 1928 both were received back into the party.

A substantial part of the proceedings of the Fifteenth Convention was devoted to the problems of economic reconstruction. At the outset the members reaffirmed their belief in the need for the rapid industrialization of Russia in order to establish a firm base for communist economy. They then reviewed the agricultural policies adopted by the previous Convention which had met in 1925, and officially recognized that the lenient agricultural measures adopted at that time had resulted in a gratifying increase in the farm land under cultivation. While the new policies were economically beneficial, it was noted that they had had adverse political effects and particularly that the leniency had resulted in an alarming growth in the class of richer peasants. The party leaders were determined to reverse this trend. Repudiating the policies of its predecessor, the Fifteenth Convention asserted that a new offensive against the class of rich peasants was necessary and urged that Soviet agricultural economy at once be adjusted to coincide with the over-all Soviet pattern envisioned for the country. As a first move in this direction the Convention took steps to strengthen the "poorest peasants" as a class by confirming the exemption of 35 per cent of them from the land tax. Several other measures designed to speed up the process of reform in agriculture were passed by the Convention—measures specifically concerned with the development of the collective farms, the Kolkhozes, and the expansion of state-owned farms, the Sovkhozes.

On the surface the decisions of the Fifteenth Convention were not especially revolutionary. Later, however, it became apparent that these superficially slight shifts, which at the time had either passed unnoticed or been misinterpreted in capitalist countries, had really inaugurated the period of forcible collectivization of agriculture which was to have such tremendous repercussions in Russia's history.

2.

THE decisions of the Fifteenth Convention eventually resulted in the total reshaping of Soviet economy. The agrarian reforms, violent and disruptive as they proved to be, were but one aspect of the shift. Without pausing to allow the country to absorb the shock of this change, the Fifteenth Convention launched the Soviet Union upon that daring and ingenious undertaking which has since come to be known as the Five Year Plan. The Russian people were thus plunged into a twin revolution which, in a sense, affected the destinies of the Russian people even more than the cataclysm of 1917. In some ways the new upheaval was a reversal of the usual revolutionary pattern. In contrast to the Revolution of 1917, which had been essentially a spontaneous movement of the masses of the people, this new revolution was deliberately instigated by the Government itself. It was a violent readjustment originating above and exerting pressure downward. The earlier uprising had been chiefly destructive in nature, a clearing away of old forms to make way for the new; the upheaval which began in 1927 was constructive both in its spirit and in its purpose. But revolution it was—in scope, in intent, and in consequences. Remembering that without this period of readjustment Russia might have fallen before the German onslaught of 1941, the future historian may well consider these events the decisive turning point in modern Russian history.

The Government's decision to swing once more into the revolutionary stream was the result of a combination of circumstances. By and large the path the Soviet Union was following was an unsatisfactory one from the standpoint of the Bolsheviks. True, under the N.E.P. the country had made rapid strides toward reconstruction of industry and agriculture, but mere reconstruction was not the goal toward which communism was driving. Politically the N.E.P. had led the nation into a dead-end road of compromise with the old capitalist principles. To many an ardent Communist this policy was little less than treason. Even after Trotsky was expelled, there was considerable dissatisfaction in the party, and some of those who had most steadfastly fought the opposition now called for a revival of militant communism. They felt that it was time to turn away from a system which strengthened the peasants and built a small farmer class of kulaks who were put in a position to dictate the policies of the Government—who might at any time if they so desired even call a halt to the development of socialism. It was the factory workers who had made the revolution; it was they who were now the backbone of Soviet power—and it was they who must always be in a position to determine the course of Russian history.

It was not denied, of course, that the N.E.P. had restored the output of Russian industry and agriculture to nearly the 1913 level. But was that enough of an achievement to justify all the horrors and privations of the civil war and the period of war communism following it? The experience of a former Duma member, Shulgin, may illustrate the Russian attitude. An émigré who had left Russia several years earlier, in 1926 Shulgin had himself smuggled into the country and traveled around secretly—or so he thought. Actually the O.G.P.U. knew of his visit but chose not to interfere with his movements. In a book he wrote subsequently, he summed up his impressions in the following words, "Everything in Russia is the same as it used to be before the revolution, only a little bit shabbier." A little bit shabbier—. It was not for shabbiness that the Bolsheviks had engineered a revolution and fought through a bitter and grueling civil war. Through all the years of their efforts they had dreamed of a land in which the ease and plenty that were the people's right could be enjoyed by them. And at the end of all that was the country to continue, because of a series of compromises with an outworn system, to be a land of want? The party leaders felt that only a determined drive toward pure socialism could remedy the situation and that only drastic changes could accelerate the rate of progress sufficiently to end the evils of scarcity.

As the Government studied the situation, it recognized that the conditions of industry were even worse than they appeared to be on the surface. No longer could Russia depend on the stream of foreign capital which in prerevolutionary days had flowed into her industries. With the nationalization of the productive system, that flow had all but stopped. A trickle remained, it is true, but the few credits from abroad that could be and were secured went immediately for desperately needed machinery and manufactured goods which had to be imported. Nothing remained for the reconstruction or expansion of the industrial plants upon which the life of the U.S.S.R. depended. Some internal loans had been floated, principally among the peasantry, but it was clear that the peasants would not much longer continue to finance industry at their own expense. Another method to achieve the industrialization of the new state was found, and the fact that its operation first necessitated breaking down the whole traditional structure of the peasant class was not sufficient to deter the Soviet leaders.

There was another important consideration which led to action at this time. Russia stood alone as the only socialistic state in the world, and its Government was constantly haunted by the fear of a "capitalist encirclement" or even of a direct attack by one or more of the capitalist powers. Great Britain and France at first seemed the most threatening potential enemies; later on Germany emerged as an even more dangerous adversary. Soviet leaders, and especially Red Army men such as Shaposhnikov, Frunze, and Tukhachevsky, well remembered the lessons of the first World War. They insisted on the urgent necessity of building powerful armament and munitions industries as speedily as possible. But the armament industries do not stand alone; to achieve this objective it was necessary first greatly to increase all industrial facilities throughout the whole Soviet Union.

The need then was clear, and since the Government itself controlled all the larger industrial plants, the Gosplan was put to work preparing a comprehensive plan for the development of Russian industry during the next five years, with the additional understanding that a Second and a Third Five Year Plan were to follow if necessary. The idea of such a planned economy was not a new one. Indeed, all the belligerent countries had turned to such planning on a greater or lesser scale during the first World War. In Russia the conditions which had caused all countries to adopt planning continued long after the war was over and after the capitalist states were well advanced in reconstruction. The Gosplan itself had been organized in 1921 to facilitate the recovery of Russian industry both from the damage resulting from the war itself and from the destruction and disorganization of the civil war. Even before that, at Lenin's suggestion, a Commission of Electrification had been set up in 1920 but because of economic circumstances it was unable to make any substantial progress. The Marxist theoreticians were not alone in their interest in the problem of building a rationalized economy; engineers and technicians were, by their training, attracted to the possibilities of such an organization. Many such plans had been suggested, but the most important and clearest blueprint for the reconstruction of Russian industry had been presented in a remarkable book written by V. I. Grinevetsky, a prominent Russian engineer of prerevolutionary training.

Grinevetsky's book, *Postwar Prospects of Russian Industry*, which was published in 1919, proposed that Russian factories and plants should be geographically adjusted to the natural resources of the country and located near the principal supplies of raw materials, in order to avoid unnecessary transportation. Basing his thesis on the practical possibilities for such a shift, Grinevetsky suggested the rapid development of two areas of great potential wealth—the Ural region and the vast territory of western Siberia which had not hitherto been sufficiently exploited. Besides the economic aspects involved in this mammoth relocation of Russian industry, it included at least one change of great military importance—the shift of productive centers far to the east out of reach of any foreign invader.

Using the ideas which Grinevetsky had expressed with convincing clarity and others which were available to them, the members of the Gosplan prepared the outline for the First Five Year Plan which was announced early in 1928 and went into operation that autumn. The following year the quotas originally set were revised upward, and it was decided "to complete the First Five Year Plan in four years"—that is, between October 1, 1928, and December 31, 1932. While the plan was not fulfilled in all details, its actual achievements during this shortened period were tremendous. In four years Russia's yearly national income rose from 27 billion rubles (1926–27 price level) to 45 billion rubles in 1932. Capital invested in industry rose from 2 billion to over 9 billion rubles. On the basis of this enormous capital investment the Soviet Union was able to move forward in a vast industrial expansion.

But the over-all figures and quantitative increases did not tell the whole story. The quality of the industrial products was usually poor and the cost of production almost invariably high. Everywhere there were waste and mismanagement, conditions which were to be explained chiefly by the shortage of skilled labor, technicians, and engineers. The reserve pool of skilled workers in Russia had always been low and after the revolution many trained engineers and technicians emigrated, reducing the supply still further. Foreign engineers were invited to supervise the building of the more important industrial plants, but they were too few personally to take care of all details of the work, and in addition they could not always be trusted by the Government. Gradually, however, the labor situation improved. Every year greater numbers of engineers and technicians were graduated from Russian schools and more and more raw peasant recruits were trained in the mechanical skills. Indeed, from one standpoint the very deficiencies in the execution of the First Five Year Plan had their positive uses. While a great deal of valuable and desperately needed machinery was ruined by newly drafted peasant boys and girls who were totally unfamiliar with mechanical processes, and while much time was wasted in adapting them to even the simplest tasks, the whole process amounted to a practical course of experimental education. In time millions of untrained youths had been poured into the creation of a reserve of machine-minded workers. More important, perhaps, was the fact that the traditional inertia of the Russian peasant had finally been broken, even though at a tremendous cost in lives, in machinery, and in money.

A vast program such as that envisaged in the First Five Year Plan demands equally vast sums of money for its execution. The capital investment required could be met in only one way—by reducing the living standards of the people. After the war and the destructive period of the civil war, Russia's economy was completely shaken. During the period of reconstruction under the N.E.P. the country recovered quickly. However, the breathing spell was not long enough to let Russia acquire real economic fat, and even by 1927 there was little surplus energy upon which she could draw. The difficulties which now arose were sharply accentuated by the dislocations of the agricultural revolution which was at the same time in progress. In the initial years of the Five Year Plan the rate of agricultural production was constantly falling; the food situation, which had been strained to the breaking point at the time of the civil war, now became even more critical; housing conditions, particularly around the vast new industrial communities where there had been no opportunity to provide new construction before workers swarmed into the districts, were appalling. Throughout this first period the emphasis of the plan was entirely on "heavy" industry, on the production of the machinery with which the plan could be carried out in its larger aspects. Within a comparatively short time there developed a "famine" of consumer goods including not only food but clothing and textiles as well. As a matter of fact, it was actually the success of the First Five Year Plan which broke the stability laboriously achieved during the period of the N.E.P. and resulted in privations comparable only to those of the period of the civil war. The situation at last became desperate, and in 1930, largely as a result of the forcible collectivization of agriculture, a famine developed in Ukraine. Starvation and all its accompanying diseases stalked unchecked through the richest agricultural region in the Soviet Union, and within the space of a few months hundreds of thousands if not millions of people died in unimaginable misery.

In spite of the almost unbelievable hardships the Russian people were called upon to bear, the Government refused to abandon its original plan of revision. It is sometimes difficult for the student to understand how any people who had passed through the cataclysms which had descended upon Russia in 1914, in 1917, and in 1920–21 could have endured the privations to which they were now subjected. That the Government was able to carry through the reorganization to a successful conclusion was, in the main, the result of its ability to combine the efforts of several groups. The Soviet leaders were aided, of course, by the coöperation of the engineers and technicians who saw in the new system an opportunity to exploit and develop the potential wealth of the nation. They had the unflagging assistance of party members and members of the Komsomol, who were inspired by the prospect of "building up socialism in a single country," of achieving the economic independence of which they had long dreamed. Recalcitrant elements were held under a discipline that was often harsh and sometimes even cruel. As a nation, the Soviet Union felt under the threat of "capitalist encirclement" and was therefore intent upon using this brief span of years to prepare for the attack which seemed imminent. The mentality of the Russian people in the early years of the First Five Year Plan was that of a nation going through a revolution and a war simultaneously. This conception perhaps explains why the people endured so much and why so little value was attached to individual rights and freedom. The Russians believed that they were battling for survival, and under those circumstances they could and did bear privations untold.

There was one more motive—narrower and more nationalistic—involved in the people's attitude. Stalin's slogan, "the building of socialism in a single country," convinced the Russian people that the era of international adventures was over and that what they were now struggling to build was for Russia alone. To work for Russia was essentially to work for their own benefit, and this conviction made it possible for Russian leaders to harness the revival of patriotic feeling, which has since flared up with such vigor, to the creation of the new communist state.

Sociologically, the most important result of the successive Five Year Plans was the transformation of Russia from a predominantly agrarian country into one 50 per cent industrialized. At the same time, this change resulted in a new relationship between the economic groups within the Soviet Union. The collectivization of agriculture did away with the class of peasants as small farmers, and the Sovkhoz and Kolkhoz members no longer stood apart as a separate segment of the population but became as much a part of the new society as the factory workers. The end result of this "deepening of the revolution" was the creation of a more homogeneous social structure which had an over-all cohesion in spite of the fact that here and there new group distinctions arose as time went on. The old cleavages which, in effect, had made Russia several distinct nations under a single head were now abolished, and by 1936 the Soviets were able to claim that they had reached the stage of a "classless" society. With the ending of the old classes and the conflicts inherent in them, the theory of class struggle, which had so long served to divide the people, became obsolete and the Soviets entered a new period of national consolidation. Paradoxically enough, the national regeneration of Russia which all groups had striven to reach had finally been achieved by militant communism.

3.

THE industrial revolution—for sociologically and economically the Five Year Plans were no less than that—began with the adoption of the First Five Year Plan in a spirit of youthful self-confidence. "Overtake and pass America" was the central and characteristic slogan of the day, and the nation bent enthusiastically to the multitude of tasks before it. But it is none too easy to sustain early enthusiasms even under the best of circumstances, and in Russia in those hectic days it was almost impossible. Delays, discouragements, setbacks, and failures of all sorts rose to plague both the planners and the workers. From time to time optimistic reports of the rise in the level of production were issued by the Government, and to the workers who suffered the unbelievable hardships of the period these reports must have appeared completely false and deliberately distorted. As time went on the gulf between the plan's bold estimate and the actual achievements seemed to become wider instead of narrower.

In retrospect, it is clear that this significant period of the First Five Year Plan established the basis for later successes, and in spite of all its shortcomings the essential work accomplished then laid the foundation for the further development of Russian heavy industry. But what is so plain today was then obscure both to contemporary students and to those actively engaged in the day-to-day work. Doubts and worries were constantly arising, and at times during the First Five Year Plan even the Soviet press was gloomy or alarmed. The most disturbing feature of the new system was the uncertainty of production. Industry appeared to function in spurts and spells, and months of feverish progress were frequently succeeded by equally long periods in which production slumped and bottlenecks developed in many crucial sectors.

The first quarter of the second year of the First Five Year Plan—from October through December, 1929—was typical of the recurring periods in which production figures showed disquieting regressions. Indeed, in January, 1930, the Soviet press was talking of serious "breaks" at various points at the economic front. For the first quarter of that year the Donets coal basin fulfilled only 94 per cent of the program set for it, which meant that industry received 500,000 less tons of coal than had been anticipated. The smelting of pig iron in the Ural region reached only 90 per cent of the planned output, and factories of the "Yugostal" or southern steel trust were only slightly higher with 92 per cent. In October, 1929, Leningrad factories turned out goods valued at 172,000,000 rubles, about $86,000,000; but the following month the output fell to 160,000,000 rubles, about $80,000,000. In general, heavy industry fell short of the quota set for it by 4 per cent, though in some factories the gap between plan and performance amounted to 10 per cent or more. Lumbering enterprises in the north of Russia fell behind by more than 25 per cent, a failure which adversely affected the balance of foreign trade, since lumber and petroleum were at that time the chief items of Soviet export.

The Soviet Government stubbornly refused to admit failure. Characteristically enough, each time a new crisis developed the Government increased quotas for production rather than adjusting them to a lower level. Wherever the situation became critical, extraordinary steps such as the formation of "shock brigades" of best workers or battalions of Komsomol members were sent in to prevent a breakdown in production. Because of the Government's single-minded insistence upon its objective and its complete disregard of the hardships and privations which the population was called upon to endure, the general rise in production at the end of the First Five Year Plan was impressive enough. In the period from 1928 to 1932 the yearly output of coal had increased from 35,000,000 tons to 64,000,000 tons; of oil from 11,000,000 tons to 22,000,000; of pig iron from 3,000,000 to 6,000,000. In 1928 less than 1,000 automobiles and only slightly more than 1,000 tractors had been produced, but in 1932, 24,000 automobiles and 50,000 tractors rolled from Soviet plants.

It is worth calling special attention to the most ambitious undertaking of the First Five Year Plan, the construction of the Dnieper River Power Station (*Dnieproges*). An American engineer, Hugh L. Cooper, was engaged to design and supervise the construction of this enormous project which was completed in October, 1932. Its annual output soon reached 2.7 billion kilowatt-hours, and its ultimate capacity was estimated as 558,000 kilowatts. This industrial unit, the pride of Soviet industry and a memorial to Russian-American coöperation, was to stand hardly ten years: during the retreat of the Red Army in the first summer of the German war it was blown up by the Russians themselves.

Of even more importance to Russian industrial development was the huge steel mill erected at Magnitogorsk in the Ural area, the construction of which overlapped into the Second Five Year Plan.

The Magnitogorsk plant, which was to become one of the cornerstones of the huge Ural-Kuznetsk *combinat* intended to make the Ural and western Siberian area a self-sufficient industrial base, was completed in the course of the Second Plan. Other industrial construction kept pace with these spectacular and daring industrial communities. Several automobile, tractor, and agricultural machinery plants at Gorky (Nizhni-Novgorod), Kharkov, Rostov, Stalingrad, and Cheliabinsk were completed during this period. To the list of important milestones in industrial development reached at this time must be added the construction of the oil pipe line from Grozny in the northern Caucasus to the Black Sea port of Tuapse, and the building of the vital Turkestan-Siberian railroad.

The First Five Year Plan was not, however, entirely a story of successes. On the contrary, there were many disturbing factors, especially the continued problem of the poor quality of goods, the low rate of production, and, as a result, the high unit cost. The Government, of course, recognized these deficiencies, but although it was aware of the situation there was little that could be done about it at first. Only gradually, during the Second and the beginning of the Third Five Year Plan, was the situation to improve, and even in 1940–41 the legacy of the hastiness with which the First Five Year Plan was started and fulfilled was still being felt. Broadly speaking, in the initial years of the Five Year Plan these difficulties were met by throwing into industry more and more labor from the almost inexhaustible reserve which had been a byproduct of the mechanization of agriculture and the release of "labor surplus" from the villages. Factories at that time worked in three shifts, and in order to do away with Sunday stops a system of "uninterrupted" or "continuous" weeks was invented and applied in 1929. In September of that year it was decreed that each worker should work for four and later for five consecutive days, after which he was given one day of rest. Since the new "week" was fluid and the rest day varied from one individual to another, members of the same family were seldom all free on the same day, and the inconveniences which arose were sometimes severe enough to break family ties. At the same time, the new system proved to have serious disadvantages in the field of industrial production which it was designed to aid. Under the continuous three-shift system, it was difficult to keep either the machinery or the factory buildings in good order, especially since no group of workers on the staggered week could function effectively as a unit. At last, having been tried in a number of forms, the "continuous week" system was abolished altogether in 1940.

An equally serious problem was the "fluidity" of labor which resulted in a constant and hampering turnover among workers in the plants. Because of poor housing conditions and, at times, because of the lack of food at the sites of new construction projects, workers were constantly on the move in search of better accommodations and better conditions elsewhere. As a result, almost no factory except those situated in long-established industrial regions like Leningrad and Moscow had a permanent staff of skilled people on whom it could rely.

The normal length of the work day was seven hours until 1940, when it was increased by an additional hour because of the pressure of external danger. The comparatively low real wages which prevailed during the First Five Year Plan were compensated for, in part at least, by a comprehensive system of unemployment, social, and health insurance. Nevertheless, though the average annual wage expressed in monetary terms rose from 703 rubles in 1928 to 1,427 rubles in 1932, because of a corresponding increase in prices the average worker was able to obtain for his wages even less food and manufactured goods than he had in 1928. Both real and monetary wages, however, improved during the Second Five Year Plan. Largely as a result of the spread of a system of piecework and bonuses, certain groups of workers reached a comparatively high standard of living by 1940. This new piecework system, "Stakhanovism" as it soon came to be called, was begun in 1935 by a coal miner by the name of Alexi Stakhanov. By the institution of "brigades" of workers who were trained in a method of teamwork based on strict division of labor, the Stakhanovites were able to produce much more rapidly than was possible when individuals worked alone, and in time their methods were applied in various forms to many branches of industry. It was sometimes observed by economists outside the Soviet Union that the Stakhanovite spirit of competition and "speed-up" was essentially more suited to the capitalist system of industrial management than to the socialist scheme. Whatever its faults or virtues may have been, it is clear now that in spite of certain technical deficiencies Stakhanovism resulted in a general upward trend in the production standards of Russia and enabled her to engage the capitalist countries on a more equal basis.

4.

THE industrial revolution put in motion by the introduction of the Five Year Plans consisted, in the industrial sphere, largely of a program of enormous and forced expansion rather than a radical revision of previous plans. The agrarian revolution which accompanied it, however, involved a complete and total readjustment of both the social and economic foundations of the N.E.P. agricultural system. The central fact of the new policy was the shift of the center of gravity from the millions of small farms—the traditional basic division of the Russian peasant economy—to enormous socialized agricultural units called kolkhozes. A social movement of such vast proportions is inevitably attended with great hardships even when the readjustment is allowed scores of years in which to develop. In Russia, compressed as it was within the space of a few years, it resulted in a social convulsion.

To rebuild agriculture according to the new plan, it was first necessary to raze the existing farm structure. The work of demolition was carried out ruthlessly and with a total disregard of the rights, needs, or desires of the recalcitrant peasants. The richer peasants, the kulaks, suffered especially. As their farms were "liquidated" and their possessions confiscated, they must have remembered the days of the revolution when they themselves were looting and dividing the estates of the landed gentry; the wheel had turned and they were suffering the same fate hardly twelve years after their own hour of triumph. Entirely aside from the violence with which it was accomplished, from the economic point of view the "dekulakization" ordered by the Government seemed at the time an act of madness. The kulaks were the most efficient group among the whole peasant class, and to knock out this mainstay of Russian agriculture seemed the certain way to bring the whole structure down in ruins. To be sure, the Government intended to move the structure to a new foundation and to replace these uncertain props with new and massive pillars. But the kulaks were eliminated before the collectives were either numerous enough or strong enough to support the whole national weight. As a result agriculture was plunged once more into chaos, and as production slumped to new lows the threat of starvation again hung over the whole country.

The new Soviet agricultural program was not a scheme completely prepared beforehand and applied at once all along the line. It was the result of a number of experiments which were carried out over a considerable time. Several plans of collectivization ranging from a free coöperative association of farmers to a strict kolkhoz economy were offered. It was proposed at first to introduce collectivization gradually, using either persuasion or comparatively mild coercive methods such as a gradual increase of taxes levied against the wealthier group of peasants. During the whole of 1928 government leaders watched the results of the experiment, and only when it became apparent that the slow progress was entirely inadequate to meet the needs of the greater over-all plans were the more stringent measures of the supporters of immediate collectivization adopted.

In the autumn of 1929, however, Soviet leaders began to speak of the necessity of speeding up the process of transferring agricultural production to a collective basis, and shortly thereafter a program of immediate expansion was set under way. The 55 gigantic Soviet farms (Sovkhoz) which in 1928–29 had included about 2,400,000 hectares were to be increased in the following year to 120 with a total area of more than 5,000,000 hectares. According to the plans proposed by the Government, the kolkhoz collectives were to be expanded even more. The 30,000 kolkhozes in operation in 1928–29 were to be increased to 100,000 in 1930, and their total area enlarged from 4,000,000 hectares to 16,000,000. The decision was thus made not only to raise the number of collectives but also to increase the size of each one. The typical collective of 1927–28, which had included the land of some twelve individual farms, was to be enlarged to take in the land previously held in from 1,000 to 5,000 individual tracts.

The final decision to prepare for a rigorous and thoroughgoing collectivization of rural life in Russia came on January 6, 1930. The whole process was to be completed in the region of the lower and middle Volga and in the northern Caucasus by the autumn of 1930 or at the latest by the spring of 1931. In other regions it was to be put into effect by the autumn of 1931 or the spring of 1932.

These huge collective farms were to be operated by the use of an enormous amount of mechanical equipment—tractors, harvesting combines, and other labor-saving machinery. Their productivity was expected, therefore, to be markedly higher than that of individual peasant enterprises. Here again, however, the element of timing defeated the theoretical schedule, for the supply of tractors and combines did not match the growth of the collectives. Until 1930 there were not more than 25,000 tractors in the whole Russian Socialist Federative Soviet Republic, and because of the lack of repair shops and the difficulties of finding experienced operators, nearly half of these chronically were in poor condition. The shortage of harvesting combines was even more acute. Although two immense factories capable of turning out 25,000 combines a year had been planned, in 1930 there were almost no such machines actually in operation anywhere in Russia. In spite of the fact that few of the new farms could be furnished with the equipment which alone could justify their organization from the economic point of view, their development was continued. Only a small number could hope to be adequately supplied at first. For most of them "columns of tractors" remained only a slogan, and the great majority had to be content to try to operate vast tracts of land with "horse and ox columns," the traditional equipment of the peasant farmer.

But still the policy of collectivization continued unabated, spurred on by the slogan, "Attack the rich peasants." Actually, of course, the burden fell upon all classes among the peasantry, and in 1928 and particularly in 1929 all except the very poorest peasants were crushed by excessive taxation and numerous direct levies. The peasants were ordered to pay by January, 1930, either in grain or cash, the total amount of taxes levied against them for the full 1929–30 period. In addition, the floating of a third Industrialization Loan was announced at the same time. The two previous loans had been subscribed almost entirely in the towns, but agents of the Commissariat of Finance were assigned the task of raising the money for the third in the villages by whatever means might be necessary. Brigades of the Union of Communist Youth and active groups recruited from organizations of the poorer peasants were ordered to aid the financial agents in their onerous duties. In actual practice the drive amounted to nothing less than the collection of an extra tax from the peasants under the rather transparent guise of a compulsory subscription to the loan. The few individuals who, after the extraction of these levies, were still capable of making further money sacrifices were compelled to make deposits in government savings banks from which withdrawals were deliberately made difficult by a series of complicated formalities.

As a consequence of the campaign to which the farm population was subjected, life in the villages returned to the conditions which had existed in 1918 under the Committees of the Poor. The prying out of excessive amounts in taxes and levies led in the course of 1929 to the practical disorganization of all the more or less well-to-do farm enterprises. With the penalties attached to the ownership of property, thousands of peasants who owned only two or three cows, for instance, chose to butcher and eat one of them rather than be listed among the richer classes. Many others were unable to endure the hardships and numbers of these, particularly those whose ancestors had settled in Russia in the eighteenth or early nineteenth century, emigrated to escape liquidation. A considerable number of Swedes and a good part of the German Mennonites were among the groups who escaped in this way. But escape was out of the question for the majority of peasants, and as they fought against the new government policy to preserve their way of life, civil strife again flared up in nearly every village. Agents of the Soviet Government were frequently attacked and sometimes killed by groups of the rich and middle peasants, and the buildings of the kolkhozes and sovkhozes were never safe from the torches of vengeful farmers. The Government's response to the opposition was a vigorous and relentless reign of terror in which all known or suspected instigators of discontent were shot. The fall of 1929 was a bloody one in the villages, and before it was over hundreds of the richer peasants had been executed.

In January, 1930, the Government determined to destroy entirely the whole class of richer peasants. In order to eliminate this class from any control of village affairs, the old village Soviets were dismissed and new ones consisting solely of poor peasants were installed. The homes of the well-to-do peasants were given to hired workers or homeless peasants, and all their herds and property were turned over to the collective farms. The expropriated peasants themselves were forbidden to join the collectives and, stripped of their possessions and without means of support, they were soon reduced to poverty. While the "dekulakization" was in full swing, hundreds of thousands of these men with their families were deported to the north and the east where they were placed in concentration camps and set to work, under the supervision of the O.G.P.U., at lumbering, canal digging, railroad building, and other heavy labor.

Since no peasant who possessed even a comparatively small amount of property could be sure that he would not eventually be classed as a kulak and treated accordingly, dissatisfaction and then despair swept through the villages. Some of the well-to-do peasants had sons serving in the Red Army and it was possibly these soldiers who by their protests were first able to secure some abatement in the violence against the peasants. The Government began to make some concessions; and those of the deported kulaks who had children in the army, in civil service, or in the factories were returned to their villages—if they were still alive. In March, 1930, *Pravda* published Stalin's famous letter, "Dizziness from Success," in which he expressed disapproval of the more violent methods of achieving collectivization and put the blame for their use on the excessive zeal of local party members. The peasants were now allowed to join the kolkhozes or not as they wished, and those who had been forced into the collectives were permitted to leave. At first there was a concerted rush to return to the old system of individual farming, and for a brief period kolkhoz membership decreased rapidly. In time, however, most of the peasants who had left the collective returned bringing with them many others who had not previously been members. The acceptance of the collectivized system was in part the result of the repeal of the more extreme regulations which had applied to the kolkhoz members—such regulations, for instance, as that providing that all property, including even a peasant's few chickens, be held in common ownership. In addition, the individual farmers who still remained outside of the new system were subjected to increasingly prohibitive taxes. Lastly, the general conditions of life in the collectives were greatly improved by the provision of more and more machinery for their operation. By 1933 the number of tractors actually in use reached the impressive total of 200,000, and 25,000 combines were in operation in the grain districts. For the first time huge parks and service stations for the repair and maintenance of agricultural machinery became generally available, and in the south, in particular, great numbers of "machine-tractor stations" were set up to serve the neighboring kolkhozes.

By 1932 the Government had won the battle of the kolkhozes—won it in the sense that the peasants had at last reluctantly accepted the new *régime*. In its broader aspects, however, the struggle was far from complete, for the advantages which had been claimed for collectivization had still to be proved. Indeed, for a considerable time the Government's success appeared to be a Pyrrhic victory, since in winning it the backbone of the Russian agricultural system seemed to have been destroyed. The first reports showed a catastrophic decrease in production particularly in the raising of livestock. The following table is illustrative of the trends which continued to baffle the Soviet planners.

LIVESTOCK IN MILLION HEADS

Years	*Horses*	*Horned Cattle*	*Sheep and Goats*	*Hogs*
1913	35	60	112	20
1929	34	68	147	20
1933	16	38	50	12

These cold statistics, perhaps unimpressive in themselves, were translated into fearful casualties among the population, for it was at this time that the loss in human life reached its most horrible proportions. The famine of 1930–31 followed close on the heels of the chaos which existed everywhere in agriculture, and in Ukraine in particular the suffering and starvation reached a scale which almost passes human comprehension.

Even this disaster did not permanently cripple Soviet economy. Within a comparatively few years the tremendous innate vitality of the Russian people once more asserted itself in the reëstablishment of a working agricultural and industrial system. On the ruins of the old peasantry, men of a new type—the *kolkhozniki*—rose to toil and strive anew for the better life which had been promised them. Then, after a respite of less than a decade and at the moment when they seemed on the verge of achieving at least a taste of freedom and comfort, the Russian people—kolkhozes, factories and all—were engulfed in a new and even more terrible catastrophe, the Armageddon of the German war.

5.

THE industrial revolution which had been inaugurated by the decisions of the Fifteenth Convention of the Communist Party, and especially the agricultural revolution which accompanied it, were watched by foreign observers with distrust and worry. The revival of militant communism which had been revealed in the new domestic policy of the Soviet Government was expected to be reflected in Soviet foreign affairs as well, and a new outburst of the activities of the Communist International seemed at the time almost inevitable. Actually, however, the internal revolution in the Soviet Union had a reverse effect on Soviet diplomacy. Instead of intensifying the revolutionary trends which had existed in Russia's foreign policy, the shift of emphasis in the internal affairs of the country was accompanied by a turn away from rabid internationalism and the growth of a moderate nationalism. For some time, however, the new orientation was cloaked in the traditionally turgid communist phraseology which has so frequently misled foreign observers. Basically, the slogan of "building socialism in a single country" signaled the abandonment—for a time at least—of any deep or far-reaching plans for the promotion of revolution abroad. The tremendous task of national reconstruction absorbed all the energies of the new revolutionary state and served to concentrate interest almost completely on domestic problems. If Leninism was the adaptation of Marxism to the era of international conflicts, Stalinism amounted to the nationalization of the revolution.

National security—which was to be attained by the strengthening of national defense and preserved by a system of international security—now became the main objective of the Soviet Government. Once again it was the decisions of the Fifteenth Convention of the Communist Party which laid the foundation of the new policy. Its resolution on foreign affairs is well worth quoting in its entirety.

"The Central Committee of the party must build up its foreign policy on the following fundamental lines. First, by carrying out a policy of international peace, which is nothing other than a struggle against the dangers of imperialistic wars. This policy of international peace is at the same time a fundamental condition for the development of socialism within the Union of Socialist Soviet Republics; second, by the strengthening in every way of the brotherly ties between the workers of the Union of Socialist Soviet Republics and those of the western European countries, as well as the laboring masses of other oppressed countries; third, by the further systematic development of economic relations with the capitalist countries, provided that the economic independence of the Union of Socialist Soviet Republics shall be secured; fourth, by the constant strengthening of the means of national defense and especially the power and fighting capacity of both the Workers' and Peasants' Army and Navy; fifth, by the accumulation of necessary economic reserves, such as grain, goods, currency, and special reserves of defense."

Since the Communist party in reality controlled the Government of Russia at that time, the party decisions actually determined the subsequent course of Soviet foreign policy. In one of its aspects, as we know, the Communist party of the Soviet Union was a member of the Communist International—was, in fact, the leading group within that body. Its decisions, therefore, could not but substantially affect the policies of the International. The Sixth Congress of the Communist International was held in Moscow from July 17 to August 28, 1928. While it had been originally intended that congresses should be called yearly, four years had elapsed since the Fifth Congress had met—a delay which was partly explained by the struggle that had been raging within the Communist party of the Soviet Union after the death of Lenin. The rise of the Trotskyite opposition in 1926 and the subsequent exclusion from the ranks of the party of both Trotsky and Zinoviev had also had serious repercussions in revolutionary circles the world over. The struggle between the Stalinists and the Trotskyites was repeated in almost all of the national Communist parties. The calling of the Sixth Congress, therefore, had been possible only after a great deal of maneuvering and countermaneuvering within the various parties. The Moscow leaders had been faced with the extremely delicate task of securing for themselves a majority of the delegates without being forced to apply such drastic measures as might result in the total breaking up of at least some of the foreign communist groups. By 1928 it was clear that they had been successful in achieving their ends, but it was also plain that, as a result, the Communist International as a whole had lost its independence, and that its non-Russian groups—which theoretically at least had enjoyed complete equality with the Russian branch—had now become satellites of the Communist party of the Soviet Union.

Since the domestic problems of the Soviet Union had monopolized the attention of the Russian Communist party, it had lost much of its original enthusiasm for internationalism. Consequently, from this time forward the Moscow leaders looked upon the Communist International as an instrument to be used in the advancement of the national interests of the Soviet Union. In reality, the International thereafter assumed the character of a subsidiary organization of the Moscow Government, charged with assisting the latter in the development of its foreign policy.

The Sixth Congress, in the resolutions passed by its membership, emphasized the growing danger of another World War which, in the opinion of many of the delegates, was likely to assume the form of an attack on the Soviet Union either by one of the capitalist powers or by a coalition. Working on this assumption, the Congress was greatly concerned with resolving the tactics to be employed by the laboring masses to avert the supposedly imminent war. After long debate the Congress passed a resolution outlining the threefold task which labor was to assume in such an eventuality. First, the proletariat of each capitalist country must continue the struggle against its own government. Second, the proletariat of the whole world must unite in the defense of the Soviet Union against the imperialism of its enemies. Lastly, it was charged with the promotion of the revolutionary movement in the colonies subject to the great powers.

In order to carry out the first of these tasks it was necessary that the proletariat of each country establish immediately a secret organization of workers' "cells" and that this network be developed especially in heavy industry and in industry concerned with the manufacture of war materials. At the outbreak of war these groups were to adopt a "defeatist program" and by vigorous propaganda were to attempt to turn the imperialist war between states into a class war between the proletariat and the middle class within each capitalist country. A special resolution carrying instructions for the development of the "revolutionary movement in colonial and semicolonial countries" was passed by the Congress. By and large, the essential core of the program proposed by the International was the development of Communist parties throughout the world and especially in the colonial countries which supplied the basic strength of the imperialist powers.

The program thus outlined by the Sixth Congress was not calculated to allay the fears of nonsocialist governments throughout the world. Indeed, from the capitalist standpoint it appeared to be alarmingly revolutionary. From the point of view of the Muscovite leaders, however, it was not intended as an aggressive policy but was meant chiefly as a measure of self-defense. Whatever the intentions may have been and however they may have been misunderstood in other countries, it is clear now that in all probability they did more harm than good to the Soviet Union.

6.

THE Soviet Government adopted a realistic attitude toward the problem of preserving the peace which the Soviet Union so desperately needed. It was possible that a militant and articulate revolutionary minority within the capitalist states might exercise a restraining influence upon imperialists who dreamed of the conquest of the Soviet Union. The Communist International was therefore assigned the task of organizing and directing such groups. At the same time the Soviet Government was well aware that the weak revolutionary parties were quite incapable of providing any positive assurance that war would not be unleashed against the Russians. Consequently, while the Soviets cultivated the radical parties for whatever help they might someday be, the main efforts of Russian officials were directed toward the prevention of war by diplomatic means. The Soviet Foreign Office characteristically approached the problem from several angles. At first Soviet spokesmen—particularly Maxim Litvinov, as Vice Commissar and then as Commissar of Foreign Affairs—stressed the necessity for total disarmament and offered a number of formulas designed to expedite such a movement. When all such suggestions failed, they attempted to secure peace by the establishment of collective security which was to be based upon a series of multilateral nonaggression treaties.

The logical instrument for the development of interlocking pacts was, of course, the League of Nations, but this organization did not at once commend itself to the Soviet Union. For a number of years Russian diplomats had pretended to ignore the League which, in the eyes of the Communists, had been designed merely to promote the political and economic objectives of the capitalist powers. As late as February, 1926, the Soviet Union refused to participate in the Geneva Conference on disarmament on the ground that she had had no relations with the Swiss Government since the assassination of the Soviet envoy, Vorovsky, on Swiss territory on May 10, 1923. A little later, however, in spite of the fact that she was not yet a member of the League, the Soviet Union decided to attempt to use the League machinery to maintain peace. On November 1, 1927, Moscow let it be known that she was prepared to participate in the disarmament proceedings and that, in the words of Soviet Prime Minister Rykov, "the Soviet Union was ready to propose, support, and carry out the most complete program of disarmament for the whole world simultaneously." The draft presented to the Conference by the Soviet delegates provided for the immediate demobilization of half of all existing armed forces, the corresponding destruction of arms and munitions, and the cessation of all military and naval construction. Demobilization and destruction were to continue progressively for four years until only such forces as were necessary for police and frontier guards were to remain. National navies were to be supplanted by an international maritime police force, and control and enforcement of the entire disarmament agreement were to be entrusted to a permanent international commission to be formed on the basis of national equality and with the participation of all working classes.

A long speech explaining and elaborating upon the various aspects of the proposal was delivered on March 19, 1928, by the Soviet delegate, Litvinov. German and Turkish representatives voiced general approval of the Soviet program, but Lord Cushendun strongly opposed the suggestion in the following remarks: "There are two kinds of war, and where there are two kinds of war, there are two kinds of peace. There are international and civil wars, and of these the civil is more horrible. It is a fair question to ask whether the Soviet Government sets its face against civil war as resolutely as against international war. . . . For years past the whole basis for the Soviet world policy has been to produce armed insurrection amounting to civil war in every country where they can exercise influence. If that is so, before we proceed much further some assurance should be given to us by the Soviet that in that respect there is to be a complete change in policy. We ought to be told whether the Soviets now have decided no longer to interfere in the affairs of other nations." The chairman of the American delegation, Hugh S. Gibson, joined in disapproving the Soviet proposal, explaining that the Government of the United States supported instead a system based upon a multilateral compact renouncing war as an instrument of national policy.

On August 27, 1928, the general Pact for the Renunciation of War was signed at Paris by representatives of fifteen states, including the British Dominions. Soviet Russia, however, was not invited to participate as an original signatory power, nor was she included in the list of states which later received the note of the United States on the subject of adherence to the general pact. Since there were no diplomatic relations between the United States and the Soviet Union, France, acting as an intermediary, formally approached the Soviets who signified, on August 31, 1928, their acceptance of the pact.

In addition to her general concern with the problem of the preservation of peace, the Soviet Union at this time was eagerly working toward an immediate and more specific goal—the restoration of diplomatic relations with Great Britain which had been severed by England in 1927. The prospects for a resumption of normal relations were brightened in 1929 by the return of a Labor Government to power. However, since Prime Minister MacDonald did not command an absolute majority in the House of Commons, it was necessary for him to proceed cautiously both in the matter of Soviet relations and, indeed, in many difficult political problems. The negotiations got under way slowly. In July, 1929, correspondence between the two governments was begun. Again the British suggested that Russian debts and guarantees that the Soviets would refrain from anti-British propaganda be discussed as part of the whole question of recognition; again the Soviet Government insisted that the question of the resumption of relations should be discussed separately and alone without preliminary discussions relating to special problems. Tentative conversations carried on between the British Secretary for Foreign Affairs, Henderson, and Soviet Ambassador to Paris, Dovgalevsky, were without result since neither side was willing to yield ground. However, after further negotiation, an agreement was finally reached on October 1. Officially, Henderson made a concession by agreeing that an exchange of ambassadors should precede the discussion of the several issues remaining between the two countries. Unofficially, it was understood that Henderson had received Dovgalevsky's assurance that the Soviet Government was prepared to give London guarantees to refrain from propaganda against the British.

This tentative agreement was, of course, subject to ratification by the British Parliament. When the House of Commons debated the question in November, 1929, Henderson declared his belief that the Soviet assurances incorporated in the agreement applied to the activities of the Communist International. Although the Conservatives in Commons voted against the measure—and the House of Lords later repudiated it—the agreement nevertheless received the support of the majority in Commons which was necessary to ratify it. As its envoy to London the Soviet Government appointed Sokolnikov, chairman of the Soviet Petroleum Trust. Sokolnikov, whose real name was Brilliant, had been a member of the party since before the revolution; although he had at one time belonged to the opposition headed by Trotsky, he later renounced these views, achieved a responsible place in Soviet councils, and as head of the Petroleum Trust was responsible for the conclusion of the agreement with English oil interests which had been signed in February, 1929. On December 20, 1929, he presented his credentials to the Prince of Wales—who was acting for the King during the latter's illness—and on the same day visited Henderson and with him exchanged formal assurances that both governments would in the future abstain from agitation against each other.

Before two weeks had passed the Soviet Government had been accused of violating its obligation. On January 1, 1930, the *Daily Worker,* the communist newspaper which had been founded only a short time before in London, published an inflammatory proclamation directed by the Executive Committee of the Third International to the English working class. This pronouncement characterized the Labor Government as lackeys of the *bourgeoisie* and called upon the workers to prepare for a revolutionary government by the organization of a network of "cells" which would unite the laboring class of Great Britain and seize power at the proper time. Confronted with this disregard of the interpretation of the diplomatic contract which he had so recently presented to the House of Commons, Henderson was left no alternative but to protest vigorously to Sokolnikov against the proclamation, with the ultimate result that relations between the two nations were again reduced to a state of suspicion and distrust.

Relations between the Soviet Union and the United States failed to improve in this period in spite of the fact that Moscow obviously hoped to establish closer contacts. If anything, Secretary of State Stimson's attempted mediation of the dispute which had arisen at this time between Russia and China, and Litvinov's blunt rebuff, had rather widened the breach between their countries. Nevertheless, Russia continued to demonstrate in a series of small gestures her friendly attitude toward America. There were a number of examples of such acts. She coöperated in the search for the lost American aviator, Eielson, in December, 1929, and January, 1930. Considerable effort was expended in locating and returning to the United States the bodies of American soldiers who had lost their lives during the period of intervention and civil war in northern Russia; in October, 1929, the remains of seventy-five men of the 339th Infantry Regiment, which had been recruited in Michigan, were carried aboard a ship at Leningrad and sent to their native land.

At the same time, the Soviet Government endeavored energetically to extend commercial relations with the United States. In connection with the launching of the First Five Year Plan and the program for the industrialization of Russia, a number of contracts had been assigned to American firms for the construction or equipping of factories in the Soviet Union, and a sizable group of American engineers had been hired to work in Russia as experts and consultants. The volume of trade continued to rise during this period and in 1929 reached the round sum of $155,000,000. However, even though trade relations proceeded on a mutually satisfactory basis, diplomatic relations remained in a state of suspension.

7.

While diplomatic relations between Soviet Russia and the western countries continued in a quiescent if not entirely satisfactory state, a period of crises arose in the Far East. Once again the difficulties had their origin in the circumstances surrounding the ownership and operation of the Chinese Eastern Railway. The agreement providing for joint operation of the railroad which had been negotiated in 1924 between the Soviet Government and the Military Governor of Manchuria, Marshal Chang Tso-Lin, had from the first functioned under difficulties. Relations between the Soviets and Marshal Chang were complicated by his undisguised animosity toward the Russian system, and his son, Chang Hsueh-liang, who succeeded him, was scarcely better disposed toward the Bolsheviks than his father had been. The Chinese authorities—both the Nanking Government and Marshal Chang Hsueh-liang—suspected the Soviets of a desire to interfere in the internal affairs of China at the first favorable opportunity.

At length, information that the Soviet Government was providing funds for General Feng Yu-hsiang, who was suspected of conspiring against Nanking, led the Chinese authorities to raid the Soviet consulate in Harbin on May 27, 1929. The results were similar to those obtained in the various other raids on Soviet property. No documents implicating Feng were discovered, but others were found which the Chinese considered evidence of communist propaganda by Soviet agents in Manchuria. Since such propaganda was in violation of the agreement of 1924, the Chinese felt justified in abrogating the treaty altogether. On July 10, 1929, they arrested more than a hundred Soviet civil servants in Harbin, among them the general manager of the Chinese Eastern, and deported them to Russia, leaving the administration of the railway entirely in Chinese hands. In addition, all institutions of the Soviet trade unions in Manchuria were closed, since they were suspected of being the principal instruments of the Bolsheviks.

Within a few days there followed a rupture of diplomatic relations between Moscow and Nanking. When it became apparent that war was imminent, international diplomatic bodies began a hasty consideration of the means to be applied in an attempt to prevent the actual beginning of hostilities. Under Article XI of its Covenant, the League of Nations had a formal right to take the dispute under advisement since China was a member. Practically, however, it was clear that intervention by the League would be ineffective, and consequently another approach was attempted. Both Soviet Russia and China had signed the Kellogg Pact of Paris, and Secretary Stimson considered that he would be justified under the circumstances in calling the attention of both governments to the moral obligations they had assumed as signatories of that agreement. Since no diplomatic relations existed between the United States and the Soviet Union, however, it was necessary that the note—which had the support of both Great Britain and France—be delivered to the Soviet Government by an intermediary, Briand, the French Minister of Foreign Affairs. The Soviets and China both responded curtly that they were aware of their obligations and that they had no desire for war. The Soviet Government, however, also announced that it would conduct negotiations only after China had agreed to the return of the expelled Soviet employees to their positions, and since the Chinese adhered to their stand the Manchurian crisis remained dangerously explosive. Both parties, in fact, began hasty preparations for war. This uncertain situation continued for several months, punctuated from time to time by border skirmishes in which—it is worth noting—companies of White Russians recruited from the refugees who had settled in Manchuria during the Russian Civil War took part on the Chinese side.

The Soviet Government assembled in Siberia a military force organized as the so-called special Far Eastern Army, but it may be presumed that from the very beginning of the conflict the Russians had depended upon a recurrence of internal strife in China and had not, therefore, wished at once to carry affairs to the stage of war. Soviet expectations of Chinese internal difficulties were soon justified, and in October there began a series of clashes between troops loyal to Nanking and the armies of the generals who had refused allegiance to the central Government. Among the opposition, the leading rôle was played by General Feng who had established contact with the radical wing of the Kuomintang. But in spite of the military and political embarrassments which resulted from the Chinese internal dissension, neither Nanking nor the

Military Governor of Manchuria was willing to accept the demands of the Soviet Union.

On November 17 Soviet troops began to advance into Manchuria from both the eastern and western ends of the Chinese Eastern Railway, and the Chinese fell back in disorder on both fronts. Red Army soldiers occupied the town of Hailar and pressed on in the direction of Harbin. In several localities in their advance they wreaked vengeance on Russian émigrés who had settled in Manchuria. Defeated decisively, Chang Hsueh-liang was compelled on November 27 to satisfy the Russian demands, and on December 3 a preliminary protocol was signed on behalf of the Soviet Government and China.

While the invasion of Manchuria was actually in progress another attempt was being made to deal with the conflict through international diplomatic channels. On November 28 Secretary Stimson addressed to the governments of Great Britain, France, Germany, Italy, and Japan a note proposing joint diplomatic intervention to maintain the Kellogg Pact and to prevent war. After an exchange of views with the governments of these countries, Secretary Stimson dispatched to China and Russia a note to this effect which bore the support of fourteen of the fifty-three signatories of the Kellogg Pact.

Litvinov, acting Soviet Commissar for Foreign Affairs, responded on December 3 with a biting protest against Secretary Stimson's interference. He contended that Soviet Russia had taken military action only for purposes of self-defense, and further that the Stimson note, which had been sent at a moment when peace negotiations were already under way, conveyed the impression that Stimson wished to exert an influence in the negotiations, a desire which could not be regarded as a friendly act. Having been thus rebuffed, Stimson took no further steps, and the incident was closed. In the meantime conferences between the Soviet Government and the Mukden authorities were continued, and on December 22, 1929, there was signed an agreement providing for the return of the Chinese Eastern to the status which had prevailed before the conflict.

Soon after the far-eastern situation appeared to have reached at least a temporary stability, a new series of important events arose in Manchuria which completely overshadowed the skirmishes of 1929. Japan, having completed the preparation of her grandiose plans for the establishment of the "Greater Asia Co-prosperity Sphere," now began the conquest of Manchuria as the first step toward the attainment of her ambitions. Paradoxically, it appears to have been the Russian venture of 1929 which demonstrated to Japan her precarious position in this area and encouraged her to move at this time. Working cautiously toward her objective by the seizure of the coveted territory piece by piece, she first occupied only southern Manchuria—an area, incidentally, which in 1907 had been recognized by Imperial Russia as within the Japanese sphere of influence. The principal protest against the Japanese attack came not from Russia but from China, which considered that her rights of sovereignty had been violated. In the League of Nations, of which both China and Japan were members at the time, there was a flurry of excitement which culminated in futility with the holding of a few meetings, the delivery of several speeches, and the appointment of committees of investigation.

When no effective action was initiated either by the League or by any of the individual powers, Japan took her second step by occupying in the spring of 1932 the northern part of Manchuria. This area included the city of Harbin, a great part of the population of which was Russian—both Red and White. Some of the anti-Bolsheviks welcomed the arrival of the Japanese and offered their services to them in the event that a war against the Soviet Union should be begun. However, Japan contented herself for the time with the installation of a puppet government in Manchuria—or Manchukuo, as the country was now renamed.

Viewed from almost any standpoint, the occupation of northern Manchuria was a threat to Russia's Asiatic interests. In 1907 Japan had specifically recognized this area as lying within the Russian sphere of influence. Entirely aside from the question of historical precedent and diplomatic commitment, however, it was clear that the presence of Japanese troops so near to the vital Chinese Eastern Railway threatened the military position of the Soviet Union in the Far East and endangered Russian commercial relations throughout the whole area. The Japanese action was a challenge which demanded an immediate decision from Moscow. If the Soviet Union were to preserve even the remnants of her control over the Chinese Eastern, she was faced with the necessity of protesting strenuously and, if diplomatic means failed, of fighting for the protection of her rights. But Russia neither desired a full-scale war nor was prepared for one. She declined to risk her position in a struggle for Asian hegemony; she took no action at all to forestall Japanese advances, and a few years later agreed to sell her share in the Chinese Eastern Railway to Manchukuo.

Although the Soviet Government was forced to adopt a position of outward acquiescence in the destruction of Manchuria, the lesson of Japan's venture in northern Asia was neither overlooked nor forgotten in Moscow. The whole episode, which inaugurated the era of instability in international affairs, was viewed as an omen of the lawlessness to follow. The failure of the League and of the great powers such as the United States and Great Britain to intervene in Manchuria, and the ominous way in which Japan left the League, casting off whatever slight diplomatic restraints remained, underscored the seriousness of the situation and once more reminded the Moscow leaders of the mortal dangers under which the Soviet Union existed.

CHAPTER XVIII.

RUSSIA AT THE CROSSROADS

(1933–1939)

I.

WHILE the results of the First Five Year Plan were in the main satisfactory, and in not a few fields even better than had been anticipated, the economic reconstruction of the Soviet Union as a whole was, in 1933, far from complete. In the industrial sphere, many of the most essential factory units had already been built but many more were either only under construction or still in the blueprint stage. While these gaps existed, the whole industrial structure lacked stability and cohesion. The railroad network, vitally important to any industrial nation and particularly to a vast country such as Russia, was still entirely inadequate to the requirements of an expanding economy. The reorganized agricultural system was in such a chaotic state that even in 1933 the Government could not be certain that collectivization was a workable principle or that it would yield adequate returns within a reasonable length of time. The people as a whole were depressed by the severe and continuous privations by which they had to pay for the fulfilment of the plan, and in spite of the wholesale deportation of kulaks—or perhaps precisely because of it—the loyalty of the peasant masses was especially doubtful.

The preservation of the peace had been the central objective of Soviet foreign policy ever since the beginning of the N.E.P., and the Russians now redoubled their efforts to avoid and prevent war. Most Soviet leaders realized that Russia dare not become involved in a war, and that any attack against her by a major power was likely to result in an economic breakdown and perhaps even in serious peasant revolts. Because they were aware of the essential weakness of Russia's position, Soviet leaders had cautiously avoided conflict with Japan in 1932, and for several years thereafter their main energies were to be devoted to avoiding every danger of war from any quarter. The resumption of relations with Great Britain had to some extent allayed the fears of an attack from that direction, but the diplomatic coolness which continued on both sides was not conducive to the growth of understanding or confidence. Under the circumstances, the Soviets sought security through the European alliances. Friendship with Germany, with whom they had first been able to come to terms, continued to be regarded by the Russians as their best insurance of peace in a threatening and unsettled world.

Hitler's rise to power in 1933 and the subsequent Nazification of Germany destroyed the cornerstone of the security framework which the Soviet Union had labored long to build. Nor was Russia the only nation caught unawares by the destruction of democratic Germany. The ominous implications of Hitler's victory and the passing of the Weimar Republic were nowhere recognized at first—not in Great Britain nor in the United States, nor even in those European states most intimately acquainted with the turns of continental politics. The Nazi party seemed an impossible assortment of selfish interests; its program a hodgepodge of revolutionary doctrine, social superstition, and transparent demagoguery; its leader a neurotic fanatic. The world looked on half contemptuously and assured itself that nothing serious would transpire. Somehow, and from somewhere, there grew a comforting legend that Hindenburg, wise old man, still knew a few tricks and that when the day came he would know how to put the impudent and revolutionary Nazis in their places. Then, too, there was fascist Italy, at that time entering its second decade of totalitarian rule quietly—or, at least, with no more bluster than appeared necessary for internal political consumption. Italy was certainly not a threat to world stability—was, as a matter of fact, an example of fascism which led the more comfortable statesmen to indulge in moderate optimism. There was as yet no understanding between the two brands of totalitarianism and since there appeared to be certain areas in which the interests of the two nations collided, it seemed not unlikely that in time the power of one dictator might well be used to balance the influence of the other in European affairs, especially in the event that either should get out of hand. Few people outside of Germany had ever read *Mein Kampf* and most of those who had were unable to accept it seriously. One other attitude should be mentioned. In some conservative circles in both Great Britain and France there was a lingering belief that Hitler's aggressiveness might someday be diverted toward the east against the Soviet Union. Not all influential men in European politics looked with gloomy foreboding on the prospect of Germany and Russia becoming locked in combat that might conceivably prove mortal to both.

The Soviet leaders themselves were concerned with the unfavorable turn of events in Germany but at first were not greatly alarmed. In the first place, until Hitler had consolidated his position in the purge of 1934 they did not consider that the Nazi government was firmly in the saddle. In addition, they too were taken in by the Italian parallel. Had not fascist Italy been one of the first European governments to grant Russia *de jure* recognition in 1924? It appears that for a considerable time Russian leaders continued to cherish some hope that the new German Government would prove to be realistic enough to continue Russo-German relations which had proved mutually beneficial. The conclusion of the nonaggression pact between Germany and Poland in 1934 was the event which finally made Soviet statesmen realize the acute menace of Nazi Germany. It was clear to them that nothing good could be expected from a rapprochement between Hitler, who did not conceal his intention eventually to try to seize Ukraine, and Pilsudski, who had already tried and might at any time be expected to repeat the attempt.

Hitler's rise to power was, perhaps, the central factor in the slow alteration in the traditional methods of conducting international relations—a change which, gradual and incomplete as it was, grew like a fire in dead wood until it burst forth in the conflagration of the Second World War. It is evident now that the whole period between 1933 and 1939 was one of mutual distrust, of lack of serious understanding on the part of responsible leaders of the various European powers, and of lost opportunities to secure and maintain peace. No nation and no individual was, of course, responsible for the chain of diplomatic failures, but those who constantly and consciously struggled to prevent the drift toward a world-encompassing destruction stand out because they were few.

As a matter of common fairness, it must be remembered that during those years the Soviet Union was perhaps the only country with a clear and consistent foreign policy and that Litvinov was one of the few diplomats who devoted himself whole-heartedly to an attempt to establish a collective security system. That his voice was not heard, and that the sincerity of the Soviet Government was doubted, was largely the result of the almost universal fear of the spread of international communism. During this time the opponents of the Soviet Union were able to make frequent and telling use of the continuing connection between the Soviet Government and the Communist International. The fact that the nature of the relations between the two bodies had undergone a far-reaching alteration since the period of the civil war was at that time realized by very few statesmen.

The rise of the Nazis to power in Europe and the danger revealed in the far-eastern crisis of 1932 were probably responsible, directly and indirectly, for the very considerable improvement of relations between the Soviet Union and the rest of the world during this time. On November 17, 1933, the long delayed *de jure* recognition was granted by the United States to the Soviet Government. This was but the first of a series of events which greatly improved Russia's position. The general betterment of Russia's relations to Europe was, to a large extent, due to the efforts of Dr. Eduard Beneš, then Minister of Foreign Affairs in Czechoslovakia, who contributed much to Russia's reappearance as a full-fledged member of the community of nations. In June, 1934, two of the three members of the Little Entente—Czechoslovakia and Rumania—granted *de jure* recognition to the Soviet Government, and in September of the same year the Soviets joined the League of Nations, being granted a permanent seat on the Council. In December the French Minister of Foreign Affairs, Pierre Laval, and Soviet Commissar Maxim Litvinov signed at Geneva an important protocol providing for the cooperation of their countries in an Eastern Security Pact. A few days later the protocol was strengthened by the adherence of Czechoslovakia.

This series of alliances appeared to have prepared the ground for a further rapprochement between the Soviet Union on one hand and France and Czechoslovakia on the other. On May 2, 1935, a treaty of mutual assistance was signed between France and the Soviet Union. The provisions of this treaty were worded so as to place the agreement between the two countries within the framework of the League of Nations. Referring to the League Covenant, each country pledged the other aid and assistance in the event of "an unprovoked attack on the part of a European state," a reference which obviously applied to Germany. Two weeks later a similar treaty was signed by the Soviet Union and Czechoslovakia. In this case, it was understood that Russia was obligated to come to the assistance of the smaller state only in the event that France had acted first to fulfill the terms of her treaty with Czechoslovakia. It may be assumed that by such an arrangement France hoped to obtain some insurance against rash action on the part of the Soviet Union. The attitude of mistrust exhibited by France in itself did not augur well for the solidity of the pact. It later became even more apparent that the French Government was not solidly behind the treaty which had been concluded with the Soviet Union, principally because influential French conservatives still retained their old suspicions of the revolutionary intentions of the Soviets and were reluctant to see any effective association with Moscow which might strengthen the radicals.

The Soviet Union, on the other hand, took the treaty much more seriously. Characteristic evidence of the Soviet attitude was revealed in the adoption of an enabling amendment to the draft of the new constitution which was then being prepared. According to this amendment, which was incorporated as a part of the Constitution of 1936, the Presidium of the Supreme Soviet was authorized in the intervals between sessions of the Supreme Soviet to proclaim a state of war not only "in the event of armed attack on the U.S.S.R." but likewise "whenever necessary to fulfill international treaty obligations concerning mutual defense against aggression." At the same time the policy of the Communist International was adjusted to the new world situation. The Seventh Congress of the Comintern which met at Moscow in July and August of 1935—the last ever held—recommended the establishment of a "united fighting front of the working class" which was to be open to all, irrespective of the political organization to which they might belong—Communist, Socialist, or Labor party. The "united front" which was thus launched was to become an important part of Russia's drive to sustain the peace and to prevent the victory of the growing "fascist"[1] menace.

2.

The Second Five Year Plan, which was officially inaugurated on January 1, 1933, was even more ambitious than the first. The annual gross output of Soviet industry, which by 1932 had reached 43,000,000,000 rubles (calculated on the 1926–27 price index), was to be expanded to 93,000,000,000 rubles by 1937, the last year of the second plan. Under the new program it was proposed to unify and consolidate the production of newly constructed industrial units and to continue the upward drive by building a series of mammoth new factories in the various industrial centers being developed throughout the nation. The railroad system was, at the same time, to be expanded to keep pace with the increasing burden it was required to bear. Recognizing that hardships arising from the shortage of consumer goods had greatly hampered the progress of the First Five Year Plan, Soviet planners now decided to lay particular emphasis on light industry. Plans which would largely have alleviated the distress of the preceding years were incorporated in the new directives, but before the revisions of policy could have any substantial effect the balance between heavy and light industry was once more upset by the ominous trend of events in the international sphere. The Soviet Union was forced again to concentrate on heavy industry in order to build up her military potential, but even though she had to abandon some of the program looking toward the satisfaction of the people's wants, the production of consumer goods nevertheless continued to increase during this period.

A number of vitally important industrial projects were completed and put into operation during the first two years of the Second Five Year Plan. Outstanding among these were the Magnitogorsk plant, the Kramatorsk heavy machinery plant, and the Cheliabinsk tractor factory. As railway transportation rose, showing a 10 per cent increase in carloadings during 1934 over the 1933 rate, several new lines such as that between Moscow and the

[1] In Soviet terminology the term "fascist" is applied not only to Italy but to Germany as well—in fact, to any brand of totalitarianism similar to either fascism or nazism.

Donets basin were laid down. A step of great importance to the economy of the whole country was the completion of the Baltic-White Sea Canal in 1933. The whole period was characterized by the enormous amount of building everywhere under way. Perhaps the best known of these projects was the construction of the Moscow subway (*metro*) in which the citizens of Moscow were particularly interested.

The critical condition in agriculture was eased somewhat at the beginning of the Second Plan. A vast amount of capital was poured into the collectives which were constantly being expanded and equipped for more efficient production. In 1933–34 alone agricultural investments totaled 5,000,000,000 rubles, most of which was spent on machinery and equipment. The extraordinary efforts previously put forth by the government to bolster the agrarian structure began to show results. The annual yield of grain crops in both 1933 and 1934 totaled more than 89,000,000 metric tons as compared to slightly more than 80,000,000 tons in 1913. The livestock situation continued to be troublesome. The number of horses continued to decline—though not at the previous catastrophic rate—but the general food situation was improved somewhat by an increase in hog production. With the mechanization and collectivization of farming thousands of peasants were released for work in factories and the pool of skilled labor available to industry was rapidly augmented. On the whole, the morale of the Russian people was moving upward. Better fed, inspired by sweeping industrial achievements of great national significance, the people entered willingly into the spirit of growth and expansion which was cultivated by the Government.

While Soviet leaders were cautious about releasing their control over the social organizations and the productive machinery of the country, some moderation in the harshness of the dictatorship now seemed possible. Since the passing of Zinoviev and Trotsky from the political scene, there had risen to positions of prominence in both the party and the Government a group of men who were interested more in the practical administration of the new system than in the abstract theories from which it had risen. Typical of the new type of leadership was S. M. Kirov, a member of the Politburo and the chairman of the Leningrad Soviet, who took the lead in urging the democratization of Soviet governmental machinery and the abolition of class distinctions. In order to achieve these reforms a number of revisions in the constitution were necessary. One step of some significance in this direction was taken on July 10, 1934, when the United Department of Political Police (O.G.P.U.) was abolished as an independent institution, its juridical functions transferred to regular courts and its administrative functions to the People's Commissariat of Internal Affairs (N.K.V.D.). In the light of subsequent events it is easy to argue that the reform was in the name rather than in the essence of the institution of political police, but it might have been originally meant as a real improvement. At the same time, several other reforms were contemplated, and the work of drafting them was begun.

The new democratic tendencies were, however, secretly opposed by at least two distinctive elements in Russia. Leftist remnants of the Trotsky-Zinoviev underground groups resisted the new moves as a relaxation of the dictatorship of the proletariat and a compromise with *bourgeois* parliamentarianism. On the other hand, the Rightists, who were principally members of the Rykov group, opposed the whole conception of the kolkhoz system as such; for them Kirov's projected reforms did not go far enough in restoring normality in Soviet life. In spite of the fact that neither of these opposition groups dared to agitate openly against the Government, Russian officials had for some time been vaguely aware of their existence, even though they did not know of the specific activities in which they were engaged. However, the results of underground agitation became increasingly apparent in the numerous acts of sabotage which occurred in industrial plants in various parts of the country, and though these acts were usually attributed officially to foreign spies, it was known that in part, at least, they were committed by members of the opposition groups.

The ramifications of the underground organizations were dramatically revealed by the assassination of Kirov on December 1, 1934. The assassin, a former member of the Komsomol, stoutly denied that he had had any accomplices, but as the investigation proceeded the Government gradually became convinced that the assassination was in some way bound up with the activities of the dissident elements. Numerous arrests were made and the circle gradually widened to include such prominent figures as Kamenev and Zinoviev. Aided by the confessions of some of the accused, the prosecution drew a systematic picture of a far-reaching conspiracy of the Trotskyite, Zinovievite, and Rightist groups, which were found to have established working alliances between themselves. In addition, some of the confessions revealed that a number of the opposition leaders had been in touch with "certain foreign powers," by which the world understood Germany, Poland, and Japan.

The preliminary examination of the accused lasted for almost two years, and it was not until August, 1936, that Kamenev and Zinoviev and eleven other leaders of the alleged conspiracy were at last put on public trial by the Military Collegium of the Supreme Court. The prosecution claimed that in addition to Kirov several other Soviet leaders, including Stalin, had been slated for assassination. The campaign of political murders, according to the Government, was only part of a larger scheme worked out in detail by the plotters. The central objective behind the "direct action" campaign was alleged to have been the overthrow of Stalin's Government and the destruction of both the Five Year Plan and the kolkhoz system. Private property was to be reëstablished among the peasantry and a semicapitalist *régime* was to be introduced in industry and commerce. Furthermore, the prosecution was convinced that the conspirators had entered into an agreement with Germany, promising the latter control of Ukraine in return for her support of the new government which was to be established in Russia after the fall of Stalin. After a spectacular trial which was fully reported in the world press, the court found most of the accused guilty, and several, including Kamenev and Zinoviev, were sentenced to death.

The trial itself and the execution of the prominent political figures which followed it evoked a strong reaction in public feeling abroad, especially in the United States. Trotsky vehemently denied any connection between himself and his avowed followers in Russia, and American Socialists and Trotskyites conducted a violent campaign of protest against the trial and the terroristic methods which they accused the Soviets of having adopted.

The attitude expressed by the dissident Leftists at this time raises a number of interesting questions. Throughout the early years of the revolution, when only *bourgeois* conspirators were being executed by the Soviet Government, no charges of cruelty had ever been made by either the Socialists or the Trotskyites. Both Trotsky and Zinoviev had supported the "Red Terror" during the period in which they were in power and, indeed, had approved extreme measures including even the taking of hostages. Only when they themselves were the objects of these violent repressive tactics did they find it necessary to protest against them.

It is, of course, true that many innocent people suffered in the purge which followed the Kirov assassination. Thousands of people must have been arrested on the flimsiest of evidence and many of them were undoubtedly hastily executed in the course of the Kamenev-Zinoviev affair. When a prominent member of the opposition had been arrested, his friends, associates, and even his secretaries frequently fell under suspicion and in some cases were imprisoned or deported to Siberia. But this application of the terror principle was nothing new; it had certainly been practiced with equally violent purpose during the initial years of the revolution. At that time it had been vindicated by the Trotskyites on the ground that extreme measures of protection were essential for the survival of the state. The same argument was advanced in 1936, and it would seem that it could have been applied to the Zinoviev case with exactly as much—or as little—justification.

3.

In spite of the political conflict which raged within the party during the period from 1934 to 1936, Kirov's reforms were not altogether abandoned; they were, in fact, largely embodied in the draft of the new constitution which was completed at the beginning of 1936. After the revisions had been codified, they were submitted to the party membership and to meetings of factory workers for criticism and discussion. Revised somewhat as a result of these discussions, they were officially approved in December, 1936. Several fundamental changes in the basic constitutional law of the Soviet Union were introduced in the new code. Both the constitution of the R.S.F.S.R., which had been adopted in 1918 and revised in 1925, and the 1923 constitution of the Soviet Union had been frankly instruments of the "dictatorship of the proletariat": by their provisions factory workers were given much stronger representation in Soviet assemblies than were the peasants, and people belonging to the *bourgeois* class were disfranchised altogether. Realizing that as a result of the readjustments arising out of the Five Year Plan and the socialization of agriculture the remnants of both the *bourgeoisie* and the individual peasant farmers had been uprooted and destroyed as a class, and convinced that the Soviet Union had reached the stage of a "classless society," Soviet statesmen now urged the passage of a body of basic constitutional law abolishing all the class qualifications which the legal code had previously contained. Throughout the nation as a whole all groups were to be granted equal rights and equal representation.

At the same time the organizational structure of the state was considerably altered. According to the original framework, the All-Union Congress of Soviets had been designated as the supreme authority. The Congress proved to be an unwieldy body whose chief function was the election of the Central Executive Committee, which roughly paralleled the "parliament" of democratic countries. By the provisions of the new constitution the All-Union Congress was abolished, and the "parliament," now called the Supreme Soviet, was elected directly by all citizens of the nation. The new Supreme Soviet, like the former Central Executive Committee, consisted of two chambers: the Union Soviet and the Soviet of Nationalities. The former body was elected by the nation according to electoral areas and on the basis of one deputy for every 300,000 of the population; the latter was elected by republics and national areas on the basis of twenty-five deputies from each union republic, eleven from each autonomous republic, five from each autonomous region, and one from each national area. The secret ballot was substituted for the show of hands which had previously been the normal procedure in all elections. The right of nominating a candidate was reserved to "public organizations and societies of the working people: Communist party organizations, and cultural societies."

There was no fundamental change in the organization of the Union itself. Each of the union republics retained, theoretically, its right to secede from the Union. Prior to 1940 there had been eleven union republics: the Russian, Ukrainian, Byelo-Russian, Azerbaijan, Georgian, Armenian, Turkmen, Uzbek, Tajik, Kazakh, and Kirghiz. To these in 1940 were added five more: the three

Baltic republics (Estonia, Latvia, and Lithuania), the Karelo-Finnish, and the Moldavian.

Neither in the first constitution of the Soviet Union nor in the earlier constitutions of any of the single Soviet republics had there been any mention of the Communist party. For the first time in Soviet constitutional history the party was, so to speak, legalized in 1936. According to one of the provisions which has just been mentioned, it was here frankly given the right, together with other "public organizations," to nominate candidates for election. In addition, in the section on "Fundamental Rights and Duties of Citizens" there appeared the following statement: "The most active and politically most conscious citizens in the ranks of the working class and other sections of the toilers unite in the Communist party of the Soviet Union, which is the vanguard of the working people in their struggle to strengthen and develop the socialist system, and is the leading core of all organizations of the working people, both public and state."

In a sense the legalization of the Communist party was an indication of the fact that it had become a permanent national institution. Paradoxically, however, it was at just this time that the party began to lose its former absolute predominance in public life. A tendency to emphasize the close coöperation between party and nonparty men now came to the fore, and it was a "bloc" of these groups which won—or, rather, was allowed to win—in the first elections held under the new constitution. The new orientation of the party may be explained as another result of the struggle which had been going on between the Stalinist and the Trotskyite groups within the party, and which had culminated in the elimination of such influential "Old Bolsheviks" as Kamenev and Zinoviev. The clash had been bitter and prolonged, and had eventually resolved itself into a split between the new nationalist generation of Communists and the older proponents of internationalism. This struggle within what formerly had been a solid and united party weakened both partisan groups, and the nationalist wing now bid for the support of nonparty support in an effort to strengthen its position.

The new constitution was hailed both by the Russians themselves and by Stalinist sympathizers in other countries as "the most democratic constitution in the world." On the other hand, both Trotskyites and *bourgeois* critics pointed out that the constitution was in reality a legal fiction of no importance whatsoever, since the dictatorial *régime* of the Communist party had not been abolished. As a matter of fact, although the secret ballot had been officially introduced, the first elections were not thereby made comparable to those customarily held in parliamentary countries, since there was only one ticket and it was made up exclusively of candidates nominated and sponsored by "public organizations." Although the nominees were subject to wide discussion both in the press and in public meetings, the deputies invariably were elected by an almost unanimous vote. On the surface it thus appeared that no fundamental change had occurred with the introduction of the new constitution.

Yet the promulgation of the new constitution *was* an important fact in the political history of the Soviet Union, and given favorable conditions it may yet play a considerable rôle in the further development of Russia. While the guarantees which it provided for the rights of individual citizens may seem to an outsider to be of little value, under the circumstances they were actually of great importance, particularly to the remnants of the old "disfranchised classes" such as the deported kulaks and clergy, whose children were now admitted to schools and for the first time became eligible for the positions of any kind both in civil service and in industry. The abolition of class distinctions and the broad, all-inclusive, national character of the constitution were important both as a principle and as an educational instrument for the people. The very existence of such a body of fundamental law—even if it were entirely a nominal existence—serves a purpose merely by instilling in the minds of the people a feeling for democratic processes. By the same token, the creation of a "bloc" composed of both party and nonparty men represents some concession to the latter group, and presumes the possibility of the formation of other "blocs" of different kinds in the future in which the emphasis may be not on the party itself but on other "public organizations" such as the trade unions, the army, or others. There can be little doubt that potentially, at least, the constitution itself is democratic. It has been called a "blueprint for the future" and in some ways it lives up to that high estimate.

4.

After the Japanese occupation of Manchuria in 1932 and Hitler's rise to power in 1933, the international political situation became more tense, more explosive, and more delicately balanced each year. At a time when armed clashes—trials of strength for the coming death grapple—were becoming more frequent throughout the world, the Soviet Union continued its almost desperate attempts to preserve world peace and, in the event those efforts should fail, to keep the Soviets out of the conflict at almost any cost. Almost any cost, for it cannot be said that Russian policy was merely appeasement or that it was entirely passive and evasive. It was, indeed, a combination of several methods applied in various ways in different situations.

As always the problem was complicated for the Russians, for they were exposed to danger in both of the principle storm centers, Asia and Europe. To begin with the Far East: In 1935 the Soviet Government had agreed to sell to the Japanese sponsored Manchukuo Government the Soviet half interest in the Chinese Eastern Railway for the rather modest price of 170,000,000 yen, the yen at that time being quoted at 28.12 cents. Upon the outbreak of the "China Incident" two years later, on July 7, 1937, and during the subsequent invasion of China by the Japanese, the Soviets officially abstained from intervention in the Sino-Japanese struggle. Unofficially, however, the Soviet Union aided China both with material and with military instructors and advisers who were sent to work with the defending armies. The situation was made additionally difficult by the fact that since 1927 the Chiang Kai-shek Government had been estranged from the communists and had harried the illusive communist state from province to province in an attempt to crush it. Nevertheless, a nucleus of the Chinese Communist Army was still in existence at the time of the Japanese invasion, and the amount of Russian aid which the beleaguered Chinese could expect depended to a large extent on the degree of coöperation which could be instituted between the communists and other political groups in China. When an understanding had been worked out on this question, unofficial Soviet aid was extended both to Chiang's army and the Communist Army, though the sympathies of the Russians were quite naturally more with the Left groups.

Even before she embarked upon the Chinese venture, Japan had signed the Anti-Comintern Pact with Germany and Italy in November, 1936. It is safe to accept this action as presumptive evidence that at that time the Japanese had intended to turn their forces against Russia as soon as China was conquered. However, in spite of a series of resounding Japanese victories, months passed and China's resistance remained unbroken. Unable to conclude the "China Incident," Japan was faced with the necessity of preparing for an attack against Russia even though her armies were still heavily committed along a winding and elastic front in Asia. By 1938 considerable Japanese forces had been concentrated in Manchuria, and Nipponese secret agents were busy in Mongolia, in Sin-Kiang, and in the Soviet Union itself. Still not in a sufficiently favorable position to attempt an all-out war against Russia, the Japanese on several occasions chose to test the strength of Russian defenses by the creation of various "border incidents." Several clashes of this kind occurred during 1938, and in the following year a full-scale battle was fought between Russian and Japanese troops on the border between Manchuria and Mongolia. In reality an undeclared war at that time existed between the two satellite states, with Russia and Japan each assisting her respective ally. The results of the tests they had sought proved disappointing to the Japanese, for their forces were thrown back with heavy losses. The Russians, however, were not encouraged by the success of this one encounter to allow the incident to develop into a war. They were determined not to become involved in any conflict which they could avoid, particularly in the Far East, since it had already become apparent to them that the immediate danger now lay upon their western frontiers.

In the west the delicate political equilibrium which had existed for a number of years was at last destroyed by Italy's Ethiopian venture in 1935. Ethiopia, however, lay geographically and socially on the fringes of civilization and both Great Britain and France—which were at the time the leading powers in the League of Nations—were reluctant to commit themselves to decisive action to prevent the destruction of the weaker state. Nevertheless both the warring states were members of the League which was, consequently, bound to take some measures to bring the conflict to an end.

Driven against its will to intervene, the League compromised by recommending the application of mild "economic sanctions," and even these were further emasculated by the League's failure to close the Suez Canal to Italian shipping. Half measures rarely reach anywhere. Convinced by the timid steps taken to restrain her that she had nothing to fear from the Western democracies, Italy protested loudly against the "sanctions" and left the League in high dudgeon. The Soviet Government would have preferred the adoption of more drastic measures against the aggressor, but since nothing else could be secured from the League, duly applied the recommended sanctions in her trade with Italy.

Soon thereafter it became apparent that neither Great Britain nor France had seriously intended to enforce even the weak restraints which had been decided upon. While the subject was still being debated in the halls at Geneva, Sir Samuel Hoare and Pierre Laval had quietly prepared a compromise plan by which Italian preponderance in Ethiopia was to be recognized by both France and Great Britain. Though it is true that the authors of the plan were subjected to withering criticism by the more ardently democratic groups in their countries when the scheme was divulged by the press, the castigation they suffered was of little avail, for Italy rapidly brought the conquest of Ethiopia to a conclusion in 1936, and soon thereafter Mussolini was able to proclaim the foundation of the African Empire upon the prostrate state.

Encouraged by the success of fascism in Africa, Spanish Rightists under the leadership of General Francisco Franco revolted against the Republican Government of Spain on July 17, 1936. Public opinion in the democratic countries had not been greatly aroused by the fate of a remote and little known African country, but the arrival of war on the European continent was a matter of direct concern to all democratic countries. France, already confronted by powerful totalitarian nations on two borders, was especially affected by the turn of events beyond the Pyrenees. The situation was further aggravated by the possibility of both German and Italian intervention in Spain in behalf of Franco; in the event that the Republican Government should be defeated, France faced the prospect of being surrounded on three sides by hostile or potentially hostile powers. When Italian and German "volunteers" and supplies began to pour into Spain, France, where the "Popular

Front" headed by Léon Blum was in power, was confronted with the necessity of making a decision upon which her own future—and indeed that of Europe—might well depend. Blum himself and the government he represented were sympathetic to the cause of the "Loyalists," but because of the critical political situation at home, and because of France's unfavorable diplomatic position, Blum hesitated. The French did eventually allow the sale of a limited number of airplanes and other supplies to the Spanish Republicans, but the British Government by its insistence on strict neutrality demonstrated measurably less sympathy toward the Loyalists than the French had shown.

Although the U.S.S.R. was geographically remote from Spain, politically she was considerably closer than the democracies. Litvinov, the spokesman for Moscow in foreign affairs, had always insisted that peace was "indivisible" and that war anywhere in the world threatened the security of all peoples. Moreover, the Spanish Communist party threw its support to the Republican Government and immediately appealed to the Executive Committee of the Comintern—that is, to Moscow—for help. The Soviet Government thereupon found itself in an extremely delicate position: it could not but be in sympathy with the Spanish communists; it was worried by the spread of fascism to Spain; it was anxious to test the sincerity of Great Britain and France. Above all, however, it was wary of becoming so deeply involved in Spanish affairs that it could be isolated and left in the lurch by the Western democracies.

One further point worried the leaders of both the Soviet Government and the Comintern. While the International at that time supported the Popular Front and within certain limits was ready to coöperate with moderate socialists and even *bourgeois* democrats, it would not and could not deal with the Trotskyites with whom the Soviet Government was just then in a desperate struggle in the Soviet Union. To meet the situation, Moscow devised a twofold policy. On the one hand, the Soviet Government instructed its agents abroad to support every effort by the League of Nations or by individual states to establish and hold a common front against fascism. At the same time, it was decided to engage in direct action of a limited nature, and "volunteers," military equipment, and other supplies were dispatched to Spain. Some Red Army leaders were not at all opposed to taking advantage of the opportunity to test Russian planes and tanks under actual battle conditions. In addition to the troops and equipment provided for the Spanish Loyalists, political advisers and N.K.V.D. agents were at the same time sent to the Iberian Peninsula. Under the pretext of advising the Spanish police on methods of combatting "fifth columnists"—a term which grew out of the Spanish war—these Russian agents also engaged in a campaign to eliminate the influence of the Trotskyites.

Limited as it was, the Soviet intervention in Spain aroused a disproportionate amount of fear and suspicion, both among certain conservative circles in Great Britain and France and among Trotskyite sympathizers the world over. In many different quarters the worth of Soviet coöperation in any kind of international committee was questioned, and since the whole diplomatic response to the Spanish situation centered in the Nonintervention Commission which had been established in London, Ivan Maisky, Soviet Ambassador to Great Britain, was hard put to it to preserve Soviet participation in the activities. Although the Soviet Union did more to assist the Loyalist cause in Spain than any other European government, even its intervention in Spanish affairs was limited to half measures, and under the pressure of inimical public opinion in France and Great Britain the help that was originally offered was gradually withdrawn. Thus, because of the failure of the democratic countries to reach any basic understanding on the issue, Franco was eventually allowed to win (the Spanish Civil War lingered on well into 1939), and his victory resulted in considerable increase in the prestige of both Germany and Italy.

The failure of Russian intervention in Spain, the deterioration of relations with France and Great Britain, and the ominous ascendancy of fascism and nazism in Europe and Africa made the Soviet Government apprehensive about the repercussions which all of these events might have at home—particularly as they might affect the activities of Russian Trotskyites and German-inspired fifth columnists, saboteurs, and spies who were known to be active in Russia. The Soviet leaders' fear and concern were evidenced by the great purge of 1937–38. In January, 1937, several members of the so-called "Trotskyite Center," including Piatakov, Radek, and Sokolnikov, were tried for their participation in a plot to overthrow the Soviet Government and for their alleged contacts with

Germany, Poland, and Japan. Of the important political figures tried, Radek alone escaped with a sentence of ten years in prison, and most of the others were executed. In March, 1938, there occurred still another mammoth public trial, that of the "Bloc of Rightists and Trotskyites," in which Bukharin, Rykov, and Yagoda, the former chief of the O.G.P.U. stood among the accused. Here again most of those on trial were eventually condemned to death.

It was Radek who during his testimony first hinted at the existence of a conspiracy in the Red Army under the leadership of Marshal Tukhachevsky. Soon thereafter Tukhachevsky and a number of other prominent army leaders, most of them civil war veterans, were arrested, tried by a court martial, and promptly executed. Marshal Voroshilov, another civil war hero and a man of only mediocre abilities as a strategist who had, however, earned the confidence of Stalin, was now put in charge of the army. Since the purge was not confined to the top leadership but affected a great number of subaltern commanders as well, in order to prevent the precipitous decline of morale it was deemed necessary to re-introduce the institution of political commissars which shortly before had been abolished at Tukhachevsky's suggestion. At the same time, the purge reached down into the ranks of civilian administration and into the Communist party itself with hardly less drastic thoroughness. Once more, as in the days of 1935–36, not only those who were themselves suspected of being leaders of the opposition were affected but also their acquaintances, their assistants, the people who served with them in their respective departments or had any contact with them. And again it was certainly true that thousands of innocent people shared the fate of the guilty.

Abroad the purge was almost universally interpreted as a sign of inner weakness in the Soviet Government and even as an indication that the communist *régime* was beginning to disintegrate. There was also a new outburst of public indignation against Russia both in Europe and in America, and especially among the liberals and Trotskyites who accused Stalin of taking revenge on his personal enemies under the pretext of guarding the integrity of the state. The confessions of the condemned men were credited by comparatively few, and it was generally suggested that they had been made under the threat of torture or as a result of a breakdown after months of duress. As always, of course, there was a great deal of uninformed talk about the alleged Dostoyevsky-like mystery of the Russian soul.

Looking back on the 1937–38 purges barely five years after the event, any humanitarian person is inclined to sympathize with the fate of the innocent victims who suffered in the general upheaval. On the other hand, the fact that when Hitler attacked Russia in 1941 he was unable to produce a well-organized and effective fifth column such as had been at his disposal in France and most of the other European countries must make us ponder. There can be no doubt that from the very beginning of the Nazi Government in Germany, the Gestapo and its "fellow travelers" were as active in Russia as they were elsewhere. It is equally apparent that the opposition of the peasants to forcible collectivization during the early experimental years in Russian agriculture had prepared the political soil for the growth of opposition groups. That the agents of these groups achieved considerable success is indicated by the series of sabotage and wrecking cases which was uncovered in numerous plants between 1930 and 1937. Since no large-scale fifth column was available for the use of the Nazis when Russia was invaded, it seems reasonable to assume that it had been smashed sometime in the interval between 1934 and 1941. If that is so, we may also assume that the purges were somehow instrumental in eliminating whatever potential fifth column may have existed.

5.

In spite of political turmoil and party intrigues and in spite of the purges and assassinations which struck down many of the guiding figures of the revolution during those five fateful and significant years from 1934 to 1939, for the bulk of Russian people life moved along on a surprisingly even keel. The purges which during these years were represented to the outside world as the essential fact of the Soviet Union, were, as a matter of fact, of much less immediate concern to the masses than had been the forcible collectivization and "dekulakization" of 1929–30. Whereas hundreds of thousands, mainly peasants, had suffered bitterly during the time of the agricultural adjustments, it was chiefly intellectuals who were touched by the political strife of 1936–38, and the number of victims, though considerable, was presumably much lower than the 1930 figures. The agrarian upheaval had dislocated the entire economy and had resulted in hunger throughout the nation, but for every party official and civil servant eliminated by the purges, hundreds of new people were prepared to step into his place and keep the government machinery functioning. In addition, at that time life was still hard and skimpy, and the ordinary Soviet citizen was so occupied with the struggle to get his share of the scant means of subsistence that he had little interest in the political disputes and intrigues that flourished around him. Among those of the younger generation whose imaginations had been fired by the great dream of socialist reconstruction, the lack of political freedom and the limitations of the rights of the individual were taken as a matter of course. Then too, by granting privileges such as the right to work and study to the children of the previously disfranchised classes, the new constitution of 1936 had strengthened the communist *régime* in at least two ways: it had added many able youths to the ranks of scholars, engineers, and skilled workers to replace those removed because of their alleged Trotskyite sympathies, and by moderating in this point its most repressive policies it had gained a considerable number of new adherents. Finally, and fortunately for the Government, there was at this time a slight but steady improvement in the supply of food and in general living conditions throughout the country, a gain which was of much greater importance to the average citizen than the political dissensions among the leadership. Encouraged by these ameliorating circumstances, and fortified by their own tenacity, the Russian people worked with determination and rising confidence.

During the years between 1934 and 1939 many of the earlier Soviet industrial projects were put into operation with the completion of the Second Five Year Plan, and still others were launched during the Third Five Year Plan which was inaugurated toward the close of this period. At the very beginning of the period the Seventeenth Convention of the Communist Party, meeting in January and February, 1934, recommended a number of revisions designed to speed up the Second Five Year Plan which had just then entered upon its second year. This revised plan, which was approved by the Central Executive Committee and the Council of People's Commissars of the Soviet Union in 1934, called for an increase in the productivity of labor, a reduction in unit costs, an improvement in the quality of goods produced, and the achievement of greater mechanization in industry, particularly heavy industry. In order to increase the production of consumer goods it was also decided to decentralize the administration of light industry by reorganizing a part of it on a regional basis instead of a national one, and by placing the major part of the responsibility upon local administrators. The geographical redistribution and reallocation of heavy industry was also speeded up. More than ever before an attempt was made to develop the Ural and Siberian industrial bases, both in order to exploit the natural resources of these vastly wealthy industrial regions and in order to shift at least part of Russia's military industries far to the east out of reach of potential invaders.

A number of huge industrial combinations were built or further developed during the Second Five Year Plan, and of these the so-called Ural-Kuznetsk *combinat* was perhaps the most important. The development of mining and the erection of metallurgical plants in the Ural area had already made substantial progress under the First Five Year Plan, when the huge Magnitogorsk project was begun and brought into partial operation in 1934. As early as at the Sixteenth Convention of the Communist Party in 1932 it had been decided to pool the iron resources of the Ural area and the coal resources of the Kuznetsk basin in western Siberia. Since the distance between these two points is more than twelve hundred miles, it was decided that coal was to be transported from the latter region to the former by rail, and that in order to use the freight cars to fullest capacity they were to be loaded with iron ore for the return trip. In spite of the magnitude of the task thus laid down, the plan was in time put into operation and worked well for several years. A little later, however, huge new coal deposits were discovered in northern Kazakhstan, which was much nearer to the Ural area, and when the exploitation of this new field had got under way the Ural projects thereby became independent of the Kuznetsk basin. In the meantime, metallurgical plants had already been begun in the Kuznetsk region, and a number of important single plants producing tractors, automobiles, locomotives, turbogenerators, and other machinery were completed in various cities on both sides of the Volga River—in Moscow, Kharkov, Stalingrad, Gorky, Ufa, and Sverdlovsk.

As the international situation grew more and more threatening, the importance of the Ural and Siberian industrial bases for defense became increasingly clear, and by the time the Third Five Year Plan was launched in 1938 the Government had decided to accelerate still more the development of industry in the east. The thoroughness of the plans worked out at this time is indicated by the fact that in addition to the new factories and plants which were built there, at a number of places structural foundations were constructed to accommodate the industrial buildings which might be transferred from the exposed western districts in the event of war.

Until this time most of the Soviet oil industry had been concentrated in the Caucasus—an area which was vulnerable to attack from either the northwest, through Ukraine, or the south through Iran and Turkey. The Soviet Government therefore considered it a most fortunate event when new oil deposits were discovered between the Volga River and the Urals. Feverish work was immediately begun to develop this new area, soon nicknamed "the Second Baku," and even in 1939 a number of oil wells had already been put into operation.

It will be evident from the above examples that Soviet industry was expanding rapidly. Just how great the increase in industrial output was will be seen in the following table.

TABLE A

Industry	*Unit*	*1932*	*1938*
Coal	million tons	64	132
Oil	million tons	22	32
Pig Iron	million tons	6	14
Steel	million tons	6	18
Automobiles	thousands	23	211
Tractors	thousands	50	176
Machinery	billion rubles (1926–27 price level)	18	33
Chemicals	billion rubles (1926–27 price level)	2	6

The above figures refer, of course, only to heavy industry. In light industry the progress was somewhat less spectacular largely because the Government was still not in a position to pay adequate attention to this aspect of the new economy. The troublesome international situation had compelled Soviet leaders to concentrate all of the national effort on the production of arms and munitions and on the development of those industries which either were essential for defense or might readily be converted to war uses. The result was that while there was a steady increase in the output of light industry, the growth was on the whole not as rapid as it was in other branches.

TABLE B

Industry	*Unit*	*1932*	*1938*
Cotton textiles	million meters	2,694	3,491
Woolen textiles	million meters	88	114
Footwear	million pairs	94	213
Paper	thousand tons	479	834
Sugar (granulated)	thousand tons	828	2,530

In the meantime, there was a parallel expansion in communications. The construction of the Moscow-Volga Canal in a sense made Moscow a seaport, and should surely rank as one of the most important undertakings of the period. Considerable railroad building was under way, the most ambitious project being the construction of a second trunk line into the Far East, skirting the northern shore of Lake Baikal in the direction of the Sea of Okhotsk. This important addition to the transportation system, however, was still incomplete at the time of the beginning of the German war. Generally speaking, the railroad network expanded rather slowly. Railway trackage, which had totaled slightly more than 58,000 kilometers in 1913, reached the figure of 83,000 in 1932, and by 1940 had climbed to an even 100,000. The carrying capacity of the railways, however, expanded much more rapidly than the mileage. While in 1931 only 132,000,000 tons had been transported by rail, this figure had risen by 1932 to 260,000,000 tons, and in 1940 reached a total of 553,000,000 tons.

The progress of agriculture was directly affected by the steady increase in the production of tractors and agricultural machinery at home and in imports from abroad, chiefly from the United States. By the end of the Second Five Year Plan more than 6,000 machine-tractor stations serving collectivized agriculture had been organized in the main farming districts of the Soviet Union—in Ukraine, in the north Caucasian area, and western Siberia. At the same time, the number of tractors operated by the stations increased from 7,000 in 1930 to 454,000 in 1941, and harvesting combines from 3,000 in 1932 to 125,000 in 1939. In addition to the technical service which the machine-tractor stations provided to agriculture, they performed an almost equally important economic and sociological function as links between industry and agriculture, and as training centers in which young men and women were made familiar with new mechanical processes.

Originally, two types of socialized agriculture had been tested by the Government—sovkhozes (state farms) and kolkhozes (collective farms). The second of these two became by all odds the more important. By 1939 there were in the Soviet Union about 4,000 sovkhozes controlling something more than 12,000,000 hectares of arable land; by the same time the number of kolkhozes had risen to 242,000, and the area included in them to more than 117,000,000 hectares. As a leftover from the period of the N.E.P. there remained 1.3 million individual farmers who still continued to cultivate privately owned land, although its area had shrunk to less than one million hectares. Originally, there had been considerable confusion about the internal organization of the kolkhozes, two different plans having been put into operation simultaneously—the one providing for strict collectivization and the other for a looser association. By the end of 1934 an intermediate form which included some elements from both of the original plans had become the prevailing type, and in 1935 there was promulgated a revised code for the kolkhozes, called the Stalin Code. Presumably this new system of organization was in part the result of the advice given by Kirov. Each kolkhoz received a special charter or deed for the land in its possession, and although the land still legally belonged to the state it was expressly provided that the farms should remain permanently in the control of each kolkhoz. Thus, the members of the more prosperous collectives were assured that the fruits of their common labor would be shared by them alone, and would not be used for the benefit of other less efficient groups.

In addition, the members were granted certain new rights within the collective. Each member was now permitted a small plot of land varying from one quarter to one hectare in size for his own personal use, and the products which were grown on such plots were to be disposed of by the holder for his own profit. Each member was also to share in the collective profit of the kolkhoz strictly in accordance with the amount of work which he had contributed. All collectives were bound to sell a certain quota of grain and other products to the Government at fixed prices, and to pay, usually in grain, the machine-tractor stations for their services. The collectives were then free to dispose of whatever balance remained of the produce on the open market.

The success of this new agricultural policy is indicated in the production figures for recent years. In 1940 the kolkhozes were able to supply 86 per cent of all market demands for grain, the sovkhozes 12½ per cent, and only the very minor remainder was drawn from individual farms. In order to relieve the cattle shortage the Government issued several decrees during 1934–35 permitting members of the kolkhozes to keep one or two cows, a certain number of hogs, and a certain number of sheep and poultry on their personal plots. These decrees had the desired result in the gradual increase in the country's livestock. By 1938 there were in the Soviet Union 30,000,000 hogs as compared to the 20,000,000 in 1913, and 63,000,000 head of horned cattle, as against 60,000,000 in 1913. While horses, sheep, and goats were also on the increase at this time, in 1938 their numbers were still below the level of 1913. During the Second Five Year Plan the total national yield of grain averaged 94,000,000 metric tons per year. In 1940 nearly 120,000,000 tons were harvested. The increase in industrial crops was even more marked. The yearly yield of cotton increased from 1.2 million tons in 1932 to 2.6 million in 1938; sugar beets from 6.5 million tons to 16.6 million tons.

The general increase in agriculture of which these examples are typical indicated that collectivized agriculture had sent down firm roots in the Soviet Union, and the further increase of agricultural production between 1938 and 1941 demonstrated that on the eve of the German attack the new system was at last about to bear abundant fruit. What may have been of more importance to the Soviet Union, especially in the light of subsequent events, was the fact that the kolkhoz members seemed to be satisfied with the results of the system which they had once dreaded and fought.

Though the economic reconstruction of Russia had not nearly reached its final stages by 1939, some stability had undoubtedly been achieved by the new *régime*. The demand for clothing and other consumer goods still greatly exceeded their production, but the situation was decidedly on the upgrade. The abolition of ration books for bread and other food products in 1935 and for manufactured articles in 1936 was a characteristic sign of the basic improvement in the standard of living. The Soviet Union had passed through the period when the attainment of a mere subsistence level was its goal and had entered the period when more abundant living seemed about to become available. The upward trend was clear and definite; it was only the shadow of war which delayed the improvement and war itself which finally reversed the process.

6.

In their campaign to undermine and destroy the prestige of Russia, the enemies of the Soviet Union all over the world contrived to use the purges of 1937–38 to even better advantage than those of 1935–36. The "capitalist" and the Trotskyite press, German and Polish "communist baiters," Roman Catholic churchmen and liberal socialists—groups who had only this one cause in common—all joined in the denunciation of "Bolshevik horrors." With malicious joy or with hypocritical pity, depending upon the sector in which the criticism was voiced, it was declared day after day that the whole administrative and military machinery of the Soviet state had been so thoroughly shaken by the purges that it was permanently and irreparably out of order. It thus became possible to urge the diplomatic isolation of Moscow on two grounds: it was first argued that any contact with the terroristic Soviet Government was an offense against political morality, and, since realistic politicians were frequently not to be swayed by moral considerations alone, it was simultaneously suggested that as the Soviets were obviously weak and racked by dissension, any agreement with them was likely to be useless anyway. Though Litvinov continued to present the Soviet position at Geneva, Russia's political and military reputation had been so thoroughly blackened in the world press that the Soviet Union entered upon 1938, the fateful year of decision, with hardly one firm friend in the community of nations.

On March 10, 1938, Hitler's troops marched into Austria. From more than one point of view this week-end enterprise was a master stroke. At that time, there seemed to be little evidence to indicate that the Austrian people themselves did not want to join the Third Reich, and although the union of two Germanic peoples had previously been opposed by the major European powers, it now began to take on the color of a natural and almost inevitable event. This belief predisposed even sincere anti-Hitler statesmen to easy acquiescence, especially since the only alternative appeared to be war, and certainly nobody was willing to die to disrupt the union of two Teutonic peoples, which had, moreover, been achieved without bloodshed. It seemed unimportant to point out that by the German annexation of Austria, Czechoslovakia had virtually been encircled, particularly since the Yugoslav Government after 1937 had entered into negotiations with Hitler and Mussolini, and by the beginning of 1938 had definitely committed Yugoslavia to neutrality—that is, to the tacit support of Hitler.

The reshuffling of power in Central Europe rapidly brought on the hour when the validity of the Franco-Czechoslovak alliance was to be tested. Torn by inner political dissension, disheartened by her failure to meet the threat which had arisen in Spain, and still distrustful of the aims of the Soviet Union, France now turned to Great Britain for guidance. In England the policy of appeasement was at its height, although from time to time Chamberlain was forced by the pressure of liberal groups to make some slight demonstration of anti-Nazi feeling. Certain of the British conservatives obviously hated the Soviets more intensely than they feared Hitler and to them the ideal policy was one which diverted Hitler's attention toward the east and thus allowed them to hope for relative quiet in Europe. Unfortunately, later events were to prove that although Hitler was indeed planning war against Russia, he first meant to round out his possessions in Central Europe. Nevertheless, he had enough cunning to move cautiously, preferring to take what he wanted piece by piece and applying wherever possible the policy of "infiltration," which he had laid down in *Mein Kampf*, before risking outright invasion. Had he attacked Czechoslovakia as a whole immediately after the annexation of Austria, it is probable that even Chamberlain would have been forced to let France honor her Czech alliance. Since this must have been perfectly clear to Hitler, he chose to achieve his purpose by manufacturing the Sudeten problem. It was then possible for him to obtain in due time the Czech "Maginot Line" along Bohemia's northern boundary and reduce Czechoslovakia to a defenseless "rump" state without firing a single shot.

When the Czechs protested against Hitler's threat to their sovereignty, the British sent to Prague a special mission headed by Lord Runciman who spent considerable time in exploring conditions and preparing recommendations on the possibilities of a compromise. That they agreed to this method proved an unfortunate decision on the part of the Czechs for, psychologically at least, it made the subsequent Munich Pact almost inevitable. It now became possible to put the blame for the explosive situation on the uncompromising attitude of the Czechs toward minority groups, and both the British and the French quickly agreed that under the circumstances it would be foolish to fight to "keep the Sudeten Germans within Czechoslovakia against their will," as the situation was summed up in appeasement circles. Even so, the Czechs continued to object and in September, 1938, it appeared that it might not be possible to avoid war. Fearful that the desired compromise might not materialize, both the British and French approached the Russians to inquire what the Soviets meant to do in the event of an open conflict. The Soviet Union made it abundantly clear that they intended to fight. Litvinov stated the case plainly in the League of Nations, and in addition Russia took the opportunity to warn Poland to keep her hands off Czechoslovakia should Hitler decide to attack. Although French opinion was divided on the question and confusion prevailed in diplomatic circles, until mid-September the French press continued to insist that France would honor her word. At this point Chamberlain decided to go to Godesberg to confer with Hitler. The weak and insecure anti-Nazi front which had been built in Europe appeared to be about to collapse completely. Since Russia was obligated to intervene only in the event that France honored her agreement, President Beneš of Czechoslovakia approached the Soviet Government through its ambassador in Prague, Aleksandrovsky, asking whether Russia would support Czechoslovakia even if France refused. Once more the answer was positively in the affirmative, but by the time it was received the Czechoslovak cabinet already had agreed to entrust the fate of Czechoslovakia to Great Britain and France. At the suggestion of Mussolini, four statesmen representing Great Britain, France, Germany, and Italy (Chamberlain, Daladier, Hitler, and Mussolini were the men) met in Munich to settle the problem. Not only was Russia not invited to participate but she was not even informed beforehand of the impending conference. Quietly and almost without consideration, the fate of Czechoslovakia was sealed, appropriately enough, by four men who late on the night of October 1 decided to hand over to Hitler the Sudeten province and the "Little Maginot Line" which was the Czechs' only defense barrier.

7.

THE Munich Pact alarmed and dismayed Russian statesmen. To them it appeared to be an open rapprochement between the Western democracies and Germany and her satellites—an agreement which could only mean that the Nazis were to be given a free hand in the east. Soviet relations with France and Great Britain at their best had never been cordial, but with the signing of the Munich agreement Soviet leaders were forced to abandon entirely what little confidence they had previously had in the sincerity and ultimate purposes of the democracies. It was evident that had Hitler been content at that time to strike directly at Russia, he would have encountered little, if any, opposition from France or Britain. But Hitler was both greedy and cautious: before attacking Russia he wanted to extract the last measure of gain from the pact and to strengthen his position by the consolidation of the whole of Central Europe. Hitler's new ambitions, however, proved to be too extreme even for Chamberlain. While it is true that when Hitler invaded Prague on March 14, 1939, he was allowed to overrun the Czech state without opposition from any of the Western powers, it is also true that from that day onward Great Britain began to prepare for war. The preparations undertaken, however, proceeded in a most leisurely fashion, and even at that late date the British Government appeared to have no realistic estimate of the danger, no accurate notion of the forces involved, and, above all, no conception of the absolute necessity for an immediate and binding agreement with the Soviet Union. Some inkling of the English attitude was revealed by the fact that British statesmen consistently underestimated both Russian and German strength, and by the fact that all of their actions pointed to a belief that the Polish army constituted a serious obstacle in the way of the Nazi Wehrmacht.

Under pressure from the Left, Chamberlain was at last forced to make at least a pretext of entering into negotiations with Russia, but he approached the task with such obvious distaste that it was apparent he expected no positive results. The week after Hitler's march on Prague a British trade delegation headed by R. S. Hudson was sent to Moscow, but its authority to act and even its right to enter into exploratory conversations were rigidly limited by Chamberlain's amazing advice to abstain from politics. Naturally enough, this abortive venture proved a complete failure. So mishandled was the whole diplomatic situation that some keen observers of the international situation, men like Ambassador Joseph E. Davies, were alarmed lest Chamberlain's tactics result in "driving Stalin into Hitler's hands."

On April 8, 1939, Litvinov resigned as Commissar of Foreign Affairs, and his portfolio was taken over by the Premier (Chairman of the Council of People's Commissars), V. M. Molotov. The meaning of the change should have been obvious to anyone who troubled to think about the matter, for Litvinov for years had been closely associated with the policy of collective security. His resignation was an open notice to the world that the Soviet Government had entirely despaired of achieving the common action for which Litvinov had so long pleaded, and was now determined to free itself of previous commitments so that it could follow the course it deemed best. Strangely enough, however, the implications of the event were not at the time fully grasped by either the British or the French. The German appraisal of the situation was much more correct. There it was understood that since Chamberlain had chosen to play the rôle of appeaser in the west at the expense of Russia, Stalin was now prepared to play the same game in reverse. Nevertheless, Stalin did not immediately close the door to negotiations with the democracies, and on April 17 Molotov proposed to the British and French ambassadors in Moscow the formation of a triple alliance against German aggression. The French representatives were willing to accept the Russian proposal, but London demonstrated no interest whatsoever in it. On May 31 in a speech before the Supreme Soviet Molotov repeated the same offer, and this time—again under pressure from Left and labor groups—Chamberlain agreed to send a special envoy to discuss the situation in Moscow. Instead of assuming the duty himself or assigning it to an important representative of the British Government, he sent William Strang, a man who then held no high official position and was not, moreover, given sufficient latitude or authority. The negotiations instituted by Strang in Moscow dragged along for weeks without achieving appreciable results. The Russians insisted that both Poland and the Baltic countries be guaranteed against indirect as well as direct aggression. The British were prepared to speak only of direct attack. Though this may well seem a minor technicality, it proved to be the point on which the negotiations broke down. The Russians were concerned about the possibility of German "infiltration" into one or more of the Baltic countries, and wished to be protected by Allied guarantees to the border states against the piecemeal dismemberment suffered by Czechoslovakia. The British position on the matter was fixed: they were reluctant to give such a guarantee for fear that Russia would then be in a position to determine by herself under what circumstances Britain would be obligated to go to war.

Since they were unable to make any headway in the conversations with Great Britain and since they were convinced that the English were merely delaying a decision, the Russians made a friendly gesture in the direction of Berlin by undertaking new negotiations concerning a trade treaty with Germany. Even then, however, the conversations with Great Britain and France were not broken off and, as a matter of fact, entered into a new stage—staff talks. Once more the Anglo-French military missions sent to Russia resorted to dilatory tactics. In the face of a constantly deteriorating diplomatic situation, the missions chose to journey to Moscow by boat through the North Sea to Leningrad, a route which was certainly the slowest possible way in an age of air travel. Conversations were begun immediately upon the arrival of the military missions, but once again a snag was soon encountered.

The Russians insisted on the adoption of a plan which would authorize them to send troops into Poland and the Baltic countries in the event of a German attack. The British, however, were afraid that such a plan would result in the opening of Europe to Russian armies, and both Poland and the Baltic states resisted any suggestion that the Red Army be allowed to enter their territory. The Russians immediately pointed out that under such circumstances no realistic or effective plan of coöperation could be devised. If, at the very moment when they were pretending to be working out a war plan, the democracies were unwilling to allow the Soviets the latitude they needed, Soviet leaders were convinced that the only way to keep Russia out of war was to choose the other alternative —to come to terms with Germany.

On August 21 there was signed in Berlin a new Soviet-German trade agreement by which the Germans agreed to advance a credit of 200 million marks to the Soviet Union. Two days later, on August 23, German Foreign Minister Ribbentrop arrived in Moscow by plane. After a conversation which lasted through the afternoon and evening a nonaggression pact between Germany and the Soviet Union was signed at 1 A.M. on August 24. According to the provisions of this pact, the two contracting parties pledged to "refrain from any violence, from any aggressive action, and from any attack against each other, either individually or jointly with other powers." Any disputes or conflicts which should in the future arise between the two contracting powers were to be solved "exclusively in a peaceful way through an amicable exchange of views." The pact was to be effective for ten years.

On August 25 Great Britain countered by signing a mutual assistance pact with Poland. The British act was a demonstration of gallantry but it was hardly evidence of a realistic appraisal of the situation. Nothing was done to prevent the final conclusion of the agreement between Russia and Germany, and on August 31, six days later, the Supreme Soviet unanimously ratified the German-Soviet pact.

CHAPTER XIX.

RUSSIAN CULTURE UNDER THE SOVIETS

(1917–1941)

I.

THE second half of the nineteenth century and the beginning of the twentieth were, as we have seen, a period of rapid and uninterrupted growth in Russian culture, an age which witnessed the blossoming of Russian literature, arts, and sciences. Having begun among the upper classes, cultural advances spread rapidly through other groups and, especially after the improvement of educational facilities which began toward the close of the nineteenth century, made notable headway with the masses. Though the first World War, of course, greatly hampered cultural activity, the real crisis in the cultural life of Russia came during the period of suffering, starvation, and sheer physical exhaustion which was ushered in by the civil war. Cultural leaders were among the most miserable victims of the cataclysm, and a full martyrology of Russian scholars and teachers who died during the famine of 1920–21 would include the names of many of the country's most prominent scientific and educational figures. After the victory of the Communists, the emigration of hundreds of thousands of men, women, and children—a high percentage of whom previously had been engaged in educational, artistic, and scientific pursuits—intensified the cultural impoverishment of the nation. Most of those who fled at this time were obliged to leave Soviet Russia because of their direct or indirect connections with the White Government or its armies; others escaped because of their unwillingness to accept the violent methods of the communist dictatorship; less frequently individuals were deported by the Soviet Government because their "idealistic" or *"bourgeois"* points of view were considered dangerous to the new *régime.* The total number of Russian emigrants may possibly have reached a million, the bulk of whom settled in European and Asiatic countries, although a considerable number found haven in America, Australia, and even in Africa. Not a few first settled in Germany, and among these thousands who were of Jewish extraction or who had democratic or socialist political inclinations were again forced to flee after the rise of Hitlerism. Some of these sought refuge in France, and after the fall of that country in 1940 were again compelled to seek safety in flight. Those who at last succeeded in reaching the United States considered themselves extremely fortunate merely to find a place where they might attempt the third or fourth reconstruction of their lives.

When they realized at the end of the civil war the magnitude of the destruction wrought by two ravaging conflicts, both Russians and foreigners gloomily predicted that Russian culture had been dealt a crippling, if not, indeed, a mortal blow, and that from a cultural point of view the Soviets had been thrown back half a century in their development. These forebodings, in the sense in which they were intended, proved to be entirely unfounded. That Russia was able to survive the holocaust and, after the first shock, to make rapid progress on a new cultural basis, is not only evidence of the enormous innate vitality of the Russian people and of their insatiable urge to knowledge and education but also an indication that the roots of cultural progress had already reached out widely among the masses of the population even before the first World War.

No less important than Russian stamina in the cultural reconstruction of the country was the vigorous policy adopted by the Soviet Government in encouraging and sponsoring the development of a great number of cultural institutions. Even at a time when the desolation and impoverishment of the civil war appeared to be on the verge of invalidating all their plans, Soviet leaders devoted some attention to the preservation of at least a part of the laboratories, schools, and museums of the country, to the maintenance of skeleton staffs in these institutions, and to the preparation of plans for their further development and extension as soon as circumstances should permit. To be sure, all education was entrusted to Marxian supervisers, and at first only the obviously "proletarian" types of culture were considered worthy of support. However, as the restraints of militant communism were relaxed during the period of the N.E.P. considerably more freedom was given to cultural and educational activities, and since the Five Year Plan was intended to abolish "classes" altogether, at a later date the "class" approach to culture was revised or abandoned in favor of a broader interpretation of cultural needs.

An interesting by-product of Soviet political federalism and an important feature of the Russian approach to the special task of reëducating the people has been the consideration given to the needs of national minorities. In the Soviet Union there is no race problem and no feeling of national inferiority or superiority. On the contrary, special care has always been taken to offer every facility for the fullest development of national cultures, not only of the principal minority groups, such as the Ukrainian, the White Russian, the Armenian, and the Georgian, but also of the smallest native tribes of the Caucasus or the Far East. It must be added, of course, that all efforts in this direction are subject to one general limitation: that the development of the varying cultures of the scores of nationalities within the Soviet Union must always be adjusted to the broad principles of Soviet education originally based upon Marxian tenets. This reservation is, however, in no sense discriminatory but applies with equal force to the Russians themselves. Though all attempts at forcible Russianization were given up after the revolution, the importance of the Russian language and of Russian culture in the life of the Soviet Union as a whole certainly has not decreased. On the contrary, because of the universal feeling of equality and because of the close social and economic coöperation existing between the various republics, the importance of Russian as a link between all the component parts of the nation has increased substantially during the past twenty years. It seems likely that the experience of the second World War will be instrumental, by welding the various national groups still more closely, in further enhancing the prestige of the Russian language as a common literary vehicle and as a common meeting ground for all Soviet peoples.

2.

THE steady progress of education in Russia from 1890 to 1914 was accomplished on the basis of the program which has already been discussed in Chapters XI and XII. Though the plan was not applied with equal effectiveness throughout the country, in general it did result in a steady yearly increase in the number of students and the number of educational institutions operating throughout Russia. In an attempt to spread and improve the organization which already existed, the Duma, in 1908, adopted a comprehensive and integrated plan providing for the training of teachers, and began the construction of schools at a rate which, had it been continued, would have enabled Russia to achieve universal primary education by 1922. Especially in the cities there was provided a program of adult elementary education, based largely on special evening and Sunday classes taught by a staff of volunteer teachers, among whom there were thousands of men and women from the intellectual class and from the universities. Although the police from time to time grew suspicious of the movement because of the obvious opportunities it provided for political propagandists, the system continued to make headway. Largely because of the success of this program, illiteracy in Russia was considerably reduced during the early years of the twentieth century. According to data collected in the census of 1897, only 24 per cent of the population of the Empire above the age of ten could read and write. In 1914 the corresponding figure for literacy was in the vicinity of 45 per cent. The figures revealed certain other facts about the condition of education in Russia: the degree of literacy was higher in the cities than in the villages; higher among men than among women; and higher among those in the younger brackets, from ten to thirty years, than among the older generations. This breakdown accounts for the fact that, in 1914, 73 per cent of the army recruits were found to be able to read and write. Taken as a whole, this evidence points to the fact that the literacy rate in Russia had continued to increase rapidly from 1890 until the disruptive effects of the civil war were felt—a significant fact that is too often overlooked by students of Russian history.

The destruction of the first World War, and especially the complete disruption which attended the initial years of the revolution, played havoc with the Russian educational system. During the civil war the collapse of educational services was intensified not only by the physical destruction of thousands of school buildings but also by general deficiencies, such as fuel shortages, which made it impossible to continue classes even in those buildings which remained standing. The loss of life during the first World War and the civil war was, of course, heaviest among the youth of military age, and, since the younger generation was also the best educated in the country, resulted in a serious setback to the educational advances which had been made in the course of the preceding years. Only with the gradual return of comparatively normal conditions and the healing of the wounds of the civil war in the years following the introduction of the N.E.P., was it possible to make any further progress in education. Almost immediately after the restoration of order, however, the upward trend which had been interrupted by the war was resumed. By 1926 the country had achieved 51 per cent literacy, surpassing the 1914 level, and from that time forward education in Soviet Russia made startling gains. By 1934 the goal of universal primary education for children of school age was at last achieved, and special efforts were simultaneously taken to "liquidate" illiteracy among the adults. As early as 1925 there were about 50,000 schools for adult illiterates, and their effectiveness may be judged by the fact that in 1940 the over-all index of illiteracy in the Soviet Union had been reduced to about 10 per cent. Among the youth of Russia illiteracy is today unknown.

Though it is true that during the early period of the revolution education suffered severe limitations because of the destruction of physical facilities, it is only fair to add that during those same years the Russians had been engaged in bold experimentation with progressive educational methods. It is worth noting that those charged with the organization of the new system were familiar with the most recent work in the development of modern pedagogical techniques and many of the methods adopted indicated that some of them had been especially influenced by the theories of John Dewey. During this experimental period a number of extreme types of "revolutionary" educational systems were adopted—such for example as "student self-government"—but after a brief trial they were, for the most part, either abandoned or modified. In spite of the fact that a few unworkable schemes were for a time seriously attempted, the whole experiment, in so far as it provided the opportunity to test a variety of new ideas, was undoubtedly beneficial.

Soviet authorities were as concerned about the progress of secondary and technical education and university training as they were about elementary instruction, and ever since the introduction of the First Five Year Plan the expansion in facilities for advanced learning has been especially impressive. Scores of new colleges have been opened throughout Russia, and hundreds of new training schools specializing in dozens of technical subjects are operated in conjunction with many of the large industrial projects. In addition to increasing the number of this type of institution which falls, more or less, within the usual educational pattern, the Soviet Union has developed a number of new types of training centers which have been adapted to her unique problems. The special courses for tractor drivers are typical of the arrangements which have been made to provide both general and vocational training—this particular one being especially designed to supply essential information relating to the collectivization of agriculture.

This general progress in education could not fail to affect the whole mentality of the new Russia. The rapid expansion of educational facilities of various kinds and in diverse fields provided the youth of Russia with the fundamental knowledge so essential to the task before them. Grasping hungrily at the elements of science and the underlying technological skills which were now made available even in remote sections of the country, they advanced at a rate that could hardly have been dreamed of before the revolution. Within a few years the Soviet Union had produced thousands of young scientists, medical and social workers, and technicians upon whom the growth of the new mechanized, socialized, and industrialized nation must and did depend.

Typical figures covering the progress of education during these years are perhaps the best illustration of the results that were achieved, though admittedly they do not satisfy all questions about the new system. In 1914 there were 104,610 primary schools with an enrollment of 7,236,000 students in Russia within the boundaries as of 1921. In 1936 there were in the Soviet Union 164,081 elementary schools with an enrollment of around 20,000,000 students. Between 1936 and 1940 around 10,000 more schools were established, and the number of children attending elementary schools in 1940 was over 25,000,000. The number of secondary schools and universities and of students enrolled increased at even greater rate. Between 1913 and 1939 the number of universities and technical schools of university rank rose from 71 to 448 and the student body increased from 85,000 to 371,000.

The publication of books is another index which points to the rapid increase in education. In 1913 there were published in Russia some 26,000 printed books, manuals, and pamphlets, and the total printings of these reached about 87,000,000 copies. In 1937, 37,000 publications were issued and a total of 673,000,000 copies were distributed. The printings of the works of individual authors, both Russian and foreign, frequently reach enormous proportions in Russia. More than 23,000,000 copies of Pushkin were printed during the first twenty years of Soviet rule, and it is not unusual for more copies of a foreign author's works to be sold in Russian than in the original language.

The educational system of the Soviet Union, which, with the exception of that part directed by the Committee on College Education, is today under the control of the People's Commissariat of Education of each of the constituent republics of the Union, has, for the most part, evolved from the basic organization developed by the Zemstvos in prerevolutionary Russia. Under the new *régime* the duties previously carried out by the Zemstvo councils have been assumed by the local soviets and adapted to the changing needs of the various communities.

The Zemstvos had, of course, a number of other functions in Imperial Russia, and among these one of the most important was the supervision of public health, the building of hospitals, and the organization of free medical care for the population. The system of medical service administered by the Zemstvos was admirably adapted to the needs of the Russian village, the ingenious program developed by the Zemstvo workers being in many ways the best in Europe at the time. The program did, however, need considerable expansion, especially since a number of provinces of the Russian Empire were not included in the Zemstvo system. Like the educational program, public health and medical service suffered greatly during the civil war. However, after the reëstablishment of order, the Soviet Government succeeded not only in restoring the wrecked facilities for medical service but also in enlarging them considerably. Under the general supervision of a "Union-Republican" Commissariat of Public Health, the local soviets took over the whole Zemstvo hospital system. Utilizing the best elements of the mechanism which they had inherited, the Soviets were in time able to build up a far-reaching and well-balanced system of socialized medicine which continued to yield increasing benefits until the day of the German attack.

The present system of health service in the Soviet Union is based upon the organization of "health centers" in all factories and other large industrial enterprises as well as in city and rural districts. Over 7,000 factory "health stations" had been established by 1940. While there were around 90,000 hospital beds in Russian urban districts in 1913, their number increased almost fivefold by 1937. Hospital facilities in rural areas had trebled between the years 1913 and 1938, the number of beds increasing from around 50,000 to around 150,000. Considerable attention has been paid to maternity institutions as well as to child care. New types of medical institutions have been developed, for example the traveling serological laboratory to combat infectious diseases in rural areas. The increase in medical facilities has a solid foundation in the rapid expansion of medical education during the Soviet period. The number of trained physicians increased from 30,000 at the time of the first World War to 120,000 in 1940.

3.

In medieval Russia and indeed throughout all Europe, Christianity was the basic moral and intellectual foundation upon which the structure of the state and society rested, and the Christian church for several centuries exercised complete and unchallenged control over the thought and action of the people. After the Renaissance in Europe, and after the reforms instigated by Peter the Great in Russia, the church began to lose its unique position, and free thought, in one form or another, increasingly challenged church dogma. The struggle was long, frequently violent, and often inconclusive, and the church doggedly disputed each newly threatened position. On the eve of the Russian Revolution, however, Christianity was still considered the fundamental moral basis of civilization, both in Europe and in Russia, though its authority was considerably more restricted than it had been during the Middle Ages. Even after one has carefully weighed and considered the events of the French Revolution and the anticlerical trends that developed in France toward the end of the nineteenth century and the early twentieth century, one is still forced to the conclusion that Russia was the first and only country with a Christian background to break with the church deliberately and openly. What is perhaps more important historically is the fact that communism's conflict with religion did not arise, like other antireligious movements, as a crusade to establish intellectual tolerance or to secure absolute freedom of thought for all mankind. On the contrary, communism sought the destruction of the authority of the church only in order to seize for itself the dominant control of social thought; the ideology of the church was to be replaced by the equally inclusive ideology of Marxism. In this sense, indeed, the *régime* established by the Communists may well be considered a new ideocracy. Not only were the principles of Marxism made obligatory for members of the select ruling group of the Communist party itself but a strenuous effort was also made to instill Marxist doctrine into the minds of the masses of the people.

Since Marxism in Russia assumed the position of an official doctrine to which all who were engaged in any field of intellectual endeavor necessarily subscribed, it is important to consider briefly the essential features of the philosophy with some special attention to its interpretation and application in the Soviet state. In this connection it is important that the philosophical core of Marxism be differentiated from its political aspects, and that the original teachings of the Marxian fathers, Karl Marx (1818–83) and Frederick Engels (1820–95), be distinguished from the later modifications of their theories. The evolution of the concepts first enunciated by them has been a constant process which has been reflected even in the variations in the name under which the movement has operated. The qualifying term "Leninism" was the first to be added, and more recently "Stalinism" has come to be used in a descriptive sense, so that today a three-word, hyphenated term, "Marxism-Leninism-Stalinism," has become necessary to designate adequately the theoretical foundation of the official Russian system of thought.

The original Marxian doctrine is a direct outgrowth of that branch of philosophy usually described as Hegelian. Deriving its theories, as it does, essentially from the dialectical logic formulated by Hegel (1770–1831), it has in time come to be known as "dialectical materialism." In its political aspect, Marxism is based primarily upon the theory of "class struggle" and upon the belief that because of the relationship of economic forces a unique and revolutionary rôle has been assigned to the working class. Because of its emphasis upon the decisive importance of economics and social change, Marxism has also been known as "economic materialism," a term that has frequently been used by M. N. Pokrovsky, the authoritative Russian historian. In still another of its aspects, that of "scientific socialism," Marxism claims to provide a formula for social progress which is equally applicable to all modern forms of society.

According to Marx, capitalism by its very nature is driven constantly and inexorably toward its destruction. Communism, the social instrument of the working class, simultaneously is rising irresistably to seize the control which capitalism can no longer exercise. The era of industrialism contains within it both the seeds of the destruction of the capitalist system, and the elements of the working class revolution. Lenin carried these original Marxist concepts still further. In his study of imperialism as the final stage of capitalism, he elaborated on the international aspects of capitalism which Marx had described, and analyzed the rôle of colonial and semicolonial countries in the development of capitalism in highly industrialized nations. Another—and perhaps more important—contribution made by Lenin was his specific definition of the active part to be taken by the revolutionary party in leading the masses of the working class in the overthrow of the capitalist state and system. According to the common interpretation of classical Marxism, the revolution, which was to be expected first in the most highly industrialized nations, was to come as an inevitable result of the dialectics of the historical process. It followed that revolutionaries need only await the day and prepare themselves to greet revolutionary events as they unfolded in history's own good time. This, essentially, was the attitude adopted both by the German Social Democratic party and by the Russian Mensheviks. Lenin, however, insisted upon the necessity of building a compact and disciplined revolutionary party which would be prepared to force the issue at the critical moment, to seize control of the situation before the dying economic system of exploitation could despoil the world in its violent death agonies.

Lenin happened to be a Russian, and when in 1917 he was confronted in his own country with the revolutionary situation he had long hoped for, he was not deterred from putting his plans into operation by the incontrovertible fact that at that time Russia was the least industrialized of all the major European countries. Somewhere, somehow, he reasoned, it was necessary to break the capitalist front, and since the opportunity had arisen in Russia, it must be exploited there. Once the ring had been broken, he thought, other nations better suited for the further development of the new system would be prepared to assume the leadership as the workers rose to power.

Thus there arose the paradox of the first communist revolution occurring in a country the socialists had always considered "semi-feudal." Both Lenin and Trotsky placed all their hopes in the immediate spread of the revolution over the European continent. Their expectations, of course, were not fulfilled, but by the time it had become clear that support was not forthcoming from outside, the Communists had already succeeded in establishing control of the Russian Government. They then had no alternative but to proceed with the consolidation of their position in Soviet Russia in order to preserve and secure this newly won bastion for the world revolution which was to follow. In the meantime, in order to prevent the complete decay and collapse of the Russian economic system, it became necessary to compromise with capitalism. This adjustment was made in the N.E.P. After Lenin's death and after the Soviet Union's recovery from the devastation of the civil war, Trotsky, representing one branch of the Communist party, continued to concentrate his interest on fomenting revolution throughout the world. By that time, however, the great majority of the Russian people were already interested mainly in the reconstruction of their own country, rather than in a political program which offered only the prospect of engaging them in interminable international adventures. Stalin's strength rested chiefly in his ability properly to evaluate these new tendencies, and he took advantage of public sentiment by organizing his government under a slogan which promised the people the ultimate success of socialism in their own country.

The distance between Stalinism and Leninism is no less than that between Leninism and Marxism. Lenin had boldly determined to drive through a revolution in a country which was insufficiently developed industrially to function properly under the new system. He was able to achieve his immediate objective but for a time the industrial weakness of Russia threatened to prevent the broader success of socialism in that country. To overcome this danger, Stalin was compelled to strengthen the industrial foundation so that it might safely support socialism. Thus, from the standpoint of classical Marxism, the Russian Revolution was actually a chain of paradoxes. In a sense, the historical process had been inverted: superindustrialism, which by all the logic of Marxist thought was to precede the revolution, in reality came last. In Russia not only did economics not determine the course of political development, but the political system was used as a lever to revise and reform the economic system. Apparently then, that part of the Marxist theory which emphasizes economic materialism proved to be inaccurate or meaningless in the Russian situation. Although in the Soviet Union lip service is still paid to the whole Marxist philosophical concept, the underlying principle of "dialectics" is the only part of the doctrine which actually functions. Stripped of moral and philosophical components, "dialectics" may serve almost any purpose. In the Soviet Union today they are used to promote a national system of political realism.

4.

Marx's hostility toward religion was made abundantly clear in his much quoted phrase describing it as the "opium for the people." Though the German Social Democrats recognized Marx's formula in principle, in actual practice they adopted a much milder program which recognized religion as the private affair of each individual. Among the Russian Socialists, the Mensheviks chose to follow the policy of the German Social Democrats. The Social Revolutionaries—who were in any case not adherents of the Marxist philosophy—in general demonstrated no hostility toward religion; indeed, some of their leaders were quite ready to grant religion an important place in the reconstruction of society. The Kerensky Government not only adopted a policy of complete religious tolerance but also was extremely cautious in curtailing any of the historic privileges which had previously been enjoyed by the Orthodox church. The Bolsheviks' attitude, on the other hand, had from the very first been militantly antagonistic. Not only was Lenin suspicious of the Orthodox church as an institution; he disliked and distrusted all religious sentiments. Since Lenin himself was prepared to apply Marx's definition of religion to the letter, atheism was made obligatory for members of the Communist party. Although it was apparent to the leaders of the revolution that it was impossible to destroy religious belief in Russia entirely and to replace it by atheism overnight, nevertheless, by sponsoring a program of atheistic propaganda, they made every effort in the early years to weaken the position of the church itself and to undermine the authority of all religion.

It is quite evident that the personal philosophical convictions which Lenin and other communist leaders held on religious questions were largely responsible for the antireligious policies of the Soviet Government. Other reasons which from time to time have been put forward as the basis for the party's attitude—such as the Soviet leaders' fear of the alleged reactionary rôle of the church—were in the last analysis of only secondary importance. The course pursued by the Soviet Government was aimed at all religious beliefs, and though the Orthodox church was the first to suffer from the communist attack, other denominations were later placed under identical government restrictions.

Even under the Imperial Government the activities of the Orthodox church had been somewhat curtailed, although it still retained a number of special privileges which were granted to no other denomination. The reëstablishment of the Patriarchate which had been abolished by Peter the Great had for years been urged by some religious leaders as a step toward regaining the independence of the church from the state, and shortly after the Revolution of 1917 a *Sobor* of the church was called for this purpose. A few days later Archbishop Tikhon was elected Patriarch, and set about his new duties under the most trying conditions of political anarchy and governmental disapproval. Although the Government had not actually forbidden religious activities, persecution of representatives of the clergy had already been begun by many of the local soviets, and in the years between 1917 and 1920 several hundred bishops, priests, and monks were either shot or starved to death in prisons. However, in spite of the fact that in January, 1918, he published a severe denunciation of communist measures, Patriarch Tikhon was not at that time molested by the Soviet Government.

By the decree of January 23, 1918, the Soviet Government officially severed the connection between the church and the state. All property owned by the churches, including the buildings themselves, was "nationalized"—that is, seized by the Government. In order to continue to use the churches for divine services, the congregations were now compelled to sign contracts with the local soviets, providing always that local leaders had not previously decided either to use the buildings for other purposes or to demolish them. It was even necessary to obtain permission from the soviets to use articles of the ritual such as the chalices and vestments, although for the time being these articles actually remained in the possession of the parishes. The churches were also forbidden by law to acquire any new property in place of that which had been confiscated. In spite of all these restrictions, however, when the first constitution of the R.S.F.S.R. was adopted on July 10, 1918, the church was still granted at least a vestige of liberty by an article which guaranteed freedom of both religious and antireligious propaganda. This clause in substantially the same form was later included in the Constitution of the Soviet Union of 1923.

In the spring of 1922 the Soviet Government issued a decree authorizing the requisition of the ritual implements of the church, with the explanation that the proceeds were to be used for famine work. This seizure of the church treasures was accompanied by a new wave of persecutions in which many priests were arrested and a number were executed, among them the Bishop of Petrograd, Veniamin. At the same time Patriarch Tikhon was incarcerated in one of the Moscow monasteries.

During this period the Soviet Government had attempted to instigate internal disorganization in the Orthodox church by supporting a group of priests, the so-called Living Church, who were engaged in a campaign urging radical revision of the church organization. In the spring of 1923 this group called representatives of part of the clergy and laity to a meeting which was then declared to be a legal *Sobor* of the Orthodox church. Although this *Sobor* accused the imprisoned Patriarch Tikhon of counterrevolutionary opinions and deprived him of his position, he was released soon afterward by the Soviet Government. Until his death on April 7, 1925, Tikhon continued to be regarded as Patriarch by the majority of the church membership. After Patriarch Tikhon's death his *locum tenens,* Metropolitan Peter, became the head of the church. When he also was imprisoned by the Soviet Government, Metropolitan Sergius became the keeper of the Patriarchal Throne, and in the summer of 1927 announced his loyalty to the Soviet state.

In 1925 the Militant Atheists' League was organized, and immediately launched a nation-wide campaign against the church. Although atheism had achieved considerable popularity by that time, especially among the younger generation, and although the membership in the churches had shown a correspondingly rapid decrease during the preceding years, the vulgar and blasphemous tone of the official atheistic propaganda seemed to repel more than it converted. By 1928 the League had recruited only 123,000 members, a figure representing less than 10 per cent of those active in the Communist party. Later on the membership increased rapidly, but the members showed, on the whole, little enthusiasm for their cause. When the Five Year Plan and the collectivization of agriculture were undertaken, an attempt was made by the Government to administer a death blow to religion. Since the Government's plan called for complete collectivization, and since it was supposed that there would be no room for church activities in the kolkhozes, Soviet authorities confidently expected the total elimination of religion in the villages. To make doubly certain of the destruction of the church, however, the Government issued on April 8, 1929, a new decree forbidding religious societies to participate in any kind of cultural or social activity except religious services themselves. On May 22, 1929, the constitution was amended to include this regulation. The new statement of the Government's position contained a significant modification. Instead of guaranteeing both *religious and antireligious propaganda,* it now proclaimed "freedom of religious *worship* and freedom of antireligious *propaganda*"—a turn in phraseology which allowed the atheists to carry on a militant campaign and at the same time prevented the faithful from engaging in any proselytizing activities. The wording of the 1929 decree was repeated in the clause on religious worship which was inserted in the new Soviet constitution of 1936.

In spite of all the restrictions raised against it, religion demonstrated a remarkable tenacity and resiliency. The chairman of the Militant Atheists' League, Emelian Yaroslavsky, in 1937 estimated that although more than half the workers in the cities considered themselves atheists, more than half the population in the villages still expressed their belief in God. If this statement is correct, it would mean that after twenty years of Soviet rule around 50 per cent of the population of the Soviet Union was still religious. However, 30 per cent would be perhaps a safer estimate. In any case it is known that in 1940 there were over 30,000 religious communities of every kind in the Soviet Union. Significantly enough, whereas during the initial years of the revolution the youth, especially the boys, had deserted the church in droves, in the 1930's it was possible to organize a Christian Youth Movement, the *Christomol,* as a parallel to the *Komsomol,* or Communist Youth Movement. Since no official statistics on religion are issued by the Soviet Government, it is impossible to say how important the new movement is numerically. No data are, of course, available on the distribution of the Christian faithful by denominations in Russia today, but it may be assumed that the Patriarchal Church is still decidedly more influential than the Living Church. In recent years Protestant denominations, notably the Baptists, have secured a sizable number of converts among the Russians. It seems likely that with the gradual relaxation of the more stringent restrictions previously placed in the way of all religious groups, membership in all denominations will show a sharp increase.

In 1937 there was a sudden and comparatively brief flare-up of antireligious propaganda in the Soviet Union, and a number of bishops and priests were arrested and tried. This time, however, the issues were not as clearly drawn as they had previously been. Although the fact that they were members of the hierarchy of the church was made exceedingly clear, the clergymen were not charged with unlawful religious activities but rather with having had connections with the espionage and sabotage groups which were then on trial or under investigation. Whatever purposes may have been behind this action, the number of church officials under suspicion at that time was not large, and no further outburst of anticlericalism has since occurred in the Soviet Union.

In recent years there has been a remarkable change in the attitude of the Soviet Government toward religion. One of the first signs of the return to a more tolerant position was the frank admission of the failure of the Militant Atheists' League and the gradual reduction in government support. A little later there came a series of events which indicated that the Government's estimate of the church's place in history was being revised. At a joint session of the Historical Institute of the Academy of Sciences and the Central Committee of the Militant Atheists' League in December, 1938, the essentially progressive rôle of the church in the historical process was admitted in general terms, and the close connection of Christianity with the development of Russian art and literature during the early periods of Russian history was specifically acknowledged. The same trends were visible in many of the official and semi-official activities of the Government. Alexander Nevsky—a prince of medieval Russia who had been canonized by the church—was glorified in the Soviet Union as a great national hero who had valiantly defended Russia against German invasion in the thirteenth century. A decade ago there were few people indeed in Russia who would openly honor Alexander Nevsky.

In 1939 the Soviets adopted a new religious policy in fact if not in legislation. Since then the Government has demonstrated an increasingly mild attitude toward the church and toward religion in general. The church, during that time, has shown itself willing to coöperate loyally with the authorities, and especially since the beginning of the German war has made every effort to assist the Government in rallying the people to meet the emergency. The cordial relations which rapidly developed between the Government and the church during the early months of the war culminated in the reëstablishment of the Patriarchate in Moscow. It was the *locum-tenens,* Metropolitan Sergius, who was elected Patriarch, on September 12, 1943. This move undoubtedly strengthened both the church and the nation. So long as the present liberal tendencies are continued in the Soviet Union, there would appear to be no reason to expect a return to the religious intolerance of the early years of the revolution.

5.

From the very beginning, the attitude of the Soviet Union was as warmly favorable toward the sciences as it was hostile toward the teachings of the church. The reasons for the Government's interest in the advancement of scientific learning are, for the most part, self-evident. In the first place, Marxism itself is considered a science by its adherents—indeed, *the* scientific form of socialism which asserts that the natural and social sciences have played an important rôle in human progress. In the second place, Marxian socialists believe that as science explores the vast unknown in which man exists and reveals more of the structure and function of the universe, it will displace religion which has, in their opinion, existed primarily as an integrated system of belief explaining the mysteries lying beyond the horizon of man's understanding. A third—and eminently practical—reason was simple necessity. The physical and mathematical sciences are the foundation upon which the social and technical progress of the Soviet Union must be constructed. Technology is, obviously, the most necessary tool in the construction of the new society, in the creation of socialism which, in Lenin's words, was to be "Soviet power plus electrification."

Even though the Marxists have, in general, been generous in aiding the development of scientific learning, their dictatorial political methods have sometimes considerably hampered scholars. At the time Marx was writing, scientists were already abandoning the extreme mechanistic conception of the world typical of the seventeenth and the eighteenth centuries, and consequently Marxian materialism was a step forward compared with the doctrine of materialistic philosophers of the period of the French "Enlightenment." However, the progress of science in the span of some hundred-odd years which has elapsed since the original formulation of Marx's doctrine has been so rapid that an entirely new approach to nature and reality is now possible. True, some of the modern scientific concepts like those concerning the nature of electricity and of atom may be interpreted in terms of the basic laws of Marxian dialectics, but on the whole no rigid philosophical schemes, be they idealistic or materialistic, can any more monopolize the development of modern science. It is characteristic of the rigidity of Marxian tenets as applied in Soviet Russia in the initial years of the revolution, that certain scientific doctrines such as the Mendelian theory and the so-called quantum theory of modern physics were for some time regarded with disfavor by the Government. It seems, however, that in the period of the bold and vigorous development of Russian science which followed, scientists were eventually able to sweep aside these and similar restrictions which hobbled them.

The obstacles which Soviet scholars encountered in the field of the humanities were much more serious, and from the beginning of the revolution the teaching of both philosophy and sociology was seriously hampered by official Marxian dogmatism. Even though in the days of summary judgments few scholars dared resist official directions and those who did were easily and quickly suppressed, the situation appears gradually to have improved as the official interpretation of the meaning of "dialectical" processes was broadened. In the initial years of the revolution, however, the teaching of history was entirely suspended in most Russian universities and was replaced by courses in sociology tailored to fit the communist interpretation of social relationships. Professors who happened to teach Russian history were in an unenviable position since as a group they were suspect as believers in nationalism and as carriers of a reactionary attitude. Among the leading Russian historians of the older generation there were only two Marxists—N. A. Rozhkov and M. N. Pokrovsky—and they were at once put in control of the new academic set-up. Under the Soviet *régime* Pokrovsky became the more important of the two, and for a number of years served as the official exponent of Marx's theories as they applied to Russian history. He was an able scholar and contributed much to the reorganization of historical archives, and was instrumental to the publication of important historical documents—among them the well-known series of Russian diplomatic papers covering the period of the first World War. His general approach to history was that of an "economic materialist," and he was an especially rabid foe of the spirit of Russian nationalism which he fought wherever he found it or suspected it. During the period in which he enjoyed the position of a virtual dictator of historical studies in the Soviet Union, Pokrovsky subjected all teachers and students in that field to a strict supervision which forced them to keep within the rigid limits he had established. Those who proved to be recalcitrant or insufficiently coöperative were frequently punished by imprisonment or exile, a disciplinary technique which resulted in the premature death of many of the ablest Russian scholars—among them Serge Platonov who, after V. O. Kliuchevsky's death in 1911, was considered the dean of Russian historians. Another noted historian, Eugene Tarle, having survived several years of exile in central Asia, returned after Pokrovsky's death to become a member of the Academy of Sciences. Today he enjoys a considerable reputation in Russia, and one of his books, dealing with Napoleon's invasion of Russia, has recently been published in English. The *régime* of academic terrorism which Pokrovsky instituted in the field of history broke down with his death in 1932. It later became apparent that his passing had come none too soon, since his activities were becoming increasingly suspect each year.

It was characteristic of the position of learning in the Soviet Union that a decision of the Central Committee of the Communist party and another by the Council of People's Commissars were necessary to establish more normal conditions in history research and teaching. According to the "theses" proposed by Stalin, Kirov, and Zhdanov, history was now to be taught as a separate subject and not as a subdivision within the framework of sociology. Russia's past was not to be deliberately distorted and maligned as it had been while Pokrovsky held the dominant position in the field, but instead the constructive elements in Russia's background were to be emphasized in order to explain the historical position of the Soviet Union in the proper light. The new policy permitted scholars to pursue their studies without exposing themselves to political retaliation, and in the years since then Russian historians have done an impressive amount of research in the rich fields around them.

Under the Soviets a number of important changes have been instituted both in the type and in the organization and administration of centers of learning. At the beginning of the revolution the emphasis was placed almost exclusively on the creation of institutions of a strictly Marxist type, such for example, as the Communist Academy which was founded in 1918 and the Marx and Engels Institute organized in 1920. At a later date, however, the Government devoted more attention to sustaining and developing older institutions like the Academy of Sciences and the prerevolutionary universities. The All-Union Academy of Sciences, which included an ever-increasing number of special research institutes in various fields, now became the leading center of scientific research in the Soviet Union. Branches were established in various parts of the country and separate academies were founded in a number of the constituent republics of the Union, such as Ukraine, White Russia, and Georgia. Since one of the functions of the All-Union Academy of Sciences was to sponsor the exploration and supervise the exploitation of natural resources in the Soviet Union, the tendency has always been to connect the activities of the Academy with the specific needs of industry in the country. Nevertheless, it should be emphasized that a number of the research institutes are still dedicated to "pure science" and that there appears to be no intention on the part of the Government to restrict or abandon this type of study.

The Soviet Government has gone to unusual lengths to provide adequately trained technicians for the rapidly expanding industries of Russia. In order to insure a steady and continuous flow of scientific personnel, a school of "aspirants" was founded at the Academy of Sciences and at each university and research institute. A considerable network of research institutes—which are even more closely connected with industry than are the academies—has recently been developed, and is one of the most interesting phases of Soviet education. In 1935 the People's Commissariat of Heavy Industry alone sponsored more than 100 such scientific institutes in which nearly 12,000 men and women were engaged in research work with the aid of some 10,000 technicians, engineers, and laboratory assistants. Obviously, such an intensive program of scientific study and research is almost certain to produce important fruits in the near future. Nor is it entirely a matter of future returns, for even today the tremendous achievements of Russian science and medicine are making enormously valuable contributions to the military success of the Soviet Union both on the field of battle and on the production front.

The readers of this book can hardly expect to find here even a brief account of the work and achievements of the leading Russian scholars of our time, but it is perhaps worthwhile at least to mention the names of a few outstanding men in various branches of science, such for example as A. N. Krylov in mathematics; V. N. Ipatiev (in the United States since 1929), A. E. Favorsky, and N. D. Zelinsky in chemistry; N. I. Vavilov in genetics; L. Mandelstam, P. Lazarev, and Kapitsa in physics; S. A. Chaplygin and A. N. Tupolev in aerodynamics; A. Karpinsky and Gubkin in geology; Vladimir I. Vernadsky and A. E. Fersman in mineralogy and biogeochemistry; and L. Berg in geography. This list could be greatly enlarged since in its present form it contains the names of only a few of the scores of prominent Russian scientists who are living today or have only recently died.

Although the study of social sciences and humanities was hampered by political restrictions at the beginning of the revolution, their position in the Soviet Union today is secure. An impressive amount of work has been done in Russia during the twenty-five-odd years of the Soviet *régime,* especially in such fields as history, archaeology, and oriental studies, and it is particularly significant that even in these "nonproductive" fields research and study have not been abandoned during the German war. The Russian Government is committed to a program which promises the widest possible distribution of educational opportunities, and in recent years it has demonstrated a growing willingness to allow at least a modicum of the intellectual freedom which such a program demands.

6.

In the winter of 1917 Alexander Blok wrote *The Twelve,* a famous poem which is perhaps the most penetrating interpretation we have yet had of the tumultuous spirit of the first weeks of the revolution. The poem, which is available in an English translation by Babette Deutsch and Avrahm Yarmolinsky, is symbolic in style, but it nevertheless provides a dramatic and realistic insight into life in Petrograd during those intense and turbulent days. It is a grim picture of chaos and destruction, of debauchery and drunkenness, of blood and misery, but it reveals beneath the shell of violence the firm and simple faith with which the workers and soldiers looked to the glorious future of international brotherhood. The twelve Red Guard soldiers patrolling the cold, deserted streets symbolize the twelve apostles, and in the poet's imagination Christ Himself leads them, although they profess themselves such convinced atheists that they are even prepared to shoot at His image.

The poem appeared during the first destructive convulsion of the revolution when only the poet's prophetic vision could have predicted its further course. Only now that the martyrdom of the second World War has revealed the self-sacrificing devotion of the Red Army and the Russian people can Blok's intuitive and prophetic interpretation be fully appreciated. Beneath the ugly violence of the revolution the poet sensed the essential core of faith in man and loyalty to high principles which today reappears in such acts as that of the church extending its blessing to the Red Army defending the nation against the German aggression. *The Twelve* is undoubtedly the highest achievement of Russian poetry during the revolutionary period. It also proved to be Blok's swan song, for in 1920 he died.

The social and political adjustments of war communism and the civil war were, of course, reflected in the transitional development of Russian literature. At the time of the revolution the established writers of prerevolutionary Russia were divided in their attitudes toward the Soviets. Leonid Andreev, whose home was in Finland which had then become a separate state, chose to remain outside of Russia, and Ivan Bunin, the winner of the Nobel Prize in 1933, emigrated. Both of them violently criticized the dictatorial methods adopted by the Bolsheviks. Alexei Tolstoy and A. Kuprin also emigrated, but after a time they felt themselves uprooted and homeless in Europe, and in 1923 the former returned to Moscow where he has since enjoyed considerable popularity. Some time later Kuprin also went back to Russia, an ill and aged man whose only desire was to return to his homeland to die.

Maxim Gorky, who because of his poor health spent the major part of his time on the island of Capri in Italy, still considered Russia his home and regularly returned for several months of each year. He at first objected to the Bolshevik program, but instead of merely adopting a negative and critical attitude toward the Government he offered his help and suggestions. He was particularly active in efforts to alleviate the special hardships suffered by Russian writers, artists, and scientists, and through this activity he in time became closely associated with the Soviet Government. Since he was himself of "proletarian" origin, and since he had demonstrated his sympathy with the revolutionary struggle of the masses in many of his novels and plays, Gorky soon became the beloved friend and teacher of many young Russian authors, especially those associated with the proletarian school. Gorky died in 1936. According to evidence later presented in one of the "purges," his death had been deliberately contrived by Yagoda, the sinister head of the O.G.P.U.

Naturally enough an effort was made by the Bolsheviks in the initial years of the revolution to create a class literature to serve the cause of the dictatorship of the proletariat. Special studios or schools of "proletarian culture" (*proletkult*) were organized to train young writers and artists of working-class origins. Even if it had been based on sound principles, such a project would have taken years to come to fruition, and since most of the recipients of the *proletkult* fellowships were soon impatient because of their isolation from the normal artistic and literary life of Russia, the attempt failed without producing any outstanding works. The most prominent poet of the period, Serge Esenin (1895–1925), certainly owed nothing to *proletkult,* although he was of peasant background himself and much of his poetry was written around life in the village. A true creative genius, he rose far above the narrow limits of the official "proletarian art."

Capable writers who could reach the people were necessary to the Government in those days of crisis and chaos, and since there were few mature artists among the revolutionaries the Government was compelled at last to seek the coöperation of a few liberal, non-Marxist authors of the older generation—men like Andrei Bely and Valeri Briusov—who were willing to support the program of the new society. Perhaps the most colorful figure of that transitional epoch was the futurist, Vladimir Maiakovsky (1894–1930), a poet of great talent who, realizing the Government's need for propaganda in the arts, boldly attempted to monopolize the field for futurism. Although both Maiakovsky and his followers succeeded in creating a distinctive style of their own in propagandistic literature and art, the average citizen's attitude toward futurism was distinctly cool if not, indeed, entirely negative. Most of the old Bolshevik leaders, including Lenin, who had been brought up on realistic art and literature, were soon weary of the new style. The first Commissar for Education, Lunacharsky, was more sympathetic than many toward modernism, but even he refused to guarantee a monopoly for the futurists.

The inauguration of the New Economic Policy brought about substantial changes in the field of literature as it had in education, and as life returned to comparatively normal conditions a more liberal approach to literature became possible. Since it was no longer deemed necessary to scrutinize an author's family background before reading his work, a number of non-Marxist writers rose to prominence during this period. Because they were willing to accept the new *régime de facto,* although they still refused to identify themselves with Marxian ideology, Leon Trotsky nicknamed this group the "Fellow Travelers." At first their work encountered passionate opposition from the more orthodox Marxists and was bitterly denounced by the ostentatiously "proletarian" writers. The public, however, tired of the ration of obvious propaganda in the guise of literature, came to their support and they were gradually accepted by the Soviet leaders. In 1925 the Central Committee of the Communist party passed a resolution granting all writers the freedom to choose whatever subjects they wanted and to develop them as they saw fit—provided only that they were willing to accept the basic principles of the proletarian dictatorship. At the time this resolution was called, with some exaggeration, the Magna Charta of Russian literature. Nevertheless, in spite of the slightly ridiculous aspects of the formality, the lifting of the more onerous restrictions on literature did have its effects, and there was a marked increase both in the quantity and quality of literary production

The most frequent subjects treated in the novels and plays published during the N.E.P. were the civil war and the national effort of reconstruction of industries and agriculture. There were also a number of books written on the familiar pattern of the historical and psychological novel. On the whole, realism was the prevailing literary style, although some authors, especially those writing of the civil war period, leaned somewhat toward romanticism in their approach. At the same time there was a healthy amount of experimentation with literary techniques, such for example, as the inverted chronology used with remarkable skill by K. Fedin in his *Cities and Years*.[1]

During this period a considerable number of writers came to the public's attention, and a few of them should at least be mentioned here. One of the most prominent was Babel, whose short stories were written in a style which showed the influence of Guy de Maupassant. Babel's best known work, *Red Cavalry,* was published in 1926, and his *Jewish Tales* in 1927. Leonov (b. 1899) is the author of *Tuatamur,* a sad and beautiful story of the period of the Mongol invasion, which was in the romantic rather than the his-

[1] All the works mentioned are available in English translation, unless otherwise stated. The English titles cited do not, however, always correspond to the original Russian titles.

torical tradition. In *Badgers,* which was published in 1925, Leonov returned to a modern theme in a story of peasant life. The reputation of A. Fadeiev was built on his colorful stories of the civil war period, of which *The Nineteen,* published in 1927, is the best known. Yuri Olesha (b. 1899) is known chiefly as the author of *Envy,* a remarkable psychological novel based on the clash between the old and the new ways of life in Russia. M. Zoshchenko (b. 1895) enjoyed a unique and universal popularity for his humorous tales and short stories, which were virtually literary candid-camera shots of everyday life. M. Bulgakov's (b. 1891) novel, dramatized under the name of *The Days of the Turbins,* the setting of which is Ukraine in 1918, at the time of civil war and German occupation, was first produced by the Moscow Art Theater and later staged in America.

It would be useless to add more names to the list, although there are certainly a number of others which should be included. We can best conclude this catalogue by remembering the best known of the Russian novels of that period—the monumental *And Quiet Flows the Don,* by M. Sholokhov, which has been compared by many enthusiastic readers to Leo Tolstoy's *War and Peace.* Although it is not as wide in scope and is definitely weaker in those sections in which the author turns from the Don Cossack life with which he is most familiar and attempts to sketch individuals from other classes, Sholokhov's novel undoubtedly has something of Tolstoy's breadth of style in historical literature.

The inauguration of the First Five Year Plan in 1928 had a direct effect on the Government's attitude toward literature. In the opinion of the Soviet leaders, the tremendous effort of the industrial revolution and of the collectivization of agriculture demanded the full and unstinting coöperation of all Soviet citizens, the concentration of their every effort on the gigantic task of securing Russia's place in the world. The mood of the period was much like that of a nation at war, and the desire of the Government to use every ounce of the people's physical and mental energy toward the achievement of the common goal is easy to understand. Nevertheless, the attempt to convert literature to the tasks of the day was fraught with danger to the personal freedom of the writer and the artist. Having learned that stringent regulations simply caused literature to dry up at the source, the authorities now contrived the principle of "social command" to serve the Government's purpose. Writers were expected to illustrate the developments of the Five Year Plan and to contribute to its fulfillment by clarifying and glorifying its aims and by firing the imagination of the people with the immense importance of the new policies. Constructive criticism of mistakes which occurred in the details of the operation of the plan were, however, allowed. But even this policy proved to be too rigid and mechanical to operate for any length of time, and the regulations were gradually relaxed. Another revision of the official policy which had considerable literary significance was the final abandonment of the Government's sponsorship of "proletarian literature." As the remnants of N.E.P. capitalism were done away with and the individual kulak farmers were "liquidated," Russia began to enter the stage of a "classless society"—or so the Government announced. Under these circumstances, it became possible to abolish the distinctions between "proletarian" and non-proletarian writers, and in 1932 all writers were accepted into a single "Union of Soviet Writers."

In 1934 the first All-Union Literary Congress met to discuss the rôle of the writer in the Soviet Union, and to establish the general principles under which creative literary work was to be done. The tendency of the time was to harness literature as closely as possible to the contemporary social and political needs. It was argued that the chief function of the true Soviet writer was to be "an engineer of human souls," and the principle of "socialist realism" was agreed upon as best expressing the essential trend which literature should follow. Soviet literary critics made it clear that while a critical attitude toward the realities of life was a characteristic feature of *bourgeois* realism, socialist realism must be constructive rather than destructive, positive rather than negative, optimistic rather than pessimistic. It was the Soviet writer's duty to accept life as fundamentally sound and beautiful. Although this limitation was not to prevent criticism of the remnants of the "ugly past" or discussion of the mistakes of socialist construction, the reader was always to be left with a feeling of faith and hope in the future of the new collectivized system.

Even though the principle of "socialist realism" somewhat widened the limits which had previously been set by the "social command" policy for literary work, it soon became evident that not all writers could adjust themselves to the new requirements. As a result, a good part of the writing done during the period of the first two Five Year Plans was decidedly dull and lifeless. On the other hand, writers whose interest and style coincided with the official interpretation of "socialist realism"—whatever was meant by that—were able to create works of force and distinction. A number of novels were written around the theme of the collectivization of agriculture and of these Sholokhov's *Seeds of Tomorrow,* which was published in 1935, is perhaps the most remarkable. It is a grimly realistic picture of civil strife growing out of the dekulakization of a Don Cossack village. In spite of the circumstances under which it was written, it is not a political pamphlet but a real work of art describing a world in which kulaks have virtues as well as vices and Communists sometimes have their foibles as well as their fortes.

Perhaps the most outstanding novel of the period—and one characteristic of the spirit of the day, although it tells a story laid in the early days of the revolution—is Nikolai Ostrovsky's (1904–36) *The Making of a Hero.* In addition to being a first-rate literary work, it is also interesting from a historical and psychological point of view, for it reveals with exceptional clarity the qualities of the new Soviet youth—their ardor, their strength of will, their realistic attitude toward life, their constructive abilities. No less interesting from the same standpoint is *The Pedagogic Poem* by Makarenko,[2] which is a semifictional diary of a teacher in a reform school. As one reads it he begins to understand the unique educational uses of Soviet youth organizations and develops a realization of some of the advantages of the Soviet system of pedagogy. In the story he follows the steps by which some of the young delinquents are brought along the way toward becoming ardent *komsomolets* and conscientious citizens.

During recent years a considerable amount of attention has been devoted to the historical novel. In his novel, *Peter the First,* which was published in 1934, Alexei Tolstoy drew a striking portrait of Peter the Great. Though he dwelt at length on the "barbaric" aspects of Russian life in early days and on the brutal features of the mighty Tsar's personality, he also emphasized his

[2] Not available in English so far as I know.

thirst for knowledge, his feeling for technological skills, and the progressive aims of his reforms. Taken as a whole, the picture is not an unfavorable one, and, indeed, the Tsar appears to be represented as an early forerunner of Bolshevism. Just before the German invasion an author of an older generation, Sergeev-Tsensky, who had won a modest following before the first World War but had never been especially prominent, wrote a monumental novel on the siege of Sevastopol during the Crimean War of 1854–55. The book, which was called *The Martyrdom of Sevastopol*[3] and was published in three parts during the course of 1939 and 1940, is in the grand historical style of *War and Peace,* although not on Tolstoy's level. It was a bitter coincidence that some of its first readers must have had before them the task of defending Sevastopol once again, this time against the Germans.

Another historical novel in an entirely different style is *Dimitri Donskoi,*[3] written by a young Soviet author, Serge Borodin. The Russo-Mongol struggle, which occurred during the time of the Grand Duke of Moscow whose name appears as the title, serves as the background for an oddly poignant story. Although the novel contains a number of realistic pictures of Russian life in the fourteenth century as well as of the life of the Mongol Horde at that time, the main stress is on the psychological growth of a number of the characters. The real hero of the story seems to be a pensive boy by the name of Andrew who has been sent to a monastery by his guardian; we have here an attempt to represent the boyhood of the famous icon-painter, Andrew Rublev. The author's method can hardly be called realistic in a strict sense, and in spite of the rather accurate historical background, the book has a definite flavor of romanticism.

7.

DURING the early years of the Soviet *régime* the graphic arts, like literature, were first plunged into a state of confusion and then passed through similar stages of futurist and *proletkult* experimentation. Soon after the November Revolution a number of prominent painters belonging to the original *World of Art* group —among them A. Benois, Dobuzhinsky, and Somov—emigrated. They were joined in exile by a group of younger Russian painters

[3] Not available in English so far as I know.

some of whom later won fame abroad—men like Grigoriev, Iakovlev, and Shukhaev. A number of those who had originally fled, however, fearing that separation from their native country would eventually result in the fading of their creative abilities, returned to Russia after having spent a few years in exile.

At the time of the revolution the younger artists, especially those associated with the futurist school led by the poet Maiakovsky, placed their art at the service of the new society. Maiakovsky himself, who was the inspiration for most of those around him, called upon his followers to abandon the strangling and outmoded traditions of the past and to create a new revolutionary art free from academic restrictions, a monumental art glorifying proletarian strength to replace the old illustrative works which were fit only to adorn the *bourgeois intérieur*. "Streets are our brushes, squares our palettes," cried Maiakovsky. His cry was more than a figure of speech, for attempts were actually made to use city squares as so many huge canvases; color was spread in tons, and even the trees on Moscow boulevards were painted red and purple. Colossal statues—mainly of plaster and clay, since no time was to be lost—were erected to honor the fathers of Marxism and the heroes of the revolution. They were later to be replaced by monuments of more enduring materials, but enthusiasm for this type of glorification waned and most of these early tributes to proletarian heroism crumbled and were lost in the débris of the revolution.

The revolution opened vast and fertile fields to the applied arts. The walls of the cities were plastered with posters of an infinite variety of colors and patterns, and in this branch of art the futurists of Maiakovsky's school soon captured the leadership. Political cartoons naturally assumed a new importance at the time, and the most popular were those done by a team of three artists who were collectively known under the name of *Kukryniks,* a phonetic combination of their initials. Among the dozens of other well-known cartoonists of the day B. Efimov became especially famous for his caricatures of figures prominent in international politics. Not only the artists who worked in the more ephemeral media, but also painters whose work had a more "academic" scope and style and whose oils had hung in museums and shows, during this period turned to the revolution for subject matter. Pictures of events in the Bolshevik uprising, scenes from the civil war, and portraits of Lenin and other Soviet leaders were produced in abundance, many of them done with mediocre attempts at modernism, others in the traditional and academic manner.

The adoption of the New Economic Policy established in the realm of art the same increased freedom it had brought to literature. A number of artists of the *World of Art* school were now given the opportunity to resume their work and in time assumed a position in their field similar to that held by the "Fellow Travelers" in literature. The inauguration of the Five Year Plans in 1928 resulted in the application to art of the "social command" policy and later that of "socialist realism"—with much the same effects as those achieved in literature.

Russian artists are perhaps less well known abroad than Russian writers and musicians, and it may be well to mention the work of a few of them very briefly here. Perhaps the leading position among Soviet painters is held by Igor Grabar (b. 1871) who was originally a Moscow associate of the *World of Art* group. A talented artist who in the course of his creative life has developed several different styles, Grabar has been called the Russian Cézanne because of the still lifes which he painted in his earlier years. He is not only a painter but has been industrious in the development of many phases of art activities in the Soviet Union, including the founding of museums and the organization of exhibitions. In addition to all his other work, he has found time to build a reputation as a historian of Russian art. Three other names stand out among the painters of the older generation: M. V. Nesterov (1862–1942), B. Kustodiev, and K. Petrov-Vodkin—although it should be added immediately that the three have little in common in their artistic manner. Nesterov, like Vasnetsov (see Chap. XII, Sec. 8), came to prominence before the revolution as a student and interpreter of medieval Russian art, especially icon-painting. Most of his early canvases dealt with religious subjects, *The Vision of the Boy Bartholomew* (St. Sergius) being perhaps the best known. Nesterov found it difficult to adjust himself to the sudden changes which followed the revolution and for a decade he produced no work especially noteworthy. In 1928, however, he painted a self-portrait which is said to be one of his finest works, and in 1932 he did a notable series of portraits of Soviet leaders. Kustodiev was a member of the *World of Art* group and in his early years became famous for his interpretations of middle-class life in Moscow. His portraits, *intérieurs,* and landscapes are all known for their rich colors. Petrov-Vodkin, who in his youth was strongly influenced by French impressionism, has a predilection for a monumental decorative style, the principles of which he seems to apply even in his still lifes.

In recent years a number of other artists have claimed the attention of critics. Alexander Gerasimov (b. 1884), who joined the Association of Revolutionary Artists in 1926, has made his reputation in portrait painting. In 1936 he completed an enormous canvas, *The Founders of the Red Cavalry,* which created something of a sensation in art circles, although his work is, on the whole, rather conventional. There is much more boldness in the work of A. Deineka (b. 1900). His best-known painting is *The Defense of Petrograd* (against the Whites in the civil war) which he finished in 1928. Although this particular work is "constructivist" in style, Deineka later turned to realism, partly because of the pressure of Soviet art criticism. The work of another artist of the younger generation, the Leningrad painter A. V. Serov, has also been favorably noticed. Among Russian engravers the best-known name is that of V. A. Favorsky. Many other artists are widely known in the Soviets, and their numbers are increasing especially rapidly because of the extraordinary energy the Government has exerted in developing the art of each of the nationalities in the Union. Like the more formal arts, the various types of folk art have been encouraged in the "decades" and national art exhibitions which are held in Moscow from time to time.

During the devastating era of the civil war there was little opportunity for the development of architecture, and consequently it escaped some of the earlier dissension which disorganized art and literature. With the beginning of the constructive period of the revolution, however, and especially after the launching of the Five Year Plans, Russian architects were given ample opportunity to contribute their full share toward the construction of the basic industrial units upon which the system was to be founded and toward the creation of suitable monumental structures for the new society. In the building of new factories and industrial projects haste, the shortage of materials, and the necessities of engineering requirements frequently overrode considerations of architectural design. But the designing of the "palaces" for the Soviet Government and the Communist party, the construction of the theaters, museums, and libraries, the planning of architectural "ensembles" of streets and squares in the new cities—all of these were claimed by the architects for their own.

In old Russia designing and building of churches constituted an important part of the work of Russian architects. After 1917 church building, of course, ceased—or at least shrank to infinitesimal proportions—and for a number of years many more churches were destroyed than built. Government building in time replaced ecclesiastical construction, and of the new projects the most ambitious was the Palace of the Soviets in Moscow to be erected on the site of the Church of the Redeemer which had been completed in 1884 and was demolished after the revolution. The contest for the design of the building was won by an architect by the name of Iofan and the construction of the palace was started in the late 'thirties. The German invasion, however, came before much progress had been made, and the work has been temporarily suspended during the war.

In addition to Iofan, other names of prominent Russian architects may be mentioned here, especially that of Shchusev who received his training before the revolution. He has worked in several fields and is popular as the creator of several monumental buildings in Soviet Russia, some of them designed along modern functional lines. Among his best known works is the famous Lenin Mausoleum in the Red Square. He also designed the Marx-Engels-Lenin Institute in Tbilisi. In the early years of the revolution when the "constructivist" style was dominant in Soviet architecture, the projects conceived by Tatlin aroused a great deal of interest—particularly his plans for the Palace of Labor in Moscow and for the Monument of the Third International in Leningrad. Tatlin's designs aimed at the replacement of the old *bourgeois* forms with new "dynamo-monumental" concepts. Conceived on the most grandiose scale, Tatlin's plans have been abandoned presumably because they were too costly and too difficult to execute.

8.

THE theater is a potent branch of art which has been defined as the bridge between literature and the pictorial arts. Because of its peculiar position it can be approached either as a pure art or as a practical medium and convenient channel for propaganda and the education of large groups of people. Small wonder, therefore, that from the very beginning of the revolution the Soviet Government was interested in using it as a uniquely effective tool for the building of the new society. The directors and producers, the actors and scenic designers, on the other hand, considered the theater an art, and for the most part were interested primarily in the expression of their own artistic beliefs—which in some cases coincided with the Government's program and in other cases did not. These two divergent conceptions resulted, as in other fields of art and literature, in a long-drawn-out and bitter conflict between official Soviet critics and advisers and the theater people themselves who in some cases continued to insist upon their right to artistic freedom.

Although the Russian people appear to have unusual innate histrionic abilities, the theater in its modern form did not take root in Russia until the end of the seventeenth century. In medieval Russia and during the sixteenth and seventeenth centuries the urge for dramatic expression found an outlet partly in the rites of folk festivals and the popular show-booths and partly in religious processions and dramatizations of Biblical episodes which were done under the patronage of the church. During the course of the eighteenth century, however, the Russians became acquainted with the forms of the western theater—including the drama, opera, and ballet—and since then the Russian theater has developed at a remarkable rate. The landed gentry first adopted the theater and many of the nobles recruited their own troops of players from the servants on their estates. Aided by the appearance of a number of exceptionally talented actors and actresses—many of whom were serfs who had begun their careers on the private stages of their masters—the Russian theater reached its first great creative period in the nineteenth century. Even at this early date it followed two major trends, the realistic and the romantic, and each developed a corps of performers skilled in the interpretive technique of their respective schools. The division has persisted even into the present, although by the end of the nineteenth century the realistic theater had become the dominant type in Russia. The Imperial Alexandra Theater in St. Petersburg and the Imperial Little Theater in Moscow achieved great renown which was based largely on a succession of great actors and actresses famed for their performances in both tragic and comic rôles. There were many other theaters in Russia in addition to the imperial ones, and one of the greatest of all modern Russian actresses, Vera Komissarjevsky, came to the fore only after she left the Alexandra Theater.

The Moscow Art Theater created by K. Stanislavsky (1863–1938) and V. I. Nemirovich-Danchenko (1858–1943) brought the realistic theater to its finest expression. Its success was based mainly on Stanislavsky's insistence that the total performance was of greater importance than the dazzling display of the talents of a few great actors and actresses, a principle that eventually resulted in a series of magnificent performances by a perfectly trained ensemble in which each player—and no one player—was the star. Stanislavsky's theater was bulging with extraordinarily talented people, and he was a great actor himself, but he demanded from every member of the cast the self-effacing restraint necessary for a flawless and luminous interpretation of the play.

When the Moscow Art Theater was founded in 1898, and for several years thereafter, little attention was paid to the artistic quality of the scenery or to the place of the pictorial artist in the production. Later, however, this weakness was corrected, and after 1909 several of the *World of Art* painters—including Dobuzhinsky, Roerich, and A. Benois—joined Stanislavsky and Nemirovich and added new beauty to the theater's productions. From the very beginning of the revolution the directors of the Moscow Art Theater affirmed their loyalty to the Government and as a result the activities of the theater continued without interruption. Season after season new plays have been added to the repertory. Among the outstanding new plays of recent years are *Days of the Turbins* by Bulgakov, and, in 1937, a dramatization of Tolstoy's *Anna Karenina* which was also shown in Paris the same year.

At the time of the revolution there were several other prominent directors and producers in Russia. One of them, Theodore Komissarjevsky, emigrated and after having spent a score of years in England, during which time he produced plays in London, Paris, and other European cities, he came to the United States and opened a studio in New York. Of those who remained in Russia, V. Meyerhold and A. Tairov are perhaps the best known. Meyerhold, although a product of the Stanislavsky school, eventually became one of Stanislavsky's bitterest opponents. He rebelled against realism and turned to "constructivist" theories in which he advocated a "biomechanical" style of acting. His attitude resembled that of Maiakovsky, and, like the poet, he attained a certain popularity with the Government during the early years of the revolution, but eventually he found himself out of sympathy with governmental policies and entirely unwilling to accept the principle of "socialist realism." He finally fell into disgrace and was prevented from continuing his work in any important group. According to reports in the American press, he was arrested in June, 1939.

Alexander Tairov (b. 1885) began the organization of his Chamber Theater (*Kamerny Teatr*) in Moscow in 1914. The revolution helped him to realize his plans for a radical revision of the relations between the actor and the audience which he hoped to achieve by doing away with the traditional three-dimensional stage. "The actor must no longer be merely a component part of the *decor*" was one of Tairov's favorite sayings. In the course of his experimentation he used many novel arrangements, such as vertical sets, "dynamic decorations," and movable surfaces in various combinations. His basic objective, in his own words, was the creation of a "synthetic theater." Tairov's "organic realism," compared to conventional and naturalistic theater, was difficult to harmonize with the principle of "socialist realism," and in 1935 he was subjected by the Soviet press to a series of blistering attacks pointing out his "errors" and "lack of ideas." In 1937 he was dismissed from his post as director of the *Kamerny Teatr*.

The cinema is even better suited than the theater for mass education and propaganda. In Russian films as in the Russian theater, however, although the Government has used the medium to disseminate the economic principles and social theories upon which it is founded, the directors and producers have consistently striven for artistic excellence. In the main they have achieved their fair share of success in the field and have contributed not a little to the development of the art of the cinema.

Of all Russian arts the film is perhaps the best known outside of the Soviet Union, and it is necessary here to mention it only in the briefest way. The three outstanding men in the Soviet cinema today are V. I. Pudovkin (b. 1893), S. M. Eisenstein (b. 1898), and the Ukrainian, A. Dovzhenko. The reputation of the Soviet films was firmly established by Eisenstein's first production, *The Battleship Potemkin,* in which there were several memorable episodes from the abortive Revolution of 1905. In 1938 he achieved an equal success in *Alexander Nevsky,* a patriotic, historical picture dealing with the defeat of the German invasion of northern Russia in the thirteenth century. The parallel with current events is so clearly drawn that after the conclusion of the Soviet-Nazi nonaggression pact in 1939 the picture was withdrawn; immediately after Hitler's attack in 1941 it was released again in the Soviet Union—where it is showing still.

9.

MUSIC, that most abstract of the arts, bears something of the same relation to the other arts that the physical sciences do to the humanities. More limited in manner and less controversial in content, music might have been expected to escape some of the effects of the revolutionary upheaval, but even though it was spared some of the political restrictions of the time, it was not to avoid the confusion in which all of the arts were caught. The disruption of the normal intellectual and psychological life of the country and the physical privations and suffering during the years of the civil war and war communism resulted in at least the temporary disorganization of musical activities. Many musicians joined the exodus of intellectuals after the revolution, and among the *émigrés* and exiles there were, of course, a number of gifted Russian composers. Paris had become Stravinsky's home even before the revolution, and some time later he chose to move on to the United States. Rachmaninov, Grechaninov, Medtner, and later on Glazunov, all preferred to emigrate. Prokofiev, on the other hand, after having spent several years in Europe elected to return to Russia.

In the initial years of the revolution there was a short-lived outburst of futurist and ultramodernist tendencies in music, but extreme musical forms had even less appeal to the masses than futuristic painting and literature. Since only a relatively small circle of sophisticated music lovers could appreciate the subtleties of the new style, the little popularity that it did attain was confined to a very circumscribed group. No more successful was the attempt to "democratize" orchestras by eliminating the "dictatorial" power of the conductor. In 1922 a conductorless orchestra known as the

"First Symphony Ensemble" (*Persimfans*) was organized, and though it was at first received enthusiastically by audiences, it soon became apparent even to the plan's supporters that this route led nowhere.

One of the most fruitful projects of Soviet music was the study of the native and traditional melodies of the people. Lasting and creative results grew out of the new interest in the folk songs and other types of "folklore music" of the Russian people and of the lesser nationalities down to and including the smallest mountaineer tribes of the Caucasus. Not only was this type of music subjected to scientific study by specially organized ethnographic expeditions but it was also given practical facilities to develop and manifest itself. Sponsored by the All-Union Government and by republican and local soviets as well, this program has given rise to a veritable renaissance of the colorful music of the many Russian nationalities. The rebirth of folk music is further encouraged by musical festivals which are arranged periodically in Moscow in connection with the "decades of folk art."

On the whole, after a rather brief period of turmoil, the main stream of Russian music was left to proceed as it would, and while modernist trends are apparent in the works of certain individual Soviet composers, the general tendency has been and still is toward the full use of the solid prerevolutionary inheritance of classical music. The reëstablishment of social order which followed the adoption of the New Economic Policy had its effect in bringing to an end the more extreme types of experimentation, and thereafter musical education and training were once more based on firm foundations. Today a great deal of attention is paid to the thorough mastery of details of mechanical technique. The number of music schools has been increasing constantly during the last two decades; in 1936 there were in the Soviet Union twelve conservatories and ninety-five "musical technicums," many of them with excellent standards.

Characteristically enough, most Soviet musical authorities, when discussing Russian music of the nineteenth century, are inclined to minimize the value of the work of the composers of the "Mighty Band" (see Chap. XII, Sec. 9), largely because of the strain of amateurism which ran through the music of all of them with the exception of Rimsky-Korsakov. On the other hand, Tchaikovsky as well as A. Rubinstein and A. N. Serov, all highly trained professional musicians, have been firmly reëstablished in the Soviet galaxy. Thus, a moderate balance has at last been restored in the very sphere in which fiery battles raged between critics who were associated with one or the other of the two schools. Today an attempt obviously is being made to profit by what is really valuable in the works of every composer of the classical period in the history of Russian music.

The name Prokofiev is certainly one of the greatest in contemporary music. Critics and musicians may continue to argue whether Prokofiev is serving "pure music" to the fullest extent and whether he should be called a "classicist" or an "impressionist." But whatever points the authorities may make on either side, it is plain to the musical public that although Prokofiev has profited by his study of the works of the composers of both the "harmonic" and the "classical" periods, especially those of Tchaikovsky and other Russian classicists, his art is modern in the best sense of the word and highly original in addition. He has composed several symphonies and concertos, some of which have been played in the United States before enthusiastic audiences. Shortly before the beginning of the war in Europe, Prokofiev composed the music for Eisenstein's historical film, *Alexander Nevsky,* and more recently an opera, *War and Peace.*

Whereas Prokofiev met with success from the very first performance of his youthful works, another Russian composer who has recently become prominent, N. Ya. Miaskovsky (b. 1881), had to wait years for public recognition. A pupil of Liadov and Rimsky-Korsakov, Miaskovsky was also deeply influenced by Glazunov. For many years his music was dismissed because it was considered too "somber" and "melancholy" but in recent years he has developed a style in which Soviet critics have discovered "optimism and faith." He has composed many symphonies, two of the best known being his *Twelfth,* sometimes called the *Kolkhoz Symphony,* which was dedicated to the fifteenth anniversary of the revolution, and the *Nineteenth,* dedicated to the Red Army. He has also written vocal music, including a collection of songs based on Lermontov's poems.

The most famous of Soviet composers and certainly the one best known in the United States is Dmitri Shostakovich (b. 1909).

Although it has been said that of all masters of music past and present he recognizes only Bach and Tchaikovsky, in his works he combines traditionalism with modernist tendencies. His opera, *Lady Macbeth of Mtsensk,* which was produced in the Metropolitan Opera House in New York in 1935, is, in his own words, an attempt "to make music as simple and expressive as possible." Incidentally, in spite of the great success of this opera on the Soviet stage, it caused the composer considerable trouble, since he was accused by communist purists of both "formalistic tendencies" and "vulgar naturalism." It was only his *Fifth Symphony,* first performed in January, 1938, which led to his complete rehabilitation. In 1942 his *Seventh Symphony* won him universal fame. It was composed during the siege of Leningrad and patriotic feeling added strength to the musical appreciation of the work.

Other contemporary Russian composers have followed divergent musical paths. N. A. Roslavets, a modernist, has been called the "Maiakovsky of music" and criticized for his "formalistic approach." Born in 1880, the son of a peasant, Roslavets was graduated from the Moscow Conservatory at the age of thirty-two. His cantata, *The October,*[4] was written in 1927, and the following year he composed a symphony, *Komsomolia,* which was well received. M. F. Gnesin (b. 1883), a pupil of Rimsky-Korsakov, is a composer devoted to an unusual array of interests. He has been especially interested in the development of Hebrew music, and in connection with his studies in this field visited Palestine in 1914 and again in 1921–23. He has also been absorbed in attempts to create a new synthesis of music and drama, and for several years collaborated with Meyerhold, composing music for a number of plays produced at the latter's studio. R. M. Glier (b. 1875) was originally a follower of Tchaikovsky, but he later fell under the influence of Borodin and Rimsky-Korsakov, especially after he had developed an intense interest in oriental music. He is the composer of the well-known ballet, *Red Poppy* (1927), in which he used as one of the themes *Yablochko,* a popular song of civil war days. A number of musicians of the younger generation are just rising to prominence. I. Dzerzhinsky's (b. 1909) operas, the *Quiet*

[4] Meaning the October, *i.e.* Bolshevik, Revolution—the November Revolution according to the Gregorian calendar.

Don and *The Upturned Soil,* both based on novels by Sholokhov, have made a name for him. Another young Soviet composer whose works have aroused considerable interest is Dmitri Kabalevsky, one of Miaskovsky's pupils.

In the Soviet Union music stands high among the arts, both in governmental favor and in public esteem. Its teachers and critics have kept alive the best of musical tradition and have encouraged an impressive amount of research into the past and a healthy spirit of experimentation in modern forms and techniques. The Government itself has been especially generous in providing facilities for the development of talented young people throughout the country. With the recent appearance of a number of highly gifted composers, Soviet music seems to be assured of a brilliant future.

CHAPTER XX.

RUSSIA IN THE SECOND WORLD WAR

(1939–1943)

I.

THE second World War was begun under circumstances differing sharply from those which prevailed at the start of the first. Russia's neutrality in 1939 was, of course, the most striking difference. In the system of alliances organized by Britain and France during the two decades between wars, Poland—a country not yet in existence in 1914—was depended upon by the allies to assume the rôle of Imperial Russia. There were other differences. Austria, now a shadow of the powerful empire of 1914, had been merged with Germany and absorbed into the Nazi economy. Hungary had been reduced to the status of a satellite nation and was firmly under German control. Fascist Italy, in 1939 as in 1914, was bound to Germany by an alliance, but this time the actions and the repeated declarations of both dictators had made it abundantly clear that the totalitarian nations would adhere to the provisions of the pact. In the second World War the conflict which led to hostilities first crystallized in the Baltic area rather than in the Balkans, but the issues were such that the Balkans could hardly hope to avoid involvement and, indeed, were sucked into the vortex in their turn.

Yet, in spite of all the obvious differences which might be enumerated, the underlying causes of the two wars remained fundamentally similar. The same aggressive spirit that had characterized Germany under the Kaiser was proclaimed in much more violent form in the tenets of Nazi ideology. Between Germany and Great Britain there had arisen the same rivalry that had culminated twenty-five years earlier in the first World War. The Russian uneasiness about the German *Drang nach Osten*—the centuries-old conflict of eastern Europe—was daily aggravated by the differences in the official ideologies and governmental systems of the two countries, though throughout the initial period of the war efforts were made by both parties to conceal them, somewhat clumsily, under the cloak of the nonaggression pact.

Whatever the surface situation may have been in the months immediately prior to the outbreak of the war, Soviet political and military leaders were fully aware of the basic tension. They well remembered the lessons of 1914. They remembered that, while it had been Austria and not Russia that had struck the first blow in the first World War, Russian mobilization had been one of the factors contributing to its spread. Had the Imperial Russian Government not resorted to calling up the army, they believed, Germany would have been deprived of a pretext for mobilization at that time, and the war might have been at least temporarily localized at the expense of Serbia. The Soviet leaders apparently resolved to apply the lessons of World War I to the new situation, and decided, rather than to step head on into an unwanted conflict, to attempt to confine it within the limits of Poland. This decision must certainly have been reinforced by their uncertainty of the British and French attitude toward the Soviet Union and by Poland's refusal to allow Russian troops to be deployed in her territory. In an insecure and uncertain situation the Soviet Government chose the road of hard-boiled realism. Its leaders were devoted first to the interests of the Soviet Union and at the time those interests were best served by neutrality.

Under the circumstances, however, while it was comparatively easy to proclaim Russia's neutrality, it was obviously difficult to define its limits, and still more difficult to keep within these limits once they were established. Moreover, the assumption of neutrality and the actions that flowed logically from such a position brought down upon the Soviet Union the almost universal condemnation of the democracies. The conclusion of the nonaggression pact with Germany and the Soviet occupation of western White Russia and western Ukraine aroused violent indignation not only in Britain and France but in the United States as well—an indignation which arose (in part, at least) from the failure of the Anglo-Saxon countries to realize the peculiarities and intricacies of the involved political background of eastern Europe. This initial strain opened a breach which was widened by subsequent events. At the time of the Soviet-Finnish War there arose an actual and immediate danger of Franco-British intervention against Russia—in Transcaucasia as well as in Finland—and the collapse of Soviet neutrality seemed then to be almost a matter of hours. Moreover, the Soviets on principle consistently objected to the British blockade of Germany which threatened their maritime commerce. During the whole period of neutrality, relations between the Soviet Union and the western democracies were so delicately poised that it was only with the greatest efforts—the result, in part, of the foresight of a few British statesmen and scholars such as Sir Stafford Cripps and Sir Bernard Pares—that the outward appearance of normality was preserved.

No less complicated were the relations between the Soviet Union and Germany. Expressions of friendship toward Germany were frequently and conspicuously displayed both in the press and in the official statements of Soviet leaders, and the Government demonstrated great caution in eliminating anything that might serve the Germans as a pretext for irritation. These moves extended to almost all official activities, from the suspension of the anti-German historical movie, *Alexander Nevsky* to the meticulous observance of every clause of the commercial treaties governing delivery of goods to Germany.

While bending every effort to avoid conflict with Germany, the Soviet Government continued to be acutely aware of the danger of a Nazi attack, and, particularly after the fall of France, took diplomatic and military steps of a precautionary nature. It was chiefly the necessity to provide for national safety which dictated the occupation of the strategic regions along Russia's western frontier. These movements along the border areas were at the same time paralleled and reinforced by internal readjustments. Considerable attention was directed to the retraining of the Red Army and to the modernization of its tactics and supply services. Industries were put on a war footing, and drastic steps were taken to increase production. The seven-hour work day was lengthened to eight hours. To stop labor turnover and to insure the productivity of war plants, workers were "frozen" in the industries in which they were employed and were forbidden to move from plant to plant without special permission. During 1940 and 1941 armament plants were moved from the exposed White Russian and Lenin-

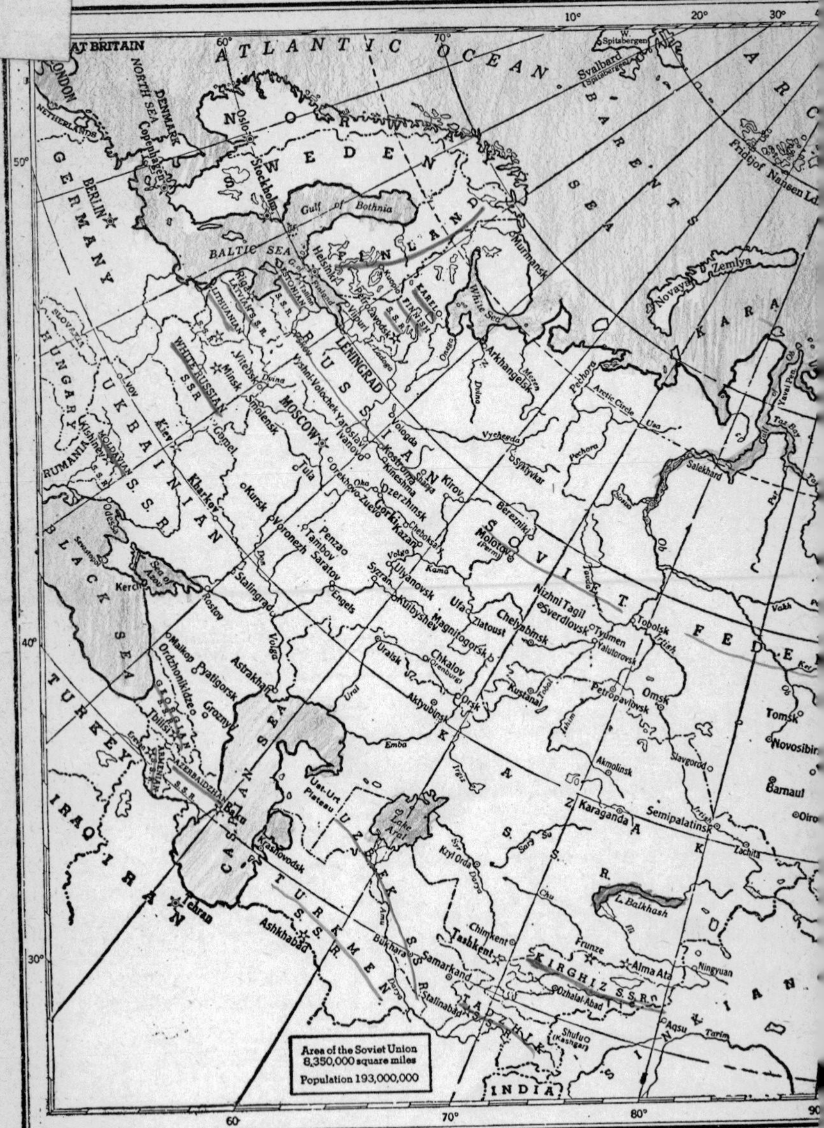

ATLANTIC OCEAN
ARCTIC
BARENTS SEA
KARA
NORTH SEA
BALTIC SEA
Gulf of Bothnia
White Sea
BLACK SEA
Sea of Azov
CASPIAN SEA
Lake Aral
L. Balkhash
GREAT BRITAIN
LONDON
NETHERLANDS
DENMARK
Copenhagen
GERMANY
BERLIN
NORWAY
Oslo
SWEDEN
Stockholm
FINLAND
Helsinki
HUNGARY
SLOVAKIA
RUMANIA
TURKEY
IRAQ
IRAN
Tehran
INDIA
SINKIANG
W. Spitsbergen
Svalbard (Spitsbergen)
Fridtjof Nansen Ld.
Novaya Zemlya
ESTONIAN S.S.R.
LATVIAN S.S.R.
Riga
LITHUANIAN S.S.R.
KARELO FINNISH S.S.R.
WHITE RUSSIAN S.S.R.
Minsk
UKRAINIAN S.S.R.
MOLDAVIAN S.S.R.
Kishinev
GEORGIAN S.S.R.
Tbilisi
ARMENIAN S.S.R.
Erevan
AZERBAIDZHAN S.S.R.
Baku
TURKMEN S.S.R.
Ashkhabad
UZBEK S.S.R.
KAZAKH S.S.R.
KIRGHIZ S.S.R.
TADZHIK S.S.R.
Stalinabad
RUSSIAN SOVIET FEDERATED
LENINGRAD
MOSCOW
Murmansk
Arkhangelsk
Petrozavodsk
Vipuri
Vitebsk
Smolensk
Gomel
Kiev
Lvov
Odessa
Sevastopol
Kerch
Kharkov
Kursk
Tula
Voronezh
Tambov
Penza
Saratov
Stalingrad
Rostov
Astrakhan
Maikop
Pyatigorsk
Ordzhonikidze
Grozny
Vyshni Volochek
Yaroslavl
Ivanovo
Vologda
Kostroma
Kineshma
Orekhovo-Zuevo
Dzerzhinsk
Gorki
Kazan
Cheboksary
Kirov
Syktyvkar
Berezniki
Molotov (Perm)
Ulyanovsk
Syzran
Kuibyshev
Engels
Ufa
Zlatoust
Magnitogorsk
Chkalov (Orenburg)
Uralsk
Aktyubinsk
Orsk
Nizhni Tagil
Sverdlovsk
Chelyabinsk
Tyumen
Yalutorovsk
Tobolsk
Kustanai
Petropavlovsk
Omsk
Tomsk
Novosibirsk
Barnaul
Oirot
Salekhard
Akmolinsk
Slavgorod
Karaganda
Semipalatinsk
Lachita
Ust-Urt Plateau
Krasnovodsk
Bukhara
Samarkand
Tashkent
Chimkent
Kzyl Orda
Frunze
Alma Ata
Dzhalal-Abad
Ningyuan
Aqsu
Shufu (Kashgar)
Volga
Don
Ural
Emba
Oka
Kama
Dvina
Onega
Mezen
Pechora
Vychegda
Usa
Ob
Irtish
Tobol
Ishim
Syr Darya
Amu Darya
Chu
Ili
Tarim
Arctic Circle
Gulf of Ob
Taz Bay
Area of the Soviet Union 8,350,000 square miles
Population 193,000,000

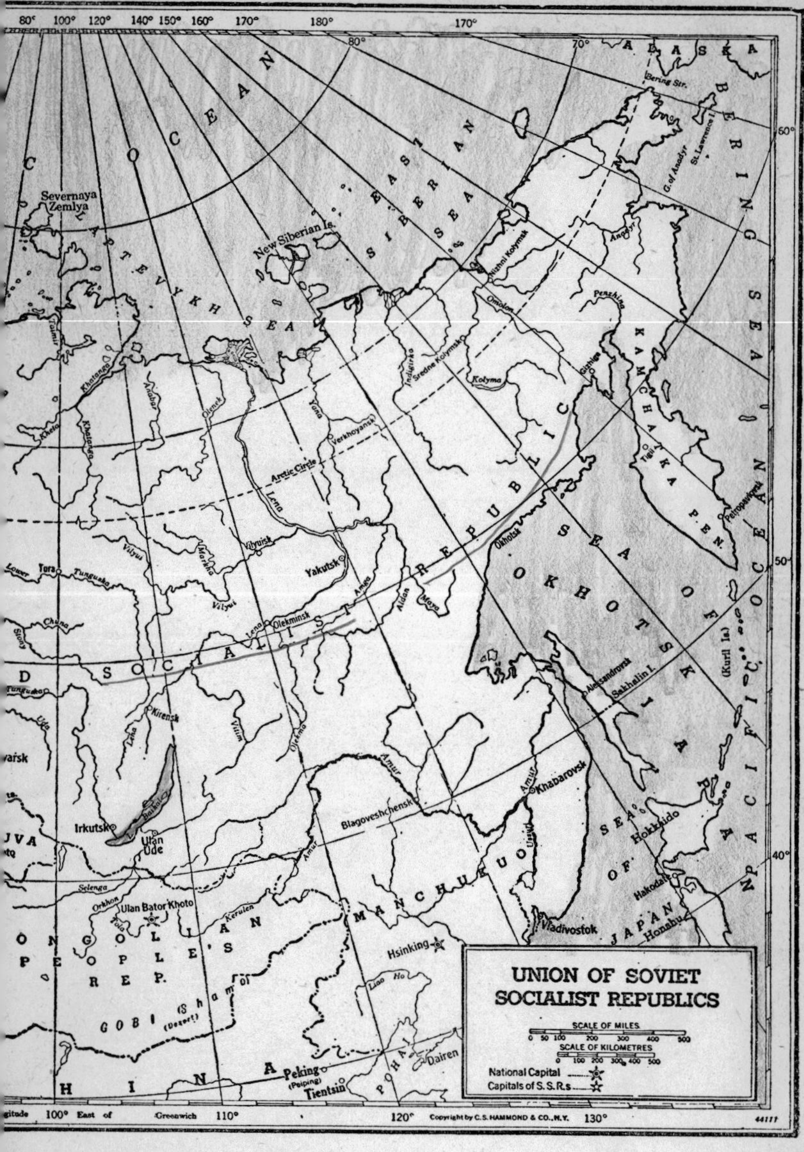
UNION OF SOVIET
SOCIALIST REPUBLICS
SCALE OF MILES
0 50 100 200 300 400 500
SCALE OF KILOMETRES
0 100 200 300 400 500
National Capital
Capitals of S. S. R.s
Copyright by C. S. HAMMOND & CO., N.Y.
44111
Longitude 100° East of Greenwich 110° 120° 130°
80° 100° 120° 140° 150° 160° 170° 180° 170°
60° 50° 40°
ALASKA
Bering Str.
BERING SEA
St. Lawrence I.
G. of Anadyr
Anadyr
Nizhni Kolymsk
Omolon
Penzhina
KAMCHATKA PEN.
Tigil
Petropavlovsk
Gizhiga
Kolyma
Sredne Kolymsk
Indigirka
EAST SIBERIAN SEA
New Siberian Is.
LAPTEV or NORDENSKJÖLD SEA
Severnaya Zemlya
Taimir
Khatanga
Kheta
Anabar
Olenek
Yana
Verkhoyansk
Arctic Circle
Lena
Vilyui
Vilyuisk
Markha
Yakutsk
Aldan
Amga
Maya
Okhotsk
SEA OF OKHOTSK
Olekminsk
Lower Tunguska
Chuna
Kirensk
Vitim
Olekma
Irkutsk
Baikal
Ulan Ude
TUVA
Selenga
Orkhon
Ulan Bator Khoto
Tola
Kerulen
MONGOLIAN PEOPLE'S REP.
GOBI (Sha mo) (Desert)
CHINA
Peking (Peiping)
Tientsin
Dairen
Liao Ho
Hsinking
MANCHUKUO
Amur
Blagoveshchensk
Khabarovsk
Ussuri
Vladivostok
SEA OF JAPAN
Hokkaido
Hakodate
Honshu
Sakhalin I.
Aleksandrovsk
(Kuril Is.)
PACIFIC OCEAN
SOCIALIST REPUBLIC

grad areas to the Urals, and along the Volga and beyond it new plants, such as the high-octane gasoline refineries at Ufa and Saratov, were rushed to completion. The Russians hoped for peace—and prepared for war.

2.

DURING the early months of the war the Russians concentrated upon the rapid rectification and strengthening of their western frontier. The German invasion of Poland on September 1, 1939, and the British and French declarations of war which followed immediately thereafter came while the Soviet Union was in a new and, geographically, a somewhat disadvantageous position of neutrality. Her immediate object, therefore, was an improvement of her strategic position all along her western borders, and her neutrality was not allowed to interfere with her attempts to achieve this end—by diplomatic moves when possible, and by military operations when no other way was open.

The attitude of the Soviet leaders at this time can better be understood, perhaps, if we reconsider for a moment the effect of the territorial changes along the western fringes of Russia which had occurred at the end of the first World War and as a result of foreign intervention at the time of the civil war. These revisions fell into several different categories. On Lenin's initiative the Soviet Government itself had granted independence to Finland in December, 1917. The Baltic area, western White Russia, and the western Ukraine had been taken from Russia by Germany as one of the conditions for granting the Brest-Litovsk peace of 1918. These regions had not been returned to Russia by the Allies after their victory over Germany. Instead, the Baltic provinces were organized as independent states, and in 1920 Poland was allowed to attack Russia and then to annex western White Russia and the western Ukraine. In the south the Allies had consented to and eventually approved the seizure of Bessarabia by the Rumanians. The Soviet Government had steadfastly refused to recognize Rumanian sovereignty in Bessarabia but in time had accepted all of the other changes. It had accepted them for a variety of reasons: first, at the time the Soviets were in such a weakened state that they had had no alternative; second, that had been the period of the Russians belief in world revolution and Soviet leaders had still pinned their hopes on the spread of communism across national borders; third, acceptance had made it possible to establish a European peace—however unstable—and since relations with Germany were friendly, there seemed to be no immediate danger of an attack on Russia by any major power.

Hitler's rise to power in Germany, however, had changed the whole international picture. Russia could no longer exclude from her calculations the possibility of the Nazification of the Baltic states. Moreover the tension which now existed between the Soviet Union and Nazi Germany had made it necessary for Russian leaders to provide for any eventuality. Ever since the early years of the Five Year Plan and the inauguration of the program of building socialism in a single country, the Soviets had felt the need for the Baltic area both for economic and strategic purposes. Leningrad, the only Baltic port left to Russia at the conclusion of the first World War, was obviously insufficient to handle all of her Baltic trade or to cope with the rapid expansion of Russian economy at the moment, much less that foreseen for the future. This situation became urgent with the outbreak of the second World War, and when Great Britain and France had refused to reconsider Russian interests in the Baltic, there remained no alternative but to attempt to snatch concessions from Germany in this area as payment for Russian neutrality. The paradox of this situation was that Russia needed these borderlands in order to strengthen her position against a future German attack. Although the Anglo-Saxon countries appear to have consistently misunderstood this need, Germany was perfectly aware of the use to which the new territory was to be put. However, she was not then in a position to bargain further, and was reluctantly forced to accept the revisions which were later to prove so crucial.

It is obvious now that in this atmosphere of mutual distrust some agreement must have been reached between Germany and the Soviet Union in regard to their respective spheres of influence in eastern Europe. Though the agreement was never made public and many of its details are still not clear, subsequent events have shown its major provisions. Germany apparently agreed to the Soviet annexation of western White Russia and western Ukraine and to the establishment of a Soviet protectorate over Latvia and Estonia. The improvement of Russia's strategic position with regard to

Finland likewise appears to have been accepted in principle. Lastly, Russian claims upon Bessarabia must have been recognized and there are reasons to believe that even certain Russian interests in Bulgaria were at first tacitly accepted by Germany.

Though the Soviet high command, in contrast to the British and French, had no illusions about the ability of Poland to withstand a determined German attack, the unprecedented speed of the German victory apparently was not foreseen. The collapse of Polish resistance made it necessary for the Soviets to move immediately, and on the morning of September 17 Red Army troops crossed the Polish frontier and raced westward in an attempt to stop the German advance as far as possible from the Russian border. In spite of the previous understanding the Germans could hardly have expected such a prompt Soviet reaction, and the appearance of the Red Army deep within Poland precipitated several minor clashes between Russian and German advance guards, the most serious of which occurred in the vicinity of Lvov. Their initial drive carried the Russians to the banks of the Vistula, but they later withdrew to the demarcation line along the Western Bug River which had been settled upon in the September agreement. By this maneuver the Soviet Union was left in control of an area whose population was predominantly non-Polish. With minor exceptions, the peasants in the occupied area were of White Russian and Ukrainian stock, and in the cities throughout the territory a considerable percentage of the population were Jews.

In the elections for the People's Assemblies of western White Russia and western Ukraine which were held on October 22, 1939, more than 90 per cent of the eligible voters participated, and of these over 90 per cent cast their ballots for the single ticket of "candidates of social organizations"—trade unions, coöperative societies, etc. Within a few days the two People's Assemblies passed resolutions expressing their desire to join Soviet White Russia and Soviet Ukraine respectively, and on November 1 the Supreme Soviet of the U.S.S.R. approved their incorporation. While the validity of the elections was questioned by some foreign observers, there can hardly be any doubt that the reunion of western White Russia and western Ukraine with their mother countries was eagerly supported by the majority of the population for both ethnic and social reasons, On the economic side, too, the peasants had every reason to welcome the division among them of the large estates of the Polish nobility, a change which was made all the more welcome by the wise decision of the Soviets not to insist upon the immediate forcible collectivization of the land.

Even before the annexation of western White Russia and western Ukraine had been legalized, the Soviet Government began a series of diplomatic moves in the Baltic states. Singly and individually representatives of Estonia, Latvia, and Lithuania were invited to Moscow to negotiate pacts of friendship between their countries and the Soviet Union, pacts which in each case included a provision granting the Soviets the right to establish and garrison with Red Army and Navy men certain naval and air bases within the territory of the smaller country. In the case of Lithuania the Russians were able to provide a token of goodwill which was enthusiastically received by the Lithuanians—the offer to return to them their ancient capital, the city of Vilno, which the Poles had seized in 1920 and which the Russians had taken over when they occupied eastern Poland. The interesting aspect of this arrangement was that though the Germans had never considered Lithuania within the Russian sphere of influence at all, circumstances forced them to yield as gracefully as possible. That they were something less than successful in saving face is indicated by the fact that they later agreed to evacuate from the Baltic area some 100,000 Germans most of whom belonged to families that had been settled in these regions for centuries. It requires but little understanding of national psychology to realize what a shock this diplomatic defeat must have been to German self-esteem.

The situation in the Baltic now seemed to have been stabilized, at least for the time being, but in June, 1940, the political status of the three Baltic states was suddenly and drastically changed again, Latvia, Estonia, and Lithuania were incorporated in the Soviet Union, each receiving the status of a constituent republic in the Union. This new move of the Soviet Union seems to have been prompted by the unexpected and alarming collapse of France before the Nazi juggernaut in May and June, 1940. The immediate reaction on the part of Soviet leaders was to hasten all diplomatic efforts to complete and consolidate the strategic occupation of the Baltic area at the earliest possible moment. Following the procedure adopted by both western White Russia and western Ukraine, a People's Government was established in each of the Baltic countries on the basis of hurriedly conducted elections which resulted in more than 90 per cent of the votes being cast for reform. These new governments almost immediately pleaded for and received admission into the Soviet Union. There has not, of course, been an opportunity to judge the validity of these elections, and to what degree they may have reflected the actual desires of the people remains to be seen.

Simultaneously an ultimatum was delivered to the Rumanian Government, and upon its expiration Soviet troops occupied Bessarabia and northern Bukovina. The parts of these two districts in which the Ukrainian population predominated were incorporated in the Soviet Ukraine, and the balance of the territory, populated chiefly by Moldavians, was organized as a constituent republic of the Soviet Union under the name of the Moldavian S.S.R.

Executed in the face of the constantly increasing irritation of the Germans, who still were in no position to offer effective opposition, this series of swift and bold diplomatic maneuvers restored within the space of a few months the western boundaries of the Russian Empire except for the Polish salient to which the Soviets laid no claim. Indeed, the new gains included in eastern Galicia and northern Bukovina a Ukrainian population which had never been part of the Russian Empire, although during the Middle Ages the area had been part of the Kievan federation. In general, from the Soviet standpoint, the revisions had resulted in a favorable realignment of the central and southern border regions and only the northern frontier remained as an immediate danger.

The rectification of that last segment, the Finnish frontier, proved to be the most difficult and dangerous issue of all. The border with Finland ran only twenty miles from Leningrad, Russia's second largest city, and only a few miles beyond the border lay the Mannerheim Line, one of the most formidable fortifications in all Europe. The Russians looked out across the frontier at a line that stretched completely across the Karelian Isthmus, that was firmly anchored on a water line at each end, that was fortified in depth and studded with massive gun emplacements facing toward Leningrad. They considered what might happen if that line were ever manned by German troops in an offensive against the Leningrad area, and decided that that threat must be removed.

But though the Soviets were inspired by a desire to improve their strategic position against a future clash with Germany, their program, ill conceived and badly carried out, nearly provoked a break with France and Britain. The initial demand that Finland cede the Karelian Isthmus to the Soviet Union in exchange for a large piece of territory north of Lake Ladoga, seems not to have been unreasonable, and in rejecting the Soviet offer the Finns now appear to have been ill advised by admirers in some of the western countries. On the other hand, in starting war the Soviet Government apparently did not take into account all of its dangerous implications. For one thing, the Russians seem not to have expected any resolute defense by the Finns, and appear to have counted on a revival of the Finnish communist movement which had been cruelly suppressed by the White Finns and Germans in the terror of 1918. At the very beginning of the Soviet-Finnish War O. Kuusinen, the leader of the Red Finns in 1918 and a prominent leader of the Communist International, hastened to organize a People's Government of Finland, but his efforts evoked no enthusiasm among the Finns. In spite of this, the Soviet Government signed a treaty of friendship with the Kuusinen Government, and continued in the war as the protector of this new government against the "White Finns." This fiction of legality, however, did not prevent the League of Nations from convicting the Soviet Union as an aggressor and depriving her of her League membership. But the League had awakened from its lethargy too late. Since for years it had done nothing to prevent increasingly violent acts of aggression on the part of Italy, Japan, and Germany, its sudden action against the Soviet Union could hardly be expected to produce the salubrious moral effect that had been hoped for. The political effects were, of course, infinitesimal.

Immediately after the beginning of the war on November 29 it became plain that the Soviet Union, overestimating the strength of communist tendencies in some sections of the Finnish population and depending upon them to arouse a crippling civil strife in Finland, had failed to amass sufficient military power to crush the resistance which was met. The Finns, united and sustained by a glowing patriotism, knew and took advantage of every wrinkle of the terrain to throw up a stout defense. Moreover, they were bolstered by expressions of sympathy and promises of equipment and volunteers which poured in from almost every country of the world, and from day to day they held on in the hope that concrete aid would soon reach them. Only Germany, still caught in the dilemma, stood aloof. In spite of the fact that the traditions of 1918 had not been forgotten, Berlin was forced to suppress all expression of pro-Finnish sympathy. Paradoxically enough, the Finnish commander-in-chief, General Mannerheim, who had asked for and received German help in his rise to power in 1918, was now compelled to display every courtesy toward the western democracies.

During the first two months of the war the Finns were able to beat off and parry most of the Russian attacks, but in February, 1940, the Red Army was reorganized to meet the realities of the situation and began waging war in all seriousness. In a short time, driving against the center of the Mannerheim Line in the depths of an arctic winter, Soviet troops literally blasted out of the ground fortifications which military men had considered all but impregnable. The Finns, having found that more promises than actual help had come from the outside world, had no alternative but to sue for peace which was concluded on March 12 on conditions less favorable to Finland than those in the original Russian demands. In addition to the Karelian Isthmus itself, the city and the district of Vyborg were annexed by the Soviet Union. Furthermore, the Finns were forced to lease the Hankoe Peninsula to Russia for a term of thirty years, a condition which they had specifically objected to during the negotiations preceding the war. A new constituent republic of the Soviet Union, the Karelo-Finnish Republic, was formed from the territory annexed from Finland and from a part of Soviet Karelia, and Kuusinen was elected chairman of the Presidium of its Supreme Soviet.

One of the most important results of the Finnish war was the disclosure to the Soviet leaders of many serious deficiencies in the organization of the Red Army. The weaknesses and mistakes were frankly recognized and discussed among army men, and under War Commissar Timoshenko feverish work was immediately begun to improve the efficiency throughout the army. Particular attention was paid to matters of organization as well as to training and tactics and the service of supplies. One of the most serious difficulties encountered had been the confusion and delay which had resulted from the conflicts arising between political commissars and army officers, since the latter were not allowed to make any important decisions without the agreement of these official political advisers. The institution of political commissars has been a matter of contention almost since the founding of the Red Army. They were first created at the time of the civil war for the dual purpose of directing the political advancement of the soldiers and controlling the army leadership. They were later abolished, then restored to power in the period immediately following Tukhachevsky's execution, and have now been eliminated once more.

For the Soviet Union the first months of the second World War were tense and difficult. However, in spite of opposition both from the fascist nations and from the democracies, the Russians were able during this troubled period to strengthen their strategic position and, to some extent, to secure their most exposed frontiers. Their action was often hasty and sometimes, perhaps, ill considered. The Russians, however, felt that there was no time to consider method but that their only concern must be to reach in the shortest possible time their first and single objective: the immediate preparation of the defense of the Soviet Union.

3.

DURING the summer of 1940 the outward air of friendship which had characterized relations between Germany and Russia began to evaporate and the realities of the underlying tensions gradually became apparent. Though not abrupt, the changes were profound in their implications—just how profound we can understand now when we remember that Hitler himself later admitted in a proclamation at the beginning of the Russian war that his decision to invade the Soviet Union was made as early as August of 1940. But for the time being the moves were veiled. In the 1939 agreement Germany had recognized the Soviet Union's interests not only in the Baltic area but also, to some extent, in the Balkans. Hitler, it appears, had felt that circumstances would force the Russians to move slowly and warily and that consequently the agreement was being bought at the cost of comparatively small German sacrifices in the Baltic area. However, the speed with which the Russians moved to absorb the Baltic states into their defense system and to consolidate their control of the whole region must certainly have alarmed German military leaders. Having disposed of France, the Germans now felt sufficiently secure to take steps to prevent the further westward expansion of the Russians, and they determined, as the first step, to exclude Russia from the Balkans. Bessarabia had been conceded to the Russians, but the annexation of northern Bukovina had seemed to the Germans nothing less than political impertinence which required immediate and strong countermeasures. Accordingly, German troops were sent into Rumania and it was discreetly made clear that they would be used to "protect" that country against any further Russian aggression. They served an additional purpose as well, for a little later these protectors compelled the protected to cede considerable slices of territory to Hungary and Bulgaria—an exchange which cost the Germans nothing and secured for them the support of two countries. As for Rumania, she was quietly promised ample compensation in the form of territory which was to be seized in the future dismemberment of Russia.

The Soviet Union was well aware of the ominous implications behind the German penetration of the Balkan Peninsula, but Russian leaders were forced to move cautiously in countering the threat. Russian foreign policy was geared to one aim—to avoid conflict with Germany altogether, or, failing that, to postpone it until the Soviets were completely prepared. Though a German attack now seemed almost unavoidable, it obviously was essential that the Russians avoid any direct provocation which would hasten the outbreak of hostilities. On the other hand, the very imminence of German attack made it all the more necessary for the Soviets to take immediate steps to insure themselves against a simultaneous blow in the east which would force the division of forces between two enormous fronts some six thousand miles apart. The Kremlin had been deeply concerned about this possibility ever since the formation of the Three Power Pact. Preliminary negotiations with Japan had been under way for some time, and on April 13, 1941, the Soviets were able to conclude an important neutrality pact with that country which to some extent reduced the hazard. Article Two of the agreement provided that "should one of the contracting parties become the object of hostilities on the part of one or several third powers, the other contracting party will observe neutrality throughout the duration of the conflict." This agreement, while it strengthened the position of the Kremlin by weakening the ties between Japan and Germany, itself contributed further to the deterioration of relations between Russia and Berlin, which were going from bad to worse. As early as in November, 1940, Molotov, the Soviet Foreign Commissar, had gone to Berlin in an attempt to iron out the diplomatic conflicts by direct and frank discussions of the situation. His mission, though distinguished by a show of cordiality and courtesy, had been fruitless, and the German push southward had continued unabated throughout the winter. With the attack on Yugoslavia and Greece in April, 1941, it appeared that all possibilities of a Russo-German understanding had vanished.

The disastrous defeat of the democratic powers in Greece and the spectacular German invasion of Crete seemed to observers to open the way for an immediate attack on Egypt. Speculation on the probable date and method ran through the world press and the Germans assiduously encouraged such beliefs as a new weapon in the war-of-nerves. As we now know, however, German plans had by this time undergone a radical revision, and under cover of the threat to drive into the Near East feverish preparations for the invasion of Russia were already in full swing. With Great Britain driven from the continent and the British Isles themselves threatened with invasion, Germany could look forward confidently to a period of comparative quiet in Europe which would make it possible to throw the whole weight of the Nazi army against the Russians. Indeed, Hitler seems to have believed it entirely possible that in England's extremity a German promise not to dismember the British Empire would be sufficient to enlist the English in a crusade against Bolshevism.

It was in line with this belief that deputy Nazi leader Rudolph Hess undertook his astounding flight to Scotland on May 10, 1941. According to a statement issued by Anthony Eden on September 22, 1943, Hess suggested that England should be allowed a free hand in the British Empire, Germany a free hand in Europe, and that Russia should be "included in Asia." However, Germany was ready to negotiate only with a "reasonable" British Government and not with Churchill's. If his terms were refused, Hitler was prepared "to destroy Great Britain utterly." The conditions which Hess stated merely amazed the British, and Hess himself was dealt with as a prisoner of war. However, even after the abrupt and ignominious failure of Hess's mission Hitler apparently hoped that his own armies would achieve a swift and resounding victory over the Russians which would demonstrate German invincibility once and for all and bring England to terms.

The motives which prompted Hitler to launch his armies against the Soviet Union at a time when he was involved in a far-flung war with Britain are at best obscure. His decision was based in part, no doubt, on his intuitive belief that the world would unite behind him to eradicate communism. The careful propagation of the fear of "Bolshevism" had carried him to power in Germany, and it must have seemed reasonable to him to expect that it would carry him on to new heights. Confidence in his ability to carry his program through to a victorious conclusion was surely fortified by the age-old German contempt for the Slavs and all their works. But beneath these ideological quirks lay a more important and concrete motive: the desire, the necessity, sooner or later, to break the Russian military machine whose very existence constituted a potential threat to Germany. It would undoubtedly have been more prudent for Germany to have postponed the attempt to remove that threat until after the conclusion of the war with Great Britain and thus to have avoided the dangers of a disastrous two-front war. But Hitler was inexorably driven to the attack by another fear. While Germany was expending her man power and material without hope of achieving an early or complete victory over Britain, the Russians, working night and day, were increasing their military and economic power at an incredible rate. It must have been clear to the German military leaders that the year 1941 might well be the last in which they could be certain of a decisive superiority, and that further delay might enable the Russians to equal or surpass them in trained men and industrial potential. They understood, further, that in 1941 the Russians were engaged in instituting reforms overshadowing those of 1905–14 which had bolstered up Russian effectiveness at that time. In both cases the reorganizations, while promising effective improvements, were incomplete. The Germans, calculating the additional strength that the completion of the reforms would release in the Soviets, decided to strike at the earliest possible moment in order to prevent the full consolidation of Russian economic power.

That the Germans confidently expected to destroy the Russian army within the space of a very few months—if not, indeed, within weeks—is clearly demonstrated in their official statements. In time it became quite clear that they had utterly underestimated the strength of the Red Army, a miscalculation which Hitler later bitterly complained was the result of Russian tricks in concealing their real military might. It seems probable that the Germans not only depended upon military successes to accomplish the destruction of Soviet power but also reckoned on the political disintegration of the state, and that in particular they had hoped to be able to take advantage of numerous peasant uprisings, especially in the Ukraine. They believed, apparently, that resentment against collectivization could be tied in with the separatist movement which had been to a certain extent nurtured in Berlin to produce a crippling civil war. It was a vain hope—a hope which might have become a reality as late as 1933 when the Kolkhoz system was still in its infancy. By 1941, however, both the physical conditions and the mood of the people had changed, and it was a German misfortune that the Nazi political advisers either misunderstood the changes or ignored them. Thus, driven by fear and enticed by false hopes, on June 22, 1941, Hitler ripped to shreds the nonaggression pact which he had signed and at dawn sent German troops pouring over the Russian border for the supreme test of the Soviet system and the ultimate trial of the Red Army.

The Red Army of the Soviet Union was not the army of Imperial Russia—neither the ill-trained army of 1905 nor the poorly supplied army of 1914. The differences were numerous and deep and were almost immediately reflected in the functioning of the whole military machine. The social gulf which had divided the officers from the men in the Tsar's army and had undermined its efficiency had been abolished; in its place there existed a unity and understanding which created and sustained fighting morale. The Red Army man was better educated than the tsarist soldier had been: while in 1905 only about 50 per cent of the men in the army could read and write and while there was still 27 per cent illiteracy among the recruits of 1914, by 1941 the Red Army was 100 per cent literate. In fact, the peacetime educational program of the Red Army was designed not only to familiarize the recruit with the technique and procedures of war but to prepare him for an important place in civilian life as well. The Soviet Army was, of course, highly mechanized, and, what is more important in modern warfare, most of its officers were thoroughly machine-minded and the personnel had been drilled to use the weapons to their best advantage. The rapid industrialization and mechanization of the Soviet Union itself had aided in this development. To take an example: about a million trained tractor drivers developed on the collective farms made excellent crews for manning divisions of Soviet tanks, and the factories in which those tractors had been produced were soon adding to the output of the plants rolling out tanks. The close coördination between scientific research, industry, and the army which had been developed through the two decades of Soviet rule was in itself a source of strength. In contrast to the pathetically inadequate production of guns and munitions which the steadily growing but still inadequate armament plants of Russia had been able to supply in 1914, the enormous industrial development of the Five Year Plans guaranteed a vast and increasing flow of equipment to the Red Army.

The Russian navy, too, was to prove an important factor in the conflict. Almost completely destroyed in the Japanese war of 1904–5, the navy had been partly rebuilt by 1914, and while it was then numerically inadequate it was modern and well equipped. The Revolution of 1917 and the civil war which followed resulted, however, in the complete disorganization and dispersal of the Russian fleet: that part of the Black Sea squadron which survived was taken over by the Whites and the Allies, and after the evacuation of Wrangel's forces in 1920 the few remaining vessels steamed into their graveyard at Bizerte. Though the Soviet Union was little concerned with the creation of a naval force during the early years of the revolution, after the beginning of the Five Year Plans the Government turned again to the construction of a small modern fleet. Numbers of destroyers and cruisers were built in Russian shipyards, and at least one battleship was laid down in Nikolaev on the Black Sea. It was not, however, completed at the time of the German invasion and was blown up by the Russians before they abandoned the port. Numerically the Soviet navy today is probably strongest in the submarine class, and though the number of such vessels constructed has been a closely guarded secret, it is known that a considerable underwater fleet is stationed in the Pacific in addition to the units operating in the Baltic and the Black

Sea. In personnel and battle training the Soviet navy, which has undergone some revision since the Finnish war, now seems to compare favorably with those of other belligerents and throughout the war squadrons in the Black Sea and the Baltic have given a good account of themselves. Units operating in the Arctic Ocean and Barents Sea along the main convoy lines from Britain and the United States have particularly distinguished themselves and have contributed substantially to the successful delivery of supplies through the Arctic ports.

During the first World War the Russians developed an embryonic air force, but like the air arm of all armies in that war it played a minor rôle in the hostilities. After the war the Soviet Government encouraged research in the field of aeronautics and made it easier for Russian scientists and mechanics to participate fully in the rapid technological developments which revolutionized the aircraft industry. The Russians produced, tested, and improved foreign and Russian-designed models of both military and commercial aircraft, and at least one of the outstanding fighting planes of this war, the Stormovik, is a Soviet development. Wide publicity was given to every phase of aviation, and a unique effort was made to enlist mass interest and participation through the so-called *Osaviakhim* (Association for Defense through Aviation and Chemical Warfare) which by 1939 had several million members. The Russians were particularly active in developing new military uses for aircraft and Russia was the first nation to perfect a technique for dropping parachutists on a large scale—a use for planes which had been discovered but not at first fully exploited in the United States. During the tense months before the start of the second World War numbers of foreign aviation experts and observers visited the Soviet Union and some of them, notably Charles Lindbergh, expressed their conviction that the Red Air Force was inefficient and obsolete—an opinion that was totally disproved early in the war. While it is true that the Germans enjoyed sheer numerical superiority in the air in their early campaigns, and made repeated announcements of the utter annihilation of the Soviet air fleet—announcements which were complete with an impressive array of astronomical figures—the Red air defense continued to be active along the whole two-thousand-mile front. Not only did Russian fighters remain to dispute German control of the air over crucial battle areas, but new models of both fighters and bombers continued to roll from Russian factories throughout the war. Their own forces augmented by a steady flow of planes from Great Britain and the United States, by the summer of 1943 the Russians had established at least an over-all air parity and in some theaters operational superiority.

On the morning of June 22 the Germans launched against the Red Army a blow which was perhaps unequaled in military history, a blow which was calculated to stun the Russians and to prepare the way for their defeat before they could properly organize their defenses. The immediate danger which faced the Red Army at that moment was enormously greater than that of 1914; in the first World War German forces were engaged on two fronts, while the onslaught of 1941 was directed at Russia alone and was backed by the whole force of the formidable German military and industrial machine. In addition the attack had been meticulously prepared and the Germans were now able to enlist and extort support from conquered and satellite countries throughout Europe—among them France, Finland, Slovakia, Hungary, Rumania, and Croatia. That the Red Army was able merely to survive a blow delivered without warning by what was then the most powerful military organization in the world, a machine bolstered by the industrial facilities of nearly the whole continent of Europe—that feat alone was a demonstration of stamina of which any people might justly be proud.

Even before the German attack, in order to strengthen the Russian administration and to coördinate the party and the governmental institutions, Joseph Stalin assumed the post of Chairman of the Council of People's Commissars, *i.e.* that of Premier (May 7, 1941). Immediately following the news of the invasion a Supreme Defense Council headed by Stalin was organized to direct the total national resistance. Made up of communist officials representing every phase of Soviet life, the council included only one military figure, Marshal Shaposhnikov, who served as an associate member and as Stalin's adviser. (In 1943 he was replaced by Marshal Vasilevsky.) Subsequently Stalin himself assumed the office of Commander-in-Chief of the Soviet Armed Forces, and still later, the title of Marshal of the Soviet Union was granted to him by the Red Army. Speaking to the nation in a broadcast on July 3, 1941, Stalin frankly warned that "a grave danger hangs over our country." Bluntly admitting the initial successes of the German armies sweeping toward the heart of Russia, he asked his listeners: "Is it really true that German fascist troops are invincible, as is ceaselessly trumpeted by boastful fascist propagandists?" To which he himself answered: "Of course not. History shows that there are no invincible armies and never have been." That bold statement sounded the keynote of Russian resistance. Coming as it did at a time when the Red Army was still in full retreat and at a time when a continuous chain of overwhelming German victories seemed to have cast a spell over the thoughts of peoples throughout the world, it did much to raise the hopes and stiffen the determination of the forces opposed to Hitlerism.

To meet the German invasion, the command of the Red Army was divided between three fronts; Marshal Timoshenko was assigned to the crucial central front, and two heroes of the civil war were put in command on either side, Marshal Voroshilov on the northern wing and Marshal Budenny on the southern sector. Russian military leaders had, of course, scrutinized every move of German strategy and tactics in the French and Balkan campaigns and were convinced that it would be futile and possibly disastrous to attempt to stop the German attack at the frontier. The time necessary to mobilize a sufficient force, coupled with the inadequacy of the Russian railroad network, would result in the piecemeal delivery of armies which would be exhausted one by one without ever being able to mount a solid defense. The Soviet war plan which had been prepared and was immediately put into operation provided for the concentration of the main body of the Red Army deep within Russian territory, and, consequently, at the time of the German attack only comparatively light forces were stationed in the frontier zone. Though these forward troops were soon in a desperate position, the Red Army commanders held firmly to the policy they had previously adopted—retreat with local counterattacks to slow the advance of the enemy and wear him down. As it moved slowly backward, the army evacuated a great part of the industrial and agricultural equipment to the remote regions beyond the Urals, and as section after section was abandoned the "scorched earth" policy was applied to destroy everything of military use which could not be removed. As retreat followed retreat the strain on morale mounted. In order to prevent any deterioration of the fighting spirit in either the army or the civilian population and in order further to facilitate the coördination of the army and civilian fighters harassing the enemy in the rear, the system of political commissars—or military commissars, as they were now called—was restored in an order of July 16.

The main force of the initial German drive was delivered in the center sector in the direction of Minsk, and by the middle of July the invading troops had already penetrated to the Smolensk region. Only then did the Russian commanders decide to make their first determined stand. The ensuing battle of Smolensk, a titanic clash which lasted from the middle of July through the month of September, was, perhaps, one of the decisive battles of the war. It was here that the Russians first succeeded in stopping the German advance, and though the halt was only temporary, it was sufficient to prevent the Germans from seizing Moscow and to doom them to a frightful winter of suffering. The battle had an additional value for the Russians for it enabled the Soviet strategists to measure the fighting abilities, the tactics, and the equipment of the two armies and provided them with the opportunity to improve their own methods and adjust them to the exacting demands of mechanized warfare.

The lack of training in actual combat conditions of modern war proved costly to the Russians on other parts of the vast front. While the Nazi machine was stalled in the Smolensk area for more than two months, the Germans scored dangerously both to the north and to the south. Moving through the Baltic states with little resistance, the vanguard of their armies finally reached the outskirts of Leningrad; in the south Kiev was occupied by September 20 and the Perekop Isthmus was forced on October 30. Though Voroshilov and Budenny showed the same valiant spirit as they had in the civil war, when it became apparent that they had not sufficiently mastered the new techniques that had developed with mechanization, both resigned their commands and were assigned less hazardous posts in the rear. By November German pincers extending through both the northern and southern sectors threatened to nullify the heroic stand at Smolensk, and for a time it seemed that Moscow itself might fall in an enormous enveloping move.

Hitler's confidence reached its height when he declared on October 3, "The enemy is already broken and will never rise again." His speech served as the signal for the start of a violent German offensive to smash the Smolensk armies and to drive on to take Moscow in a direct frontal assault. At this juncture there came another shift in the Russian command; Timoshenko was transferred to the southern front and Zhukov was assigned the heavy task of holding the lines around Moscow. Throughout November the Germans launched a series of ferocious, battering attacks against both the central and the southern fronts. At the high point of their advance in the south on November 22, they were able to bludgeon their way into Rostov, but a week later the Russians recaptured the city in a counterdrive that stopped the invaders at the gateway to the Caucasus. Meanwhile, the position of Moscow seemed hopeless as the German army piled up at the approaches of the city and sent troops swinging around the capital to cut communications with the rear. In the bitter Russian winter hundreds of thousands of soldiers stormed backward and forward over the ringing ground as the great armies struggled for a mortal grip. And there, almost within artillery range of the spires of the Kremlin, with victory on its fingertips, the German army was stopped.

On December 6 a carefully prepared and brilliantly executed counteroffensive was hurled at the numbed, ill-clad Germans. Armed with special winter equipment designed to function efficiently at temperatures far below zero and clothed in uniforms adapted to the Russian climate, Red Army men were able to take advantage of every weakness in the German army and to exploit every crack they were able to open in the Nazi lines. The noose that had been drawing around Moscow was cut and Soviet troops, pressing on relentlessly on the heels of a frozen and dejected German army, forced them to fight a bitter retreat which lasted until the spring thaws ended the campaign in March, 1942. Having suffered tremendous losses and endured one of the cruelest ordeals in modern military history, as the first stage of the war ended the Germans were at last able to establish the center of their forces on the line running from Rzhev to Viazma.

4.

THE war deeply affected Russian national consciousness, much more deeply and in many more ways than the first World War ever had. The very nature of this devastating "total" war differentiated it from all previous conflicts of modern times; even the first World War, in spite of its violence and magnitude, today seems "Victorian" when compared with the second. The present war is not only a battle between armies but also, in its widest sense, a struggle between peoples, and the blows that fall upon the civilian populations are nearly as heavy as those exchanged by the armed forces.

In the first World War it was not military defeat which forced Russia out of the war. The disintegration which brought her to sue for peace began, not in the army, but in the rear among a people lacking in the complete unity essential to the successful prosecution of a long and wearying conflict. The Russian Empire was riddled with divisions. At the head there was the political conflict between the Tsar and the Duma; among the people there was a rising social unrest fed by the fires of the class struggle; as the war dragged on, throughout the whole empire there was noticeable an apathetic spirit, a serious lack of a central national patriotism. Among the peasants, in particular, there existed a lack of concern with the problems and possible consequences of the war. "We are from Kaluga. The enemy will never reach us," was a saying typical of millions of the population. Underlying this tepid attitude was the insufficient realization of the scope of the danger. It seemed inconceivable then that the Germans ever would or ever could subjugate Russia, and the possibility was made all the more remote by the fact that the Germans were at the same time heavily engaged with the Allies in Europe. Because of these divisions the nation as a whole did not provide sufficient moral support for the armies which, however, still continued until the eve of the revolution to fight valiantly on all fronts. The lack of national unity was also a contributing factor in the failure of the Government to supply adequate arms and equipment to the troops, a failure which counted heavily against them at the beginning of the war though the deficiency was somewhat made up toward the end of 1916.

By 1941, however, conditions within the Soviet Union had been greatly altered and the changes were reflected in the response of the population at large as well as that of the troops. To begin with, a political conflict—one between Stalin and the Supreme Soviet, for example—was simply impossible since both represented the will of a single all-powerful party. Furthermore, twenty-five years of life under a system of planned national economy had had its effect; organized governmental propaganda and the conditions of life and work themselves had developed a deep sense of interdependence in all citizens, factory worker and kolkhoz member alike. Every Moscow housewife understood that the loss of the Ukraine would very soon mean less food for her table, that the seizure of Baku would mean a shortage of kerosene in Moscow. She knew, and the members of the collective farms beyond the Urals knew, that if the Germans should ever cut off the flow of petroleum, the tractors would in time stand useless in the fields and Russians would be without bread. For years before the beginning of the second World War the Government had been warning the people of the precarious isolation of "the only socialist country in the world," and had been preparing them for the possibility of an attack by one or more "capitalist powers." However, in the months following the conclusion of the nonaggression pact with Germany the Government's stand had been confusing. In trying to avoid any move which the Germans might seize upon as a pretext for an attack, the official press had represented Soviet-German relations as fundamentally sound. In addition, the belief was frequently expressed in official statements that, even if war should come, the invaders would be hurled back and the decision would be won on enemy territory. This shift in the Government's position, while it had not obliterated the effects of the teaching of the preceding two decades, had to some extent disarmed the Russian people. When the German blow did fall, it came like a bolt out of the blue, completely unexpected and much more stunning than it might otherwise have been.

In the crisis, however, the Russians rallied quickly. A nationwide drive for volunteers for the civilian and army services was immediately organized among the youth, and both young men and women responded enthusiastically to the call. Factory workers voluntarily increased their working hours and speeded up their machines in order to increase the production of military equipment and munitions. The reaction of the peasants appears to have been somewhat slower on the whole. The village population, however, soon learned the real meaning of war from the German occupational authorities who instituted a *régime* replete with the seizure of hostages, the deportation of Russian workers to Poland and Germany, and the requisitioning of all available food supplies. Tales of what the Germans had done in White Russia traveled fast to the east to warn the people of central Russia of what an enemy victory held in store for them. The excesses of the conquerors did more than all the Soviet propaganda to solidify the Russian will to resist.

As the Germans advanced eastward and absorbed more and more Ukrainian and Russian territory, they had to use a number of Russians for the civilian administration of the conquered towns and villages. A number of Ukrainian separatists and Russian monarchist émigrés who had followed the German armies eastward were assigned minor posts in the German administration of the occupied territories, and some native inhabitants either voluntarily agreed or were drafted by the Germans to serve as mayors, clerks, police officers, or other petty officials. Most of those who agreed to such service belonged to the remnants of the *bourgeois* or kulak classes. However, their number was on the whole small, and, as far as can be judged from the evidence available, they enjoyed little, if any, prestige among the population. Wherever military reverses forced the Germans to retreat, the fate of the "collaborators" was certain and bloody. The population which had suffered at their hands was always ready to paint them out, and the vengeance exacted by the guerrilla fighters especially can well be imagined.

All in all, by the fall of 1941, the national unity of the Russian people had been firmly cemented. All groups joined with the Government in promoting a great revival of patriotic feeling. The most famous Soviet authors—men like Alexei Tolstoy, Ilya Ehrenburg, Eugene Petrov, and others—volunteered as war correspondents, and many of them, including Petrov, lost their lives at the front. Artists, contributing their services through their organizations, designed and produced posters on every phase of military and home-front activities. The revival of patriotism had for several years been reflected in literature (the rise of the historical novel), in education (especially in the teaching of history), in art (particularly in motion pictures), in the army (the emphasis on the glorious traditions of the Russian army) and in religion (the milder attitude toward the church). The movement now reached its peak. The war was universally referred to as the "sacred patriotic war" or "the Second War of the Fatherland"—the first being that of 1812. There soon appeared a series of new novels and plays on the war theme, many of them hastily written and mediocre but some of a remarkable literary quality. The writing of the day uniformly stressed the importance of national unity and appealed to the people to forget the old class divisions. In some of the novels and plays a former tsarist officer, for example, would be represented as throwing his whole strength into the war on the side of the Red Army (as in Constantine Simonov's play, *The Russian People*). In others, on the other hand, the old-fashioned commander of civil war days was shown to be unequal to the tasks of modern war and the new type of machine-minded officer was presented as the ideal (as in A. Korneichuk's play, *The Front*). But whatever particular situation or event served as the basis for their work, the artist and the intellectual strove always to aid in some way in the prosecution of the war.

Evidence of the rise of the spirit of nationalism was to be found in almost every organization and every field of activity. The changes in army attitudes were, perhaps, as characteristic as any. The glorification of Russian history was emphasized in the creation of new military decorations for exceptional deeds of heroism—the Orders of Alexander Nevsky, Kutuzov, and Suvorov, for example. An equally revealing change occurred in January, 1942, when the army newspaper, *Red Star,* replaced the old revolutionary slogan which it had long carried on its front page, "Proletarians of the whole world, unite," with the grim motto, "Death to the German invaders." Significant, too, was the reception accorded the drive for national unity by all religious groups. Metropolitan Sergius and the heads of the Living Church, the Baptists, the Judaic Congregations, and the Moslems sent greetings to Stalin and invoked blessings upon him as the national leader. Many religious groups organized and took an active part in drives to collect money for the war effort and to promote subscriptions to war loans. The amount of money collected from these sources was considerable, which, in itself is some indication that the material position of the churches had improved during the years immediately preceding the war in spite of the legal restrictions still in force. The response of the factory workers and kolkhoz members, was, of course, no less adequate than that of other groups. They contributed generously to the financial support of the war and were a large factor in the success of the war loan of the spring of 1943, which was early oversubscribed. In addition, their organizations plunged into the effort on the home front, taking an important part in such civilian activities as the evacuation of children, the care of the wounded, the housing of refugees, etc. Women were quick to volunteer to replace the men who had been called to the armed services from agriculture and industry, and displayed magnificent courage and determination in undertaking difficult and dangerous tasks. Throughout the country, in city and village and farm, the people showed themselves to be willing and coöperative in the performance of every duty—from heroic assistance to the army in the defense of Leningrad and Stalingrad to the day-to-day job of caring for children in nurseries.

In spite of careful governmental planning and in spite of the help, especially from America, which the Soviet Union received through Lend-Lease channels, the civilian population had to endure severe deprivation and hardship. Because of the loss of enormously rich agricultural regions such as the Ukraine and, in 1942, the northern Caucasus—the latter was held by the Germans for only a brief period, but, unfortunately for the Russians, a period coinciding with the harvest—the supply of basic foods was dangerously reduced. Especially in north Russia shortages became alarming, and to insure the distribution of food even on a subsistence level it became necessary to institute strict rationing. Since all industrial facilities were turned over to the production of military supplies immediately after the invasion, the scarcity of clothing and other consumer goods soon created additional hardships. Even though the controls set up by the Soviet Government have functioned much more efficiently than those instituted in 1914–17, it seems certain that the actual suffering of the civilian population has been far greater in this war than at any time during the first World War.

In spite of all the shock and strain, the terror and the pressure to which the Soviet people have been subjected, they have displayed a remarkable devotion to the cause of the nation. There has nowhere been a suggestion of revolt by any large national or social group, and nowhere evidence of even passive resistance such as that which developed early in the last war. Though this is being written while the war is still in progress (December, 1943), it seems safe to say that the social fabric of Soviet Russia has proved immensely stronger than that of tsarist Russia. Its strength, in part at least, is psychological. The rising spirit of Soviet nationalism is all embracing, a patriotism which includes all the nationalities within the Russian state, threatens none, and seems to inspire all of them equally in the defense of the Soviet Union. Today one can speak of Soviet nationalism in the broadest, general sense as the mature development of a feeling of national responsibility.

5.

Before Hitler's attack on Russia, relations between the Soviet Union and the Anglo-Saxon countries had been characterized, as we have seen, by mutual distrust and suspicion. The first result of the German invasion was the immediate installation of the Soviet Union in the camp of the Allies; whether formally recognized or not, the logic of the situation at once made Russia an ally of Great Britain. Circumstances forced the two countries to coördinate their efforts against a common enemy, and, as events transpired, for the next two years it was the Soviet Union that had to bear the full brunt of the German assault. It is possible that even after the internment of Rudolph Hess, the Germans hoped that Great Britain might tacitly, if not openly, accept his message and refrain from interference with the German offensive in Russia. If they did entertain such hopes, they were quickly disillusioned. Within the space of hours Winston Churchill had declared his country's complete solidarity with Russia. Sir Stafford Cripps was immediately sent to Moscow to establish a working contact with the Soviet Government, and on July 12, 1941, a solemn agreement for joint action between the two governments was signed.

A secondary result of the German war in Russia was the beginning of a measure of relief for the bomb-shocked, weary English people. As the Germans thrust deeper into Russia, they threw all their available forces to the east, and London and other shattered British cities were spared, for the time being at least, the devastating bombing raids of the preceding months. The average Briton could not but feel gratitude to the Russians who, by their determined stand, had provided some respite for Great Britain. It is true there remained conservative circles in which an attitude of fear and coldness toward the Soviets was much in evidence; early in September, for example, a member of the British Cabinet, J. T. C. Moore-Barbazon rose to express the hope that the Red Army and the German army would exterminate each other. However, such churlish statements were comparatively rare, usually confined to ultraconservative groups, and never representative of the opinion of the general British public.

In the United States—at that time, of course, not officially in the war—public opinion changed more slowly. President Roosevelt, however, at a press conference two days after the German attack made it clear that the United States would help Russia. The Treasury Department immediately released a part of the Soviet funds which had been frozen in the United States at the time of the Russo-Finnish War, and on October 30 a billion-dollar loan was granted to the Soviet Union for the purchase of armaments and supplies. There remained, nevertheless, a very tangible difference between the British attitude and the American attitude toward Russia. The United States was still at peace, officially; she was remote from the war, psychologically and geographically; bombs had never fallen on an American city. Consequently, the turn in public opinion toward Russia did not come as quickly as it did in Britain, nor was it as far reaching. For a long time Russia was considered in a special category—not so much as an ally but rather as an enemy of our enemy. Later, after Pearl Harbor and the German declaration of war against the United States, and after Russia's continued heroic resistance had had time to develop a feeling of admiration in wide sections of the American public, the rapprochement with the Soviets found broader and more genuine support. In time a Russian War Relief group was organized to carry on work paralleling that of the British and China War Relief organizations and its drives met with considerable success. By the fall of 1942 Russian War Relief was receiving very general public support, and in most cities throughout the country it had been sufficiently well received to make it possible to pool all the national relief drives in a single combined effort.

Just as it was not easy for the United States and, to a lesser extent, for Great Britain wholeheartedly to accept Russia as an ally, Russia found it difficult to adjust her attitudes to the new situation. Soviet leaders could not at once rid themselves of the fear that the Anglo-Saxon countries intended to attempt to use Russia as a pawn, and statements such as that of Moore-Barbazon and occasional articles in irresponsible publications were fuel for their suspicions. In a speech on July 3, 1941, Stalin expressed the hope that in her war of liberation Russia would have "loyal allies in the peoples of Europe and America," but he was careful to avoid any definite commitments in regard to the Anglo-Saxon countries. Russia needed Britain's help, and when the trickle of supplies which she received in the beginning gradually began to assume important proportions, she was grateful. The supplies were necessary, and all Russians accepted them with thanks. But as time went on they hoped for more direct support; they began to expect a more active military effort on the part of Great Britain. However, Russia expressed complete willingness to come to terms with both Great Britain and the United States by adhering to the Atlantic Charter of August 14, 1941, as well as by signing the Declaration of the United Nations of January 1, 1942.

As Russian defenses stiffened toward the end of the first year of the Soviet-German war, British and American confidence in the seriousness of the Russian effort grew. The warming of relations encouraged the visit of Foreign Commissar Molotov to both London and Washington in June, 1942. In London a twenty-year treaty of alliance was signed by Great Britain and the Soviet Union, a treaty which provided not only for common action between the two countries during the war but also for their collaboration afterward for "the organization of security and the economic prosperity of Europe." In Washington Molotov met with less success than he had in London; the United States avoided a formal alliance with the Soviet Union, in all probability because of her reluctance to recognize Soviet control over the Baltic states. That did not mean that the Government would not continue to support the Russian military effort; the Soviets were included in the Lend-Lease plan and an agreement to that effect was signed by both countries. Indeed, from then on supplies were shipped both through Murmansk and Iran in constantly increasing amounts, and by July, 1943, the United States had achieved the goal of moving a million tons of equipment a month over the Iran route alone.

It appears, however, that the main purpose of Molotov's visit was to secure the opening of the so-called second front in Europe. On this subject neither President Roosevelt nor Prime Minister Churchill could do more than express their desire to establish such a front before the year was out, but both Stalin and Molotov seem to have considered that statement a definite commitment. The misunderstanding which seems to have arisen here resulted in considerable disappointment in Moscow when the summer came and went without the Allies having taken any action. In his letter of October 4, 1942, to Henry Cassidy, an American correspondent in Moscow, Stalin said bluntly that "the aid of the Allies to the Soviet Union has so far been little effective," and recommended that "the Allies fulfill their obligations fully and on time." The landing of Allied troops in North Africa in November, 1942, somewhat improved the situation, since it was recognized in Moscow that thenceforward German attention would necessarily be divided and that the African campaign was certain to result in psychological if not material help to Russia. The North African landing was not, however, accepted by the Russians as a full-fledged second front and they continued to remind the democracies that the promise of an invasion of Europe had not so far been realized. On February 23, 1943, in a speech on the occasion of the twenty-fifth anniversary of the founding of the Red Army, Stalin pointedly emphasized the fact that "in view of the absence of the second front in Europe the Red Army alone is bearing the full weight of the war."

The American Government, on the other hand, sometimes found conditions in Russia not completely to its liking. Admiral Standley, the United States Ambassador in Moscow, in a public statement on March 8, 1943, expressed his dissatisfaction with the Soviet Government's reluctance to exchange information on the conduct of the war. He complained, too, that American aid to Russia—through Lend-Lease, Russian War Relief, and other channels—could not be sufficiently appreciated by the Russian people because the Russian Government told them little about it. This charge was objected to by many Americans, including such men as Senator Connally, Representative Bloom, and Edward C. Carter, president of Russian War Relief. They declared their belief that the Russian people had been well aware of American help; they reported that every shipment of medical supplies and clothing received from Russian War Relief had been duly acknowledged. The appearance of American airplanes and tanks on the Russian front, they observed, certainly could not have been kept secret from the Red Army men even if Soviet leaders had any such intentions, and it was well known that some American foods—lard, for instance—had already become exceedingly popular with Moscow housewives. The incident, though not important in itself, made an unfortunate impression in both countries. It is, however, perhaps significant that in order to avoid a repetition the Soviet Government has since gone to considerable lengths to publicize American aid through the press and the radio.

As the war progressed and as the democracies began to be more active in its prosecution, there was a noticeable improvement in the relations between the Soviets and the Anglo-Saxon countries. In his order of the day on May 1, 1943, Stalin took cognizance of the Allied successes in Africa. The capture of Tunisia, which constituted a German rout similar in some ways to that at Stalingrad, and especially the landing in Sicily in July seem to have convinced the Russians that the Allies were waging war in all earnestness. They were convinced of the sincere intention of the democracies to open a second front, though the question of when it should be done continued to be a sore point.

6.

On April 26, 1942, Hitler unequivocally declared that the decision of the war must fall on the eastern front, and Russia was thus warned that a renewed German drive was imminent. In spite of the substantial successes which they had achieved during the campaigns of the preceding winter, the Russians did not minimize the dangers that now threatened them. The concentration of almost the whole of Europe's man power and industrial facilities in Hitler's hands made the German army the most formidable military machine in the world. R.A.F. raids over Germany and France which were later to take a heavy toll of German production were still in an experimental stage, and the German industrial system had nowhere shown any signs of disorganization. In 1942 it is probable that German and German-controlled production of armament and munitions was rising to its peak, and, in spite of substantial German losses in men and material in the campaigns of 1941, the Russians could reasonably expect the German army to be stronger in 1942 than it had been a year before.

The Red Army, however, had also been gathering strength during the preceding year. It had acquired valuable experience both in defensive and offensive warfare; a substantial percentage of the troops was battle-trained, and the leadership was everywhere in competent hands. Russian industries in the safe areas of the Urals were now pouring out equipment, and British and American aid in material was beginning to be felt on a larger scale. More important, perhaps, was the strengthening of national morale which had resulted from the successes of the preceding winter. The elimination of the "military commissars" on October 9, 1942, was a concrete demonstration of the Soviet leaders' belief in the new spirit, a spirit of mutual confidence between the army and the nation as a whole.

In order to postpone if not forestall altogether the expected German offensive, the Red Army command determined in the spring of 1942 to launch an attack of its own even if it had to be a very limited one. On May 12 Timoshenko struck in the direction of Kharkov. Though he suffered heavy losses without being able to take the city, he did succeed in forcing the Germans to call up reserves and reinforcements from other sectors and thus temporarily upset German plans in that area. In the meantime, however, Russian defenses were being overrun along other parts of the wide front. The Germans took a part of eastern Crimea which gave them control of the Kerch Strait and of the near by iron mines and at the same time completed the isolation of Sevastopol. However, it was not until the end of June that they were able to begin their major drive and by that time it had become necessary for them to settle upon more limited objectives than those of 1941. Instead of attacking along the whole front from the Baltic to the Black Sea, they now had to concentrate their forces in the south alone. Caucasian oil and not the annihilation of the Red Army became their important objective, and a break-through to Iran which might eventually have led to a union with the Japanese became a dream to be hoped for only in the event of the total and unexpected collapse of Russian resistance.

The main German blow was delivered against the Don area between Voronezh and Rostov. The German plan was an ambitious one, and had they succeeded in the opening drive all along the line, they would have provided themselves with a number of possibilities, the most likely of which would probably have been a deep and dangerous flanking movement against Moscow itself. However Voronezh, at the very northern end of the front, held against their heaviest assaults, and the German offensive consequently could develop only in a southern and southeastern direction—against the Caucasus and the lower Volga. That, in turn, posed other problems: in order to protect their western flank while they drove into the Caucasus, it was necessary that the Germans establish complete control over Crimea. To do that they were forced to undertake at any cost the complete reduction of the last Russian bastion in Crimea, Sevastopol. If for no other reason than the fact that the Germans had secured complete control of the air in that area, Sevastopol was a doomed city from the very beginning of the siege. It was a fortress that could be taken—but only at a fearful price. The Germans had to take the city, and the defenders were determined to resist to the last man, for they knew that by their resistance they could inflict heavy losses on the enemy and delay him beyond all possibility of his reaching his major objective that year. The besiegers threw an enormous weight of armament against the city, and as the days dragged on into weeks it became apparent that for the second time within a century, against hopeless odds, Sevastopol was throwing up an incredibly stubborn defense which would remain forever a saga of Russian heroism. The Russians fought for the city foot by foot and stone by stone. When Sevastopol fell, it was a heap of rubble, a tombstone.

The Crimea having been wrenched from Russian control, the Germans were now free to continue their desperate drive for the Caucasian oil fields. On July 24 the hard-pressed Russians were again forced out of Rostov, and the advancing German troops, reinforced by an army that had swung down through Crimea and crossed the Kerch Strait, slogged on into the northern Caucasus. They seized the important Maikop oil fields—but only after they had been wrecked and put to the torch by the Russians—and menaced both Ordjonikidze (Vladikavkaz) at the northern entrance of the vital Georgian military road across the Caucasian Mountains, and the Grozny oil fields from which the Russians drew a large part of their petroleum supplies. The Black Sea port of Novorossiisk fell, and with both Sevastopol and Novorossiisk in German hands the Russian Black Sea squadron was forced back on Batum, a poor harbor with insufficient facilities for a naval base. With the Soviet troops staggering backward all along the southern front, it seemed that nothing could prevent the victorious Germans from overrunning the Grozny fields and continuing their advance to their ultimate goal in Baku. The Germans, themselves, however, were not as confident of their position as some observers. Before they had begun their advance they had removed the Russian armies in the Crimea as a menace on their western flank; now, as their lines lengthened into the Caucasus, the unconquered lower Volga salient threatened their eastern flank. Just as it had been necessary to destroy Sevastopol it now became necessary to reduce another Russian bastion, a city on the Volga—Stalingrad.

The story of the defense of Stalingrad will in the future belong to the epic poet rather than to the historian. It is a story of unbelievable endurance in the face of overwhelming odds, of bloodshed and sacrifice on a scale unequaled in modern military history. So tenacious was the Russian resistance and so determined was Hitler to break it that the conquest of that one city lying in a bend of the Volga at last became a cardinal point of German military honor. As if hypnotized by the magnitude of the task they had set for themselves, all through the fall of 1942 the Germans sent division after division, wave after wave crashing against the citadel. Retreating from house to house and then from room to room, extracting a terrific price in blood for every foot of the shell-torn streets, the Russians were at last forced into a rubble-strewn strip of land no more than a few hundred yards wide. Backed up into that narrow corner, Red Army men withstood every attack the Germans could hurl at them. And in that corner, in those ruins, their commanders prepared the destruction of the army surrounding them. North and south of the city Russian troops began hacking at the flanks of the attackers. The German command dismissed these attacks as desperate sallies designed to relieve the pressure on the center and flung still more men against the tight little knot of resistance still clinging to the icy bank of the Volga. The jaws of massive pincers moved around the German army, and, apparently before the Nazi command was aware of the danger, closed around 350,000 exhausted German troops. Methodically the Red Army, under the command of Marshal Zhukov and General Rokosovsky, proceeded with the annihilation of this tremendous force, destroying it piece by piece within this bristling ring. In January, 1943, some 90,000 Germans surrendered—all that was left of the mighty German army that had stood before Stalingrad.

Some Russian military writers have called the victory at Stalingrad a threefold revenge for the 1914 defeat at Tannenberg. It was at least that. Looked at in the light of subsequent events, the battle of Stalingrad was surely the turning point of the 1942 campaign, probably one of the truly decisive struggles of the war, and, perhaps, in a larger sense, the dividing line between two worlds.

While the battle of Stalingrad was in progress, the Russians had been able to mount attacks in several other sectors. In time the drives which they developed near Voronezh and near Ordjonikidze threatened all of the German armies on the southern front and finally forced them to retreat in order to avoid a catastrophe similar to that which had overtaken them at Stalingrad. In the extreme north, too, the Russians took advantage of the changed situation to improve their position around Leningrad. In January, 1943, they succeeded in retaking Schluesselburg on the shore of Lake Ladoga and in driving the Germans back from the Leningrad-Vologda railway. While these operations were not sufficient to relieve Leningrad from siege, they did establish at least one rail link with the rear and thus improved somewhat the desperate condition of the people within the city. Meanwhile the Red Army continued offensive action all along the southern front. Rostov was again recaptured, and, striking boldly at the retreating German armies in the Donets region, the Russians rushed westward until by the end of February, 1943, they had occupied Kursk, Belgorod, and Kharkov. As the Russian armies swept on from these newly captured strong points, it seemed for a time that the Germans would be forced to continue their retreat to the Dnieper. The Russians, however, overreached themselves. The recaptured railways upon which they depended for the movement of much of their supplies all had to be laboriously reconverted from the narrow European gauge to which the Germans had adapted them, and in their rapid sweep across the Donets the Russians outran the work of reconversion and dangerously weakened their extended lines of communications. Meanwhile, feeling that the Allied threat of an invasion of western Europe could not materialize that summer—even the Tunisian operation was still making but little headway—Hitler was free to throw sufficient reserves into the Donets fighting to stop the Russians and force them back from the advance positions which they had not had time to fortify.

This resurgence of German power compelled the Russians to attempt to drain some of the Nazi armies from the southern front by the creation of a "second front" of their own in the Lake Ilmen and Velikie Luki sector. In this new Red Army drive the Russians scored an important success by eliminating the powerful triangle of German fortresses in Rzhev, Gzhatsk, and Viazma which throughout the winter had remained a potential threat to Moscow. Though the advance toward Smolensk, perhaps the most important and best-fortified German defense point in the north, gradually bogged down, the Russian offensive had succeeded in preventing the Germans from shifting important reserves southward to exploit their advantages in the Donets. The Nazis were able to muster enough strength to retake Kharkov and Belgorod by the end of March, but all their attempts to force a crossing of the Donets River collapsed after three weeks of severe fighting. By the beginning of April the eastern front was once more stabilized and both armies took advantage of the period of the spring thaws to rest and prepare for renewed summer offensives.

The second winter campaign was thus even more fruitful for the Russians than the first. Though the Germans had been able to hold strategically important Novorossiisk and the Taman bridgehead, they had lost practically the whole of the north Caucasus with its vital oil deposits and its agricultural riches. Germany's southern drive which had begun with such smashing victories had in the end become little more than a costly adventure involving the loss of an enormous amount of material and a disastrous expenditure of man power. The Russians, on the other hand, during the winter had improved their position along the whole length of the front. In the north they had broken the strangling German encirclement of Leningrad. In the center they had blunted the most dangerous German salient thrust toward Moscow and had thrown the invaders back onto the defense in the Smolensk area. By cutting the Moscow-Kharkov railway at Kursk, they had prevented the Germans from using it to strengthen their two most powerful advance positions, Orel and the recently recaptured Kharkov. On the extreme southern front the Russians had sealed the German armies in Novorossiisk and the Taman bridgehead and had themselves taken up positions which menaced the Nazi foothold in the Caucasus and Crimea. In the brief interval of enforced rest between winter and summer violence, the Russians were able to face the future with a confidence based on growing strength. The Germans were haunted by the ever-increasing necessity to finish quickly a task which had already grown beyond all expectations and whose end seemed ever more remote.

7.

THE circumstances surrounding the outbreak of the second World War and the developments of the first two years of the conflict revealed clearly enough that, contrary to the expectations of many, the division of forces had been drawn on the basis of nationalities rather than classes, that national boundaries rather than international class lines separated the opposing groups. The emphasis on Russian patriotism reflected Soviet recognition of the national character of the war and foreshadowed other adjustments which the Soviet Union could be expected to make to meet the situation. The Communist International was, of course, a symbol of the revolutionary interpretation of international class solidarity; with the working out of the pattern of the war and with the improvement of relations between the Soviets and the Anglo-Saxon countries it more and more became an anachronism. It had ceased to conform to the realities of Russian national policies and remained only as a source of irritation and worry to the democratic allies in the war. It had, in fact, become a positive detriment to the Russian war effort for its continued existence furnished substance for Nazi propaganda at home and abroad, and provided some pretext for the continuation of alliances such as the Anti-Comintern Pact to which smaller neutral countries like Spain could still adhere. Useless in the immediate struggle and dangerous to the continued growth of friendly relations between the Allies, the Communist International was ripe for the dissolution which awaited it.

We have already seen (in Chap. XVIII, Sec. 1) that the Seventh Congress of the Communist International in 1935 revealed a curtailment of the activities and a marked diminution of the fighting spirit of that body. For various reasons, principally the fear of Trotskyite opposition, no more congresses were allowed to convene, and in the years after 1935 the Executive Committee of the International more and more assumed the character of a subsidiary organ of the All-Union Communist party. It was brought forward when and if the foreign policy of the Soviet Union required its support, and even in these relatively infrequent occasions—notably in the case of the Soviet-Finnish War—its activities often resulted in more harm than help. As a result of this progressive disuse of the body, the Presidium of the Executive Committee of the Communist International on May 22, 1943, moved the dissolution of the whole organization. After emphasizing the important rôle of the International in accomplishing historically necessary functions, the Presidium concluded that, since in the present war the division definitely did not correspond to class lines but was rather a conflict between the Hitlerite military machine and an anti-Hitlerite coalition, the International no longer served an essential political purpose. The national Communist parties which had previously been affiliated with the International were advised to shape their policies in accordance with their own judgment of the national situation. The resolution was then submitted to the various Communist parties throughout the world and with their approval the International had ceased to exist.

To those not intimately acquainted with the events of recent Russian history the news came as a bombshell. The Nazi propaganda machine, always quick to recover, immediately attempted to parry the blow by trumpeting that the resolution represented nothing more than lip service to Russia's uneasy allies, that the move was only a cover for the intensification of communist penetration in all countries, and that, even if the International were temporarily abolished, it would certainly be revived after the war. Even in the Allied countries the announcement was received with mixed feelings and doubts were frequently expressed as to the sincerity of the move. Though this is being written too soon after the event to allow definite predictions, it is possible to offer some comments on the circumstances surrounding the dissolution. The Presidium's resolution follows logically the sequence of trends in Russian political and social developments since the beginning of the First Five Year Plan. In a sense, it brings to a conclusion the whole Stalin-Trotsky controversy, and may well be considered an aftermath of the trials of 1936–38 which resulted in the elimination of Zinoviev and the other leaders of the old internationalist group. Just as clearly the move away from internationalism is in complete agreement with the total Russian attitude toward the war. Finally—and perhaps most significant for the democracies—the adoption and wide publicizing of such a resolution, even if it should prove less than completely sincere, is evidence of an important change in the Soviet spirit which may have tremendous consequences in the postwar world.

Coincident with the weakening and final dissolution of the Communist International and paralleling the growth of Soviet nationalism came the revival of Pan-Slavism. Apparently buried forever with the imperial *régime,* the Pan-Slav movement dramatically reappeared in Moscow, perhaps as an inevitable corollary of the shift in Soviet policies from an international to a national base. Having abandoned the communist lever as a method of influencing world politics, Russia now reverted to her old technique of seeking friends beyond her borders among her kin. To say that the Soviets "reverted" to Pan-Slavism is perhaps misleading, for between the present movement and that encouraged by tsarist Russia there are essential differences. Whereas religious affiliations between Imperial Russia and the Orthodox Slav peoples of the Balkan Peninsula were once the firmest ties, today the ethnic and cultural affinities are the primary links.

However, the present-day Soviet leaders are not entirely neglecting the religious aspects either, and the reëstablishment of the Patriarchate in Moscow (September 12, 1943) cannot fail to produce a favorable impression among the Orthodox peoples of the Balkan Peninsula. In any case, the basic and fundamental difference between the old and the new Pan-Slav movement is political. The Pan-Slavism of Imperial Russia was an instrument of the conservative political elements of the time. The present movement, on the other hand, is built on a democratic foundation and has enlisted the support of democratic groups in all Slavic nations.

The real founder of modern Pan-Slavism was, of course, none other than Hitler himself. By his propagation of the doctrine of German racial superiority over the Slav, by his brutal attempts to reduce the Slavic peoples to an amorphous mass of German serfs through the systematic extermination of all cultural leaders in Bohemia, Poland, and Serbia, Hitler himself drove the Slavs toward unity to protect themselves against this self-anointed master race. Nazi fanaticism sank to unprecedented depths in Russia when the Germans officially sanctioned the senseless looting of museums and laboratories and the wanton destruction of historic and artistic shrines dear to the Russian people. The slaughter of actual and potential leaders of Russian resistance was, of course, a major tenet of the Nazi plan of conquest. It was characteristic of the Soviet Government to attempt to differentiate between the Nazi Government and the German people, but the Russian people, millions of whom had been driven from their burning homes and subjected to unthinkable German atrocities, could not long be expected to resist the growth of a violent hatred against the Germans as a people.

The Nazi persecution of the whole Slav people thus prepared the ground both in Russia and in other Slavic countries for the organization of close coöperation. Spokesmen for all Slavic peoples participated in the first All-Slav Congress which met in Moscow as early as August, 1941, and among the organizers and speakers were many prominent Slavic writers, historians, and artists. The emphasis at this meeting was naturally on the cultural ties which bound all the peoples represented in an ethnic unity, and it is with this theme that the Pan-Slavism has continued its steady development. Its literary organ, the magazine *The Slavs* (*Slaviane*), is published in Russian, but it has the active support and collaboration of important leaders of other countries, including President Beneš of the Czechoslovak Republic.

As always, Russo-Polish relations presented a delicate problem and at once became a stumbling block in the way of Slavic unity. There is a long history of Polish antagonism toward the Russians, and it is only natural that the older resentments had been increased by the recent Soviet occupation of eastern Poland in September, 1939. On the other hand, Russia could not well forgive the Polish attack of 1920 which had resulted in the Polish annexation of a considerable part of western White Russia and western Ukraine. The reoccupation of that territory in 1939, from the Soviet point of view, represented nothing more than the recapture of land which had been forcibly taken from Russia during the turmoil of the civil war. In addition to these specific points of contention, the general tone of relations between the two countries during the interval between 1921 and 1939 had been anything but friendly, and at times had been especially complicated by Soviet antireligious moves and by the violent opposition of Polish Catholicism to every aspect of communism.

When the German attack placed Russia on the side of the Allies, to whose camp Poland had, of course, belonged from the beginning of the war, some sort of working agreement between the Soviets and the Polish Government-in-Exile became imperative. A preliminary arrangement, in which such thorny problems as that of the frontiers were avoided, was signed on July 30, 1941. Two weeks later representatives of the two countries concluded a military agreement which provided for the formation in Russia of a Polish army to participate in the common struggle against the German invader. Relations seemed to be progressing on a mutually satisfactory basis and in Moscow on December 3, at the end of a friendly conference with General Sikorski, head of the Polish Government-in-Exile, Stalin took the opportunity to declare his belief that a strong Poland was essential for a lasting European peace.

Relations between the two nations were not, however, to continue on the same smooth course. The Polish army provided for in the agreement was to be recruited among the Polish officers and men who had been taken prisoner by the Red Army at the time of the occupation of "Eastern Poland" in 1939. These men who had been interned at various places—mostly in Kazakhstan—were released upon the conclusion of the military agreement, and immediately set about the organization of the army which was to be equipped with supplies from Great Britain. But it was difficult for either side to forget the injuries of the past, and within a short time friction had once more developed between the Soviet Government and the Polish leaders. At last, toward the end of January, 1942, it was decided to transfer the newly-formed Polish army to Iran where it would operate under British jurisdiction. The whole incident left an unfortunate impression with both nations, and the Russians were particularly disappointed since they had hoped for the immediate participation of the Poles in the war on the eastern front.

Though the Soviet Government tended to become increasingly suspicious of the Polish Government-in-Exile, every effort was made to build and preserve close relations with the Polish people themselves. In this connection it was significant that many of the Poles who had been interned in Russia or who had taken refuge there proved to be of a more democratic spirit than some of the Polish émigrés in London. In 1942 a group of refugees in Russia formed the Union of Polish Patriots and in Moscow began the publication of a Polish language newspaper called *Free Poland.* This group, one of whose leading members was the writer Wanda Wasilewska, as an essential part of its program urged the closest possible coöperation of the Poles with the Soviet Union. In London, meanwhile, the feeling of some groups of Polish émigrés was mounting against the Soviet Union and early in 1943 a number of them started a campaign in both the British and American press urging the Allies to guarantee that the 1921–39 eastern frontier of Poland would be restored after the war. This campaign evoked bitter resentment in the Soviet Union, and in February *Pravda* published an article by the prominent Ukrainian playwright, A. Korneichuk, warning that the Ukrainians and the White Russians would never agree to a return to Polish domination. In April, 1943, relations were further strained by the demand of the Polish Government-in-Exile for an international investigation of alleged Russian atrocities against Polish prisoners which the Germans claimed to have unearthed in territory occupied by them some two years previously. This last episode led on April 26 to an official breaking-off of relations between the Soviet Government and the Polish Government-in-Exile. In some Allied circles the fear was expressed that the Soviet Union would then recognize the Union of Polish Patriots as the legal government of Poland in order to use it as a pawn in the political game, but though the Union offered its support to the Soviets, it was never given official recognition.

In addition to the difficulties with Poland, further Pan-Slavic complications arose in Yugoslavia. The anti-Axis guerrilla movement which developed in that country immediately after its conquest by the Germans was not, unfortunately, united in the struggle against the invaders but had divided into two rival groups whose leaders vied with each other for control of the patriot forces. One group, headed by General D. Mihailovich, operated under the auspices of the Yugoslav Government-in-Exile. The other, known as the "Partisans," led by Josef Broz, known as Comrade Tito, established connections with the Soviet Government, and, while not officially communist, was more radical than the first. Within its ranks, too, both Serbs and Croats were active, while Mihailovich's movement represented a narrower aspect of Serbian nationalism. Of the two, the Partisan movement seems to have developed a wider range of action and may be expected, in addition, to establish better relations with the people of Bulgaria, a country which preserves its prewar form of government under Axis domination, though a considerable part of the population is in opposition. In two other Slavic countries, Slovakia and Croatia, the puppet governments established and propped up by Axis armies can hardly count on the support of any measurable part of their populations, and Slovenia was, until the Italian capitulation, divided between Germany and Italy. In the event of an early or sudden Axis collapse, popular revolutions may be expected to sweep all of these countries, and it is in that period that the Pan-Slav movement will be given its real test. But whatever happens throughout the Slavic world, it seems certain that in its cultural aspects at least the Pan-Slav movement will continue to assume increasing importance even after the termination of the war.

8.

By the spring of 1943 the circumstances of the war in all its international phases had turned greatly in favor of the Allies. On May 9 the Tunisian campaign was brought to a successful conclusion, and along the whole northern coast of Africa the Allies stood ready to launch the Mediterranean assault against Hitler's European fortress. Once again Winston Churchill went to Washington to discuss with President Roosevelt the larger aspects of the war in a meeting in which particular attention could now be given to

Japan and the Pacific operations—a subject which automatically excluded Russia from the discussions. In regard to the situation in western Europe, the conferees seem to have agreed not to hurry the landing of troops in France or Holland, but to concentrate first on an attempt to shatter German industry and weaken German resistance by air attack. There followed almost immediately a series of powerful air raids by R.A.F. bombers and American Flying Fortresses aimed principally at the industrial centers of the Ruhr. In July, 1943, British experts estimated that in the Ruhr alone nearly 1,000,000 homes had been destroyed by bombs and that German authorities had been forced to evacuate no less than 3,000,000 people from the area. This interference with the labor supply in the most concentrated factory area in Europe, coupled with the certain destruction and damage to the plants themselves, must have had a paralyzing effect on the delivery of essential military supplies from the whole region.

No actual invasion of western Europe, however, had yet begun, nor were there signs that one was imminent, and Hitler must have believed that he still had time for another attempt to deal the Russians a crushing blow before the second front could materialize. Accordingly, as soon as the weather permitted in April and May the Germans made several attempts to improve their positions around Novorossiisk and the Taman bridgehead. These attacks were beaten off by the Russians without drawing off any of their forces on the central front where, they knew, the Germans had concentrated the bulk of their mechanized divisions and their air force. While the two armies piled men and material along this front, Soviet fliers kept up a series of harassing raids over railway yards and German centers of communication in the rear, and German bombers made several attacks on the automobile plant in Gorky (Nizhni-Novgorod), on the high-octane gasoline plant in Saratov, and on other Russian industrial centers.

It seems that in preparing for the campaign the Germans also planned to drive a political wedge into the Russian lines. Lacking a fifth column inside Russia, Hitler attempted to create one in Germany by organizing a Russian "anticommunist" army for a crusade against the Bolsheviks. Ever since the spring of 1943 there have been recurring reports in the press that a former Red Army general, taken prisoner by the Germans in 1942, had agreed to organize a "Russian army of liberation." His name was subsequently given as General Vlasov. His agents delivered a number of addresses before Russian émigré audiences in Paris and in other European cities in which they claimed that Vlasov's army, recruited chiefly from the war prisoners, totaled several hundred thousand men. By the end of 1943 this "army" had not merited mention in the communiqués issued by either side, and it may safely be assumed that, if it ever existed at all, the "army" was never more than a group of would-be staff officers drawing salaries from the German treasury.

On July 5 the main German offensive rolled ahead on the full front from Orel to Kharkov. Since Orel lay well forward on a German salient driven into the Russian lines, the Nazis once again could attempt to break through in an effort to flank Moscow, and, should that fail once more, they would still, perhaps, have an opportunity to swing south in an encircling movement against the Russians in the exposed Kursk salient. But this time, instead of adopting their usual tactic of retreating while they wore down the enemy, the Russians were determined to stand firm on their lines and meet the attackers head on. It was a momentous decision, for, if it should have failed to hold fast, the Red Army would certainly have suffered tremendous losses and might well have been thrown into a critical disorganization. For nearly ten days furious battles raged along the front with enormous quantities of aircraft and tanks being hurled into the fray by both sides. During the first few days the Germans inched forward around both Orel and Belgorod, but the Russians were able to seal off the wedges driven into their lines and to prevent their enlargement. By July 15 the German attacks had dwindled with the apparent exhaustion of the Nazi troops, and then it was that the Red Army seized the initiative on the Orel front and surged forward in the Soviet's first summer offensive.

The immediate object of the Red Army was the elimination of the Orel salient, the recapture of Belgorod and Kharkov, and the reëstablishment of the rail connections between Moscow and Kharkov, which would enormously facilitate the movement of supplies to the whole central front and enable the Russians to mount massive drives southward toward the Crimea. After three weeks of heavy fighting the Russians were able to announce the successful conclusion of all preliminary drives in this theater: by August 6 both Orel and Belgorod were in their hands, and two weeks later Kharkov fell to the Red Army troops. The Russian successes were, however, tempered by the fact that the Germans had engaged in an incredible orgy of systematic destruction in every town and city they had been forced to abandon. In Kharkov, for example, fully 65 per cent of the buildings had been burned and blasted to rubble before the Russians reoccupied the city, and many of the structures which still remained on their foundations were so seriously damaged that they were not habitable. Orel was reduced to a shambles as unrecognizable as Kharkov.

The senseless physical obliteration of thriving, vigorous Russian cities was not, perhaps, the most shocking aspect of the German retreat. The shattered and pitiful survivors who remained to greet the Red Army related tales of terror and starvation under the German occupation that would have been completely unbelievable without the mass of corroborating evidence everywhere at hand. A detailed description of the havoc and horror which the Russians uncovered in these cities was reported by Alexander Werth in a despatch to the *New York Times,* and reports of similar atrocities continued to appear with sickening regularity. Interestingly enough, it has been revealed, the churches in Orel—which were almost the only places in which even a few of the Russians were allowed to gather by the German occupation authorities—became rallying points for the city's inhabitants.

After the first stage of the Soviet offensive had been completed, the Red Army leaders chose the natural barrier of the Dnieper as the next goal. Many foreign observers at this time expressed fear that the Russians were overextending themselves, and almost all seemed certain that the Dnieper line was to be the extreme limit of any possible Russian summer offensive. The approach to the Dnieper was an exceptionally difficult operation which required for its success almost perfect synchronization and coördination of effort. In the north sector it was necessary to storm such formidable German bastions as Briansk and Smolensk; in the center important railroad junctions such as Konotop and Poltava had to be brought under control; in the south the liberation of the Donets coal basin was both an economic and strategic necessity.

The Red Army proved equal to these tremendous tasks. Methodically, one by one, the strong points of German resistance were eliminated on each segment of the front. Step by step the Russians advanced along the huge front from Smolensk to Rostov, and as they moved forward in the center, they simultaneously dealt blows to the hard-pressed Germans both in the north, around Velikie Luki and Lake Ladoga, and in the south, in the area around the Taman Peninsula. In addition, a series of daring amphibious operations was undertaken by the Russians at Novorossiisk and along the northern shore of the Sea of Azov. In time, each of these subsidiary drives assumed individual importance of its own, the northern one potentially endangering the German grip on Leningrad and the Baltic coast, and the southern one menacing the German hold in the Crimea.

By October 1 the Russians had reached the Dnieper line on a wide front from Kiev to Zaporozhie. By taking Smolensk they had not only assumed control of the upper part of the river but had spread westward beyond it. Between Smolensk and Kiev their troops had everywhere surged to a line just short of the Dnieper, and the Gomel fortress was almost the only Nazi strong point remaining in the area. To the south the Russians had not only reoccupied the Donets basin but by seizing the Taman Peninsula had also closed the door to the Caucasus. The Germans still clung desperately to a line running from Zaporozhie on the bend of the Dnieper to the Sea of Azov, for they well knew that in the event of a Russian break-through in this sector all the German forces in the Crimea would be bottled up.

As they were forced to abandon city after city the Germans continued the same orgy of demolition they had begun in the earlier stages of their retreat. They even developed new techniques of brutality. Motivated apparently by a desire to collect as much man power as possible for work in German factories, they attempted to drive westward with them the entire population of a number of Russian cities. In some cases they were successful, as for example, in Novorossiisk, a city which the Russians found almost empty when they regained it. Sometimes, however, as in the case of Poltava, the Russian advance was so swift that the Germans were compelled to abandon great herds of men and women whom they were driving away.

At this point most foreign observers and military experts expected the Russian offensive to be halted, at least until late in the fall. It was argued that the Germans obviously had strongly fortified the Dnieper line and its extension overland from Zaporozhie to Melitopol, and it was thought that they would be able to make a strong stand all along it. Indeed, it was reported via Stockholm that Hitler had issued an order to the German troops in Kiev and Melitopol to hold on where they were at all costs. Finally, the approach of the rainy season was thought unfavorable to any further Russian advances, especially since the Russians would have to replace the railways recaptured from the Germans in order to readjust them to the wide Russian gauge.

Although logical enough in themselves, these considerations proved to be only partly valid, and the interval between the second and third stages of the Russian offensive was a very brief one. On October 7 the Red Army crashed through the Dnieper line above Kiev, at Pereiaslav and in Kremenchug, and established three firm bridgeheads on the western bank of the river. Concerted German efforts failed to throw the Russians back, and the Red Army gradually succeeded in expanding the base westward at each of these points. This, of course, was only the beginning of another gigantic operation, but the implications of these initial Russian gains were quite obvious.

As the autumn weeks rolled on into the winter the Red Army slashed into the German lines all along the Ukrainian front. The Zaporozhie-Melitopol barrier was smashed and Russian troops, swooping onto the Perekop Isthmus, bottled up a sizable Nazi force in the Crimea and drove on to the mouth of the Dnieper. Southward and westward from the bridgehead at Kremenchug the Soviet forces approached Krivoi Rog to threaten the remnants of the Nazi forces clinging to the banks of the Dnieper at the great bend. Other powerful Russian forces pounded westward from Kiev until they had overrun Korosten and Zhitomir. Here, however, as the Soviet troops pressed to within seventy-five miles of the old Polish border, the Germans rallied in a desperate effort to prevent their southern armies from being trapped or driven southward into Rumania, and in bitter battles forced the advance guards of the Red Army out of newly recaptured Zhitomir as well as Korosten. Still farther to the north Gomel fell and the advancing Russians trod upon the heels of the Nazis sloshing through the icy mud toward Zhlobin and Mozyr.

As the snow fell along the northern part of the Russian front in the third winter of the war, the Red Army was poised for a series of drives from Leningrad to the Black Sea. In Leningrad itself there were rumblings of an offensive that might be mounted to free the city entirely from the threat of the German armies so long encamped in a semicircle around it. From Velikie Luki a salient stabbed westward in the general direction of Riga, a constant threat of an attack that might cut off the whole northern segment of the German armies. In the center the Russians could choose either the Gomel spearhead or the wider base extending from Kiev for a winter offensive skirting the frozen Pripet Marshes toward the line of the Bug. In the south the Red Army could launch an attack across the broad deltas of the Dnieper and the Bug toward Bessarabia and the Rumanian frontier.

In Russia, in Italy, in burned-out Berlin itself—everywhere the Nazi Government faced more troubles. True, German arms were still capable of delivering searing blows, still able to man far-flung defensive lines around the heart of the Fatherland, but that was at once Germany's strength and weakness. Although she might at frightful cost be able to stand off defeat for a time, the strategic offensive which had brought her victory and conquest seemed now lost to the Allies.

9.

The Allies, who were still somewhat skeptical of the offensive strength of the Red Army, were favorably impressed by the Russian campaigns carried through in the summer and fall of 1943. The Russians, on the other hand, could not but be pleased by the Anglo-American conquest of Sicily and their subsequent amputation of the foot of the Italian "boot." The eastern and western theaters of war were thus slowly being drawn together, and the possibility of their being merged somewhere in the Balkans in the not too distant future now began to occupy the minds of the Allied statesmen. Obviously the coördination of the military efforts and the political actions of all the Allies was now an urgent necessity. Although there already existed a fundamental unity of purpose between the nations allied against Nazi Germany, and although it was well understood in all capitals that the logic of the situation had made the synchronization of the grand strategy an absolute imperative, the actual conclusion of such a working agreement was repeatedly thwarted.

In spite of the "self-liquidation" of the Comintern, certain isolationist and Roman Catholic groups in the United States still retained their fears of the possible spread of communism in Europe, especially in the event that the Red Army achieved a swift and decisive victory on the eastern front. On the other hand—and precisely in the same quarters—there were recurring spates of rumors of an impending "deal" between the Russians and the Germans. There were few occasions that one or the other of these attitudes would not fit. Every time the Red Army splintered the German lines there arose a flood of fears that the Communists would be the first to get to Berlin—with dire and disastrous consequences for the world. If the Russians but halted to reorganize their supplies for a new stage of operations, there was immediately talk of Moscow's unwillingness to send its armies beyond the old borders and of the alleged understanding which was rumored to have been made with Germany.

The Russians, in turn, had their own apprehensions. They felt that while both the United States and Great Britain had given them substantial support in the form of material supplied through Lend Lease, the Allied military participation in Europe was still insufficient. They reasoned that while more than two hundred German divisions were concentrated on the Russian front, the Allied armies faced perhaps five—certainly not more than ten—Nazi divisions in their drive from Naples toward Rome, and that the total potential strength of German troops concentrated in north Italy was limited to twenty-five divisions. The Russians, therefore, continued to insist on the opening of a "real second front" in Europe, the launching of a major offensive which would draw no less than fifty divisions from the eastern front. The Red Army was confident that when perhaps a quarter of the German man power had been withdrawn from the east to forestall an attack from the west, they would be able to slice through the weakened Nazi lines and bring the war to a speedy conclusion.

Another delicate point which the Allies found difficult to resolve was the problem of arriving at a common agreement on the method of handling Germany politically. The slogan of "unconditional surrender" announced by President Roosevelt and Prime Minister Churchill at the Casablanca Conference did not seem to the Russians to be a realistic policy to apply in the situation. They had chosen to follow a distinctly different path themselves, and they made it clear they would have preferred to see the Allies attempt other—and to their way of thinking, more efficient—methods to undermine German morale. There was, perhaps, a more fundamental divergence beneath this question of tactics. While both Great Britain and the United States declared that it was their intention to smash Germany utterly and possibly to dismember her after the war, the Russians must have entertained serious doubts as to the advantages they might expect from such a program. In the opinion of some foreign observers, the Soviet Union was justified in questioning such a conclusion to the war, for should Germany be completely destroyed as a political entity, the Russians would be left alone to face an enormously powerful Anglo-Saxon bloc which would then be in a position to dictate policy to all other nations, including Russia.

On July 21, 1943, the formation of a "Free Germany Committee" was announced in Moscow. Its manifesto was signed by thirty-three more or less prominent Germans, including five former members of the Reichstag. Although the Committee included several known German Communists, it was not, to all appearances, a partisan organization. Its president was the German poet, Erich Weinert, and Lieutenant Count Heinrich von Einsiedel, a great-grandson of Bismarck, was listed as one of the vice-presidents. Even though there was no evidence that the Soviet Government had given its official support to the Committee, the significant fact that the announcement was prominently displayed in the Soviet press was sufficient to arouse speculation abroad. The manifesto of the "Free Germany" group read in part as follows: "Facts prove relentlessly that the war is lost for Germany. If the German people will find enough courage at the proper time, and prove by their actions that they want to remain a free nation and are determined to free Germany of Hitler, then they will win the right to decide for themselves their fate, and other nations will recognize them."

In addition to this first organization of German civilian exiles, a "Union of German Officers" was formed somewhat later in Russia. Composed of prisoners of war who had become convinced that the Nazis had led Germany to a military debacle, this group called upon the army to dissociate itself from the National Socialist dreams of world conquest which had brought Germany to the very brink of disaster. Speaking as it did with the authority of the military tradition of its members, this group seemed even better adapted than the first to the task of breaking German morale and splitting the high command away from Hitler.

Faced with a *fait accompli* in this Russian approach to the German problem, the western democracies were compelled somehow to make a hasty readjustment to their attitude toward the anti-Hitler Germans. The United States was, apparently, reluctant to commit itself to any definite policy and allowed the matter to pass without any official notice. The British Government, however, followed the Russian lead, by allowing the formation on British soil of a committee of German anti-Hitler émigrés with objectives similar to those of the group formed in Russia.

At the Anglo-American parley in Quebec in August, 1943, no Russian delegate participated in the conversations. Although certain sections of the American press seemed to have found sinister implications in the alleged Russian unwillingness to attend the conference, Stalin, in a characteristically blunt statement, announced that because of the special nature of the meeting the Soviet Government had not been invited to participate. This was taken to mean that problems relating to the war in the Pacific constituted an important part of the agenda, and that Russia was exercising caution in an effort to avoid impairing the delicately poised neutrality existing between the U.S.S.R. and Japan. Apparently, however, this explanation was incomplete, for about the same time Russia's veiled displeasure was revealed in her removal of her ace diplomats from London and Washington. Ivan Maisky was replaced in London by Fedor Gusev, former Russian Minister in Ottawa, and Andrei Gromyko was assigned the post previously held by Litvinov in Washington. In both cases capable and experienced diplomats who were closely associated with the policy of international coöperation were displaced by able young men whose training identified them with the realistic and nationalistic Russian spirit of more recent years. The hint, if one was intended, was somewhat blunted by the Soviet comment that no ulterior purpose should be read into the shift, and that the Soviet Government had recalled both Maisky and Litvinov to Moscow only in order to take full advantage of their constant advice and assistance during a difficult period.

Not long afterward, in September, United States Ambassador Admiral Standley was called from Moscow to Washington to report on the Russian situation. He subsequently resigned his post for what he said were personal reasons. He was replaced on October 1 by W. Averell Harriman, who, because of his previous connection with the Lend-Lease program, was *persona grata* with the Russian Government. The appointment on September 25 of Edward R. Stettinius, formerly Lend-Lease Administrator, as Under-Secretary of State was also a move which created a favorable impression in Moscow.

As early as the Casablanca Conference both President Roosevelt and Prime Minister Churchill had expressed their desire to arrange a personal meeting with Marshal Stalin in order to eliminate, through direct, frank discussion, any misunderstandings which might still remain among the Allies. After the Quebec Conference they reiterated their suggestions. The Russians, although they appeared eager to come to an agreement with the Allies, proposed that before the meeting of the heads of the governments a conference of the foreign secretaries take place to prepare the ground. Assuming that London would be the logical place for the meeting, both Great Britain and the United States readily agreed to such a conference. The Russians, however, insisted that it be held in Moscow. Their demand was motivated partly, perhaps, by considerations of prestige, and partly by Foreign Commissar Molotov's desire to be in a position to avail himself of Stalin's advice should unexpected problems arise at the parleys. After some hesitation, London and Washington accepted the Russian proposal and preparations were immediately begun for a conference in Moscow in October.

In the weeks following this discussion the Russians became noticeably more coöperative, especially in the diplomatic problems connected with the Mediterranean theater of war. When Italy declared war on her former ally, Germany, on October 13, the Russians joined with the United States and Great Britain in accepting

Italy as a cobelligerent, and a joint declaration signed by President Roosevelt, Prime Minister Churchill, and Marshal Stalin was published to that effect. The Russians also agreed to participate in the Mediterranean Commission, sending a Vice-Commissar of Foreign Affairs, Andrei Vyshinsky, as delegate. They also insisted, unexpectedly, that the Commission be given full authority instead of being only a "fact-finding" body as had originally been planned by both Great Britain and the United States.

Just before the scheduled conference of foreign secretaries in Moscow, the new calm prevailing in Allied relations was somewhat ruffled by a series of ill-considered statements issued by five United States senators returning in October from a tour of the principal theaters of the war. The British took exception to a number of their remarks; and a proposal to investigate the workings of Lend Lease appeared to be directed at Russia, especially since an obvious attempt was made to connect the investigation with a demand that the Soviet Union lease Siberian bases to the United States in order to facilitate the prosecution of the war against Japan. The question of the bases was quickly dropped, and the Senate later adopted a resolution favoring the participation of the United States with other Allied powers in a system of postwar coöperation.

The Moscow Conference began auspiciously. On October 18 Cordell Hull and Anthony Eden arrived in Moscow, each with a staff of experts. In addition, Hull was accompanied by the new United States Ambassador W. A. Harriman, and by Major General John R. Deane, head of the newly created American military mission. The following day the third Lend-Lease agreement between Great Britain, the United States, and the Soviet Union was signed in London, with Canada participating for the first time. The same day the conferees set to work in Spiridonovka House in Moscow and, with two sessions a day, the conference proceeded for two weeks. At the conclusion of the meetings representatives of all the participating powers hailed the success of the conference with an enthusiasm which could only have reflected the deep satisfaction each of them felt.

The results of the Moscow Conference were set forth in a joint declaration at its conclusion. This statement asserted that the united action of the four great participating powers—the United States, Great Britain, the U.S.S.R., and China—"pledged for the prosecution of the war against their common enemies, will be continued for the organization and maintenance of peace and security." To this end the four governments declared that they "recognized the necessity of establishing at the earliest practicable date a central international organization, based on the principle of the sovereign equality of all peace-loving states, and open to membership by all such states, large and small." It was further declared that the four governments would "consult with one another and, as occasion requires, with other members of the United Nations, with a view to joint action on behalf of the community of nations." In an especially significant section the governments agreed "that after the termination of hostilities they will not employ their forces within the territories of other states, except for the purpose envisaged in this declaration and after joint consultation."

The results of the Moscow Conference seemed to have satisfied all the parties concerned, and preparations started immediately for the meeting of the heads of the governments—President Roosevelt, Prime Minister Churchill, and Premier Stalin. The Big Three met in Teheran, Iran, on November 28, 1943, in the building of the Russian Embassy. They conferred for four days after which, on December 1, they signed a joint declaration in which they expressed their determination "that our nations shall work together in the war and in the peace to follow. . . . And as to the peace, we are sure that our concord will make it an enduring peace." As to the war, it was stated that: "We have reached complete agreement as to the scope and timing of operations which will be undertaken from the East, West, and South. . . . We shall seek the cooperation and active participation of all nations, large and small, whose peoples in heart and mind are dedicated, as are our own peoples, to the elimination of tyranny and slavery, oppression and intolerance." Altogether it was an announcement to the effect that the Allies now considered themselves more firmly united and more ready to tackle the common tasks before them than at any time since the beginning of the second World War.

10.

By the end of 1943 it was obvious that the Allies had at last wrested the initiative from the Axis and that Germany, while still capable of tremendous resistance, had been driven into a defensive position. The Allies, though still geographically separated by vast distances, disposed of greater forces, and, what was especially important in this war of mechanized weapons, their production of armament and supply had exceeded that of the Axis and continued to grow steadily. The only escape left to Germany lay in an effort to prolong the war in the hope that internal dissensions might divide the Anglo-Saxon countries and the Soviet Union before victory could be achieved.

A major clash between the Anglo-Saxon democracies and the Soviets before the end of the war now seems hardly possible. But the task before the Allies does not end with the military victory. If this war is to result in any lasting peace, the Allies must create some stable international organization capable of withstanding world social and political stresses; they must, at the very least, evolve some permanent agreement which will make a third world war forever impossible. Nothing less can truly be considered an allied victory.

Today a beginning has been made in the solution of this most urgent world problem. Between Great Britain and the Soviet Union there exists a twenty-year agreement providing for military assistance during the war and coöperation during the reconstruction. In the United States and in the Soviet Union there is a growing appreciation of the problems and the aspirations of each nation. All three countries have, as signatories of the Atlantic Charter, signified their intention to seek a just and enduring peace. The Moscow Conference of the foreign secretaries of the three countries held in October, 1943, as well as the Teheran declaration, seem to have sealed their close agreement. And yet nobody at this time can predict the development of national relations in the postwar world. At least one generalization can, however, be flatly stated: Fundamentally, there is no basis whatsoever for a conflict between Russia and the United States at any time in the future.

The position of the Soviet Union is clear for those who will try honestly to understand it. Having been attacked by the Germans, it is but natural that the Russians want to restore their boundaries as they existed on the eve of the attack. No victorious nation would accept less, and especially since she has already borne the full weight of the war for more than two years, the Soviet Union expects from the Allies full recognition of her right to get back what the Germans took from her. For her this is the first condition of European stability for future generations.

Again, it is only natural that Russia expects to have a voice in the organization of the peace. She particularly hopes to have a share in the reorganization of both the Slavic and non-Slavic states along her western frontier from Poland to the Balkans since any repetition of the *cordon sanitaire* plan is for her a matter of utmost concern. This does not, of course, mean that the Soviet Union will demand the annexation of those states. Much depends upon the spirit in which international relations are determined in the postwar period. If Russia is satisfied that the Allies do not intend to prepare the ground in Europe for a future anti-Soviet coalition, considerations of strategic frontiers will not then play an important role in Russian politics. If, however, Russia feels that no real stability has been created in Europe, she may well insist upon such strategic frontiers and "spheres of influence" as seem to her essential to her own security. Russia has been devastated and bled white by war more than any other nation. By July, 1943, an estimated 5,000,000 Red Army soldiers had already been killed or permanently crippled. The mortality among Russian prisoners in the camps of Germany and her satellite nations has reached fearful proportions. As an example: according to reports in the press, within the space of a few months more than 20,000 Russian prisoners were starved to death in Finland alone. To all this must be added civilian casualties. It is probable that no less than 5,000,000 civilians were killed or starved to death in the Soviet territories occupied by the Germans. Russia cannot under any circumstances afford war in the near future. She must and will do everything within her power to establish the conditions of peace.

The people of the Soviet Union have tasks sufficient to occupy them for years to come. Material losses have been staggering; they have included everything from the rudest peasant cabin to the famous Dnieper dam and were particularly heavy among railways, factories, and industrial installations of all kinds. It will require the full energy of the nation, the government, and the people to accomplish the necessary work of reconstruction. Like all nations, the Soviet Union will be faced by the task of reconverting her industrial facilities to the production of peacetime goods. In spite of the rapid growth of Russian industry since the beginning of the First Five Year Plan, in 1941 the Soviet Union was still behind most other industrial countries in per capita production. Beyond all the other postwar tasks, Russia faces the problem of achieving a vast expansion of her existing industries especially in the field of consumption goods. It must surely be plain that the attention of both the Soviet Government and the people is certain to be concentrated chiefly on internal reconstruction for many years to come.

No change in the basic principles of the Soviet economic system may be expected. Soviet socialism—state management of both industry and agriculture—having proved its validity in the war, will probably remain in force. However, the fact that Russian economics will remain collectivist in no way postulates the inevitability of a conflict with the capitalist countries. Since the inauguration of the program of building socialism within a single country, socialism has become part of Russia's national *régime,* and as such most certainly can coexist peacefully with capitalist *régimes* in other countries. It is necessary only that each side recognize the freedom of the other to establish and develop whatever system it deems necessary for itself, and that each firmly resolve not to interfere in the domestic affairs of the other. These concessions seem small enough to be freely given by any nation and yet are sufficient to insure the maintenance of peace and prosperity for the years to come.

SELECTED BIBLIOGRAPHY

ABRAHAM, G., *On Russian Music* (New York: Charles Scribner's Sons, 1939).

CHAMBERLIN, W. H., *The Russian Enigma* (New York: Charles Scribner's Sons, 1943).

DALLIN, D. J., *Soviet Russia's Foreign Policy, 1939–1942* (New Haven: Yale University Press, 1942).

FISCHER, L., *The Soviets in World Affairs*. 2 vols. (New York: Jonathan Cape & Harrison Smith, 1930).

HINDUS, M., *Mother Russia* (Garden City, New York: Doubleday, Doran & Co., 1943).

KARPOVICH, M., *Imperial Russia* (New York: H. Holt & Co., 1932).

KAUN, A., *Soviet Poets and Poetry* (Berkeley and Los Angeles: University of California Press, 1943).

KLIUCHEVSKY, V. O., *A History of Russia*. Translated by Hogarth. 4 vols. (New York: E. P. Dutton & Co., 1911–26).

KORNILOV, A. A., *Modern Russian History*. Translated and extended by A. S. Kaun (2d ed. 1943; New York: A. A. Knopf, 1926).

LONDON, K., *The Seven Soviet Arts* (New Haven: Yale University Press, 1938).

MASARYK, T. G., *The Spirit of Russia* (London: George Allen & Union, 1915).

MAYNARD, SIR JOHN, *Russia in Flux* (London: V. Gollancz, Ltd., 1941).

——, *The Russian Peasant* (London: V. Gollancz, Ltd., 1942).

MILIUKOV, P. N., *Outlines of Russian Culture*. Edited by M. Karpovich. 3 vols. (Philadelphia: University of Pennsylvania Press, 1942).

MIRSKY, PRINCE D. S., *A History of Russian Literature* (New York: A. Knopf, 1927).

——, *Contemporary Russian Literature* (New York: A. Knopf, 1926).

NEWMARCH, R., *The Russian Arts* (London: H. Jenkins, 1916).

PARES, SIR BERNARD, *A History of Russia* (2d ed. 1928; New York: A. A. Knopf, 1926).

——, *Russia* (New York: Penguin Books, 1943).

PLATONOV, S. F., *History of Russia*. Translated by E. Aronsberg, edited by F. A. Golder, New York: The Macmillan Company, 1925).

POKROVSKY, M. N., *History of Russia*. Translated and edited by J. D. Clarkson and M. R. M. Griffiths (New York: International Publishers, 1931).

SCOTT, J., *Behind the Urals* (Cambridge, Mass.: Houghton Mifflin Company, 1942).
——, *Duel for Europe* (Boston: Houghton Mifflin Company, 1942).
SHOTWELL, JAMES T., general editor, *Economic and Social History of the [First] World War, Russian Series.* 12 vols. (New Haven: Yale University Press, 1928–1932).
SIMMONS, E. J., *An Outline of Modern Russian Literature* (Ithaca, N. Y.: Cornell University Press, 1943).
STRUVE, G., *Soviet Russian Literature* (London: Routledge & Sons, 1935).
SUMNER, B. H., *A Short History of Russia* (New York: Reynal & Hitchcock, 1943).
TIMASHEV, N. S., *Religion in Soviet Russia* (New York: Sheed & Ward, 1942).
VERNADSKY, G., *Lenin: Red Dictator* (New Haven: Yale University Press, 1931).
——, *Political and Diplomatic History of Russia* (Boston: Little, Brown & Co., 1936).
VERNADSKY, G. and KARPOVICH, M., *A History of Russia.* Vol. I, *Ancient Russia,* by G. VERNADSKY (New Haven: Yale University Press, 1943).
WALLACE, D. M., *Russia* (London, 1912; New York, Cassel & Co., revised and enlarged edition).
WEBB, S. and B., *Soviet Communism* (2d ed. 1938; New York: Scribner's Sons, 1936).
WHITE, D. FEDOTOFF, *The Growth of the Red Army* (Princeton: Princeton University Press, 1944).
WILLIAMS, H. W., *Russia of the Russians* (New York: Scribner's Sons, 1914).
YUGOW, A., *Russia's Economic Front for War and Peace* (New York: Harper & Brothers, 1942).

INDEX